MW00681728

WATERSIDE *ESCAPES*

Great Getaways By Lake, River & Sea

By Betsy Wittemann & Nancy Webster

IN THE NORTHEAST

Wood Pond Press
365 Ridgewood Road
West Hartford, Conn.

Readers should bear in mind that prices and hours, especially in restaurants and lodging establishments, change seasonally and with inflation. Prices quoted in this book are for peak season. They are offered as a relative guide, rather than an absolute.

Places in this book are assumed to be open year-round, unless otherwise specified. But schedules vary. Readers should call or write ahead to avoid disappointment.

The authors have personally visited the places recommended in this edition. There is no charge for inclusion.

Readers' comments and suggestions are welcomed by the authors.

First Printing, April 1987.
Second Printing, April 1988.
Third Printing, October 1989.
Fourth Printing, March 1991.

Cover Design by Bob Smith the Artsmith.

Cover Photo by Nancy Webster: Camden (Me.) Harbor from back porch of Smiling Cow gift shop.

Edited by Richard Woodworth.

Library of Congress Catalog No. 87-050272.

ISBN No. 0-934260-68-0.

Contents

About the Authors

Betsy Wittemann has lived close to water most of her life. Born in Bridgeport, Conn., she attended college in New Rochelle, N.Y. (both on Long Island Sound). She worked as a newspaper reporter in Rochester, N.Y., on Lake Ontario, and taught school in Athens, Greece, where she traveled to several islands of the Aegean. She worked as a journalist in Hartford, Conn. (a Connecticut River town), and lived for two years beside the Atlantic Ocean in San Juan, Puerto Rico, where she was the associate editor of a travel magazine. She now is a feature editor and travel writer for the Journal Inquirer in Manchester, Conn. She and her family live in Glastonbury, Conn., another Connecticut River town. She is the co-author, with Nancy Webster, of the *Daytripping & Dining in New England* books and of *Weekending in New England.* Her travel articles have appeared in several newspapers in the Northeast. She is a Pisces.

Nancy Webster grew up in Montreal, a city on the St. Lawrence River. She spent summers in St. Andrews-by-the-Sea, N.B., and at a girls' camp and a cottage with her family on Lake Memphremagog, Que. During her college years at McGill University, she waitressed at summer resorts on the Gaspe Peninsula, in the Muskoka Lakes region of Ontario and at Jasper Park Lodge on Lac Beauvert in the Alberta Rockies. She worked in London, England, and for a Greek ship owner in Montreal prior to her marriage to an American newspaper editor. She since has lived in Geneva, N.Y., in the Finger Lakes area; in Rochester, N.Y., near Lake Ontario and the Barge Canal, and in West Hartford, Conn., where her family's home is near the lake that gives Wood Pond Press its name. Besides the books she has written with Betsy Wittemann, she is the co-author with her husband, Richard Woodworth, of *Getaways for Gourmets in the Northeast, Inn Spots and Special Places in New England* and he Restaurants of New England. She is an Aquarius.

To Our Readers

A room overlooking the harbor, a table with a water view, a stroll along the docks — is there anyone who doesn't like to be near the water?

In our fifteen years of researching and writing travel books, we have been struck by the universal love for the water. Because we enjoy waterside places as much as you, we decided to find and share the best destinations for getaways beside the water throughout the Northeast.

Naturally, we have included many coastal areas: from Chincoteague and Chesapeake Bay along the Eastern Shore of Virginia and Maryland to the Maritime Provinces of Canada. But that's just the start. We also have selected several lakes — from Sebago in Maine to Seneca in New York State. We have two chapters focusing on the Connecticut River and one each on the Niagara and the Hudson. We look at canals in Bucks County, Pa., and at coves on Cape Cod. Of course there are islands: Block, Nantucket, Martha's Vineyard and Cape Breton, to name four — the Champlain and the Thousand Islands, to name more.

In every chapter we have emphasized the restaurants, the inns, the bed and breakfasts that are close to — or have views of — the water. We tell you where you can rent or moor a boat. We advise you about harbor cruises and whale watches, steer you to the best beaches, and find for you the scenic waterfront drives. We cover maritime museums and nautical attractions, fishing excursions and bird-watching places. We even tip you off to campsites and rental cottages. As in our other books, *Weekending in New England* and the *Daytripping & Dining* series, we tell you where to shop, picnic and play.

Every book becomes our favorite, we suppose, but *Waterside Escapes* has captured our enthusiasm like none before. We have been delighted by all that we have found: from the precious Victorian B&Bs within sound of the surf in Cape May, N.J., to spectacular ocean beaches at the tip of Long Island. We've idled in a canoe on crystal-clear Highland Lake in Maine and savored a picnic high on a bluff above the Hudson River. We've cracked open lobsters on rocks in a Vinalhaven restaurant and dressed for dinner in an elegant inn in Bar Harbor. We've revisited former haunts like the Finger Lakes and St. Andrews-by-the-Sea, and discovered treasures like Chester in Nova Scotia and the Cabot Trail. And we have enjoyed every minute of it.

Each place included in this book comes with our personal recommendation. Some we like better than others; that becomes apparent in the descriptions. But after more than a year of traveling around the Northeast to update this second edition, we think we have some wonderful secrets to share. If you have comments, we invite you to share them with us. We wish you good reading and many happy escapes by the water.

Betsy Wittemann and Nancy Webster
March 1991

Wild ponies graze near Chincoteague National Wildlife Preserve.

Chincoteague Island, Va.

The Indians called it "the beautiful land across the water." Oldtime residents say theirs is a tranquil, loving community. And visitors are prone to superlatives in describing this scenic, fascinating place.

Chincoteague, a diminutive strip that's home for an active fishing community, is the postmark for its larger barrier-island neighbor, Assateague Island, a 37-mile ribbon of sand that crosses the Maryland state line and ends just south of Ocean City. It is the longest stretch of accessible, undeveloped land along the northern East Coast.

Think of Chincoteague and you'll likely think of oysters and the wild ponies made famous by Marguerite Henry's book, *Misty of Chincoteague.*

Chincoteague oysters — pronounced "arsters" by the natives — are gathered to this day by watermen of the old school. Crabbing and clamming are other leading pursuits in what remains an active fishing community.

Wild ponies roam the Chincoteague National Wildlife Preserve, swimming the Assateague Channel during the annual Pony Penning Days that draw thousands of spectators in late July.

But there's more, much more, to raise Chincoteague's permanent population of 3,500 to 20,000 or more on summer weekends.

"Most people come here for the nature," reports Jacklyn Russell, executive secretary of the Chamber of Commerce. The Chincoteague National Wildlife Preserve, a prime Atlantic flyway habitat, harbors more than 260 species of birds. They're among the most exotic we've seen this side of the famed J.N. "Ding" Darling National Wildlife Preserve on Florida's Sanibel Island. Sika deer, whitetail deer, river otters and the occasional dolphin vie with the ponies for visitors' attention. Hiking and biking trails, nature programs, safaris and channel cruises beckon those partial to birding and wildlife.

Backed by fragile, shifting, man-made dunes, the beach is one of the East's most prized. With access to its 37 miles of sand limited by available parking facilities, it's also one of the few where you can find your own isolated plot on the busiest holiday weekend for swimming, surfing and surf fishing.

"This is Cape Cod the way it used to be," says local innkeeper Priscilla Stam, a much-traveled Boston native who will always be a "come-here," as off-islanders are called. "It's the most New Englandish Southern place there is." Chincoteague, pretty much a two-street town, is home to artists and craftsmen known for their fine carved decoys. It has no high-rises nor honky-tonk. The only jarring notes are the mile of billboards rising one after the other from the marshes along the causeway entrance to the island (a never-ending source of consternation among the come-heres) and at the entrance to the refuge a McDonald's, the only corporate come-here.

Otherwise unspoiled and not yet yuppified, Chincoteague coexists with the space age. Rockets are launched periodically by NASA from the neighboring Wallops Island Flight Facility, one of the world's first. The NASA Visitor Center here stands in contrast with the U.S. Fish and Wildlife Service's visitor centers a dozen or so miles away on Assateague.

That's part of the appeal of Chincoteague to families, who take over its motels and campgrounds in summer to enjoy the beach plus wildlife and space-age diversions. Older people prefer the quieter pace of spring and fall, which lingers past Thanksgiving.

Getting There

Chincoteague is an island in Chincoteague Bay, just inland from the Atlantic Ocean on the south side of the Maryland-Virginia state line. The wildlife refuge is at the southern end of Assateague Island, a barrier beach stretching north to Ocean City, Md. Chincoteague is reached by Route 175 off Route 13, which runs from Wilmington, Del., to Norfolk, Va., and is crossed by U.S. Route 50 via the Chesapeake Bay Bridge out of Annapolis, Md.

Where to Stay

Although the peak season is summer, the tourist season here runs from March to December. Accommodations are not particularly numerous and vary widely between motels and campgrounds, with a sprinkling of inns and B&Bs and many rentals of summer homes whose Washington and Baltimore owners use them in spring and fall.

On or Near the Water

Island Motor Inn, 711 North Main St., Chincoteague 23336. (804) 336-3141. Indisputably the area's best waterfront setting and positioning are offered by this eight-year-old motel, whose 48 air-conditioned units on three stories are about the only ones to face the water head-on. A bit off the tourist path, the site is quiet and nicely landscaped. You can sit on your balcony, enjoy the antics of shore birds, and look west across "The Gut," which laps at lawn's edge beneath you, and onto Chincoteague Bay just beyond. (The view is fine from each, though rates rise by the floor). Rooms are spacious, recently redecorated, and have a vanity dressing area and mini-refrigerator off the bathroom. A lighted swimming pool is in front, and there's an observation platform with deck chairs and a hammock at the side. A two-story addition houses a library-conference room and an indoor hot tub and exercise facility. Doubles, $68 to $125.

Refuge Motor Inn, Maddox Boulevard, Box 378, Chincoteague 23336. (804) 336-5511 or (800) 544-8469. The closest accommodations to the refuge are in this weathered wood structure nestled in the loblolly pines, with an observation deck, balconies and patios, a nicely landscaped swimming pool (half covered, so it can be enclosed for use in winter) and jacuzzi, laundry room, sauna, picnic tables and hibachi grills. Of the 68 rooms off an interior hallway on two floors, the thirteen considered deluxe have attractive sitting areas. Many are being upgraded, most in a country style, with bleached pine furniture and appropriate touches like geese on the shower curtains and egrets on the lamps. Room 207, for instance, is done in nautical style, with a blue and white striped sofa and a wall border of sailboats. Its balcony is shaded by a big pine tree. Most beds are queensize and, given the shade from the pines, rooms are cool and dark. The motor inn is run by the Leonard family — Art Leonard, a decoy carver, shows his private collection of decoys in the **Rookery,** a good gift shop off the lobby, and the inn is headquarters for the safari and boat tours run by his sister, Donna Leonard. Doubles, $75 to $90.

Year of the Horse Inn, 600 South Main St., Chincoteague 23336. (804) 336-3221. Decorated rather whimsically, this little inn with three upstairs bedrooms, all with balconies overlooking Chincoteague Sound, is owned by Carlton Bond. There's also a two-bedroom apartment with a porch. All rooms have private baths, air-conditioning and cable TV; there's another TV and comfortable seating in the lobby. We especially liked the mural in Room 3, done in sunset hues by artist Nancy Armour of the Island Gallery and enhanced by four cutout wooden egrets. This room has a small efficiency kitchen. The wicker room is another favorite. Continental breakfast of fresh fruit and cinnamon rolls is served; most guests take it on a tray to their private balcony overlooking the water. The side garden is filled with inanimate critters like flamingos, herons and pelicans. Doubles, $70 to $95. Closed December and January.

Waterside Motor Inn, 544 South Main St., Box 347, Chincoteague 23336. (804) 336-3434. This three-story affair sits sideways to the water, so the view of Chincoteague's notable sunsets from the balconies of most of the 45 rooms is across land. The best view here is from the waterside pool at the rear, directly beside Chincoteague Channel, or from the fishing and crabbing pier out in the channel. An "adult solar health spa" offers a large jacuzzi with a view of the sunset. Most rooms have two double beds, two chairs flanking a round table, a refrigerator and a dressing area with vanity. Doubles, $62 to $92.

Assateague Inn, off Chicken City Road, Box 1006, Chincoteague 23336. (804) 336-3738. Twenty-one efficiency units make this a favorite of families, who enjoy balconies as well as picnic tables on a deck built over a marsh beside a small saltwater creek, one of the serpentine waterways that slice through the island's salt marshes and loblolly pine forests and are locally called "guts." Each has a queensize sofabed or two loveseat sleepers, a sturdy wood dining table that takes up nearly half the living room, a kitchenette, and a bedroom with a queensize bed. An apartment is available (three-night minimum), as are six standard motel rooms, four of them in the back and lacking a water view. An indoor hot tub in a free-standing building accommodates eight people, and there's an outdoor pool. Doubles, $55 to $77.

Other Choices

The Garden and the Sea Inn, Route 710, New Church 23415. (804) 824-0672. With its noted dining room a destination in itself, this new inn in the

French country tradition, built in 1802 as Bloxom's Tavern, now has two upstairs guest rooms of the utmost elegance. Washington attorney Jack Betz and his interior-designer wife, Victoria Olian, planned to add four more rooms (one a suite) in the oldest house in New Church, which they moved to their property. In the meantime, you may stay in the Chantilly Room or the French Garden Room, the first with a wicker queensize sleigh bed and the second with a headboard draped in lace. The modern bathrooms, with gold fixtures, have bidets and pedestal sinks. A dressing table draped in paisley fabric, lace and ribbons, a deep green rug patterned with flowers, painted furniture, squares of colored glass around the windows — these are rooms to escape to. An augmented continental breakfast of fresh orange juice, fresh fruit, cereals, muffins and croissants is served, and you may also have afternoon tea with homemade brownies. The owners plan to set up a small boutique in the lobby to sell French things, and offer three Sunday afternoon chamber music concerts a year. Doubles, $85 to $105; two-night minimum on weekends. Open April-October.

Miss Molly's Inn, 113 North Main St., Chincoteague 23336. (804) 336-6686. This seven-bedroom Victorian bed and breakfast is famous as the place where Marguerite Henry stayed while writing "Misty of Chincoteague." Owners Jim and Priscilla Stam are a font of information about their antiques-filled inn, which they were originally restoring for a family summer home. Then everyone in the family moved west, says Priscilla with a laugh, so they decided to open to the public. Jim makes breakfast, usually served on the spacious screened porch in back — a choice of four juices, maybe melon with blackberries or baked grapefruit with grand marnier, quiche, apple strudel with a yogurt-almond sauce, or Louisiana crunch cake. Priscilla serves afternoon tea (iced, in summer) with cheese, crackers, cookies and cake in the formal dining room, the table centered by an antique etched-glass condiment set. A portrait of Miss Molly, daughter of the home's original owner and with whom Marguerite Henry stayed, is at the foot of the stairs (Miss Molly lived in the house until she was 84). Bedrooms, all nicely done in antiques in the Victorian style, are on the second and third floors, and most share baths, although more private baths were in the works. The Blue Room has a kingsize bed and a private bath. Porches and decks are all over, and from the second-floor deck in back you can see the water. In the front parlor, with its lace curtains and tasseled red valances, is an 1886 Victrola with its original diamond needle. When we stopped in, one couple was listening to a Garrison Keillor tape on the back porch, and Bach was resounding through the rest of the house. Doubles, $69 to $105.

The Little Traveller by the Sea, 112 North Main St., Chincoteague 23336. (804) 336-6686. The Stams of Miss Molly's also own this delightful, rather more up-to-date, six-room inn in an antebellum pillared house across the street. Baths are shared here, too, except for the Witlatch Room with a small private bath. This is another house with a fascinating history — it was built for two brothers who married two sisters and then had it split into two houses. The Stams joined the two houses with a fabulous fireplaced garden room filled with comfortable places to sit and lots of plants and magazines, facing a lovely rear courtyard that has a trickling fountain. Breakfast is taken at Miss Molly's. Doubles, $65 to $99.

Channel Bass Inn, 100 Church St., Chincoteague 23336. (804) 336-6148. In his two decades overseeing this well-known inn, innkeeper-chef James Hanretta has upgraded the accommodations in both decor and price. All ten rooms, one of them a suite, on the second and third floors have private baths and are furnished in elegant Colonial style. The largest rooms are two kingsize on the third floor; one queensize room has a small sitting area. Neutrogena soaps and shampoos grace the bathrooms, artworks enhance the walls and robes are in the closets. Guests gather in a pleasant parlor on the main floor, and there's a small garden off the dining room. Breakfast is available a la carte on weekends at staggering prices. Continental is $12.50, the chef's specialty souffleed pancakes are $12 to $15, and eggs benedict, $20. The minimum is $12.50 per; no wonder one local of our acquaintance was set back $64 at breakfast for two. Big spenders also go for the chef's three-day cooking vacation, a demonstration and eating spree that starts with Sunday night lodging and goes through Wednesday breakfast, $850 each. Doubles, $120 to $210; suites $240.

Dove Winds Apartments, Beach Road, Box 916, Chincoteague 23336. (804) 336-5667. Twelve mini-townhouses, like condo units, and a two-bedroom cottage are rented by the week, mini-week (Monday-Thursday) or weekend (Friday-Sunday). The units are simply furnished with a daybed in the living room, a kitchen, a downstairs bathroom with shower and two small bedrooms upstairs. Guests furnish their own sheets and towels. The complex includes barbecue grills and a heated indoor pool, but not much outside space. Rates, week $420; mini-week, $150; weekend, $200.

CAMPING: Camping is one of Chincoteague's attractions and especially popular with families. **Tom's Cove Park,** Beebe Road Extension, is Virginia's largest campground; when full, its population outnumbers the 3,500 fulltime residents of Chincoteague. It offers waterfront facilities, a view of Assateague Island, a saltwater swimming hole and pine-shaded sites — very close together, as is the area's norm. **Maddox Family Campground,** Maddox Boulevard, bills itself as closest to the beach and has a pool and a mini-golf course. **Pine Grove Campground,** off Deep Hole Road, is secluded and quiet and has a beautiful waterfowl pond. There is no camping on the Virginia end of Assateague Island, but the National Park Service has two campgrounds and seven backcountry campsites in the **Assateague Island National Seashore** in Maryland. Also in Maryland, **Assateague State Park** offers a campground with bathhouses.

RENTALS: Owners of many second homes on the island rent them out in summer. **Island Property Enterprises,** Main Street at Bridge, 336-3456, is the oldest and largest rental agency. Others include **Vacation Cottages,** Box 547, East Side Drive, 336-3720, and **Bay Company Inc.,** 127 Maddox Blvd., 336-5490. Summer rentals range from $250 to more than $750 a week.

Seeing and Doing

Chincoteague National Wildlife Refuge, (804) 336-6122. Established in 1943 as a wintering area for migratory waterfowl, the refuge occupies the Virginia end of Assateague Island and is maintained by the U.S. Fish and Wildlife Service. Some 1.3 million visitors a year make it the nation's third most popular wildlife refuge. More than 260 species of birds have been identified on the refuge. Whitetail deer and the small Sika deer, an oriental elk released here in 1923, also populate the pine forests of the island's interior. The most popular inhabitants undoubtedly are the wild ponies, the only wild herds still grazing east of the Rockies.

The Chincoteague Refuge Visitor Center provides information, brochures and interpretive activities, including guided walks and auditorium programs. Particularly interesting is the Tom's Cove Visitor Center operated by the National Park Service, with "Please Touch" exhibits and a fascinating display in glass jars of varieties of sand from Key West to Utah.

A good overview is provided by driving the main refuge road, past Swan Cove and Tom's Cove, to the Tom's Cove Visitor Center. On visits in early December and May, we saw herons, egrets, cormorants, mute swans and untold geese, plus white-tailed deer and wild ponies coming and going. Local guide Donna Leonard pointed out things we otherwise might have missed, including a baby snapping turtle, endangered Delmarva Peninsula fox squirrels and Sika deer. The best place to see the ponies is around Tom's Cove, especially from the 1.6-mile-long Woodland Trail. A 3.2-mile Wildlife Loop around Snow Goose Pond is reserved for walkers and bikers until 3 p.m. daily, when it opens for vehicles. During the ten days of Waterfowl Week at Thanksgiving, visitors can drive up Assateague Island on the 7.5-mile Service Road for a better look at migratory waterfowl.

The refuge is open daily from 5 a.m. to 10 p.m., May-September; 6 a.m. to 6 p.m. in winter. Visitor center, 9 to 4; interpretive programs daily in summer, weekends and some weekdays in spring and fall. Admission is $3 per car or $1 per person on bike or foot.

THE BEACHES. Fragile manmade dunes shield the glorious sands of Assateague, producing some of the nicest and most remote beaches on the East Coast. Folks generally park near the Tom's Cove Visitor Center and hike to their favorite spot along the horseshoe-shaped, five-mile long Tom's Cove Hook beach or the ten-mile unsupervised Wild Beach to the north. Certain sections are designated for surfing and surf fishing (no saltwater license required). Beach capacity is limited by parking; when lots are filled, one car is allowed in when another leaves. On weekends, officials recommend arriving before 10 or after 2 and promote bicycling. "Biking not only helps you avoid parking problems, but also helps alleviate them," the park brochure notes.

WILDLIFE TOURS. The Leonard family of the nearby Refuge Motor Inn has the concession for refuge tours. A narrated, fifteen-mile wildlife safari along service roads not otherwise open to the public is offered at 10 a.m. daily in summer (tickets, $5). The tour in an odd-looking, custom-made bus attached to a pickup truck is billed as lasting an hour and a half, but usually takes an extra half hour "because our guides are so knowledgeable and point out so many species," says Donna Leonard. Twice each evening in summer, her brother, Art Leonard, leads a narrated 90-minute cruise on the Osprey through Assateague Channel (tickets, $8). It offers the best closeup view of Assateague Lighthouse; the occasional dolphin is spotted cavorting offshore.

THE PONIES. Their origin is debatable (legend has it that their ancestors swam ashore from a Spanish ship that was breaking up in a heavy storm), but the wild ponies inhabiting Assateague and Chincoteague date to the 17th century. To prevent overgrazing on the refuge, the herds are limited to 150 in Maryland and another 150 in Virginia. The latter are maintained by the Chincoteague Volunteer Fire Company, which sponsors an annual two-week carnival that culminates in the famous roundup and swim called Pony Penning on the last Wednesday and Thursday in July. Firemen turn cowboys as they round up the horses to swim across Assateague Channel to Memorial Park in Chincoteague, where some are sold (average price in 1990, $406) at auction. On Friday, the rest swim back to Assateague. Upwards of 40,000 visitors turn out to watch. At other times, the ponies are best viewed from the Woodland Trail in the wildlife refuge, the beach road beside Tom's Cove, the wildlife safari, and in the Refuge Motor Inn's corral behind McDonald's restaurant, the last commercial enterprise before crossing the bridge to Assateague.

BICYCLING. Biking, as the refuge brochure puts it, is a good way to get around Chincoteague and Assateague. A bike path leads from the town to the refuge visitor center, circles Wildlife Drive, and continues to the Tom's Cove Visitor Center. The Woodland Trail is also open for biking. Bike rentals average $1 an hour from the **Refuge Motor Inn** and **T&T Riding Rentals,** both along Maddox Boulevard. T&T offers everything from one-speeds to mopeds.

BOATING. Chincoteague Bay and Assateague Channel are shallow, so sailing is discouraged. Bottom fishing is good. Several small motels cater to fishermen and rent boats. Clamming and crabbing are popular in the shallow waters, guts and marshes. Skiffs and scows powered by eight-horsepower outboards are available at **R&R Boat Rentals, 207 North Main St.**

Island Museum of Chincoteague, Maddox Boulevard, 336-6117. Formerly known as the Oyster Museum (and as such, the only one of its kind), this still focuses on oysters. But its guiding light, Nicki West, says it's "really a history museum, a museum of Chincoteague." Oysters, their predators and equipment used by watermen for several generations are the dominant theme. A good audio-visual diorama details the oyster industry, and you're told it's not true that you should eat oysters only during "r" months. Oyster shells from across the world and shell byproducts (like buttons) are shown. Among "oddities" are shells found implanted on an inner tube, a pipe, a fuse and a chisel. Also on display are the postcard collection of a New Church woman and famous newspaper front pages ("Snow in Miami," from the Miami Herald). We were fascinated by the press clippings of the 1962 winter storm that flooded Chincoteague. Open daily 11 to 4:45, Memorial Day to Labor Day; rest of year, weekends sporadically. Adults $1, children 25 cents.

NASA Visitor Center, Wallops Island, 824-1344 or 824-2298. Since 1945, the National Aeronautics and Space Administration has launched 12,000-plus rocket research vehicles and nineteen earth satellites from its Wallops Island Flight Facility. In keeping with the area, the small visitor center is rustic and low-key, lacking the glitz of the Kennedy Space Center in Florida. A few model rockets are poised among picnic tables outside. Inside, you'll find a collection of spacecraft and flight articles, exhibits on the space flight program, movies and video presentations. A moon rock sample from the Apollo 17 mission and the practice suit of Apollo 9 astronaut Russell Schweickart are highlights from the manned space era. Also part of Wallops Island is the National Oceanic and Atmospheric Agency's weather satellite tracking station. Open Thursday-Monday 10 to 4, daily in summer. Free.

Chincoteague Memorial Park, East Side Drive. Called the best-kept secret on the island is the small town park with a playground, picnic tables and a cross in memory of deceased watermen. The cross was built from the mast of an old ship. The park is at its busiest during Pony Penning Days, when the ponies arrive here after swimming across Assateague Channel.

Sunset Watching. As in the few other East Coast areas where you can see the sun setting over the water, sunset watching is something of a local tradition. For an unobstructed view, regulars head "down the marsh" along South Main Street to Captain Bob's parking lot, where the boat trailers are gone by sunset and the vista is unimpeded. Nearby, you might spot yellow crowned night herons nesting in the trees.

SHOPPING. Hand-carved decoys are the area's leading sales item. "Cigar" Daisey is the resident carver at the Refuge Waterfowl Museum, open daily in summer on Maddox Boulevard. Other leading decoy carvers include Herb Daisey, Reggie Birch and Russell Fish. The Chincoteague Decoy Carvers Association numbers 27 active members. Their works are on sale at their homes

7

and in many shops. **Decoys, Decoys, Decoys** at 324 South Main St. has an amazing selection.

Two of our favorite shops are almost across the street from each other on Maddox Boulevard. At **Island Arts** at 124 Maddox, Nancy Richards West displays her own fine paintings of nature, carvings of Russell Fish, photographs of Julie West (her sister-in-law and co-owner), handpainted clothing, handsome pottery and the fantastic wall sculptures of George Wazenegger. Nancy Hogan Armour sells her paintings at **Island Gallery & Gifts,** 131 Maddox. We like her depictions of the wild ponies, as well as those of herons and other birds.

Next door to the Island Roxy Theater, which shows fairly new movies, is **The Corner Book Shop** at 201 South Main, a great place for browsing. As well as all the *Misty* books, there are many nature books. In back, you'll find an excellent selection of sheet music. **Country Fare** at 109 Main St. has a collection of trolls not to be believed, plus lovely Christmas ornaments, ribbons, lace and, of course, decoys. At **Count Your Blessings** on Main Street we liked the carvings of Steve Merritt, especially one of a snowy egret. More country things like dolls are for sale here. The **Osprey Nest Art Gallery** at 117 South Main St. features the works of owner Kevin McBride, including his posters done annually for Pony Penning Days. Decoys, baskets by local weavers, handsome cards and much more are available. You'll find Pony Tails taffy in many stores on Chincoteague. Watch it being made at the **Pony Tails** shop on Beach Road. The peanut-butter version is especially good. You'll also find a million bathing suits and T-shirts here, as well as many Christian books and tracts. One of the largest gift shops is **The Brant** on Maddox Boulevard, with something for everyone and an entire second floor devoted to wicker baskets. It also has two shops in Landmark Plaza.

Where to Eat

Fine Dining

The Oyster Catcher, 518 South Main St., Chincoteague. (804) 336-5316. "This is a very personal restaurant," owner Neal Thornton said as we stopped in for a tour of his new quarters about half a mile up Main Street from his original tiny place. No children under 16 are welcome (and Thornton, the PhD son and grandson of watermen, who left academia in the 70s, does not welcome the impolite as well). In fact, his theme is "We cater to adults, serving adult food in adult surroundings. Minimum age: 16." That translates to an excellent and reasonable wine list (chardonnays $9.50 to $24) and food on the order of oysters bienville, shrimp-winged scallop barque, and Italian baked clams. We loved the fluffy New Orleans onion pie ($2.50) and the piquant shrimp remoulade ($6) to start, and relished the oyster wheel (a sampler of four baked oyster entrees) and the seasonal soft-shell crabs, sauteed with unsalted butter and capers. Entrees run from $10.50 to $17.50 (for filet mignon). The delicious French bread that Neal bakes himself has a sourdough taste. Both the tender leaf-lettuce salad and the sweet and sour salad made with sauerkraut and bean sprouts are fine accompaniments. A homemade pear ice is a lovely finale. The new restaurant bears the owner's fine collection of Audubon prints in the Audubon Garden Room, painted a pretty Williamsburg Market Square green; beyond it is a garden where roses are trained to grow over a pergola, water trickles in a fountain, and where lunch was to be served starting in 1991. More tables are in the Fireplace Room, and there's a wine bar. Polished wood tables, some made by the owner's late uncle, are topped with soft linen dishtowels in lieu of napkins, and classical music plays. You might end your "adult" meal with a sweet butter tart or Venetian chocolate cake, and finish with a glass of Cockburn's tawny port. Dinner by reservation, nightly 6:30 to 8 or 8:30. Closed in mid-winter.

The Garden and the Sea Inn, Route 710, New Church. (804) 824-0672. It's off island, but innkeepers and those in the know make the twenty-minute trek to New Church for some of the best meals around. Washington attorney Jack Betz and his interior-designer wife, Victoria Olian, both admitted francophiles and second-home owners in Chincoteague, have fashioned a small inn of distinction. Victoria, the chef, a graduate of the Academy of Cuisine in Washington, uses as many Eastern Shore products as she can, both in her $23.50 four-course prix fixe menu and on the a la carte side. When we visited, lucky diners could start with chilled fresh asparagus soup, go on to fresh soft-shell crabs sauteed with capers, lemon and garlic in the Grenoble style and finish with home-baked strawberry shortcake with Eastern Shore strawberries. Entrees ($14.50 to $19.50) on the a la carte menu included veal scaloppine Normandy and grilled drum filet with garlic-mayonnaise sauce. The dining room is sophisticated as can be, with pink stemmed glassware, shell patterned silver, china in the delicate "Plantation Blossom" pattern and a collection of Toby jugs on the mantel. We especially like the blond wood Queen Ann-style chairs and the incredible window treatments. A good selection of award-winning Virginia wines is included in the list. Dinner, Tuesday-Saturday from 5:30, Sunday from 1.

Nonnie's, 432 South Main St., Chincoteague. (804) 336-5822. Her sons are watermen, so the fish at Marcy Pearce's rustic Italian restaurant is fresh as can be. Her decade-old restaurant on the first floor of a downtown house is billed as "the small restaurant for adults," meaning it's off-limits to children. The L-shaped dining room has macrame curtains, beamed ceilings and provincial decor. Interesting sauces enhance the entrees ($11.95 to $20.95), perhaps quail grilled with provencal herb butter, tuna with salsa verde, and breast of duck with citrus sauce. About twenty pastas are listed ($10.95 to $18.95), from linguini topped with clams, to shrimp and chicken in a spicy Portuguese sauce to sea scallops and crabmeat with mushrooms and tomato cream sauce. A new menu item features chilled chicken, shrimp or salmon with their sauces over hot pasta, each creating an unusual room-temperature dish. Homemade pastries are served for dessert. Dinner nightly except Sunday in summer, 6 to 9:30; weekends in spring and fall. Closed November-April.

Channel Bass Inn, 100 Church St., Chincoteague. (804) 336-6148. "Our restaurant is very small, very intimate, and very expensive," chef-owner James Hanretta advises in a letter to potential guests. Patrons are likely to be impressed or enraged, depending on their predilections and their pocketbooks. As one local innkeeper tells his guests, meals at the Channel Bass are "memorable, especially when you get the check. But there are people who like to conspicuously consume, and this is the place to do it." About eighteen people are seated nightly on the half hour at seven well-spaced tables amid Wedgwood china and ornate crystal in the hushed dining room. Hanretta says his cooking is exotic, a blend of Spanish basque and French continental. Among appetizers ($15 to $19), we shared oysters basque, plump, spicy and piquant and more than enough for two. The broiled seafood espagnol ($39), a house specialty, had rather the same tasting basque sauce and abundant seafood, all excellent except for an overdone lobster tail. The medallions of backfin crab ($36) were thick and succulent, accompanied by saffron rice that otherwise is $8 extra, as are vegetables (tossed salads are $12). Nothing beyond a hard roll comes with — no complimentary canape nor truffles with the bill. Nor was the chef's presence made known, although we were assured he cooks every breakfast and dinner single-handedly. We were dismayed that smoking was allowed — the smoke drifting over our table from the party of four at the next table did nothing to enhance the meal or our mood. We nursed a $28 Dry Creek chardonnay, about the cheapest on the wine list, and passed up coffee and dessert (Swiss mocha cheesecake ($12) and strawberries continental, flambeed with cognac and grand marnier and topped with chocolate sauce, $25 for two. Our $154 tab was more impressive than the meal. Dinner by reservation, Wednesday-Sunday 6 to 9.

By the Water

A.J.'s on the Creek, Beach Road, Chincoteague. (804) 336-5888. "Chincoteague oysters and clams are naturally salty — we don't salt them, nature does," advises the menu here. A heron statue in bullrushes beside a globe in the corner watched as we lunched on the assorted fried veggie platter, enough for four at $6.95, and scampi spaghetti with a good side salad dressed with artichoke vinaigrette, mushrooms and strips of salami ($3.95). Garlic is not used sparingly here in dishes like shrimp scampi. Dinner entrees run from $9.95 for linguini with a white clam wine and cream sauce to $16.95 for New York strip steak. Barbecued beef ribs, seafood-smothered flounder, crab imperial and veal dishes are house specialties. White tablecloths, black chairs and booths, and a vaguely Italianate decor characterize the main dining room; there are a few rustic tables outside for dining by the creek. Lunch daily, 11 to 4:30, dinner 4:30 to 10.

The Chincoteague Inn, 100 Marlin St., Chincoteague. (804) 336-6110. This place has been around for years, so the first-timer doesn't expect the rather glamorous renovation into an airy dining room with bare wood tables angled toward the water and a spiffy cocktail lounge with mauve upholstered chairs. Decor is simple so as not to detract from the view. A large screened outdoor deck by the water was added in 1990. Popular with families, the menu offers children's portions and specializes in seafood entrees, from $8.95 for clam strips to $15.95 for a baked seafood feast or the locally ubiquitous filet of flounder stuffed with crab imperial. Like the menu, the short wine list holds no surprises. Open daily in summer, 11:30 to 9 or 10.

Etta's Family Restaurant, East Side Drive, Chincoteague. (804) 336-5644. White lights outline this long gray house overlooking Assateague Channel. There are picnic tables on a side deck, and inside, votive candles flicker on glass-topped pink tables flanked by walls of pine paneling and pinkish print wallpaper. Etta and Mac MacDowell specialize in seafood platters ($8.95 to $15.95), but you can also get a crab cake sandwich, hot roast beef sandwich with gravy or fried chicken. For dessert, try the turtle cheesecake, made with candy turtles. Lunches are in the $2.25 to $4.95 range. Rib-eye steak with two eggs is the priciest breakfast item at $5.95. Open Wednesday-Monday, 7 a.m. to 9 p.m.

Shucking House Cafe, Landmark Plaza, North Main Street, Chincoteague. (804) 336-5145. The sister operation of the **Landmark Crab House** next door, this is popular for breakfast or lunch by the water. We tried the french toast special with scrapple or bacon ($2.95) and an order of corned beef hash to start the day on a porch right over the water. At lunchtime, sandwiches are in the $2.50 to $4 range. Similar bargains are offered at the Saturday breakfast buffet and the Sunday chicken and dumpling buffet. Open daily, 8 to 3.

Other Choices

The Beachway, Maddox Boulevard, Chincoteague. (804) 336-5590. We defy anyone not to fall for the homemade desserts, temptingly on display in a circular glass case near the entry of this attractive restaurant that's been going strong since 1964. How about almond-amaretto cheesecake, Jack Daniels pecan pie or grand marnier orange tart? Somehow these did not seem appropriate at breakfast, when we sampled the oysters benedict ($6.75, and mediocre at best) and half a honeydew melon, cinnamon toast and a cup of cappuccino (on top of which they put — horrors — whipped cream). The new Garden Room is a colorful solarium with custommade inlaid tables that match the wallpaper. Two more formal dining rooms have tablecloths. Lamb chops, a whole rock cornish game hen with sliced peaches, paella and a 30-ounce prime rib set the dinner menu apart from the norm (entrees $8.95 to $21.95). Bouillabaisse for two is a house specialty. Open daily in summer, 8 a.m. to 9 p.m.

The Village, Maddox Boulevard, Chincoteague. (804) 336-5120. Some tables get a view of the creek at this restaurant, which under new owners is the favorite of many locals. Dining is by candlelight in two rooms, and there's a mellow lounge where we paused for an after-dinner drink after finding other places too noisy or closed. The menu is a bit more inspired than others of its ilk, from fried oysters to seafood platter, seafood-stuffed tomatoes to veal with crab imperial. You also can get beef liver with sauteed onions, fried chicken or filet mignon. Prices range from $8.95 to $16.95, and there's a children's menu. Dinner nightly from 4.

Bill's Seafood Restaurant, 303 South Main St., Chincoteague. (804) 336-5831. For local character, this oldtimer is the place to go. Watermen and NASA base workers start their day here at 5 a.m.; businessmen end theirs with a coffee klatch about 4 p.m. In between, Pam and Ronnie Malone offer a mixed bag of local favorites, from baked ham with raisins to surf and turf ($7.95 to $13.95). Homemade crab cakes, Chincoteague onions with ham, soft-shell crabs and broiled seafood platter are among the favorites. Vegetables are true to the Southern tradition of coleslaw, string beans, applesauce and mashed potatoes. Meals are served at booths and pine tables, and there's a full service bar. Open daily except Wednesday, 5 a.m. to 9 p.m.

Island Creamery Ice Cream & Yogurt, 137 Maddox Blvd., Chincoteague. (804) 336-6236. The very bright and Friendly-ish Island Creamery Family Restaurant next door is, well, good for families. We prefer this spacious haunt, where the delicious aroma from the waffle cones being made on eight waffle irons at the entrance nearly bowls you over. Ice cream comes in untold varieties, old South pecan, strawberry cheesecake and key lime and watermelon sherbets among them. Plain, sugar and waffle cones are priced from $1.29 to $2.49; a banana split is $3. You can partake inside or out. Open daily, 10 to 10.

Barbara's Take-Out, 212 South Main St., Chincoteague. (804) 336-3125. Maybe you've overdosed on seafood and feel like something a bit different. This little takeout spot, with two picnic tables just outside, might fill the bill. Subs, salads, pizzas that the locals line up to take out and pastas (of the traditional sort) are the fare. Pizza is $8, extras $1 and slices $1.25. Barbara Eve also dishes up some super desserts like heath bar pie, caramel apple pie and, in season, homemade strawberry shortcake. Her delicious chili with rice and biscuits is $2.95, and she makes soups like California medley, which mixes cheese and a lot of vegetables. The Italian bread is homemade to order. Open Tuesday-Sunday, 11:30 to 8; to 6 in winter, also closed Sunday.

FOR MORE INFORMATION: Chincoteague Chamber of Commerce, Maddox Boulevard at the Rotary, Box 258, Chincoteague, Va. 23336. (804) 336-6161.

St. Michaels waterfront from veranda of Hambleton Inn.

St. Michaels-Oxford, Md.

You're sitting on your veranda on a balmy September evening. Gone are the crowds of summer sailors who make St. Michaels the second busiest transient harbor on Chesapeake Bay. Yet to come are the hunters who flock to this area every fall.

Egrets and ospreys can be seen and ducks heard; Canada geese are all around. Tall Southern pines sway in the breeze. The foliage tends to magnolia, holly and boxwood trees. The homes are pillared and porched. You detect a drawl in the natives' speech.

There's an unmistakable Southern air about St. Michaels and Oxford, its neighbor across the Tred Avon River, as well as about remote Tilghman Island between the Choptank River and Chesapeake Bay.

This is Tidewater territory. It's also the Mason-Dixon line, said the woman who checked us in at the Harbourtowne Resort. "People think that with my accent I'm from Virginia, but no, I was born and raised on the Eastern Shore."

Both St. Michaels and Oxford date back to the 1600s and played key roles in the developing nation and its boatbuilding interests before yielding their importance to Washington and Baltimore. For years they languished, relatively undiscovered by tourists and bypassed by the masses headed for Ocean City beaches, but beloved by the watermen who make their livelihood from the bay.

The opening of the Bay Bridge out of Annapolis in 1954 forever altered the Eastern Shore's lifestyle. It wasn't until James Michener penned *Chesapeake* in the area that this choice piece of real estate really took off, however.

"When I moved here there was one B&B and now there are eight," said ex-Connecticut resident Richard Grunewald, a local businessman. There also are new inns, motels, restaurants, shops and, of course, more than enough boatsmen, sportsmen and visitors to fill them. Oxford and Tilghman Island remain less changed, and zoning regulations have been tightened in the St. Michaels area to keep its waterfront unspoiled.

The focus of western Talbot County — which has an incredible 602 miles of shoreline — is St. Michaels, its landlocked harbor located half way up the Miles River from Eastern Bay toward Easton, the historic county seat. Hidden beneath the clapboards of modernized houses are logs or bricks dating to the 18th century. When the British bombarded this strategically important town from the Miles River one night in 1813, townspeople blacked out the lamps and hung lanterns in the treetops to confuse the invaders. The ploy worked and the British overshot; only the now-famous Cannonball House was hit, and St. Michaels earned a place in history as the town that fooled the British. Today, visitors take historic walking tours through one of America's earliest seaports, enjoy the Chesapeake Bay Maritime Museum and share the harbor with the 20,000 boats that put into St. Michaels annually.

The wildlife that lures hunters and the waters that attract mariners will appeal to you, too. So will the abundance of Eastern Shore oysters and crabs as well as the Tidewater's unhurried lifestyle.

Getting There

St. Michaels is located on the east side of Chesapeake Bay, about 40 miles due east of Washington, D.C. Main approaches are U.S. Route 50 via the Chesapeake Bay Bridge out of Annapolis, Routes 13 and 301 out of Wilmington, Del., and Routes 13 and 50 out of Norfolk, Va. From Route 50 near Easton, take the St. Michaels bypass to Route 33, which leads to St. Michaels and Tilghman. Take Route 333 from Easton to Oxford. To get from St. Michaels to Oxford, use the Bellevue-Oxford ferry.

Where to Stay⎯⎯⎯⎯⎯⎯⎯⎯⎯⎯⎯⎯⎯⎯⎯⎯⎯⎯⎯⎯ *CCC*

Because of its location and its wealth of fish and game, the tourist season is longer in St. Michaels than in more northerly areas (November and December, for instance, are peak periods). Most lodging facilities are open year-round. Many impose surcharges for weekends.

By the Water

Black Walnut Point Inn, Box 308, Tilghman Island 21671. (301) 886-2452. We found the ultimate water escape at this new B&B, which has a 57-acre monopoly on paradise at the end of Tilghman Island. Water (the Choptank River on the east and south and Chesapeake Bay on the west) surrounds the landscaped grounds and wildlife preserve on three sides and you almost feel you're out in the ocean. The point is so secluded it's not surprising to learn that this once was the summer retreat for the Soviet embassy. The state acquired the property in 1986 and ultimately leased it to Tom and Brenda Ward to run as a B&B. In the charming main house, part of which dates back to before the Civil War, they offer four guest rooms, two with private baths and one with a beamed ceiling and windows on three sides. We stayed in the Choptank Cottage, with spacious bedroom, tiny sitting room and screened porch, and waves lapping at the rocky shore outside — just like the summer cottage of your dreams. Other cottage accommodations raise the total number of rooms to seven. The main house has a parlor with TV, VCR, games and grand piano, a summery sun porch with rattan furniture, a chandeliered dining room and a room off the kitchen where guests may help themselves to lemonade, iced tea, soft drinks or wine from the refrigerator, and find wine glasses and an ice machine. In the morning, Brenda serves a continental-plus breakfast with choice of juice, fresh fruit, cereal and homemade muffins. Outside are a freeform swimming pool, roses blooming around it, and a lighted tennis court, a swing and rope hammocks —

once you stretch out in a hammock by the bay, you won't want to get up. Tom may be persuaded to pilot guests around the island on a champagne tour in his speedy commercial fishing boat. The Wards are outgoing hosts and energetic innkeepers, their rooms have a lived-in look, and the place has a casual, laid-back feeling that's perfect for a getaway beside the water. Doubles, $85 to $105; cottage rooms and suites, $105 to $135. Closed in January.

The Inn at Perry Cabin, 308 Watkins Lane, St. Michaels 21663. (301) 745-2200 or (800) 722-2949. Laura Ashley this, Laura Ashley that — more Laura Ashley than you've ever seen in your life. You name it and Sir Bernard Ashley, her widower, has used it in his first American innkeeping venture (he just opened an inn in Wales and has plans for eleven more on this side of the Atlantic). Many millions were spent in redoing this inn for its 1990 reopening, even after multi-million-dollar refurbishings by previous owners of what started as a cabin for Commodore Oliver Perry ("we have met the enemy and they are ours") after the War of 1812. From the dining room to the lounges to the bedrooms, all is plush, plush, plush. Stressing service, Sir Bernard is quoted as saying his philosophy is to welcome guests as he would to one of his homes. But home was never like this. In 1990, the original six bedrooms had expanded to nineteen, most with views of the water (the inn is situated scenically at the edge of Fogg Cove), and by summer of 1991 a new wing added 23 more. We toured the inn just before it was to open to the public, and were stunned by the stripes, flowers, flounces, ruffles, fancy window treatments, beautiful colors, wallpaper, borders, painted furniture — this is decoration to the nth degree. Bedrooms have sitting areas, televisions, baskets of fruit, coffee-table books and magazines, pleated lamp shades, terrycloth robes and, in the modern bathrooms, that most British of luxuries, heated towel racks. Most rooms have views of the cove, and those on the first floor have doors to the gardens. On the second floor, some have balconies. Rates include a full breakfast; this is taken in the yellow-hued breakfast room with its willowware collection displayed in a glass case. There are three lounges, all filled with lovely antiques and spectacular flower arrangements; one is set aside for use by house guests only. French doors lead to a brick terrace, where comfortable chairs invite sitting and looking at the water. House guests may take tea here — a proper British one with little tea sandwiches, scones and sweets. All in all, this is a perfect spot for those who love to be pampered and can afford it. Doubles, $185 to $385.

St. Michaels Harbour Inn & Marina, 101 North Harbor Road, St. Michaels 21663. (301) 745-9001 or (800) 955-9001. We first thought it a luxury condominium complex, this contemporary structure commanding a superb location at the head of the busy St. Michaels harbor. Not a sign identified it, two months after it had opened in 1986, and only a chance encounter with a local businessman who mentioned he liked the restaurant at the new hotel led us to investigate. We're glad we did, because this is the kind of full-service inn that St. Michaels needed on the waterfront in the center of town. The L-shaped, three-story structure has 46 guest rooms, 32 of them two-room suites facing the water. And what suites they are! Each has a living room with sofabed, desk, kitchenette (just a sink and refrigerator — no cooking here) and color television, and a bedroom with two queensize beds, remote-control TV and a large bathroom with double vanities and thick towels. French doors lead from each room onto a private terrace or balcony with good-looking chairs and a table overlooking the harbor. After a day of exploring St. Michaels, what luxury it is to have a drink on your balcony before dinner, then after dinner to be able to watch the show of your choice on the bedroom TV while your spouse (this was playoff time) watches a baseball game in the living room. Smaller quarters on the third floor have rooms with one queen bed; some have kitchenettes. The pleasant **Lighthouse Restaurant** has many tables beside the water and serves three meals a day (see Where to Eat). A small outdoor pool beside the harbor has a jacuzzi and a new pool bar for beverages and snacks, and overnight docking slips are available for 60 boats. An aqua center with paddleboats, rowboats and day-sailers was in the works for the marina. A shuttle boat takes guests to points around the harbor. Doubles, $99 to $149; suites, $159 to $249.

Harbourtowne Golf Resort & Conference Center, Route 33, Box 126, St. Michaels 21663. (301) 745-9066 or (800) 446-9066. The first new lodging facility in St. Michaels in the 1980s, this was patterned after a similar development at Hilton Head. Hence the resort-like resemblance with an eighteen-hole, Pete Dye-designed golf course, Olympic-size pool, tennis courts, conference facilities and posh homes all around. Situated a couple of miles west of town and a mile off the road through the luxury 573-acre planned community known as Martingham, this is smack up against the rocky Miles River shore on a peninsula with water on three sides. The Grand Heritage Corp. took over management in 1990 and began a major upgrading program. First to be finished in 1991 were 25 renovated rooms scattered throughout the complex, each with fireplace, four-poster bed and overstuffed furniture. We stayed earlier in one of the second-floor rooms of the original 48-unit complex. They are nicely secluded in several cedar buildings, have brick walls up to vaulted ceilings, spacious dressing areas and private balconies overlooking a tree-lined inlet and lagoon populated by flocks of birds. Some of the 30 villas in five buildings on the point are right on the shore, the most coveted having water on three sides. The rooms here, with double or kingsize beds, are plush but smaller than was ours in the older section. The large **Harbourwatch** dining room in the main conference center has water views and a new outdoor deck right on the water. The menu was in transition with a new executive chef at the helm in 1991, and we were assured the food would be more of a priority than it had been when we dined here. A full breakfast is included in the rates. Lunch daily and Sunday brunch, 11 to 2; dinner, 5:30 to 9. Doubles, $119 to $126.

Wades Point Inn on the Bay, Wades Point Road, Box 7, St. Michaels 21633. (301) 745-2500. Very Southern looking, this imposing white brick plantation-style home at the end of a long lane is surrounded by attractive grounds and backs up to Chesapeake Bay about five miles west of St. Michaels on the way to Tilghman Island. The original house was built in 1819 by Baltimore shipwright Thomas Kemp. A summer wing was added in 1890 and it has operated as a guest house in the old Bay tradition ever since. "We've been updating it but want it to stay comfy and homey," said effervescent innkeeper Betsy Feiler, who's owned the inn with husband John since 1984. Lately they've put their energy and money into the new Mildred T. Kemp Building, which has twelve motel-style rooms with modern baths, most with waterfront balconies and some with kitchenette facilities to encourage families. Each is furnished simply but differently with down comforters, plush carpeting, and interesting window treatments. The main house has fourteen guest rooms, two with private baths, and several more with wash basin in the rooms. Most rooms here are interestingly if sparely furnished, and the annex is candidly described as a "sophisticated Girl Scout house." The summer wing is what you'd expect to find around Tidewater: rooms with high ceilings (and windows) open off the long corridor, the entrance to each containing a screen door inside the regular door, which guests tend to leave open for cross-ventilation on summer nights. The main parlor is comfortably furnished with two sofas, a piano, a tapestry over the fireplace and more books than a Southern gentleman could possibly have read. The large Bay Room is sensational, with columns and arches, a fireplace, wonderful wicker furniture, bleached floors topped with colorful patterned rugs and windows on all sides onto the water. Here is where guests linger over a continental breakfast of fruit, juice, cereal, muffins, croissants and french rolls. A rear porch looks onto the bay, where Betsy says guests catch the biggest crabs off the dock (she'll boil them for you). There's great fishing and you'll marvel at the deer and birds along the inn's mile-long nature walk. Doubles, $60 to $90, $95 to $135 in Kemp Building. Two-night minimum stay on weekends in season.

Robert Morris Inn, Morris Street at the Strand, Box 70, Oxford 21654. (301) 226-5111. Built prior to 1710, the home of the important Robert Morris family has been expanded several times since it housed Robert Morris Jr., who was to become a close friend of George Washington and financier of the Revolution. But it remains a study in Colonial architecture and the fame of its dining room and tavern extends far beyond the Eastern Shore. Best of all, for those who seek a Southern experience beside the water, is **Sandaway,** the inn's lately refurbished riverfront mansion with sumptuous rooms, many with porches looking onto the lovely Tred Avon River. Surrounded by shady lawns leading to the river, Sandaway offers several riverfront cottages, a small beach and a view of the Tred Avon Yacht Club. The 19th-century house has a small den with TV and seven spacious rooms lavishly furnished with antiques, including kingsize canopy and pencil-post beds, large private baths and rocking chairs on screened porches facing the water. Rooms in the 18th-century, mansard-roofed main inn are more historic but well appointed and all now have private baths; one of the nicest, Room 1 with a river view, has a four-poster bed, a sofa and upholstered chair near a working fireplace of English bricks, and hooked rugs over the sloping, wide-board floor. The handmade nails, hand-hewn oak pegs and original Georgia white pine flooring are typical of the Colonial detail throughout the inn. All told, the Robert Morris offers thirty-four rooms, sixteen in the inn and eighteen in or around Sandaway. Innkeeper Jay Gibson says the inn caters to couples, especially those who like a restrained, historic atmosphere. Doubles, $70 to $160; weekday rates include continental breakfast.

Victoriana Inn, 205 Cherry St., Box 449, St. Michaels 21663. (301) 745-3368. Tiny sachets are on the beds, candies of the season are at bedside, fresh flowers are in the rooms and all is frilly and lacy in this aptly named B&B facing the harbor. Innkeeper Janet Bernstein — who lives here and generally is more in evidence than other innkeepers in town — provides thoughtful touches: velvety towels folded up in baskets, embroidered pillows, toiletries, a collection of glass animals on the parlor mantel, a sensational oriental piece in the upstairs hall, samplers, dolls and Victorian antiques all around. A small sun room has a TV and VCR. A front porch in gray and white wicker overlooks lovely flower gardens, one of the biggest magnolia tree we ever saw, a little fish pond where Janet's pet frog hangs out and, of course, the boats in the harbor. The most coveted room is the one on the main floor with a four-poster canopy bed, private bath and fireplace. The other four rooms on the second floor share two baths, and beds vary from twins to queensize. Breakfast is sumptuous: fresh fruit and juice, perhaps corned beef hash or eggs benedict, and at least two homemade breads. Doubles, $85 to $125.

Hambleton Inn, 202 Cherry St., St. Michaels 21663. (301) 745-3350. A wicker-filled porch facing the harbor runs the length of the second floor of this 1860 B&B, which is very Southern and elegant in feeling. Opened in 1986 by

Aileen and Harry Arader, it reflects the design flair of Mrs. Arader, who used to own the suave Aileen Arader Boutique. The five guest rooms, each with private bath and harbor view, may have king or queen four-poster beds with pillow covers matching the wallpaper and St. Michaels Pottery accessories; one has a working fireplace and all are ever-so-decorated. Nautical types like the Schooner Room or the Crow's Nest Room at the top, which has a bird's-eye view of the harbor. A continental breakfast is served. Doubles, $80 to $95.

Two Swan Inn, Foot of Carpenter Street, Box 727, St. Michaels 21663. (301) 745-2929. This inviting B&B couldn't have a nicer location, its spacious treed lawn sloping to the harbor in full view of all the boating action. Once the home of the Miles River Yacht Club, the 19th-century house was renovated by innkeepers Susan and Andy Merrill in 1984. They offer four guest rooms, one with fireplace and an adjoining bath. Two other harborview rooms and a smaller side-view room share a bath. What Susan calls a sturdy continental breakfast might include baked apples and coffee ring. Swans are the decorating motif and you wouldn't be surprised to find one on the lawn, which is great for lounging. The inn has boats and bikes for guests' use. Doubles, $70 to $115. No smoking.

The Tilghman Island Inn, Coopertown Road, Box B, Tilghman Island 21671. (301) 886-2141. A modern resort with motel units, restaurant, lounge and marina — this is an "inn" in transition. Yet it's good for those who want creature comforts and a waterfront location where Knapps Narrows joins the Choptank River and Chesapeake Bay. New management has been renovating the twenty rooms, each with two double beds and full baths. Also available are suites with kitchen areas. Caribbean-style rattan furnishings characterize the **Narrows Lounge.** The paneled **Captain's Table** dining room looks onto the marshes and inlet; an open umbrellaed deck overlooks the bay. Also part of the ongoing renovations are a clubhouse by the pool and an airy lobby. Doubles, $95 to $110.

Other Choices

The Parsonage Inn, 210 North Talbot St., St. Michaels 21663. (301) 745-5519. This striking-looking inn on the main street was extensively renovated from a former church parsonage. Check the unusual brick exterior with its many inlay patterns, the Victorian gingerbread trim over the porches and the steeple-type roof above. Four rooms were fashioned from the parsonage and three with separate entrances were added motel-style at the rear. All with private baths including Victorian pedestal wash basins and brass fixtures, they have king or queen beds, plush carpeting and thick towels, Queen Anne-style furniture and Laura Ashley linens and accessories. Three have working fireplaces, a couple open onto an upstairs deck and two have television. Oriental rugs and fine Victorian furniture enhance the cozy fireplaced parlor and a large formal dining room, where freshly ground coffee, fruit, cereal and muffins are served by innkeepers Sharon and David Proctor. A patio has lovely wicker furniture, the landscaping is perfect and the decor reflects the sure touch of owner Willard Workman. Doubles, $72 to $84.

Kemp House Inn, 412 South Talbot St., Box 638, St. Michaels 21663. (301) 745-2243. In 1982, this was the first B&B to open in St. Michaels, and it's said that Gen. Robert E. Lee stayed here long before that. Built in 1805, it has six guest rooms, two on each floor, plus a cottage out back, but no common facilities other than a rocker-lined front porch and a back yard. Period furnishings and candles are in each room, which have four-poster rope beds with trundle beds beneath, patchwork quilts and down pillows. Four rooms have washstands and

W/C, others washstand only, and guests share shower rooms on the second floor. Four also have working fireplaces, which are lit on cool nights. Continental breakfast with hot pastries is taken on trays in the room or outside on the porch or lawn in summer. Doubles, $55 to $95.

Oxford Inn, 1 South Morris St., Box 627, Oxford 21654. (301) 226-5220. New innkeepers George and Susan Schmitt raised the roof — literally — of this old watermen's tavern and inn that had seen better days. They added a third floor to produce fourteen guest rooms, all but four with private baths. Rooms vary considerably in size and decor, but even the new rooms were built to feel old. Electric candles in the windows and attractive quilts add to the historic air. The third-floor front corner room called Tavern Hall is especially appealing with four window seats, a walnut spool bed and an armoire. The second-floor sitting room is equipped with TV, VCR with a collection of sailing tapes, games, fresh fruit and decanters of sherry. Continental breakfast includes fruit, cereals, muffins and breakfast cakes. Doubles, $75 to $135.

The 1876 House, 110 North Morris St., Box 658, Oxford 21654. (301) 266-5496. A pleasant front veranda facing Oxford's quiet, tree-shaded main street leads to the interior of this Victorian B&B with three guest rooms. The common room, outfitted in pinks and blues, has a fireplace and period antiques. A continental-plus breakfast, including soft-cooked eggs and English muffins, is served by innkeepers Eleanor and Jerry Clark in a formal dining room. Ten-foot ceilings, oriental rugs and wide-plank floors are featured in the guest rooms. The master suite has a queen-size poster bed, private bath and dressing room. Two other rooms, one with a sitting room, share a bath. Doubles, $75 to $85.

RENTALS. Grand View Rentals, Box 217, Neavitt 21652, 745-5069, offers fully equipped housekeeping cottages with screened porches and one or two bedrooms on the waterfront. This is a hot spot for real estate and rentals, and many brokers are located in the area. One of the longest established is Benson & Wales, 208 Talbot St., St. Michaels 21663, 745-2936.

Seeing and Doing

Although steeped in maritime tradition, St. Michaels may be too recently rediscovered to have the tourist sights and guides usually associated with such an area. We found no visitor information center and only a couple of brochures with information about the town, although quaint black signs with white lettering at street corners point to some attractions.

On or Near the Water

Chesapeake Bay Maritime Museum, Navy Point, St. Michaels, 745-2916. Founded in 1965 and built on mounds of crushed oyster shells, the expanding museum is the town's major tourist attraction, drawing about 100,000 visitors annually. British-born curator Richard Dodds ranks it among the nation's ten largest, but notes that presently it's bigger in property (eighteen acres) than in collections. That may change when the future Watermen's Village is developed, detailing life in a typical bay village of a century ago.

For the moment, the museum has the largest floating fleet of historic Chesapeake Bay boats in existence, including a skipjack, log canoe, oyster boat and crab dredger. They're maintained in a traditional working boat shop, where you get to see craftsmen at work and view a small display of primitive boat-building tools.

The focal point is the 1879 Hooper Strait Lighthouse, one of only three

18

cottage-type lighthouses remaining on the bay; its move to St. Michaels was the impetus that inspired the museum. You learn what a lightkeeper's life was like and pass some interesting exhibits of fog signals, lamps and lenses as you climb to the top level for a bird's-eye view of the St. Michaels harbor. The Waterfowling Building contains an extensive collection of decoys, guns and mounted waterfowl, all so important in this area. The 18th-century corn crib houses gunning boats now outlawed for use on the bay. The Chesapeake Bay Building traces the area's geological and social history.

Among other sights are the Small Boat Exhibit Shed, a bell tower, a Victorian bandstand where concerts are still staged in summer, and a small aquarium whose "exhibit population depends on what the museum staff catches as well as what inhabitant has dined upon another," according to the museum guide. It's that kind of a low-key place. The museum shop is exceptionally good, containing many books, cookbooks for sailors, decoys, needlepoint coasters and Chesapeake Challenge, an intriguing game.

Museum open daily in summer, 10 to 5; rest of year, 10 to 4; January to mid-March, weekends only. Adults $5, children $2.50.

Patriot Cruise, Navy Point, St. Michaels, 745-3100. The best way to see and savor this part of the Eastern Shore — most of its meandering shoreline is very private and far from view — is by boat. Baltimore native David Etzel, his wife and two young daughters run the area's only excursion boat, giving a leisurely 90-minute cruise up the Miles River. The new two-deck boat with bar carries 200 passengers. Dave advised beforehand that he points out "birds, houses, duck blinds, whatever I see." We saw the Mystic Clipper in the distance, various kinds of bulkheading to prevent shore erosion, several osprey nests on channel markers, the ruins of St. John's Chapel, and some mighty impressive plantations and contemporary homes. We learned that the Miles River is not really a river but a brackish tidal estuary of the bay, and that James Michener wrote "Chesapeake" in a rented house along the river. The river was originally called the St. Michaels, Dave said, but the Quakers dropped the "Saint" and local dialect turned Michaels into Miles. Our only regret was that the boat didn't go closer to the sights the guide or the taped narration were pointing out on the eleven-mile round trip. Cruises daily at 11, 1 and 3 (minimum fifteen persons), mid-April to mid-November. Adults $6, children $3.50.

Oxford-Bellevue Ferry, Foot of Morris Street at the Strand, Oxford, 745-9023. America's oldest ferry (established 1683) crosses the Tred Avon River between Oxford and Bellevue. It's the shortest way to get from St. Michaels to Oxford and, again, the scenery conveys a feeling of the Thames and Great Britain, to which this area was so closely allied. The main ferry holds nine cars; a smaller, older one is pressed into service weekends and in summer. Continuous crossings are provided every twenty minutes, June to Labor Day, Monday-Friday 7 a.m. to 9 p.m., weekends 9 to 9; Labor Day through May, service stops at sunset. Car and driver, $4 one way, $5.75 round trip.

SAILBOAT CHARTERS. Eastern Bay Charter, Mill Street, St. Michaels, 886-2489, offers three-hour day sails along the Miles River on board the 40-foot schooner Farewell. Two to six people can board at 9, 2 or 6 for $35 each. **Eastern Shore Yacht Charters,** Tilghman Street, Oxford, 226-5000, rents day and overnight sailboats and power boats, up to 44 feet in size.

St. Michaels Town Dock Marina, St. Michaels, 745-2400. Outboard runabouts, sailboats and bikes are available for rent or charter on the Town Dock. A thirteen-foot, 30-horsepower outboard rents for $55 for two hours ($250 deposit required); sailboats start at $55 for four hours.

Other Attractions

St. Michaels Walking Tour. A self-guided walking tour with map is provided by the St. Mary's Square Museum and the St. Michaels Business Association. It covers the meandering waterfront, including the footbridge from Cherry Street to Navy Point (one wishes there were more footbridges to get from point to point), the Talbot Street business section and St. Mary's Square, an unusual town green laid out away from the main street and apt to be missed unless you seek it out. The map identifies 23 historic houses (none open to the public), churches and sites; you'll likely find equally interesting things along the way.

The St. Mary's Square Museum, On the Green, St. Michaels, 745-9561. One of the town's oldest Colonial houses was moved to this site, restored and furnished. It is joined to the 1860 Teetotum Building, so named because it resembles an old-fashioned top. The display areas of local memorabilia and history are open weekends from 10 to 4, May-October. Donation.

Oxford. The Strand at Oxford's north side, facing Bellevue across the Tred Avon River, is the only real beach we saw in this area. Few people swim in Chesapeake Bay or its estuaries because of sea nettles that sting everything but the palms and feet, we were told. Once Maryland's principal port, Oxford is a lovely, tree-lined town in which the presence of water on all sides is felt more than in St. Michaels. Never in one small area have we seen so many sailboats, yachts and marinas. Besides marinas and restaurants, there are a few shops, several historic buildings, and the Oxford Customs House and the small Oxford Museum, both open Friday-Sunday from 2 to 5.

BIKING. The flat, meandering country is good bicycling terrain. Favorite day trips by bike or car are across the old Tred Avon River ferry to Oxford, which has an ever-so-British yet Southern feeling, or out to a different world on Tilghman Island, where much of the Eastern Shore's famed seafood is caught and the watermen are ubiquitous. Another scenic byway is Route 579 to Bozman and Neavitt. Bicycles are available at **St. Michaels Town Dock Marina,** 745-2400, ($3 an hour, $16 all day), or the **Oxford Mews Bike Boutique,** Morris Street, Oxford, 820-2222.

SHOPPING. Most of the area's shopping is found along narrow Talbot Street in St. Michaels, and much of it has to do with the area's position as a waterfowl center (the annual mid-November Waterfowl Festival draws 20,000 people to neighboring Easton and is considered the best of its kind in the country). We like **Paper Moon** for its interesting imported costume jewelry, contemporary American Indian silver jewelry, its unusal picture frames and carved animals. Beside it, **Bleachers** has jazzy clothing to appeal to the young at heart. Contemporary clothing is found at the **Aileen Arader Boutique.** At **Whimsies,** where everything is whimsical, we loved the baskets filled with birds and flowers, and the switchplates covered with bunnies. **The Book Yard** has more crafts than books, some quite handsome. Wild and wacky jewelry and clothes are found at **Nina's.**

At **St. Michaels Pottery,** you'll prowl through room after room of wicker, brass, lamps, shades, baskets, kitchen gadgets, lucite items and, of course, lots of pottery. **The Calico Gallery** has a large selection of local art posters and a resident decoy carver. Resort-type clothes are found at **Shaw Bay Classics.** At the **Connoisseur Shop,** which just doubled its space by expanding into the shop next door, Louise Clifford sells everything from cookbooks to soup mixes, and lots of local food products as well as the usual gourmet cooking things. We picked up some dynamite jalapeno-stuffed olives. **Woodworks, Etc.** has a fine selection of decoys, and at the **Blue Swan,** we liked the nautical Christmas ornaments. One of us, who likes food spicy enough to bring tears to the eyes, thought she was in seventh heaven when she found **Flamingo Flats.** This little shop must have every hot, spicy sauce or relish ever bottled, including many from the Caribbean.

In Oxford, two shops on Tilghman Street are special: At the **Sign of the Rudder** we found local books and prints, pretty pillows, colorful banners and windsockets, and a good selection of cards. **The Tender Herb** is filled with dainty things, many having to do with herbs, of course. Artworks and decoys abound.

Where to Eat

Windows on the Water

The Inn at Perry Cabin, Watkins Lane, St. Michaels. (301) 745-2200. Long the largest and most elaborate dining place in town, this once-sprawling restaurant and lounge has been downsized and upscaled by its new owner, the Laura Ashley interests. A serene, peaked-ceilinged dining room seats about 75 at round white tables skirted to the floor, with hurricane lamps, gold-rimmed china, silverplated cutlery, burgundy fabric chairs and a grape-hued carpet. Expansive windows amd french doors look out onto a terrace and treed lawns leading to Fogg Cove. Dinner guests have cocktails and complimentary hors d'oeuvres as they study the menu in a parlor-lounge dressed in rosy rust and green chintzes. They place their order and are ushered to their table when the first course is ready. That could be a chilled terrine of goose foie gras with champagne aspic, a gateau of crab with asparagus and Indian queen corn, roast quail with white beans and home-grown tomato, or warmed Maryland oysters with apples, cucumbers and salmon caviar ($7.25 to $11.95). Or perhaps a clear butter bean soup with dumplings and cilantro or white corn bisque with fresh crab and sorrel. For main courses ($17.95 to $27.50, with most at the lower end of the scale), chef Scott Hoyland might offer steamed fillet of rockfish with fennel, rhubarb and dried beans; grilled sea scallops with cabbage pudding, tomato concasse and fried salsify; beignet of soft-shell crab and lemon pasta with coriander and asparagus; Maryland rabbit with grilled summer squash and smoked bacon, and roasted rack of lamb with pickled vegetables, lentils and garlic confit. A short but choice wine list is priced from $18 up; many wines are available by the glass. For dessert, you might find sweet potato cheesecake with macerated granny smith apples, steam beer sorbet with fresh fruit coulis or four variations under "just chocolate." Coffee and after-dinner drinks are taken back in the lounge. The lunch menu is fairly similar to that at dinner, with a few sandwiches and prices in the $10 to $15 range. Lunch daily, noon to 2:30; dinner nightly, 6 to 10.

Bay Hundred Restaurant, Route 33 at Knapps Narrows, Tilghman Island. (301) 886-2622. A deceptive, small gray building beside the water houses a funky lounge with jukebox and video games and beyond, a dining porch that serves up what many consider the area's best food. It's certainly among the most interesting, prepared from scratch by chef-owner Donelda Monahan, who uses seasonal seafood and local produce. Dinner entrees run from $10.95 for zuni stew (a bean, rice, cheese and vegetable concoction inspired by the Pueblo Indians) to $18.95 for crab cake with sirloin steak. We enjoyed a special of soft-shell crabs with green beans and shrimp with zucchini, peas and tomatoes over fettuccine. Start with cajun coconut shrimp and end with a dense grand marnier pudding, the signature dessert for which Bon Appetit magazine requested the recipe. The house salad dressing — a mayonnaise base with curry, thyme, onion and vinegar — is so popular the restaurant sells it by the pint. Although service can be erratic, the view of the passing boats and the colorful lights from the drawbridge compensates — this is like dining on the Intercoastal Waterway. The wine list, heavy on California vintages, is one of the area's best. The decor of green linens, fresh flowers and candlelight is quite elegant. Accents are assorted glass jars containing flowers, tools on the walls and other knickknacks given to Donelda and husband Jamie by a supportive community. Homemade soups, salads and sandwiches are featured at lunch. Open daily, 11:30 to 9:30.

The Tilghman Island Inn, Coopertown Road, Tilghman Island. (301) 886-2141. Chef Chuck Reeser has added an innovative touch to the fare served in this pleasant, white-linened dining room done up in rose and green, with works by local artists on the barnwood walls. There's a good view of boats and, around the corner and beyond the jaunty outdoor deck, a glimpse of Chesapeake Bay. Chuck, who studied in Paris, blends French, Japanese and Eastern Shore cuisines on his menu, which changes every two months. We started with zesty blackeye pea cakes served with tomato salsa and a crab bisque so thick that a spoon could stand vertical in it. The crab imperial and the grilled soft-shell crabs were excellent. Other choices on the dinner menu ($12.95 to $15.95) ranged from fettuccine primavera to medallions of pork with two mustard sauces, grilled breast of duck with a hot pepper jelly glaze and a mixed grill of tuna, swordfish and rockfish, with a different sauce on each. Homemade ginger-pear ice cream made an excellent ending. Dinner nightly, 6 to 9:30 or 10; closed Monday and Tuesday in off-season; Sunday jazz brunch buffet, noon to 3.

The Crab Claw, Navy Point, St. Michaels. (301) 745-2900. The first tourist attraction in St. Michaels, this self-styled "tradition" has been operated very successfully since 1965 by Bill and Sylvia Jones, whose daughter Tracy says "we feel responsible for the development of St. Michaels." Certainly they are responsible for feeding hundreds of diners at all hours (except at 9:30 one slow September weeknight when we tried to get in and were told the kitchen had just closed). The knotty pine main room looking onto the harbor has open windows to let in the breeze, a vaulted ceiling crossed by a mishmash of beams, large tables where you sit family style, a bare floor and mallets for cracking crabs. There's more dining in a back room, and in summer you can eat by the water at picnic tables and a raw bar, watching the staff steam crabs and shuck oysters. The menu is all seafood, except for hamburgers and fried chicken, and the placemat tells you how to tackle your crab. Fried hard blue crab ($6.95) is the house specialty, but crab also is served in soup, cocktail, salad, backfin crab cake, soft crab sandwich, crab fluff, imperial and even a crab dog ($2.75). There are platters from crab cakes and soft crabs ($10.95) to mixed seafood ($16.95). Beer and liquor are available. The seafood is fresh and priced right, and the atmosphere casual and fun. Open daily 11 to 10 "most of the time." Closed December-February. No credit cards.

Lighthouse Restaurant, St. Michaels Harbour Inn and Marina, 101 North Harbor Road, St. Michaels. (301) 745-9001. A commanding water view is offered from an angled dining room decked out in mauve cloths with pink runners and blond wood chairs. The crab cakes here are acclaimed, although the menu ($13.50 to $18) also has such continental twists as salmon en papillote and beef wellington. We liked the scampi Chesapeake sauteed in garlic wine butter but missing the advertised cilantro, and the night's special of two oysters, clams and shrimp stuffed with crab imperial; good rice and crisp long green beans accompanied. A sorbet cleanses the palate following appetizers like hearts of palm vinaigrette, oysters sassafras or clams casino. At breakfast, we enjoyed a stack of apple pecan pancakes while watching the harbor activity. Three meals daily, dinner to 9 or 10.

Longfellow's, 125 Mulberry St., St. Michaels. (301) 745-2624. Outside decks with white molded chairs and an interior with large windows take full advantage of the harborfront location at this contemporary restaurant. Inside, the ceiling covered with white and blue beach umbrellas adds to the nautical feeling. Hot crusty rolls and undistinguished salads came with our dinners of six stuffed oysters, incredibly rich and topped with crab and a cheese sauce, and Napoli Nice, a pasta dish topped with succulent soft-shell crabs. Entrees ($10.95 to $16.95) are also accompanied by a vegetable of the chef's creation — in our case, rather oddly, more pasta with vegetables. Desserts are primarily homemade vanilla ice cream in many guises; we shared an ample creme de menthe parfait, served with a shot of liqueur on the side. Open daily, 8 a.m. to 9 or 10 p.m.

Town Dock Restaurant, 305 Mulberry St., St. Michaels. (301) 745-5577. The locals like this small place, which dates to the 1830s when it was one of the area's first oyster shucking sheds. We found the inside rather dark for lunch, but the picnic tables we had to ourselves outside on the dock were fine. We tried the 1+1+1, a sampler of three soups ($2.50), crab bisque (so floury as to taste almost like library paste), a spicy seafood jambalaya and a vichyssoise. The fried oyster sandwich with steak potatoes in garlic butter ($5) and a shrimp and crab salad ($6.50) were fair but filling. The dinner menu is vaguely continental (caesar salad, chicken florentine, wiener schnitzel and cioppino), priced from $12 to $14.50 for rack of lamb. Desserts range from chocolate decadence with raspberry puree to Bailey's Irish Cream cake and bananas foster. Open daily, 11 to 10.

The Bridge, Route 33 at Knapps Narrows, Tilghman Island. (301) 886-2500. Taking its name from the adjacent drawbridge (said to be the busiest in the world), this attractive restaurant on two levels has some great views, especially from two small alcoves with four or five tables right over the water and a small upstairs crow's nest with glass on all sides. The unusual polished tables made by a previous owner contain inlaid ropes topped with polyurethane. Artifacts and treasures unearthed off the coast of Key West also figure prominently in the decor. In season, oysters (all you can eat) are $6.95 with any lunch or dinner entree; they also come in fritters, a deep-dish pie, fried or baked stuffed. Entrees are priced from $9.95 for chicken to $18.95 for filet mignon. Locals like to sit outside at picnic tables under a canopy and chomp on fresh crabs and shrimps steamed by owner Jim Stansbury. Lunch and dinner daily.

Harrison's Chesapeake House, Route 33, Tilghman Island. (301) 886-2123. Run for nearly a century by four generations of the Harrison family, this vast restaurant, motel and sport-fishing center is a legend on the Eastern Shore. Most of the 48 overnight accommodations in the inn and motel have seen better days, but the yellow and green hotel-style restaurant divided in three sections is especially well liked by families and bus tours. It seats 220, the hostess said, but "it feels like 4,000 on a Saturday night." Beyond is a covered deck near the water with a bar and carry-out area. Letters posted on the wall of the wicker-filled front porch, where diners wait for a table, testify to owner Buddy Harrison's hospitality. The menu is typically Eastern Shore, with dinner entrees from $8.95 for ham steak to $15.95 for seafood extravaganza (five seafoods) and the house specialty, fried chicken and crab cakes. Large bowls of applesauce, coleslaw and stewed tomatoes come with the seafood dishes. Open for three meals daily.

Other Choices

208 Talbot, 208 North Talbot St., St. Michaels. (301) 745-3838. This welcome addition to the St. Michaels dining scene opened in 1990 in the space formerly occupied by the late St. Michaels Inn and restaurant. Culinary Institute-trained chef Paul Milne and partner Candace Chiaruttini present what she calls casual gourmet dining in their own venture following a stint at the King's Contrivance restaurant in Columbia, Md. Dinner entrees ($15.50 to $19.50) might be scallops sauteed with bouillabaisse butter, fresh rock fish with wild mushrooms and oyster cream, sauteed calves liver, rack of lamb with roasted garlic and, one winter's evening, New Zealand venison with roasted vegetables and gooseberry black-pepper game sauce. For starters, how about a napoleon of assorted smoked fish with crispy wontons and wasabi sauce or oysters baked with prosciutto, champagne cream and pistachio nuts? Finish with one of Candy's desserts: lemon tart, apple-pecan pie, tirami su or homemade ice cream. About 70 diners can be accommodated in four small dining rooms of a mid-19th-century house decked out in brick and teal green with white tablecloths. Lunch, Wednesday-Friday 11:30 to 2; dinner, Tuesday-Saturday 5 to 10; Sunday, brunch 11:30 to 3, dinner 4 to 9.

The Masthead, 101 Mill St., Oxford. (301) 226-5303. "We don't own a crab steamer or deep fat fryer," the owners of this hard-to-find restaurant behind the Oxford Boatyard advertise. They contend that simple food, innovative recipes and fresh vegetables are a welcome alternative to the ubiquitous fried fish and steamed crabs. There's no view; the main dining room consists of small tables dressed in white and blue and set apart in unusual carpeted alcoves. Stained-glass windows, mismatched chairs, numerous sailing pictures and a long copper bar in the adjacent pub complete the decor. Dining is by candlelight. Owner Leigh Duncan Marquess's menu is ever-changing, with starters like cream of asparagus soup, house pate and tomato tortellini filled with beef in a creamy garlic sauce. Entrees ($10.95 to $22.95) might be grilled swordfish with sesame mayonnaise, sea scallops tossed with rigatoni in vodka cream sauce, chicken sauteed with mushrooms and amaretto, filet mignon with a blue cheese mustard sauce, and rack of lamb baked in Guinness stout and served with currant-horse-radish sauce. Derby pie is the specialty dessert, along with cheesecakes and fruit tarts. Weekend brunch, a local tradition, brings choices from crab benedict to cheeseburgers. Lunch, Monday-Friday 11:30 to 2:30, April-December and winter weekends; dinner, 6 to 9:30 or 10; weekend brunch, 11 to 3.

Robert Morris Inn, Morris Street at the Strand, Oxford. (301) 226-5111. No dining reservations are accepted at this landmark inn with a large and popular restaurant. Lunch in the Tavern is an experience straight from the 18th century, the staff in Colonial costumes amid walls of brick, floors of Vermont slate and the Morris coat of arms above the fireplace. Many like to start with a hot buttered rum or the 1710, a mixture of amber rum and fruit juices in a Colonial glass that you get to keep ($7.75). A basket of corn muffins (which crumbled all over the table) preceded our crab soup, a house specialty chock full of vegetables, and a paltry dish of three mushrooms stuffed with crab imperial for $6.50. More filling was a delicious and pure oyster stew ($4.50). You can order anything from a crab cake sandwich platter to prime rib on the extensive lunch menu, $4.95 to $14.95, or mix and match appetizers as we did. The dinner menu is even more extensive — from assorted juices (95 cents) to prime rib supreme topped with crabmeat ($20.95), a combination we certainly wouldn't order. As you'd expect, crab is the specialty — from soup to crab cakes, crab Norfolk, crab imperial and a variety of seafood platters. Desserts run from cheesecake to assorted parfaits. The formal, carpeted and chandeliered dining room has well-spaced tables, stenciled chairs and four impressive murals. Lunch, Wednesday-Sunday noon to 3; dinner, Wednesday-Saturday 6 to 9.

Oxford Inn and Pope's Tavern, South Morris Street, Oxford. (301) 226-5220. This old watermen's tavern has been renovated and upgraded by new owners, the Schmitt family, two brothers and their wives. Etched sailboats are in the windows, a model of the Muskrat boat and a local mural enhance the bar with its elaborate high tin ceiling. Dining is at glass-covered tables enlivened with different colored cloths in the tavern and a smaller room. The dinner menu ($12.95 to $18.95) ranges from potato skins to steak and chicken kabobs. Stuffed flounder, crab cakes, seafood capellini, shrimp scampi and crab or shrimp norfolk are specialties. Desserts include an English sherry trifle topped with fresh cream and walnuts. Lunch daily, 11:30 to 2; dinner, 6 to 9 or 10; closed Tuesday.

The Bakery, 102 Talbot St., St. Michaels. (301) 745-3366. This new restaurant serving breakfast and lunch is an addition to the Talbot Street Shoppe & Bakery. The bakery is still in back, but chef Carl Langkammerer adds wonderful soups, Buffalo wings, sesame chicken fingers with mandarin and pecan marmalade, sandwiches in the $3.50 to $4.95 range, and entrees like broiled salmon steak with fresh chives and lemon-yogurt sauce. Nothing is over $7.95. We enjoyed a shrimp and crab salad with fresh thyme dressing, and the crab cakes (secret recipe) made by Helen Fields, a longtime St. Michaels cook, touted to be the best around. At breakfast you might order lump crab crepes with creole sauce and what one patron said were the best pancakes he had ever eaten (strawberry, apple, cinnamon or blueberry, $3.95). The chef has an herb garden in back, the coleslaw is made from scratch and is delicious, the only thing fried is the french fries, and smoking is discouraged. Traces of owner Courtney Barry's former antiques operation in the space are on the walls; otherwise decor is fairly plain with rose-colored paper mats on polished tables, fresh flowers in old campaign bottles, and some tables with sewing machine bases. A limited selection of beer and wine is available. Open 7:30 to 5 in season, fewer hours off-season.

Morsels, 205 North Talbot St., St. Michaels. (301) 745-2911. Although Sherry and Ron Thomas are known for gourmet goodies to go, they serve inside at a handful of small tables or outside on the brick alleyway. You also can get theme dinners on weekends, a different theme each week. We were tempted by the Island Night: the menu included coconut bean soup, platters of spiced beef pastries and crab cakes, West Indian shrimp and scallops primavera, and key lime pie. Other themes include French, German and glasnost (East European), which featured homemade gypsy soup, Polish beans and East German meat loaf. The prix-fixe dinner, including soup, salad and choice of several entrees, ranges from $8.95 to $11.95. Up to 28 people can partake in-house, and the meal is available for takeout. At lunch, we enjoyed sampler plates ($4.75) of the day's five salads (curried tuna, chicken Tangier, Greek chicken with pasta, tabouleh and March hare) and eyed a good-looking crab cake sandwich ($4.75). Hours, Monday-Thursday 11 to 3; Friday and Saturday, 11 to 3 and 6 to 9; beer and wine license.

FOR MORE INFORMATION: Talbot County Chamber of Commerce, 805 Gouldsborough St., Easton, Md. 21601. (301) 822-4606.

National Aquarium is backdrop for boats in Baltimore Harbor.

Baltimore Harbor, Md.

"Harbor of History," it's called by the operators of excursion boats that ply thousands of visitors daily along the Baltimore waterfront in a variety of craft. They might also call it a harbor of fun. Baltimore's lately transformed harbor has an abundance of both.

For history, consider that the guardian of the harbor, old Fort McHenry, is where Baltimore turned back the British in the War of 1812. Had the city not withstood the challenge, the course of American history might have been altered. And Francis Scott Key's "Star Spangled Banner," written as he watched the bombardment by dawn's early light, might not have become the National Anthem. The past lives on across the harbor from Fort McHenry in Fells Point, still a working urban seaport community.

Baltimore's harbor area is making history today. Little more than a decade ago, it was a wasteland of rotting piers, warehouses and railroad yards, and the city in general was the butt of jokes around the country. Today, the restored Inner Harbor — the horseshoe-shaped recreation area where the Patapsco River moves from downtown out to Chesapeake Bay — is alive with new buildings, boats and people in a transformation that has had Baltimore starring on the covers of national magazines.

The focus is hometown developer James W. Rouse's Harborplace, the twin pavilions of shops and restaurants that sparked the renewal of both harborfront and downtown in a joint public-private revitalization effort considered to be the best managed in the nation. On either side of Harborplace, landscaped promenades lead to the Maryland Science Center, the National Aquarium, the Pier 6 Concert Pavilion, and the emerging Brokerage and City Fish Market entertainment and shopping centers. Pedestrian skywalks link the harbor with a dozen new and renovated hotels, a vast convention center, a Festival Hall where ethnic festivals are staged most summer weekends, and Charles Center.

No wonder Baltimore Harbor now attracts 21 million visitors a year, more than Disney World.

They come to be near the water, of course, and to enjoy a bit of history, in the past and in the making. They also come to have fun — amid the festival atmosphere of Harborplace, the attractions of the lately expanded National Aquarium and the Maryland Science Center, the nightclub offerings of the hotels and the Brokerage, the name entertainers at the Concert Pavilion, and any number of watercraft from pedal boats to Tall Ships.

So come along with us and the millions of others attracted to Baltimore's Inner Harbor. Rarely will you find so many things to see and do — most of them fun-oriented — in such a compact and appealing area.

Getting There

Baltimore is a major transportation center served by airlines and trains. Interstate 95 passes under the harbor via the new Fort McHenry Tunnel. Also serving the city are Interstate 83 from the north and Interstate 70 from the west. Well-marked exits lead to downtown, where unusually good (and numerous) signs steer you to the Inner Harbor and other points of interest.

Where to Stay

For a city that had only a few hotels a decade ago, Baltimore now has an abundance. Some 4,000 hotel rooms have been added since 1984 in the downtown area, most of them near the Inner Harbor. You can get around to Inner Harbor-downtown attractions by walking the promenades and pedestrian skywalk system, taking a water taxi (see below) or the new Baltimore trolleys, which traverse two routes along Charles Street and the Inner Harbor (fare 25 cents).

Hotels

Harbor Court Hotel, 550 Light St., Baltimore 21202. (301) 234-0550 or (800) 824-0076. Opulent, personalized, an exclusive retreat — all characterize this elegant, European-style hotel that opened in 1986. Its understated six-story brick facade fronts onto the Inner Harbor opposite the Maryland Science Center, beneath a towering condominium complex of which it is a part. Each of the 203 guest rooms, including 25 specialty rooms and suites, is a study in luxury with custom-designed furnishings and such amenities as oversized desks, stocked miniature dry bars, bathrooms with large tubs and television sets, separate makeup areas and bathrobes for guests. The eighth-story penthouse suite contains two bedrooms, a wood-burning fireplace, grand piano, wet bar and whirlpool tub, and rents for a cool $1,500 a night. Meals are served in the cheery, aptly named **Brightons** or the sumptuous **Hampton's,** considered by some the city's best dining room (see Where to Eat). Guests gather around the ebullient concierge in the library off the lobby, full of rare books from across the world, or in the **Explorers Lounge,** colorful with handpainted African scenes and exotic objets d'art. Doubles, $190 to $210; weekends, from $129.

Hyatt Regency Baltimore, 300 Light St., Baltimore 21202. (301) 528-1234. Opened in 1981 shortly after Harborplace, which is just across the street, the glitzy Hyatt with its trademark six-story atrium and outdoor glass elevators was the forerunner of the city's hotel boom. Such is the boom's pace now that — can you believe it? — the Hyatt underwent renovations six years later, which said more for the competition than for the state of the Hyatt. Located fully in the thick of things, the hotel offers an action-packed view — if you're lucky enough to snag one of the booked-far-in-advance harborview rooms. Each of the 487 guest rooms is spacious and furnished in typical Hyatt style. The outdoor swimming pool and three tennis courts atop a roof over the fifth floor are surprisingly popular, given all the attractions around and on the harbor. The lobby is a beehive of activity (especially on the Friday when we arrived to a noisy happy hour with orchestra and a multitude of partakers). Hotel guests get to admire the harbor every time they go up or down the glass elevators; transients have to be satisfied with the view from the fifteenth-floor rooftop restaurant and lounge, **Berry and Elliot's,** where every table in a two-level dining room looks across the harbor (dinner entrees, $17.25 to $19.25). More casual fare is available downstairs in **Wok 'n Roll.** Doubles, $180 to $210; weekends, $139 to $159.

Stouffer Harborplace Hotel, 202 East Pratt St., Baltimore 21202. (301) 547-1200. The carpets in the elevators at this deluxe hotel that opened in 1988 say "Have a Pleasant Saturday" — or Friday, or whatever day it happens to be. In what appears to be quite a feat, they're changed daily at midnight, the concierge advised. The hotel has 562 guest rooms and 60 suites on floors 6 to 12 above the Gallery at Harborplace. Most in demand are those (about one-fourth) facing the harbor. The hotel has an indoor pool and a health club with whirlpool and sauna. It offers direct access to the 75 high-style Gallery shops and restaurants, as well as its own appealing lounge and restaurant — appropriately called **Windows.** The lounge is blessed with a harbor view, while the gray and cream-colored dining room settles for a look at Light Street from several levels. The menu features "crab cuisine" among dinner entrees from $11.95 to $21.95. Doubles, $185 to $225; weekends from $109.

Sheraton Inner Harbor Hotel, 300 South Charles St., Baltimore 21201. (301) 962-8300. Quieter and more sedate than its older neighbor, the Hyatt Regency (which obstructs part of the Sheraton's view of the harbor), this smart hotel opened in 1985 a long block away from the water. Some guests find its restfulness more appealing than the hubbub of the Hyatt. About one-third of the 339 guest rooms in the fifteen-story structure angled away from the harbor have water views; best are the end rooms that face the harbor head-on. Most have spacious sitting areas; the motif here and in the lobby is muted earth colors, beige walls and rich paneled accents. An indoor health facility contains a sauna, spa and pool, and there's a no-smoking guest floor. The **Lobby Lounge** has a piano bar, and local seafood and regional cuisine are offered at **McHenry's.** Doubles, $139 to $230; weekends from $99.

Brookshire Hotel, 120 East Lombard St., Baltimore 21202. (301) 625-1300 or (800) 647-0013. This new, 90-suite hotel fashioned from a parking garage is especially good for families or those who, like us, want room to spread out. Do not be misled by the designation "harbor suite" — the view from ours, and most others, was blocked by buildings across the street. But the suite was spacious, containing a comfy living room, a kitchenette with a grinder for the fresh coffee beans supplied, an ample bedroom, two telephones, two TVs, and a complimentary morning paper. We also liked the Swiss chocolates and cordial left at nightly turndown. The hotel's obscure rooftop restaurant, **JaFe,** serving an interesting cross of Japanese and French cuisine, is well-regarded by those in the know. Doubles, $149 to $199; weekends from $109.

Harrison's Pier 5 Clarion Inn, 711 Eastern Ave., Baltimore 21202. (301) 783-5553. Appealing looking in red brick with an aqua roof, this new low-rise hotel is surrounded by water on three sides. It was opened by the Harrison family, whose restaurant on Tilghman Island is a Maryland Eastern Shore tradition. A bit removed from the harbor action (though linked to it by water taxi), Harrison's has its own assets: free parking, easy access to the water from the landscaped grounds, grassy areas, colorful outdoor seating areas and the **Patio Deck** for light dining, and a trademark Chesapeake Bay lighthouse at the end of the pier. A 40-foot skipjack is berthed in the middle of the tiled, three-story lobby atrium surrounded by shops. Each of the 71 rooms is named after a Chesapeake Bay sailing vessel. Georgian mahogany furniture, oversize bathrooms, fresh flowers and nightly turndown service are featured. Most rooms overlook the water but, alas, only a few have balconies for really enjoying the view. The three-level, glass-walled **Eastern Shore Restaurant** is a super location for dining in the Harrison family tradition (dinner entrees, $12.95 to $19.95). Steamed crabs and other raw bar items are available in summer at the **Crab Deck** aboard two restored 19th-century Chesapeake Bay buy boats docked at Pier 5. Doubles, $150 to $185.

Inns and B&Bs

Admiral Fell Inn, 888 South Broadway, Baltimore 21231. (301) 522-7377 or (800) 292-4667. Located across the street from the working harbor, this is one of the nicest city inns we've seen, located a bit off the tourists' path in up-and-coming Fells Point. The brick exterior of the three-building complex that was restored in 1985 into an inn gives little indication of its past dating to 1790 as, variously, a seafarer's hostelry, the home of a Baltimore mayor, a vinegar bottling plant, a dance hall and a house of ill repute. Inside, all is deluxe, from the fireplaced drawing room in deep hunter green and red where you check in at an antique partners' desk to the comfortable library with its honor bar to the small four-story atrium letting in light to all floors. Each of the 38 rooms is named for a famous Baltimore resident (like Edgar Allan Poe) or visitor, with a biography of its namesake on the wall. Owner Jim Widman is from Savannah, Ga., and his background shows in the rooms: rice-carved or pencil-point canopied beds, Federal period antiques or reproductions, and TVs hidden in armoires. Each room is different in size and shape, and you'll be struck by the various color schemes as well as by the art displays beside the atrium shaft on each floor. The goal is to make guests feel they are visiting the home of a wealthy friend, says Jim. Those in the front rooms facing Broadway may be kept awake into the wee hours, as we were, by nighttime revelers from a visiting foreign ship; the inn's location puts it in the thick of the action on summer weekends. A quiet refuge, the inn's basement dining room features new American and continental cuisine from a menu that changes weekly for lunch and dinner. There's outdoor dining on an enclosed courtyard. Entrees are priced from $13.95 for linguini with pesto to $19.95 for veal oscar or angus tenderloin filet. Adjacent to the restaurant is a properly historic-looking pub. Guests enjoy free van transportation throughout Baltimore. A complimentary continental breakfast is served with the morning newspapers in the library. Doubles, $89 to $120.

Celie's Waterfront Bed & Breakfast, 1714 Thames St., Baltimore 21231. (301) 522-2323. Here is one smashing B&B, taking full advantage of its Fells Point location but well hidden from public view. Only a small sign and a locked gate mark the entry to a long, mysterious-looking corridor that appears European and leads into the spacious home that Celie Ives shares with overnighters. Newly built from the ground up for an opening on Valentine's Day in 1990, this romantic and luxurious place is long and narrow in the rowhouse tradition. It offers seven guest rooms on three floors, a rear brick terrace and garden oasis with a trickling fountain, a private courtyard and an atrium, balconies, and a fourth-floor rooftop deck with seating all around for enjoying the view of the harbor and city. All rooms have private baths (four with whirlpools), telephones, clock-radios (no TV, but one was planned for a downstairs common area), air-conditioning, and king or queensize beds. Some have fireplaces and balconies. They are lavishly furnished with antiques and bear such touches as interesting art, fresh flowers, terrycloth robes, duvet comforters and flannel sheets. Celie persuaded a woman from Center Sandwich, N.H., to custom-design stunning lamp shades for each room to match her fabrics. In the morning in the downstairs dining room, Celie puts out a continental breakfast buffet of fresh fruits, orange juice and fresh-baked pastries from local bakeries, which guests can enjoy there or in the living room, or take to their rooms, balcony, rear garden or rooftop deck. Enthusiastic Celie makes a good tour guide to Baltimore, from her helpful restaurant book to the array of local lore she's stashed on a shelf amid the plants in the long upstairs hallway. Doubles, $95 and $125. No smoking.

Ann Street Bed and Breakfast, 804 South Ann St., Baltimore 21231. (301) 342-5883. Another Fells Point winner is this B&B in two side-by-side, 18th-century houses with four guest rooms and twelve fireplaces, including one in a bathroom. Joanne and Andrew Mazurek spent ten years renovating the houses before opening in 1988, and they're still not finished (they were planning a sitting room and a dining room for the ground floor of one house at our visit). The rooms are suitably historic, painted in Williamsburg colors with beamed ceilings, reproduction furnishings, wreaths, wing chairs and such. Guests enjoy a great garden in back, with black wrought-iron furniture amid prolific flowers. Breakfast when we were there involved homemade muffins, juice, strawberry waffles and broccoli quiche; the day before Andrew made pancakes and a potato-onion-garlic dish. Doubles, $75 to $85.

Seeing and Doing _____ ◠◠◠

Baltimore's Inner Harbor is "a masterpiece of planning and execution," in the words of the American Institute of Architects, which honored it in 1984 as "one of the supreme achievements of large-scale design and development in U.S. history."

Around the Harbor

Harborplace, Pratt & Light Streets. The James Rouse-designed marketplace put the Inner Harbor on the map when it opened in 1980 and again for its gala tenth anniversary celebration in 1990. Patterned after Rouse's Faneuil Hall Marketplace in Boston and precursor of his South Street Seaport in New York, this in one way is better than either since it takes full advantage of its waterside location — especially its restaurants, many with outdoor cafes. Harborplace consists of two glass-enclosed, two-story pavilions linked by a promenade along the harbor. Otherwise, the 135 boutiques and eateries are fairly typical of their genre, with 45 higher-style shops in the Pratt Street Pavilion, and the souvenir shops and most of the 46 specialty eating places, gourmet markets and the mammoth Food Hall in the Light Street Pavilion. Twelve restaurants are located in the pavilions. Outside on a plaza between the two, free performances are given day and night by a variety of entertainers, from jugglers and mimes to Scottish bagpipers and brass bands. One noontime when we were there, hari krishnas chanted on the grass as a Fuji film blimp floated overhead. Harborplace is at the heart of the harbor and is linked by overhead pedestrian skywalks with hotels and downtown, so it's a busy place most of the time. Shops are open daily

10 to 9:30, Sunday noon to 6 or 8. Most restaurants are open daily until 10, midnight or later; a handful of small eateries open at 8 for breakfast, but most open with the shops.

The Gallery at Harborplace, Pratt and Calvert Streets. This 1988 addition to Harborplace, across the street from the Pratt Street Pavilion, is much more upscale than its partners. Indeed, its five-story atrium layout is one of the best we've seen, since everything from escalators to benches is user-friendly. Shops range from Williams-Sonoma to Brooks Brothers, Ann Taylor to Carroll Reed, the Coach Store to Godiva Chocolates. The restaurants in the fourth-floor Food Court are more serene than those in the Light Street Pavilion, offering seating at dark wood tables near the windows. The second-floor **Gallery Grill** is pleasant in pink, even if the menu is pedestrian.

National Aquarium in Baltimore, Pier 3, 501 East Pratt St., 576-3810. The crown jewel of the Inner Harbor is the colorful and architecturally striking National Aquarium in Baltimore, described by Time magazine at its opening as the most advanced and most attractive in the world. Although Congress did not contribute to its funding, it did designate it a national aquarium before the $21 million first phase was finished in 1981. Three-fourths of its visitors come from outside Maryland and say they were drawn to Baltimore primarily by the aquarium. Such is its appeal, both to generalists and specialists, that every morning people queue up in long lines for entry every fifteen minutes. We visited late on a Friday afternoon, entered immediately and had the place fairly much to ourselves, which is the best way to see it.

The seven-level aquarium is so big that, as one enthusiast noted, you don't walk around it, you walk around in it. Its two large tanks are rings, and you move via escalators and moving sidewalks through the hole in the middle of the rings as fish swim in circles around you. Seals in an outdoor pool and two beluga whales inside the entrance set the stage for things to come. Many people dawdle at the first major attraction, the Open Ocean tank; actually the pool is visible from many points throughout the building, above and underneath, and by the time you've finished the average two-hour tour you may consider its sharks tame stuff. As the recorded glug-glug, squeak and grunt sounds of surf, sea creatures and birds are heard, you wend your way upward through an unusually enlightening mix of descriptions and live displays: the Tidal Marsh, where two fast-moving crabs prance in front of a sign, "No Crabbing or Fishing;" an informative eight-minute slide show called "The Bay at Risk," after which you'll want to join the effort to save the bay; the puffins on the North Atlantic sea cliffs, imported by the director from Iceland; the busy Pacific Reef, populated by colorful fish which you'll try to identify from their pictures above the tank.

The open South American rain forest at the top, enclosed in the 64-foot pyramid of glass that is the structure's most striking architectural feature, provides a tropical-jungle refuge for free-roaming birds, reptiles and amphibians. You're apt to come face to face with a friendly parrot in a ficus tree or be joined by a golden ringed trumpeter hopping onto your platform. On the way back down past the 335,000-gallon coral reef that's among the nation's largest, you'll enjoy a circular parade of fish swimming both ways. One turned and seemed to wink at us, as spotted eagle ray, silver tarpon and shark teams played follow the leader. You may even see a scuba diver floating amid the fish, handing out dinner. On the ground level is a good museum shop, specializing in fish and water-related items from necklaces to glassware, stationery to stuffed whales. Nearby is **Puffin Place,** with inexpensive gifts and T-shirts for children. There's also a food-service area for refreshments.

The aquarium's much-heralded $35 million **Marine Mammal Pavilion** opened in December 1990 in a companion building on Pier 4, connected to the existing building by an enclosed skywalk. Five Atlantic bottlenose dolphins and three beluga whales perform up to five times daily in the 1,300-seat Meyerhoff Amphitheater, which surrounds a 1.2-million-gallon pool.

Summer hours, Monday-Thursday 9 to 5, Friday-Sunday 9 to 8; Sept. 15 to May 14, 10 to 5 daily except Friday, 10 to 8. Adults $10.75; children $6.50.

Maryland Science Center, 601 Light St., 685-5225. The first major attraction at the Inner Harbor, the science center that features live exhibits and hands-on displays has been growing in stature since. Go on a Saturday morning and you'll think all the kids age 10 and under in Baltimore (and their parents) are there, playing games with computers, learning about energy, watching gerbils and the like. There's a good exhibit about Chesapeake Bay, and we enjoyed a traveling exhibit on dinosaurs. At our latest visit, the 400-seat **IMAX Theater** was detailing the life of a beaver family on its 50-by-75-foot screen, and the acclaimed **Davis Planetarium** had a show on "The Pseudoscience Circus," offering scientific explanations for unexplained phenomena. There are films and demonstrations throughout the day, and the shop here is great fun for kids. Open daily in summer 10 to 8; rest of year, Monday-Thursday 10 to 5, Saturday 10 to 6, Sunday noon to 6. Adults $4.50, students $3. Planetarium, $2 additional; IMAX Theater, $3.

Top of the World, World Trade Center, Pratt Street, 837-4515. The 28-story, I.M. Pei-designed tower is the tallest pentagonal structure in the world. Its 27th-floor observation deck is a popular place called Top of the World — these Baltimoreans are proud, indeed. From five sides you get a panoramic view of the city and the harbor, and some of the exhibits on Baltimore prove interesting. Open daily 10 to 5, Sunday noon to 5. Adults $2, children $1.

U.S. Frigate Constellation, Constellation Dock at Pier 1, Inner Harbor, 539-1797. The first commissioned ship of the U.S. Navy was launched from Baltimore in 1797 and returned to the city in 1955, where it ended up occupying a starring position at a specially designed pier in the Inner Harbor. The oldest warship afloat, it has two months' seniority on Boston's U.S. Frigate Constitution. You can relive the past aboard what envious French sailors back in the 18th century nicknamed the Yankee Racehorse. Go down the old, steep stairs to three decks below, where you'll marvel at the cannons on the gundeck and peer at the barrels in the cargo hold. "Mind your head," warns a sign on the stairway to the crew's quarters, where you stoop to look into tiny bunkrooms with berths, a chair and a bureau. This vessel sure looks, smells and feels old. Open daily in summer, 10 to 8; late spring and early fall, 10 to 6; rest of year, 10 to 4. Adults $2, children $1.

Baltimore Maritime Museum, Pier 4, Pratt Street, 396-3854. The submarine U.S.S. Torsk and the Lightship Chesapeake, a floating lighthouse, are open for self-guided tours at the end of the pier in what is loosely called the Baltimore Maritime Museum (there being no museum as such that we could find). Instead you board the football-field-length World War II sub, known as the Galloping Ghost of the Japanese Coast, and get an idea of what dungeon life beneath the sea was like. Nearby is the Lightship 116, which served 40 years anchored in coastal waters, mostly off the mouth of Chesapeake Bay, its beacon lantern atop the mainmast a welcome sight to ships' captains negotiating difficult waters. Both operated by the City of Baltimore, they are open daily except Tuesday and Wednesday from 10 to 8 May-October, 9:30 to 4:30 rest of year. Adults $3, children $1.50.

Pier Six Concert Pavilion, Pier 6, 727-5580. Summer evening concerts are enjoyed under the stars or beneath the soaring fabric, tent-like structure at water's edge. Performers have included the Baltimore Symphony Orchestra, jazz artists like Gap Mangione and Maynard Ferguson, and such name entertainers as Dionne Warwick, the Kingston Trio and Peter, Paul and Mary.

Harbor Tours

The Inner Harbor is a continuing and colorful pageant of excursion boats, sailboats, yachts and paddle boats, many available for hire. The choices are legion:

Water Taxis, Harborplace. One of the easiest, most fun ways to get around the Inner Harbor is by water taxi, in this case pontoon boats. They're used both for sightseeing and shuttle service between Harborplace, the Maryland Science Center, the National Aquarium, Pier 5, Little Italy, Fells Point and the Canton Waterfront Park. They run roughly every fifteen to twenty minutes, daily mid-April to mid-October, from 11 to 9 or later. Unlimited use on the day of purchase costs adults $3.25, children $2.25.

Paddle Boats, opposite Pratt Street Pavilion, Harborplace. Many of those colorful little boats that one sees bobbing around the inner harbor are pedaled by their occupants, and we hear it's hard work. But they're obviously popular, with waiting lines up to twenty minutes for the 80 available boats. Two-passenger boats rent for $4.50 a half hour, $7.75 an hour; four-passenger boats, $7.75 for a half hour.

Trident Electric Boat Rentals, opposite Pratt Street Pavilion. Lazier types will enjoy the electric-powered two-seaters, which rent for $9.95 per half hour ($14 for three-seaters), plus $1.50 for every five minutes overtime. Posted rules are strict; most important is one that says, "Never go left of the aquarium," out into the busy river. The larger vessels have a difficult enough time dodging all the little boats.

The Baltimore Patriot, Constellation Dock, 685-4288. This two-deck (enclosed below, open but covered above) boat gives a 90-minute, sixteen-mile ride out the Patapsco River past the Port of Baltimore to Fort Carroll and back. Try to sit on the right-hand side since that's the way both the live and taped narration are focused, as we discovered too late. The trip is unusually informative and, on a hot day, refreshingly cooling. Capt. Robert C. Webster was a font of knowledge on local lore and harbor goings-on. He pointed out the Procter & Gamble plant where 28 percent of the Ivory Soap bars are produced, a freighter "offloading" into the Domino sugar plant, the six-sided island Fort Carroll and the Dundalk Marine Terminal, which he credited as the principal reason the port had gone from the tenth to the fifth busiest in the nation. Here the Queen Elizabeth II sometimes docks, eleven giant cranes can lift massive tractor-trailer boxes in two minutes and 50,000 cars are unloaded from ships onto carriers ("last week we watched them offload 4,000 Mercedes-Benzes, all gassed up and with the keys in the ignition," the captain drooled). You pass Federal Hill, Fort McHenry and Fells Point, and see the progress of the expanding harbor: the International Yachting Center, the new Anchorage Marina with 1,200 slips priced at $12,000 and up, the site of the Harbor Keys condo development and more. There's lots of activity and we never knew an industrial-city port could be so fascinating. Departures hourly May-September from 11 to 4; late April and October, 11, 1 and 3. Adults $5.50, children $2.75.

The Baltimore Defender and Guardian, both 85-passenger vessels, are operated by the same company from Memorial Day to Labor Day. They provide shuttle service to Fort McHenry and Fells Point, where passengers disembark for tours. They run every half hour from the Inner Harbor from 11 to 5:30. Adults $3.30, children $2.20.

The Bay Lady, 301 Light St., 727-3113. This 550-passenger showboat offers 90-minute lunch and three-hour dinner cruises, as well as moonlight cruises on weekends. Very popular are the dinner cruises, where you enjoy a buffet dinner (roast beef, chicken and seafood), live bands and a musical revue, and everyone usually comes back singing and dancing, according to participants. Lunch cruises, Tuesday-Sunday 12:30 to 2, $16.95; dinner cruises, Monday-Thursday 7 to 10, $22.50, Friday-Sunday, $26.95. Moonlight cruises, Friday and Saturday 11:30 to 1:30, $9.95. Reservations recommended.

Clipper City, Finger Pier, 539-6277. Baltimore's Tall Ship, billed as the largest in America licensed to carry passengers, gives three-hour sailing excursions at noon and 3 Tuesday-Sunday, moonlight cruises or reggae steel nights Friday and Saturday from 8 to 11, and a Sunday sunset cruise from 7 to 10. Adults $12 to $32 (for champagne brunch), children $2.

Skipjack Minnie V, Harborplace, 522-4214. The 24-passenger skipjack, part of America's last fleet of oyster boats on Chesapeake Bay, catches oysters in the winter and harbor sightseers in summer. Tour lengths and schedules vary, Tuesday-Sunday in summer, weekends May and September. Adults $5 to $10, children half price.

Schooner Nighthawk, 1715 Thames St., Fells Point, 327-7245. Three-hour cruises leave from Fells Point at 7:30 p.m. Wednesday, Friday and Saturday, May-October. There are also a two-hour midnight mystery cruise on Saturday, a crab cruise on Sunday evening, and a champagne brunch sail Sunday from 11 to 1:30. Rates $25, midnight cruise $15.

Other Attractions

Fort McHenry National Monument and Historic Shrine, foot of East Fort Avenue, 962-4290. "There are 79 million acres of National Park System," says the sign at the Visitor Center entrance. "Welcome to 43 of them." Although small, it's powerful, this star-shaped citadel at the entrance to the harbor where Baltimore held off the British in 1814, and even the most cynical cannot help but be moved. Local poet-lawyer Francis Scott Key was inspired to write "The Star Spangled Banner" after watching the historic bombardment from a ship on the river. Visitors are usually inspired to join in song with the recorded U.S. Naval Academy Chorus as the window curtains part, revealing the unfurled flag at the end of an informative fifteen-minute movie in the Visitor Center. A park ranger then leads a 25-minute tour through the fort, which was restored to its pre-Civil War appearance after serving as the world's largest hospital for returning veterans following World War I. Open daily June-Labor Day, 8 to 8; rest of year 8 to 5. Adults $1.

Little Italy. Out Pratt Street just east of Pier 6 is Little Italy, perhaps the most famous of Baltimore's neighborhoods and the heart of its older restaurant district. The four corners at Fawn and South High streets bulge with four leading Italian restaurants and sidewalk cafes.

Fells Point. Just beyond Little Italy is the original Baltimore harborfront, now considered unique in America as a surviving Colonial working seaport community. Listed on the National Register of Historic Places, Fells Point shelters 350 original structures from the 18th century, and nearly half its residents are working seamen. It's rapidly being gentrified with restaurants and shops, but maintains a mixed character. The Art Gallery of Fells Point is juxtaposed next to the decrepit Port Mission; in the middle of the street is the Broadway Market, one of six municipal offspring of the downtown Lexington Market, the nation's oldest. Brown's Wharf is a nicely restored complex of shops and restaurants between Thames Street and the waterfront. Savor the past in some of the seamen's bars, the old houses along Ann and Bond streets, and the commercial establishments along South Broadway and Thames Street. Fells Point will be the Georgetown of Baltimore within a few years, if local restorationists have their way.

Federal Hill. Already a Georgetown of sorts is this nationally designated landmark area just south of the Inner Harbor and the original site of Baltimore's pioneering "dollar-housing" homestead program. For a mere dollar bill, the city sold rundown houses in the 1970s to purchasers who pledged sweat equity. Some of the results can be seen on Federal Hill, where 19th-century red-brick row houses have been transformed into places of charm (and are re-selling for $100,000 to $300,000). You can walk the quiet residential streets above the Inner Harbor and rest at the hillside Federal Hill Park, which grants a panoramic view of the recreational harbor and the industrial port beyond.

MUSEUMS. A Museum Row embracing two centuries of Baltimore history is emerging within a three-block radius of Jonestown, at the edge of Little Italy a few blocks from the Inner Harbor. It brings together the **Star Spangled Banner Flag House and 1812 Museum,** the 234-foot **Old Shot Tower** and four of the six Baltimore City Life Museums clustered around a courtyard: the **Carroll Mansion** where a signer of the Declaration of Independence lived, the **1840 House,** the **Courtyard Exhibition Center** tracing Baltimore's rebirth, and the unusual **Baltimore Center for Urban Archaeology.** Farther away are the prized **Baltimore & Ohio Railroad Museum,** the **Babe Ruth Birthplace,** the **H.L. Mencken House,** the **Edgar Allan Poe House**, the **Peale Museum** (said to be the oldest original museum building in the U.S.), and the outstanding **Baltimore Museum of Art,** which claims the nation's largest Matisse collection.

Festival Hall, 1 West Pratt St., 659-7000. Weekend ethnic festivals celebrating the diverse heritages of one of America's most diverse cities are conducted in the summer. A Ukrainian Festival with arts and crafts exhibits, songs and dances, music, food and drinks was on when we were there.

Downtown. Pedestrian skywalks and nicely landscaped promenades lead from the harbor through hotels, office buildings and shopping malls to Charles Center, Baltimore's first revitalization showcase. From there it's a short walk up quaintly posh Charles Street, past the restored Brown's Arcade, to Mount Vernon Place. The first Washington Monument is the focus of four tree-shaded squares that provide a verdant front yard for fashionable townhouses, the Walters Art Gallery and the Peabody Conservatory of Music.

Where to Eat ⎯⎯⎯⎯⎯⎯⎯⎯⎯⎯⎯⎯ ⨍⨍⨍

Baltimore was described as the gastronomic metropolis of the universe by Oliver Wendell Holmes. Visitors cherish its crabs and oysters, and have packed into such institutions as Danny's, Haussner's, Obrycki's Crab House and the restaurants of Little Italy for years. The revitalized Inner Harbor has a panoply of eateries popular with tourists; otherwise, locals point to a few standouts pioneering their way out of a sea of sameness in dining choices.

Interesting Dining

Hampton's, Harbor Court Hotel, 550 Light St., Inner Harbor. (301) 234-0550. Restaurant reviewers swoon over this small, sumptuous hotel dining room, one going so far as to write that he had his most memorable meal in ten years of travels here. The room is a high-ceilinged beauty of upholstered chairs and swagged draperies in luscious coral colors. The new American fare is pricey ($19 to $31) but worth it for entrees like grilled swordfish with a three-herb pesto, Lake Superior trout poached with artichokes and sundried tomatoes, veal pillows stuffed with wild mushrooms and pinenuts, blackened buffalo steak and grilled pheasant with pecan rice. Baltimore's ubiquitous crabmeat is presented with a light touch here — as fillips to stuffed oysters, stuffed avocado, creamed bisque with corn and oysters, and garnishes for dover sole and Maine lobster. The pastries on the dessert table live up to their billing as an extravaganza. So does the Sunday champagne brunch. Dinner, Tuesday-Saturday 5:30 to 11; Sunday, brunch 10:30 to 2:30, dinner 5:30 to 10.

Pierpoint, 1822 Aliceanna St., Fells Point. (301) 675-2080. Nancy Longo, our favorite Baltimore chef and seafood cookbook author, left Something Fishy and turned up in 1990 at this delightful bistro she owns with two partners. Early on, the Baltimore Sun reviewer said of Pierpoint: "it might do for Maryland cuisine what Chez Panisse did for California's." The sleek boxcar-size space seats 58 at tables of gray marble, with black lacquered chairs, small votive candles flickering in etched glass and arrangements of fresh flowers all around. From her small open kitchen, young Nancy turns out a short but tantalizing menu of what she calls "Maryland-terranean cuisine," involving a repertoire of some 600 items that change frequently. For dinner, we started with the specialty bruschetta ($1.95), a fabulous thick bread laden with garlic and parmesan, and overheard great things about the fresh tuna tapenade, the potato and herb tart, and the warm Eastern Shore rabbit sausage with wilted greens and cider vinaigrette. For main courses ($12.50 to $22), we liked the Maryland-style cioppino simmered in rich crab stock and the soft-shell crabs served with homemade red and green tomato salsa. We found Nancy's favorite smoked crab cakes wonderful, but remain partial to the unsmoked (she will serve them either way). Crisp matchstick potatoes, an interesting slaw of brussels sprouts, snap peas and tiny new potatoes accompanied the various dishes. A sensational raspberry sorbet with chocolate chips and a heavenly blueberry tart, topped off with good decaf cappuccino, ended as fine a meal as we've had in Maryland. Why the restaurant's name? It's located two blocks from the pier and three blocks from Fells Point, so Pierpoint was a natural, says Nancy. And her restaurant is a natural for those into exciting cuisine. Lunch, Tuesday-Saturday 11:30 to 3; dinner 5 to 10 or 11, Sunday 4 to 10; closed Monday.

South By Southwest, 629 South Broadway, Fells Point. (301) 558-0906. Everything is for sale in the small front room with the coyotes in the window and the incredible decor inside, through which you pass to get to the dining room. You also pass by the tiny open kitchen in which chef Stephanie Campbell from New Zealand puts out some interesting fare. This is officially a gallery as well as a restaurant, which explains the sales philosophy. But most people come to this casual, laid-back establishment for the food: entrees ($8 to $18.50) like high plains crab cake (touched with mild green chilies and served with calabacitas and dirty rice), spicy chicken in a tortilla topped with cheese, broiled swordfish with red hot sauce served with black bean-corn salsa, mesquite sirloin strips and the "especial," acorn squash stuffed with black beans, sour cream and cheese ($8 or $15 with crab imperial), which tastes better than it sounds. Start with fifteen-bean soup, slightly spicy with a touch of hickory smoke, stuffed mushrooms or quesadillas. The owner's girlfriend makes the key lime pie, coffee toffee chocolate cake and bird of paradise cake for dessert. The bleached wood tables in the small rear dining room are topped with little Indian rugs; those in the larger second floor dining room sport colorful runners. The bathroom at the head of the stairs contains a tub full of cactus. Lunch, Friday and Saturday noon to 4:30; dinner nightly, 5 to 11. BYOB.

L'Auberge, 505 South Broadway, Fells Point. (301) 732-1151. Copper pots hang from the ceiling and forest green print wallpaper above cherry wainscoting dresses the walls of this intimate auberge, hidden behind a burgundy canopy, an etched-glass and wood door flanked by little gas lights, and windows that have been blocked to the outside world. The interior is sophisticated and warm with floral china, crisp linens and fine crystal at well-spaced tables. Chef Georges Chaubron and his wife Janet present classic fare that customers say is the best French food in town. Main courses are priced from $13.50 for three veal and sweetbread dishes to $19.50 for chateaubriand with two sauces. Duck, stuffed pheasant and pepper steak are favorites. The signature pate dishes and salmon roll dotted with shrimp mousse make good starters. Salads are special, and desserts like a fresh raspberry tartlet and a liquor-laced genoise layered with chocolate and meringue prove irresistible. Lunch, Tuesday-Friday 11:30 to 2; dinner, Monday-Saturday 5:30 to 10 or 11.

Henninger's Ale House, 1812 Bank St., Upper Fells Point. (301) 342-2172. The visitor might dismiss this as another corner tavern nestled among the rowhouses of Fells Point, but locals know it for some of the best food in town. Two resident innkeepers praised its short, changing menu of seafood: perhaps grilled swordfish with dijon-tarragon cream sauce, blackened mahi-mahi with lime butter, sesame-coated red snapper and sea scallops provencale. Entrees are priced from $10.25 for chicken to $16.95 for filet mignon with port and green peppercorn sauce. The place is small (only nine white-linened tables, bentwood chairs and votive candles), plus an adjoining tavern where the choice of ales is surprisingly limited. Interesting stained-glass windows shaped like fanlights are over the regular windows in front. Dinner, Tuesday-Saturday 5 to 10 or 11.

Something Fishy, 606 South Broadway, Fells Point. (301) 732-2233. This upscale place with the amusing name provided a great meal at our first visit. After original chef Nancy Longo left to open her own restaurant, the culinary excitement lessened, but still attracts those who like their seafood fresh from the adjacent market. Owned by Martin's Seafood, the state's largest, Stevi Martin oversees a place that's simple yet elegant — seven pedestal tables for four and a small Victorian bar in front and a rear skylit dining room with cathedral ceiling, track lights, bare wood tables and bow chairs, plus two new dining rooms next door, upstairs and down. Today's "fishy fare" supplements a menu with not many surprises. At our latest visit, the day's soup was gazpacho and the appetizer smoked salmon mousse with roasted garlic and dijon sauce. Dinner specials ($16.95 to $20.95) included sauteed soft-shell crabs, broiled rock fish with sweet red onion butter, grilled marlin with Smithfield ham and mushrooms, and broiled flounder with black bean sauce. Crab cakes that our Baltimore relatives consider the city's best, shrimp scampi, seafood linguini and a smattering of meat dishes also are offered. Among desserts are lemon mousse, pistachio torte, almond cream roll and chocolate pate. Lunch, Tuesday-Saturday noon to 4:30; dinner, 5:30 to 10 or 11, Sunday 3 to 9.

Red Star, 906 South Wolfe St., Fells Point. (301) 327-2212. A something-for-everyone menu with food that's a cut above. That's the consensus of habitues at this crowded bar and solarium dining room with brick walls, heavy blond wood tables and a noise level that can be deafening. The short, handwritten dinner menu lists such entrees ($12.95 to $15.95) as broiled mahi-mahi with macadamia nuts and mango beurre blanc, sauteed scallops with morels over fettuccine and veal scaloppine julienne. You also can order anything from an omelet to bobolis, from Willie's chili to a soft-shell crab sandwich. The dessert special might be cheesecake with fresh blueberries. Open Monday-Saturday, 11:30 to 11 or midnight.

Bertha's, 734 South Broadway, Fells Point. (301) 327-5795. "Eat Bertha's Mussels," say the ubiquitous bumper stickers, and everyone seems to at this dark and kooky place with brick, tile and wood floors and a zillion wine bottles overhead. The featured mussels come in a number of ways — perhaps with garlic butter and capers, or with sauces of spinach, tarragon and garlic or anchovy, tomato and garlic, or with Lancaster cream. Prices are $6.35 to $8.45 (for assorted sauces). You also can get three Mediterranean rice dishes including paella, a crab cake platter, shellfish royale and oysters, $9.95 to $17.95, plus soups, salads, omelets and sandwiches. Scottish trifle and pecan-butter tarts are among the desserts. Welsh rarebit and creamed chipped oysters are offered for Sunday brunch, and afternoon tea in the British tradition is served from 3 to 5 for $6.95 (reservations required). Otherwise, it's "turn right and seat yourself," as the sign inside the door advises. Open daily from 11:30 to 11, weekends to midnight.

Regi's, 1002 Light St., Federal Hill. (301) 539-7344. Billed as an American bistro serving homemade soups, salads, pastas, entrees and sandwiches, this small establishment overseen by Regi Elion is popular with those who like things pure. The bar on one side opens onto the main dining room of tile tables and folding chairs; a little dining room is tucked behind the bar. The all-day menu is supplemented by specials for dinner: things like Portuguese clams and sausage over linguini, a codfish cake platter, steamed mussels puttanesca and Tuscan chicken oven-baked with potatoes and tomatoes and served with asparagus ($6.75 to $12.75). Regi is known for such accompaniments as lemon-dill rice, baked zucchini with bacon and a cauliflower puree as well as her soups, perhaps Lee Bailey's all-vegetable, "Bawlmer" crab or mulligatawny. For lunch, try a Philly cheese steak or oyster po'boy sandwich. Open daily from 11:30 to 11 or midnight; Sunday brunch, 11 to 3.

Sisson's, 36 East Cross St., Federal Hill. (301) 539-2093. Across from the Cross Street municipal market is a lively establishment that owner Hugh Sisson started in 1980 as a beer hall, expanded into an upscale Cajun restaurant and lately added a small pub-brewery that makes English-style ales and stouts. You pass through a narrow, crowded stand-up bar to get to the rear dining room, where you sit on church pews at tables covered with copper beneath a large map of the world; dozens of labels of beers and ales are connected by strings to their homes on the map. There's a more elegant side dining room with brick walls and copper tables, and upstairs are two more rooms with linened tables, fresh flowers and votive candles. The blackboard menu features cajun specialties in the style of Paul Prudhomme — blackened steak or redfish, shrimp etouffee, chicken big mamoo (in a spicy tomato sauce over spinach fettuccine) and cajun sampler, $12.95 to $16.95. The seafood file gumbo and bourbon pecan pie are highly rated. Lunch, Monday-Friday; dinner nightly, 5 to 11, to 1 on weekends.

Bandaloops, 1024 South Charles St., Federal Hill. (301) 727-1355. What the owners call "casual gourmet" food is served in a skylit atrium and three other dining rooms on two floors. Brick walls, original wide-board floors and baskets hanging from beamed ceilings create a pleasant backdrop for interesting salads, appetizers, sandwiches and entrees ($13.50 to $17.25) like cajun shrimp and oysters over linguini, Mexican chicken, salmon with five flavors, and tournedos. Steamers and oysters are available at the upstairs bar on weekends. Open Monday-Saturday, 11:30 to 11.

Cafe Vienna, 1041 Marshall St., Federal Hill. (301) 539-5550. Chef Fritz Hofer closed his popular Fritz's at Fells Point restaurant in 1990 to take over the atrium space formerly occupied by Alley Oops! near the Cross Street Market. The airy dining room with a wraparound balcony offers German fare plus specialties like leg of venison with mushrooms and bacon, selection of wild game and game birds served with cranberries and red cabbage, and a house platter of sauteed veal and pork (entrees, $12.95 to $18.95). Lunch daily, 11 to 3; dinner, 5 to 11; Sunday brunch, 10 to 3.

Harborside Choices

Bay Cafe, 2809 Boston St., Canton. (301) 522-3377. You want water, boats, sunshine, a young crowd, action? Get them all at this new place east of Fells Point, facing Fort McHenry. When we were there, water taxis cruised back and forth from Harborplace to the Bay Cafe, luring patrons with handbills and bargain prices. As if they needed more customers. The Saturday afternoon we were there the patio was closed for a private party with a calypso band, and the inside was standing-room only, though there seemed to be a few seats in the upstairs dining room with its soaring ceiling. Could the attraction be the food? It's a mixed bag of raw bar, sandwiches, burgers, gourmet pizzas and a dozen dinner entrees priced from $14.95 for broiled scallops over rice to $24.95 for lobster tail stuffed with crab imperial, served by a staff clad in fluorescent Caribbean shirts. The draw is more likely the large lounge, the jaunty patio and the views — of water and people. Open daily, 11 to 10 or 11.

The Rusty Scupper, 402 Key Highway, Federal Hill. (301) 727-3678. The Rusty Scupper chain always seems to have a corner on waterfront views, and this one is no exception. It's superbly situated right on the water at the foot of Federal Hill, across from all the harbor action. The lengthy menu is typically Rusty Scupper, embracing everything from prime rib and mesquite-grilled salmon to shrimp tempura and pastas ($11.95 to $19.95). Only certified angus beef is served. Lunch and happy hour on the outdoor decks are popular; it's a busy singles spot at night. Lunch daily, 11:30 to 2; dinner, 5 to 10 or 11.

Francie's, 1629 Browns Wharf, Fells Point. (301) 327-6500. The Haussners of local restaurant fame got the best Fells Point waterfront location for their casual new eatery run by daughter Francie. The all-day menu runs from Buffalo wings and baked brie through pastas, sandwiches and salads to entrees from $8.95 for meat loaf to $22.75 for three Maine lobster tails, taken at shiny green tables in a brick and wood dining hall with wraparound windows onto the water. Tourists give way to pub-crawlers at night. Open daily, 11:30 to 10.

Gordon's Crab House, Brown's Wharf, Fells Point. (301) 276-8660. All kinds of nautical memorabilia hang from the ceiling of this rustic, earthy restaurant opened in 1990. Brown butcher paper covers the tables, the better to enjoy hot steamed crabs in many guises, from an award-winning backfin crab cake sandwich ($6.25) to crab imperial ($11.95). Crab out on steamed garlic crabs or the broiled/fried seafood platters bringing some of everything for $15.95. Open daily, 11 a.m. to 11 p.m.

Phillips Harborplace, Light Street Pavilion, Harborplace. (301) 685-6600.

The largest and most crowded restaurant at Harborplace is this offshoot of the Ocean City seafood establishment that started as a beachfront takeout in 1957. Particularly appealing is the sidewalk cafe looking onto the water and the National Aquarium. The enormous menu typical of its genre offers oysters on the half shell, cream of crab soup, shrimp salad and crab cake sandwiches. Among entrees ($11.95 to $22.95) are eight versions of crabmeat, four seafood platters and five lobster dishes. Service is fast (those waterfront seats are coveted); at night you can wait for a table at the piano bar. If you can't wait, head for **Phillips Seafood** for takeout or **Phillips Express** in the Food Court. Open daily, 11 to 11.

Tandoor, Pratt Street Pavilion, Harborplace. (301) 547-0575. In happy contrast to Phillips and many of the standard seafood emporia is this lovable Indian restaurant, with a gorgeous second-floor view of the harbor. Dining outside on a warm spring night, we could have sworn we were at Disney World, such was the spell cast by the twinkling white lights of Harborplace and the constant parade of boats and pedestrians. The shrimp biriyani and Tandoori platter were standouts, compared with the mundane offerings of most of other Harborplace dining options, and we only had to wait ten minutes for a waterside table. Lunch and dinner daily.

Paolo's Ristorante, Light Street Pavilion, Harborplace. (301) 539-7060. An instant winner in the Harborplace sweepstakes was this offshoot of a Georgetown establishment that opened in 1990. It advertised "pizza, pasta and pizzazz" in stylish digs marked by an open kitchen, marble tables set with pink napkins and fresh flowers, an appealing outdoor area, a large bar and a quieter dining area in back with black marble tables amid lots of lovely oak trim and paneling. Paolo's features pizzas from the city's first wood-burning oven and pastas ($8.95 to $13.95) like grilled sirloin on fettuccine tossed with pesto, roasted red peppers, Bermuda onions and mushrooms. From the oak wood-fired grill come such entrees ($8.95 to $16.95) as grilled sirloin salad on seasonal greens, garlic fennel sausage over linguini, grilled jumbo shrimp, herb-grilled chicken breast with sundried tomatoes, veal hunter style and tournedos. Open daily from 11; weekend brunch, 10:30 to 4.

Other Harborplace restaurants run the gamut from Food Hall eateries of every description — some with innovative fare and no lineups — to the trendy American Cafe. Other choices include the **Bamboo House,** with oriental food and a sleek canopied and open-air pavilion; **Taverna Athena,** with an appropriate blue and white Greek look; **Mariner's Pier One,** and **City Lights.**

For the ultimate in grazing, don't miss the food stalls at the downtown **Lexington Market.** Purists and those seeking local color find it more to their liking than Harborplace. Another choice is the **Cross Street Market** on Federal Hill, where we made a stand-up lunch of prime raw oysters ($6.50 for a half dozen) and fried oyster sandwiches on plain white bread ($3.50).

FOR MORE INFORMATION: Baltimore Area Convention & Visitors Association, One East Pratt St., Baltimore, Md. 21202. (301) 659-7300 or (800) 282-6632.

Mules pull passenger barge along Delaware River canal.

Delaware River/Bucks County, Pa.-N.J.

When William Penn came upon Bucks County back in 1682, it so reminded him of Great Britain that he named it after Buckingham, the shire in which he was born.

The resemblance still is clear: A rolling countryside dropping down to the wide Delaware River, just as England's does along the Thames River west of London. Crossroads pubs and stone houses that would look at home in the Cotswolds. Narrow, winding roads eliciting rural discoveries at every turn. Even the place names are similar: Solebury, Warminster, Chalfont, Wycombe. Such is the influence of the area's English Quaker settlers.

Although the area straddling the Delaware River became a stagecoach stop on the old York turnpike linking New York and Philadelphia, it retained its rural heritage and, to this day, remains a surprisingly unspoiled refuge amid the sprawling megalopolis.

The tranquil, idyllic setting of river and hills attracted a colony of painters known as the New Hope Artists early in the 20th century. Since then it has lured thousands of visitors, most of them to New Hope, a chic town whose mystique far exceeds its size (about 1,500). Lately, the New Jersey river towns of Lambertville, Frenchtown and Milford are attracting tourists as well.

The arts colony, antiquing and the Bucks County Playhouse are prime attractions. So are several concentrations of small inns and uncommonly good restaurants.

In the midst of it all is the Delaware River, narrow and deserted as it cuts beneath hillsides and cliffs of strange-colored layers of rock at Upper Black Eddy, majestic and lazing at New Hope and Lambertville, mysterious and historic at Washington Crossing. Towpaths and canals flank the river on both sides, and islands occasionally part the river in the middle.

41

River Road (Pennsylvania Route 32) undulates along the west bank through sharp turns and the odd hamlet a slow 30 miles from Washington Crossing north to Upper Black Eddy. On the east bank, New Jersey's Route 29 speeds motorists the same distance through utterly rural terrain spelled by an occasional town.

The river, the canals and the towpaths lure people for all kinds of rest and recreation — canoeing, rafting, fishing and swimming in the water; bicycling, jogging, strolling and dining alongside. We focus here to the river and immediate environs, acknowledging that other attractions could entice you away.

The river offers so many pleasures, however, that we seldom have time or inclination to yield to the temptations beyond.

Getting There

This area along the Delaware River in Pennsylvania's Bucks County and New Jersey's Hunterdon County lies 30 miles north of Philadelphia and 60 miles southwest of New York City. Interstates 95 and 78 plus the Pennsylvania and New Jersey turnpikes are nearby. U.S. Route 202 is the main approach to New Hope and Lambertville.

Where to Stay

Travelers have paused for rest and sustenance at inns and B&Bs along the river since Colonial days. Today, the numerous but small lodging places are booked far in advance, particularly in summer and on weekends, and you won't find any large chain motels except for a Holiday Inn west of New Hope. Many inns require two-night stays on weekends (three nights for holiday weekends), and have lower weekday rates when the area isn't nearly so busy. The area could use more inns, New Hope Information Center director Marianne Speiser concedes, and visitors would enjoy a few riverfront motels.

Larger Inns

The Inn at Lambertville Station, 11 Bridge St., Lambertville, N.J. 08530. (609) 397-4400 or (800) 524-1091. In 1985, this area gained a fine, large inn on the riverfront. Following their success with the restored Lambertville Station restaurant, Dan Whitaker and his Philadelphia partners set to building the architecturally impressive, three-story luxury inn on land that had long been an eyesore at the west entrance to Lambertville. More than $3 million went into the inn, and it looks it, from the open three-story-high lobby to the most elegant of suites. You check in at a counter resembling the ticket office of an old train station, perhaps tarry for tea or a drink from the honor bar in the towering lobby (which is higher than it is wide) and get your bags up the elevator to your room. Prized antiques are in the 45 guest rooms, each named for a major city and decorated to match. Ours was the corner New York Suite, high in the trees above a rushing waterfall that lulled us to sleep. The bed is turned down at night and chocolates are left, the bathroom has a whirlpool tub, and around the L-shaped room are heavy mahogany furniture, leather chairs facing the fireplace and TV, handsome draperies, ornate mirrors and fine art. A light continental breakfast with carrot-nut muffins arrived at our door with a newspaper the next morning. Other rooms that we saw were equally impressive, all individually decorated by antiques dealer Phil Cowley, who spared no expense. Though no rooms face the river, occupants on the south side beside the woods hear the sounds of Swan Creek spilling down from the canal; those on the north side view the lights of Lambertville and New Hope glimmering on the river. The large Riverside Room, which does face the river with windows on three sides, is used for conferences and Sunday brunch ($17.95 for quite a spread). Doubles, $75 to $110; suites with fireplaces and whirlpool baths, $150.

1740 House, River Road, Lumberville, Pa. 18933. (215) 297-5661. If the Inn at Lambertville Station is the welcome new guy on the block, the 1740 House is the sprightly oldtimer, highly popular and booked far in advance. Its serenity, its quiet location in a quaint hamlet beside the Delaware and its motel-style privacy appeal to repeat visitors who book the same rooms year after year. Opened in 1967 by well-traveled New Yorker Harry Nessler and his late wife, the 1740 House was built to look old, each room in two wings opening from a front corridor and extending to patios or balconies perched out back at canal's edge. Individually decorated, the 24 spacious rooms have king or twin beds, bathrooms with showers or tubs, comfortable chairs with reading lights, nightly turndown service, and no television or phones to intrude. You help yourself to a buffet-style breakfast in the cheery garden dining room; there's always a hot dish like scrambled eggs or creamed chipped beef. A three-course dinner with choice of three entrees is available to house guests; you order when you make your dinner reservation and bring your own wine. You'll want time to enjoy the peace and quiet of the river from your balcony or porch, catch some sun around the small pool, read in a couple of small parlors, meander up River Road to the center of Lumberville and walk the canal towpath or cross the footbridge to an island park in New Jersey. Doubles, $72 to $93. No credit cards.

Centre Bridge Inn, River Road, Box 74, Star Route, New Hope, Pa. 18938. (215) 862-2048. Wonderfully situated beside the Delaware across from the pleasant New Jersey village of Stockton, this striking white structure with red shutters built in Colonial Williamsburg style has a large restaurant-tavern and nine sumptuous guest rooms. Fires destroyed inns that had occupied the site since 1705, so this is of early 1960s vintage. After checking in downstairs in the restaurant, you return to the main floor and are let in through a locked door to an enormous formal vestibule, with a fireplaced parlor on the river side. Ahead are a pair of two-room suites, one with a foyer leading into the main room with queensize canopy bed, two plush blue chairs on thick carpeting, TV set, cedar-lined bath and private riverview deck — "our nicest room," according to our guide. The other suite in front has a queen brass bed and sitting room with sofa, loveseat and TV. Upstairs are seven more rooms, many with canopy beds and three with TV. All are air-conditioned, have private baths, and are notable for colorful Schumacher wall coverings. A continental breakfast is served in the suites, the parlor or outside on a deck off the main floor, which has one of the best views of the river anywhere. Doubles, $80 to $125.

Evermay-on-the-Delaware, River Road, Erwinna, Pa. 18920. (215) 294-9100. A three-story gold and tan Victorian mansion set back on a broad lawn facing the river, Evermay is the bed-and-breakfast and gourmet-dinner venture of Ron Strouse and Fred Cresson, who were known for their cuisine at the Sign of the Sorrel Horse in Quakertown. Evermay's twenty guest rooms, all with private baths, are furnished in fine Victoriana. We found ours in the Carriage House a bit cold and spare, despite the presence of fresh flowers and a large bowl of fresh fruit. Some inn rooms retain the original fireplaces; walnut beds, oriental rugs, marble-topped dressers, fancy quilts and lacy pillows are among the furnishings. Downstairs in the double front parlor, where afternoon tea is served at 4, a fire often burns in the fireplace and decanters of sherry are at the ready. An excellent continental breakfast is served in the conservatory dining room at the rear; we liked the incredibly flaky croissants and a magnificent compote of fresh fruit. Prix-fixe dinners of five or six courses with a choice of two entrees are served Friday-Sunday at 7:30. We remember with relish an extraordinary fall dinner of lamb noisettes and poached Norwegian salmon, beautifully presented with exotic accompaniments. Doubles, $70 to $135.

Hotel du Village, River Road and Phillips Mill Road, New Hope. Pa. 18938. (215) 862-9911. A Tudor English manor house dispenses renowned French nouvelle cuisine and a converted stable to the rear contains twenty air-conditioned guest rooms and suites with private baths. Old-fashioned beds and quilts are the rule. Guests have access to two tennis courts and a pool on the lovely grounds that were part of a land grant from William Penn. An impressive country estate was built on the property in the late 19th century, and from 1917 to 1976 it was the site of the Solebury School's Lower Campus. Algerian chef-owner Omar Arbani and his wife Barbara converted it into a restaurant and inn in 1978. Across River Road is the canal and next door are the spectacular grounds of Lenteboden, home of bulb specialist Charles Mueller. A complimentary continental breakfast is served. Doubles, $85 to $100.

The Logan Inn, 10 West Ferry St., New Hope, Pa. 18938. (215) 862-2300. The oldest building in New Hope and one of the five oldest inns in the country, this 1722 structure was restored in 1988 by Steve Kates into what is billed as an intimate luxury inn. Its sixteen air-conditioned rooms on two floors have private tiled baths, phones and television sets hidden in cabinets and armoires. Most of the furniture is Shaker reproduction, and each room has Colonial pieces, antiques, wall-to-wall carpeting and prints of a local artist on the walls. Down comforters and all-cotton sheets are on the beds, many of them canopy fourposters. We found Room 7, the southwest corner, quite spacious and comfortable, but as for Room 6 across the hall, no thanks. It's haunted, the manager said; it seems the bathroom mirror is always mysteriously splattered, the room is always cold, despite its southeast exposure, and whenever anyone takes a photo, nine times out of ten it doesn't come out! The other rooms are fine, however. The Logan is one of the few area inns that welcomes children, providing trundle beds and cribs. A complimentary breakfast is served in the airy greenhouse **Garden Room,** one of a number of dining areas — most popular in summer is the front courtyard covered by a canopy and great for watching the passing action. Three meals a day are served, and there's a tavern menu. Doubles, $95 to $125.

Hacienda Inn, 36 West Mechanic St., New Hope, Pa. 18938. (215) 862-2078 or (800) 272-2078. Another place good for families, this motel-inn-apartment-restaurant-bistro complex has a variety of accommodations. "I built it all myself," says owner Pamela Minford; "this was all swamp down here when we started in 1962." You'd never know it today. A series of white structures with bright yellow shutters in the heart of town offers small rooms beside the village's only heated swimming pool, gallery rooms, studio rooms, luxury rooms, suites and hideaways, a total of 30 in all. Twelve have fireplaces and one a jacuzzi. Those we saw were unexpectedly plush in an old-school way, had lots of space and their furnishings varied from twin beds to queen canopies, loveseats to sectionals. All have private baths, phones and TV. Some have terraces overlooking Ingham Spring Creek. Room rates include a $20 credit toward dinner in the inn's large restaurant or bistro. Doubles, $75 to $135.

Small Inns and B&Bs

Bridgeton House, River Road, Box 167, Upper Black Eddy, Pa. 18972. (215) 982-5856. This onetime wreck of an apartment house built in 1836 has been transformed with sweat and love by Bea and Charles Briggs into a comfortable B&B with a glorious location beside the river. Although smack up against the road, the inn has been opened to the rear for a water orientation. Lovely stenciling, fresh or dried flowers, a decanter of sherry and potpourri grace the dining room. A rear parlor and upstairs balconies look onto a landscaped courtyard beside the canal. Most of the ten guest rooms overlook the water, each exceptionally fashioned by Charles, a master carpenter and renovator, and interestingly decorated by Bea. Some have four-posters and chaise-lounges; all have private baths, country antiques, colorful sheets, fresh flowers and intriguing touches. Our main-floor room had a private porch with rockers and lovely stenciling. The dramatic new penthouse suite is Bucks County's ultimate, with its twelve-foot cathedral ceiling, a kingsize bed, black and white marble fireplace, marble bathtub, backgammon table, black leather chairs, a stereo-TV center and a full-length deck. A full breakfast brings fresh breads or muffins and a hot dish like cheddar cheese omelet or scrambled eggs. Doubles, $75 to $115; suite, $130 to $165. No smoking.

Chestnut Hill on the Delaware, 63 Church St., Milford, N.J. 08848. (201) 995-9761. The river lazes past this 1860 Victorian house, considered the grandest in town, and a great place to view it is from the long lineup of rockers on the veranda just a shady front yard away. Linda and Rob Castagna offer five guest rooms, two of which can be joined as a suite. Two have private baths and the rest share. The Pineapple Room has a reading area and color TV, as does the suite. Guests are served an ample breakfast at the large lace-covered table in the dining room — perhaps German apple pancakes "or whatever I'm in the mood to do," says Linda. Apothecary wall units in a formal drawing room in the Eastlake tradition contain books, gifts and potpourri. Next door is the Country Cottage by the River, a self-contained suite with living room, fireplaced bedroom and kitchen, renting for $125 a night (two-night minimum) or $600 a week. Doubles, $70 to $85. No smoking.

Isaac Stover House, Route 32, Erwinna, Pa. 18920. (215) 294-8044. This 1837 Victorian Federal mansion across the road from the Delaware was acquired in 1988 by radio-TV personality Sally Jessy Raphael, who has furnished it with theatrics and whimsey. The collections from her globe-trotting travels are showcased in typical Victorian clutter through the seven guest rooms, five with private baths. The owner's favorite, the third-floor Cupid's Bower, is a confection of pink ruffles and lace. Wizard of Oz paraphernalia marks the fireplaced Emerald City Room, a beauty in deep greens. A poofed valance borders the ceiling of the Amore Room, which has a river view and the inn's only queensize bed. A big potted plant with fake flowers adorns the Secret Garden room. The Bridal Suite, all lace, has its own sitting room with a small TV. Swags, tassels, stuffed animals, oriental tapestries, crystal chandeliers — you name it, it's bound to be somewhere here. Although you won't likely see the owner — she gets here only a couple of times a month, says innkeeper Susan Tettemer — you can see her picture in the bathroom of the Loyalty Royalty room, and others are scattered throughout the house. The red velvet chairs and settees, moire draperies, lace antimacassars and silk pillows from Burma are a sight to behold in the formal parlor, where Balinese shadow puppets and a tapestry from Malta are showcased above the marble fireplace. There's an upstairs television nook with books and games, and a front porch is outfitted in white wicker and black wrought iron. Cookies, fruit, beverages, wine and cheese are put out in the afternoon, and truffles are at bedside. In the morning, Susan serves a hearty repast (perhaps potato-cheese frittata, crepes or an asparagus omelet) amid crocheted tops, lacy cloths and crystal chandeliers in a pretty breakfast room. Doubles, $150 to $175; suite, $250.

Pineapple Hill, 1324 River Road, New Hope, Pa. 18938. (215) 862-9608. This 18th-century Bucks County farmhouse is one of the few places in which to stay south of New Hope. The pineapple motif, symbolizing welcome, appears throughout the house, and candles are lit in the windows to add to the warmth. The five guest rooms are clustered in separate areas on the second and third floors, affording privacy for families or couples traveling together. One is a suite with bedroom, sitting room and bath. Three of the four other guest rooms have private baths. Rooms sport country or primitive antiques, stenciling, displays of pewter and perhaps a corner cupboard filled with china or walls covered with quilts. Guests gather for breakfast in a large fireplaced common room, where innkeeper Linda Chaize offers things like eggs strata or different kinds of pancakes. Out back are lovely gardens and a wonderful swimming pool built in the stone ruins of a barn, and beyond is the towpath by the canal. Doubles, $70 to $120. No smoking.

Seeing and Doing

Many are the attractions and varied the appeal of the Delaware River and the narrow canals on both sides. Built in the 1830s, the Delaware Division Canal was used for floating coal and limestone from Easton through New Hope south to Bristol. During its 60-mile course, barges dropped 165 feet through 25 locks and under 106 bridges. New Hope was the only point on the canal where four barges could pass at once, and after 1854, barges shuttled across the Delaware River to Lambertville and the Delaware & Raritan Canal, and thence to Princeton, Newark and New York. The last shipments of coal and manufactured goods were floated down the canal about 1930. These days, there is rarely enough water in the canal for the traditional canoeing except in the immediate New Hope area. Pennsylvania's Delaware Division Canal has become the Theodore Roosevelt State Park and a National Historic Landmark. Most of New Jersey's Raritan canal also is a state park.

On or Near the Water

Walk the Towpath. We thoroughly enjoy walking the canal towpaths along the river, particularly the Pennsylvania portion between Lumberville and Phillips Mill and particularly in spring when the daffodils are abloom. Start in Lumberville at the footbridge to Bull's Island, a New Jersey state park. The Black Bass Hotel's friendly duck may greet you, the gardens and back yards of English-type manor houses are sure to intrigue, and everywhere are wildflowers, singing birds, joggers, picnickers and other strollers. A footbridge leads to the Cuttalossa Inn, where the outdoor terrace appeals for lunch or a drink; you can stop at the Centre Bridge Inn for a drink, or cross the highway bridge to Stockton, N.J., to pick up a picnic lunch at Errico's Market and a bottle of wine at the incredibly well-stocked Phillips wine store. Just downriver is Phillips Mill, an ever-so-British looking cluster of stone houses hugging the River Road, and the colorful grounds of **Lenteboden,** the business and residence of Charles Mueller, the bulb specialist whose gardens full of daffodils, tulips and hyacinths herald the arrival of spring. Like almost everything else along the towpath, they're free and open for the exploring. A word of caution: the towpath walk is lulling and may take the better part of a day; unless you have a car meeting you at the end, you'll have to walk back or hitch a ride, as we did (and it took almost an hour before anyone stopped).

Canoeing, Rafting and Tubing. The river is so popular for these pastimes that in 24 years, owner Tom McBrien has turned his **Point Pleasant Canoe & Tubing** enterprise in Point Pleasant, Pa., into the East's largest water recreation facility. Tubing is the biggest operation, with up to 3,500 people a day renting inner tubes for floats of three to six miles (adults $12, children $10). Canoeists are transported up to Tinicum, Upper Black Eddy or Riegelsville for trips downriver of six to twelve miles ($15 to $20 per person). The season is April-October, daily Memorial Day to Labor Day, weekends in spring and fall, 297-8823. McBrien says there's nothing like floating or paddling down the Delaware, watching fish leaping and osprey feeding, and pausing for a swim in the warm, clear waters. At our last visit, he was expanding activity at his Upper Black Eddy and Martin's Creek bases and was planning to open the Delaware Canal's first floating barge restaurant.

Boat Rides. Gen. George Washington advised: "Be sure to take the ferry by Coryell's as it is the swiftest, surest route." We can't say **Coryell's Ferry** is the swiftest, but it is the surest way for the public to see the New Hope section of the river. Capt. Robert Gerenser, whose name is attached to much activity and enterprise in New Hope, gives scenic half-hour excursions with an informative narrative on a pontoon boat from 22 South Main St., New Hope, 862-2050. Rides leave hourly on the hour from 11 to 5, spring through fall. Adults $5, children $3. Occasional excursions are offered by **Wells Ferry Boat Rides,** 14 East Ferry St., New Hope, 862-5965.

Fishing. Considered one of the best fishing rivers in the East, the Delaware is known to harbor more than 30 species, including trout, bass, muskies and pike. Whenever we visit in the spring, the shad seem to be running and the fishermen are out in force, in boats or in hip boots just offshore in the Lumberville-Bull's Island launch areas. All the activity is a sight to behold from the balcony at the 1740 House.

New Hope Mule Barge Co., New and South Main Streets, New Hope, 862-2842. Mule-drawn barges bring back the past for hundreds of visitors daily on the old Delaware Canal. The barges have been hauling tourists since 1931 after the canal's commercial usage ended. Spanish-Colombian Leo Ramirez and German George Schweickhardt have owned the four-barge operation since 1976. At their outlying farm they care for nine mules that draw the barges two miles up the river past Colonial homes, artists' workshops, gardens and countryside to the Route 202 bridge and back. A musician-historian relates canal lore and strums folk songs. The one-hour excursion costs $6.95 for adults, $4.25 for children. May 1 to Oct. 15, daily at 11:30, 1, 2, 3, 4:30 and 6; April and to Nov. 15, reduced hours Wednesday, Saturday and Sunday.

Covered Bridges. Thirteen of 36 covered bridges built in Bucks County remain standing, crossing creeks and canals. A self-guided driving tour available at the information center gives locations and details for each.

Washington Crossing Historic Park, Pa., 493-4076. History was made here in 1776 when George Washington and 2,400 troops crossed the Delaware on Christmas night to attack Trenton. Now it's a large state park in two sections.

The northern Thompson Mill section is two miles south of New Hope. It features **Bowman's Tower,** a 110-foot-high stone observation point with an elevator (admission, $2). From the top of the site where sentries watched enemy troop movements you get a panoramic view of river and valley. Around the tower is a 100-acre **Wild Flower Preserve,** with 26 acres of trails and habitat areas plus a headquarters building with gift shop and displays. Across River Road is the 1702 **Thompson-Neely House,** requisitioned in 1776 as a battle headquarters and now a museum, as well as a grist mill and picnic areas.

Four miles south is the park's southern section and visitor center. Here a 25-minute film tells the story of how George Washington and his half-frozen troops regrouped at this location from encampments stretching from New Hope to Yardley to cross the river and capture Trenton. The film ends rather abruptly, we thought. Then you can take a walking tour and enter three historic buildings for $3. Included are the **McConkey Ferry Inn,** where Washington is believed to have eaten dinner the night before the Battle of Trenton, the 1816 **Taylor House** and the Thompson-Neely House to the north. One area of this park has a picturesque lagoon populated by incredible numbers of Canada geese and other birds, surrounded by picnicking facilities.

Across the Delaware River bridge is New Jersey's **Washington Crossing State Park,** which has a visitor center, the **Ferry House Inn,** an overlook area, nature trails, an open-air theater for the Summer Festival of Performing Arts, the **George Washington Memorial Arboretum** and the **Nelson House** museum.

The biggest event of the year is the annual reenactment of Washington's crossing of the Delaware at 1 p.m. on Dec. 25. The dress rehearsal about two weeks earlier offers a quieter preview.

Parks generally open daily; hours vary.

Around the Towns

Walk New Hope. New Hope, a compact village, is made for walking. That's fortunate, because in summer things get really congested; outlying lots charge an average of $4 for parking, and it's best to leave your car. The small information center in the 1839 jail-town hall at South Main and Mechanic streets logged a staggering 6,577 visitors one August. A short New Hope walking tour guides you to the East Ferry Street landing and mill complex, the hub of early village life (now including Martine's restaurant, Farley's New Delaware Bookshop and the Bucks County Playhouse), the historic Logan Inn, the 1784 **Parry Mansion Museum** (open for tours, May-October, Friday-Sunday 1 to 5; adults $4, children 50 cents) and the old houses of West Ferry Street (they're among the town's 243 properties included in 1985 on the National Register of Historic Places). We'd also suggest strolling along the Delaware Canal park and gardens, through the alleys filled with art galleries, and along the streets lined with more shops than we can possibly enumerate. Take our word: if it's for sale, someone in New Hope or environs carries it.

Walk across the Delaware River bridge from New Hope to **Lambertville,** an up-and-coming riverside town of interesting shops (many featuring antiques) and restaurants.

For the ultimate rural small-town experience, walk through tiny **Lumberville** and savor the past, including the historic Black Bass Hotel and Gerald Gordon's **Lumberville Store,** which dates to 1770 and encompasses the post office, an art gallery, food and sandwiches, books and bicycle rentals.

Wine Bars and Pubs. A favorite pastime of many is stopping at a wine bar, something of an early local phenomenon. The **Boat House** wine bar at the Porkyard in Lambertville is nearest the water; the **Swan Hotel** at 43 South Main St. is a large and extraordinary bar with much atmosphere and food service. Nearby is **The Elephant and Castle,** 74 South Union St., an English pub and restaurant with four British ales and hard cider on draught. Another popular spot for English pub food and a pint of bitter is the **Ship's Inn** in Milford.

New Hope & Ivyland Railroad, 32 West Bridge St., New Hope, 862-2332. The 1891 New Hope train station with its witch-hat peak has been restored as part of a museum that includes a 1906 wooden baggage car and the Freight House Gift Shop. The steam locomotive and vintage 1920s Reading Railroad passenger coaches take passengers on a nine-mile, 50-minute round trip up Solebury Mountain to Lahaska and back. New owners were planning frequent trips daily starting in spring 1991 from the New Hope Station. Adults $6.50, children $3.25.

Bucks County Carriages, West End Farm, Route 32, New Hope, 862-5883. Shawn McCook offers horse-drawn carriage rides around New Hope daily from March-November. A twenty-minute ride costs $8.50 per person. Horseback rides also are available.

Bucks County Playhouse, 70 South Main St., New Hope, 862-2041. The old town mill that backs up to the river ceased operating in 1938. It was purchased by local citizens who turned it into a summer stock theater, which debuted in 1939 with Edward Everett Horton in "Springtime for Henry." The 457-seat theater runs an ambitious 30-week schedule from May 1 to late December, Tuesday-Sunday in summer (with Wednesday and Thursday matinees) and differing schedules in spring and fall. Tickets, $13 to $15.

ART GALLERIES. The number of galleries doubled in two years lately in New Hope, long a noted art colony, in the more recent concentration around Lahaska and in newly blossoming Lambertville. The New Hope-Lambertville Gallery Association lists twenty galleries in the area.

ANTIQUING. "The East Coast mecca for antiques" is how one advocate describes the area. The largest concentration is in Lahaska, where the Lahaska Antique Courte, for instance, claims twelve distinctive shops and the Bucks County Antiques Dealers Association lists six more. Others are in New Hope, Lambertville and small towns on both sides of the river.

Where to Eat

Dining is a big deal along the Delaware, and the choices are legion. Some restaurants do not have liquor licenses, but allow guests to bring their own.

North of New Hope

The Frenchtown Inn, 7 Bridge St., Frenchtown, N.J. (201) 996-3300. Opened in 1986 by Robert and Holly Long, this outstanding restaurant draws rave reviews. Robert Long's food is inventive and superb, the service friendly yet flawless, and the setting comfortable. Arriving for a Friday lunch without reservations, we found the front dining room with its planked ceiling, brick walls and carpeted floors full. So we were seated in the more austere columned dining room in the rear, outfitted with pink and green wallpaper, crisp white linens and Villeroy & Boch china. Everything on the menu looked great; we can vouch for an unusual and airy black bean soup, the selection of pates and terrines ($5.75 — small but very smooth and good), the corned beef sandwich on brown bread and a sensational salad of duck and smoked pheasant with a warm cider vinaigrette ($7.75), loaded with meat and mixed greens like radicchio and arugula. A layered pear-raspberry tart with whipped cream was a perfect dessert. On the spring dinner menu, the seven entrees ran from $17.75 for sauteed sea scallops on a bed of mixed beans with curry oil and croutons of saffron rouille to $24.75 for rack of lamb with triangles of seared confit lamb and a mousseline of eggplant en cocotte. Robert Long was chef at the Tarragon Tree in Chatham, N.J., and worked in Paris before finding his culinary niche in Frenchtown. Lunch, Tuesday-Saturday noon to 2; dinner, Tuesday-Friday 6 to 9, Saturday 5:30 to 9:30; Sunday, brunch noon to 2, dinner 5:30 to 8:30.

The Inn at Phillips Mill, North River Road, New Hope, Pa. (215) 862-9919. For charm and good food, this quaint gray stone building right next to a bend in the River Road is tops. Looking as if it had been transported from the British Cotswolds, the 1750 structure has a copper pig above the entrance — a symbol of the stone barn's origin as a gristmill that stood next to the village piggery. Architect Brooks Kaufman and his innkeeper wife Joyce transformed it into a country French restaurant, plus a cozy inn with five cheerily decorated guest rooms upstairs. The dining setting could not be more romantic: candles augmenting light from the fireplace in low-ceilinged rooms with dark beams, and arrangements of flowers all around. The chef's terrine and escargots with garlic butter are favored appetizers. We liked the sauteed calves liver in a cider vinegar and the steak au poivre, chosen among ten entrees from $14.50 to $18.50. A dessert of vanilla mousse with big chips of chocolate and a chocolate fudge sauce made a worthy ending. Dinner nightly, 5:30 to 9:30 or 10. BYOB; no credit cards.

Centre Bridge Inn, River Road, New Hope, Pa. (215) 862-2048. The downstairs tavern-dining room with beamed ceilings, stucco walls and huge open fireplaces could not be more attractive, nor the glass-enclosed porch overlooking the river more inviting. Outside by the river is a brick patio with white wrought-iron furniture and a circle of granite tables around a fountain. Here is the ultimate waterside setting, and if some think that the food doesn't necessarily measure up to the surroundings, who cares? The short continental menu is relatively unchanging: appetizers about $9.50 for house pate, escargot en croute and shrimp and lobster mousseline; entrees ($22.95 to $31.95) like roast duckling montmorency, veal champignon, poached lobster cardinal, steak au poivre and rack of lamb persille. Cappuccino and international coffees are available, and we recall a happy evening sipping after-dinner drinks at the bar as a pianist entertained. Dinner, Monday-Saturday 5:30 to 9:30 or 10, Sunday 3 to 9.

Cuttalossa Inn, River Road, Lumberville, Pa. (215) 297-5082. Another place where the food may not live up to the surroundings is the venerable Cuttalossa, but it's not for lack of trying. New owner Marilyn MacMaster, something of a showperson, travels the world to find new recipes. And the setting is tough to beat: an 1833 stone landmark, with three history-filled dining rooms inside and a large outdoor terrace beside a millstream and waterfall, where we'd gladly have an al fresco lunch anytime. The dinner menu mixes continental and American ($18 to $26): crab imperial, duckling bigarade, and veal cacciatore and oscar; stir-fry scallops and asparagus with ginger butter, baked salmon with crunchy cream cheese and cucumber sauce, and prime rib. You might start with smoked oysters with raspberry vinaigrette and finish with homemade strawberry cheesecake. Stop for a drink in the outdoor bar, illuminated at night by twinkling white lights; with the woods and the stone buildings and the roar of the falls in the background, it's rather magical. Lunch, Monday-Saturday 11 to 3; dinner, Monday-Saturday 5 to 9 or 10.

Black Bass Hotel, Route 32, Lumberville, Pa. (215) 297-5770. The food here goes up and down with changing chefs, but there's no beating the river view goes up and down with changing chefs, but there's no beating the river view from the rear dining rooms, full of historic memorabilia and atmosphere. At our latest visit, the food was said to be very good again, and the Sunday brunch for $22.50 was considered one of the best around. We like this place for lunch, when you can see outside to feast on the scenery. Many favor the Charleston Meeting Street crab, a menu fixture ($12.95), but you can get a poached seafood and grapefruit salad with poppyseed dressing or old-fashioned chicken and dumplings, priced from $6.95. Dinner entrees range from $17.95 for chicken pojarski with paprika sauce to $24.95 for aforementioned crab. Chocolate chip cheesecake and rum cream pie are good desserts. Lunch, Monday-Saturday noon to 3, dinner, 5:30 to 9; Sunday, brunch 11 to 2:30; dinner 4:30 to 8:30.

Golden Pheasant Inn, River Road, Erwinna, Pa. (215) 294-9595. The glamorous plant-filled solarium once was the setting for a memorable meal, so after the Golden Pheasant had declined, we were glad to hear it was purchased by French chef Michel Faure, who was well regarded at the nearby Carversville Inn and Philadelphia's Le Bec Fin. He and his wife Barbara, who oversees the front of the house, have restored the two dark inner Victorian dining rooms to an elegant country French look of the 1850 period, a vast improvement, and were renovating six upstairs guest rooms when we visited. We'd still choose the solarium, where you can see the canal and the trees illuminated at night, for one of Michel's dinner creations: perhaps his renowned lobster bisque, pheasant pate or croustade of wild mushrooms with bordelaise sauce for appetizers; filet of salmon with champagne and shrimp sauce, medallions of pork dijonnaise or entrecote au poivre for entrees ($19.95 to $26.95). For dessert, try the fresh raspberry puree with Belgian white chocolate mousse. Dinner, Tuesday-Sunday 5:30 to 9 or 10.

Olde Mill Ford Oyster House, 17 Bridge St., Milford, N.J. (201) 995-9411. When a restaurant has an adjacent fish market, you can bet the seafood will be fresh. That's one reason the Oyster House is highly regarded across the area. Another is the prices, with the most expensive entree (shellfish stew) going for $17.95. The menu is quite simple: dishes like shrimp in beer batter, New England baked scallops and stuffed flounder with shrimp sauce. The many nightly specials might include crab Norfolk, beer-braised rabbit, and roast duckling with sweet potatoes and brandied peach orange sauce. A local woman makes the pies, and there's an ice cream crepe with chocolate rum sauce. The three small dining rooms, plain but fresh looking, have oriental rugs and blue and white tablecloths. Fetch your wine from the Milford Liquor Store next door; with a selection of 250 you will surely find what you want. Dinner, Wednesday-Monday 4 to 9 or 10. Closed Tuesday and month of January. BYOB; no credit cards.

Meil's Restaurant, Bridge and Main Streets, Stockton, N.J. (609) 397-8033. The prices are right and the menu extensive at this cramped little bakery and restaurant, which moved here in 1990 from Lambertville. There are picnic tables in front, which we eyed for lunch on a warm January day. We sampled a classic salad nicoise ($6.50) and a not-so-classic huevos rancheros ($7.95), the salsa lacking fresh coriander and with an unexpected and unwanted ton of chili between the eggs and the tortilla. All kinds of interesting salads, sandwiches and egg dishes are featured at lunch, when something called "Day after Thanksgiving" (you must know what that means) tops off the menu at $9.95. Night brings some of the daytime fare as well as hefty pastas and fourteen main courses from $11.95 for meatloaf platter to $18.95 for shrimp scampi. The place packs in the hungry; you also can get almost anything from buttermilk biscuits and blueberry muffins to beef stew and chicken pot pie to go. Breakfast daily, 9 to 3; lunch, to 3; dinner, 4:30 to 9 or 10. No credit cards.

The Bridge Cafe, 8 Bridge St., Frenchtown, N.J. (201) 996-6040. Casual country fare is available in this little train station converted to a bakery and deli-cafe. There are five tables with a river view, and a tiny brick patio by the river. Lunch on an asparagus-mushroom-cheese quiche or knockwurst with kraut, or perhaps a smoked turkey and brie croissant sandwich ($4 to $7 range). Get scones for English tea, or a cup of cappuccino. Everything from salads to pies is available for takeout. Open Tuesday-Sunday, 7 to 6 in summer, to 5 in winter.

Great American Grill and Food Store, Routes 32 and 611, Kintnersville, Pa. (215) 847-2023. Folks in upper Bucks County like this vast place for casual family fare in informal surroundings. Behind the store is a large dining area where patrons doodle with crayons on the paper-covered tables, munch on greasy popcorn and sample finger foods. The varied menu offers everything from sandwiches to pasta to ribs at lunch and dinner. One night we had pork ribs ($7.95) and grilled chicken with a saute of vegetables ($10.95), washed down with a $20 bottle of Robert Mondavi fume blanc. The cheapest white wine, it came in an ice-filled pail. Open daily, 11:30 to 9 or 10.

In Town, Near the River

Hamilton's Grill Room, 8 1/2 Coryell St., Lambertville, N.J. (609) 397-4343. Hidden at the end of an alley in the Porkyard complex beside the canal and towpath is the culinary star of Lambertville. Former Broadway set designer Jim Hamilton and his daughter, Melissa, opened to immediate acclaim in 1988. "I designed the place," said Jim, an architect who designs other restaurants, "and Melissa established the food service." He installed an open grill beside the entrance and built the wood-fired pizza oven himself. Melissa produced a menu featuring Mediterranean grill fare. Patrons dine at tables rather close together in the grill room, the Bishop's Room beneath angels and clouds surrounding a huge gilt mirror on the ceiling, the new gallery (taking space from the art gallery next door) and, in season, outdoors around the fountain on the courtyard. Seafood is the specialty, the shellfish delivered twice weekly from Boston and the other fish coming from Philadelphia. Our convivial winter's meal began with grilled shrimp with anchovy sauce and a crab cake with wilted greens and sweet red pepper sauce, chosen among appetizers priced from $4.75 to $9.50. Entrees range from $13.75 for roasted chicken with herbs to $18.75 for grilled ribeye steak. We sampled an exceptional grilled duck on bitter greens with pancetta and honey glaze and a rather tough marinated lamb brochette. The oversize plates were filled with fanned razor-thin sliced potatoes and grilled zucchini and green and red peppers. The dense chocolate almond meringue torte was almost too rich, and two biscotti came with the bill. The warm salads and pastas are interesting here. While the main grill is BYOB (our white wine was served with ice in a pail), Hamilton's serves its regular menu at the **Wine Bar** across the courtyard on weekends for folks who want full liquor service. Dinner, Tuesday-Saturday 6 to 10 or 11, Sunday 5 to 10. BYOB.

Lambertville Station, 11 Bridge St., Lambertville, N.J. (609) 397-8300. The once-abandoned 2 1/2-story train station has been transformed into a stylish Victorian restaurant and lounge that fairly ooze atmosphere. Diners on several levels of the glass-enclosed Platform Room can watch geese glide by on the Delaware Raritan Canal and tiny lights reflecting off the water. With good-size drinks, our party of four sampled the unusual appetizer of alligator strips ($7.95), which you dip into a mustard and green peppercorn sauce — novel but interesting, and so popular that now it's offered as a main course as well, sauteed with lemon butter for $15.75. Among entrees ($11.25 to $19.95), the jambalaya was spicy, the boneless roast duck was properly crispy and had a raspberry sauce, the seafood fettuccine was more than ample and the veal medallions with jumbo shrimp in garlic butter were excellent. The honey-mustard dressing on the house spinach salad was super. Lime-almond cheesecake and key lime mousse pie were good desserts. The Sunset on the Delaware special, served weekdays from 4 to 6:30, is considered one of the best bargains around: soup or salad, entree and dessert for $9.95. A Victorian lounge is on the mezzanine. Lunch, Monday-Saturday 11:30 to 3; dinner, Monday-Thursday and Sunday 4 to 10, Friday and Saturday 5 to 11; Sunday brunch, 10:30 to 3.

The Landing, 22 North Main St., New Hope, Pa. (215) 862-5711. The only restaurant with a river view in the heart of New Hope is tucked back off the main street in a small house with windows onto the water and a rear patio with a great view of the river. Two small dining rooms on either side of a bar also offer what many consider the best food in town. The limited menu appeals, from beef carpaccio and smoked duck slices on a green peppercorn vinaigrette for appetizers, grilled yellowfin tuna with sundried tomatoes and venison medallions with bacon and rosemary for main courses ($17.95 to $22.95). You might find grilled flank steak with jerk spices and tropical fruit salsa, cajun crayfish ravioli, beer-batter chicken or a quiche of brussels sprouts and sundried tomatoes on the lunch menu. Desserts are to groan over: cranberry-walnut tartlet, truffle torte with grand marnier and chocolate macadamia cake. Lunch daily, 11 to 4; dinner nightly from 5. Closed Monday and Tuesday in winter. No smoking.

Mothers, 34 North Main St., New Hope, Pa. (215) 862-9354. If you can get by the spectacular desserts in the glass case at the entrance and put up with the usual crowds waiting for a table, you'll be rewarded with some of the most interesting food in town. The choice is staggering. At dinner, for instance, you could snack on sesane walnut chicken wings, beef sate or fried chestnut balls with cranberry dipping sauce. Or you could get pork ravioli or a duck and sweet potato pizza. Or a dijon leek duck with cornbread stuffing, Indian chicken curry, Jamaican filet mignon, tuna with pistachio-lime butter or teriyaki tofu. Or, for dessert, chocolate-strawberry cake, mocha-hazelnut cake or an almond meringue filled with rum butter cream, almonds and chocolate. And that's just for dinner; you can imagine what they do for breakfast and lunch. Prices aren't inexpensive (dinner entrees, $15.50 to $19.50), but you can mix and match. There's full bar service, the minimum dining charge is $3.50, and the menu warns that "Momma don't allow no cigar or pipe smoking here." The several small dining rooms, all tile and brick with beamed ceilings, are lively and intimate, and there's courtyard dining in back. Breakfast, Monday-Friday 8 to 2, weekends 9 to 2; lunch, 11 to 5; dinner, 5 to 10 or midnight.

Martine's, 7 East Ferry St., New Hope, Pa. (215) 862-2966. Originally a salt store that was part of the first village center built around a ferry, this mid-18th century structure combines American history and a French bistro atmosphere. The small upstairs dining room is country French with beamed ceilings, small-paned windows, simple wood chairs and delicate stained-glass lamps hanging over handsome tile tables; the downstairs pub has tile booths and a fireplace. The outdoor cafe is popular in season. The classic French menu has some trendy touches: sauteed pork tenderloin with oriental orange sauce and roast duckling with maple-pecan bourbon glaze. Dinner prices run from $16.50 for grilled chicken breast nicoise to $22 for seafood paella. Interesting salads and pastas are featured at lunch, as are omelets and croissants at breakfast. The fancy wine list contains good values. Breakfast, lunch and dinner daily.

Havana, 105 South Main St., New Hope, Pa. (215) 862-9897. The best burgers in town are featured on the all-day menu at this trendy place with a canopied sidewalk cafe, a windowed front dining room and a noisy bar with live entertainment nightly behind. The tropical, fluorescent pink and green decor and the food attract a younger crowd. Hickory-grilled burgers are served seven ways, one of them with smoked mozzarella and sundried tomatoes ($7). Among sandwiches are Philly cheesesteak, grilled tandoori chicken on Indian fry bread, Peking duck in pita and Mexican chicken fajitas ($5 for BLT to $10 for hickory-grilled swordfish on French bread). They're more interesting than the salads, but there are plenty of light entrees and more substantial fare on the daily lunch and dinner specials, listed on sheets as lengthy as many a restaurant menu. Dinners go from $6 for pierogies or black beans and rice to $16.50 for bouillabaisse or grilled salmon with creme fraiche and golden caviar. Desserts are rich, rich, rich. Open daily, 11 a.m. to midnight.

Hacienda Inn, 36 West Mechanic St., New Hope. (215) 862-2078. Since Pamela Minford renovated her age-old Spanish restaurant from heavy red and black to lighter Southwest decor, locals think this is much improved. The main floor is a ramble of rooms with beige-linened tables, chrome-back chairs, mirrored walls, cactus plants and a collection of handsome clocks for sale. The extensive menu lists "gourmet entrees" from $8.95 for fried chicken to $17.95 for baby rack of lamb with mint sauce or jelly. Pamela says her namesake seafood au gratin, deviled crab and prime rib are perennial favorites. At our visit, she was renovating the downstairs into **El Patio Bistro,** with what she said would be a trendy all-day menu of Southwest appetizers, pizzas and chargrilled light entrees, at prices under $7.95. Lunch daily, noon to 2; dinner from 5; fewer hours in winter, but Bistro open noon to midnight year-round.

Wildflowers, 8 West Mechanic St., New Hope, Pa. (215) 862-2241. "Dedicated to yesterday's charm" is this little restaurant and garden cafe backing up to Ingham Spring Creek in downtown New Hope. That translates to low prices and Bucks County home cooking. Entrees, all $7.50, include Yankee pot roast, baked flounder parmesan, baked Virginia ham and American meatloaf. The varied menu offers sandwiches ranging from peanut butter and jelly to cream cheese and walnut, and Gus's pickles from the Lower East Side. Fruit cobblers are the featured desserts. Enjoy inside or out, on the rear garden patio beside the creek. Flexible hours, daily noon to 8, weekends to 11.

New York Delicatessen & Appetizing, 12 West Bridge St., New Hope, Pa. (215) 862-5514. Get the real thing — from bagels to overstuffed sandwiches to latkes to knishes — at ex-New Yorker Marvin Berman's new deli and takeout. Bins of pickles and display cases full of luscious desserts are as much part of the decor as the few tables, a marble counter and a mural along a rear wall. Our informant said her corned beef sandwich with mustard on Jewish rye bread and coleslaw ($5.95) was the best she'd had in ages. The breakfast special brings two eggs, homefries, toast and coffee for $1.95. Or try the smoked fish feast with choice of three fish, $19.95 for two or three. Open daily, 8:30 to 6. No credit cards.

South of New Hope

Odette's, South River Road, New Hope, Pa. (215) 862-2432. For many, this is the ultra Bucks County dining experience: big, lavish, theatrical. The rear outdoor terrace, the glassed-in room facing it and another room above afford gorgeous views of the river. Taped classical or live music from a superior piano bar, beautiful flowers, and formal table settings and service contribute to a perfect atmosphere in which to see and be seen. Three hundred people can be seated in the various dining rooms or in the lounge, and owner Rocky Barborone offers a new cabaret. The menu changes seasonally. You might start with margarita shrimp or crabmeat ravioli in sherry cream sauce for appetizers ($6.95 to $8.95). Main courses ($14.95 to $24.95) could be poached salmon with lemon and macadamia nut butter, stuffed pork chop with apple-walnut butter, veal citron or cioppino. Chocolate fudge cake and fruit tortes are among the mainstays on the dessert tray; the wine list is pricey. Seafood enchilada, chilled filet with caper sauce and tri-color tortellini with cheese, sundried tomatoes, goat cheese and olives are lunch possibilities ($7.95 to $8.95). Lunch, Monday-Saturday 11:30 to 3; dinner, 5 to 10 or 11; Sunday, buffet brunch 11 to 3, dinner 3 to 9.

Forager House, 1800 River Road, New Hope, Pa. (215) 862-9477. Contemporary decor with track lighting, purple napkins on white linen, well-spaced tables and good-looking prints along the walls distinguish this restaurant. So does the food, which tends to be in the vanguard — Forager House was the first to bring Spanish tapas to Bucks County, and varying Thursday-night ethnic or regional dinners are an annual winter tradition, billed in 1991 as "recession fighters at only $14.50." The changing menu of chef-owner Dick Barrows typically ranges from Thai chicken curry with pineapple chutney to mesquite-grilled sirloin with smoked onion demi-glace, $17.50 to $18.75. Baked goat cheese salad and lobster ravioli are possible starters. Desserts might be a Viennese chocolate torte, fresh fruit sorbet or meringue glace. The wine list is good and fairly priced. Dinner, Wednesday-Saturday 6 to 9 or 10; Sunday, brunch 11 to 2:30, dinner from 5.

The Black Tulip, 1253 River Road, Washington Crossing, Pa. (215) 321-3339. New in 1989 was this country French restaurant, its pretty covered outdoor patio overlooking the river across the road. The two attractive small dining rooms with fireplaces and beamed ceilings are intimate and carefully appointed with stunning imported china; you'd never guess that this once was a hot dog stand. Chef-owner Henri Zerbib's menu is short and to the point: eight entrees ($18 to $24) like salmon filet with beurre blanc sauce, duck breast with grapefruit sauce, veal tenderloin with tomato and black olives, and tournedos with madeira sauce. Start with ragout of veal and mushrooms or hearts of palm with balsamic vinaigrette. Finish with a chocolate mousse terrine or hazelnut roulade. The three pasta dishes at dinner turn up on the lunch menu; you'll also find quiche, veal scaloppine, steak au poivre and the like, $9 to $13.50. Lunch, weekdays 11:30 to 2:30; dinner, 5:30 to 9:30 or 10:30, Sunday 4 to 8:30 or 9. Closed Tuesday. BYOB.

FOR MORE INFORMATION: New Hope Information Center, South Main Street at Mechanic Street, Box 141, New Hope, Pa. 18938, (215) 862-5880. Bucks County Tourist Commission, 152 Swamp Road, Doylestown, Pa. 18901, (215) 345-4552. Lambertville Area Chamber of Commerce, 4 South Union St., Lambertville, N.J. 08530, (609) 397-0055.

Ornate Victorian houses face oceanfront at Cape May.

Cape May, N.J.

Cape May, America's oldest seaside resort, is an oasis of exuberant Victoriana not far from the Mason-Dixon line.

Near the end of a peninsula between the Atlantic Ocean and Delaware Bay where South Jersey fades away, this late bloomer has been reborn into a remarkably diverse charmer that is the closest thing to a Key West up north. Some of the similarities are unmistakable: a salubrious ocean setting with water on three sides, unsurpassed Victorian architecture, a spate of period bed-and-breakfast inns, outstanding restaurants and, by northern standards, something of a southern air.

Time had forgotten Cape May since the late 1800s when it was the playground for presidents and personages from Ulysses S. Grant and William Harrison to Bret Harte and Henry Ford. Fires, new transportation modes and changing lifestyles took their toll; Atlantic City and other more accessible resorts left Cape May languishing as a country town out of the mainstream.

Not until 1970 when a group of citizens banded together to save the landmark Emlen Physick House from demolition did Cape May's fortunes turn. Along came the U.S. Bicentennial spurring an interest in history and, as local tour guide James Corson tells it, "ours was still standing all around us." Having declined the honor a few years earlier, Cape May in 1976 was designated a National Historic Landmark city, one of only five in the nation, and its future would be forever altered — and preserved.

The Mid-Atlantic Center for the Arts, founded to save the Physick Estate, has left its imprint on the entire community. Two of its longtime officers, Tom Carroll and Marianne Schatz, restored neighboring landmarks into museum-quality guest houses, launching a bed-and-breakfast phenomenon that was a model throughout Cape May and elsewhere.

If B&B is now part and parcel of the Cape May experience, so is Victoriana.

Some 670 structures from the late 1800s, the largest concentration anywhere, have been preserved. They range from gingerbread cottages to ornate showplaces, from slivers of guest houses to block-long hotels. And everywhere there are front verandas — seemingly all of them in use from late afternoon to sunset or later. So immersed is Cape May in its past that it celebrates an entire Victorian Week in mid-October, not to mention a weeklong Tulip Festival, a Dickens Christmas Extravaganza, Victorian dinners, and Victorian house and inn tours. Even the city's welcome center is in an 1853 church.

The Cape May area is one of America's best birding spots, and in season the bird-watchers outnumber beachcombers, fishermen, souvenir shoppers, restaurant-goers and even Victorianophiles.

Such is the annual crush of tourists that one local newspaper wag suggested a spring Festival of Lawns. With tongue firmly in cheek, he wanted to celebrate the last view of grass before it disappeared beneath the influx.

Getting There

Cape May, located at the southern end of the Garden State Parkway, is about 90 miles southeast of Philadelphia. From the Delmarva peninsula, it can be reached by ferry from Lewes, Del.

Where to Stay

The city of 5,000 year-round residents offers more than 3,000 rooms, many of them in efficiency motels and rooming houses. Because bed and breakfast is so integral to the Cape May experience, we concentrate on some of the more than 90 in town. Most have minimum stays of two or three nights, do not permit smoking and allow access only via the unique combination locks installed in the doors (many of these are museum-quality homes and curious passersby would be an intrusion). Breakfasts tend to be lighter in summer, more formal and filling the rest of the year. The Cape May ritual is for the innkeepers to serve afternoon tea or beverages as well as breakfast, mingling with their guests all the while.

Bed and Breakfast

The Mainstay Inn, 635 Columbia Ave., Cape May 08204. (609) 884-8690. The Mainstay and the Abbey are the two that led the way, and are the most likely to be filled weeks, if not months, in advance. Tom and Sue Carroll began the B&B movement in Cape May at the Windward House, now under new ownership, and purchased the Mainstay in 1975. The fourteen-foot-high public rooms in the 1872 Italianate villa are furnished in Victoriana right down to the sheet music on the piano. Especially notable is the ceiling of the entrance hall, where a stunning combination of seventeen wallpapers makes a beautiful accent. Rooms in the inn and in the pleasant 1870 Cottage next door are named for famous visitors to Cape May like Stonewall Jackson. Lace curtains, stenciling, brass and iron bedsteads, armoires and rockers decorate the twelve guest rooms, nine with private baths and some with copper tubs. The Henry Ford room has its own small porch and the Bret Harte room (with many of his books in a case) opens onto the entire second-floor veranda. Should you not mind a very steep ladder with a wavering rope for a railing, climb to the tower on the third floor, where, with cushions on two sides and windows on all four, you can get a good view of town. The inn and the cottage, both with wide verandas and rocking chairs, are separated by a brick walk and a handsome trickling fountain; the front gardens are brilliant with flowers. Sue Carroll's recipes for her breakfast and tea goodies are so sought after that she has published a small cookbook called "Breakfast at Nine, Tea at Four." In summer, breakfast is continental-plus, served buffet-style on the veranda; other seasons it is formal sit-down around the table for twelve in the dining room. Ham and apple pie, strawberry french toast and chicken-pecan quiche are among the offerings. Tours of the Mainstay ($5) are given Saturday, Sunday, Tuesday and Thursday at 4, after which participants are invited to join inn guests for a formal tea. "Young children generally find us tiresome," the inn's brochure advises sensibly. This is, as Tom Carroll says, "a total Victorian experience." Doubles, $85 to $140; three-night minimum in season and most weekends. Open mid-March through mid-December.

The Abbey, Columbia Avenue and Gurney Street, Cape May 08204. (609) 884-4506. Relax on the porch of the Abbey, and you'll likely be a supporting player in someone's video, slide or snapshot. A constant stream of tourists gawk at, and take pictures of, this elegant Gothic villa with its 60-foot tower and incredible gingerbread trim, all painstakingly painted green with deep red and ivory accents. Jay and Marianne Schatz, corporate and academic dropouts, purchased the 1869 Abbey, built as a summer home for a coal baron, in 1979. It's their fourth restoration, and they've done a splendid job. The parlor, library and dining room on the main floor, with ornate twelve-foot ceilings and eleven-foot windows (decorated with lace curtains and striking lambrequins, designed by Marianne) are filled with priceless items, including the largest freestanding bookcase (which comes apart in 27 pieces) we've ever seen. In the dining room, with its Teutonic sideboard, fourteen people can sit around the banquet table; says Marianne, "we have the noisiest breakfasts in town." That's partly because Jay keeps guests regaled both with his stories and his selection of hats from a closet that holds a choice of more than 250 — perhaps an Australian bush hat or a "Hagar the Horrible" beauty. A continental-plus breakfast is served in summer. In spring and fall, you might have pink grapefruit juice, a dish of fresh peaches and whipped cream, an egg and ham casserole with garlic grits on the side, and buttered English muffins. Marianne also makes a great quiche with a Bisquick crust. The Schatzes preside at 6 o'clock over beer, wine and popcorn on the porch or in the parlor. On the second and third floors, seven bedrooms, all with private baths and interesting period light fixtures, are named for cities. We stayed in the Savannah, a sweet room with white enamel bedstead, oriental carpets, a white wicker sofa with purple cushions and a small refrigerator in the bathroom. Tours of the first floor ($3) are given Thursday-Sunday at 5. In 1987, the Schatzes opened the cottage next door as an adjunct, offering seven less formal guest rooms, all with private baths, and a couple of parlors and verandas. Doubles, $75 to $150; three to four-night minimum stay in season. Open April-October.

The Queen Victoria, 102 Ocean St., Cape May 08204. (609) 884-8702. At the head of the stairway to the second floor is a basket of amenities and essentials labeled "In Case You Forgot." It's typical of the thoughtful touches offered by Joan and Dane Wells in their luxurious and lately expanded inn. The original 1881 property has twelve rooms, eight with private baths. In 1989, they turned the Victorian house and carriage house next door into eleven luxury suites with queensize beds, sitting rooms or areas, whirlpool baths, fireplaces and television. Furnishings in both guest and public rooms are not so high Victorian as in other inns. "We try to feature comfortableness," says Dane. Each house has a parlor, one in the original building with a piano and a fireplace and the new one with TV, games and jigsaw puzzles. Pantry areas are stocked with the makings for popcorn, tea, sherry and such. The library in the original inn contains volumes on architecture, art and history collected by Joan when she was executive director of the Victorian Society in America. Baked eggs, a spinach or corn casserole and homemade breads are served for breakfast at a long table beneath a portrait of Queen Victoria in the dining room of the main house and in a dining room outfitted similarly in the new addition. Doubles, $85 to $180.

The Manor House, 612 Hughes St., Cape May 08204. (609) 884-4710. After all the Victoriana, the Manor House comes as a refreshing change of pace. The impressive, gambrel-roofed house with warm oak and chestnut foyer and striking furnishings seems almost contemporary in contrast. "We're not trying to be high Victorian," explains Mary Snyder, innkeeper with her husband Tom. "This is more homey and we want people to feel comfortable." Guests spread out for punch or tea in a living room with a striking stained-glass-front player piano or a library with two plush loveseats in front of a fireplace. Upstairs are nine guest rooms, seven with private bath, furnished in antiques, brass and wood beds, handmade quilts and light Victorian print wallpapers. Two back rooms on the third floor catch a glimpse of the ocean. The Snyders offer a choice of two entrees at one of the town's more elaborate breakfasts — perhaps frittatas, corn quiche, "asparageggs" or breakfast pizza. They're accompanied by Mary's crumb buns and non-stop monologue by Tom, who rivals the Abbey's Jay Schatz as a standup comic and sometimes conducts walking tours of town when he isn't singing with his barbershop quartet. Doubles, $98 to $145.

The Angel of the Sea, 5-7 Trenton Ave., Cape May 08204. (609) 884-3369 or (800) 848-3369. Rising somewhat starkly in an undeveloped area a half block from the ocean and away from the historic district, this new gray and mauve B&B with colorful gardens in front claims to be Cape May's most deluxe and charges accordingly. The 27 rooms in two turreted Victorian buildings have all the amenities: private baths (many with pedestal sinks and clawfoot tubs), antique queen or double beds, ceiling fans, reproduction furniture, and handcrafted wood-slat ceilings and wainscoting. Many have interesting angles and niches. Some third-floor rooms have ocean views but lack the balconies that enhance some on the second floor; everyone gets to share the main-floor verandas. Resident innkeepers are Greg and Laurie Whissell (she's the daughter of owners John and Barbara Girton, who poured more than $3 million into the two buildings). Laurie bakes at least three kinds of cookies and breads for tea at 4, offers wine and cheese at 5:30, and serves a full breakfast in a dining room with high-back, red velvet chairs at four tables for six. Breakfast the morning we were there included fresh fruit buffet, apple crisp, cinnamon-walnut pancakes, country vegetable frittata with bacon and toast, and blueberry-apple coffee cake. Family photographs lend a personal touch to the the living room, the inn's only common room, where Bill the cockatoo in a fancy cage makes his presence known. Doubles, $125 to $230.

Columns By the Sea, 1513 Beach Drive, Cape May 08204. (609) 884-2228. Facing the ocean head-on is this twenty-room summer "cottage" built by a Philadelphia physician in 1910. It has fluted columns, Colonial revival accents and something of the look of an Italian palazzo townhouse, according to innkeepers Barry and Cathy Rein. Beyond a huge, brick-floored porch full of white wicker is a grand entry with a three-story staircase and a parlor on each floor. Inside, all appears dark and high Victorian, yet the spacious rooms and the views give a sense of airiness. The master suite contains a bed that was President Truman's at the Blair House; its enormous bathroom with a clawfoot tub and a shower stall in the corner is the size of many a bedroom. All eleven rooms have private baths. Costumes, dolls, old prams, chests, valises and such are part of the clutter. The main-floor parlor appointed in white wicker looks out toward the ocean. Breakfast is served beneath a high ceiling in a rather extravagant dining room with a lace-covered table, candelabra, majestic sideboards and wood paneling to about five feet high. Pineapple bread pudding, blueberry blintzes, quiches and souffles might be the fare. Tea time brings hot and cold hors d'oeuvres, and port or sherry and baked goods are put out in the late evening. Doubles, $95 to $145. Open May-December.

Wilbraham Mansion & Inn, 133 Myrtle Ave., Cape May 08204. (609) 884-2046. A heated indoor swimming pool is an attraction at this purple, gold and green mansion built in 1840 and restored into a B&B in 1988. Pat and Rose Downes offer seven rooms and two suites with private baths and air-conditioning. Off a hall of vivid silver and fern wallpaper, rooms vary in size and are appointed with antiques, wicker, much lace and baskets, some with washcloths and towels tied up in ribbons. The large oval pool, surrounded by stained-glass windows, is the centerpiece of a rear addition built in 1900. Afternoon tea and wine are served on the terrace around the pool. Guests also have use of a formal dining room, two parlors and a small TV room. The full breakfast might involve eggs in champagne, baked pancakes and honeyed sausages. The Downeses offer five-day spa retreats for businesswomen, including aerobics, swimming, beauty consultations and nature walks. Doubles, $75 to $135.

The Brass Bed, 719 Columbia Ave., Cape May 08204. (609) 884-8075. Guests are welcomed into an attractive enclosed sunporch or a delightful small parlor with an old victrola and a desk topped by an old Corona typewriter, two pairs of spectacles and a small globe. Eight guest rooms with 19th-century brass beds, period wall coverings, oriental carpets and lace curtains are offered by John and Donna Dunwoody. Two rooms have private baths and two have half baths. "We did the total restoration ourselves," advised Donna, rolling her eyes skyward. The result is cozy and homey. Egg and cheese strata, deep-dish french toast or banana pancakes might be the fare for breakfast, served at a long table in the dining room. Doubles, $80 to $115.

Motels

Sandpiper Beach Inn, Beach Drive and Grant Street, Cape May 08204. (609) 884-4256. Locally considered to be the nicest of the lot, this family operation run by Ruth and Bob Escher is pleasantly restrained in architecture and luxurious in accommodations. Many of the 60 rooms are two-room efficiencies with sitting rooms, balconies and two TVs; the third-floor suites with vaulted ceilings and oceanfront views are most in demand. Rooms contain queensize or two double beds and modern oak furniture. All have balconies, from which you can see the ocean and "all the way through to Delaware," says Bob. Doubles, $118 to $128; two-room efficiencies, $122 to $132. Open May-October.

La Mer Motor Inn, Beach Drive and Pittsburgh Avenue, Cape May 08204. (609) 884-9000. This appealing, low-key motel with shingled roof has 62 units on two floors in a rather out-of-the-way location along the ocean on the north side of town. We stay here because of the prices, the facilities and the second-floor rooms facing the ocean; the pool and breakwater block the view of those on ground level. The spacious rooms have been redecorated and some have kitchens. There are a new children's playground, a miniature golf course, barbecue area, laundry facilities and an adjacent restaurant and lounge called

60

Water's Edge (see Where to Eat). Doubles, $107 to $124. Open May to late October.

Periwinkle Inn, 1039 Beach Ave., Box 220, Cape May 08204. (609) 884-9200. The former Stockholm Motor Inn was renovated into the Periwinkle, an oceanfront motel with 50 rooms and efficiencies. Half face a garden courtyard and an attractive pool area, and the ocean view from most is marginal at best. Two bi-level units with upstairs bedrooms and balconies do face the ocean. Doubles, $102 to $122; efficiencies, $120 to $170. Open mid-April to mid-October.

Montreal Inn, Beach Drive at Madison Street, Cape May 08204. (609) 884-7011 or (800) 525-7011. Opened in 1966 with 27 units, this oceanfront motel has grown to four floors with 73 units, plus a restaurant and lounge, a package store, large pool, sauna and mini-golf layout. The Montreal connection is unclear, but the values are — especially in the off-season, when we got a fine room for $44. The only minus was the noise of a carousing group of fishermen in a unit next door. Doubles, $73 to $119. Open March-November.

Hotels

The Virginia Hotel, 25 Jackson St., Box 557, Cape May 08204. (609) 884-5700. Built in 1879 as Cape May's first hotel, the Virginia was reopened in 1989 as what general manager Curtis Bashaw, son of the owner, calls a deluxe "boutique" hotel — one that B&B innkeepers gladly recommend for those who want contemporary amenities. Upstairs on the second and third floor are 24 guest rooms varying in size and shape. They are equipped with modern baths, telephones, and remote-control TVs and VCRs hidden in built-in cabinets, and are furnished in a simple yet sophisticated manner. Two premium rooms at the front of the second floor have private balconies. Room service is available, as are beach towels, tags and chairs. The main floor has a parlor, where a pianist plays dinner music at night, a small lounge and an elegant restaurant called **The Ebbitt Room,** serving lunch and dinner daily. Chef Joe Lotozo, who gave us some of our best meals in Cape May at the old Bayberry Inn, has toned down his fare to appeal to a hotel clientele. Among entrees ($15.95 to $21), we liked the shrimp margarita flamed in tequila and the pan-roasted quail with grapes and green peppercorns. Upside-down fig cake and pecan praline cheesecake were good desserts. Doubles, $135 to $220; two-night minimum on weekends.

The Chalfonte, 301 Howard St., Cape May 08204. (609) 884-8409. Cape May's oldest hotel (1876) and in many ways its most revered is somewhat hard to find — a block from the ocean at the edge of the historic district — and we bumped into it quite by accident on a walking tour. Owners Judy Bartella and Anne LeDuc are upgrading both the public rooms and guest quarters. Although the rambling three-story hotel has 103 rooms, only 78 are rented. They're conceded to be rustic and threadbare in the endearing manner of an earlier era. Each has a sink, but most of the baths are down the hall; eleven have private baths. The front porch is lined with rocking chairs, and one TV and two phones are available for guests' use. Four generations of the Dickerson family have been cooking Southern food served family style in the long, echoing dining room since 1876. Helen Dickerson, head chef for more than 40 years and now in her 80s, is assisted by her daughters, Dot Burton and Lucille Thompson. Helen's cookbook, "I Just Stop Stirrin' When the Tastin's Good," typifies her style. The Virginia country breakfast ($7) includes spoonbread and biscuits. Four-course Southern dinners with a set menu and all the trimmings are $21 and gentlemen are requested to wear jackets. There's nightly entertainment in the King Edward

Bar. "This is really still like a large boarding house," Judy Bartella concedes, and guests keep returning for the experience. Doubles, $84 to $135, MAP. Breakfast daily, 8:30 to 10, Sunday to 11; dinner, seatings at 6:30 and 8. Open summer through September, weekends in October.

Rentals

Somewhere In Time, 202 Ocean Ave., Box 1334, Cape May Point 08212. (609) 884-8554. Victorian on the outside and contemporary inside, this is an appealing complex of nine air-conditioned apartments located away from the hubbub in summery Cape May Point and available by the half-week or week. Decor is crisp and refreshing, with platform beds, built-in cabinets, high-tech closets with shelves, well equipped kitchens and, bonus, they're easy to keep clean. Four have ocean views, and the rest get a glimpse. Most in demand are those on the third floor with decks catching the sea breeze. One two-bedroom apartment on the main floor has a porch in front and a deck in the rear. Martha Marcus, innkeeper with her husband Joel, is responsible for the lovely English gardens with lounge furniture and picnic tables at the side. The Marcuses pamper their guests with caring touches like souvenirs — a canvas bag bearing the inn's logo at our visit. The facility is good for families or couples wanting to be on their own in style. Minimum stay is a week in summer, three nights in June and September. Studio, $775 a week; one-bedroom suite, $775 to $875, two-bedroom $1,100. Open Memorial Day to late October.

HOUSE RENTALS. Many summer houses are available for rent, particularly in the Cape May Point area. Rentals top out at about $900, although some condominiums charge more than $1,000 a week. The major agent for summer rentals is Tolz Realtors, 1001 Lafayette St., (609) 884-7001 or (800) 444-7001.

Seeing and Doing

Besides enjoying the beach, which is as far as a few unknowing souls get, there's enough in Cape May and environs to keep one busy for days. No wonder the minimum-stay requirements don't bother most; many come for a week or more and return season after season. Incidentally, Cape May's season — from Memorial Day to mid-October — is extending every year as new events are staged and more inns and restaurants stay open longer.

Cape May is best seen and appreciated by walking or bicycling along the beach and through the tree-lined historic district, which consists of a compact area generally east of Washington Street between Franklin and Congress streets. Columbia Avenue and Hughes Street and their cross streets are at the heart.

Touring Cape May

There are no Gray Line bus tours here — only old-fashioned trolley tours and walking tours sponsored by the Mid-Atlantic Center for the Arts (MAC), which seems to have a hand in just about everything that's good in town.

Guided Trolley Tours, MAC, 884-5404. Leaving regularly from Ocean Street opposite the Washington Street Mall, tours take half an hour and cover the Historic East End (the best tour if you only have time for one), the Historic West End and Historic Beach Drive. Our guide, tenth-generation resident Jim Corson, told about the town's bad luck with hurricanes and fires and pointed out his house, "which cost more to paint this year than it did to buy in 1904." He explained that the Washington Inn was moved three times, showed how Victorian cottagers were trying to outdo each other (including his favorite house, the Abbey, where the original owner was not content to compete only with his neighbors but also with himself on every side), and pointed out the largest mansion in town, the George Allen House, and its prized outhouse, a two-seater with cupola. His comments made our subsequent wanderings much more informed. Moonlight trolley rides (unguided) also are given at 8 o'clock many evenings for $3. Historic tours, adults $4, children $1. Operating early spring to late fall.

Walking Tours. Following maps or instinct, you can explore on your own, but the guided walking tours offered by MAC are more entertaining and informative. Geared to those who like to see history close up, the 90-minute tours are led by knowledgeable residents, who share insights into Victorian traditions and customs. Tours of two distinct areas on either side of Ocean Street leave from the Washington Street Mall information booth weekends and some weekdays at 10 a.m. and 7 p.m. Adults $4, children $1.

Mansions by Gaslight. Four of Cape May's finest homes are open for self-guided tours Wednesdays from 8 to 10 p.m., mid-June to mid-September. Included are the Physick House, the Mainstay Inn, the Abbey and the Humphrey Hughes House. MAC's shuttle bus runs a continuous transit loop starting from the Emlen Physick House, where tickets are purchased. Adults $12, children $6.

Victorian Sampler Tours. Five Cape May B&Bs and guesthouses offer self-guided tours on Mondays and Saturdays in summer and Saturdays in spring and fall. A different group of houses is opened for each tour. Trolley transporation is included. Tickets, available at the MAC office or at one of the participating houses, cost $10 for adults, $5 for children.

Jewels in the Crown Tour. New in 1990, this tour opens four of Cape May's oldest hotels, the Chalfonte, Congress Hall, Inn of Cape May (formerly the Colonial) and the Virginia. Hours vary weekly, sometimes Sunday mid-day or late Tuesday afternoon, and may include tea at the Chalfonte. Adults $10, children $5.

Christmas Inns Tours. Six year-round B&Bs are decked out in their Yuletide finery, each in a way that tells a part of the Christmas story: an elegant Christmas setting at Alexander's, a children's Christmas at the Brass Bed, vintage fashions for the holidays at Windward House, the sounds of Christmas at the Humphrey Hughes, the legends of Christmas at the Duke of Windsor, and a floral Christmas at the Bedford. Afternoon semi-guided tours are offered weekends in December; adults $12, children $4. In 1990, four inns opened for evening tours, featuring Victorian decorations at Columns By the Sea and ghosts of Christmas at Wilbraham Mansion. Tour times vary, Thursday-Sunday throughout December; adults $8, children $3.

Carriage Rides. Costumed drivers from Cape May Carriage Co., 884-4466, take visitors on half-hour, horse-drawn carriage rides around Cape May's historic district. Carriages leave daily except Sunday from 10 to 2 and 6:30 to 10:30 from Ocean Street at Washington Street Mall. Adults $6, children $3.

Sightseeing by Air. For a different perspective, get above it all on a sightseeing tour by Cape Air Inc., Cape May County Airport, 886-8805. Up to three people may be accommodated in a Piper Warrior on a 25-minute ride (price, $45).

Emlen Physick House and Estate, 1048 Washington St., 884-5404. The place where Cape May's restoration effort started (and now the headquarters of MAC, the group whose arts offerings funded the restoration) is open daily for guided tours in summer and weekends in spring and fall. The eighteen-room house was designed by Philadelphia architect Frank Furness in 1879 for a young physician (an eminent surgeon's grandson, who never practiced and never married) and his mother. Many of the original furnishings have been retrieved and returned to the house. The family parlor has the original fireplace, sofabed and pipe organ. A crazy tureen in the corner of the formal parlor was a housewarming present. The upstairs library has striking Japanese wallpaper, even on the ceiling. Tapestry curtains, porcelain lamp fixtures and chandeliers are all around. We liked best the owner's bachelor bedroom beside a sunken marble bathroom; right next door is Mother's bedroom, her fan collection framed over the fireplace. Don't miss the costume collection across the hall. The tours take about an hour and fifteen minutes or longer, our informant advised, if you get "a long-winded tour guide." On weekends, the tour of the 8.5-acre estate also includes the Carriage House, now home of the venerable Cape May Colony Art League. Adults $4, children $1.

Cape May Firemen's Museum. In Cape May you're not surprised to stumble across yet another museum, this one opened in 1986 by the Cape May Volunteer Fire Company in front of the fire headquarters at Washington and Franklin streets. The small establishment houses a 1929 Hale pumper, badges, alarm boxes and other memorabilia pertaining to fires in a city in which fires have played an important role. Open daily. Free.

On or Near the Water

BIRDING. Cape May lies on the heavily populated Atlantic Flyway and more than 400 species of birds, plus the entire migration of monarch butterflies along the East Coast, heads south through Cape May Point. Spring and fall are the peak migration seasons, but many species stay year-round. Off Sunset Boulevard south of town is **South Cape May Meadow,** a 180-acre wildlife preserve and migratory bird refuge owned by the Nature Conservancy. A U-shaped trail across the meadow into the dunes, with grazing cattle at the side, is one mecca. A more popular one is **Cape May Point State Park,** where a platform beside a pond provides a pleasant and cooling spot to watch for birds and listen to the surf. A professional hawk counter and hawk banders can be seen at work, and a scoreboard is posted in the hawk-watch area charting the number of species counted the previous day and the year to date. Another bird-watching spot is **Higbee's Beach Wildlife Management Area,** 600 acres of dune forest along Delaware Bay. The **Cape May Bird Observatory,** run by the New Jersey Audubon Society, conducts bird walks in the fall. Just north of Cape May off Stone Harbor Boulevard is the **Wetlands Institute and Museum,** surrounded by a 6,000-acre salt marsh. Included are an observation tower, a touch museum called Wetlandia, saltwater aquaria, a gallery with changing art and crafts shows, library and marsh trails.

Cape May Point State Park. Located near the lighthouse in the quaint summer colony of Cape May Point, this is a favorite with birders, naturalists and those who like to walk the dunes, beaches and three miles of trails. MAC is restoring the 1859 lighthouse and developing a maritime museum on its small grounds. Some visitors say not to miss the small museum containing information about birds and beach erosion (a particular problem around Cape May). The hardy can climb the 199 tower stairs to the Watch Room Gallery just below the lantern for a panoramic view (tower admission: adults $3, children $1). Do walk out to the World War II bunker built with guns to guard Delaware Bay from enemy attack. Today it is an open "fortress" with benches and picnic tables above the surf. The beach here is unprotected and swimming is discouraged, although some sunbathers ventured into the water the late-September afternoon we visited. Nearby, St. Peter's-by-the-Sea, a tiny gray Episcopal chapel with fancy trim, crouches behind the dunes that line the beachfront.

Sunset Beach, Cape May Point. At the end of Sunset Boulevard is a sheltered beach with free parking and a small hodgepodge of snack bars and souvenir stands. Just offshore is the shell of the USS Atlantis, one of twelve concrete ships built during World War I and brought to the Point in 1926 to serve as a breakwater; it ran aground in a storm and has been trapped ever since. The beach often yields Cape May diamonds, stones of pure quartz that are found only here; they can be polished, cut and set to make attractive jewelry. We latched onto someone who seemed to know what he was doing and he showed us how to seek out the good stones from the bad; otherwise, we'd never have known.

SWIMMING. The aforementioned beaches, including Higbee's, are more secluded than Cape May's strand, but the latter is where the action is. Most inns and motels give their guests beach passes; the beach is patrolled in season so no one gets on free. A boardwalk flanks the beach and provides a view of the goings-on.

FISHING AND BOATING. More than 30 species of fish inhabit the waters of the Atlantic, Delaware Bay and the inland waterways that separate the barrier resort islands from the mainland. Entered in Cape May's year-long fishing tournament are everything from winter flounder to mako sharks; the Canyons, said to be one of the world's great white marlin areas, are easily accessible. Boat rentals and charter boats are plentiful, and launching ramps are available along the waterway and Delaware Bay. The center of fishing activity is Fisherman's Wharf, where the commercial fleet unloads beyond the Lobster House restaurant. Boating is concentrated on the inland waterway near the Cape May Bridge at the north end of town.

Cape May by Boat. Another of MAC's tours is a 90-minute guided cruise aboard the Big Blue Sightseer Cruiser from Otten's Harbor in Wildwood. MAC furnishes a guide to point out local architecture as the boat circles Cape May and Cape May Point. Dolphins often are seen cavorting off Cape May. Tour runs summer Sundays at 10:30 a.m.; adults $7, children $3.50. MAC also sponsors a **Sunset Cruise** Fridays at 7 p.m. on the same boat to show Cape May as those arriving from Philadelphia by steamboat in the 1870s would have seen it. Tickets for both cruises must be purchased in advance at the Physick Estate or the Trolley Station, Beach Drive at Gurney Street.

Miss Chris Fishing Center, Third Avenue and Wilson Drive, 884-3939, includes three party boats, two charter boats and one speedboat ride, the last around Wildwood at 35 miles an hour. Daily fishing trips of four and eight hours are available, $16 to $25. The Lady Chris gives dinner cruises Sunday-Thursday at 6 to Urie's restaurant in Wildwood, where the meal is taken (tickets, $29).

Cape May Fishing & Sightseeing Center, 1286 Wilson Drive, 898-0055, offers four-hour whale-watching cruises daily at 9, 1 and 6 for $22. The cruises have "an 80 percent sighting rate on whales and 100 percent on dolphins," the captain informed. The 105-passenger boat also has a dolphin-watching breakfast cruise at 9 a.m. and a 6 o'clock evening dolphin cruise.

Capt. John Wilsey of **Cape Island Sailing Cruise,** 884-8347, offers leisurely afternoon or evening sails, viewing Cape May from the ocean and from the bay on a 23-foot trimaran or a 37-foot boat.

Other Activities

ARTS AND ENTERTAINMENT. Theatre By the Sea, 884-2787, presents professional theater on its outdoor stage in an amphitheater surrounded by hedges and towering trees, nightly except Sunday in summer. A typical season might include "Deathtrap," "George M!" and "Godspell," presented in rotation two nights a week (adults $10). MAC sponsors a summer **Vintage Film Festival** with favorites from the 1930s and '40s, Monday evenings at 7 and 9:30 at the Chalfonte Hotel. For eighteen summers, band and choral concerts have taken place Wednesday, Saturday and Sunday evenings at 8 at the Victorian Bandstand. For those interested in more mundane pursuits, the Arcade at the boardwalk offers the usual diversions.

SPECIAL EVENTS. From **Crafts at Tulip-Time** in late April to the **Christmas Candlelight House Tour** the weekend after Christmas, Victorian Cape May is alive with scheduled activities and events. **Victorian Week,** a ten-day extravaganza encompassing two weekends in mid-October, celebrates the Victorian lifestyle in great variety. It includes house tours, fashion shows, evening stained-glass tours, crafts and antiques shows, a dance workshop, Victorian vaudeville and theater, a Victorian dinner and gala, a restoration seminar, a workshop on becoming a B&B innkeeper, and even an "incredible condos" tour. **Victorian dinners** for $35 are served in high style to 24 guests five times a year in the Emlen Physick House. A **Victorian Fair** is a mid-June highlight.

SHOPPING. Shopping is big business in Cape May, and the city's famed Washington Street Mall — one of the nation's first to be closed to traffic in 1971 — is filled with pedestrians, particularly on inclement days. The small City Center Mall even has an atrium and an escalator (one-way, up). Newer is the quirky little Carpenter's Square Mall off Carpenter's Lane.

You'll find all kinds of stores, from swish to tacky. Our favorites:

The Whale's Tale is a nifty ramble of rooms containing everything from wind sockets to coffee mugs to shell magnets to an extraordinary collection of cards. The owners' previous emphasis on gourmet cookware has been eclipsed, since their offspring arrived, by children's games and accessories.

McDowell's Gallery of Gifts is literally that, its walls between marble floors and high ceilings brightened by colorful kites and wind sockets. There's an interesting assortment of jewelry, glass, crafts, wood products and games.

The Victorian Pink House Gift Shop, a local landmark, is open only mornings and evenings; the afternoons are for restocking. It has an incredible array of Victoriana. "We look back on the past with pleasure to things that were pleasurable," owner John Miller said in explaining it all. The lace baskets, nosegays, Victorian cards and much more are pure nostalgia.

If you like kitties or bunnies, stop at **Whiskers** where they are the theme for cards, pictures, tags, jewelry, pottery and even light-switch plates. The Washington Street Gallery has Cape May and beachy posters; we almost sprang for a photo poster called "99 Bottles of Beer on the Wall" for a nephew. **For the Birds** and **Donegal Bay Co.** stock international fashions and gifts. **Swede Things in America** offers just what it says, mainly small items but some furniture.

The **Cape May Linen Outlet** has good bargains, especially in placemats. We saw some pretty Laura Ashley sheets. It's a small store, so don't expect a large selection.

66

Where to Eat _____ ✺✺✺

The choice in Cape May is staggering and the prices generally quite reasonable, all the more so at many places that do not have liquor licenses but allow you to bring your own wine. Many are open seasonally, with reduced hours in the spring and fall.

Near the Ocean

Restaurant Maureen, 429 Beach Drive. (609) 884-3774. Consistently good food and flawless service are high points of this sophisticated place run by Maureen and Stephen Horn on the second floor of what was once a bath house and saloon. Particularly inviting is the enclosed porch with a smashing view of the ocean, all pristinely white with pink napkins; inside is a long chandeliered dining room. The Horns have attracted quite a following after seven years in Philadelphia and nine in Cape May. Shrimp Madagascar, salmon sauvignon, shellfish Brazilian, duck framboise and sliced lamb with a sauce of scotch, mint and mustard are among the entrees ($18 to $23). We liked the zesty sauce of ginger, soy and scallions that accompanied the shrimp oriental. You might also start with lobster ravioli or Steve's crab cake with a puree of red pepper. Finish with a dessert from the pastry cart. Dinner nightly in summer, 5 to 10; fewer days in off-season. Open mid-April through October.

Es-Ta-Ti, 429 Beach Drive. (609) 884-3504. Downstairs beneath Restaurant Maureen is this northern Italian restaurant, occupying the space the Horns formerly used for Summers, a casual restaurant attracting beach-goers. This is quite a cut above, offering a melange of Mediterranean dishes. Seafood items dominate the short menu, priced from $17.50 for flounder stuffed with crab to $23 for grilled lamb sorrento. Penne with lobster, plum tomatoes and fennel is one of the good pastas. Start with garlic and crab soup or anchovies Catalan served on toasted French bread. Finish with tirami su or creme caramel. The decor is contemporary in black and white. Dinner nightly, 5:30 to 10; weekends in off-season. Open March-October.

Water's Edge, Beach Drive and Pittsburgh Avenue. (609) 884-1717. This sleek, hotel-style dining room in front of La Mer Motor Inn is outfitted with banquettes and booths dressed in white cloths and has an outdoor deck with the ocean beyond. Chef Neil Elsohn and his wife Karen, who is hostess, offer some of the best and most inspired food in town. On one occasion, we enjoyed an appetizer of strudel with escargots, pignoli and an ethereal garlic cream sauce before digging into poached filet of Norwegian salmon with lime and salmon caviar, and sauteed sea scallops with tomatillos, cilantro and grilled jicama. On our second visit, we grazed happily through appetizers and salads, including scallop chowder, spicy pork and scallion empanadas with pineapple-ginger chutney, fusilli with grilled tuna, oriental vegetables and Szechuan vinaigrette and grilled chicken salad with toasted pecans, grilled red onions, mixed greens and citrus vinaigrette. Main courses are priced from $17 for pan-fried flounder with cornmeal breading and frangelico to $28 for medallions of lobster with champagne and caviar beurre blanc. In summer, a lounge menu is served in the spacious bar. The brunch menu contains some exotic items, nicely priced from $6.25 to $11.50 and quite salubrious when taken outside. Lunch in summer, 11:30 to 3; dinner nightly, 5 to 9:30 or 10; closed Wednesday in off-season.

The Mad Batter, 19 Jackson St. (609) 884-5970. For more than fifteen years, some of the most creative meals in town have been served here in the covered

67

sidewalk cafe, the large dining room divided into two parts or on the rear porch amid white garden furniture, statues and greenery. We found the sidewalk cafe warm enough for candlelight dining on an early May night — a special treat, what with the view of the passing scene, the roar of the surf muted by classical music, and food so assertive that we returned the next morning for breakfast. But the fare depends on the chef; we came for lunch a year later and found the food so bland as to be beyond redemption. Locals say the fare is better now that Mindy Silver is back as executive chef, and lunch and brunch were touted as being as good as ever. We enjoyed her dancing devil shrimp stir-fried with pecans, kumquats and black bean sauce. A fettuccine tossed with snails, asparagus and baked garlic was sensational. Entrees on the changing dinner menu range from $14.50 to $21. Breakfast produced a gorgeous fruit plate and excellent whole wheat peach pancakes. Breakfast-brunch-lunch, daily 8 or 9 to 2:30; dinner, 5:30 to 9:30 or 11. Open late March-November, closed Monday in spring and fall. BYOB.

McGlade's On the Pier, 722 Beach Drive. 884-2614. Chef Mickey McGlade calls this the best-kept secret in Cape May. It is indeed hidden behind Morrow's Nut House near Convention Hall, and only because of an innkeeper's tip did we find it. But what a view of the ocean! And what food! We went for breakfast and thoroughly relished a shrimp and garlic omelet ($6.25) and Uncle Tuse's bacon, tomato and cheese omelet ($6), from a large menu on which everything had zip. The omelets were accompanied by fresh fruit garnishes and great hash-browns with lots of onions. A surprise treat was the school of dolphins that passed just off shore on their way to and from breakfast; although folks were watching from the breakwater, we on the canopied rear deck had the best view of all. The waitress advised that the dolphins pass each morning and afternoon. At lunch, the crab cakes ($5.95) are superb, and the salads are as enticing as the breakfast fare. We know innkeepers who come here for a casual dinner by the water to feast on shrimp butter rosa (with mushrooms and garlic over linguini), grilled salmon steak or the triple threat salad of crab, shrimp and lobster (entrees, $8.50 to $11.25). For interesting food, affordable prices and that glorious view, McGlade's can't be beat. Open daily in summer, 7 a.m. to 9 p.m.; otherwise, breakfast and lunch, 9 to 3. Open May-September. BYOB.

The Lobster House, Fisherman's Wharf. (609) 884-8296. One of the largest enterprises we've seen, this includes an enormous restaurant, an outdoor raw bar, the schooner American, a take-out counter and the best seafood market around. The inside is jammed for lunch and dinner; once we lunched on the 143-foot-long schooner anchored on the inland waterway, and felt somewhat on display for those at window tables inside. The schooner menu is unfortunately limited and boring; most people go there for drinks, and we found the tuna melt and shrimp salad croissant mundane at best. Better is the raw bar — crab soup for $2.95, twelve steamed crabs for $6.75, and a clambake dinner for $11.50. Even better is the Dockside Take-out, offering goodies from the seafood market like snapper soup ($2.25), soft-shell crab sandwich ($4.95 and delicious), and dinner for two (two crab cakes, four shrimp, half a pound of sea scallops, a pint of coleslaw and french fries, $11.95). The last made a good, quick lunch on the dock as we watched the boats parade by. Inside, the oversize menu offers something for everyone in the old-school tradition, from fried oysters with pepper hash to fisherman's platter. The house specialty is baked crab imperial. Lunch, daily 11:30 to 3; dinner, 5 to 10, Sunday 4 to 10.

The Cove Restaurant and Seaside Deck, south end of Beach Drive. Picnic tables on the porch of this casual establishment are covered with oilcloth. The porch, almost over the water, affords a superb view of the Cape May lighthouse. Crab cake sandwiches, Manhattan clam chowder, platters of fried seafood with french fries and coleslaw are inexpensive. We enjoyed breakfast here — especially the creamed chipped beef on toast ($4.85).

The Sunset Beach Grill at Sunset Beach, Cape May Point, also has a deck on the water. Breakfast sandwiches are $1.65 and $2.75 (depending on one egg or two) and come with bacon or ham, peppers or mushrooms. Chili dogs, pizza steaks, burgers, ice cream and lemon ice float are other menu items.

Away from the Water

410 Bank Street, 410 Bank St. (609) 884-2127. What could be more magical than dining in an outdoor courtyard, surrounded by plants, tiny white lights and Victorian lamps? That's the joy of this restaurant, whose owners also run Frescos for seafood and pasta next door. Here they offer a gumbo of New Orleans, Caribbean and French dishes, many grilled over mesquite wood but all with Cajun-Creole overtones. We loved the special seviche and blackened quail for appetizers, and found both our entrees of blackened redfish and snapper with pecan sauce, served with crisp vegetables and rice pilaf, too much to eat. After all, we had to save room for the key lime pie, which was the real thing. So is everything else, from Cajun crawfish popcorn to possibly the best bread pudding you'll ever taste. If you can't eat outside, settle for one of the screened porches or the small, intimate dining rooms adorned with New Orleans posters inside the restored 1840 house. Appetizers are in the $5.50 to $7.50 range; entrees, $18.95 to $24.95. Dinner nightly, 5:30 to 10. Closed November-April. BYOB.

Frescos, 420 Bank St. (609) 884-0366. Some reviewers find this northern Italian bistro even better than its parent next door. The pasta dishes ($10.95 to $15.95) are Cape May's most extensive, ranging from fusilli puttanesca to tagliatelle al pesto. Other entree choices ($15.95 to $21.95) include fresh trout amandine, jumbo shrimp stuffed with crabmeat, osso buco and veal scaloppine. Among delectable desserts are a key lime cream-filled cannoli and a rum-soaked sponge cake with mascarpone cream and grated chocolate. The main dining area is intimate, with crayons on the tables for doodling on the paper overlays covering the white tablecloths. The narrow wraparound porch has tables for two far enough apart for privacy. Dinner nightly, 5:30 to 10; Thursday-Sunday, mid-October to New Years. Closed January-April. BYOB.

The Washington Inn, 801 Washington St. (609) 884-5697. Considered far and away the best of the larger restaurants in town, this historic white building is surrounded by banks of impatiens and inside all is elegant. Dining is in several areas, including a pretty wicker-filled front veranda done up in pink and candlelight, a Victorian greenhouse, dark interior rooms and a Victorian lounge. The fairly extensive menu starts with scallops sauteed with smoked salmon and cheese, crab cakes with a roasted red pepper sauce, clams casino and a sampler of four of the most popular appetizers ($11.95). Entrees ($13.95 to $19.95) include flounder stuffed with crab imperial, baked snapper, seafood fricassee, three chicken and three veal dishes, Kansas steak with wild mushrooms and twin filet mignons. The new basement wine cellar won the Wine Spectator Grand Award. The wine list is reasonably priced, and diners like to finish with international coffees. Dinner nightly, 5 to 10; fewer nights in off-season. Closed in January.

Globe Restaurant, 110 North Broadway, West Cape May. (609) 884-2429. "Global cuisine" is the theme at this new restaurant where flags fly out front, globes hang in the entryway and maps of the world adorn the walls. It is run by two of New York's top former chefs, Michael Colameco, who had been at the Ritz-Carlton and the Tavern on the Green, and his South Korean wife, Heijung Park, pastry chef at the Hotel Pierre. Part of the offbeat menu represents their ethnic Italian and oriental specialties. But they draw inspiration from around the world, producing items like chilled peach soup, salad nicoise, blackfish in potato crust, crab cakes with coriander and lemon mayonnaise, and grilled swordfish with tomato salsa. Specialties are lamb tagine, a Moroccan dish; chicken pot pie with corn and cheddar, and a shrimp burger, fashioned from six ounces of shrimp and served with Maui onion rings. Prices are moderate (appetizers, $5 to $7, and entrees, $12 to $18) and the decor in several dining rooms is casual; the owners designed it as "a family restaurant for the 1990s." Dinner nightly in summer, 5 to 10; Wednesday-Sunday in off-season. Open mid-May to mid-October. BYOB.

Dillon's Restaurant, 524 Washington St. Mall. (609) 884-5225. This family restaurant is billed as a place for folks to "eat good food, laugh out loud and enjoy." Occupying the quarters of the former A Ca Mia, it has a garden cafe inside and an enclosed side porch. The northern Italian cuisine has given way to good old chicken dijon, veal francaise, barbecued ribs, shrimp and scallops fra diavolo, prime rib and strip steak ($12.95 to $15.95, with salad included). Popcorn shrimp, Buffalo wings, potato skins and mozzarella sticks are the appetizer fare. Salads come in an edible tortilla shell, and sandwiches are priced in the $5 range. Lunch daily, 11 to 5; dinner, from 5.

Tomasello Wine Cellar & Restaurant, Carpenter's Square, 31 Perry St. (609) 884-6662. The outdoor terrace is the place to be at this tiny wine-tasting room and restaurant owned by Tomasello Winery, a long-established producer of 26 varieties from a vineyard near Atlantic City. With a bottle of premium chardonnay for $12 picked after a sampling at the tasting counter, we enjoyed a lunch of chef's salad and spinach salad among choices including a cheese plate and sandwiches, priced from $5.75 to $6.50. The menu gets fancier at night, when entrees run from $14.95 for chicken francaise to $17.95 for jumbo shrimp with shallots, tomatoes and oyster mushrooms served on capellini. Finish with chocolate mousse cake or key lime pie. A good value is the champagne brunch, $16.95 prix-fixe. Brunch, Monday-Friday 10 to noon; champagne brunch, Saturday and Sunday 10 to 3; lunch, Monday-Friday 11 to 4; dinner nightly, 5:30 to 10:30. Open mid-May to mid-October.

La Toque, 210 Ocean St. (609) 884-1511. A stained-glass rendering of a chef is in the window of this intimate French bistro, crammed with glass-topped, pink-linened tables and a partially open kitchen. Fresh croissants and breads, authentic french toast, soups and salads, creative dinners and desserts are the fare. Omelets with a croissant are in the $5 to $7 range, depending on the filling (crabmeat and salmon are two). The seafood linguini or the California sandwich make a good lunch. Dinner entrees from $15.95 to $18.95 include blackened redfish, shrimp francaise and tournedos with jumbo lump crabmeat and hollandaise sauce. Danish apple cake, raspberry cheesecake and chocolate raspberry cake are some of the good desserts. Breakfast and lunch served til closing, dinner from 5.

FOR MORE INFORMATION: Cape May Chamber of Commerce, 609 Lafayette St., Cape May, N.J. 08204, (609) 884-5508, or Mid-Atlantic Center for the Arts, P.O. Box 340, Cape May, 884-5404.

Boardwalk parallels ocean beach at Spring Lake.

Spring Lake, N.J.

Quiet. Unhurried. Gracious. And very pretty. That's the way we think of Spring Lake, almost an anomaly on a New Jersey coastline that is more apt to be noisy, crowded and honky-tonk.

This town on the north Jersey Shore, south of Asbury Park and north of Bay Head, must have had some hard-headed members on its zoning board over the years. Houses are large, imposing and architecturally interesting. Lawns are in pristine condition. Flowers bloom. And neon signs are nonexistent.

Yet the attractions for the tourist are clearly here: a beautiful ocean strand and a wide, well-maintained, two-mile-long boardwalk; a charming lake crossed by two rustic wooden bridges and surrounded by a small green park in the center of town; wide, flat tree-lined streets perfect for bicycling; good restaurants, and a fine selection of accommodations from Victorian B&Bs to breezy summer hotels.

Summer is the season. Oh, some of the places open as early as March (most not until May) and many remain open into October, but June, July and August are prime time. When New York and Philadelphia and Pittsburgh become steamy, Jersey's exceptional coastline beckons. Of course, in some spots, it's hard to find the reason for cottages are cheek-by-jowl, the bands blare and the beer flows.

Here in Spring Lake, a calm, cool difference is apparent. Settled by upper-class Irish families, and still called the Irish Riviera, the town is welcoming to those who choose — and can afford — to come. Seasonal rentals are not inexpensive and short-term ones are hard to find. High priced beach badges ($8 per day on weekends; $7 during the week) deter casual daytrippers and hordes of kids.

You will notice the difference dramatically if you drive north on Ocean Avenue from Spring Lake to Belmar, the next town, in the evening. A large pair of brick pillars is the line of demarcation. After you've passed through you're in a world of fudge and taffy, frozen custard, and a McDonald's on the beach. You'll see crowds of college and young working people (group rentals) strolling around with beers in hand. Rock music is blaring from tiny cottages, cars and the beach.

Spring Lake will have none of that. There is a tranquility to the town. Of course, you can head south to Brielle or Point Pleasant Beach to find party boats for deep-sea fishing; you can go out to see the trotters at Freehold or the thoroughbreads at the Monmouth Park Jockey Club; you can shop in pricey stores or even "slum it" at the amusement ride area in Point Pleasant. You can do all those things, but you may not need to.

You may just want the beach, the boardwalk and the lake. You may be so relaxed you don't need any diversions beyond sunny weather and good food, both of which we've found in abundance here. You may want to schedule a weekend for a "second honeymoon" — the town is perfect for strolling hand in hand — or a week for a summer vacation. You may even want to bring some elderly relatives or friends with you (they'll love it).

Spring Lake has been a dignified summer resort for more than 80 years and it looks as if it's going to stay that way for many more.

Getting There

About 35 miles due south of New York City, Spring Lake is about 75 round-about miles by car. Take the Garden State Parkway south to Exit 98 and Route 34 south to the second traffic circle; there, follow Route 35 south to Spring Lake, watching for Warren Avenue, which will bring you into town. Frequent train service is provided from New York City.

Where to Stay

No Jersey Shore town except Cape May offers a wider selection of bed-and-breakfast facilities than Spring Lake. These are fun for singles and couples; families with children are usually wiser to select a larger summer hotel where amenities like pools, tennis courts, shuffleboard and ping-pong help to keep the troops entertained.

On or Near the Water

The Normandy Inn, 21 Tuttle Ave., Spring Lake 07762. (908) 449-7172. This Victorian B&B is clearly the cream of the crop, both for its location, just a half block from the ocean, and the purity of its restoration. Susan and Michael Ingino left an ice-cream business in Bayville in 1982 to take over this imposing olive green mansion with seventeen bedrooms in the main house and two more in a carriage house out back. All have private baths and air-conditioning. They have been beautifully decorated and sport such items as brass beds, oak bureaus and pretty floral wallpapers, one a reproduction of that in the home of Robert Todd Lincoln. Room 102 has a huge walnut bed with four-piece matching bedroom set and gas fixture lights (which, of course, have been electrified). Deep red carpeting splashed with roses makes for a dramatic entry in the downstairs public rooms, and the red velvet furniture in the front parlor adds to the setting. Guests enjoy a full breakfast in a cheerful breakfast room on the main floor (for those not staying here, the privilege costs $6.95 per person). White wicker furniture on the broad front porch beckons; from a few rooms there are distant views of the ocean. Doubles, $92 to $132.

Sea Crest by the Sea, 19 Tuttle Ave., Spring Lake 07762. (908) 449-9031. This large white Victorian B&B is right next door to the Normandy Inn, a few steps closer to the beach and boardwalk. Purchased in 1990 by an affable couple, Carol and John Kirby, it has been stunningly redecorated and updated. Rooms are whimsical and fun, from Casablanca under the eaves on the third floor, which you enter through a beaded curtain, to Flamingo Grove, a cozy second-floor room with flamingos on the pillowcases. "I'm a flamingo person," says

Carol. The Kirbys serve a continental-plus breakfast at a communal dining-room table; buttermilk scones, yogurt and granola are often on the menu. Tea is served on the porch in the afternoon and guests sometimes gather around the player piano in the living room and sing. Doubles, $90 to $120.

Ashling Cottage, 106 Sussex Ave., Spring Lake 07762. (908) 449-3553. Halfway between ocean and lake, this charming Victorian B&B was built by George Hulett in 1877 with lumber from the dismantled Agricultural Exhibit of the Philadelphia Exposition of 1876. Hulett was responsible for many of Spring Lake's late 19th-century homes; this he built for his own use. Now Goodi and Jack Stewart lend their own special flair to innkeeping at this ten-room charmer. We love the bright pink impatiens that hang in the glassed-in solarium where guests take their breakfast (served buffet style in the nearby breakfast room). Here are wicker tables and chairs and a white, pink and blue color scheme that is delightful. A large comfortable parlor with color TV is a great place to relax. Goodi and Jack offer impromptu wine get-togethers and a pleasant side yard where guest may use a gas grill for a simple picnic. Two rooms have views of the water; most rooms have private baths, one of them a sunken bathroom, and the peach room is popular. All have furniture with a period feeling. Doubles, $65 to $105. Open April-December.

The Breakers Hotel, 1507 Ocean Ave., Spring Lake 07762. (908) 449-7700. Smack on the ocean, this completely updated Victorian hotel has a wraparound porch overlooking the water and many rooms with water views. All 65 recently renovated guest bedrooms have private baths. Some suites feature whirlpool baths, and all rooms have air-conditioning, color TV, refrigerator and telephone. There is a pool. The main dining room with shell-back chairs affords a great ocean view. Doubles, $130 to $160; suites, $175 to $240.

The Warren Hotel, 901 Ocean Ave., Spring Lake 07762. (908) 449-8800. This large brown and white turreted hotel, with bright yellow and white striped awnings and American flags displayed in front, is less than a block from the ocean. It is also being spruced up. As of 1990 the majority of guest bedrooms had been renovated along with the public rooms on the main level. White wicker furniture with bright green cushions and a green patterned carpet make the lobby crisp and inviting; the all-white dining room — right to the tablecloths and napkins — is stunning and cool. College students are waitresses, bellhops and elevator operators, among others, and are cheerfully accommodating. Outdoors, a pool area with bar, tennis court, shuffleboard court and nine-hole putting green are available for guests; next door is the popular **Beach House** (see Where to Eat). Doubles, $170 to $236, MAP in July and August. Open May to mid-September.

The Beacon House, 104 Beacon Blvd., Sea Girt 08750. (908) 449-5835. For a dozen years now Ernie and Ginny Westphal have been operating two large white, green-shuttered houses — with an attractive pool between — in neighboring Sea Girt, just a short walk from the town's lovely beach and boardwalk. Everything is green and white, cool and clean and the place is one of the most attractive offerings in the area (if you can get a room). We peeked into one triple (most of the 26 rooms have three singles or a double and a single bed) where all of the four-poster beds were covered with white puff quilts with a pink and green stencil design. Room 6 in the west building has twin beds in one room and a single bed in a little adjoining room — perfect for a family with a child. Guests breakfast on croissants, muffins and danish pastry along with juices and coffee in a large breakfast room in the west building. A wicker-filled lobby has television. The Beacon House is just across the street from The Parker House (see Where to Eat). Doubles, $84 to $100. Open Memorial Day to mid-September.

Other Good Bets

La Maison, 404 Jersey Ave., Spring Lake 07762. (908) 449-0969. This cocoa-colored, eight-room B&B is most attractive, although located a few blocks back from the beach. It is, however, only a short walk to the center of town. Owned by Nelson and Barbara Camp, it has resident managers and guests enjoy a large, awning-trimmed front porch, a comfortable parlor and an elegant dining room where a full continental breakfast is served. Guest bedrooms are on the second and third floors and, while not huge, have beautifully color-coordinated linens and updated private baths. Doubles, $97 to $137.

The Stone Post Inn, 115 Washington Ave., Spring Lake 07762. (908) 449-1212. This large rambling old hotel is run by an energetic former bank officer, Julie Paris, and her two teen-age daughters. The huge front parlor with its grand piano is sometimes the setting for intimate weddings, but weekenders focus more on the charming breakfast room where Julie turns out homemade muffins and breads (corn and banana when we visited) and fresh fruits such as ample bowls of strawberries with sweetened whipped cream. The runners in town for the annual Memorial Day Weekend Spring Lake Five, a major road race, sipped their tea enviously while the rest of us indulged. Rooms, most decorated in a flouncy Victorian mode, are spread through the second and third floors of the house. Some have private baths and some share hall baths. Straw hats trimmed with flowers are tacked to each bedroom door. Doubles, $70 to $90. Open year-round.

Victoria House, 214 Monmouth Ave., Spring Lake 07762. (908) 974-1882. Maggie Galisch, a former nurse, changed careers to become an innkeeper in the late 1980s at this B&B. There are ten rooms with private and shared baths, five on the second and five on the third floor. Stained-glass windows in the stairwell indicate that the house dates from 1882; gingerbread accents and carpenter gothic shingles add more clues. A buffet breakfast, perhaps with quiche or an onion tart, is set out with muffins, coffee cake, fruit juices and hot beverages in the dining room. Doubles, $65 to $95.

Villa Park Guest House, 417 Ocean Road, Spring Lake 07762. (908) 449-9698. Alice and David Bramhall are welcoming hosts at this small hostelry with five guest rooms a bit off the beaten path in Spring Lake. The walk to the beach is a few blocks, but the friendly warmth of this house highly recommends it. A comfortable living room and an oak-filled dining room where breakfast is served add to the comfort. From her wondrous kitchen Alice dishes up some fine breakfasts for guests: bacon and eggs, french toast or apple nut pancakes. Doubles, $65 to $85.

The Chateau, 500 Warren Ave., Spring Lake 07762. (908) 974-2000. This splendidly kept-up Victorian brick house with veranda and pretty hanging plants plus a more modern addition is in a residential area at the foot of the lake, not far from village shops. It has been operated for some 40 years by the same family. An inviting green and white lobby, plus individual patios for many of the 40 rooms, make this a good choice. Accommodations range from double rooms to efficiencies and two-room suites. All have refrigerators, and deluxe suites offer marble bathrooms with soaking tubs, remote-control TVs, fireplaces and wet bars. Doubles, $99 to $109; suites, to $150; three-night minimum stay required in July and August. Open April-October.

Seeing and Doing ﹏﹏﹏﹏﹏﹏﹏﹏﹏﹏﹏﹏﹏ _ᏟᏟᏟ_

This is not an area filled with historic monuments, art colonies and museums. This is the beach, and most people spend their days on or near it. There are also good shopping, deep-sea fishing, biking and the like. A car tour around Spring Lake and Sea Girt is highly recommended.

THE OCEAN. The Atlantic is the draw and the beach at Spring Lake, while suffering yearly ravages and erosion, is still quite good. Small dunes anchored by beach grass and flowers are touted, but they're too small to look much like dunes to anyone who's seen the National Seashore on Cape Cod. Two pavilions (one at the south end, one at the north end of the stretch) sell refreshments and beach badges. Badges ($3.25 per day) are necessary from mid-June through Labor Day; most hotels and guest houses include them in their rates or sell them at a discount to overnight guests. A saltwater pool is located at each of the pavilions, but we are told that only Spring Lake residents may use them. The beach at Sea Girt (the next town south) is nice, but quite a bit smaller; badges must also be purchased for about the same price as in Spring Lake. Again, nearby hotels or guest houses usually provide them free or for a small fee. The beach at Point Pleasant is backed by a boardwalk with amusement-park rides; that at Bay Head has no boardwalk and huge weathered "cottages" overlook it. Again, badges must be purchased.

THE LAKE. Spring Lake's lake is quite pretty, with weeping willows planted in areas along the bank and two rustic bridges to walk across. Benches overlook the lake at comfortable intervals. Evening strolls are popular, and the ducks and swans are fun to watch. The lake is said to be spring-fed.

Sea Girt Lighthouse, corner Ocean and Beach avenues, Sea Girt. This is the only lighthouse on this portion of the Jersey Shore. Perched atop a brick house, the light began to beam in 1896 and continued until 1955. It has been restored but is not open to the public. However, it makes a nice background for photographs.

St Catharine's Church, West Lake Drive at Third Avenue, Spring Lake. This Roman Catholic church, a smallish replica of St. Peter's in Rome, is very ornate and worth a visit.

Spring Lake Trolley. A jaunty orange and green trolley ferries tourists and others around Spring Lake. The 30-minute route is covered from 11 to 7 daily, Memorial Day until Labor Day. A ride is 50 cents and you can hail the trolley and get off any place along the route.

Amusement Parks. Jenkinson's Park at Point Pleasant Beach is a typical, old-fashioned amusement area with rides for adults and children, taffy, fudge, fried dough, pizza by the slice and so forth. Kids love it.

Historic Allaire Village, Allaire State Park, off Route 524, Allaire Road, Allaire, 938-2371. Several historic buildings can be visited in this restored area, which recreates a 19th-century community. Historic Allaire was a community producing bog iron, which was cast into shapes of cauldrons, stoves, pipes and other objects. Bog iron ore is a renewable source of iron oxide deposited in decaying vegetation in swampy areas. At the height of the community, some 400 people lived and worked here. On a rainy day, we found it quite interesting to wander the paths and visit the buildings. Several exhibits show the iron ore smelting process. Parking fee, $3 weekends, $2 weekdays. Buildings open daily 10 to 5, May to Labor Day; Wednesday-Sunday in off-season. Closed January-March.

DEEP-SEA FISHING. Party boats in search of blues, flukes, sea bass and mackerel go out year-round from Brielle and Point Pleasant. **Bogan's Boat Basin,** at the Manasquan River Bridge just off Route 35, Brielle, 528-8377, has the largest fleet of party boats. Capt. John Bogan, who started his trips more than 50 years ago, overseas the Paramount, Jamaica, Paramount II and Jamaica II. Cost is about $20 for a half day, about $30 for a full day. Night trips are also offered. The nearby bait and tackle shop is open daily and if Capt. John is in, he'll give you other advice (such as good restaurants in the area). Party boats also leave from Point Pleasant Beach, just off Route 35. Half-day fluke trips and half-night blues trips are available.

BOAT RIDES. Sightseeing and dining cruises are offered aboard two small replicas of riverboats, the **River Belle** and the **River Queen,** which sail the Manasquan River and Barnegat Bay. The River Belle has daytime and evening buffet cruises as well as afternoon and evening sightseeing cruises. For information call 528-6620 or 892-3377.

BICYCLING. The flatness of these towns makes them especially appealing to cyclists. Bicycles can be rented from **Point Pleasant Bicycle,** 2701 Bridge Ave., 899-9755. Some hotels and guest houses also rent or lend bicycles to guests. Bikers are allowed on boardwalks from 6 to 10 a.m.

OTHER SPORTS. Golf. Public golf courses include the Bey Lea Municipal Golf Course on Bay Avenue, Toms River, and the Bel-Aire Golf Club, Allaire Road and Highway 34, Wall.

Horse racing. Monmouth Park, Oceanport Avenue, Oceanport, 222-5100, has been bringing thoroughbred racing to New Jersey for more than 40 years. The season is early June through August with ten races daily Monday-Saturday.

SHOPPING. The main shopping street is Third Avenue, with a few shops also found on Morris Avenue. Because of the town's Irish heritage, it is worthwhile to stop at the **Irish Centre,** 1120 Third Ave., to check out the handmade Irish woolen sweaters and other native crafts — everything from Waterford crystal to christening dresses. **The Butcher Block,** a gourmet grocery with deli-bakery, is also on Third, as are the **Ladybug Boutique,** a good gift shop; **Another Angle** for fashionable women's duds, and the **Third Avenue Chocolate Shoppe** for candy and stuffed toys. The lately expanded **Fireside Book Shop** at 1212 Third is chock-full of hard cover and paperback books and also has a lending library.

A SPECIAL PLACE. Ocean Grove, an oceanfront religious community that still clings to its Methodist past, is a twenty-minute drive north of Spring Lake via Route 71. Look at all the tiny gingerbread houses and the larger gingerbread boarding houses and hotels. Read the street names: Pilgrim's Pathway, Mount Tabor Way, Mount Carmel Way. Visit the auditorium where religious meetings are still held weekly throughout the summer. On Thursday and Saturday evenings performers such as a gospel singer or an orchestra playing Mozart are scheduled. The auditorium is being restored and is on the National Register of Historic Places. Next to Ocean Grove (when we were in college the kids called it "Ocean Grave") is Asbury Park, which, we're told, is going to be restored. Wait until it is.

ANNUAL EVENTS. The **Spring Lake Five** is a five-mile run that annually attracts top runners from the New York metropolitan area. It is usually held on Memorial Day Weekend and more than 4,500 runners take part. Another popular event is the annual **House Tour** usually scheduled on a weekday in June. Eight to ten lovely Spring Lake homes are open to the public.

Where to Eat ⟋⟋⟋

There is a disconcerting aspect to eating at the Jersey Shore. Most restaurants don't take reservations, resulting in waits up to two hours on Friday and Saturday nights. Plan to arrive before 7 or after 9:30 when the crowd is usually thinner. Also check whether the restaurant has a liquor license. Several do not, but let you tote your own bottle of wine.

By the Water

The Yankee Clipper, Ocean Avenue, Sea Girt. (908) 449-7200. Ask anyone in the area where you can dine with a view of the ocean, and this will be the response. The view from huge windows in the main **Surf Room** on the upper level is fantastic. Downstairs, the **Sand Bar Pub** has a view of the water from the windows in front, but it's not nearly as dramatic. Nevertheless, the pub is popular, especially with all the beachers who throw T-shirts on over their bathing suits and cross the road for a cooler or a quick lunch. A big barrel of peanuts greets you at the door to the pub and beer drinkers scoop them up by the handful. The decor is wood (tongue-in-groove paneling around the side), brass and plants around a bar in the center of the room. Our party of three had tasty lunches of clams on the half shell, tacos and a roast beef on rye; prices range from $4.50 to $11 and you can have breakfast here. A special pub drink is "Surf's Up," vanilla ice cream with melon liqueur and rum. Surf Room, lunch, Tuesday-Saturday 11:30 to 2:30; dinner, 4:30 to 9; Sunday brunch, 11:30 to 2:30. Pub, open year-round 11:30 to midnight.

GaBrielle's at the Brielle Yacht Club, Brielle. (908) 528-7750. This attractive luncheon and light dining spot overlooks the Intracoastal Waterway, where there's lots of activity, especially by day. Set yourself up on the outside patio with a bar or inside in a bright room with pink formica tables, deep green placemats and deep green napkins stuffed into the glasses. The black lacquered chairs with textured pink upholstered seats add an air of sophistication and the waitresses, even at noon, are clad in black trousers, white shirts, bow ties and cummerbunds. At lunch, entrees ($5 to $12) range from melon crown (half a cantaloupe filled with seafood or chicken salad, surrounded by fresh fruit and cottage cheese) to fish and chips. At night you can still get sandwiches but might opt for sea scallops alfredo, prime rib, or surf and turf in the $14 to $17 range. **The River Watch** is the yacht club's fancier dining spot; it doesn't have the view but the tablecloths are white and entrees (many seafood selections) rise in price to $17 to $20. GaBrielle's, open daily 11:30 to 10. River Watch, dinner 6 to 10.

The Beach House, 901 Ocean Ave., Spring Lake. (908) 449-9646. Operated by the Warren Hotel and located just across the street from the beach, this is the most popular spot for dining (and drinking) in Spring Lake. The turreted, brown-shingled Victorian building (check the crazy chimney architecture on the roof) attracts a crowd for lunch, happy hour, and dinner. The bar in front and the two picnic tables outside have the best view of the ocean and boardwalk just across the street. Two pleasant dining rooms with pressed-oak furniture and black and white tiled floors are in back. A wraparound, glassed-in porch on the side of the building also offers great views at small tables for two. No reservations are accepted for dinner at the Beach House and the lines can be discouraging. The creative menu usually includes a half dozen appetizers, such as country pate with cornichons and French bread croutons and iced jumbo shrimp with horseradish sauce and tarragon mayonnaise. Usually two salad choices are offered: possibly sliced tomatoes with red onions in basil and olive oil or watercress and endive with a walnut vinaigrette. Entrees ($12 to $17) include breast of chicken stuffed with ham and Swiss cheese, shrimp baked with spinach and feta cheese, and loin lamb chops with fresh mint sauce. There is always a hamburger choice on the dinner menu, priced at about $5.50. Lunches are heavy on salads and sandwiches (a jumbo hot dog with caraway sauerkraut is $4.25). Lunch daily, noon to 5; dinner, 6 to 10 or 11. Open May-September.

The Wharfside, Channel Drive, Point Pleasant. (908) 892-9100. Overlooking the busy Manasquan River channel, this restaurant is one of several owned in New Jersey and Florida by Jack Baker. Another is the **Lobster Shanty** next door. Popular with tourists, these restaurants provide standard water lovers' fare: a good range of seafood, a water view, bustling conviviality and rational prices. The Wharfside is usually packed. We managed to be seated within twenty minutes by arriving just before 7 on a Saturday evening. Orange shell-motif lamps hang in both restaurants and rough pine wood booths are also standard. The Lobster Shanty is a bit more open, with a slightly better view. The menus are virtually identical and include such items as baked scallops, seafood florentine, baked whitefish, and shrimp and scallop combo, priced in the $11 to $15 range. Corn fritters and garlic bread come to the table in a basket and are quite tasty; the meal also includes coleslaw, a potato choice, and a tossed salad mixed at table by a "salad bar waitress" and served with the house dressing, Italian. There is a small section for outdoor dining. Open daily, noon to 9:30.

The Old Mill Inn, Old Mill Road, Spring Lake Heights. (908) 449-1800. Overlooking its own mill pond (they call it "a lake") and with especially good water views from the Waterview Room, the Old Mill Inn has become a classic on the Jersey Shore. It was rebuilt and enlarged following a fire in 1985 and is as popular as ever. This is a large place with three dining rooms, a staff of more than 200, and a cafe and bar with live entertainment some nights. Lunches ($6 to $10) stress quiches, salads and pastas. In the evening try seafood entrees like shrimp with crabmeat stuffing, fisherman's platter or coconut shrimp. Other choices on the large menu priced from $15 to $25 include steaks, prime rib, veal chop bercy, garlic chicken and pasta. The wine list is extensive. Open daily, 11:30 to 10 or 11; Sunday brunch, 11 to 3.

Other Choices

The following restaurants do not boast a water view but the food is fine — in many instances better than what can be found at water's edge.

Whispers, 200 Monmouth Ave., Spring Lake. (908) 974-1212. RoseAnne and Don Del Nero are the energetic force behind this restaurant, located in the Hewitt Wellington, a condominium hotel in Spring Lake. Arguably the most inventive place in town, the kitchen produces choices like cashew chicken salad, a beef wellington sandwich and a quiche of the day for lunch ($5.50 to $8) and dinner entrees like chicken campagne, tournedos cabernet and salmon fumet ($13 to $19). The much-admired veal Evelyn, named for Don's mother, is milk-fed veal sauteed with shallots and artichoke hearts and finished in a light white wine cream sauce. RoseAnne is in the kitchen; her husband manages the front of the house. The pink and rose decor is elegant. Reservations are hard to come by at times. Lunch daily except Monday; Sunday brunch; dinner on weekends. BYOB.

The Sandpiper, 7 Atlantic Ave., Spring Lake. (908) 449-6060. Located on the lower level of an inn not far from the beach, the Sandpiper is highly rated. The pink and white color scheme seems appropriate for the Victorian-era inn and a pianist who plays during dinner adds an elegant touch. Chef Mark Head puts out a creative repertoire including such specials as grilled tuna with tomato and fresh basil or a mixed grill of tuna, chicken and barbequed shrimp. Smoked salmon ravioli might be available as appetizer or entree and there's always a pasta. Entrees range from $14 to $20. Dinner nightly in season, 6 to 9 or 10.

Pagano's, Ocean Avenue (corner Park), Bradley Beach. (908) 775-0795. Once a simple pizza restaurant, Pagano's expanded in 1989 to include a dining room where excellent dinners are served at reasonable prices. Pasta is homemade and there is a good selection of seafood, veal and chicken along with favorites like fettuccine carbonara, eggplant parmigiana and linguini Bolognese, all in the $7 to $9 range. Shrimp francaise, veal francaise and chicken breast florentine are among other entrees, priced from $11 to $14. It's a pleasant ride along the ocean to reach Pagano's and you can dress casually. You can also get a pizza to go from the other side of the place, which operates as it always did. Dinner nightly, 4 to 10; pizza, Monday-Wednesday 3 to 10, Thursday-Saturday 11 to 10. BYOB.

Evelyn's, 507 Main St., Belmar. (908) 681-0236. Evelyn Longstreet was a real character in these parts and even after her death, her restaurant thrives in nearby Belmar. Completely renovated in 1990 by owner Steven Cross, the place has a fish market up front, tile floors, black and white checked oilcloth tablecloths and a real "seafood at the shore" atmosphere. Seating is in light wood booths near the bar or tables out back and a young waitstaff is enthusiastic. The place gets mobbed by 7 on weekends so plan your visit accordingly. Corn muffins and warm biscuits are delivered with drinks. There is even a private label wine, Oyster White or Oyster Red. You can get clams, shrimp, oysters, crab and lobster cocktail from the Oyster Bar, a variety of cold appetizers including a smoked bluefish plate, and — if you are splurging — beluga caviar with Dom Perignon for $125. But other prices are down to earth, in the $13 to $18 range for such entrees as Evelyn's original stuffed shrimp balls, broiled fish (listed alphabetically from bluefish to tuna with more than twenty options), lobsters and — for landlubbers - chicken or steak dishes. Evelyn's clambake ($23.95) comes with Manhattan or New England clam chowder plus the usual. Cheesecake and bread pudding are among the signature desserts. It's good fresh food, nothing fancy. Lunch, Tuesday-Saturday 11:30 to 5; dinner, 5 to 9, Sunday noon to 9:30.

Rod's Old Irish Tavern, 507 Washington Blvd., Sea Girt. (908) 449-2020. This is a fun, pub-atmosphere place, popular for both lunch and dinner. Green and white checked cloths, bentwood chairs and green carpeting — plus a very large bar — add to a goodtime Irish feeling. The all-day menu is filled with snack-type fare, such as salads, nachos and fried zucchini, soups, burgers and deli sandwiches, plus "Saloon Specials" like open-face hot turkey or sirloin steak sandwiches. Entrees include chicken dishes, seafood and pasta in the $10 to $15 range. Daily specials are listed on the blackboard. Open daily, 11:30 to 10.

After hours, yuppies and others gather at the huge white and green **Parker House** in Sea Girt for drinks on the porch, in the bar, or downstairs where there's a happy hour with music just about every day. **The Osprey** in Manasquan attracts a happy-hour crowd as well.

FOR MORE INFORMATION: Spring Lake Chamber of Commerce, 1315 Third Ave., Box 694, Spring Lake, N.J. 07762. (908) 449-0577.

Montauk Lighthouse is at tip of Long Island.

Montauk/Long Island, N.Y.

For many of us, Long Island conjures up images of asphalt and anguish, crowds and crush. It isn't exactly the place we imagine for long luxurious days on the beach, for relaxing dinners, for restful moments. Except for the Hamptons, of course — where the image is of money, money, money.

Still, the geography intrigues us: that long sandbar jutting out into the open ocean. And at the very tip of the island, stretching as far as it can into the shining Atlantic, is Montauk. What a piece of real estate! Crowned by one of the country's first lighthouses at its very end, blessed by an ocean strand that seems to stretch to infinity, home to an inland lake that is safe harbor to gorgeous sailboats and other vessels, Montauk is just the place for summer days and summer nights.

Unlike its pricier neighbors, much of Montauk is affordable. Motels have been built close enough to the beach that visitors can roll out of bed and onto the sand, and most are only two or three stories high. Beach parking is free at many points for those not staying right at the water's edge. Good restaurants, lots of water activities, state and county parks and a little bit of history all contribute to Montauk's draw. And, if you want to leave Manhattan behind one steamy weekend — as New Yorkers do — you can take the train all the way out.

Resort status came relatively late, not until 1920 when entrepreneur Carl Fisher decided to turn Montauk into a "Miami Beach of the North." High on Signal Hill he built the Tudor-style Montauk Manor, which for many years was a popular luxury hotel in spite of its distance from the ocean (it's been con-dominiumized of late). Somewhat braver and smarter developers built motels right along the sandy beaches.

Montauk Village is a bit of Hyannis with a slice of New York. Good Jewish delicatessens serve up lox and bagels and kippered herring. Visitors walk into the IGA store in bathing suits and plastic thongs. Dressing for dinner means climbing into jeans or a denim skirt. Everyone, it seems, is on vacation.

80

Montauk Village is on the ocean side. A few miles across, on Long Island Sound, is the harbor that boaters know. (One of Carl Fisher's more successful ideas was to dredge out what is called Lake Montauk and make a huge protected anchorage.)

Few visitors get this close to the tip of Long Island without going all the way. Follow Route 27 to the end of Montauk State Park, where you can take a variety of paths down to a rocky beach for views of the great lighthouse at land's end.

There's history here, too. Indians were the earliest settlers, but as far back as the 17th century the gently undulating grasslands were used as grazing land for cows and sheep owned by inhabitants of towns farther west. Montauk goes so far as to claim to be the birthplace of the American cowboy.

The best part about Montauk is the sense one has of being close to the end of the world. Sea grapes and beach plums line the roads, the dune grass bends in the wind, the ocean is everywhere. The pretentiousness of the Hamptons ends at their borders. Here in Montauk the relaxed attitude is refreshing.

Getting There

Montauk is about 135 miles east of New York City. The Long Island Rail Road schedules service from Pennsylvania Station directly to Montauk, a trip of a little more than three hours. One-way passenger tickets are $9.50. The train station is located just north of the center of the village, and there are many motels right in town and on the beach, so once here, you don't need a car.

From points south and west, motorists take the Long Island Expressway to Exit 70, then Route 111 south to Route 27. From New England, take the Cross Sound Ferry (car and driver, $26; each passenger, $8) from New London, Conn., to Orient Point. Drive Route 25 to Greenport to catch a ferry to Shelter Island. Cross that island on Route 114 to another ferry to Sag Harbor. From Sag Harbor drive to East Hampton to pick up Route 27 to Montauk. A car, with passengers, is $5.50 one way on each of two ferries to and from Shelter Island. Cross Sound ferries run hourly through the summer and car reservations should be made in advance. Call (203) 443-5281 in Connecticut or (516) 323-2525 on Long Island. Shelter Island ferries run on demand; get in line and wait your turn.

Where to Stay

You will probably want to be on the ocean — or the inland lake — and that's quite possible as long as you commit to three- or four-night minimums during the summer. During slower seasons like 1990 you could find vacancies for one or two night, but you had to wait until a week ahead, or take a chance on finding them when you got to Montauk. If that is your plan, go early in the day and reserve your room.

Several motels with oceanfront terraces, and many with pools, line the beach. Most are cooperatives, which means the units are individually owned, but they operate as motels. Inns and B&Bs haven't been developed in Montauk. What's available serves quite well the needs of visitors: a clean bed, a shower, and access to the magnificent beach.

The Panoramic View, Old Montauk Highway, Montauk 11954. (516) 668-3000. The French family built this gorgeous, terraced, hillside complex in the late 1950s and are still in charge. A half dozen buildings — all white clapboard with green roofs — are set into a steep hill leading down to 1,000 feet of private ocean beach at this spectacular spot. Located on the road that hugs the ocean, the Panoramic View is enormously popular both for its location and the service that is rendered guests. All 120 accommodations have a terrace with an ocean view. The plantings are particularly pleasing; we were charmed by white begonias in the shape of a whale and masses of impatiens near the check-in area. You can stay in a one-and-one-half-room unit with bedroom and small kitchenette, or an oceanfront house with wood-burning fireplace, two bedrooms and two baths, accommodating six. Barbecue grills are tucked discreetly into the shrubbery. A free-form heated swimming pool is halfway down the hill between the road and ocean. Rooms are mostly paneled and have wall-to-wall carpeting, air-conditioning, cable TV, telephones and VCRs. If there is a negative, it is the steepness of the walk back up the hill after you've spent a day on the beach. Avoid it by staying in the closest building, Salt Sea. Rates are quite rational and off-season weekends are bargains (doubles, $144 to $208 for two nights, including a 5 p.m. departure). Doubles, $116 to $178 daily in season (minimum stay, five days). Open early April-October. No credit cards.

Montauk Yacht Club Resort Marina, Star Island, Montauk 11954. (516) 668-3100 or (800) 932-4200. Under new ownership in 1990 and managed by Brock Services, Ltd., this full-service resort is built around what was once a working lighthouse overlooking Lake Montauk. While not on the ocean, the inn has a great marina setting on Star Island, which juts out into the lake, connected by a causeway; boaters can pull their craft right up to the dock and spend a few luxurious days ashore. Of a total 107 accommodations, 84 are in the main complex and another 23 are in "villas" — five houses that were renovated by the hotel in the early 1980s and are located a short walk along the water from the main area. Rooms are in weathered contemporary buildings with large decks or patios, most of which are waterfront. All have kingsize or two double beds. The villa area — with its own pool — features larger rooms, lush lawns and a quieter, away-from-it-all feeling. Nine tennis courts (four lighted), an indoor pool with jacuzzi and sauna, game rooms, and a small beach where sunfish may be rented for sailing make this a place to play. Bellhops are dressed like yacht club commodores in the luxurious and tasteful lobby. The fine restaurant is **Ziegfeld's,** the lighter indoor-outdoor casual spot is **Follies,** so named because Florenz Ziegfeld once owned a portion of the property. Courtesy vans take guests to the ocean beach. Doubles, $250 to $275; two-night minimum in season. Open April-November.

Gurney's Inn and Spa, Old Montauk Highway, Montauk 11954. (516) 668-2345 or (800) 847-6397. Probably the best-known place in town and the oldest, this sprawling hillside complex celebrates its 70th anniversary in 1991. A bit glitzy with its Italianate statuary and wrought iron, Gurney's attracts a well-heeled crowd in search of eternal youth (which it attempts to provide through its spa program and special calorie-conscious meals). Altogether 125 rooms are located in a half dozen buildings, plus four fireplaced cottages on the beach. The beach is that next door to The Panoramic View, but at Gurney's the climb is not quite so steep. There are a heated indoor saltwater swimming pool, Finnish rock saunas, Russian steamrooms, Swiss showers, gymnasiums and equipment. Now a time-sharing cooperative, the inn includes suites, staterooms, studios and cottages. Guests take two meals a day in the spacious, oceanview dining room that is part of the large administrative complex at the top of the hill. It may all appear a bit much, right down to the Sevilles and limos in the parking area, but Gurney's certainly throbs with activity mid-season. Doubles, $270 to $350 MAP.

Hartman's Briney Breezes Motel, Old Montauk Highway, Montauk 11954. (516) 668-2290. This contemporary two-story motel complex with large swimming pool is across the street from the ocean. Most terraced rooms have ocean views from wooden decks and the complex is immaculately maintained by owners Herman and Sheila Hartman. All units include kitchenettes and have one or two bedrooms; because of this and the location they are often booked for a full week. Cable TVs, HBO and air-conditioning are standard. Doubles, $120; two-room apartment accommodating four, $170 to $180; weekly, $760 for two, about $1100 for four. No credit cards. Open late March to mid-October.

The Beach Plum Motel, Old Montauk Highway, Montauk 11954. (516) 668-4100. This is another attractive motel complex along the Old Montauk Highway, just west of the village. Nestled on a hill, the Beach Plum overlooks the Atlantic and offers studio, one-bedroom efficiency apartments and cottages. You can walk across the street and down to a fine ocean beach. Doubles, $120 to $145; two-bedroom cottage for four, $200.

The Royal Atlantic, South Edgemere Street, Montauk 11954. (516) 668-5103. Located right in town — and on the ocean — this is for the visitor who wants to be within walking distance of restaurants, nightlife and the beach. The large two-story complex with a pool sits right on the sand; across the street, with its own pool, is its sister motel, **The Royal Atlantic North,** (516) 668-5597. Accommodations range from regular and oversize rooms to three-room suites accommodating four. All 152 units have carpeting, TVs, in-room coffee makers, and refrigerators plus terraces overlooking the ocean or pool. Units at the Royal Atlantic North also have kitchenettes. A lounge and restaurant are open to the public. Doubles, $115 to $145; suites, $145 to $175. Open April-October.

East Deck Resort Motel, Ditch Plains Road, Montauk 11954. (516) 668-2334. This low-key, one-story family motel was one of the first in Montauk. Located east of town on a quiet and gorgeous stretch of beach, it is raised from the sand a few feet and surrounded on all sides by one vast deck where guests lounge and chat. If you want privacy, do not choose this resort, for its convivial, open, communal spirit is its strength. Absolutely basic furnishings — linoleum covered floors and 1950s dinette tables, for example — make these units perfect for sweeping out the sand and keeping the dinner hour as simple as possible. An Olympic-size pool out back is a plus and teenagers love the surf at the beach. If you don't bring a surfboard along, you may find yourself buying one in town. The 30 accommodations include studio and one-bedroom efficiencies, motel units and one-bedroom apartments with private decks. Prices are relatively low for Montauk, but we're not talking about luxury here, just a basic spot at the beach with location, location, location. Suppose it rains? Well, there are all those paperbacks in the public parlor next to the office. Doubles, $90 to $115.

Malibu Motel, Elmwood Avenue, Montauk 11954. (516) 668-5233. We have stayed at this motel and found it quite satisfactory. The two-story, U-shaped building is across the street from the beach and Al and Anneliese Issing, the owners, take great care in keeping things shipshape. All 32 rooms have wall-to-wall carpeting, cable TV, refrigerators, and most have balconies. There are a few efficiencies as well. The smallish size makes it seem less crowded and there is a lawn area out back with grill and picnic table, plus an outdoor shower for rinsing after the beach. Doubles, $80 to $95.

CAMPING. Hither Hills State Park, off the Old Montauk Highway, Montauk, is an exceptional situation for campers: a wonderful ocean beach, a bathhouse and a playground for children. But it's hard to get in because it's so popular. The 140 sites are booked through a toll-free reservation system that applies to all New York State campgrounds. Call (800) 456-2267 no more than

90 days in advance of the date you want and no less than seven days. New York State residents pay $11 per night for a campsite; out-of-staters, $13.

Seeing and Doing

THE BEACH. The beach runs the entire length of the south shore and it's one of the best in the Northeast. Both sand and surf are found in abundance and in some places there are dunes. If you're a serious surfer you'll probably want to go to **Ditch Plains Beach,** east of Montauk Village, off Route 27. If you'd like to have the amenities of **Hither Hills State Park,** pay the day rate of $4 and enjoy. In many of the beach areas, if you can find parking along the road, you're welcome to it, free of charge — a refreshing attitude.

The Montauk Lighthouse, end of Route 27. George Washington commissioned the building of the lighthouse at Montauk Point back in 1795; it was finished two years later and — white, with red cummerbund — is symbolic of the area. It appears on almost everything: T-shirts, posters, signs and even a beer called Montauk Light. Perched above the rocks and churning waves of the Atlantic at the tip of Long Island, it's a beautiful place to visit. This is land's end and you feel as if you're at the end of the world. A $3 parking fee allows visitors to explore the environs, buy a bite at the snack bar and walk down one of several paths to the beach.

There's an additional fee (adults $2, children $1) to get into the lighthouse, where a small museum and a gift shop are located in the base. Want to climb to the tower? That'll be another 25 cents, please, and a line forms quickly. We like the appropriateness of the items in the gift shop — almost all are lighthouse-oriented. Erosion control is necessary to prevent the lighthouse bluff from being eaten away more than it has been (200 feet in 200 years). The information on the "Save the Lighthouse" project may even move you to donate.

BOATING. Uihlein's Boat Rentals on West Lake Drive Extension at Montauk Harbor, 668-3799, rents a wide range of craft, from skiffs to T-birds. You can arrange for water-skiing as well.

FISHING. Calling itself the "Sport-fishing Capital of the World," Montauk claims to have had more world-record fish caught in its waters than any other port. **The Viking Fishing Fleet,** West Lake Drive Extension, Montauk Harbor, 668-5700, boasts four supercruisers for half-day and full-day fishing for giant cod and pollack, blues, blackfish, porgies, fluke and tuna. The Viking fleet also runs a passenger ferry to Block Island, New London, Mystic, Newport and Martha's Vineyard.

The **Marlin V** makes two half-day trips daily (8 a.m. and 1 p.m.) from Salivars Dock, 668-5343. It also goes out on a sunset cruise ($10 each) daily at 7.

Some charter boats leave from Tuma's Dock off Flamingo Road in Montauk Harbor. Also check out the Captain's Cove Marina on West Lake Drive, from which many charters leave.

Surfcasting is permitted free at Montauk County Park in Montauk. Bluefish and striped bass are caught in the northern area of the park.

WHALE WATCHES. The Okeanos Ocean Research Foundation, a non-profit research and educational organization, offers one or two whale-watch trips daily from the Viking Dock, 728-4522. Adults $25, children $15. An Okeanos information center was opened in 1990 on the lower level of the Montauk Chamber of Commerce building in the center of the village on the plaza. Here are artifacts, videos and information about the foundation's work with all types of marine mammals and sea turtles.

HORSEBACK RIDING. There's a real business in horseback riding on the beaches and trails at the east end of the island — possibly a carryover from when Montauk was the land of cowboys, or perhaps from Long Islander Teddy Roosevelt's Roughrider days. From the **Deep Hollow Ranch** on Route 27, 668-2244, 90-minute rides leave on the hour from 9 to 6 and cost $25. It's a good idea to call for reservations and you should wear jeans. **Rita's Stable,** 668-5453, offers sunset beach rides on the bluffs overlooking the ocean as well as half-day backpack rides and lessons.

Golf and Tennis. The newish Montauk Downs State Park off South Fairview Street in the village has an eighteen-hole golf course, driving range, several tennis courts, restaurant and changing facilities.

Second House Museum, Montauk Highway (Route 27), Montauk. Built in 1797 and virtually as old as the lighthouse, this was one of the original three houses in Montauk (the first burned to the ground; the third is part of the Montauk County Park). They were used by cattlemen and their families while caring for the herds of sheep and cows brought out to Montauk to graze. The weathered Cape is a charmer, and visitors are treated to a tour by a Montauk Historical Society member. They view candle molds, a cranberry scoop, a courting couch and a number of other artifacts and furnishings from the 18th and 19th centuries. A rope handrail leads to the second floor, where five bedrooms are furnished in period style. On the first floor, a small room attached to the kitchen is furnished as a school room, for it was in this house that Montauk's children were first schooled. After the sand, the sun and the fun of Montauk, visiting Second House is a nice change of pace. The gorgeous lawn, the herb and flower garden maintained by local garden clubs and the ambience of it all are refreshing. We spread our cloth and had a picnic here. Open daily except Wednesday in summer, 10 to 4.

Montauk County Park, Route 27, Montauk. 668-5022. This large county park, stretching from Montauk Highway north to the beach on Block Island Sound, offers several diversions. A large, rambling wood building houses park offices and a portion of Third House, constructed in 1806, plus photographs of Teddy Roosevelt and his Rough Riders who were stationed at Montauk following the Spanish-American War. The photographs, which are real gems, aren't as well-preserved, displayed or documented as they should be. Also on the site are an Indian Museum that's more or less open daily, pleasant picnic areas, a large pond for freshwater fishing and a bicycle hostel. Guided walks are offered free on summer weekends and there are several miles of nature trails. Only county residents may camp in the park.

SHOPPING. Gosman's Dock at the mouth of the harbor is more than just a restaurant complex (see Where to Eat). It is a village of shops, some of them quite tony, such as **Summer Stock,** which sells high-priced and sophisticated items; **Capt. Kid,** a children's clothing shop (we love the name); the **Irish Country Loft,** for items Irish, and — best of all — **The Fish Shop,** for all sorts of things with fish motifs, from ashtrays and pottery to sweatshirts, all extraordinarily tasteful.

In the village, check out **A Little Bit of Everything** on the Plaza. A ten-year-old could spend the day here. You'll find sunglasses, beach umbrellas, puzzles, footballs to throw on the beach, mugs, mirrors, magic, you name it. **The Bookshop** has mostly romances for the beach. And the **Montauk Beach Shop** has, well, beach things.

Where to Eat _____ _✏✏✏_

Surfside Inn, Old Montauk Highway, Montauk. (516) 668-5958. This guest-house and restaurant, situated above the road and across the street from the beach, has a sweeping ocean view that is one of its draws. Add a charming deck and main dining room, inventive cuisine and cheerful service, and you have a winning combination. We had a lovely lunch here one hot Saturday when we would have sweltered anywhere else, but were cooled by a constant breeze on the outdoor deck. Here, white wrought-iron tables and chairs beneath striped blue and white Molson umbrellas offer a good vantage for enjoying the water view. Linda and Jim Burnds have been renovating and upgrading since they took over in 1983. The main dining room has mismatched wooden chairs, floral cloth-covered tables and a good view. Blackboard specials supplement the menu at lunch and dinner. We had warm Thai chicken salad with a chile lime dressing (and could have had duck, beef or shrimp in a similar guise) and a spicy peanut flavor that was quite good, and a hefty hamburger that was all of its promised half pound in size. Other items included broiled scallops, shrimp and broccoli or shrimp and sugar snap peas over linguini, and stir-fry vegetables over rice. For dinner, regular items include a boneless marinated shell steak ($17.95), which is extremely popular, and lots of fresh fish. Lunch prices are $4 to $12 and dinner entrees, $15 to $20. Open for lunch and dinner.

Dave's Grill, West Lake Drive, Montauk Harbor. (516) 668-9190. Dave Marcley opened this small but smashing spot on the pier area off Lake Montauk in 1988. It's so popular that unless you're in place before 7, you'll probably be cooling your heels for a while in the summer. Dave is in the kitchen, keeping quality high. Inside are brightly painted booths with aqua and white predominating and a few small tables; outside is a modest deck with a half dozen tables and a view of the harbor a short distance away. Dinner appetizers ($4 to $8) include such delights as tomato and zucchini soup with fresh basil, topped with parmesan and fresh mozzarella, or fried calamari served with a cool vegetable salsa. Among entrees ($17 to $20) at our visit were grilled yellowfin tuna with basil pesto and toasted pinenuts and fresh spinach linguini with sea scallops and chorizo sausage. A regular dinner item is rack of lamb with glazed honey mustard sauce. Desserts are wild: a chocolate bag full of ice cream and whipped cream and served with a raspberry sauce for two or the espresso and rum soaked ladyfingers in the tirami su, surrounded with a mousse of mascarpone cheese and kahlua and layered with grated chocolate. Open daily except Wednesday for lunch and dinner, late spring to fall.

The Inn at Napeague, Montauk Highway, Amagansett. (516) 267-3332. For over twenty years, Monty and Muriel Grossman (and lately son Mark) have been catering to the tastes of summer people; before that Monty was a chef at Quo Vadis in New York City. The "inn" is a rather plain little gray roadside building that warms up once you're inside. A stone fireplace, captain's chairs, wood tables and bare floors set the mood. The dunes are on view across the road from the window tables, but the water is out of sight. Muriel is the hostess and Monty and Mark hold forth out back. Among appetizers ($3 to $7) are clam chowder, clams on the half shell, mussels mariniere, stuffed eggplant parmigiana and fettuccine alfredo; a hot antipasto plate for two is $9.95. Entrees are priced from $14 to $23 for broiled lobster and sirloin steak. They include veal parmigiana, frog's legs provencale, steak au poivre, duckling a l'orange flambe and lots of fresh fish from the docks. If you still have room, you might try caramel custard, rice pudding or peach melba for dessert. Dinner nightly, 5 to 10 or 11, Sunday to 9. Open late April to mid-November.

Gosman's Dock, West Lake Drive at the mouth of Montauk Harbor, Montauk. (516) 668-5330. The location of this complex with several spots in which to dine makes it one of Montauk's most sought after. It overlooks the inlet leading to Lake Montauk and the harbor, providing spectacular views of the passing parade of sail and motor boats. A large group of seagulls hangs around looking for a handout — and usually a couple of swans do, too. On a popular weekend night you might have to sit first at one of the breezy outdoor tables with a drink before a table is ready inside. The food is respectable, if predictable. The all-day menu includes lobsters of various sizes ($9.95 for a chicken lobster to $27.50 for a two-pounder), seafood salad and fried soft-shell crabs as well as chowders, clams on the half shell and such. Other restaurants here include the self-service **Clam Bar,** where you can get shrimp, lobster or clam rolls, corn on the cob, steamers, and fish and chips, and eat your repast at a red and blue Cinzano-umbrellaed table in a courtyard; the long and narrow **Inlet Cafe,** where tables are set in a row so that each has a good water view and you can get shell steaks, lobster in the rough or mesquite-grilled swordfish ($15 to $20), or upstairs at **Topside,** which may have the best views of the action below. This outdoor deck is off-limits to children and is open from noon until dark for items like surf and turf or marinated yellowfin tuna in the $14 to $18 range. Other areas, daily noon to 10. Seasonal.

Trail's End, Edgemere Avenue, Montauk. (516) 668-2133. This family-owned restaurant is unpretentious from the outside, to say the least, and its green and pink neon sign at night gives one pause. But it's an unusual and rather fun spot, actually advertising itself as the oldest restaurant in Montauk. Open for dinner only, the restaurant is located in an older house with a front porch where, on nice nights, dessert can be taken. Out back behind a high hedge is a courtyard with umbrellaed tables. The main dining room is two distinct areas with a bar and open floor area toward the rear. Tablecloths are gray over white with burgundy napkins; flame-shaped lights on the walls give a soft ambiance and there is a low-key, almost old-world quality here. You can order a la carte or, for $4 more, get a complete dinner. The eclectic menu includes such entrees ($10 to $25) as blackened tuna, prime rib with Yorkshire pudding, double-cut baby lamb chops, a half roasted Long Island duckling with grand marnier sauce, roast turkey and honey-dipped chicken. The homemade lobster bisque came well-recommended but had too many chunks of pepper and morsels other than lobster for our taste. A bread basket has homemade sweet breads like date nut bread and corn bread in addition to French bread. Salads are extra. We had a very pleasant and relaxed meal, if not a stunning culinary adventure, here. A plus is that it takes reservations, which many Montauk restaurants do not. Dinner nightly.

The Boathouse, South Emery Street, Montauk. (516) 668-5574. Margaret and Bob Lachmann have been operating this waterfront spot on Fort Pond for a decade. Coveted tables are those on the wraparound porch but from inside, and even from the bar — where it's fun to perch on a stool for a pre-dinner drink — you get a good view of the water and the sunset if the time is right. The emphasis is on seafood and the feeling is nautical, including the navy or red knit shirts worn by the waitstaff (and for sale at the cash register as you leave). Local fish specials change nightly; other entrees ($10 to $15) range from the boneless roast Long Island duck, a house specialty, to the combination seafood platter, shrimp scampi, soft-shell crabs and broiled, steamed or stuffed lobster. Start with escargots in mushroom caps, oysters on the half shell or steamers ($4.95 to $7.95). Finish with mud pie, key lime pie or homemade cheesecake. Out front are paddleboats and rowboats to rent; at one side is a miniature golf course. At lunch there are sandwiches, burgers, hot dogs and salads. Open daily, noon to 10. Seasonal.

The Lobster Roll Restaurant, Montauk Highway at Napeague Beach, Amagansett. (516) 267-3740. A short distance down the highway from Montauk, this unpretentious but enormously popular restaurant has a sign on top that screams "Lunch!" The Terry family celebrated their 25th season here in 1990. This is a typical shore restaurant with the emphasis on lobster rolls, fried clams, chowder, hot dogs, burgers and a few specialty sandwiches. There's outdoor dining at umbrellaed tables on a deck on two sides with a view of, alas, the highway; inside are booths with wood slat benches. Wine and beer are served, the featured wine being that from the Long Island winery, Bidwell's. The menu lists some of the better-known patrons of the place, including Woody Allen, Christie Brinkley, Rodney Dangerfield, Bill Murray and Kathleen Turner, which might be a turnoff, but here it's not. The prices are right; the namesake lobster roll with big chunks of lobster is $6.95. You also can get bowls or platters featuring lobster salad for $9.95 and $13.95 respectively. Open daily in summer, 11:30 to 10 p.m.; weekends only in off-season. Open May-October.

Duryea's Lobster Deck, Tuthill Road, Montauk. (516) 668-2410. New in the summer of 1990, this self-service, BYOB outdoor lobster/chowder/crab spot is the perfect place for enjoying seafood in the rough. Round glass-topped tables under solid green umbrellas and comfortable white plastic chairs are arranged on a deck of several levels descending to the water's edge. The establishment's credibility is enhanced by its adjoining wholesale seafood and ice company, which has been here for years. We loved our lobster salad rolls, chock full of lobster on dense, sesame-studded rolls, served with good, carroty coleslaw and potato chips for $7.95. Top price on the all-day menu is $10.95 for the 1 1/8-pound steamed lobster served with coleslaw and roll and butter; a one-claw lobster goes for $8.50. You also can get clam chowder, steamed mussels, a crab salad plate and, for landlubbers, hot dogs or hamburgers. Open daily in summer for lunch and dinner, weather permitting.

Cyril's Fish House, Montauk Highway, Amagansett. (516) 267-7993. Also new in 1990, this indoor-outdoor spot was opened by Cyril Fitzsimons, an Irishman who came to the New World via Spain. There's a prominent bar off the highway where the fresh fruit frozen drinks are a specialty; then you can sit on a large outdoor deck or in a smallish dining room out back. Check the blackboard for daily fish specials. The menu lists such items as grilled tuna and fried clam sandwiches, lobster salad roll, sesame-grilled shrimp, fried calamari and lobster in the rough, all served with french fries or potato salad. Cyril is an affable fellow and the locals praise the food. Open daily, noon to 10, May-October.

John's Pancake and Steak House on the main drag in Montauk is a good breakfast spot and advertises homemade donuts. For gourmet and picnic items, try the **Four Oaks General Store** in Montauk Harbor. **Montauk Light** is the premium light beer sold in the area; you can buy it at the IGA store. Homemade ice cream cones are available at the **Montauk Ice Cream Club** in the center. There's also a **Ben & Jerry's** on West Lake Drive at the harbor.

FOR MORE INFORMATION: Montauk Chamber of Commerce, Box CC, Montauk, N.Y. 11954. (516) 668-2428.

Roundout Belle takes passengers onto Hudson River.

The Hudson Highlands, N.Y.

The Hudson River, tidal and navigable from New York to Albany, is the most interesting river in the Northeast. Endlessly fascinating, its traffic ranges from tiny sailboats to huge oil tankers. It was on this river that the steamboat got its start: Robert Fulton sailed the Clermont from New York to Albany in 32 hours in the early 1800s. But it was Henry Hudson who, back in 1609, explored the mighty stream from its mouth as far north as Albany and put it on the map.

Some of the river's splendor comes from the beauty of its banks: in the Hudson Highlands area, of which we write, the river winds between steep western slopes and rolling eastern farmland. Because of its navigability, villages sprang up early and several grew into cities. The Hudson was so important a passageway for the Colonists that its defense became critical in the Revolutionary War; at the winding turn in the river known as West Point a contingent of the Colonial Army was stationed. Later, in 1802, the U.S. Military Academy was founded on that strategic site, high above the Hudson.

In the 19th century, the magnificent views and high vantage points along the Hudson attracted the rich, who built castle-like homes and mansions to which they retreated in the summer. Today some are opened to the public as museums, among them the homes of Eleanor and Franklin Roosevelt, the artist Frederick Church and Frederick Vanderbilt, one of the Commodore's grandsons.

The extraordinary light that plays over the Hudson River Valley attracted artists in the same century that it attracted the wealthy. Those whose landscapes celebrated the wonders of nature — not only with the river as the focus, but in the western United States as well — were said to belong to the Hudson River School.

Interest in the river is high today, after a difficult period in the middle of the century when the Hudson, like many other rivers in America, became polluted, and many of its towns and cities seemed to be declining. A cleanup of the water was spearheaded by an active environmental group headquartered in Pough-keepsie. Renovations of historic buildings in towns along the Hudson, the presence of several attractive inns and restaurants, and a wonderful variety of things to see and do — many of them on the river itself — draw travelers to the Hudson River Valley as never before.

This Hudson is humbling and awe-inspiring. It is moody, one day glistening in the sunlight, and another, brooding darkly under low gray clouds. Its waters may be tranquil one moment, stirred to whitecaps the next.

If there is any frustration in a trip to the Hudson Highlands, it is in not being able to see or reach the river often enough. The moments when you do, therefore, become all the more dramatic, and you will take with you memories of a place unlike any other we know.

Getting There

The area included in this chapter lies between the Bear Mountain Bridge to the south and the Kingston-Rhinecliff bridge to the north. It encompasses both sides of the river, the western side along Route 9W between Highland Falls/West Point to the south and Kingston to the north; along Routes 9 and 9D to the east, from Garrison-on-Hudson to the south to Rhinebeck and Rhinecliff to the north. Amtrak trains run along the riverside. The region is reached by the New York Thruway and Interstate 84.

Where to Stay _____ ♫♫♫

The area has too few interesting hotels and inns, particularly near the water. You can stay in any of the places suggested here and quite easily access the entire area. No one town is best in terms of location, but for the charm of being close to the river and having interesting shopping available, we like Cold Spring.

On or Near the River

The Hudson House, 2 Main St., Cold Spring 10516. (914) 265-9355. At the foot of Main Street, right across from the river, the Hudson House offers both smashing views and cozy, country charm. Billing itself as the second oldest inn in continuous operation in New York State, it was renovated with taste in 1981. A red, white and blue decorating scheme is carried out with homespun fabrics and mini-prints. Several of the fifteen guest rooms have a river view and those on the second floor also have small porches for sitting and enjoying it. The wallpaper matches the dust ruffles on the beds; there are overhead ceiling fans, simple pine bureaus and bare polished wooden floors. Tin molds (some heart-shaped) adorn the walls, and all rooms have modern baths. A pleasant dining room across the front of the main floor offers breakfast, lunch and dinner and river views. Across the street is the town park and gazebo; it is agreeable to walk along the waterfront, or to sit on a park bench and watch the river traffic. Continental breakfast is included in the rates. Doubles, $95 to $125.

3 Rock Bed and Breakfast, 3 Rock St., Cold Spring 10516. (914) 265-2330. Perched atop a rocky bluff with stunning vistas of the Hudson River on three sides is this new B&B. Owner-builder Peter Hold offers three suites with queensize beds and whirlpool baths, all of the latter with dramatic river views. The accommodations are spacious and comfortable, but what sets this apart are the common facilities: a modern living room with huge fireplace, a two-story breakfast room full of windows onto West Point across the river, and a third-floor reading room with a 180-degree view and a telescope for taking it all in. Outside is a wraparound veranda, looking across a landscaped lawn toward the river below. This is the site of private parties and weddings, to which 3 Rock caters, often renting out the whole place for long weekends. For lucky overnight guests who can fit in between groups, Peter serves a continental breakfast of fruit, rolls and cheese. Doubles, $100 to $140. No smoking.

Jacob Kip River House, 103 Rhinecliff Road, Rhinebeck 12572. (914) 876-8330. This 300-year-old house has been the home for several years of Katherine Mansfield and Norman Shatkin, who in 1989 opened four rooms to visitors on the second floor. Three of these bright, floral rooms share a hall bathroom; the Master Suite has a separate dressing room, its own bath and a gorgeous river view. All bedrooms have a four-poster canopy or antique bed. Guests enjoy the use of a fireplaced parlor and a front porch with an unimpeded view of the water. Amtrak trains also rush past down by the water's edge. Breakfasts are big: eggs in Canadian bacon cups, at our visit. Doubles, $60; suite, $85.

Hotel Thayer, West Point 10996. (914) 446-4731 or (800) 247-5047. Located on the grounds of the U.S. Military Academy, the Hotel Thayer sits high above the Hudson River and offers splendid river views from some of its 197 rooms. Still, one does not seek it out for the river as much as for its proximity to the activity of the academy. It is quite large and bustling, catering to the thousands of tourists who visit West Point annually, who might just drop in to look around or eat a meal, or who may stay here while visiting a son or daughter. A bit overwhelming are the large bus groups, particularly during the fall foliage season, which is also football season. Sunday brunch is said to be quite good. Doubles, $64 to $84; two-bedroom suites, $150.

Other Choices

Pig Hill Bed & Breakfast, 73 Main St., Cold Spring 10516. (914) 265-9247. Wendy O'Brien's eight-room inn located in a 150-year-old building on Cold Spring's main drag is a charmer. All sorts of pigs — brass, stuffed, wooden — adorn the walls. There's lots of antique furniture and "almost everything is for sale," says the energetic innkeeper, who loves seeking new things to dress her place up. Farm-fresh breakfasts are served at the harvest table in the main-floor breakfast room or in your bedroom. Four guest rooms on the second and third floors have private baths and four share. Some have fireplaces or enameled stoves and all are decorated colorfully and whimsically with bright comforters everywhere. Out back is a pleasant sitting area, away from the madding crowd. Wendy will prepare picnics for guests with a day's notice. Doubles, $90 to $140.

Olde Post Inn, 43 Main St., Cold Spring 10516. (914) 265-2510. This friendly inn is a few steps from the train station and Manhattanites often come by rail for the weekend. Barbara and Jim Ryan have owned it since 1989, and the resident manager is Barbara's sister, Mary Leber. The new owners are keeping a concept begun by the founders, music on weekends — in this case jazz on Fridays and Saturdays in a special basement room well-equipped for the purpose. Six air-conditioned guest rooms share two baths. A continental breakfast with homemade muffins, croissants, fresh fruits, coffee and juice is served in the dining room, which has original open-beam ceilings and wide-plank floors. A large comfortable living room, a patio and a garden are available to guests. Doubles, $60 to $75.

The Bird & Bottle Inn, Nelson Corners, Route 9, Garrison 10524. (914) 424-3000. Built in 1761, this inn offers Colonial charm. The starkly simple, main-floor dining room and tap room (see Where to Eat) are a popular destination for weekend drivers. Set at the end of a dirt road just off busy Route 9, the white-trimmed, yellow inn has two guest rooms and a two-room suite on the second floor, plus a cozy cottage on the grounds. Decorated in early American style with antiques, the rooms have working fireplaces and private baths. The emphasis is clearly on food, however, and room rates on weekends include full breakfasts and dinners. Doubles, $195 MAP; suite or cottage, $215.

The Beekman Arms, Route 9, Rhinebeck 12572. (914) 876-7077. Dating from 1766, the Beekman Arms bills itself as America's oldest inn. Both George Washington and Aaron Burr are said to have slept here, and we think they would have been comfortable. The inn has been added onto several times so has a rambling quality, with dining rooms on different levels and true Colonial flavor. One addition we find a bit incongruous is a greenhouse dining room that stretches across half the front of the building. Bedrooms are smallish in the main inn. Up the street is the **Delamater House,** also owned by the inn, a charming confection of a place in the American Gothic (gingerbread) style. Stay there if you can. Also available behind the Delamater House are a couple of buildings of more recent vintage done very tastefully. Our huge queen-bedded room had country pine built-ins and a working fireplace, plus a decanter of sherry as a welcoming gesture. Continental breakfast is served for guests of the Delamater House in a courtyard area in the center of the complex. Most of the inn's 54 rooms have private baths, phones and television. Doubles, $65 to $100.

Plumbush, Route 9D, Cold Spring 10516. (914) 265-3904. Known for fine dining for more than a decade (see Where to Eat), the Swiss-born owners of this elegant inn opened three guest rooms, all with private baths, in 1986. The Washington Irving Room and the Marquesa are located off a wicker-filled (and not very warm) sitting room on the second floor; the Hendrik Hudson room, also on the second floor, is set apart and has a more settled feeling. Decorating has been done with a Victorian touch; there are oriental rugs and queensize beds. The Marquesa, which is considered a suite, has a sitting area filled with red plush sofas and chairs. Because of the popularity of the restaurant, inn guests may find staying here somewhat busy, although the guest rooms do have a feeling of being away from the world. Continental breakfast is served to guests in their rooms. Doubles, $95; suite, $135.

Seeing and Doing _____ _ʍʍ_

The Hudson Highlands area can keep you busy for days. Attractions include mansions and historic homes, the Rhinebeck Aerodrome where vintage airplanes are flown in air shows on weekends from May to October, the Storm King Art Center, a maritime museum, hiking trails and nature walks, West Point, antiques and crafts shops, and boat trips on the Hudson. Things are not centrally located, but we keep our focus close to the river and think every visitor should get out on the water at least once.

On the River

The Hudson River Maritime Center, Rondout Landing, Kingston, 338-0071. Begun as a small storefront exhibit hall in 1980, the center is gradually growing and is the only waterfront educational center on the Hudson. A small museum is worth a walk-through (it doesn't take long and proceeds go to a worthy cause). Old photographs showing Hudson River activity, a model of the steamer James W. Baldwin, poster-size color photos of the steamer Alexander Hamilton, and a videotape on the steamship era are interesting. A small gift shop offers river-type souvenirs. Next door is a boat-building shop. Open Wednesday-Monday, 11 to 5, May-October. Adults, $1.

The Rondout Belle, Rondout Landing, Kingston, 338-6280. This small excursion boat takes sightseers on Sunday brunch cruises from noon to 2 and dinner cruises periodically during the summer (both $26.50). It offers cruises to the Rondout II lighthouse on Saturdays. Adults $12, children $6.

Trolley Rides, Trolley Museum of New York, Kingston, 331-3399. Forty-minute trolley rides along Rondout Creek, which enters the Hudson nearby, are offered on an antique trolley from the Trolley Museum, a stone's throw away. Open daily, noon to 5 in July-August, weekends in late spring and early fall. Adults $1.50, children $1.

Hudson Highlands Cruises and Tours Inc., Highland Falls, 446-7171. The jaunty, canopied M.V. Commander takes passengers out on the Hudson daily between West Haverstraw and Peekskill, with stops at West Point. A favorite cruise leaves the West Point dock at 12:30 daily, sailing past Constitution Island, and returning at 2. Cruises, May-October; reservations required. Adults $6, children $5.

Hudson River Cruises, Rifton, 255-6618. All-day cruises from Kingston to West Point and back, with a 90-minute stop at West Point, are offered a couple of times a week in the summer. The M.V. Rip Van Winkle leaves the Kingston dock at 9:30, reaches West Point at 1, and returns to Kingston by 5. It's possible for passengers to take a one-hour tour of the U.S. Military Academy while at West Point. Other excursions take passengers out on the water for a couple of hours of sightseeing or for lunch, and there are music cruises as well. Adult prices range from $12 to $20.

Hudson River Yacht Tours, 152 South Saw Mill River Road, Elmsford, 592-6010, offers a chance to charter a yacht and sail the river for two to six days. This is a luxurious way to see the mighty Hudson, with the group staying overnight in an inn or resort.

Shearwater Cruises Inc., Mountain View Road, Rhinebeck, 876-7350. Marty Ward, who has her U.S. Coast Guard captain's license, teaches sailing on the Hudson. She also offers two-hour pleasure sails where passengers may participate in the sailing of the boat if they wish. Two to eight persons are accommodated aboard the 28-foot yacht and snacks, luncheon or dinner may be included. All trips must be reserved in advance. Adults $25, children $10 for basic two hours sail.

Constitution Marsh, a nature sanctuary in Garrison, is reached from Route 9 via Indian Brook Road, an unmarked dirt road one quarter mile south of Boscobel. There are several nature trails and a boardwalk through the marsh. The walk from the parking area to the boardwalk is an easy half hour. Owned by the Taconic State Park Commission, it is managed by the National Audubon Society. Open daily, 8 to 6.

Manitoga, Route 9D, Garrison, 424-3812. This sanctuary and contemporary house were created through the vision of the industrial designer and landscape architect Russel Wright. Today the 80-acre site is open to the public primarily as a nature sanctuary with several marked trails. At two spots in particular visitors have fabulous vistas of the Hudson River. Among the trails is an access route to the Appalachian Trail, a portion of which cuts through the property. Open Wednesday-Friday 10 to 4, weekends 10 to 6 or dusk. Adults $2.

Riverfront Access. If you just want to see the river from close up, not sail on it, you have fewer options than you'd probably like. The waterfront park at Cold Spring is particularly attractive and you can see the imposing stone walls of West Point on the opposite shore. West Point is also visible from Garrison's Landing. The Beacon waterfront is being revived. In Kingston, you can see the Hudson from Kingston Point Beach at the end of Delaware Avenue. It's rather a seedy drive to get there and the beach isn't extraordinary, but it is sandy, there are lifeguards and changing areas, and there's a boat launch area as well. We saw windsurfers on a cool Sunday morning in September. The West Point docking area, located below the academy grounds (the road is quite simple to find), is also a good place from which to view the river.

The Houses

Several magnificent houses high above the Hudson offer wonderful river views. They also are of great interest in themselves.

Franklin Delano Roosevelt Home and Library, Route 9, Hyde Park, 229-8114. The boyhood home of Franklin Delano Roosevelt is the most intimate of all of the great homes to be seen in the Hudson River Valley. Roosevelt's father bought the house in 1867, and had it redesigned in 1915 to add the south wing. It is an intensely personal place, left just as it was when the President died in 1945, and is an incredible peek into what life was like for this extraordinary man. The small Snuggery on the first floor, where his mother Sarah organized her household, is revealing. The enormous living room with massive fireplaces at each end was where the family played, rested, read and entertained. Upstairs are the bedrooms, including that in which young Franklin was born, all remarkably unassuming and homey. His Presidential office, used as a Summer White House, is on the main floor and viewed from outdoors. Visitors may press a button and hear the President's voice.

Nearby is a pleasant shuttered stone building that is the **Roosevelt Library and Museum.** Established in 1939, it contains an exceptional exhibit of the President's "First Fifty Years." Starting with the wicker bassinet used for him as a baby, and including touching letters in his childish hand to his mother, as well as from the Groton School and Harvard, the entire exhibit is absorbing. Outside in the rose garden are the graves of Franklin and Eleanor Roosevelt and their famous little dog, Fala.

Not far distant is **Val-Kill,** 229-9115, which was used by the First Lady as a retreat while her husband was alive, and more or less full time after his death until her own in 1962. Visitors are introduced to the Val-kill site and to Mrs. Roosevelt through a twenty-minute audio-visual presentation in a building known as the playhouse. Also on the property are the Dutch Colonial house used by Eleanor until she died, and the larger white building, the Factory, erected by her and her friends for use by local craftspeople who made early American furniture here for some years. The First Lady's home is most memorable for the photographs covering the walls, tables and just about every possible space. They provide a glimpse into a life devoted to people.

Roosevelt home and library, open daily 9 to 5; adults $3.50, children free. Val-Kill, open daily 9 to 5, May-October, weekends spring and fall; free.

Vanderbilt Mansion, Route 9, Hyde Park, 229-9115. A short distance north of the Roosevelt site and with an enchanting view of the Hudson River, this 54-room mansion was the home of Frederick W. Vanderbilt, grandson of Commodore Vanderbilt. Frederick's brothers built the Marble House and the Breakers in Newport, R.I. and the guide told us that this was the most modest of the Vanderbilt mansions built during the gilded age. An Italian renaissance palace created by the architectural firm of McKim, Mead and White, it was used during the spring and fall by Frederick and his wife, Louisa, a social woman who entertained — didn't they all? — lavishly. The circular plan of the first floor, with a dining room that could be turned into a ballroom, and where the Roosevelts' only daughter Anna was once feted, is in marked contrast to the home of F.D.R. Perhaps it's the marble that makes it seem so formal; this is a pretentious place that just doesn't appear lived in. The surrounding property, however, is especially nice. A road leads down to the riverfront, where there are picnic tables and ample parking. The "guest house" of sixteen rooms is now a visitor center. A short slide presentation precedes a visit to the house. Open daily, 9 to 5. Adults $2, children free.

Boscobel, Route 9D, Garrison, 265-3638. One of the leading museums of the decorative arts of the Federal period, Boscobel was saved from the wrecker's ball — through the generosity of Lila Acheson Wallace, co-founder of the Reader's Digest, among others — and opened as a house museum in 1961. Located on 45 acres high above the Hudson, Boscobel was the dream of States Morris Dyckman, a descendant of early Dutch settlers, who with his wife began construction of the house in 1804. His heirs lived in the house until 1888, after which it gradually declined and was almost torn down by the middle of this century. Thanks to Mrs. Wallace, it lives today as a handsomely reconstructed monument to the Federal period. It is filled with outstanding examples of New York Federal furniture, including pieces by Duncan Phyfe and other leading furniture makers of the day. The house's exquisite gardens (thousands of tulips and flowering fruit trees in the spring), its fabulous views of the river, and its outbuildings, including a gate house where spinning is demonstrated, all work together to make a worthwhile place to visit. Open Wednesday-Monday, 9:30 to 4; closed January and February. Adults $5, children $2.50.

Mills Mansion, Old Post Road, Staatsburg, 889-4100. This is an example of one of the great estates built by financial and industrial leaders at the turn of the century. Ogden Mills, whose wife Ruth Livingston Mills inherited the property, had the prestigious architectural firm of McKim, Mead and White remodel and enlarge the home that occupied the gorgeous site above the river. Completed in 1896, the new house was very different from its former self, with two large wings and balustrades, pilasters and floral swags added as exterior ornament. Inside the decoration is in the style of Louis XV and Louis XVI, rich with marble fireplaces, oak paneling and gilded ceilings. The mansion was given by Mills's daughters to New York State. The parklike grounds are marvelous and the views of the Hudson quite stunning; you can walk to the water's edge. Open Memorial Day-October, Wednesday-Saturday 10 to 5 (after Labor Day, noon to 5), Sunday 1 to 5. Free.

Washington's Headquarters, 84 Liberty St., Newburgh, 562-1195. You drive through what looks like a war zone in downtown Newburgh to reach the spot where George Washington had his headquarters from April 1782 to August 1783. The large grassy piece of land, with a magnificent view of the Hudson River, is in marked contrast to the surrounding depressed neighborhood, although some reconstruction is taking place. The typical Dutch farmhouse belonged to the Jonathan Hasbroucks. Hasbrouck's widow and daughters were required to move out so that Washington, his wife Martha and their retinue could move in. While Washington was in residence, we were told by our guide, he had fifteen to eighteen dinner guests daily, which is when he conducted business. The table was set up in a large parlor with a Dutch jambless fireplace; in the corner today is a table with reproductions of the dinnerware and implements he used. Martha apparently always breakfasted with the general, and a small breakfast table in their bedroom is a reminder. The rest of the house included an office for George's aides de camp, the general's private office, a sleeping room for his assistants and a very English front parlor. Next door is a brick museum building full of American Revolutionary and Hudson River artifacts. Acquired by New York State, the house became the first public historic site in the nation in 1850. Open Wednesday-Saturday 10 to 5, Sunday 1 to 5, April-October. Free.

Special Attractions

U.S. Military Academy, Route 218N, West Point. Both Ulysses S. Grant and Robert E. Lee were West Point graduates and the leadership of every major war in which the United States has been involved since the Revolution has included many West Point-trained officers. The place oozes history and as you stroll about, perhaps witnessing a parade or a drill, any latent patriotism probably will be rekindled. Cadets (both male and female) are in uniform, whether it be dress attire or the black shorts with yellow stripes and white T-shirts used for tennis and jogging. There are always quite a few of them jogging, no doubt attempting to keep in the magnificent physical condition that is required of them. Visitors are welcome at West Point, and there's lots to see — from statues of great military figures (Eisenhower and MacArthur among them) — to the cadet chapels, a wonderful museum and the ruins of Fort Clinton. Best of all is the "million dollar view" from Trophy Point, a view of the Hudson looking north as it cuts through the Highlands and the Catskills. On our visit we picked up sandwiches and drinks at the Snack Bar next door to the PX, carried them to Trophy Point, and had a picnic lunch while enjoying the view. The Information Center for West Point is located just outside the Thayer Gate in the town of Highland Falls; from there, guided tours may be arranged. Frequent, hour-long shuttle bus tours are quite informative. Academy grounds open daily, 8 to 4:15.

Storm King Art Center, Old Pleasant Hill Road, Mountainville, 534-3115. More than 200 sculptures, some 100 of them exhibited outdoors on 200 acres of rolling fields, form the core of this magnificent contemporary art collection. A popular day-trip destination for New Yorkers, the center manages to show off huge contemporary pieces to great advantage on its splendid grounds. Visitors like to stroll about, stopping to admire the sculptures from many angles, and to enjoy the views of the surrounding countryside. Artists represented include such greats as Alexander Calder, David Smith (thirteen of whose works formed the nucleus of the collection), Isamu Noguchi, Alexander Liberman and Mark diSuvero. Stop at the main stone building (which has exhibition galleries as well) and pick up a map of the outdoor sculpture area. Changing exhibitions in the galleries are of interest, as are the paintings, graphics and smaller sculptures. There is a picnic area. Wear comfortable shoes for climbing about the hillsides. The sculpture park is open daily except Tuesday, noon to 5:30, April-November; museum building open May 21 through October, same hours. Donation, $2.

SHOPPING. The area is not rich shopping territory for visitors, although there are antiques shops here and there. The village of Cold Spring is full of interesting boutiques and shops. Among them are **Salmagundi Books Ltd.,** a really good bookstore, and the **Hudson Valley Visitor Center,** where you can pick up interesting craft and art items made in the area as well as informational brochures and maps.

Where to Eat _____ _лслс_

The area is home to the renowned Culinary Institute of America, which operates four fine restaurants. And there are other special finds.

Culinary Institute of America, Route 9, Hyde Park. (914) 471-6608. The esteemed school for chefs moved from New Haven, Conn., to this former Jesuit seminary high above the Hudson in 1972. Home to 1,850 students enrolled in the 21-month associate's degree program, the school contains extraordinary facilities for would-be chefs, including nineteen commercially equipped production kitchens, five bakeshops and eight instructional dining rooms. Four student-staffed restaurants are open to the public and are highly recommended.

American Bounty was opened in 1982 to present American foods and wines. The high-ceilinged restaurant at the main building's east end is handsome with etched-glass doors and cream and green draperies with a pineapple motif, gathered back from high arched windows. A dramatic and gorgeous arrangement of America's bounty is arranged in front of the glassed-in kitchen window where you can see duckling turning on the rotisserie as white-clad students work in the final course of their schooling. The menu changes with every meal. For starters at lunch ($4 to $5), who could decide between chilled shellfish timbale with olive oil vinaigrette and basil sauce or grilled Maine belon oysters with creamed leeks? Entrees ($12 to $15) might be marinated and grilled duck breast over greens with fried ginger and root vegetables or a seafood medley in saffron broth. Desserts are also exciting: chocolate-dipped strawberries on orange custard sauce, for example, or Florida lemon and lime cake ($3). American wines and beers are offered to sip with the meal. In the evening, when dining is by candlelight, prices escalate a bit, but the concept is the same. Lunch, Tuesday-Saturday noon to 1; dinner, 6:30 to 8:30. Reservations required.

The **Escoffier Room** at the CIA has been around longer, and is very elegant and classic French in style. Gold and white latticework walls, handsome brass chandeliers and comfortable black chairs and banquettes put you in the mood for a fancy lunch or dinner. Lots of tableside preparation is to be expected and you will not be rushed. Possible entrees are braised chicken in beaujolais nouveau with pearl onions and mushrooms, or lamb chops in a potato crust. At lunch, entree prices are $12 to $16; at dinner, $15 to $25. Lunch, Tuesday-Saturday noon to 1; dinner, 6:30 to 8:30. Reservations required.

The Culinary Institute's new **St. Andrew's Cafe** is for those watching their diet, their weight, their nutrition. The emphasis is on healthful foods as the young chefs learn to prepare dishes low in fat and sodium in response to the fitness craze. Dinner entrees are in the $9 to $12 range. A typical appetizer is terrine of roasted peppers and grilled eggplant with parmesan croutons; an entree might be grilled tuna with pineapple salsa and broccoli, and dessert could be light lemon bavarian with tropical fruit sorbet. Lunch, Monday-Friday 11:30 to 1; dinner, 6 to 8.

Finally, the CIA's **Caterina de Medici** room specializes in regional Italian cuisine. The prix-fixe luncheon costs $16 and dinner is $24. A typical dinner included cheese-filled risotto croquettes with tomato sauce, a soup with semolina dumplings and herbs in broth, ravioli Bolognese, small veal cutlets in cream mushroom sauce, a mixed green salad with olive oil-vinegar dressing and a ricotta cheesecake with candied fruits. There are several choices for all courses. Lunch, Monday-Friday at 11:30, dinner, Monday-Friday at 6.

Plumbush, Route 9D, Cold Spring. (914) 265-3904. Celebrating its fifteenth anniversary in 1991, Plumbush is touted as one of the area's best restaurants. Its Swiss owners, host Gieri Albin and chef Ans Benderer, concoct an elegant dining experience inside the striking plum-colored house with gold trim. The five Victorian dining rooms range in style from dark wood paneling to elegant rose-splashed wallpaper. The oak-paneled bar is dark and intimate, and a porch has been enclosed for dining in winter. In summer there is also dining on a wraparound porch. Dinner may be ordered a la carte or prix-fixe for $32. Appetizers ($5.25 to $7.50) include shrimp in beer batter with pungent fruit sauce, country terrine with cumberland sauce or mussels and cucumbers with dill sauce. House specialties among entrees in the $25 range are medallions of veal with chestnuts and shiitake mushrooms, brook trout with a sauce gribiche, broiled or poached Norwegian salmon, and roast rack of lamb with an herb sauce. Swiss apple fritters are a dessert mainstay, supplemented perhaps by chocolate praline mousse or frozen orange souffle grand marnier. Lunch entrees in the $8 to $11 range include quiches, sauteed chicken filets with mushrooms and ginger and vol-au-vent with wild mushrooms. Lunch, Wednesday-Monday noon to 2:30 (no lunch in winter); dinner, 5:30 to 9:30. Closed in January.

Bird & Bottle Inn, Nelson's Corners, Route 9, Garrison. (914) 424-3000. This was the inn selected for location scenes in the movie "Kiss Me Goodbye" with Sally Field, which may or may not mean anything to you. The ambience is strictly Colonial, in keeping with the history of the structure built as a tavern in 1761. Wide-plank floorboards throughout the main floor and a stark simplicity set the scene in the main dining room, with its white tablecloths, and the more intimate tavern rooms. The five-course, prix-fixe dinner varies from $35.50 to $45.50, depending on choice of entree. You might start with a vegetable tart or a smoked three-fish terrine; have roast duckling, salmon filet or rack of lamb as your main course, and finish with the famed Bird & Bottle cheesecake. Dinner, Wednesday-Friday 6 to 9, Saturday seatings at 6 and 9, Sunday 4 to 7; Sunday brunch, seatings at noon and 2.

Mariner's Harbor, off Route 9W, Highland. (914) 691-6011. For proximity to the water, you can't do better than this popular but difficult-to-find restaurant on the western bank of the Hudson. There's a huge deck and if you arrive early enough to get a table there on a warm summer night, you'll have the entertainment of the river to enjoy. Boaters in shorts and T-shirts favor this spot; they can pull right up. We watched a shell, symmetrically powered by the pull of eight pairs of arms and oars, gliding along the opposite shore — no doubt the crew from one of the many colleges in the area. On this side of the river, ducks swim up close to the deck, begging for handouts. The interior is fairly casual with pine paneling and simple tables with captain's chairs. Seafood is featured (entrees in the $15 range) and the special of the evening when we were there was seafood-stuffed trout. Everything from shrimp and lobster to scallops and sole is available, adequately if not inventively prepared. It's the location that counts here. Open daily, 11:30 to 11.

Rondout Golden Duck, 11 Broadway, Kingston. (914) 331-3221. This enormously popular Chinese restaurant just a block or so from the water at Rondout Landing in Kingston is considered one of the best in the region. Chef-owner Paul Wong has been cooking in China and this country for more than twenty years and the menu notes he does it all without additives like monosodium glutamate. Dinner specials include Szechuan, Cantonese and Mandarin foods — plus a few dishes from Shanghai. Among the offerings in the $10 to $14 range are crispy chunked chicken and shrimp imperial, pan-fried noodles (a house special), Szechuan sauteed scallops and shrimps, and chicken with garlic sauce. A whole Peking duck is $24.95. The dozen lunch choices include shrimp with Chinese vegetables, roast duck with mixed vegetables and the ever-in-demand moo goo gai pan. Open Monday-Friday 11 to 10, Saturday 3 to 10, Sunday 11:30 to 9.

Ship to Shore, Rondout Landing, Kingston. (914) 331-7034. A young couple, Ricky and Michelle Polacco, originally opened this bar with a sandwich menu to an appreciative audience; later they added a greenhouse room in the back and a dinner menu. Located in the Rondout area not far from the maritime museum, this is a pleasant spot for lunch or dinner, its small tables covered with sprightly flowered cloths and a popcorn machine merrily at work at happy hour. Soup of the day was chicken with barley when we were there; sandwiches served with chips and garnishes are $5. You can also get burgers. Dinners range from $5.50 for fish and chips to $18 for lobster tails. Broiled sea scallops on pasta and shrimp scampi are among the choices. Desserts are homemade. Lunch, Monday-Saturday 11 to 5; dinner, 5 to 10, Sunday 3 to 9.

Vintage Cafe, 91 Main St., Cold Spring. (914) 265-4726. This funky place is located off a courtyard and set back from the main drag in Cold Spring. It is very well regarded, thanks to Chris and Cathy Carl's attention to good food. The decor is eclectic with mismatched tables and chairs. Special menus — like a Mexican night — are sometimes offered. Lunch entrees ($4.50 to $8.50) might be fettuccine gorgonzola, blackened swordfish or avocado salad with navel oranges and cilantro dressing. At dinner ($11 to $14), how about fresh smoked salmon on fettuccine, prime ribeye steak served cajun style, or beef tips and cajun sausage with mushrooms and fettuccine? You can start with Hudson Valley goat cheese, sundried tomatoes and almonds and end with an apple tart and creme anglaise. Lunch, 11:30 to 2; dinner nightly, 6 to 9:30. Closed Tuesdays in winter. No credit cards.

Breakneck Lodge, Route 9D, Cold Spring. (914) 265-9669. At the foot of Breakneck Mountain, which rises 1,400 precipitous feet above the Hudson River across from Storm King Mountain, stands this German restaurant of the old school — a "true" place, if ever there was one. Owner Ludwig Link's wife does most of the baking, and two German chefs turn out old-world specialties for a rather considerable operation. Large windows framed the Hudson as we lunched in an old-fashioned room that was a mixture of brick walls, stained-glass crests hanging in room dividers, and captain's chairs at tables covered with woven blue mats over yellow cloths. Lunch prices are not cheap ($6.50 to $13) — after all, you do have that million-dollar river view. But we enjoyed a good lentil soup, included with our entrees of grilled knockwurst with sauerkraut and whipped potatoes and the day's special of venison ragout with burgundy and onions, served with homemade spaetzle and red cabbage. At night, a large menu ranges from $13 for baby beef liver to $17 for pork chops with cheese and ham, garnished with asparagus tips. Warm bread pudding, linzer torte and apple strudel are among desserts. Lunch daily, noon to 2:30; dinner, 5 to 9 or 10, Sunday noon to 8.

Other recommended restaurants include two in Rhinebeck: **Le Petit Bistro,** a small and well-rated French restaurant, open for dinner only, and the dining room at the **Beekman Arms,** old and Colonial and charming.

FOR MORE INFORMATION: Hudson River Valley Association, The McCabe Carriage House, 42 Catharine St., Poughkeepsie, N.Y. 12601. (914) 452-4910.

Powerboat heads toward Whiteface Mountain from Lake Placid Manor.

Lake Placid, N.Y.

Think of Lake Placid and you think of the Olympics, Whiteface, skiing, skating, sports — and snow.

Think again. Lake Placid, as its name suggests, is a tranquil mountain lake and a summer resort of long standing. Though famed as a winter sports capital, it's actually busiest during summer and early fall.

Lake Placid (the lake that adjoins the village) and Mirror Lake (the in-town lake that first-time visitors invariably think must be Lake Placid) give the village a watery presence that distinguishes this from other Eastern mountain towns. And the scenic mountains all around distinguish Lake Placid from other water places.

Located on a lofty plateau 1,744 feet above sea level, the village of 2,800 hardy souls is ringed by the highest of the Adirondacks' High Peaks, Mount Marcy, Algonquin and Whiteface among them.

Nature's endowments influenced Lake Placid's development as one of the premier summer and winter resorts in the Northeast. Grand hotels were built overlooking Mirror Lake. In 1904, the Lake Placid Club imported 40 pairs of skis from Norway and introduced winter sports to North America. Within less than three decades, Lake Placid was chosen to host the 1932 Winter Olympic Games, the first in North America. Its Olympic stature was reinforced in 1980 when it again hosted the Winter Olympics — best remembered for the "miracle of Lake Placid." People danced in the streets after the upstart American hockey players defeated the Soviets on their way to the gold medal.

Lake Placid has acquired an enviable Olympic heritage, both in sports personalities and venues. The town has placed more than 60 competitors on Olympic teams, on every Winter Olympic team and in every event. The visitor's first out-of-the-ordinary sight is apt to be the ski jump towers, rising like high-tech grain elevators southeast of town. Upon entering town, one senses the importance of athletics — from stores to clinics to doctors specializing in sports injuries. And in the heart of town, beneath flags of all participating countries flying alongside the Olympic Arena, in the middle of summer is a pile of, well, snow. Some guess that it's mounds of ice shavings from the skating rink, but young and old alike pause to make a few snowballs or cool off on a hot day.

The mountains and the athletic atmosphere make Lake Placid a mecca for mountain climbers, hikers and cyclists. The lakes and rushing streams make it popular with boaters, swimmers, fishermen and anyone else who likes to be near the water.

There are boat excursions, paddle boats, gorge trips, carriage rides around Mirror Lake, sailplane rides over the lake, and concerts by the lake. The village's charming little library backs up to the lake, and when the excellent Lake Placid Sinfonietta presented a 1990 program "Down by the Water" featuring musical compositions inspired by water, many concertgoers attended in boats.

The village is in the heart of Adirondack Park, an area of forever-wild wilderness larger than Massachusetts. This is where the Adirondack great camps and lodges are centered, and the home of the Adirondack chair and birchbark furnishings. The Adirondacks exude a sense of place. At the heart of it all is Lake Placid.

Getting There

Lake Placid is located in the northeastern Adirondacks, about 130 miles north of Albany and 125 miles south of Montreal. Most motorists approach from the south via I-87 (the Northway); take Exit 30 at Underwood for Route 73, 28 miles northwest to Lake Placid.

Adirondack Trailways buses serve Lake Placid from Albany, New York City and Montreal. Amtrak is available from Westport, N.Y. Lake Placid Airport has daily charter services and a weekend commuter service to New York City. TW Express airplanes from metropolitan centers serve nearby Saranac Lake's airport.

Where to Stay

The renowned Lake Placid Club, founded in 1895 by Dr. Melville Dewey of Dewey Decimal System fame, closed years ago. Its new owner, Lake Placid Resort Partnership, plans a $100 million infusion to develop it as a world-class resort. The main lodge would be restored as a hotel and restaurant by the firm, part of Scotland's noted Gleneagles group. Plans to build condominiums before restoring the hotel were delaying the required approvals.

The area offers resorts, many motels, ski chalets and a growing number of small B&Bs. Here we concentrate on those on or near Mirror Lake or Lake Placid. Throughout this chapter, note the distinction between Mirror Lake, the small lake in the village, from which power boats are banned, from Lake Placid, the larger, less accessible lake that leads up to the base of Whiteface Mountain.

Lodging rates vary dramatically between high season (summer and winter) and off-season.

Mirror Lake Inn, 35 Mirror Lake Drive, Lake Placid 12946. (518) 523-2544. In the last decade, this four-diamond resort facing Mirror Lake has become Lake Placid's ultimate in taste and luxury. Though the main inn was destroyed by fire in 1988, its successor built by owners Ed and Lisa Weibrecht looks as if it's been there forever. The resort has 128 rooms, sixteen of which are suites in the main building. A few are in two houses by the lakeshore and in a hilltop conference center; the rest are in two motel-style structures behind the inn and connected to it by enclosed walkways. The public spaces, which are uncommonly plentiful, are sights to behold. Especially appealing are the fireplaced library, a paneled room with stained glass and heads of stuffed animals. Complimentary tea, cookies and tea breads are served in a corner sitting area, off which is a plush sunroom-lounge with big windows toward the lake. Every table in the swank, formal **Averil Conwell Dining Room** has a water view, and casual fare is served at **The Cottage** beside the lake (see Where to Eat). Downstairs is a new salon and spa, complete with exercise room, sauna, a huge whirlpool and a 60-yard lap pool with a waterfall at one end. The sixteen Placid suites, all with jacuzzi baths and all different, are luxurious indeed. They range from large rooms with sitting areas and private balconies to split-levels, each with a living room and a spiral staircase leading to a kingbedded loft. Less regal are the majority of rooms in the two motel-style buildings, one topped off in 1989 with third and fourth floors. Every room faces the lake and most have private balconies, kingsize beds, bathrooms with hair dryers, wet bars and mini-refrigerators, clock-radios, TVs, padded hangers and photos of old Lake Placid. Rooms in two houses by the lake are closest to the water, but are older, smaller, furnished in early American style and are billed as the most economical way to enjoy the ambiance of the inn. Although most guests tend to gather around the outdoor pool, the inn's beach is good for swimming, and rentals are available at the boathouse. Most rates are quoted MAP; rooms also are available without meals. Doubles, EP: $88 to $160; MAP: $144 to $252, suites $286 to $486.

Whiteface Inn Resort, Whiteface Inn Road, Box 231, Lake Placid 12946. (518) 523-2551 or (800) 422-6757. This golf and lake resort a mile or so off the highway has been upgraded over the last dozen years by Montreal-based owners. Its location on 360 acres of woods and golf fairways, with 1,200 feet of frontage along the quiet shores of Lake Placid facing Whiteface, give it probably the best waterfront setting of any public facility in the area. There's no more choice a spot for waterside seclusion than in one of the 25 lakefront log cabins, nicely scattered about the lawns in a park-like setting. Built in the 1920s and refurbished in 1988, they combine the best of old and new. All are done in rustic Adirondack style and have a fieldstone fireplace, small refrigerator, TV and phone, country furnishings and stoneware lamps. Also available are twelve pool-side "cabanas" that we and our guide called motel units, seven multi-roomed cottages with common living rooms, and twenty condominium units rented by the night (many other condos away from the inn are occupied by owners). The olympic-size swimming pool just above the lake is perhaps the area's most appealing, with lots of terrace and lawn space for lounging. There's swimming in the lake, of course, and watercraft can be rented from the large boathouse. Four tennis courts, a scenic eighteen-hole golf course and groomed cross-country ski trails are offered. Meals are served in a summertime cafe-bar called the **First Tee Terrace** beside the putting green and in the main **Adirondack Room** (see Where to Eat). Doubles, $102, EP; cabins, $140 for one room to $252 for two bedrooms with kitchen; condos, $296 to $380. Five-night minimum for lakefront cabins in peak season.

Lake Placid Manor, Whiteface Inn Road, Lake Placid 12946. (518) 523-2573. Adjacent to the Whiteface Inn resort and sharing its setting, this is less glitzy and more rustic, more Adirondack — "a small, personal hotel tucked in the woods at the edge of beautiful Lake Placid," in the words of the inn's brochure. The site is hilly and heavily wooded, with lots of ups and downs to get from parking lot to inn and restaurant to cottages and to the shore. You enter via a great porch full of white wicker facing the lake from on high, adjacent to an open deck with umbrellaed tables for outside dining. Inside are a pretty dining room serving three meals a day (see Where to Eat), a paneled and fireplaced living room like that of an Adirondack great camp, and a particularly striking bar and lounge in which all the posts and beams are birch and all the furniture is twig. Elsewhere in the main lodge built in 1882 as a private home and camp are thirteen guest rooms of assorted shapes and sizes. We liked the front upstairs corner room with a kingsize bed, diamond-paned windows onto the lake, a small sitting room, a full bath with Crabtree & Evelyn toiletries and a dressing area, good reading lamps and a birchbark wastebasket. Underneath the main floor are more lakefront rooms with picture windows for taking in the view and a lounge area on the lawn outside. Twenty-one rooms are available in five cottages, ranging from primitive to deluxe (in the Swiss Cottage). Throughout, most rooms have large walk-in closets (after all, oldtimers used to spend the whole summer in the great camps), frilly curtains, cable TV and Adirondack twig furniture. Manager Robert Hardy has been upgrading about four rooms a year. Down at the lakeshore are a small beach with a big deck for sunning, a raft and a swimming area. Doubles, EP: in lodge, $55 to $140; in cottages, $40 to $120.

Lake Placid Hilton, 1 Mirror Lake Drive, Lake Placid 12946. (518) 523-4411. Don't be deceived by the address. Most of this 176-room hotel is located across Main Street in a five-story, U-shaped highrise built around a swimming pool. Standard hotel rooms (they call them super deluxe) have private balconies, but Mirror Lake can barely be glimpsed across the rooftops from the lower floors. Here is where the action is, around the indoor and outdoor pools, in the Dancing Bears lounge, the meeting and banquet facilities, and the Terrace Room restaurant. We far prefer the motel-style rooms by the lake, 44 cheaper units in an older building across the street and 29 of the most expensive right beside the lake — six in a three-story building from which one could fish off the balconies and the rest hidden from public view in a one-story strip under the parking lot, facing grass and docks at water's edge. Doubles, $92 to $142.

Golden Arrow Motor Inn, 150 Main St., Lake Placid 12946. (518) 523-3353. It ain't the Hilton, but this Best Western is located right on the shore of Mirror Lake and appeals more to water-lovers. The lobby with soaring windows framing the view gives an indication of what's in store. Half the 130 rooms face the lake a stone's throw away. The two four-story buildings screen the sights and sounds of Main Street from those on the striking, pure-white sand beach below, a popular place for swimming, paddleboating and canoeing. The recently renovated rooms are furnished in typical motel style; some have fireplaces and jacuzzis. There's plenty of action in the indoor pool, fitness center, the lounge and nightclub. Doubles, $98 to $128.

Holiday Inn-Grandview Hotel, 1 Olympic Drive, Lake Placid 12946. (518) 523-2556. High on a hill overlooking town and Mirror Lake, this 199-room motor inn has a view that lives up to the name of its hotel predecessor. Front rooms on the second, third and fourth floors have lake views; those in back face the High Peaks. The newer mini-suites are angled for the best views. There are also chalets with fireplaces and jacuzzis. Other attractions are an indoor pool, health spa with sauna and whirlpool, four tennis courts and a trout stream for fishing. Three meals a day are served in the attractive Greenhouse Restaurant. Formal dining is offered at the inn's **La Veranda** (see Where to Eat), a summery house across the street. Doubles, $126 to $166; mini-suites, $186.

The Interlaken Inn and Restaurant, 15 Interlaken Ave., Lake Placid 12946. (518) 523-3180. Exceptionally attractive from the outside with gardens and terraces all around, this in-town inn is on a residential side street linking Mirror Lake and Lake Placid, both within easy walking distance. It's attractive inside as well, personally run by innkeepers Roy and Carol Johnson and their offspring. A big stuffed goose sits in a basket full of flowers at the entry; inside the front hall are teddybears in a sleigh and on the stairs, and Cabbage Patch Kids in a crib. Straw hats or wreaths are on the doors of the twelve guest rooms, all with private baths. Each room is delightfully decorated with antiques, baskets, lace and Victorian outfits, shoes, dolls and such. Room 7 has a partial-canopy king bed done up in frills, a small sitting room, a private porch and a full bath; over the bed is a birdhouse with a bird popping out and flowers spilling around. Most rooms come with thick carpeting, tin ceilings, clawfoot tubs, handsome quilts, potpourri, Caswell-Massey toiletries and decanters of port. A pleasant breakfast porch has wrought-iron tables and ice-cream parlor chairs, and a full breakfast is served. Tea with goodies is put out in the late afternoon. There's a small bar as well. Prix-fixe dinners are served nightly at 7 in the elegant Victorian dining room (see Where to Eat). Doubles, $100 to $150, MAP.

Lakeshore Motel, 54 Saranac Ave., Lake Placid 12946. (518) 523-2261. Set well back from the road close to the shore of Lake Placid is this pleasant 23-room motel run for a dozen years by Sue and Larry Praeger. "We're the only ones right on the lake," said Sue. We were skeptical until we saw the other motels, which are on an end of the lake that is too shallow for swimming. Here, redwood chairs are at the ready for guests to relax on the lawn, facing straight up Lake Placid toward Whiteface. They can swim off a sandy beach, borrow rowboats and barbecue in a picnic area. The rooms are color-coordinated, each with two double beds, cable TV, a little refrigerator and tasteful art. The newer rooms closest to the lake in the two-story section with balconies are most choice; older efficiency units are in a one-story section across the way. Doubles, $59 to $99.

Placid Bay Motor Inn, 70 Saranac Ave., Lake Placid 12946. (518) 523-2001. Right down the street from the Lakeshore Motel, this two story motel near the road backs up to the shallow waters and lacks the straight-up-the-lake view of its neighbor. A lawn extends to the bay filled with lily pads and a little island, but a swimmer would sink in the mud. Not to worry, there's a pleasant, L-shaped swimming pool alongside; also picnic tables, barbecues, a rowboat and a canoe. About half the nineteen motel rooms yield a water view; the ones we saw had two double beds with vivid yellow velvet spreads, green shag carpeting and a TV. In a kitchenette unit, the kingsize bed was smack up against the stove, with a table for two in the middle of the room. Larger kitchenettes, suites and two cottages accommodate five to eight. "We've never considered ourselves fancy," said owner Denise Dramm. "We're a family place with personal service, kind of like home without the work." Doubles, $60 to $88; larger units, $68 to $200.

Wildwood on the Lake, 88 Saranac Ave., Lake Placid 12946. (518) 523-2624. Twelve of the 30 units here face Lake Placid and are quite appealing with private decks or balconies and a view onto the shady lawn. All rooms have two double beds, two chairs, a table, TV, telephone, a small refrigerator and a coffee maker. This part of the lake is too shallow for swimming, but there's a quite charming little pool by the road, filled with lake water that trickles down a waterfall, with a slide and a small beach at one end. There's also a small heated pool up a hill beside some poolside units with private balconies, and an indoor hot tub and sauna. Owners Horst and Edith Weber are responsbile for the Tyrolean look of the place. A cottage overlooking the pool has a lovely kingsize room and balcony, while a fireplaced cottage with kitchenette has accommodations for up to eight. The lakeside lawn is a beauty (many people enjoying reading in loungers when we visited), and there's a game room for rainy days. Doubles, $66 to $86; cottages, $66 to $104.

Stagecoach Inn, 370 Old Military Road, Lake Placid 12946. (518) 523-9474. Although well away from the lakes on a bypass road, this 1830 house that served as a hotel until the late 1800s is now the largest and most comfortable B&B in town. Innkeeper Lyn Witte offers nine rooms, five with private baths and two sets of two rooms that share a bath each. The place is full of interesting touches: a stained-glass panel of a stagecoach in the dining room, a yellow birch staircase rising from the living room onto a yellow birch mezzanine, pine cone lampshades on the chandelier, and snowshoes, stuffed trout and deer heads, and Indian art on the walls. The upstairs rooms are furnished as in the Adirondack lodges. Newer rooms in a four-year-old addition have wicker furniture and narrow-slat wood wainscoting. Lyn was cleaning up from a breakfast that included a cheese and broccoli strata when we stopped by; other offerings could be cheese souffle or scrambled eggs and sausage. Doubles, $55 to $80.

Hotel Marcy Suites, 122 Main St., Lake Placid 12946. (518) 523-1818 or (800) 447-1818. Once a mere hotel, this is now the only all-suite property in Lake Placid, offering 23 suites on each of four floors. It claims to have the most reasonable rates and largest rooms in town. Each suite has a bedroom with a king bed or two doubles in front and a sitting room with a pull-out couch. The upper rooms are more expensive, having been renovated; they afford glimpses of Mirror Lake across the downtown rooftops. The hotel has a large lounge with a fireplace, big-screen TV and a breakfast area. Doubles, $49 to $99.

Rustic Lodges and Camping

Solitude, West Shore, Lake Placid 12946. (518) 523-3190. "I never get tired of this scene," said Elva Kelsall as she led us around her 62-acre lakefront property. "There's not a sound, the solitude is almost tangible." The octogenarian and her adopted son operate what must be one of the more unusual bed and breakfasts around. A classic Adirondack camp, it isn't for everyone. For one thing, you can't get there by road; Rick Kelsall picks guests up in his water taxi at Paradox Bay for the fifteen-minute boat ride up the lake to a wilderness area facing Whiteface. For another, you must bring in your groceries for lunch and dinner. Mrs. Kelsall provides a continental breakfast with her homemade granola for those staying in the three rooms sharing one bath in the main house and in cottages without kitchens. For years, alto soloist Elva Kelsall and her husband Joe ran a music camp here and though most of the music is gone, the camp feeling remains. Rooms in the main house and the fourteen cabins plus a bunkhouse are best described as basic and rustic. Guests without kitchen facilities may use the original camp kitchen; liquor is discouraged. Linens and towels are provided. The boathouse is a good place to take in the unforgettable view of lake and mountains. "Rest, Relax, Refresh, Rejuvenate, Reflect," says the brochure, and Solitude would be a good place for that. We met a woman who had come back three times in one summer. But, we reiterate, the degree of rusticity is not for everyone. In the off-season, Mrs. Kelsall lives in Princeton, N.J., with her 97-year-old husband, a still-active voice teacher, where she takes reservations at (609) 452-2139. B&B, $65 nightly. Cottages, from one to four-bedroom, $350 to $565 weekly. No smoking.

Adirondack Mountain Club Lodges, Box 867, Lake Placid 12946. (518) 523-3441. The two AMC lodges are surrounded by the High Peaks and appeal particularly to hikers. During the day, visitors explore the high-country environment and return in the evenings for homemade meals, frequent educational programs and overnight lodging. **Adirondak Loj,** a year-round outdoor center, is off Route 73, eight miles southeast of Lake Placid. It houses 46 guests in four private rooms, four family bunkrooms and an eighteen-person coed bunkroom. Linens and hot showers are provided. MAP rates, $36 to $54 per person; trail lunch $4. **Johns Brook Lodge,** a back-country base camp, takes more effort to reach — a 3.5-mile hike into the midst of the mountains west of Keene Valley, to be exact. The young staff is known for "the best meals in the High Peaks." The lodge accommodates 28 guests in two small family bunkrooms and two coed bunkrooms. There's running water but no showers, and guests bring sheets or a sleeping bag. MAP rates, $36 to $38. The AMC also offers a wilderness campground with 34 campsites ($9), thirteen lean-tos ($13) and two self-service cabins for six to twelve people ($45 to $100).

High Peaks Base Camp, Springfield Road, Box 91, Upper Jay 12987. (518) 946-2133. This facility has a B&B lodge with private rooms (doubles, $40 and $45), dorm rooms ($15 per person), tent sites with showers and toilets ($3 per person) and one-room cabins for one to four people ($30). The Wood Parlor, a family restaurant, is open daily for three meals. The facility also has a newly stocked, spring-fed fishing pond.

RENTALS. Vacation rentals are handled by real estate agents like W. Terry Horrocks Inc., 13 Main St., 523-4162. Others are available from Vacation Rental Management, Box 809, 523-3365, and The Water's Edge, condos at 1 Victor Herbert Road, 523-9861.

Seeing and Doing

The lakes and the mountains in such close proximity make a fortuitous combination — to our minds, the best of its kind in the Northeast. One can fish, hike, climb the High Peaks or play golf in the morning; go boating, swim or tour the Olympic sites in the afternoon, and go to a cultural event in the evening — all within a few miles of Lake Placid.

Touring Lake Placid

Holly the Trolley, 523-4431. If you don't have your own wheels or prefer not to use them, this 32-passenger, open-air trolley is one of the best ways to see the town. The 60-minute narrated tour operates hourly between hotels, Olympic sites and around Mirror Lake with numerous stops so passengers can get on or off. Daily in season, 10 to 6. Adults $2.

Lake Placid Carriage Rides, Mirror Lake Drive and Hilton Corner, 523-2483. Horse-drawn carriages take many a couple or two on a pleasant excursion around Mirror Lake. Operating 10 a.m. to 11 p.m. daily, June-September. Adults $7, children $5.

Adirondack Adventure Tours, 126 Main St., Lake Placid, 523-1475. This tour outfit offers a variety of trips by van, canoe, bicycle or what have you. The three-hour Lake Placid Sports and Sightseeing Tour covers the Olympic and local historical sites at 9 and 1:30 daily; adults $18. There are moonlight canoe tours on Mirror Lake at 9 and 10 p.m., $25 per person and the guide paddles. Pond-hopping by canoe through the St. Regis Lakes is an all-day outing, $150 for two including transportation, portage, guide and lunch. Hiking, fishing, biking, whitewater rafting and horseback trail tours can be arranged.

Lake Placid Sightseeing Tours, Hilton Plaza, 523-4431, has 2 1/2-hour bus tours departing from major hotels and motels to see historic and Olympic sites. Adults $19, children $14.

Walking Tour. In summer, everyone seems to be walking (or jogging or biking) around Mirror Lake. The 2.5-mile loop allows one to see both the lake, fine homes and the downtown area close up. You pass by the storied Lake Placid Club (planned for restoration) and Mirror Lake Inn. In town, take Parkside Drive by the beach and the toboggan slide. Head up Main Street, admiring glimpses of the lake between shops and through their rear windows. A pleasant vantage point is Bandshell Park, with its Paul White Bandshell across from the beautiful Episcopal Church.

The **Peninsula Nature Trails** off Saranac Avenue, behind the Howard Johnson Motor Lodge, is an arboretum in which forest growth is marked for identification. Its network of trails reaches to the edge of Lake Placid lake.

BOAT TOURS. Paddle boats, canoes, rowboats and sailboats may be rented at several places along Main Street, including P.K.'s Boats Inc., for use in Mirror Lake, where power boats are banned. **Lake Placid Marina** offers hour-long, sixteen-mile cruises of Lake Placid in an enclosed tour boat. Boats pass three large islands, many awesome private estates and the base of Whiteface Mountain. Most of the lake frontage is accessible only by boat, leaving much of the wilderness in its pristine state. Tours at 10:30, 1, 2:30 and 4 daily in summer. Adults $5.50, children $3.50. **Capt. Marney's Boat Rentals,** 3 Victor Herbert Road, 523-9746, offers fishing boats, speed boats, water skiing and canoes. **Jones Outfitters,** 37 Main St., next to the Bandshell on Mirror Lake, has canoe and kayak rentals as well as trips and guide service. Sunfish, sailboards, kayaks and canoes can be rented from **Syd & Dusty's at the Club Beach,** across from the Lake Placid Club on Mirror Lake.

BIKING AND BIKE TOURS. The biggest place in town is **High Peaks Cyclery,** 18 Saranac Ave., 523-3764. It has all kinds of rentals and information on guided or self-guided tours. Mountain bikes can be rented at **Sundog Ski & Sports,** Main Street, 523-2752, for $3 an hour, $14 a day. Higher prices are charged at **Syd & Dusty's Performance Sports,** 110 Main St., so shop around.

FISHING. The state record lake trout was hauled out of Lake Placid in 1986. Rainbow trout and bass are also caught, and Mirror Lake is popular for small-scale fishing. Nearby mountain streams like the Ausable River are renowned for fly fishing.

HIKING AND MOUNTAIN CLIMBING. The Adirondack Mountain Club as well as local sports shops have information on trails and tours. The AMC's summer information center is on Cascade Road, six miles southeast of Lake Placid. Many of the High Peaks trails start at the Adirondak Loj, eight miles southeast of the village. The casual visitor would barely get a leg up on the 46 High Peaks, which take most mountaineers years to conquer all. But in our younger days the men in our party managed to climb to the summit of Mount Marcy, New York's highest, while the women shopped in Lake Placid and brought a steak back to the campground for the evening's dinner.

Airplane Rides. Adirondack Flying Service, Lake Placid Airport, 523-2473, gives two twenty-minute scenic flights: one over the Olympic venues, village, Whiteface Mountain and Cascade area, and the other over the Adirondack High Peaks, including Mount Marcy. Adults, $20; two-person minimum. **Sailplane Rides,** Lake Placid Airport, 523-2473, offers half-hour flights aboard its Grob 109 motor glider for $45 per person.

Olympic Site Tour

The Olympic Regional Development Authority, 523-1655 or (800) 462-6236, oversees the sites of the 1932 and 1980 Winter Olympic Games, the major of which are open to the public. The Lake Placid Olympic Site Tour, sponsored by Eastman Kodak Co., is a self-guided driving tour of the Olympic facilities, available from mid-June through early October at a reduced price: adults $12, children $4. Among the facilities:

Olympic Center, the largest ice complex of its kind in the world, is the main landmark in the center of town. Four ice surfaces are housed under one roof, and at least one is open for public ice-skating in the summer (the shavings from the rinks help make the pile of snow that stops passersby in front of the arena). When we visited, a main-floor location was being readied as the site of the new **Lake Placid Winter Olympic Sports Museum.**

Olympic Jumping Complex, off Route 73 at the southeast entrance to town, is notable for two towers that look a bit like high-tech grain elevators from afar. Ski jumpers train and compete year-round on special surfaces that simulate snow conditions when wet. You can take a chairlift (or drive around) to the 90-meter ski jump tower, where a glass-enclosed elevator rises 26 stories to a wrap-around observation room affording a panorama of the Lake Placid area and the High Peaks. At the tower's base is a grandstand-type affair where you can watch jumpers plummet down the in-run and soar off the jump onto a plastic-covered outrun. At the foot of the jumping complex is the new Kodak Sports Park, the official U.S. Freestyle Ski Team aerial training center. In summer, aerialists perfect their technique, jumping off plastic-covered ramps and being propelled 50 feet into the air. They do twists and flips before landing skis first in a seventeen-foot-deep pool of water, to the delight of the crowds that are always present, whether during daily practices or special competitions. Open daily, 9 to 4 or 5; adults $5, children $4.

Olympic Sports Complex at Mount Van Hoevenberg, off Route 73 farther southeast of town, includes the only bobsled run in the country and its companion luge run. A mile long and with sixteen turns, it's said to be the most perilous in the world. A trolley takes visitors up a service road to the top every fifteen minutes; our driver volunteered that the run was redone in 1989 because the athletes said it had become too fast and too dangerous. You can walk down the inside of the bobsled run or return by trolley. Displays and films of bobsledding are shown in the bobsled finish building at the base. Open daily, 9 to 4; adults $3, children $2.

Whiteface Mountain Highway and Chairlift, Wilmington. Opened in 1935, the easy, eight-mile drive up the north face to the 4,867-foot summit of Whiteface offers spectacular vistas. You can see the Montreal skyline, Lake Champlain and Vermont's Green Mountains on a clear day. The two-lane road has only two hairpin turns as you near the top of the only Adirondack High Peak accessible by car. It ends at a stone castle with a cafeteria, gift shop and parking area. The last portion of the trip up New York's fifth highest peak is accomplished by climbing a stone stairway or riding a 276-foot-high elevator, cut through the top of the mountain and reached through a cold, dank tunnel. The latter is not for the claustrophobic. At the top, you can clamber up and around the rocks to the summit, surprisingly unencumbered by any fences.

The way to see the Whiteface ski area, the lower east face of the mountain that was the site of the Olympic competitions and still known for good but often windblown skiing, is from the base parking area off Route 86. Two chairlifts take sightseers to the top of 3,600-foot Little Whiteface. Highway open mid-June to Labor Day, 8 to 6; from May 18 and to Oct. 8, 9 to 4; adults $4, children $3. Chairlift. daily 9 to 4, June 16 to Columbus Day, 9 to 4; adults $4, children $3.

Olympic Training Center, Old Military Road at Church Street. The $13 million training center dedicated in 1990 has two clusters of housing for 200 athletes and one of two U.S. Olympic Committee gift shops in the nation selling items with the Olympics logo. The gymnasium complex includes three basketball courts, weight rooms and facilities for volleyball and handball, plus outdoor playing fields. The center is expected to attract record numbers of summer athletes to Lake Placid because of the additional space and sports programs.

Other Attractions

John Brown Farm, John Brown Road, Lake Placid, 523-3900. This state historic site represents the last home and burial site of abolitionist John Brown — remember the song: "John Brown's body lies a-mouldering in the grave?" The unassuming farmhouse is furnished as it was in the 19th century and includes documents and mementos of a man who came to the Adirondacks in 1848 and whose ideas rank with those of the world's great thinkers. A self-guiding farm trail passes through the grounds. House open Wednesday-Saturday 10 to 5, Sunday 1 to 5, early May to late October. Free.

High Falls Gorge, Route 86, Wilmington, 946-2278. Proclaimed as "the ancient valley of foaming waters," this privately owned gorge drops 120 feet in a cascading series of falls, potholes and whirlpools just off Route 86. A large gift shop and restaurant are at the entrance. Visitors take a half-hour walk a quarter of a mile down and back along groomed paths, railed platforms and steps. A self-guiding tour map and recorded messages detail some of the interesting geology and plant life. Open daily, 9 to 4:45 in summer, to 4:15 rest of season. Open Memorial Day to Columbus Day. Adults $3.95, children $2.

GOLFING. Golf Digest writer called Lake Placid's courses "a formidable lineup." The town-owned **Craig Wood Golf & Country Club,** off Route 73 east of town, welcomes the public; greens fees for eighteen holes, $16. **Whiteface Inn Resort** offers an exceptionally scenic, eighteen-hole championship course beside woods and Lake Placid; greens fees, $29. In 1990, the **Lake Placid Resort Partnership** reopened 27 of the 36 holes of the former Lake Placid Club courses.

ENTERTAINMENT. Lake Placid considers itself the summer entertainment capital of the Adirondacks. Concerts like New Kids on the Block were presented in 1990 at the Olympic Center. Two major horse shows are scheduled in late June and early July. Ice skating, hockey, freestyle skiing and ski jumping competitions are held throughout the summer.

Lake Placid Center for the Arts and Fine Arts Gallery, 523-2512, offers live theater ("Dames at Sea" and "Same Time Next Year" in summer 1990), concerts, dance performances and films. The gallery exhibitions are open free Monday-Friday 10 to 5 and weekends 1 to 5, year-round.

You'd expect to find music in the air in a town with a Paul White Bandshell, a street named Victor Herbert Road and the former summer home of Kate Smith. **The Lake Placid Sinfonietta,** founded in 1917 at the Lake Placid Club, is considered one of the best small orchestras in the East. It presents six formal concerts in the Lake Placid Center for the Arts, eight free community concerts and six special events. The free events include Wednesday evening Cushion Concerts in July and August at the Paul White Bandshell beside Mirror Lake.

Many concertgoers attend by boat. David Gilbert, conductor of the Greenwich Symphony, conducts the eighteen-piece orchestra.

Shopping

If you want athletic equipment or clothes, you will be sure to find it in Lake Placid. **High Peaks Cyclery** at 18 Saranac Ave. is a sports store deluxe; we're told that if the folks at L.L. Bean don't have it, they refer people to H.P.C. But there are lots of other goodies, and Eastern Mountain Sports and Benetton are the only chain stores.

We loved the **Adirondack Store & Gallery** at 109 Saranac Ave., where we wandered around the birchbark baskets, the twig furniture, the balsam pillows and the pine cone china used at the Lake Placid Club. The **Adirondack North Country Crafts Center** at the Lake Placid Center for the Arts, 93 Saranac Ave., is a treasure trove of the works of more than 150 area artisans. Beautiful quilts, jewelry and pottery are shown; we admired a metal armadillo that we would have liked to put in our garden, but its $300-plus cost discouraged us.

We also liked the Mexican imports at **Guadalupe's** at 47 Saranac Ave., though they did seem a bit out of place in the North Country. The pastel-colored rugs of various sizes were especially attractive.

Ruthie's Run at 11 Main St. is about the best place for clothes of the Geiger ilk and a choice of zillions of sweaters. **The Bookstore Plus** has a selection of regional books, as does **With Pipe & Book** almost next door. The latter has used books, as well. For a snack, stop in the Alpine Mall at 125 Main St. In front is the **Alpine Strudel & Croissant Shop** with all kinds of strudels, or a raspberry or blueberry croissant. Out back is the tiny **Cafe on the Lake,** a pleasant place for soups, salads, bagels, frozen yogurt, ice cream and the like with two tables on a deck overlooking Mirror Lake.

The Market, 97 Main, is a well-stocked gift shop with some local art. It used to be a food market run by Jack Shea, 1932 Olympic speed-skating gold medalist who spearheaded the 1980 Olympics; his son Jim, a former Olympic cross-country skier and biathlon coach, runs the adjacent **Mirror Lake Liquor Store. La Boutique Suisse** has handsome clothes, and if you'd like a stained-glass hockey player, stop in at **The Studio.** Want a pair of racy socks? **The Country Store** at 71 Main has tons of them, above which is the motto "Help Stamp Out Bored Feet." At **Potluck Specialty Foods & Delicatessen,** 3 Main St., try one of the golden walnut cookies ($8.50 a pound) or a myrtle. Subs are $5.50 and a Po' Boy sandwich $3.75. Take one out for a picnic by the lake.

Where to Eat ⎯⎯⎯⎯⎯⎯⎯⎯⎯⎯⎯⎯⎯⎯ _ᏟᏟᏟ_

Lake Placid offers endless places to eat, many of them of the traditional tourist variety. Lately, more upscale restaurants have been sprouting up.

Water Views

Lake Placid Manor, Whiteface Inn Road, Lake Placid. (518) 523-2573. Go here for the Adirondack great camp experience, plus a smashing view of Lake Placid. The stylish, two-level dining room has striking floral service plates atop tables dressed in beige and white, heavy windsor chairs, oriental rugs and large windows all around. The deck out front, with jaunty umbrellaed tables, is positively idyllic for lunch. Chef David Gotzmer offers a dozen entrees ($15 to $19.95), including pork tenderloin with cassis sauce, poached Norwegian salmon with a Granny Smith apple-cucumber sauce, baked red snapper with pineapple sabayon sauce accented with cumin, roast duckling with Malmsey maple-orange sauce and a baked pear, and rack of lamb with steamed kale and fresh oregano. A house salad accompanies. Start with a shellfish bisque, eggplant strudel, or sauteed prawns with lime and lager. Finish with the strawberry double chocolate fool or frozen orange custard with raspberry sauce (the recipe for the latter was requested by Gourmet magazine). Come early or stay after for a drink in the lounge, surely the epitome of an Adirondack bar. Five salads and entrees like blue crab cakes and tricolor tortellini with pesto and veggies are offered at lunch, $4.50 to $10.95 (for a salad of king crab and shrimp with avocado and rouille sauce). Breakfast, lunch and dinner daily. No smoking.

La Veranda, 1 Olympic Drive, Lake Placid. (518) 523-3339. This high-style restaurant is part of Serge Lussi's Holiday Inn enterprises. There's no denying the charm of the summery house on a hilltop with a glimpse of Mirror Lake through the trees. It takes its name from the wonderful front veranda, full of rattan tables and chairs that must be popular commodities on warm evenings. Inside, past the bar built around a fieldstone fireplace, is the main Hearthside Room, with fabric panels on the upper half of the room. Upstairs is the beautiful Birch Room, trimmed in birch logs, which also has a fieldstone fireplace. Peach and white linens are topped with the original service plates that came with the house. Although known for French cuisine, the chef in 1990 added a few Italian dishes, which makes for confusing reading with Italian interspersed throughout the French menu. Among entrees ($12.95 to $24.95), you might find souffle of fresh salmon, sauteed dover sole with lime butter, broiled quail with grapes, rack of lamb persille and tornedo alla rossini. Start with Italian soup of the day or French onion, Italian snails or chilled terrine of trout with tarragon, the house insalata or caesar salad for two. Four pastas are offered as main courses. For dessert, we hear good things about the floating island, meringue glace, chocolate mousse cake and tarte tatin. For a place of its aspirations, the wine list is thin, and friends found dining here a bit hushed and stiff. Dinner nightly, 5 to 10. Open late May through September.

Mirror Lake Inn, 5 Mirror Lake Drive, Lake Placid. (518) 523-2544. The murals of early Lake Placid on the walls of the **Averil Conwell Dining Room** were done by the local artist of that name, who died in 1990. At age 94, she had restored the paintings saved by rescuers from the inn's fire in 1988. The expansive room on two levels has windows facing Mirror Lake across the road and every table gets a view. Long-stemmed wine glasses top the white-linened tables. Co-owner Lisa Weibrech was the U.S. women's national luge champion in 1977 and is into fitness and health, which accounts for the special wellness menu and spa specialties offered at dinner. Regular entrees ($15.95 to $22.95) include shrimp dijonnaise, salmon piccata, roast duckling with orange-grand marnier sauce, filet au poivre and Adirondack mixed grill. The chef has an herb garden and the inn does all its own smoking for the smoked seafood plate and smoked trout, scallops and shrimp offered as appetizers. Peanut butter or walnut pies are favored desserts. A pianist entertains on weekends. In the morning, recorded classical music is the backdrop for an extensive breakfast buffet taken by the sunny windows. The full buffet was $8.95, but we were quite satisfied with the continental buffet ($4.95) with lots of fresh fruit, cereals and muffins. Breakfast daily, 7:30 to 11; lunch, 11:30 to 3; dinner, 6 to 9. Dress code.

Also run by the inn, **The Cottage Cafe,** 523-9845, across the street is right by Mirror Lake, with windows onto the water and a popular side deck that catches the breezes beneath the shade of birch trees. It's perfect for lunch and light supper. On a sunny afternoon, three of us enjoyed the roast beef sandwich special ($4.95), the knockwurst dog ($3.50) and a gloppy taco salad ($5.95). Heaping sandwiches and salads are the rule, but you also will find nachos, baked brie served with fresh fruit and french bread, a fruit and cheese boat, quiche and daily specials. Lunch daily in season from noon to 3 or 3:30, supper 4 to 9.

The Artist's Cafe, 1 Main St., Lake Placid. (518) 523-9493. Named for a previous owner who was an artist, this little cafe tucked down and around a park beneath a storefront is convivial as can be. The bar and small dining room are intimate, to say the least. For more privacy (and a great water view), try for one of the three tables with oil lamps flickering on the enclosed lakeside porch. We'd heard the seafood selections were better than the meat, so our party dined on broiled swordfish, scampi sauteed with garlic and cognac and shrimp tempura, chosen from a short menu priced from $6.95 for ground sirloin to $15.95 for surf and turf. Nachos, "Mexiskins," fried mozzarella sticks and homemade onion rings comprise most of the starters. The concise wine list is priced from yesteryear — $9.95 to $13.95 (for a Parducci chardonnay). Lunch daily, 11:30 to 3; dinner, 5 to 10.

Adirondack Room, Whiteface Inn Resort, Whiteface Inn Road, Lake Placid. (518) 523-2551. The main dining room here is all in soft blues and woods, the tables spaced comfortably apart and bearing most unusual twig candlesticks. The front Lakeside Dining Room has windows facing Lake Placid. The big stone fireplace in the middle is used by both rooms, and there's even a twig picture frame. The short continental menu, priced from $15.75 to $21.25, includes entrees like chicken boursin, veal normande, steak au poivre and, the most expensive items, shrimp gamberetto and seafood alfredo. Listed under Adirondack specialties are lamb chops, roasted crisp duck with a ginger-raspberry sauce, and fresh trout prepared with a beurre blanc. The best deal is the Friday night clambake, when steamers, lobster, corn on the cob and Boston cream pie are $15.75. A typical golf club menu is served at lunch in the **Adirondack Cafe-Lounge,** which opens onto the pleasant **First Tee Terrace.** Lunch daily, 11:30 to 2; dinner, 5:30 to 9 or 9:30.

Other Choices

Lindsay's, 237 Main St., Lake Placid. (518) 523-9470. Tucked away at the rear of the Woodshed restaurant is this lovely room with paneled wainscoting and peach napkins standing tall in the wine glasses. Rear windows look onto a brick-walled patio with flowers and birch trees illuminated at night. Tiffany-style lamps hang from the high beamed ceiling. Chef-owner Terry Ziff bills his fare as "the taste of elegance." The contineal menu runs from $15.95 for petite New York steak supreme to $24.95 for dover sole florentine or moularde duck with orange-currant sauce. Veal oscar, sweetbreads madeira, quail normandy and tournedos with bearnaise sauce are other possibilities. Start with tortellini with lobster and prosciutto in basil sauce, escargots or shrimp dijon. White chocolate mousse is the dessert specialty. The same kitchen serves the **Woodshed** restaurant in front, which is more rustic with bare floors and farm implements on the barnwood walls. The family fare is priced from $6.95 to $13.95. Dinner at Lindsay's, nightly 6 to 10; fewer nights in off-season.

The Interlaken Inn and Restaurant, 15 Interlaken Inn, Lake Placid. (518) 523-3180. The dinner menu changes nightly at this small inn, where the intimate Victorian dining room is enhanced by lavish lace, walnut paneling and the original pressed-tin ceilings. Tables are set with gold-colored service plates upon white and burgundy linens. Innkeeper Carol Johnson is the chef, assisted

112

by her Culinary Institute-trained son. Their busy schedule accounts for the single seating at 7 p.m. with a prix-fixe menu for $20. The meal the night we were there was chilled melon-peach-champagne soup, garden salad with apples, walnuts and a raspberry vinaigrette, and a choice of sole meuniere, chicken cordon bleu, smoked pork loin with peach chutney or veal marsala. Twice-baked potatoes and a medley of baby vegetables accompanied. A blackberry-strawberry double chocolate fool was the night's dessert, but grand marnier souffle could be on the docket. Dinner by reservation, Tuesday-Saturday at 7.

Charcoal Pit Restaurant, Sara-Placid Road (Route 86), Lake Placid. (518) 523-3050. The parking lot always seems to be packed at this local institution on the west side of town. With good reason. Everyone says the food is excellent, it's fairly priced and the atmosphere is a cut above what you'd expect from a place that's been around since 1957. We're partial to the greenhouse room, pretty in pink and green with a solarium along one side looking onto splendid illuminated gardens that outshine even the notable sunsets. Traditionalists like the original, darker dining room, where tiny white lights outline the crossbeams, the linens are pink and burgundy, and plants are everywhere. Owner Jim Hadgis is Greek, which accounts for such items on the oversize menu as Greek lamb chops, chicken oregano a la grecque, and Greek shrimp (as well as a painting of a Greek wedding by local artist Averil Conwell and a stunning stained-glass piece representing Greek mythology). But he says prime rib is the biggest seller, followed by fish, veal and rack of lamb. Altogther, some 30 possibilities run from $12.95 to $21 (for steak au poivre). Chateaubriand bouquetiere is a special-occasion dish, $46 for two. The dessert cart might harbor banana-chocolate chip or Heath bar crunch pies. The two dozen wines are priced in the teens. Dinner nightly, 5 to 10. Closed one or two nights in off-season.

Alpine Cellar, Wilmington Road, Lake Placid. (518) 523-2180. On the lower level beneath and to the rear of their eighteen-room motel, Wolfgang and Monique Brandenburg (he German and she Swiss) run a very personal, stylish and well-regarded Bavarian restaurant. The decor is charming, from the painted ceiling and stucco walls to collections of elaborate steins, Tyrolean plates, and copper pots on the fireplace mantel. A small back dining room features pictures of the Alps, and the lounge is a haven of luxury with leather chairs inset with leather diamonds of various colors. The place is made to order for skiers, but summer visitors are impressed by the gardens and the collection of birdhouses in back. One can feast quite well on Swiss fondue, bratwurst or a couple of assorted Bavarian platters for $12.95 or less, or get more fancy with four kinds of schnitzel, sole ludwig, orange roughy, trout amandine, sauerbraten and duckling with green peppercorn sauce and red cabbage ($12.95 to $15.95). All entrees come with house salad, homemade bread, and choice of potato pancakes, spaetzle or rice pilaf. The wine list ranges from New York to Germany to California to Australia, and all bottles are under $21. Save room for apple strudel, the dessert specialty, or a fruit tart or cheesecake. Dinner nightly, 5 to 10. Open mid-May through October and mid-December through March.

Villa Vespa, 85 Saranac Ave., Lake Placid. (518) 523-9959. The Vespa family bills this as "a nice little Italian restaurant," which you could say it is. But you also could say it's fairly big, bright and noisy. One wall is covered with Olympic sports logos, for owner George Vespa is an avid skier and Olympics fan. This made a convivial place for dinner for a group of seven spanning three generations. We sampled everything from basic spaghetti with meatballs and excellent pasta primavera to breast of capon with spinach and seafood marinara. The salad bar was varied and the entree portions hearty, some served with sides of homemade pastas. The Vespas make their own breads, soups and even their pickled beets and dill pickles. Pastas range in price from $8.95 to $13.95 and entrees from $12.95 to $15.95. Desserts include black forest cake, Kentucky derby pie, raspberry pie and homemade cheesecake. Most of the wines are priced in the low teens. Dinner nightly, 4 to 9:30. Closed April and late fall.

The Hungry Trout, Route 86, Wilmington. (518) 946-2217. Who wouldn't like a place with a name like this? The spacious, main-floor dining room is pleasant in beige and brown amid fly-fishing decor, antiques and windows onto the Flume Falls and mountains. Fresh rainbow trout ($13.95 to $16.95) comes six ways: baked, charbroiled with bearnaise sauce, blackened, pan-fried, stuffed with crab or taliaferro (baked with mushrooms, onions, peppers, artichokes and tomatoes and seasoned with Italian spices). With these, owner Jerry Bottcher recommends a bottle of pescevino soave, an Italian wine in a bottle shaped like a fish, which may be taken home as a souvenir. The rest of the menu runs from $11.95 for grilled chicken to $18.95 for extra-large prime rib. The appetizer sampler plate includes three of the most popular: crab-stuffed mushrooms, clams casino and scallops florentine. The longtime chef, who said his name was Tag ("that's how everybody knows me"), is partial to desserts like deep-fried ice cream, mud pie and southern pecan pie. Downstairs is the new **R.F. McDougall's** lounge, a "civilized saloon" with a sports bar and TV, casual fare priced from $8.95 to $14.95, and a children's menu. Dinner nightly, 5 to 10.

Desperados, Saranac Avenue, Lake Placid. (518) 523-1507. This colorful Mexican restaurant in a new shopping center is amusingly promoted as "a desperate place operated by desperate people." Actually, the owners also have the well-regarded Casa del Sol in Saranac Lake. Their new venture is an extraordinary rainbow of colors amid a mix of tables and booths. Papier-mache skulls and nice artworks are scattered about the long, narrow room behind a mod bar up front. Check out the paintings of the owners clad in Southwest attire on the restroom doors. The all-day menu is unbelievably priced — huevos rancheros and three other egg dishes for $4.25, and seafood chilaquiles, seafood tostada and shrimp chimichanga topping the price list at $6.50. The Mexican roulette, fresh roasted jalapenos stuffed with shrimp and cheese, is a popular appetizer, and the ceviche tempts as well. Orange sherbet layered with tequila and grenadine is the dessert of choice. Open daily, 11 to 10; Sunday, 5 to 10.

The Great Adirondack Pasta Company, 57 Saranac Ave., Lake Placid. (518) 523-1614. The owners of this new pasta, steak and seafood establishment also own the Artist's Cafe and the Great Adirondack Steak & Seafood Company in downtown Lake Placid. Here, as in the others, the atmosphere is casual and the menu aims to appeal to all tastes. Pasta prices range from $8.95 for pasta primavera to $10.95 for shrimp primavera. You can get calzones (one with lobster is $11.95), or a variety of meats and fish from $8.95 to $13.95 (for surf and turf). Nightly specials might involve broiled salmon with orange hollandaise sauce or whole shrimp wrapped in boneless breast of chicken. The ultimate combo must be T-bone steak, shrimp and lobster tail for $10.95. Start with fried calamari or mozzarella sticks. Finish with cannoli, kahlua cheesecake or chocolate chambord cake. The very limited wine list mentions three whites and three reds for under $12.95. Dining is in a front room with bare tables, vaulted ceiling and skylights, or in a rear dining room with glass-covered, green checkered tablecloths and red napkins. Dinner nightly, 5 to 10.

FOR MORE INFORMATION: Lake Placid Commerce & Visitors Bureau, Olympic Arena, Lake Plaid 12946. (518) 523-2445.

Tour boat passes beneath Canadian span of Thousand Islands Bridge.

The Thousand Islands, N.Y.-Ont.

The quaint overhead "welcome" signs at the entrance to each village in the Thousand Islands region are distinctive:

Alexandria Bay's sign lights up in neon, a garish reminder of the resort heritage of this touristy village, which, though somewhat tacky, is endearingly so. The signs for Clayton and Gananoque are old-fashioned wood, reflecting a more low-key tradition. The small sign at the entrance to the hamlet of Rockport has a homemade look, evidence of a simpler way of life.

The Thousand Islands region is a watery venue of rocky, forested islands straddling two nations and marking the beginning of the storied St. Lawrence River as it leaves Lake Ontario to flow northeast to the Atlantic Ocean.

Some of the Thousand Islands — actually they number nearly 1,800 — are mere rocks with a tree, too small for habitation or more than a single cabin. Others are large enough for many cottages, and busy Wellesley Island contains a Victorian village, several state parks, a major resort and hundreds of summer homes. The largest, Canada's charming Wolfe Island, supports a year-round farming population of nearly 1,500.

The region's vacation centers are as varied as the islands themselves. The focus on the American side is Alexandria Bay, or Alex Bay as it's called; here is an old-fashioned, once-moneyed resort in the genre, perhaps, of the Jersey shore. To the west is Clayton, its poor-boy cousin, a mecca for fishermen and campers.

The Canadian side is more low-key and more scenic. Its focus is Gananoque (GAN-a-NOK-kwee, or Gan, as the locals call it), an up-and-coming town of inns and restaurants. To the east, tiny Ivy Lea and Rockport retain the look of a generation ago. In the heart of the area, Wellesley Island in New York and Hill Island in Ontario provide the bridge and highway links between the two nations and two very different shores.

Fishing and boating are the islands' chief attractions for many. Bass, northern pike and muskies keep the anglers happy, and no fewer than 75 sightseeing excursion boats ply the river waters.

You can rent a houseboat or ride on a tour boat. Watch ocean-going freighters pass along the St. Lawrence Seaway. View the islands from the Skydeck tower or a helicopter. Attend vesper services by boat. Take a shuttle boat to shop at the Boateak on Bluff Island or a ferry to dine at an inn on Wolfe Island. Camp in a cabin on Canoe Island or a tent on Mary Island, and island-hop between campsites in Canada's St. Lawrence National Park.

You can visit North America's largest inland Shipyard Museum, see first-rate theater at a playhouse beside the water, take in the wonders of the Wellesley Island nature center, reminisce in the Victorian homes and ambience of Thousand Island Park, step back in time on Wolfe Island, and enjoy the local Thousand Island salad dressing and River Rat cheese.

And everyone ogles Boldt Castle, the $2.5 million monument to a man's love and a broken heart on Heart Island, an omnipresent landmark off Alexandria Bay.

Just as the islands and towns vary, so do the people who visit or populate this busy summer vacation area. All types can find their place among the myriad islands and attractions of the mighty St. Lawrence.

Getting There

The Thousand Islands region is located approximately 100 miles north of Syracuse, 200 miles east of Toronto and 100 miles southwest of Ottawa. The closest nearby cities, Watertown, N.Y., and Kingston, Ont., are each about 30 miles away. Interstate 81 and the Trans-Canada Highway 401 are the main access routes to the area. The two soaring spans of the Thousand Islands International Bridge connect the American and Canadian shores (toll, $2).

Prices are quoted in local currency. Recently, American funds have stretched about fifteen percent farther in Canada, but Canada's new GST tax eats up part of the difference.

Where to Stay⎯⎯⎯⎯⎯⎯⎯⎯⎯⎯⎯⎯⎯⎯⎯⎯⎯ ⟋⟍⟍⟍

What you do and how you enjoy the Thousand Islands likely will depend on your choice of accommodations, which range from resort to motel to cabin to campsite. The area is highly seasonal, and generally battens down the hatches for the winter.

Resorts

Pine Tree Point, Alexandria Bay, N.Y. 13607. (315) 482-9911 or (800) 253-9229. This 35-year-old resort, on a 40-acre peninsula thick with pines, has what we consider the most enticing public setting in the islands. Still personally overseen by the founding Thomson family and situated off by itself away from town, the 83-room complex has a main inn with 21 guest rooms, a cocktail lounge and dining rooms (see Where to Eat), plus cottages and motel-style buildings (many with idyllic waterfront balconies), a picturesque outdoor dining terrace with a smashing view down the St. Lawrence, a quiet cove for boats and a shady area with a tepid swimming pool and a jacuzzi. The corner Victorian room and the 22 balconied Cliffs units at water's edge are most prized, though ours suffered somewhat from wear and outdated decor. But even the more modest rooms without water views have television and share the verdant setting. Doubles, $60 to $100; suites, $140. Open May to mid-October.

Riveredge Resort Hotel, 17 Holland St., Alexandria Bay, N.Y. 13607. (315) 482-9917 or (800) 365-6987. Following a 1988 fire, Jim Donegan's Riveredge motel re-emerged in the Islands' most glamorous reincarnation: a four-story behemoth with two atriums, elevators, a concierge floor with loft suites and turndown service, corner jacuzzi rooms, a fourth-floor "gourmet" restaurant and valet parking. (The last is a necessity because parking is limited and casual visitors are discouraged.) Rooms are Alexandria Bay's most luxurious, with Chippendale-style furniture, concealed TV, two chairs and a table and private balconies — flawed, we think, because only a railing separates each from the next and you can see every other balcony on the floor, which seems to make for convivial gatherings. Ten rooms face the St. Lawrence head-on; the rest have side views of the river, although those on the west side look across a small harbor to downtown Alex Bay. The fourth-floor concierge suites have sitting rooms with loft bedrooms up a spiral staircase, two TVs and three telephones (we've heard that the lofts can get rather warm). The indoor pool area has a large jacuzzi and sauna, and there's an outdoor pool by the marina. Doubles, $118 to $168; loft and jacuzzi suites, $188 to $248.

Glen House Resort and Motel, Thousand Islands Parkway, Box 10, Gananoque, Ont. K7G 2T6. (613) 659-2204. The Canadian side's largest resort, this rustic complex sprawls in motel-style on either side of the main turn-of-the-century Glen House along the quiet riverfront, well away from the parkway. Most of the 80 nicely furnished rooms with color TVs have water views. There are a heated pool at river's edge, an indoor pool and sauna, and a dining room and cocktail lounge with panoramic views. Doubles, $75 to $125.

The Edgewood Resort, Box 218, Alexandria Bay, N.Y. 13607. (315) 482-9922 or (800) 766-6576. Occupying its own 75-acre peninsula across the bay from downtown, the Edgewood has 160 rooms in a variety of motel-style buildings clustered around a lively central clubhouse. The 100 waterfront rooms are as sought-after as those at the more sedate Pine Tree Point, but those away from the water could be anywhere. The heart-shaped pool, three cocktail lounges and nightly entertainment set a young-at-heart theme, and the weekend specials — a Friday night seafood buffet for $21.95 and a Sunday brunch for $13.50 — pack them in. The resort stayed open year-round starting in 1990-91. Doubles, $75 to $135.

Bonnie Castle Resort, Holland Street, Box 219, Alexandria Bay, N.Y. 13607. (315) 482-4511 or (800) 955-4511. Under the auspices of Baldwinsville muffler-chain owner Don Cole, the old Holland estate has blossomed into "the showplace of the Thousand Islands" (its words). Now there are allied enterprises — the Bonnie Castle Downs with harness racing and a country music festival, and the Bonnie Castle Greens, a golf driving range and not-so-miniature mini-golf course with eighteen holes depicting U.S. attractions like Boldt Castle and eighteen depicting Canadian, including a 40-foot-high sky deck, linked by a suspension bridge. The emphasis at the resort is on romance and big-name entertainment (the Nichols brothers and David Grayson shows, when we visited) in the **Showplace of the Stars** nightclub. The circular **Chandelier Terrace** dining room, right over the water, is glamorous and glitzy in black and white, the nightclub is noisy and the bar between the two is crowded. We were reminded of Atlantic City, without the jingle of the slot machines, but could they be next? A "luxury hotel" (its words) is really a motel with 100 spacious rooms (each with wet bar, some with heart-shaped tubs) set back from the river overlooking parking lots, a pool and roofs of a boatyard and marina. Only six of the 34 new units around a courtyard face the water, but all have heart-shaped jacuzzis and walls and ceilings splashed with mirrors. Some have balconies onto a red-tiled Florida room with a whirlpool and a gazebo in the midst of a small freeform pool. And — spare us, please — there's a tanning bed in the beauty center. A replica of the Statue of Liberty is on the grounds. Doubles, $99 to $175.

Thousand Islands Club & Conference Center, Wellesley Island, Alexandria Bay, N.Y. 13607. (315) 482-2551. This venerable Mediterranean-style resort has undergone several incarnations in its 86 years, recently as a Treadway inn and then as the Thousand Islands Resort; it is slowly emerging again as the Thousand Islands Club and Conference Center, thanks to a multi-million-dollar expansion and refurbishing by new owners, a group of investors from Syracuse. They first renovated the aging public rooms, then built 64 contemporary villa units that could be mistaken for condos along the golf course greens. They closed the 44 rooms in the main hotel during the 1990 season for badly needed renovations. Expanded marina facilities, an eighteen-hole golf course, tennis and a large heated pool are attractions. The large dining room has been stylishly done over (see Where to Eat), and there's nightly entertainment. Doubles, $99 to $129. Open mid-April through Christmas.

Inns and B&Bs

Trinity House, 90 Stone St. South, Gananoque, Ont. K7G 1Z8. (613) 382-8383. Longtime sailing friends who often sailed in the Thousand Islands while vacationing from Toronto, Jacques O'Shea and Brad Garside opened this appealing B&B in a 130-year-old house, whose bricks imported from the Trinity district in Scotland account for its name. In 1990, they added a cafe with lounge and veranda to supplement their basement art gallery and shop. The six guest rooms, all with private baths, are named after favorite islands. Jacques collects the oriental sconces that adorn some of the rooms, which are handsomely furnished with oriental and Victorian touches. A screen of cranes in the downstairs hall is a masterpiece. Next door in the old jail is "The Lock-Up," a suite with kitchen accommodating four. Guests enjoy a striking parlor with a shiny black floor, white rug and sofas, the small cafe and a private rear deck beside a lovely garden. Works of area artists, collectibles and gifts are showcased in the excellent downstairs gallery. Fresh fruit and homemade muffins are served for breakfast. Doubles, $85 to $105; suite, $125. Closed February and March.

The Athlone Inn, 250 King St. West, Gananoque, Ont. K7G 2G6. (613) 382-2440. A red brick and gingerbread structure built in 1874 houses the region's best-known dining room (see Where to Eat) and four elegant guest rooms, each sumptuously furnished in Victoriana with poster beds and sitting areas. At the side are six well-appointed motel rooms. Each room has an eagle over the bed, television, good reading lamps and enough personal touches to show that innkeepers Gerald and Barbara Schothuis care as much for their overnight guests' comfort as they do for their diners' palates. Doubles, $75 to $90.

Glenwood Manor Inn, 279 King St. West, Gananoque, Ont. K7G 2G7. (613) 382-3368. Gananoque's most sumptuous accommodations are found in this 1872 Italianate villa. Innkeeper Kathy Pfeiffer, a former Toronto interior designer who spent summers as a child helping her grandmother run an inn in her native Hungary, decorated the six guest rooms to the hilt. The bridal suite features a marble fireplace, an elaborate canopied kingsize four-poster outfitted in lovely chintzes and lace, and a double whirlpool bath. A third-floor suite has a built-in bed for a child in an alcove between a sitting room and a back bedroom. Soft floral wallpapers and fabrics are color-coordinated, of course, with fancy sheets, delicate pillows and duvets, and Caswell-Massey toiletries. A second-floor common room is graced with a fireplace, shelves of books and two sofas. Complimentary breakfast might include juice and fresh fruit, almond-chocolate chip muffins, french toast or eggs benedict. The public can partake of high tea ($6.50) on the rear veranda on summer afternoons. Doubles, $125 to $200.

The Gananoque Inn, 550 Stone St. South, Gananoque, Ont. K7G 2G6. (613) 382-2165 or (800) 267-3911. Nicely situated on the river a few blocks south of downtown, this complex has 30 rooms in the 100-year-old main structure plus twenty motel units. Most popular are the fourteen new waterfront units, as well as the inn rooms with brass beds and balconies. Private baths, TV and air-conditioning are modern touches in a building that otherwise shows its age. The best riverfront view in Gananoque opens up from the dining room and a pleasant outdoor cocktail deck with tables topped by yellow umbrellas. At noon, the food is standard. We enjoyed a reuben and a chef's salad topped, appropriately, with Thousand Island dressing. At night, the two large dining rooms are gussied up with tall orange napkins in orange water glasses on white linen; each table had a potted begonia wrapped in tinfoil when we visited. A large cocktail lounge is done in a rustically old-school motif. Doubles, $80 to $120; suites, $120 to $175.

Bach's Alexandria Bay Inn, 2 Church St., Alexandria Bay, N.Y. 13607. (315) 482-9697. Super-keen fishing enthusiast Virginia Bach had been coming here for years from New Jersey to participate in her favorite sport. In 1986 she took the plunge and bought the old Dixie Inn, now running it with her son Robert — and, ironically, has little time to go fishing anymore. This is Alex Bay's first real B&B and the somewhat rundown Victorian house, the village's oldest extant building, is being nicely redone. Four of the six guest rooms have private baths. The enthusiastic mother and son serve continental breakfast with homemade rolls and breads in the morning and afternoon lemonade or tea in the living room or on the wicker-filled side veranda. Lots of lace, little dolls, antiques, an 1856 encyclopedia set, a Persian rug and new carpeting are caring touches; so are the fresh flowers, champagne in summer, Gilbert & Soames amenities and bottled water. Virginia scorns linens from a linen service (as do we) and provides pretty Laura Ashley sheets and properly large, thirsty and colorful towels. She recently opened a small gift and antiques shop in back. Doubles, $65 to $125. Open late April to November.

Wellesley Hotel, Thousand Island Park, Wellesley Island, N.Y. 13692. (315) 482-9400. The ever-so-quaint, Victorian-relic community of Thousand Island Park is home of the old Wellesley Hotel, which has a lobby full of wicker, an acclaimed dining room (see Where to Eat), and a second floor of Victorian boutiques with a wing of basic guest rooms of the old school. New owners Windsor and Eileen Price have upgraded four rooms with private baths, and plan ultimately to redo more on the third floor. The rooms are fresh and simple, with rose stenciling, painted floors, and a couple have adjoining sitting rooms. Doubles, $60 to $80. Open mid-June to Labor Day.

Thousand Islands Inn, 335 Riverside Drive, Clayton, N.Y. 13624. (315) 686-3030. Built in 1897 across the main street from the river, this three-story place is popular with fishermen and advertises all kinds of fishing packages. The seventeen rooms vary; thirteen have private baths and television and the rest are "just sleeping rooms," according to the manager. The pleasantly rustic dining room has received Silver Spoon awards. Doubles, $40 to $55. Open mid-May to mid-October.

Two others B&Bs are of interest. **Featherbed Shoals,** Box 11, RD 1, Cape Vincent, N.Y., 13618, (315) 654-2983, offers four guest rooms, two with private baths, during July and August in a good-looking summer home on the riverfront. Doubles, $50. For an unusual, rustic experience, you can stay in the cabins of the 3,000-ton icebreaker **Alexander Henry,** part of the Marine Museum of the Great Lakes, 55 Ontario St., Kingston, Ont. K7L 2Y2, (613) 542-2261. Rooms vary from captain's and officer's cabins with private washrooms to crew cabins with bunks and sinks. Doubles with continental breakfast, $31.50 to $52.50. Open May-August.

Motels

Capt. Thomson's Resort, 1 James St., Alexandria Bay, N.Y. 13607. (315) 482-9961. The Thomson family, which also owns Pine Tree Point and the adjacent new Captain's Landing floating restaurant here, runs this motel, where the riverfront (Main Channel) rooms are blessed with an unbeatable location right over the water with a view across to Boldt Castle. As you watch all the boating activity or take in the sunset, the waves lap at the rocks and birds land on your private balcony (and at one point the hook — with worm — on the fishing line of the young lad fishing from the balcony next door swung around and imbedded itself in our balcony as well). The 117 rooms are spacious and comfortable; ours had a full bathroom with an extra sink, but also had those skimpy linen-service towels that you can almost read through. There's a pool out front beside the parking lot and restaurant. Doubles, $75 to $109. Open late April to late October.

The Ledges Resort Motel-Boatel, Box 245, Alexandria Bay, N.Y. 13607. (315) 482-9334. Its location set back from the riverfront near Pine Tree Point rates this 24-unit motel a cut above many of the Bay's others. The swimming pool has a water slide, and guests can fish from the docks. Doubles, $78 to $88. Open May to mid-October.

Fishermen's Wharf Motel, 15 Sisson St., Alexandria Bay, N.Y. 13607. (315) 482-2230. All rooms are within 25 feet of the waterfront in this downtown motel overlooking the town pier. Rooms are modern and comfortable, but some do not face the water and late-night noise can be a problem, especially on weekends, when young carousers make merry in downtown Alex Bay. Doubles, $55 to $110. Open late April to late October.

Torchlite Motel, Peel Dock Road, Wellesley Island, Alexandria Bay N.Y. 13607. (315) 482-3550. Eighteen comfortable motel and efficiency units are available at this secluded waterfront location, on Wellesley Island almost under the American span of the Thousand Islands International Bridge. The view is what sells the place, although a free continental breakfast and a pool help. Doubles, $59 to $79. Open May-October.

West Winds Motel & Cottages, Route 12E, RD2, Box 56, Clayton, N.Y. 13624. (315) 686-3352. Sloping lawns down to the river, an attractive pool and fairly sprightly motel furnishings make this a good bet in the Clayton area. Twelve motel units have one or two beds, and there are eight good-looking efficiency cabins and housekeeping cottages, two near the water. Doubles, $52 to $58; cottages for four to six, $470 to $595 per week. Open mid-May through September.

RENTALS. Island cottages and houses can be rented, through private auspices or real-estate brokers. Efficiency cabins by the week or month abound on both the American and Canadian mainlands; rentals are generally $250 to $600 a week. R. Kemp Realty at 39 Church St., Alexandria Bay, (315) 382-9241, and at 507 Riverside Drive, Clayton, (315) 686-3409, is the islands' largest realtor.

Houseboats can be rented for $850 to $1,695 a week from Remar Rentals, 510 Theresa St., Clayton; Houseboat Holidays Ltd., R.R. 3, Gananoque, or St. Lawrence River Houseboat Rentals, Holiday Point, Wolfe Island, Ont.

Camping

STATE PARKS. Some of New York State's finest parks are in this area and offer campsites among their facilities. **Wellesley Island State Park,** (315) 482-2722, is by far the largest, with 429 campsites and a public golf course. From a marina here you can rent a boat to get to campsites on Canoe or Mary islands. One of the more pleasant sites is **Keewaydin State Park,** (315) 482-3331, a 179-acre former private estate sloping down to the river west of Alexandria Bay and boasting an Olympic-size pool and a marina among its amenities. (It's also the headquarters of the Thousand Islands regional state park office, where camping reservations are computerized through Ticketron).

Those who prefer not to rough it in tent or camper may rent cabins by the week at DeWolf Point and Canoe Island. At **DeWolf Point State Park,** (315) 482-2012, where one of our families spent many a happy vacation in the 1950s, fourteen two-room cabins for four are scattered along the Lake of the Isles shoreline. They're basic and bare, with nothing more than a refrigerator, bunk beds and two electric lights. Weekly rentals are $82 and they are fully booked for the summer through a January lottery drawing.

Limited camping is offered in **St. Lawrence Islands National Park,** Canada's smallest national park, which consists of nineteen islands and Mallorytown Landing on the mainland northeast of Rockport.

A number of large, privately owned campgrounds are available as well.

Seeing and Doing   *∩∩∩*

The water, and the islands, are the lure. The passing traveler might wonder what the attraction is, since you really have to get onto the river to see the islands and sense their mystique.

On the Water

BOAT TOURS are *the* thing in the Thousand Islands, and more than 75 tour boats from six cruise lines offer trips up to 52 miles long as often as every hour in season. Sometimes it seems there are more tour boats than private craft in this area seemingly made for powerboats (sailing vessels are far less in evidence — more noticeable are the enormous lakers and ocean-going freighters plodding to and from the Great Lakes through the St. Lawrence Seaway via the American Narrows off Alexandria Bay).

Tour boats vary in size and duration of trip (from 90 minutes to five hours). Some, particularly **Ivy Lea** and **Rockport** lines in Canada, boast of small boats that go where the larger ones can't. The three-decker **Gananoque Boat Line** vessels and the large **Uncle Sam Boat Lines** and **Empire Boat Tours** boats out of Alexandria Bay let people move around for various vantage points. High points are the millionaires' row cottages around Alex Bay, the Canadian palisades area where the greenish waters are 250 feet deep, and some of the smaller, fancily landscaped islands containing a single home and boathouse.

Youngsters might get bored after awhile, but we enjoyed hearing all the tidbits about who owned the houses and islands. Uncle Sam's Seaway Island Tour, upwards of three hours long and encompassing both Canadian and American channels between Alex Bay, Rockport and Clayton, is perhaps the most interesting tour. You also can take lunch and dinner cruises, and take a boat cruise to Cherry Island for a tour of Casa Blanca, a turn-of-the-century mansion. Basic tour prices are in the $8 to $12 range and include unlimited stopovers at Boldt Castle.

Boldt Castle on the appropriately named Heart Island was to be the testament of the love for his wife of George C. Boldt, a Prussian immigrant who became the most successful early hotel magnate in America, owning the Waldorf-Astoria in New York and the Bellevue-Stratford in Philadelphia. He had spent $2.5 million on a six-story, 150-room Rhineland-style castle with enormous boathouse and power plant when she died in 1904 — mysteriously. No one ever tells the cause, although our young boat guide suggested cancer. Work was stopped and visitors wander through the huge, empty rooms, imagining what might have been. The castle is reached by boat tours or shuttles from Alex Bay. Open daily, 10 to 6, mid-May to early October. Adults $3, children $1.75.

You also can see the Thousand Islands by water taxis, day sailing expeditions, U-Drive Boats, helicopter tours and the 350-foot Thousand Islands skydeck on Hill Island (adults, $3.95). The best auto route is along the Thousand Islands Parkway on the scenic Canadian side, with beautiful vistas and frequent picnic spots; the American side, alas, is almost devoid of river views from the main road.

FISHING is popular, from Alexandra Bay ("bass fishing capital of the world") to Clayton. Our boat tour guide said 85 species, from pan fish to sturgeon, have been caught, and the world's biggest muskie was landed in the Shoals region. Numerous guides lead fishing parties on chartered boats.

Half Moon Bay Vesper Services. Since 1887, non-denominational vesper services have been conducted by visiting ministers in a secluded bay off Bostwick Island near Gananoque. The congregation arrives and remains in small boats, including canoes, for an hour of hymns and meditation at 4:30 p.m. on summer Sundays amid a natural water setting gouged in granite by the glaciers. Water taxis leave by reservation, (613) 382-8058, at 4 from the Bay Street Dock in Gananoque.

A fun day trip is by ferry to **Wolfe Island,** largest of the Thousand Islands, and then on to Kingston, Ont., the Islands' largest city. We started from Cape Vincent, N.Y., arriving at 1:55 for the 2 p.m. ferry, only to be told by the Customs official that the boat operator had left two minutes earlier — "2 o'clock, according to his watch." A half hour later, we boarded the next ten-vehicle ferry ($5) run by the same family since the 18th century. It was a ten-minute ride to the island, which is a time warp of rolling farmlands, waterfront cottages, a little village called Marysville and about 1,100 permanent residents. A free, much larger provincial ferry completes the twenty-minute ride to **Kingston,** an up-and-coming university town of museums, suave shops and good restaurants (Chez Piggy, the River Mill and Zona Rosa are three of the best).

Waterside Attractions

Thousand Islands Shipyard Museum, 750 Mary St., Clayton, 686-4104. Started in 1964 as the outgrowth of the oldest antique boat show, this non-profit institution has grown into the largest freshwater maritime museum in the country. Boating enthusiasts have a field day exploring the rambling riverfront buildings containing all manner of wooden boats, the local St. Lawrence skiffs, old birchbark canoes, exotic yachts, runabouts, outboard motors and such. The more than 150 small craft show the ingenuity of builders in adapting to the tricky St. Lawrence waters, our informant said, and you'll marvel at the importance boating has had here over the years.

One yacht in the Cleveland Dodge launch building rests on blocks so visitors can peer under as well as in via ramps. The Stroh beer family's commuter boat was being readied to go back in the water when we visited. There's a fine shop with books and nautical gifts.

Considered a sleeper with great potential as a destination site, the museum is well worth the $4 admission charge. Open daily 10 to 5, mid-May to mid-October.

Minna Anthony Common Nature Center, Wellesley Island State Park, N.Y. Eight miles of trails and walkways crisscross through 600 acres of wooded wetlands, marshes, swamps and rocky knobs for closeup views of varied wildlife — perhaps a thorny porcupine in a tree, or beavers splashing in ponds or white-tailed deer loping into the woods. The center's staff offers special trail hikes and nature walks. Perched on a plateau of the reddish-brown Potsdam sandstone characteristic of the area, the museum includes live collections of fish, reptiles and amphibians, plus mounted waterfowl and a beehive with live bees.

WATER DRAMA. The Thousand Islands Playhouse, fashioned from the old Gananoque Canoe Club building, is right on the river in Gananoque. Since 1982, it has been producing five plays a season in a 350-seat theater, with comedy the theme in 1990. The cast is professional, curtain is at 8:30 and tickets, $14. Also popular but less well known are the **River Barge Productions** in Clayton's Old Town Hall, hour-long touring shows featuring New York and North Country actors in an original musical titled "The Slick of '76," a look back at the 1976 oil spill in the Thousand Islands, and a new environmental musical cabaret.

Thousand Island Park. Established in 1875 as a church colony, this slice of Victoriana at the west end of Wellesley Island is on the National Historic Register and reminiscent of the campground at Oak Bluffs on Martha's Vineyard. It's worth a visit for a look at the colorful old cottages and the spacious green, and a stop at the boutiques upstairs in the restored Wellesley Hotel or at the Guzzle, an old-fashioned ice cream parlor across the street.

The **Thousand Islands Wild Kingdom** on the north side of Gananoque is of particular interest to youngsters. A baby black panther from India, snow monkeys from Japan, and a Siberian tiger are among the more unusual of the zoo's 250 animals, birds and reptiles, viewed from a nature walk blending cages and animal pods with the landscape. Open daily, 9 to 7; adults, $6.

SHOPPING has not been among the area's strengths, although things are picking up. Alex Bay is full of ice cream parlors, candy stores, trinket, T-shirt and curio shops, and an arcade. But it also has **Riverbank Gallery** with good local art, **Sunshine Peddlar** with nice country crafts including handblown glass hummingbirds that we admired, and casual and resort wear at **Bay Trading Company Store, Chez Therese** and **Hilda's Place, Too.** Local items and historical memorabilia are on view and for sale at **Cornwall Brothers Store,** run by the local historical society.

On Wellesley Island, the small and unusual boutiques upstairs at the Wellesley Hotel in Thousand Island Park show promise. The Hill Island discount stores leave much to be desired, and Gananoque holds few bargains, though some Americans are intrigued by Canadian stores and you may buy English china and woolens at prices lower than in the States.

On Route 12 between Alex Bay and Clayton is **Captain Spicer's Gift Shop,** with appealing gifts and a fine selection of marine and local art. The **Gold Cup Farms** store at 528 Riverside Drive in Clayton is a favorite; we passed on the squeaky fresh cheese curd but bought the local River Rat cheddar cheese (the extra-sharp is great) and tried a couple of the sensational truffles that come packed in an egg carton.

For a different experience, shop at the **Boateak,** a shop above owner Cookie and Matt Tomaivoli's boathouse on Bluff Island off Clayton. Reached via a shuttle boat by appointment, it features American arts, crafts and antiques, including Sid Bell wildlife jewelry, stuffed animals and pierced lampshades.

Where to Eat

Dining in the Thousand Islands region sticks to the surf-and-turf syndrome with, surprisingly, Maine lobster and prime rib heading the list. Local fish is rarely on restaurant menus; even Thousand Island dressing is seldom mentioned. For the best dining, knowledgeable locals head for Wolfe Island and Gananoque.

The Best for Food

The General Wolfe Hotel, Wolfe Island, Ont. (613) 385-2611. People on both sides of the border consider this little-publicized spot tops for dining in the Islands. And the fact that it's on an island, reached by a free twenty-minute ferry ride from Kingston and a short walk from the landing, adds to its appeal. The exterior looks like a typical Canadian village roadhouse/hotel, but the large, two-level dining room with a glimpse of the water is country-pretty in pink and white. Czech hotelier Miroslav F. Zborovsky is known for his ambitious, oversize continental menu that ranges widely from $14.95 for salmon steak bearnaise, coquilles St. Jacques and frog's legs to $24.95 for surf and turf. Those in the know go for his specials of the day, a complete table d'hote dinner for a bargain $21.95. You might start with French onion soup and caesar salad, select from a choice of sirloin steak, roasted pheasant, rack of lamb or filet of sole pontchartrain, and end with French pastries and coffee. Wines are pleasantly priced by Ontario standards. Lunch is a treat as well, especially the prix-fixe special with soup or salad, shish kabob or Hungarian goulash, vegetables and sherbet for $8.95. Upstairs are six simple bedrooms (one a two-bedroom apartment with a sunken living room), renting for $25 to $45 a night. Lunch daily, 11:30 to 3:30; dinner seatings at 5:30, 6:30, 8 and 9. Closed Monday, September-May.

The Athlone Inn, 250 King St. West, Gananoque, Ont. (613) 382-2440. Favored by gourmands for more than two decades is this charming Victorian inn, personally run by Dutch chef-owner Gerald Schothuis. His two ornate, high-ceilinged dining rooms are handsomely appointed in burgundy and pink with rose and white china, cream-colored lace curtains, a large tapestry and velvet draperies between the two rooms. Chef Gerald calls his dinner menu French-continental, with the emphasis decidedly on the French. Start with his house pate or French onion soup before trying the likes of poached salmon with hollandaise, dover sole meuniere, scallops and mushrooms in wine sauce, veal cordon bleu or entrecote Paris (entrees, $14.95 to $19.95). Meringue glace, pear

124

helene and parfait Athlone (vanilla ice cream with Bailey's Irish Cream and whipped cream) are worthy endings. The wine list is mainly French. Although the prices are higher than most in the area, so are the results. Dinner nightly, 5 to 10; closed Monday, October-April.

Glenwood Manor Inn, 279 King St. West, Gananoque, Ont. (613) 382-3368. Almost across the street from the venerable Athlone is a promising newcomer, which opened in 1986 in a magnificently restored 1872 red-brick house as the Grand McCammon and took its new name in 1989. Suave in peach and mint green, two dining rooms linked by a grand piano and a veranda for outdoor dining overlooking the rear gardens are the setting for the highly regarded fare of chef Yvonne Belohouhek, a Czech who won two gold medals for Canada in 1990 at an international gastronomic competition in Prague. For starters, consider smoked arctic char, zesty Thai marinated shrimp or smoked chicken with mangos and pecan dressing. Entrees ($13.75 to $20.50) could be filet of salmon with curry-lime vinaigrette, chicken breast with seafood mousse in port sauce, pork loin stuffed with duxelle and glazed with dates, and roast pheasant with herb-cranberry stuffing and a wild mushroom confit. Finish with mango mousse cake, double chocolate fudge cake or apple crumble with ice cream. Lunch, June-September, daily 11:30 to 2; dinner nightly except Monday from 5:30.

Golden Apple Inn, 45 King St. West, Gananoque, Ont. (613) 382-3300. A gray stone building with gray and yellow trim dating to 1830 has been home to a local dining tradition since 1928. Only since Sil and Shirley Fernetich took over from longtime owners in 1988 has the menu changed. The two older dining rooms in particular are terribly quaint, and the expansive garden terrace with yellow wood umbrellas couldn't be nicer. Old-fashioned, home-style cooking and meals are the rule: roast leg of lamb with mint sauce, steaks, prime rib and roast chicken with dressing and gravy, accompanied by vegetables or stewed apples, sticky buns and tea biscuits, followed by cream pies or ice cream. You get the idea, and traditionalists love it. The new owners have added continental items and livened up the menu to mixed reviews; they also expanded the hours and started accepting credit cards. Complete dinners are $11.95 to $25.95; a la carte lunches (which, except for the salads, are more like dinners), $6.95 to $15.95. There's a standard beverage list. Lunch daily, noon to 3; dinner, 5 to 9. Open May-December.

The Wellesley Hotel, Thousand Island Park, Wellesley Island, N.Y. (315) 482-9400. Thank goodness for this charming summery spot in a restored 1903 hotel. Reopened in 1984, it has the American side's most interesting restaurant, redecorated in teal and rose in 1989, some small boutiques upstairs, a new pub and four guest rooms. Candles glow, classical music plays, formally attired staff serve and there's a wondrous blend of the up-to-date with yesteryear. Chef Myla Seitz, who says she can't stand anything boring, offers an exciting, always changing menu. Our dinner began with a complimentary dish of vegetables: olives with fennel seeds, pasta salad with pecan shrimp, carrots in raspberry vinaigrette, celery with liver pate and marinated cauliflower, followed by an assortment of breads and a mixed salad of exotic greens with choice of creamy tarragon, roasted shallot or honey-sage vinaigrette dressings. The specials of tempura shrimp and squid with a lime mayonnaise and blue corn pasta with avocado-tequilla-blood orange sauce ($17.95) and Hawaiian monkfish wrapped in spinach and leek leaves with sesame-hoisin butter sauce ($18.95) were accompanied by snow peas and a garlicky zucchini-almond concoction. You might find smoked bluefish and bacon soup to start, and a fresh pear and date cobbler topped with cream to finish. The wine list is reasonable and well-chosen. The downstairs pub has a 150-year-old bar imported from Albany and serves snack food. Lunch, Tuesday-Saturday 11 to 2 in mid-summer; dinner, Tuesday-Saturday 5 to 9; Sunday brunch, 11 to 3. Open mid-June to Labor Day.

Wild Goose Restaurant, 506 Riverside Drive, Clayton, N.Y. (315) 686-5004. So successful was Ellen Burr with her seasonal restaurant down the street that she moved in 1990 into larger quarters that we knew as Bamford's. Food supervisor for the area school district, she spends her summers cooking for receptive customers in a colorful dining room with a floral motif, trellises on the walls, Tiffany-style lamps and on an outdoor deck facing the river. Her menu is creative: dinner entrees ($10.50 to $22) like pork tenderloin in phyllo with dark rum and apples, veal with asparagus and brie, chicken and scallops au gratin, and lobster tripoli. Start with chilled raspberry bisque, chilled shrimp and sliced melon with honey-garlic sauce or tabouleh with feta cheese and red grapes. Raisin-walnut pie is the dessert specialty. Luscious salads and sandwiches are the rule at lunch. Lunch and dinner daily in summer. Open Memorial Day to mid-October.

Candlelight Inn, off Route 180, Omar, N.Y. (315) 686-4042. Since 1988, people have beaten a path to chef-owner Mitchell Workman's off-the-beaten-path location in the hamlet of Omar (just south of Fishers Landing, between Alex Bay and Clayton). Mitchell transformed a former tavern into a spacious establishment seating 125 in three simple, relaxing dining rooms. He prepares everything from scratch, features natural ingredients and is revered for his sauces. Roast pheasant and roast duck are his specialties, but the short menu offers a choice from $10.95 for eight-ounce prime rib to $18.95 for baked stuffed lobster. The Candlelight twist: mix and match any of seven sauces with seafood, chicken or poultry, or combination thereof. Dinner, nightly 4:30 to 10 in summer; closed Tuesday in off-season and January-April.

On the Riverfront

Pine Tree Point, Alexandria Bay. (315) 482-9911. We can think of no better setting for a Sunday jazz brunch than the outdoor terrace surrounded by pines and water or, for dinner, the small Sunset Room off the larger Voyageur dining room at Pine Tree Point. Here, amid half a dozen tables, we watched freighters pass and the sun set as we warmed up at the salad bar and sampled an adequate rack of lamb and a filet mignon, each garnished with grapes and a good, zesty mix of tomatoes and zucchini. We thought the highly touted pastry cart ordinary, but liked the creme de menthe parfait, big enough for two and a bargain at $1.75. Choices ranged from $13.95 for chicken piccata to $21.95 for rack of lamb. At our latest visit, we enjoyed the $19.95 seafood buffet on Friday night, an all-you-could-eat extravaganza of appetizers (the smoked salmon with proper accompaniments was excellent), hot dishes like grilled tuna and king crab legs, excellent roast beef and lamb, and a table of mediocre desserts. Lunch, noon to 2; dinner, 6 to 10.

Captain's Landing, 2 James St., Alexandria Bay. (315) 482-7777. We ate dinner here, and breakfast, too — such is the appeal of this floating barge with a new restaurant right at water's edge. As you approach, you think you're about to enter a shingled house on a pier between two sections of the Capt. Thomson motels. Inside, you know you're right on the water when the restaurant pitches slightly as waves from a passing freighter roll in. The Thomson family's newest hit, this has a pleasant candlelit, two-level dining room (all tables with views of the water) on the ground floor and a an upstairs lounge with old postcards inlaid in the tables. Both levels have small decks at one end and a couple of open alcoves for outdoor dining. The dinner menu ($12.95 to $17.95) is short but sweet; we enjoyed poached salmon bearnaise and pork cutlets with a good mushroom-leek sauce, accompanied by a Napa chardonnay. And, because of a kitchen delay on the salmon dish, we took them up on their offer of free desserts (raspberry sherbet and a dense chocolate chambord cake, which went particularly well when mixed together). At breakfast we enjoyed eggs benedict at a table for two in our own outdoor alcove beside the water. Breakfast, 7 to 11; lunch, 11:30 to 2; dinner, 5 to 9 or 10. Closed mid-October to end of April.

Jacques Cartier Dining Room, Riveredge Resort Hotel, 17 Holland St., Alexandria Bay. (315) 482-9917. Alex Bay's most glamorous hotel claims its most glamorous restaurant, a fourth-floor beauty in blue and white with windows onto the water on three sides. Elaborate rattan chairs are at tables set with Steuben crystal, alstroemeria and frosted-glass oil candles. A team of three chefs prepares an expensive menu ($17.95 to $23.95, except $14.95 for chicken brochette). Items like roast duckling and roast rack of lamb are done on a French rotisserie in a space open to the room, handsomely bordered with blue and white tile. Other choices range from seafood newburg in puff pastry and lobster thermidor to filet mignon and steak diane. Appetizers include smoked duck with cumberland sauce and calamari sauteed with Italian tomatoes; desserts run to chocolate and strawberry gateau and grand marnier torte. The good wine list includes several of New York State's finest. Dinner nightly, 5:30 to 10 or 11; weekends only in winter.

Windows on the Bay, Riveredge Resort Hotel, Alexandria Bay. This is the main-floor restaurant of the Riveredge, and successor to the old Pancake House whose grounds it occupies. It's a pleasant, L-shaped room with heavy wood tables set with pink woven mats and a more casual, varied menu than that offered upstairs. For breakfast, we found the strawberry pancakes ($3.95, with a choice of four varieties of syrup) to be quite good, but the coffee stayed only lukewarm in the little glass hottles. We'd return for lunch, the only meal served outside on the waterside deck, and we'd probably order the cobb salad for $5.95. Open daily, 6:30 a.m. to 10 or 11 p.m.; pancakes available until 2 p.m.

Boathouse Restaurant & Tavern, Rockport, Ont. (613) 659-2348. Right on the water in the placid hamlet of Rockport is this restaurant with indoor tablecloth dining in two rooms and an idyllic canopied deck at water's edge. People came and went by boat as we lingered on a sunny Saturday over a hamburg plate ($4.95, with fries and cucumber coleslaw) and a good but not very ample caesar salad ($5.95). The kitchen can get fancy with specials like prime rib soup and cucumber cup filled with shrimp and crab. At night, the short menu runs from $10.95 for deep-fried Icelandic cod to $19.95 for steak au poivre, again supplemented by interesting specials. Thousand Island cheesecake (layers of chocolate and vanilla) is the signature dessert. Lunch and dinner daily, 11 to 11; weekends from 9 a.m. Closed mid-October to late April.

All-American Choices

The Clipper Inn, Route 12, Clayton. (315) 686-3842. Residents like the Simpson family's modern restaurant beside the highway east of Clayton. The interior is contemporary with stained glass, skylights, hanging plants and cane and chrome chairs at blue-linened tables. The American-continental menu offers something for everyone, from potato skins and nachos or shrimp cocktail to veggie alfredo, veal parmesan, chicken Alaska, frog's legs and sole oscar to kahlua parfait and key lime pie. Entrees are $8.95 to $23.95. Dinner nightly, 5 to 10. Closed January-March.

The Ship Restaurant & Lounge, 29 James St., Alexandria Bay. (315) 482-9500. Pat and Mike Simpson of the Clipper Inn have taken over this nautical restaurant with a motel in back. The food is pricey, rising rapidly from $9.95 for chicken livers into the high teens and twenties for filet mignon, Alaskan king crab and lobster. There are seven pastas, five chicken and four veal dishes. Strawberries romanoff and peanut butter ice cream pie are favored desserts. Dinner nightly, 5 to 10.

Cavallario's Steak and Seafood House, 24 Church St., Alexandria Bay. (315) 482-9867. A longtime favorite of the locals is this large establishment with valet parking and ersatz medieval decor inside and out. The extensive menu includes pastas, snapper with crabmeat, stone crabs, shrimp creole, and caesar salad with sliced steak amid a host of meat specialties, but Frank Cavallario says "most of the people come here for lobster and prime rib." Entrees are $12.95 to $26.50. The Cavallario family also runs **Chez Paris Restaurant** next door, which may account for the "Recommended by Frank Cavallario" signs in its windows. His nephew owns **Casa Di Pasta,** an appealing Italian eatery across the street, as well as the adjacent **Riverboat Restaurant** and **River House Inn.** Dinner nightly, 4 to 11. Closed November to mid-April.

Admirals' Inn, James and Market Streets, Alexandria Bay. (315) 482-2781. For casual dining, the wraparound sidewalk terrace here is popular. The menu is like most of the others in town (that is to say, uninspired), but you can find almost anything traditional from spaghetti to surf and turf ($8.95 to $25.95). Lunch and dinner daily, 11:30 to 10 or 11.

Harbor Inn Diner, 625 Mary St., Clayton. (315) 686-2293. Across the street from the Shipyard Museum is this little spot, where we had a good lunch of monkfish chowder, vegetable quiche and spinach salad, accompanied by a mason jar full of iced tea, the biggest drink we ever saw for 85 cents. There are seats at the counter, a few tables topped with red and white checked cloths, and a collection of old tools, bottles and such on the walls. At breakfast, Texas french toast is $2.95 and there's a choice of 21 omelets from $3.25 to $4.45. At lunch you can get a jumbo hot dog for $2 or a garbage sandwich, whatever that is. Dinner entrees ($5.95 to $8.95) include the likes of ziti with meatballs, fried clams, and liver and onions. The pies, like rhubarb and raspberry, are homemade and delicious. Breakfast, lunch and dinner daily.

FOR MORE INFORMATION: Thousand Islands International Council, Box 400, Alexandria Bay, N.Y. 13607, or Box 69, Lansdowne, Ont. K0E 1L0, (800) 847-5263. Alexandria Bay Chamber of Commerce, Box 365, Alexandria Bay 13607, (315) 482-9531. Gananoque Chamber of Commerce, 2 King St. East, Gananoque, Ont. K7G 2L7. (613) 382-3250.

Youngsters cavort in waters of Havana Glen.

Watkins Glen/Finger Lakes, N.Y.

"The Glen Is Back," the advertisements all around New York's Finger Lakes region proclaim.

They refer to the Watkins Glen International racetrack, which is busy once again following its revival from a bankruptcy that nearly destroyed the illustrious resort status of the village of Watkins Glen when the track closed in 1980.

The ads might just as well refer to the Watkins Glen area as a whole. The area, blessed with a scenic location at the foot of the most sparkling of the Finger Lakes and overshadowed between booming Ithaca to the east and Corning to the southwest, is a slumbering giant reawakening.

It's long had its natural attractions — Seneca Lake, towering waterfalls, awesome gorges and placid glens. In the last decade or so, it has developed an unusual concentration of small wineries. And now the home of auto road racing is back on track for race-car enthusiasts.

Although the Glen remains synonymous with racing, there's much more. The Syracuse Post-Standard headlined a section-cover article in 1990, "Watkins Glen: Not Just a Place to Race."

There's a new dynamic in an area that had seen better days. Timespell, a million-dollar outdoor laser and sound show, draws upwards of 1,000 people a night into the lower depths of the Watkins Glen State Park gorge. The lakefront is enlivened with the opening of Seneca Market, an array of shops and eateries in an old machine shop complex, and the completion of a new 150-slip marina and a 330-foot-long fishing pier crowned with a Victorian gazebo. A new excursion boat cruises Seneca Lake. And the downtown is spruced up with plantings, cobblestone walkways and Victorian-style street lamps.

The problem of housing visitors adequately is just being addressed. Schuyler County, of which Watkins Glen is the county seat, had 35 lodging facilities, but all were built prior to 1960 and most look it. A couple of dozen small bed-and-breakfasts have popped up in the last ten years. But until a private developer builds the planned Watkins Glen waterfront hotel — or a savvy chain motel operator enters this area where the only non-indigenous establishments are a Burger King and a Pizza Hut — visitors will find the lodging and restaurant pickings surprisingly thin.

That's unfortunate, because, as Sandy Schmanke, co-owner of the Red House Country Inn in nearby Burdett, says: "The southern Finger Lakes are a paradise untapped." And Watkins Glen is at the heart of it all.

Getting There

Watkins Glen is at the southern end of Seneca Lake, longest of the Finger Lakes, about 80 miles southeast of Rochester and 75 miles southwest of Syracuse. From the New York Thruway, take Route 14 south from Geneva. Watkins Glen also can be reached from the south via Route 14 off the Route 17 expressway at Elmira-Horseheads.

Where to Stay

Accommodations are varied but limited, considering the vast numbers of visitors to this area in summer and early fall .

Motels and Lodges

Glen Motor Inn, Route 14, Box 44, Watkins Glen 14891. (607) 535-2706. The only reasonably modern, full-service motel in the area, this has 40 units in two buildings separated by a swimming pool and a third building one level higher. Located down a sharp hillside and shielded from the highway above, they overlook a parking area and the lake in the distance below. Thirty units have balconies, and all have color cable television. Rooms are relatively small and spare; we had to bring in a chair from the balcony in order to seat a guest. Run by five generations of one family, the motel started with a two-bedroom flat rented for $3 a couple in 1937, says owner Helen Franzese, who's proud that twelve Franzese grandchildren work in the motel or the adjacent restaurant and cocktail lounge. She's also proud of the racers pictured in the motel-restaurant lobby; "we've been catering to celebrities since the first race in 1948," says she. "I'm the momma to all the racers." Doubles, $58 to $73. Open mid-March through November.

Rainbow Cove Resort Motel and Restaurant, off Route 14, Box 171, Himrod 14842. (607) 243-7535. Twenty-four rooms in two structures have patios or balconies and access to pleasant, shaded grounds leading to the lakefront across Plum Point Road. Our room in the "economy" one-story section built about 1950 was smaller than the rooms in the "deluxe" two-story section built about 1970. Having access to the lake and an impressive pool behind the restaurant are distinct pluses; the folksy atmosphere remains from yesteryear. The restaurant (see Where to Eat) is known for good prix-fixe dinners served family style at 7 p.m. for $9; at breakfast, others are likely to join your table as well. Longtime owner Dot Plubell may tell you the story of how the original house and the Four Chimneys winery homestead up the road were part of a Hollywood retreat envisioned by Mary Pickford and Douglas Fairbanks Jr. Doubles, $50 to $65. Open May 10 to Oct. 23.

Chalet Leon Motel-Resort, Route 414, Box 388, Watkins Glen 14891. (607) 546-7171. Hector Falls is right beside this eleven-room motel and eight rustic cottages above Seneca Lake. The two-story motel has large rooms with full baths and television; the cottages have showers but no tubs. The roar of the falls lulls to sleep all except those in the one northside room to which we were assigned. Steep paths lead to the three cascades of Hector Falls, to picnic tables and all the way down to the lakefront, which has a dock, beach and a canoe. To start the day, you may help yourself to coffee, tea or hot chocolate in the main building. Doubles for motel, $49 to $66, cabins $40 to $55, weekly $195 to $250.

Seneca Lodge, South Entrance to Watkins Glen State Park, Watkins Glen 14891. (607) 535-2014. In the late 1940s, lawyer Donald Brubaker quit his practice and bought the former White City Tourist Camp, added a log restaurant-bar and called it Seneca Lodge. He and his sons have run it since. The complex across from the state park's South Entrance bears a faint resemblance to a national park lodge. Nestled in the woods away from the road are twenty older motel units in two strips opening onto shared front decks, two A-frame housekeeping chalets and twenty cabins that have seen better days. To the rear are tennis courts and an appealing spring-fed swimming pool; to the front are a crowded lodge-style restaurant and an enormous bar popular with racers. There also are 26 new motel units away from the hubbub. Our older motel room was large and comfortable. Everything appealed until we found the TV set received only two channels and those marginally, a large neighboring family noisily barbecued hamburgers on our common deck, and another young group partied outside our window until 2 in the morning. Doubles in cabins, $26; motel, $46; chalets, $75 to $90 daily, $400 to $500 weekly. Open April-Thanksgiving.

Longhouse Motel, Route 14, Box 111, Watkins Glen 14891. (607) 535-2565. The Mobil and AAA raters like this unpretentious, thirteen-unit motel high above the lake, and so do we. There's plenty of space for relaxation: on deck chairs outside each unit, on lawn chairs facing each other in a gazebo, and on loungers beside the small pool and hot tub. The spacious rooms are better furnished than most in the area, including refrigerators and air-conditioning. Owners Bill and Carol Franzese offer a complimentary breakfast of coffee, tea, donuts and occasionally homebaked goodies. When we stopped, an addition of six to ten larger rooms was in the planning stages. Doubles, $60 to $65. Open March-November.

Captain's Quarters Motel, Salt Point Road, Watkins Glen 14891. (607) 535-2816. The ride up the rutty driveway (and especially the steep drive down) is hair-raising, but the view from some of the eleven motel units and five cabins makes it worthwhile. Retired Marine Corps captain Gus Beligotti treats guests as if they were in his home, and in a sense they are. He has a private bar in his house-office, where guests are welcome to join him for a beer or two. Motel rooms have two double beds, full baths, TV and a shared balcony for taking in the view. Cottages sleep four to seven. Down the driveway and across the road are docks for swimming, fishing and picnicking. Doubles, $50; cottages, weekly $295 to $390. Open April to November.

Montour House, 401 West Main St., Montour Falls 14865. (607) 535-2494. Former Keuka Lake restaurateur Walter Jones moved his French Quarter restaurant to Montour Falls in 1986 as the first step in a $1.5 million restoration of the 1854 Greek Revival hostelry into a European-style luxury hotel with 30 large guest rooms, a restaurant and a gift shop. The restaurant and gift shop failed, only nine guest rooms and suites were completed, and new management took over in 1990 to run this as a B&B for a group of local investors. The spacious rooms on the second floor are as plush as any in the area with thick carpeting, wing chairs, remote-control TV in cabinets, telephones, and a washstand in most bedrooms. The astounding thing is that all share a large men's room and a large ladies' room with a couple of toilets, stall showers and a bathtub. Most of the rooms have space for facilities, but they had not been completed at our latest visit; one corner suite had a washstand in the corner of a large closet and a single chair in a small sitting room. Manager Louis Devillers, an Elmira businessman, turned part of the main-floor bar into a sports lounge, and provided space for the Watkins Glen Racing Museum collection. He hoped to reopen the restaurant, but at our visit was only serving continental breakfast to house guests at the front end of an eerie upstairs corridor. Doubles, $40 to $50; suites, $45 to $60.

Inns and B&Bs

The Red House Country Inn and Store, Picnic Area Road, Burdett 14818. (607) 546-8566. Joan Martin and Sandy Schmanke left careers in Rochester to open their charming B&B inn in an 1844 farmhouse in the Hector National Forest. Indeed, they and their guests are the only humans in this preserve full of birds and wildlife. Three goats, four dogs, a donkey and chickens are part of the entourage; so is a fine gift shop, one of two the pair operate (the other is the Country Store along Route 14 in Hector). Five lovingly furnished guest rooms share four baths, two up and two down, each outfitted with perfumes, powders and soaps. Guests sip sherry in the living room, make snacks in a guest kitchen and savor the restful life on a wicker-filled veranda. By reservation from November through April, the innkeepers will serve dinner (for a bargain $18, country vegetable chowder, cheese muffins, salad with poppyseed dressing, roast Long Island duckling with fresh raspberries or beef bourguignonne, and butter pecan tarte or six-inch-high Viennese cheesecake, plus Hazlitt wines and dessert sherry). Breakfasts include local melon with raspberries, pumpkin or lemon yogurt bread, eggs with slab bacon and scones with the partners' own jellies and jams. Chairs are scattered around the five acres of lawns and flowers; there's a sparkling new swimming pool with a cabana. Party games are the entertainment at night. Doubles, $55 to $85. Smoking discouraged.

Reading House B&B, 4610 Route 14, Rock Stream 14878. (607) 535-9785. Four guest rooms, ample common rooms and rural property with two farm ponds and all manner of fruit trees commend this rambling white B&B opened in 1990 by Rita and Bill Newell. A view of Seneca Lake that makes Bill think of his native Hudson River area doesn't hurt. Built in 1820, the Federal-style farmhouse has been expanded and embellished with Greek Revival and Victorian touches. A stunning quilt made locally almost covers an entire wall of one of the two nicely furnished parlors. Upstairs, two rooms have private baths and two share a huge bath. We like best the large, front-corner room with a quilt and matching pillows in deep teals and crimson. Colorful area rugs and dried flowers enhance all the rooms. The Newells prepare a bountiful breakfast: juice, fruit salad and cereal followed perhaps by mushroom omelets, cheese quiche, frittata, buckwheat pancakes with local sausage or french toast made with french bread. Then they and guests may take slices of bread to feed the small fish that crowd their ponds. Doubles, $45 to $50. No smoking. No credit cards.

The 1819 Red Brick Inn, Route 230, RD 2, Box 57A, Dundee 14837. (607) 243-8844. The winemaker and general manager of Glenora Wine Cellars, Raymond J. Spencer, bought this striking red Federal farmhouse with fifteen-inch-thick brick walls specifically to open a B&B in 1984. Guests have the run of two antiques-filled parlors, an upstairs Vintage Room for games and reading, and a family dining room in which breakfasts featuring grape juice, sausages made by Ray's father, and eggs or pancakes are served. They also can view in his cool, clean cellar the Barrington Champagne Co., which he thinks is the smallest commercial winery in the state and the first devoted exclusively to the "method champenoise" production of sparkling wines. "A purer, more natural wine will not be found anywhere," says he; tours and tastings are by appointment only. Two of the four upstairs bedrooms have private baths. The Burgundy Room has a huge oak bedstead and rocking chairs; the Bordeaux has lovely hand-stenciling and a grapevine wreath. All the rooms are tastefully decorated and accented with grape art and handmade quilts. Doubles, $60.

Willow Cove, Glenora-on-Seneca, 77 South Glenora Road, Dundee 14837. (607) 243-8482. Who could want a more fortuitous location, directly on the expansive lakefront in a family compound with the waterfalls of Glenora Glen as a restful backdrop? George and Joan Van Heusen have run a B&B since 1984 in a house built in 1828 as the Glenora Inn. You'd barely know it, although the four third-floor guest rooms sharing two baths remain as they were when her grandparents bought it in the 1920s. Fresh fruit, cereal, muffins and coffee cake are served at a huge, lace-cloth-covered table in the formal dining room or outside on an open porch. Above the lower floor is a large living room with fireplace and a super porch for viewing the lake. The third-floor Canopy Room has windows stretching to the floor and you can hear the waterfall behind the house across the road. Rooms are simply but nicely furnished. Guests may use the spacious lawns and the picnic table with a grill beside the water. Doubles, $45. No credit cards. Smoking restricted. Open April into November.

Glenora Guests, 65 North Glenora Road, Dundee 14837. (607) 243-7686. Just up the road from the lake, with a good view and access to the water below, is the columned home of Tess and Jack Wilgus, who opened it as a B&B in 1984. "Our home is their home," says peppy Tess, who chats with guests while sharing a bottle of Glenora wine in the large, handsome living room or on the pleasant front porch looking down to the lake. Two double rooms and a single share one bathroom; they are furnished in homey style. "Jack always says the rooms are small but the breakfasts are big," says Tess with a laugh as she reels off a typical menu: juice, potatoes, bacon and sausage, scrapple, omelet and "sweet sticky buns for dessert," plus homemade tomato relish and seasoned cottage cheese. The upstairs den is comfortable for TV-watching. Doubles, $50. No smoking.

Country Gardens, Route 414 at Mathews Road, RD1, Box 67, Burdett 14818. (607) 546-2272. This new B&B is aptly named; the gardens at the side entrance and in the rear are almost too perfect for words. Guests enjoy a terrace with two tables under umbrellas, a small pond, bird feeders, colorful flowers and a view of vineyards beyond the garden or, on the other side of the house, a panorama of Seneca Lake. Inside, Nancy and Howard Key offer three guest rooms, one on the first floor with private bath and two upstairs sharing. The exposed beams give a hint that this was once a tavern; rooms are handsomely furnished with antiques. Guests gather in the country kitchen in the new section of the house as the hosts prepare a full breakfast on weekends, a continental breakfast during the week. Doubles, $45 to $60. Smoking restricted.

Peach Orchard B&B, 5296 Peach Orchard Road, Hector 14841. This turn-of-the-century farmhouse was restored from "disaster" condition by Mary and Bill Musolf, two of the many New Jersey residents lately discovering the charms of the Finger Lakes. They ended up with a cheery parlor with TV, a double bedroom with brass bed and private bath on the main floor, and three upstairs bedrooms sharing a bath. The Musolfs serve a full breakfast including eggs, bacon, sausage, pancakes and homefries. They offer guests wine, crackers and cheese upon arrival and give them a doggy bag of homemade muffins as they leave. At the entrance is a small gift shop and outside in back is a pleasant patio. Doubles, $40 to $52. No smoking. Open May-October.

Vintage View B&B, Route 14, Box 245, Watkins Glen 14891. (607) 535-7909. Guests here share the warmth and hominess of a circa 1865 farmhouse as well as Heidi and Al Gerth's working vineyard above Seneca Lake. The view is more of vineyards than lake, however. The Gerths offer a swimming pool and a summer kitchen with a barbecue grill. The four bedrooms share two baths, and there's a small cabin. A full breakfast is served in the morning. Doubles, $30 to $70. No smoking.

Camping and Cottages

Campgrounds are numerous. **Warren W. Clute Memorial Park** at the south end of Seneca Lake has complete facilities. Run by the village (303 Franklin St., Watkins Glen 14891, 535-4438), it offers tent and trailer sites by the day, week or season. South of town, fourteen campsites are available at **Havana Glen Park,** Route 14, Montour Falls, 535-9476, and 106 wooded and open sites are available at the **Watkins Glen KOA,** Route 414 South, Watkins Glen, 535-7404. Sites along the canal leading to Seneca Lake are available through **Montour Marina and Campsites,** Route 14, Montour Falls, 535-9397. North of town are **Paradise Park Campground,** Route 14A, Reading Center, 535-9969, and the municipally owned **Smith Park & Campground,** Peach Orchard Point, Hector, 546-9911, with lakefront campsites by the day or week.

Six housekeeping cottages on the lake at Willow Point, Hector, are offered by **Pedlar Village,** Box 369, Watkins Glen, 546-6856. Large one-room cabins equipped for light housekeeping and up to six people are available from **Rustic Log Cabins,** Box 18, Hector, 546-8489.

Realtors specializing in lakefront properties include Shoemaker Real Estate, Franklin and Fourth Streets, Watkins Glen, 535-6613, and Watkins Glen Real Estate Co., 1005 North Decatur St., Watkins Glen, 535-2944.

Seeing and Doing _____ ᒧᑌᑌᒪ

The lake and the glens are foremost for many.

The longest and deepest of the Finger Lakes, Seneca Lake is flanked by hillsides that reach their peak at the southern end around Watkins Glen. Their steepness has prevented much of the cottage and commercial mishmash that mars the shoreline of more crowded Finger Lakes (namely Canandaigua and parts of Keuka).

"Seneca Lake is quieter and less developed because of the cliffs," notes Mary Ellen Andrews, executive director of the Schuyler County Chamber of Commerce. "We rather like it that way."

The hillsides also make perfect growing sites for the vineyards and orchards that crisscross their slopes, creating an unforgettable canvas. Creeks that slice through crevices as they rush toward the lake have forged waterfalls and glens, no fewer than 400 in the southern Finger Lakes alone.

The Lake and the Glens

Watkins Glen State Park, Route 14, Watkins Glen, 535-4511. This is the biggest and best-known of all the gorges. Stone walkways and trails traverse the gorge, which drops 700 feet in two miles from the park's upper entrance to the tunnel entrance in downtown Watkins Glen. Sometimes called the eighth wonder of the world, it has sheer, 200-foot-high cliffs, rock caverns, grottos and eighteen waterfalls and cascades that create the greatest pageant of waters in the East. It's an easy, though sometimes wet and slippery walk with 832 steps, most at the lower end. For those who want to walk only one way, a shuttle bus ($2) runs between the two entrances every fifteen minutes until 6 p.m. A shorter version of the walk goes as far as the South Entrance. At the South Entrance, the state park has 302 campsites in forests above the gorge as well as an Olympic-size swimming pool with a reported capacity of 2,000 people, for those who like crowds. The pool costs 50 cents for adults, 25 cents for children. Park open daily from 8 a.m. to 10 p.m., mid-May to mid-October. Parking fee, $3.

Timespell, Franklin Street, Watkins Glen, 535-4960. Watkins Glen State Park comes alive at night in a $1 million sound and light extravaganza in which the audience is guided part way into the darkened gorge. With considerable pomp and circumstance, the show traces the history of the gorge through an inspiring (if overly dramatic) documentary. Dinosaurs and lighting effects are splashed onto the darkened cliffs and waterfalls, and Aaron Copland music resounds from a sound system all around. Most visitors find what is advertised as the only outdoor show of its kind worth the tab, especially since the laser images became animated in 1986. Two shows nightly, first at dusk, second 45 minutes later, May-October. Admission, $4.75.

Other Falls. Four nearby falls and glens have their devotees, too. **Chequagua Falls** tumbles 186 feet — just eight feet short of Niagara — into downtown Montour Falls, presenting a startling sight at the end of the village's Main Street. Just south of Montour Falls is **Havana Glen,** a village park with 37 waterfalls. Here the visitor emerges after a two-minute walk from the parking lot into an open glen where youngsters wade in a pool and cavort behind a 75-foot-high waterfall. Along Seneca Lake are two other glens and falls, which are less accessible to the public. **Hector Falls** tumbles 165 feet in several cascades above and below Route 414 next to the Chalet Leon motel in Hector. The privately owned **Glenora Glen** meanders through cascades and swimming holes from Route 14 down to one last waterfall in the lakefront hamlet of Glenora.

Captain Bill's Seneca Lake Cruises, foot of Franklin Street, Watkins Glen, 535-4541. Hour-long boat cruises have been popular for years on the 50-foot mock steamer that lives up to its name, Stroller IV. They've been augmented lately by a sprightly blue and white double-decker vessel with a capacity of 150, the Columbia. It offers a two-hour lunch cruise, a three-hour dinner cruise, a late-evening cocktail cruise lasting close to midnight on weekends, and even a Monday night teen dance cruise (which we, on our balcony at the Glen Motor Inn, could hear coming from a long way away). Capt. Bill Simiele still gives 50-minute cruises with a minimum of eight customers on the Stroller IV, hourly from 10 a.m. in summer. Columbia cruises by reservation: Lunch, Tuesday-Friday noon to 2, $15; dinner, Tuesday-Friday 7 to 10 and Saturday-Sunday 6 to 9, $29; Sunday champagne brunch, noon to 2, $15. Stroller IV, adults $5.75, children $2.75. Season, May 15-Oct. 15.

BOATING. Sailing and powerboating are favorite sports in the Finger Lakes. Boaters can use 150 slips in the new Watkins Glen marina, located next to Captain Bill's. Powerboats and sailboats may be rented from Glen Harbor Marina, Fourth Street at the canal. Montour Marina, one of the few civic projects of its kind, offers 175 docks and campsites shaded by willows, as well as access to Seneca Lake through the Seneca Lake Inlet canal. Paddleboats are available from Seneca Lake Paddleboat Rentals in Clute Memorial Park.

SWIMMING. Swimmers who eschew the pool at Watkins Glen State Park will find the real thing — meaning cool, clear and deep water — in Seneca Lake. Fortunately, its waters are more accessible than are many of the Finger Lakes. The village operates W.W. Clute Memorial Park, named after the founder of the local salt industry that remains here and there in evidence, at the south end of the lake. A stony beach (all the Finger Lakes shores are lined with rocks and gravel), a wooded picnic area and campsites across Route 414 are offered. Just up the lake in Hector is a secluded town beach and forested picnic grove at Smith Park, at the foot of Peach Orchard Point.

FISHING. Fishermen prize the lake trout, rainbows and Atlantic salmon among 35 varieties of gamefish that thrive in the depths of Seneca Lake. Catherine Creek, which spills through the area, also is known for its rainbows. Capt. Harvey R. O'Harra, 535-2390, conducts full or half-day fishing charter trips ("fish guaranteed") on a 25-foot cruiser. Capt. Al Gerth also gives full or half-day charters through Vintage View charters, 535-7909.

The Wineries

Seneca Lake's deep waters and steep hillsides have produced a winegrowing region that has been called "the American Rhineland." Since New York's Farm Winery Act of 1976 allowed vineyardists to bottle and sell wine, sixteen wineries have opened around the southern half of Seneca Lake alone, those on the west side clustering in the highest density outside the Napa Valley. They vary in size and stature, but all are relatively small and specialize in European and California-style viniferas rather than the fruity blends for which the Finger Lakes had been noted. All are open for wine tastings and sales (most for a price — refundable with purchases — ostensibly to discourage freeloading tipplers).

Seemingly the largest is **Wagner Vineyards** in Lodi, where owner-entrepreneur Bill Wagner has parlayed a spectacular vineyard setting overlooking the lake into an architecturally striking octagonal winery and the adjacent Ginny Lee Cafe, an enclosed platform with an open deck perfect for sipping wines with lunch or a snack.

Actually a larger producer in terms of volume, not varieties, is across the lake. **Glenora Wine Cellars** specializes in prize-winning white viniferas and offers an audio-visual presentation followed by a tasting in the new, expanded showroom. The new winery at the **Hermann J. Wiemer Vineyard** is very small and very serious, and has many national awards to show for it.

Up the lake, the **Four Chimneys Winery** at Himrod produces organic wines, including an Eye of the Bee blend of Concord grape and honey. This unusual commune-style establishment has a new gourmet restaurant (see Where to Eat) and hosts weekend chamber music concerts in August and September, which are followed by elegant candlelight dinners and wine tastings at $55 a head in the adjacent Chateau farmhouse.

Castel Grisch, which really looks like a chalet, is a new Swiss-run winery close to Watkins Glen on the lake's west side. It offers tastings in a new showroom and meals in a large, European-looking cafe and restaurant with outdoor deck overlooking Seneca Lake (see Where to Eat).

Two small wineries on the east side of the lake also are worth a visit. **Rolling Vineyards** in Hector, close to Watkins Glen, offers one of the best lake views, although there's no outdoor deck from which to enjoy it. Nearby, the rustic tasting room of **Hazlitt Winery** is full of memorabilia and antiques from five generations of Hazlitts, who staked their claim here in 1852 and now produce quality wines from grapes grown only at their farm.

Other Attractions

Bird and wildlife watching is offered in **Queen Catherine Marsh,** an 890-acre state-owned wetland, fish and wildlife preserve. It's accessible by boat, foot or car off the east side of Route 14 between Watkins Glen and Montour Falls.

Hiking and camping are popular in the **Finger Lakes National Forest,** which embraces 13,000 acres of wildlife and forestry management land in Hector. It has 25 miles of trails (part of the 650-mile Finger Lakes Trail network) for hikers and horseback riders. Nine primitive campsites are available at the Blueberry Patch Campground, a wooded area next to five acres of blueberries.

Watkins Glen International, Box 500, Watkins Glen, 535-2481. The widely known Watkins Glen auto races, which started on the village's hilly streets in 1948 and became world-famous for its annual Grand Prix in October, a three-day weekend of Formula One racing and humper-to-bumper partying, ended in bankruptcy in 1980. A subsidiary of Corning Glass Works bought the hilltop racetrack four miles southwest of town in 1983 and invested more than $1 million in badly needed renovations. Six major racing weekends are scheduled from June through September. The racing crowd, upon which the town so depends, is a mixed blessing. Upwards of 150,000 fans descend upon the area and fill the business coffers while disturbing the area's peace and quiet, imbuing the village with a schizophrenic character. Race schedule and prices vary.

Watkins Glen Grand Prix Circuit Tour. New in 1990 were historical signs placed along the original 6.6-mile route of the Grand Prix race, which started and ended in front of the Schuyler County Courthouse and went up hill and across dale. Using a brochure available from the Chamber of Commerce, you can trace the original course used from 1948 to 1952. As the brochure claims, for those who were here in the early days, it is a sentimental journey and for those who have never been here, it is a lesson in motor racing history.

Racing memorabilia abounds in nearly every restaurant and tavern hereabouts. Part of the displaced **Watkins Glen Racing Museum** collection was given space in 1990 in the lobby and lounge of the Montour House in Montour Falls. A collection of motor racing books is housed in a special alcove at the Watkins Glen Public Library.

SHOPPING. The choices are limited, unless you go on wine-buying sprees as we do at the area vineyards. The much-ballyhooed new **Seneca Market,** a keystone of the lakefront development envisioned by the Watkins Glen Tomorrow plan, is supposed to reflect the interests of the Rouse Company that designed it. The old three-story Frost Machine Shop building at the foot of Franklin Street and an adjacent courtyard and shed have a handful of farm-market stands, fast-food eateries and souvenir shops of the ilk that appeal to youngsters. The festival atmosphere, however, has been overshadowed by a large **Corning Glass** outlet, the market's anchor store.

Another big store of interest to tourists is **Famous Brands Clothing Outlet** at 412 Franklin St., with good discounts on Woolwich, Levi's, Wrangler, Lee and the like. Best of the gift shops along Franklin Street is **Noel Gifts,** which has everything you'd ever want to put on a Christmas tree (one tree is covered with Mickey Mouse-Walt Disney stuff), lovely dolls and assorted gifts. **Wrap It Up** and **What Did You Bring Me?** are other gift shops. For candies and more than twenty kinds of homemade truffles, head for **Seneca Sweets.**

Out of town, follow Route 14 to Glenora and **Orchard Ovens,** a wonderful farm stand with the makings for a great picnic, run by the founders of Glenora Wine Cellars across the road. We couldn't resist the corn chowder and a piece of fabulous grape pie made by Mary Beers. Or head up Route 414 to Burdett and **Family Fare,** where Joan Wickham of the former Wickham Vineyards offers gifts and gourmet foods in a delightful little house built by her husband's grandmother as a tea room and ice cream shop. Beyond is the **Red House Country Store,** which lives up to its name in looks and contents.

Where to Eat ⎯⎯⎯⎯⎯⎯⎯⎯⎯⎯⎯⎯⎯⎯ ♪♪♪

Until lately, this area has been woefully lacking in good dining facilities. You can imagine the situation when some townspeople said the best dinners were to be had at a pizza parlor. Wineries are spearheading a resurgence, however.

Food with a View

Castel Grisch, 3380 County Route 28, Watkins Glen. (607) 535-9614. Founded by a Swiss couple who live in a beautiful manor house glimpsed as one enters the property, this new cafe and restaurant has had its ups and downs. The setting is dynamite: two large dining rooms dressed in red and blue with full-length windows onto a partly canopied, partly open deck strung with tiny white lights. Beyond is a view of Seneca Lake beneath steep hillsides. When we visited, Austrian chefs were producing what they called a limited menu: soups including Hungarian goulash, sandwiches, a winemaker's plate of cheese and meat, spinach and Swiss cervelat salads, and appetizers. Dinner entrees were priced from $8.50 for spaetzle (Bavarian noodles with ham and onion) to $16.50 for filet mignon. Veal or scallops with mushrooms and wine sauce were listed as the specialties. We liked the sound of some of the day's specials: Louisiana chicken soup, lamb and mushroom fettuccine, spinach tortellini in gorgonzola tomato sauce and German bratwurst. Desserts include grape nut pie and Bavarian strudel. Live music is scheduled most weekends. Open daily, 11 to 10. Closed January and February.

Ginny Lee Cafe, Wagner Vineyards, Route 414, Lodi. (607) 582-6574. The once tent-covered deck with view across vineyards and lake is idyllic as ever, even if it has been enclosed with a permanent structure to ward off the elements and even if the food isn't as creative as when we first visited. Gone were the weekend dinners and the scallops seviche and fettuccine primavera we recall so fondly. Never mind. The French bread with herb-flavored butter, the turkey croissant and a chef's salad laden with cheese, ham and turkey strips made a fine lunch. We lingered over a bottle of Wagner seyval for $6.50. Extraordinary as ever were the fuzzy navel peach pie and cinnamon-flavored coffee, which you might need to get through the rest of the afternoon. Open Monday-Saturday 11 to 4, Sunday 2 to 4:30 and brunch, 10 to 2; weekends in off-season.

Montage, Glen Motor Inn, Route 14, Watkins Glen. (607) 535-9776. The Franzese family has long been proud of the lake view from their spacious motel-style dining room and ebullient hostess-owner Helen Franzese likes to tell you about all the racing celebrities they've entertained over the years. (The sign at the head of the stairs says it's "time for a pit stop in the Victory Lane Lounge" below.) The view from expansive windows may surpass the fare, which ranges from $9.50 for broiled lake trout to $18.95 for filet mignon. Whet your appetite with a pepperoni and sharp cheese plate, antipasto platter or fried calamari. Seafood au gratin, lobster saute, grilled pork chops and Italian-style steak and peppers are favorite entrees. Lunch, Monday-Saturday 11:30 to 5; dinner nightly from 5, Sunday from noon. Open mid-March through November.

Rainbow Cove Restaurant, Plum Point Road, Himrod. (607) 243-7535. The family-style dinners served nightly at 7 have a loyal following among motel guests and residents, who say the food is well prepared and the best bargain around ($9 per, children $5). The dining room looking across the lawn toward Seneca Lake is a mishmash of fancy Victorian draperies and oilcloth-covered tables. But the food is down-home good and plentiful, served on heaping platters and with seconds offered. The fixed menu changes daily: Tuesday is baked chicken night with mashed potatoes, gravy, rice, carrots, marinated beans, peas, pumpkin bread and fruited Jello. When we stayed, regular visitors from Westchester County were looking forward to the Wednesday night fare of lasagna and baked pork chops, finished off with sherbet. The roast beef and apple pie dinners offered Thursdays and Sundays are most popular hereabouts; the baked ham with scalloped potatoes on Mondays and Fridays is a close second. No liquor is served. Dinner at 7. Open May 10 to Oct. 23.

Lakeview Inn, Route 14, Rock Stream. (607) 535-7101. Most travelers would never stop at this unpretentious roadhouse, but those in the know say it's a winner, particularly for weekend suppers. The Friday night fish fry ($5.25) is surpassed only by the Saturday night prime rib ($10.95 to $12.75), which is the best around, we're told. Thursday is pasta night; the menu offers spaghetti with tossed salad and Italian bread, $4.95. Except for Saturday night, meals are simple and unadorned, but the salad bar is something else. You can see the lake from the screened porch or an open deck. Open Tuesday-Saturday, 4 to 8 or 9.

Other Choices

Wildflower Cafe, 301 North Franklin St., Watkins Glen. (607) 535-9797. Area food circles were abuzz following the opening in 1990 of this trendy little cafe, which attracted celebrity local chef Bernard Navarra from Ithaca, where he'd put Joe's Restaurant back on the culinary map. Fifty patrons can be seated at a mix of booths and pine tables beneath a pressed-tin ceiling, with posters enhancing the brick walls. Navarra is into fresh seafood and grilling, thanks to a stint at San Diego waterfront restaurants. We can vouch for his California pizza ($5.95), big enough that three shared it as an appetizer and still took part home in a doggy bag. Among entrees ($9.95 to $14.95), we enjoyed the salmon alfredo and a special of fettuccine with anchovies, mushrooms and more, but could have passed on the salad made entirely of iceberg lettuce and the chicken sauteed with fresh vegetables (the same ones that had graced the pizza and an appetizer of fresh vegetables with dip — a bit of veggie overkill). The Glenora Glen seyval blanc was a bargain (as are most local wines in restaurants hereabouts) and the apple crisp with whipped cream was fine. The price was right, the ambience spirited and casual, and the menu more appealing than most in the area. Lunch and dinner, Monday-Saturday 11:30 to 10 or 11.

La Cote d'Or, 3586 Route 14, Himrod. (607) 243-5855. This little prize was opened by the folks from Four Chimneys Winery in the fall of 1990. It takes its name from Seneca Lake's heritage as the Gold Coast, when it was home to movie stars after black and white films were launched in Ithaca. It takes its spirit from winery owner Walter Pederson and his Korean-born chef, Dongmee Smith, wife of his winemaker, both known for their gourmet flair. One side of the restaurant, transformed from a roadhouse, is elegant with white linens and indirect lighting; it specializes in contemporary French and regional cuisine, with a prix-fixe meal priced in the high $20s. The other side is a more casual Victorian wine bar done up in brass and hunter green. The menu changes weekly, but Walter said a typical dinner would start with appetizer and salad (perhaps a hot salad topped with fish) and include a choice of four entrees, ranging from game to vegetarian. A tray of local cheeses and desserts follows. The Victorian wine bar follows a tapas theme, including appetizers and simple meals. Open Friday-Tuesday, lunch noon to 2:30, dinner 5 to 9. Closed January-March.

Chef's, Route 14 South, Watkins Glen. (607) 535-9975. "Smoking or non-smoking, folks?" barked the waitress as we arrived for breakfast. She seated us at a table, poured coffee and went on to the next party. "Smoking or non-smoking, ladies?" Our griddle cakes ($1.80) and a western omelet ($3.10) arrived almost as we placed our order. The old-school waitresses at this diner-grown-large are as much the show as the food, which is basic, bountiful and downright cheap. The 120-item menu lists dinners from $4.50 (meatloaf with gravy, made from Grandma's recipe) to $12.95 for surf and turf. When Tony Pulos took over the business in 1949, he couldn't afford a sign so kept his predecessors' name. We learned from John Pulos that his father's long hours at the diner had put him through Hobart College, that John is on the Hobart board of trustees and that Chef's is the "official restaurant" of the Hobart soccer team, as it seems to be of so many people in Watkins Glen. They call it "a little piece of culinary Americana," and rightly so. Open daily from 6 a.m.

Seneca Lodge, South Entrance to Watkins Glen State Park, Watkins Glen. (607) 535-2014. No reservations are accepted and you may have to wait in the congenial Bench and Bar Tavern Room and listen to an authentic nickelodeon while waiting for dinner here. Some locals think it traditionally has had the best food in town; it certainly is the "real Watkins Glen," as one writer put it. The former emphasis on natural foods and vegetables "for a way of life harmonious with the natural order of the universe" was less in evidence at our latest visit. We found the salad bar uninspired, the fresh breads good, the lamb kabob and chicken kiev too much to eat, and the vegetables cooked beyond redemption. But the spacious and rustic lodge-style dining room is pleasant enough, dimly lit and full of local color — tables full of tourist brochures on one side, vintage posters of Formula One racers in a side room — and some of the prices ($7.25 to $16.95) are from yesteryear. Breakfast, 8 to 10 or 11; lunch, Monday-Friday 11:30 to 2; dinner nightly, 6 to 9. Open May-October.

FOR MORE INFORMATION: Schuyler County Chamber of Commerce, 1000 North Franklin St., Watkins Glen, N.Y. 14891. (607) 535-4300.

Old Fort Niagara (N.Y.) is on view across river from town park gazebo.

Niagara-on-the-Lake, Ont.

Think of Niagara and most people think of Niagara Falls. But there's much more to Niagara than the falls. Devoted locals cling to the belief that the real Niagara is Niagara-on-the-Lake, a once-sleepy hamlet blossoming into a world-class cultural resort at the point where the Niagara River meets Lake Ontario.

Though a scant dozen miles distant from touristy Niagara Falls, Niagara-on-the-Lake is a world apart. Here is a lovely, sedate town dating to the late 1700s when it was the first capital of Upper Canada. However, the British relocated the capital to Toronto before the War of 1812. Shipping interests moved west with the opening of the Welland Canal linking Lakes Erie and Ontario. The town's role later in the 19th century as a lakeside summer resort and home of a Canadian version of Chautauqua, the traveling cultural and spiritual program, was short-lived.

Niagara-on-the-Lake languished until the summer of 1962, when a local attorney began mounting George Bernard Shaw plays. They were the precursor of the Shaw Festival, which now produces a variety of plays of Shaw and his contemporaries in three theaters from April through October. Theater-goers came from near and far for the plays, but also found a quaint town of great beauty and architectural merit, steeped in history and British Loyalist tradition. Within a distance of fifteen miles are some of the finest parks in the world and at least 43 scenic or historic sights, according to one tour guide.

Niagara-on-the-Lake — or NOTL, as it's abbreviated, and Niagara, as it's called — is bordered on two sides by water. On the north is Lake Ontario, from the shores of which on a clear day you can see the skyline of Toronto 30 miles distant. On the east is the Niagara River, whose shores gradually fold into the majestic gorge ending at Niagara Falls. On the other two sides are scenic parklands and more vineyards and orchards than we've encountered before in such proximity.

141

The falls are a must-see, of course. Americans have long considered the Canadian side of the falls and its surroundings more scenic and well kept up than the American side. But head up the Niagara River Parkway to Niagara-on-the-Lake and you'll find that NOTL is nicer yet.

The parkway lives up to its billing as 35 miles of remarkable scenery, interspersed with historic houses, gorges and glens, and glorious gardens. The view of the Niagara River from Queenston Heights reminds some of Europe. The "lake effect" tempers the climate and helps produce abundant fruit and award-winning wines. The Welland Canal offers views of ocean-going vessels, and the early harborfront lives on in Old Port Dalhousie.

All the while, Niagara-on-the-Lake remains poised beside river and lake, secure in its own charms and welcoming visitors to share them.

Getting There

Niagara-on-the-Lake is situated on the south shore of Lake Ontario, across the Niagara River from New York State. It's roughly 30 miles north of Buffalo and 85 miles south (by road around the lake) from Toronto. Both cities are major ports of entry for air, rail and bus passengers.

Motorists arriving by the New York Thruway or Ontario's Queen Elizabeth Way take the Niagara River Parkway or Route 55 to NOTL.

Where to Stay

While Niagara Falls caters to families and honeymooners, NOTL is very much an adult place, and most small children would not enjoy it. Its appeal to people of culture and affluence is reflected in its accommodations.

Near the Water

The Oban Inn, 160 Front St., Box 94, Niagara-on-the-Lake L0S 1J0. (416) 468-2165. If you want to be near the water in historic surroundings, the Oban Inn is for you. The landmark facing Lake Ontario across a strip of golf course has been around since 1824 and looks it. The best of the 23 rooms are considered to be those in the adjacent Oban House looking onto the lake. On the second and third floors of the main inn, twenty rooms go off a long, narrow corridor. They vary in size from cramped twins to lakefront rooms with queensize beds and chairs or sofas facing the TV. Vivid wallpapers, period furnishings, complimentary toiletries, clock-radios and telephones are the norm. The open, plant-filled veranda facing the lake atop the main-floor dining room is available for all guests to enjoy. Three meals a day are served in the historic restaurant, lounge and dining terrace (see Where to Eat). Doubles, $95 to $135.

Queen's Landing, Byron Street, Box 1180, Niagara-on-the-Lake L0S 1J0. (416) 468-2195. The town's largest hostelry opened in 1990 atop a slope overlooking the river across the Niagara-on-the-Lake Sailing Club's busy marina. Doug McLeod, owner of the Pillar and Post, which started Niagara's inn boom in the 1970s, gave the four-story structure (six stories in back, facing the water) a Georgian facade. So it looks as if it's been around awhile. Although billed as "the inn at Niagara-on-the-Lake," this is more a hotel in the classic Williamsburg style, from the two jazzy elevators to the conference rooms and health facility, complete with one long lap pool and a "swim-ex" that lets one swim in place against the waves. The 135 rooms have TVs, minibars and tiled marble bathrooms, each with an unusually large complement of toiletries and some with jacuzzis. A few rooms have fireplaces. Doubles, $135 to $225.

The Old Bank House, 10 Front St., Box 1708, Niagara-on-the-Lake L0S 1J0. (416) 468-7136. You can glimpse Lake Ontario through the trees of a lakefront park from this B&B's shady front veranda, which reminds us of those in Cape May, N.J. Part of the first Bank of Upper Canada branch, you wouldn't realize that now, for it has been skillfully converted into the town's largest B&B, with eight rooms and "suites." Rooms vary widely. Four upstairs with wash basins share one bathroom with a separate w.c. We chose the Gallery Suite off the veranda, a double-bedded room containing the only private bathroom with combination shower-tub, a small sitting area and a dressing room that doubled as a kitchenette with a mini-fridge, an electric kettle for coffee and even a teapot. We were glad it was air-conditioned, for most of the windows wouldn't open. Two other rooms also have private baths with showers and private entrances, and the Rose Suite has two bedrooms, a sitting room and "four-piece bathroom ensuite," as full private baths are called in Ontario. The formal living room is so spacious that tables can be set up for sixteen for breakfast with room to spare. British-born Marjorie Ironmonger, innkeeper with her husband Don, prepares a hearty English country breakfast. Following juice and perhaps fruit crisp or melon in creme fraiche, you might be served scrambled eggs, corned beef crepes with cream sauce, cheese strata or welsh rarebit. Doubles, $88 to $125.

The Kiely House Heritage Inn, 209 Queen St., Box 1642, Niagara-on-the-Lake L0S 1J0. (416) 468-4588. Set on an acre of lawns beside a golf course overlooking Lake Ontario, this pillared Georgian house built in 1832 has extra-large verandas on two stories, front and back. The rear veranda is so big it contains both a screened porch and an open porch facing spectacular gardens, where roses bloom into November along with rare specimens not found elsewhere in Canada. A tunnel once linked the house with Fort Mississauga across the way, but the middle has since collapsed, new innkeepers Heather and Ray Pettit advised. All thirteen guest rooms have private baths and five have fireplaces. The six smallest are in a wing at the side. One large guest room with canopy bed is in the original kitchen, which has a kitchen-size fireplace, rich wood paneling and deep wallpaper, and a loveseat looking out at the gardens. Room 8 upstairs is lighter with a 1930s art deco look, a fireplace and a private veranda. The main floor offers half of a double parlor (the other half has been sectioned off for the innkeepers' quarters) and a cheery breakfast room with watercolors on the walls. The Pettits serve a continental-plus breakfast of juice, seasonal fruits, cereal, homebaked scones and muffins. Doubles, $75 to $145.

South Landing Inn, Kent and Front Streets, Queenston L0S 1L0. (416) 262-4634. Good values as well as good views are offered from this historic inn and new motel-style annex in Queenston, Niagara's hilltop neighbor. The values are rooms priced half again lower than they would be in NOTL; the views are of the Niagara River from the inn's front verandas and the annex's private decks. The main house, built as an inn in the early 1800s, is the town's oldest building. Its five rooms have private baths, are furnished in Canadian pine, and have TV and air-conditioning. Since 1987, guests have enjoyed eighteen rooms on two floors of the annex across the street. Four suites on either end are most prized, particularly those on the river end with private decks. The standard rooms have two double beds and private baths; those on the second floor have ceiling fans and better views over and around the main inn toward the river. Innkeeper Tony Szabo proudly shows the remarkable needlepoint pictures, one a large portrait of the Rockies, done by his wife Kathy and now gracing the second-floor foyer of the main house. Breakfast is available in a simple little restaurant on the main floor. Doubles, $80; suites, $95.

George III Hotel & Pub, 61 Melville St., Box 1011, Niagara-on-the-Lake L0S 1J0. (416) 468-4207. The rooms pictured in a glass case in front of this unassuming riverfront hostelry don't do them justice. They appeared quite basic, so we were surprised to find eight fairly spacious rooms, individually outfitted with pretty wallpapers, attractive quilts, clock-radios, cable TV and private baths. Four rooms have balconies facing the river across the Niagara Sailing Club marina; Room 8 at the end has a big side balcony that those in smaller rooms get to use as well. There's a separate entrance for the rooms from the downstairs pub, and a continental breakfast is served in the upstairs foyer. Long ago a house of ill repute patronized by visiting sailors, the operation is now leased out by Doug McLeod, owner of four of the town's inns. Breakfast is served all day in the pub, where lunch items and light entrees range from $4.25 to $9.25, and a few heavy entrees are priced from $14.95 to $21.95. Doubles, $95 to $120.

Villa McNab, 1356 McNab Road, Niagara-on-the-Lake L0S 1J0. (416) 934-6865. Who'd expect to find a Spanish-style villa with tiled red roof and white statuary around a fountain on spacious lawns down a side road ending at Lake Ontario? One built by a Dutchman, no less? Englishmen Bob and Beryl Owen bought the house and opened it as a B&B in early 1990. They had run a hotel in Lancashire for eleven years, so were suited to the task and were adding a third guest room when we visited. The villa is built around an enclosed atrium harboring an indoor swimming pool and many exotic plants. In separate rooms on either side are a jacuzzi and a sauna. The Owens share these facilities plus an ornate dining room with red velvet chairs and a fireplaced, Spanish-looking sitting room with their guests. The spacious bedrooms all have private baths, antique queensize beds, remote-control TVs and two chairs with reading lamps. A continental breakfast comes with, and what Beryl calls a full "cardiac arrest" breakfast is available for $5 additional. Doubles, $95.

Fisher Farm Homestead, 14820 Niagara River Pkwy., Niagara-on-the-Lake L0S 1J0. (416) 262-5627. A substantial house across the street screens the Niagara River gorge from view from this new B&B, but guests here can cross the parkway for a look or borrow bicycles to tour the new river bike path. Guests also enjoy a swimming pool in the side yard, well back from the parkway, and a patio behind the large house. William and Charlotte Urquhart and daughter Sarah offer two guest rooms with private baths. One with a queensize bed is at the main-floor rear; the other is upstairs and has a king bed with lace-edged dust ruffle and an appealing writing alcove. Guests have use of a spacious, comfortable living room. The Urquharts serve a continental-plus breakfast of fresh fruit, cereal, muffins and croissants in a formal dining room graced with colorful placemats by local designer Angie Strauss and paintings by a Connecticut artist. Doubles, $74 and $89. Open May-November.

The Royal Anchorage, 186 Ricardo St., Box 233, Niagara-on-the-Lake L0S 1J0. (416) 468-2141. The town's only motel faces the river opposite the sailing club marina. Even it bills itself as a hotel, though its 1950s-style, L-shaped motel look gives it away for what it is. Most of the 21 units have one double or two twin beds; the two highest-priced have two double beds. ("We're the economy lodging in town," the manager noted.) They are furnished in pine, with TV, vinyl chairs, draperies matching the bedspreads, and striped carpeting. The dining room-lounge offers snacks and a patio bar,. Doubles, $70 to $75.

Other Choices

Prince of Wales Hotel, 6 Picton St., Niagara-on-the-Lake L0S 1J0. (416) 468-3246 or (800) 263-2452. The Wiens family bought a sixteen-room hotel in the center of town in 1974 and have carefully expanded to 105 rooms behind a meandering brick facade that looks more residential than commercial. Period furnishings, brass beds and floral chintzes enhance all the guest rooms, which have high ceilings, mini-bar refrigerators, TVs and gleaming white bathrooms with bidets and hair dryers. Rooms vary in size from standard to suites. The most elegant hotel in town, this offers an indoor pool, a basement health club, a paddle tennis court on the second-floor roof and a rooftop sun deck. Light fare is available in the **Three Feathers Cafe** and the **Queen's Royal Lounge.** Full meals are provided in the dining room (see Where to Eat). Doubles, $120 to $190.

The Pillar and Post, King and John Streets, Box 1011, Niagara-on-the-Lake L0S 1J0. (416) 468-2123. From a turn-of-the-century canning factory to a basket manufacturer to a restaurant and crafts center. That's the history of this hostelry, which was converted into the town's first new inn in the early 1970s and has grown in campus-like fashion around a central pool and courtyard, into a thriving facility with 92 rooms, a lounge, a gift shop and a restaurant (see Where to Eat). Gorgeous flowers surround the inn, which occupies a residential location off by itself at the far edge of town. Bellboys in breeches and waitresses in period costumes lend an historic touch. Some of the rooms appear historic as well, like the deluxe queensize room we saw with a beamed ceiling, huge fireplace, a sofa and wing chairs, all dark and cozy. Other rooms are brighter and newer, in attached, motel-like buildings. All rooms have private baths, toiletries and mini-bars, and many have canopied four-poster beds, fireplaces, handcrafted pine furnishings and patchwork quilts. Although the Pillar and Post appeals anytime, its ambiance and fireplaces make it particularly cozy in autumn and winter. Doubles, $132 to $195.

Moffatt Inn, 60 Picton St., Box 578, Niagara-on-the-Lake L0S 1J0. (416) 468-4116. Given its in-town location and extra amenities, this is an uncommon value locally. The 22 rooms are individually decorated, up-to-date and arranged for privacy. The two buildings, one dating to 1834 and the other fairly new, flank a garden solarium that doubles as a guest lounge and as part of the **Coach and Horses Tea Room and Bar,** a separate operation. Our room on the second floor front had a queen bed, a pleasant smallish sitting area with TV, telephone and a modern bath with Finesse toiletries and hair dryer. We also liked the four rooms on the main floor sharing a side patio and a small garden. All rooms have unusual carved wood doors and brass headboards. Doubles, $75 to $99.

Gate House Hotel, 142 Queen St., Box 1364, Niagara-on-the-Lake L0S 1J0. (416) 468-3263. This sleek, mirrored hotel in black and white emerged in 1989 after a total renovation of what had been a small inn. It's best known now for its contemporary Italian **Ristorante Giardino** (see Where to Eat), but the nine guest rooms are anything but slouches, well worthy of the BMWs and other fancy wheels parked outside. It's obvious that no expense was spared, from the marble entryway to the striking artworks in the halls. We were shown a room done up in teal and black with two double beds, German and Italian furnishings, and a bathroom with double sinks, a bidet and Auberge toiletries. Modern black headboards behind the beds, black lamp shades and black loveseats are apt to be accents. Rooms have TVs and all the usual amenities in contemporary European style. A continental breakfast is included in the rates. Doubles, $165.

Royal Park Hotel, 92 Picton St., Niagara-on-the-Lake, L0S 1J0. (416) 468-5711. This hotel facing the Shaw Festival Theater was so new that it was still getting its act together when we visited in September 1990. Twenty-eight rooms were open, with plans for fourteen more. The deluxe room we saw had a

145

queensize four-poster bed, TV in an armoire, Niagara's ubiquitous mini-bar, and a bathroom with a double jacuzzi and no shower; the regular rooms were rather small, and a couple of single rooms had one bed against a wall and a bath with shower only. The dining facility is in part of an old house that belonged to the founder of the Niagara Historical Society and somehow was incorporated into the new building. It's unusually pretty in pink, burgundy and blue, with blue moire upholstered chairs and curtains and floral wallpaper. The menu was in transition, but poulet madagascar, sole amandine and prime rib with Yorkshire pudding were expected to be regulars (entrees, $14.95 to $17.95). Camembert romanoff with strawberry sauce was a featured appetizer. One of the desserts was coupe Festival — ice cream with tropical coco rum sauce. An outdoor patio appealed for lunch. Doubles, $120 to $160. Lunch and dinner daily.

BED & BREAKFAST. Besides the hotels and inns mentioned here, 65 bed-and-breakfast homes are registered with the local Chamber of Commerce. All are inspected and licensed, have three or fewer guest rooms, and the hosts live on the premises, so guests feel like part of the family. Most do not have signs or brochures. Contact the Chamber at (416) 468-4263 and for a $5 booking fee you will be matched to a B&B that meets your needs. An estimated 35 other B&Bs do not register with the Chamber. Even with all these rooms, the town is often fully booked weeks ahead for weekends during the Festival.

CAMPING. The Niagara Parks Commission operates two campgrounds. Just west of St. Catherines on the shore of Lake Ontario is **Charles Daley Park** with 65 campsites, a playground and limited facilities. **Miller Creek Campgrounds**, fourteen miles south of the Horseshoe Falls, has 52 campsites tucked into a quiet wooded area. **Shalamar Lake Niagara,** Niagara River Parkway, Niagara Falls, 262-4895, is a family trailer park with tenting, laundry facilities and a pool.

Seeing and Doing _____ *ᏙᏙᏙ*

The Shaw Festival is the attraction for most here. We were impressed as well by all the water pleasures as well as the myriad historical, sightseeing, winery and farm-market attractions.

Shaw Festival, Box 774, Niagara-on-the-Lake L0S 1J0, (416) 468-2172. Ten plays of George Bernard Shaw and his contemporaries are staged in three theaters from April through October. One of the world's largest permanent ensembles of actors led by artistic director Christopher Newton explores classic plays in a modern way for contemporary audiences. The 861-seat Festival Theater, built in 1973, showcases the larger epic works and musicals. The 345-seat Court House Theater presents smaller Shaw works and the more intimate American and European dramas of the period. The 353-seat Royal George Theater houses mysteries, musicals and Shaw plays at lunchtime. Monday is an off day, but you can usually choose from plays at noon, 2 and 8 on other days in peak season. Regular ticket prices range from $20 to $42.

Touring

It's best to have a car, both to get around town and to see the sights.

The **Niagara River Parkway,** a 35-mile-long drive along the river between Niagara-on-the-Lake and Fort Erie, is incredibly scenic and generally tranquil, except near the falls. The northern end from NOTL south to Queenston is the most lovely, with orchards and substantial homes on the west side and treed parklands to the river on the east. Picnic tables and river vistas abound.

Meandering beside the parkway is the wonderful new **Niagara River Recreation Trail,** a paved path for bicycling, jogging and walking, which gets lots of use, naturally. The Georgian-style **McFarland House,** restored and furnished to the War of 1812 period, backs up to the river and is open to the public for tours and tea. The **Gen. Isaac Brock Monument** dominates the Queenston Heights Park, just above the historic little riverside town of Queenston. South of Queenston, in rapid scenic fashion, come the **Niagara Parks School of Horticulture** gardens, a 100-acre riot of outdoor color in season; the famed **Floral Clock,** formed by about 20,000 plants that change every year, and the **Niagara Glen Nature Area,** an unexpected treat with picnic tables overlooking the gorge and nearly three miles of trails along the gorge wall and river bank. It's a 45-minute walk down and back, but worth it for the flora and fauna and rock formations. (Park naturalists guide free nature walks in season.) Beyond are the **Niagara Whirlpool,** crossed by a Spanish cable-car ride, and the **Great Gorge Adventure,** a boardwalk along the fierce rapids, reached by elevator and tunnel. The **Canadian and American Falls** are best viewed from the Canadian park system, if you don't get up close via the **Maid of the Mist** boat tour. Why anyone would pay to go up the three high-rise towers, we don't know. Whenever our family visited Niagara Falls over the years during the time we lived fairly nearby in Rochester, N.Y., we took a quick look at the falls and then headed for the super swimming holes and picnicking areas of Dufferin Islands sequestered just south, away from the crowds.

Other Drives. Niagara Boulevard along the lakeshore and outer Queen Street are waterside streets lined with beautiful homes. Almost every street in what's called the Old Town harbors architectural treasures as well. Just west of town between Niagara Boulevard and Lakeshore Road lies Chautauqua Circle, where new homes have sprung up among the Victorian gingerbread cottages built during the heyday of the Chautauqua campground here. Lakeshore Road cuts through vineyards and orchards, seldom yielding a view of the lake, although you can detour down any of the Fire Line roads that end at the water. Other than the Niagara River Parkway, we think the area's most scenic route is Route 81 along the Niagara Escarpment. It's a twisting, hilly, mostly rural road full of surprises, with very different vistas and topography from those of the flatlands below.

BICYCLING. Bicycles are not only a pleasant but at busy times the most practical way of getting around town. Cyclists get to savor the architectural and landscaping treasures on every side street, which motorists are prone to miss and most pedestrians don't get to. You also can bike along the Niagara River Recreation Trail, a paved path between parkway and river. Bicycles are available for rent from Old Town Sportswear, 112 Queen St., 468-3595, for $6 an hour, $20 a day. **Niagara Cycle Tours,** 338-7682, organizes day-long bicycle tours of the wineries and NOTL on Saturdays and the River Trail along the Niagara Parkway on Sundays. Cost: $20.

STROLLING. Niagara-on-the-Lake seemingly was made for strolling, perhaps because of its age and penchant for a slower pace. The main street, Queen changing to Picton, is peopled by pedestrians at all hours, enjoying the shops and historic sites — not to mention the six-foot-high flowering plants hanging in baskets from the light poles and the prolific gardens all around. Detours onto the side streets and parallel streets are worthy diversions. Simcoe Park and Queen's Royal Park where the river meets Lake Ontario are full of treats.

Double Deck Tours, 3957 Bossert Road, Niagara Falls, 356-7633, offers bus service three times daily between NOTL and Niagara Falls. The red double-deckers leave at 11, 3:15 and 5:15, across from the NOTL Chamber of Commerce on King Street. They can be used as regular buses or to connect with narrated package tours of the Niagara Falls area. At 1 p.m. daily, the bus gives a fifteen-mile scenic tour of historic sights around Niagara-on-the-Lake, with a stop at Hillebrand Estates Winery. Trips daily, mid-May to mid-October.

Niagara Riverboat Company, Olde Boatworks off Ricardo Street, Niagara-on-the-Lake, 468-4291 or 468-5154. The Senator, a 72-foot-long passenger boat, takes up to 150 passengers on sightseeing cruises plus dinner, dance and Sunday brunch cruises. The best thing about the 90-minute afternoon sightseeing cruise we took was the cooling breeze on a warm day. The boat goes at a snail's pace upriver nearly to Queenston, but there's very little narration and you can't see much, even from the open upper deck covered by a blue canopy. The steep hillsides and woods that make the Niagara River Parkway above the Canadian shore so pleasant block views from the river. Near tour's end, you do get a good view of boats anchored in the river at Youngstown and of historic Fort Niagara, a commanding presence across the river from NOTL. Perhaps one of the dinner ($40), moonlight dance ($10) or Sunday brunch ($20) cruises would provide more diversion. Sightseeing cruises, most days in summer at noon, 1:30, 3 and 4:30. Adults $10, children $5.

Recreation

SWIMMING. Swimming facilities are sadly lacking, which may be why so many prosperous residents have their own pools. We found a little beach in NOTL's riverfront Queen's Royal Park, but nobody was swimming ("pollution," the natives advised, though we've seldom seen such clear, appealing water and have never hesitated to swim in Lake Ontario). A small lakefront beach and picnic area also are available at Ryerson Park off Niagara Boulevard in the Chautauqua section. Good swimming of the pond and creek types is available in Dufferin Islands, part of the Niagara Parks Commission just above the falls.

FISHING. Lake Ontario is full of salmon and trout, pike and muskies. Shore or bank fishing is popular at Queenston along the Niagara River, from some of the parklands surrounding NOTL, and from Old Port Dalhousie near St. Catherines. Fishing licenses, available through the Ontario Licensing Bureau at 23 Queen St. or most sporting goods stores, are required.

GOLFING. Of the two dozen golf courses in the Niagara Region, three are in Niagara-on-the-Lake. Most historic is **Niagara-on-the-Lake Golf Club,** a nine-hole course by river and lake that's said to be the first in North America. The public is welcome; greens fees, $14 weekdays, $17 weekends. Other, cheaper nine-hole courses are **St. Davids** and **Queenston.**

Other Attractions

Historic Sites. As the first capital of Upper Canada and one of Ontario's oldest towns, Niagara is full of history. Forty historic points of interest are noted in the town's "Historic Guide," a handy pamphlet and map. We won't begin to duplicate it, but will steer you to the **Niagara Apothecary,** the restored first pharmacy at Queen and King, and **St. Mark's Anglican** and **St. Andrew's Presbyterian** churches around Simcoe Park. The locally prized **Niagara Historical Society Museum** at Castlereach and Davy streets, the first in Ontario built solely for use as a museum, houses room settings, displays and more than 20,000 artifacts; open daily 10 to 6, May-October; adults $2, children $1. The **McFarland House,** a mile south of town along the Niagara Parkway,

148

is a restored Georgian house open daily 11 to 5 in summer; adults $1, children 50 cents. **The Laura Secord Homestead** in Queenston houses a fine collection of early Upper Canada furniture and artifacts appropriate to the woman known as the Paul Revere of Canada; summer tours every half hour, 1 to 6; adults $1.

Fort George, Niagara Parkway, NOTL, 468-4257. Dating to 1797, this was the principal British fort on the Niagara Frontier. It helped prevent the Niagara area and all of British North America from falling into American hands in the War of 1812. Now a National Historic Site following reconstruction in 1939, it's worth touring for a look at the officers' quarters, soldiers' barracks, blockhouses, carpenter shop, powder magazine and the other trappings of a major fortress. In the summer there are fife and drum drills and infantry and cannon firings at various times. Open daily 10 to 6 in summer; closed except by appointment from November to mid-May. Adults $2, children $1.

The Welland Canal, just west of town at the entrance to St. Catherines, is one of Canada's engineering marvels and the second most visited attraction in the region after Niagara Falls. Opened in 1932, it is the fourth in a series of canals built since 1829 so Great Lakes ships could bypass the falls to go between Lakes Erie and Ontario. Huge lakers and ocean-going vessels are raised and lowered a total of 325 feet in a series of eight locks. The best vantage point is the lookout platform at the new Welland Canal Viewing Center, which opened in 1990 at Lock 3 (just off the QEW at Glendale Avenue, Route 89). The site contains an information center, audio-visuals, the new St. Catharines Museum, a canalside restaurant and the Welland Canal Gallery, which has a large, hands-on working model of the canal's lock system. You learn that ships go up and down in each lock in about ten minutes, but take twelve hours to navigate the canal's length. Call 685-3711 for the day's schedule to time your visit with that of a ship.

Old Port Dalhousie, Lakeport Road, St. Catherines, shows how the old harborfront used to be when this area was the terminus for the first three Welland Canals. The old port (locally pronounced Duh-loo-zi) is an up-and-coming area of craft galleries, shops, restaurants and such fashioned from old dry docks, mills and ship chandleries. The Royal Canadian Henley Regatta takes place every August in the Henley Basin. An old carousel in Lakeside Park offers rides for five cents. Boat tours from the harbor into the Welland Canal are offered by Garden City Cruises. In the evenings, hundreds of white lights illuminate the lively harborfront, often a sea of people enjoying the Good Times Emporium, Chandler's Brew Pub and outdoor eateries, taverns and dance halls. **Marie's Lobster House** at 1 Lock St. is an institution, selling lobster by the pound, $16.95 to $99.95 (for six pounds) when we were there; "your waitress will gladly shell your lobster if you so desire," the menu advised.

SHOPPING. A large branch of **Crabtree & Evelyn,** which looks right at home along Queen Street, is the town's only chain store. A number of sophisticated, one-of-a-kind shops are found along Queen and a couple of side streets.

Gifts and crafts from twenty Third World countries as well as Canadian native people are for sale at the fascinating **MCC Global Crafts,** 126 Queen St. It's the Niagara self-help outlet for the Mennonite Central Committee, and you'll find baskets, brassware, jewelry, rugs, wall hangings and more.

The **Old Niagara Bookshop** has plenty of local lore and Canadiana. **Leisure Threads,** which specializes in embroidered leisure ware, shares a building with **Queen Street Gallery,** purveyor of contemporary Canadian crafts. **Loyalist Village** offers distinctively Canadian parkas, gloves, clothing, shearling hats — all that heavy gear for northern winters — as well as cottons and jewelry. **Just**

Christmas is just that. **Captain's Quarters** has classic clothing, as does **Classic Casuals.** Two stores of interest to those partial to the British Isles are **Glens of Scotland** and **Irish Design.**

Greaves Jams & Marmalades, which occupies a prime downtown corner at 55 Queen St., looks just as it must have 50 years ago. Bins of jams, shelves of jams, boysenberry, peach, raspberry, red and black currant — you name it, they have it, and they use no pectin, preservatives or coloring.

The chocolate aroma is almost overpowering at **Maple Leaf Fudge,** which offers flavors from Irish cream and rum-almond to amaretto. At **Niagara Fudge,** you can choose from 35 kinds, including chocolate ginger studded with chunks of fresh ginger. It's $7.98 a pound, and one man produces it all right there on the marble table.

Barb Zimmermann's work appeals at **Lakeside Pottery,** 755 Lakeshore Road, especially her pots in a celedon green tint. She also does nice soup bowls, piggy banks, jewelry and buttons.

Many of the watercolors and vivid floral designs you see around town emanate from **Angie Strauss,** a shop-home-studio that's a riot of color and good taste at 178 Victoria St. Her staff of 25 Mennonite women put Angie's designs on everything from high-fashion sweatshirts in the $50 range to gifts, cards, wine labels and kitchen accessories. We acquired a couple of refrigerator magnets and a large print at a fraction of the cost of one of her lovely originals ($2,000), and thus qualified for a pair of free sweatpants at the **Last Few** store across the street, where discontinued patterns are sold.

FRUIT STANDS. The prolific Niagara orchards are a fruit bowl for the rest of Canada. Country markets and stands, some of them run by local Mennonites, line almost every road. Our favorites:

Kurtz Orchards Family Market, Niagara Parkway at East-West Line, is the biggest and most commercial market, but don't be put off by the tour buses out front. Jean and Ed Kurtz still maintain the family touch, albeit part of it is for an amazing number of Japanese, who represent the biggest share of their mail-order business. On our visit two busloads of Japanese tourists had just disbarked, and many of the signs at the market were in Japanese as well as English. They have varieties of jams and plum butter with crackers for sampling, a Candy Shack, many specialty foods, baked goods like almond raisin bread (a local specialty with marzipan in the middle), and drinks like apple or cherry cider and peach nectar.

Rempel Farm Market, 1651 Lakeshore Road, sells its own choice selection of fruits and vegetables, including "washed and defuzzed peaches" and the biggest radishes we ever saw. Debbie Rempel's bakery produces the best raspberry squares ever (99 cents); we took home a rempelberry pie ($7.50) made of raspberries, blackberries, rhubarb and apples.

Harvest Barn, Highway 55 at East-West Line, is a large country market selling everything from fresh produce to home-baked breads, pies, cornish pasties and steak and kidney pies ($1.79). We made a picnic out of the salad bar ($2.59 a pound, supermarket style).

The Wineries

The Niagara Peninsula has become one of North America's leading wine producers in the last fifteen years. It is known for its rieslings and chardonnays, as well as a local eiswein ("ice wine") made from grapes that are pressed frozen in winter, producing a sweet dessert wine that could become as Canadian as hockey, in one wine writer's estimation. The vineyards are concentrated on the flatlands and on what locals call "the Bench" of the Niagara Escarpment (the seat of the long, tiered ridge shaped like a bench above Lake Ontario.

Reif Winery, the closest to river and town, is known for wines in the German style, particularly dry riesling and gewurtztraminer. All North American grapes were uprooted in favor of European vinifera and premium French hybrids on the 130-acre estate behind the winery.

Licensed as Ontario's first cottage winery in 1975, **Inniskillin Wines Inc.,** is considered by many to be Canada's finest winemaker. Visitors may take a 45-minute tour and taste wines in a 1930s barn, the ground floor of which has been transformed into a sparkling showroom. The second floor is used for changing art exhibits and sit-down "festival tastings."

Hillebrand Estates Winery calls itself Canada's most award-winning winery and its largest estate winery. Associated with sister wineries in Germany's Rhine Valley, it is known for its lively and informative tours, given year-round. Its showroom looks like a big retail wine store, which it is.

Wines in the German style are featured at the **Konzelmann Estate Winery** by Herman Konzelmann, his wife and son, who just returned from studying in Germany to join his parents as winemaker. The dry riesling and gewurtztraminer are especially good here, and you can see the rows of grapes, all labeled, growing primly outside along the lakeshore.

A bit farther afield but worth the trip is **Vineland Estates,** Niagara's most picturesque winery at 3620 Moyer Road, Vineland. Sequested astride the Bench of the Niagara Escarpment with a view of Lake Ontario in the distance, this small operation produces much-acclaimed chardonnays and rieslings. It also runs a wonderful new limited-menu restaurant, the Boardwalk Room and outside deck, and a cottage for B&B.

Where to Eat

Near the Water

The Oban Inn, 160 Front St., Niagara-on-the-Lake. (416) 468-2165. The Oban is considered the quintessential Niagara experience, and was when we had dinner there on our first visit to NOTL to see a Shaw play back in the '60s. It seemed a bit dated then. Now, hundreds of inn experiences across North America later, the Oban appears updated dated, sort of 1950ish with a 1990s twist. The menu still offers for dinner entrees ($18.75 to $21) the traditional prime rib with Yorkshire pudding and Dover sole, fried or broiled, with tartar sauce. But you'll also find more contemporary fare like poached salmon with a delicate hollandaise sauce and cucumber vinaigrette, pork medallions with calvados sauce and apple chutney, and twin filets with cracked peppercorn sauce. The staff wears tartan vests, reflecting the inn's start as a private home built by one Captain Duncan Milloy from Oban, Scotland. The Shaw's Corner piano bar is festive and filled with festival memorabilia, the large tavern draws locals year-round for English fare, and the outdoor terrace — surrounded by flowers and offering a view of Lake Ontario — is popular in summer for lunch, tea and drinks. Lunch daily, 11:30 to 2; tea, 3 to 5; dinner, 5:30 to 8:30. No smoking in dining rooms.

The Queenston Heights Restaurant, Queenston Heights Park, Queenston. (416) 262-4276. We figured this oldtimer, operated by the Niagara Parks Commission, would be charming and quaint in the Oban Inn style. How wrong our expectations! The dining room is glamorous, the cuisine contemporary and the view — well, you'd think you were high on a slope gazing down at the Rhine.

From the heights above the river, you can see all the way down the Niagara to Lake Ontario. Everything appealed on the menu at a summertime lunch on the expansive outdoor terrace until we discovered that the power had gone off and only cold meals were available. One of us made a lunch of two appetizers: a tomato and eggplant salad ($4.25) and smoked salmon carpaccio ($7.50), garnished with shavings of romano cheese, herbs and flowers. The other settled for a sandwich of smoked turkey breast with cranberry mayonnaise stuffed inside a whole wheat croissant ($7.95). A glass of the local Inniskillin brae blanc was a good choice from a wine list with a page each of Canadian whites and reds. From the dessert cart we picked a magnificent chocolate-strawberry charlotte with curls of chocolate ($4.50) as we savored the afternoon sunshine. A tad expensive at lunch, the menu seems more reasonable at night, especially considering prices in NOTL. Entrees ($14.95 to $19.50) include shrimp and scallop linguini, grilled swordfish with roasted peppers and tomato, roast peppered pork loin with apples and pecans in brandy sauce, and rack of lamb with dijon mustard, herbs, garlic and eggplant antipasto. The formal main dining room is Tudor in feeling with a high timbered ceiling, armchairs at well-spaced tables, and a painting of Niagara Falls above a huge stone fireplace. The expansive windows looking to the north are the dominant feature, and most diners can't take their eyes off the view. Open Monday-Saturday 11:30 to 9; tea, 3 to 5; Sunday brunch, 11 to 3.

Queen's Landing, Byron Street, Niagara-on-the-Lake. (416) 468-2195. This new Georgian-style hotel's two-level dining room, with large windows toward marina and river, is pretty in powder blue. The dinner menu is regional-contemporary, offering starters ($3.50 to $9.75) like a selection of homemade pates with Niagara fruit chutney and hazelnuts, escargots garnished with oyster mushrooms and tomato petals, and smoked salmon with two sauces. Main courses range from $16.50 for filet of pickerel garnished with artichokes and morels to $32.50 for fresh lobster with morels. Other choices might be grilled Atlantic salmon on a sauce of rose wine, rabbit basted in white wine and mustard, and rack of lamb on a bed of spinach with roasted garlic madeira sauce. Dessert could be fresh fruit flan, amaretto ice cream and fresh berries in brandy, or a trio of chocolate mousses on vanilla sauce. The quite expensive wine list features Canadian whites and reds. Light alternatives, such as caesar salad with grilled chicken and baby shrimp, supplement the pricey lunch menu (entrees, $10.50 to $17.85). Some of the dining room specialties as well as light fare turn up on the lounge menu, attractively priced from $6.50 to $10.75. Although some townspeople give this high praise, we must note that scores of Eastern innkeepers here for a regional meeting in the fall of 1990 reported that their food service was sadly lacking. Lunch daily, noon to 2; tea, 3 to 4:30; dinner, 5 to 9; lounge menu, 11 a.m. to 1 a.m.

Harbour Inn, 35 Melville St., Niagara-on-the-Lake. (416) 488-3881. This is one of the few restaurants in town with a direct water view. Dating to 1894, it has brown fabric walls, tweed and chrome armchairs, Tiffany lamps and folded white napkins amid a setting of nautical prints, nets and shells. Garlic bread topped with melted Swiss and cheddar cheese is a house specialty for $2.95. Dinner entrees run from $11.95 for fettuccine marinara to $22.95 for surf and turf. They average about $16 and include sole a la romanoff, scampi with sambucca, medallion of pork on spaetzle, and pepper steak. Oysters rockefeller, steamed mussels and clams casino are among appetizers. Desserts include coconut snowballs, chocolate-strawberry cheesecake and pecan pie. Lunch daily, 11:30 to 2:30; dinner, 4:30 to 9. Closed January-April.

Away from the Water

The Buttery, 19 Queen St., Niagara-on-the-Lake. (416) 468-2564. After the obligatory dinner at the Oban Inn, our second meal in town was lunch at the Buttery. The conspicuous outdoor terrace fronting on the main street drew our attention, and the casual tavern menu sealed the deal. That menu includes a trio of Colonial soups served with homemade bread, salads, sandwiches and such offbeat fare as welsh rarebit, cornish pasties, salamagundi and croques monsieur. Served daily from 11, the tavern menu also includes crepes, curries, steak and kidney pie and spare ribs, priced from $7.65 to $15.50 (for filet mignon). Inside are a couple of dark dining rooms notable for pierced-copper tables. One is a banquet hall that hosts weekend medieval banquets, four-course theatrical events called Henry VIII feasts ($37.50 per person Friday, $38.50 on Saturday). The regular dinner menu ($15.95 to $20.95) is a mix of Canadian and continental entrees of the kind to draw tourists, ranging from chicken chardonnay and lobster newburg to steak teriyaki and chateaubriand. Tavern menu, daily from 11; tea, 2 to 5; dinner, Tuesday-Sunday 5:30 to 10 or midnight.

Ristorante Giardino, Gate House Hotel, 142 Queen St., Niagara-on-the-Lake. (416) 468-3263. From the casual to the sublime, it's just a couple of blocks to the fanciest new restaurant in town, one that would seem more at home in Toronto or New York. It's ultra-chic in black and white, full of mirrors, marble and other accoutrements of contemporary Italian design. Huge windows look onto the gardens and lawns. Two long-stemmed wine glasses and a white napkin rolled up in a black paper napkin ring are at each place setting, along with octagonal, black-edged service plates. At dinner, antipasti possibilities ($8 to $9.50) range from braised escargots with garlic and polenta to ravioli filled with prosciutto and mascarpone cheese in a sauce of basil and pinenuts. Among entrees ($21 to $29.50) are steamed salmon with red wine and basil sauce and provimi veal liver Venice style. We sampled lunch, which consisted of five prix-fixe offerings for $13, including soup or salad, entree and dessert. A plate of crusty Italian bread arrived with a bottle of the house Inniskillin brae blanc wine ($14). One of us enjoyed an intense, silken shrimp bisque, followed by a rolled pasta with spinach and ricotta cheese. The other sampled the trio of Italian pastas: spaghetti with Italian bacon and parmesan cream sauce, gnocchi with four different kinds of cheese, and fettuccine tossed with vegetables and herbs. Dessert was a thin slice of carrot cake with vanilla ice cream and fresh strawberries — imported from California, which struck us as strange, given all the fresh fruit in season around Niagara. Good cappuccino ($2.50) and coffee finished a memorable repast. Lunch daily, noon to 2; dinner, 5:30 to 9. Closed Monday and no lunch November-March.

Fans Court, 135 Queen St., Niagara-on-the-Lake. (416) 468-4511. In the opinion of local diners-out, this unpretentious Chinese restaurant shares top billing with Ristorante Giardino as the town's best place to eat. Past a pleasant outdoor patio are a couple of nondescript rooms, where tables are set simply with silverware and chopsticks atop peach cloths amid a backdrop of oriental art and music. For starters, we chose deep-fried wontons ($2.80) and an intriguing sounding radish and pork soup ($2.50) that bore little evidence of radish. For main courses ($9 to $16.80), we tried the shrimps and scallops in a phoenix nest and double-cooked pork tenderloin. There were no noodles for dipping, no soy sauce or salt and pepper, no Chinese tea, and we had to pay extra for steamed rice, to boot. Open daily, noon to 9.

Prince of Wales Hotel, 6 Picton St., Niagara-on-the-Lake. (416) 468-3246 or

(800) 263-2452. A window table in the hotel's lovely main dining room in deep blue and white, **Royals,** is a great place for people-watching — especially during pre-theater dinner, as folks pass between inns, shops, parks and restaurants. Full-length windows face the hotel's lush flower beds and Simcoe Park across the street. Decor is elegant and restrained, the walls covered in rusty-pumpkin suede, the tables set with octagonal silver service plates, and a prevailing color scheme of white and blue. A small salmon and spinach terrine, "compliments of the chef," preceded our appetizers, a good spinach salad ($4) and an oversize portion of sliced smoked venison with English cucumbers, tomatoes and a roasted garlic vinaigrette ($7). Among entrees ($16 to $23) were an excellent roasted rabbit with prosciutto, spinach, garlic and tomato and a more ordinary medallions of beef tenderloin bathed in cream, cognac and peppercorns. From a wide dessert choice came a plate of raspberry sorbet with three ice creams (vanilla, pistachio and caramel), garnished with fresh blueberries and raspberries and plenty for two ($4.25). Piano music wafting in from the main entryway helped make the occasion festive. The hotel offers lighter fare in its **Queen's Royal Lounge** and casual **Three Feathers Cafe.** Lunch daily, noon to 2; dinner nightly, 6 to 9 or 10; Sunday brunch, 11 to 2:30.

The Pillar and Post, King and John Streets, Niagara-on-the-Lake. (416) 468-2123. Bricks, beams and barnwood siding create a decidedly Colonial feeling in the spacious restaurant of this inn, reflecting its start as a cannery and a basket factory. Captain's chairs flank tables covered with beige linens and striking large white service plates — the plates and the wildflower placemats used for breakfast are for sale in the adjacent Country Treasures gift shop. The dinner menu mixes a dollop of nouvelle touches amid the classic prime rib with Yorkshire pudding and grilled New York steak with madeira sauce. Among entrees ($19.95 to $24.50) are cherrywood smoked trout, buckwheat fusilli with smoked venison sausage and roasted bell peppers, sauteed veal tenderloin with artichoke hearts and rack of lamb stuffed with apricots. Among desserts are apple, cranberry, pear and strawberry tarts with fresh creme anglaise, carrot and zucchini cake with cream cheese icing, walnut flan with grand marnier sauce, and pear, sour cream and ganache gateau. Lunch daily, noon to 2; tea, 3 to 5:30; dinner, 5 to 9, winter 6 to 8.

The Luis' House, 245 King St., Niagara-on-the-Lake. (416) 468-4038. Have breakfast at Bella's, the locals advised. So we did, one rainy morning when we and a lonely gent were the only customers in two large dining rooms about 8:30. Why they advised us, we're not sure. There were only two choices: continental breakfast ($2.95) and Bella's Breakfast ($4.95). The latter produced muffins, coffee and a choice of eggs, pancakes or homemade salmon fish cakes with a grilled tomato, served with bacon, ham or sausage. Bella is Portuguese, and somehow we expected favorites from Portugal to show up on the menu. Not so, except for "veal scalopen a la Portuguese with mushroom sauce" at dinner. Otherwise the table d'hote dinners range from $16.95 for filet of sole with tartar sauce or grilled lamb chops to $17.50 for surf and turf. Tomato juice or soup, potato, vegetable and coffee or tea come with. Hamburgs, sandwiches, salads and entrees like steak and kidney pie, homemade lasagna and chicken a la king are the fare at lunch, $3 to $6.95. Decor is bare-bones, with paper mats on wood tables, homespun curtains, old posters and pictures, and lots of mirrors and chandeliers. Breakfast daily, 8 to 11; lunch, 11:30 to 3:30; dinner 5 to 9:30.

FOR MORE INFORMATION: Chamber of Commerce, 153 King St., Box 1043, Niagara-on-the-Lake L0S 1J0, (416) 468-4263.

Boat docks beside Victorian Goodspeed Opera House.

The Lower Connecticut River, Conn.

As it travels south, the Connecticut River cuts a wider swath — and dominates the countryside more. From Middletown to Old Saybrook, it is a major factor in the life of towns that developed on its shores. Essex is, in fact, a sailing center, its harbor filled with graceful craft that sail the waters of Long Island Sound, into which the river flows. (An Essex resident was a member of the crew of Stars and Stripes, winner of the America's Cup in 1987.)

Connecticut's river towns have quite a heritage. Many were settled in the 1600s, so their sense of history is strong and much of their real estate is impressively aged. Essex is almost "museum quality," its main street lined with Colonial homes and an 18th-century inn that is one of the nation's oldest continuously operating hostelries.

East Haddam is home to the famed Goodspeed Opera House and a vintage bed-and-breakfast inn. Day excursion boats cruise from here down the river and across Long Island Sound to several Long Island ports.

Chester, connected by a tiny car ferry to Hadlyme on the eastern bank of the river, has nifty shops, fine dining and experimental drama at the Goodspeed-at-Chester theater. Across the river, high above the water, is Gillette Castle, the incredible edifice that was home to actor William Gillette.

Deep River, Ivoryton and Centerbrook are other river areas awakening to their tourism potential. Ivoryton especially has fine dining and good places to stay.

Bed and breakfasts are springing up, good restaurants abound, and shops and antiques stores attract weekend browsers from early spring to late fall (hardy souls who really like quiet pick winter).

Because Connecticut is our home state, and because we love this section of the river, we're excited about the developments. We hope you will be, too.

155

Getting There

The area occupies a stretch along the river about 20 to 40 miles southeast of Hartford. Route 9 is a divided highway from I-91 in Cromwell, just north of Middletown, to I-95 in Old Saybrook, just south of Essex. It parallels the river and brings visitors to all the towns along it.

Where to Stay _____ ⟋⟍⟍

Bishopsgate Inn, Goodspeed Landing, East Haddam 06423. (203) 873-1677. This 1818 Colonial with a soft beige facade, cocoa trim and a red door was taken over in 1987 by a Brooklyn couple, Dan and Molly Swartz. But the theatrical bent established by the former innkeeper continued since Dan ran a performing arts center prior to becoming an innkeeper. The six guest rooms (two downstairs, four up) are furnished mostly with period pieces — many of them antiques from the Swartzes' Brooklyn brownstone. A suite with bath, sauna, its own entrance and a deck is comfortable. All of the other five rooms have private baths and four have working fireplaces. Full breakfasts are served in the former 1860 kitchen, which has a little fireplace and baking oven. Guests dine at two four-foot trestle tables in the period kitchen where stuffed french toast is an especially popular choice. They also relax in a downstairs living room and a second-floor parlor. Doubles, $80 to $100.

Riverwind, 209 Main St. (Route 9A), Deep River 06417. (203) 526-2014. This rosy peach inn was renovated and opened by Barbara Barlow, a former junior high school teacher who grew up in Smithfield, Va., and expanded with a four-room addition. The 1850 main house, which was in dilapidated condition before Barbara applied her talents to it, is now the coziest and most original place imaginable. The daughter of a farmer who raises hogs in Smithfield, she has one standard item at her country breakfasts, Smithfield ham. This is accompanied by biscuits, often cut into the shape of pigs, homemade breads and jams, fruit, coffee and tea. They are served at a wonderful old harvest table beneath a candlelit chandelier in a fireplaced room filled with antiques. In the inviting front parlor, a unique lighting fixture, which seems to be a cross between a weathervane and a chandelier, has animal cutouts holding candles; there are a piano with all sorts of sheet music, hooked and woven rugs, quilts, and comfortable sofas and chairs. A wicker-filled, enclosed front porch appeals in summer. All four bedrooms in the original house — one on the first floor and the other three up a steep flight of stairs — are enticingly decorated. The new addition has large, beautifully decorated rooms, all with private baths. The Champagne and Roses Room is perfect for the most romantic of getaways. Barbara gained more than an addition: she married the builder, Bob Bucknall, and now the two of them are innkeepers. Doubles, $85 to $145.

The Copper Beech Inn, Main Street, Ivoryton 06442. (203) 767-0330. Although known primarily for its dining room (see Where to Eat), the Copper Beech Inn has thirteen guest rooms. Four are in the sprawling white main house, and nine in a carriage house restored in 1986. Those in the main house have been decorated in country fashion with TLC and good taste by Eldon and Sally Senner, who added their own antiques and the quilts of her mother. The old-fashioned baths have been kept intact to lend a feeling of nostalgia. A suite decorated in rich shades of blue has a canopied kingsize bed, a loveseat and a chaise longue; there's a large table for two in the front dormer window. Out in the Carriage House, where original supporting beams have been exposed, rooms have an elegant country atmosphere with contemporary touches. Some have cathedral ceilings; each has a large jacuzzi tub and french doors leading to a deck. Several queensize beds are canopied; others are four-posters. A complimentary buffet breakfast is served in one of the three dining rooms, which has a view of the great copper beech tree for which the inn is named. Doubles, $100 to $150 in inn, $120 to $160 in Carriage House.

The Griswold Inn, Main Street, Essex 06426. (203) 767-0991. Built in 1776 as Connecticut's first three-storied structure, the "Gris," as it's fondly called, oozes charm. Its first-floor dining rooms (see Where to Eat) are fascinating; its tap room with steamboat-Gothic bar, potbellied stove and antique popcorn machine is a place to linger. The 22 guest rooms in the main inn, the annex and a house are less charming — just simple, old-fashioned and, in some cases, rather small. One upstairs room facing the street in front has beamed ceilings and sloping floors, a marble-topped table, and a small bath with shower. Suites are a bit classier: the Oliver Cromwell features a living room with two sofas, coffee table and fireplace, a four-poster bed in the bedroom, a kitchenette and a small porch from which you can look over rooftops to the busy river. A Garden Suite has a loft, fireplace and wet bar. A continental breakfast buffet of juice, coffee and danish pastry is served in the dark paneled Library (our favorite dining room) where the table next to the fireplace is favored in chilly weather. If atmosphere is what you want, you'll enjoy staying here. Doubles, $80; suites, $95 to $165.

Saybrook Point Inn, 2 Bridge St., Old Saybrook 06475. (203) 395-2000 or (800) 243-0212. New in late 1989, the Saybrook Point Inn is situated at the entrance of the Connecticut River on Long Island Sound. And it is a great location. You feel as if you're surrounded by water, and right next to the restaurant is the inn's marina with boats bobbing at their slips. In weathered gray with white trim, the inn's facade has a perfect nautical look, but inside all is elegant and stylish. We love the black rug with bright floral squares in the lobby. The 62 spacious guest rooms are most comfortable, each furnished in 18th-century style reproduction mahogany furniture, with Italian tile floors, refrigerators and state-of-the-art telephones that will do everything but mix your drinks. Many rooms feature working fireplaces. Master suites also have gracious dining areas, full wetbars, whirlpool baths, separate showers and plush terrycloth robes. A complete spa includes whirlpool, steambath, sauna, indoor pool and fitness equipment. You can arrive by land or sea, with more than 100 slips available for tying up. This is truly an elegant place to stay. Doubles, $135 to $195; suites to $495.

The Ivoryton Inn, 115 Main St., Ivoryton 06442. (203) 767-0330. This dark gray inn with yellow trim and awnings was taken over in 1989 by musician Ed Bant and his wife, Birta. A main-floor lounge — where jazz groups play on weekends — was completely redone and the 28 rooms were also in the process of renovation. All have private baths and telephones. In addition, the small but attractive restaurant was being worked on, and there's a comfortable lobby. The location makes the inn accessible to the town of Essex as well as the Goodspeed Opera House in East Haddam. Doubles, $85 to $100.

CAMPING. Wolf's Den Family Campsites, Route 82, East Haddam 06423, (203) 873-9681, rents 225 sites from May-October. For something different, camp on an island in the Connecticut River. You park your car at Gillette Castle State Park and paddle a canoe to **Hurd State Park** or **Selden Neck State Park,** both on islands accessible only by boat. Each has room for about 50 campers at $2 each. Island campsites must be booked in advance with the Office of Parks and Recreation, Connecticut Department of Environmental Protection, 165 Capitol Ave., Hartford 06106, (203) 566-2304.

Seeing and Doing

There is plenty to keep a weekender — or a week-long visitor — busy in the lower Connecticut River Valley. You'll want to get out onto the water — or at least as close as possible. There are special museums to visit, and be sure to leave time for shopping.

On the River

Camelot Cruises Inc., Marine Park, Haddam, 345-8591 or 345-4507. Cruises to Long Island have long been pleasurable summer trips. The **M/V Island Clipper** and **M/V Yankee Clipper,** both 500-passenger excursion boats, sail down the Connecticut River and across Long Island Sound to Greenport or Sag Harbor, N.Y. Trips to Sag Harbor go daily except Wednesday and Thursday, when the destination is Greenport. Boats leave Haddam at 9, arrive in Long Island at noon, leave Long Island at 3 and return at 6. The price is $24.75. Two-hour narrated paddlewheeler trips are offered daily at noon, 2 and 4 in summer on the new Tom Sawyer. Adults $11, children $5.50.

Harborpark Cruises, Route 9, Middletown, 526-4954. The Deep River Navigation Company offers luncheon, afternoon and cocktail cruises from summer to late October, leaving from Harborpark. The daily schedule includes a one-hour luncheon cruise at noon ($5); a two-and-a-half-hour cruise at 2:30 ($9) and a 90-minute cocktail cruise at 5:30 and 7 ($6).

Boat launching is permitted at the Chester Town Landing, off Parker's Point Road, and the Town Dock at the foot of Main Street in Essex.

Steam Train and Riverboat, Valley Railroad Company, Essex, 767-0103. You can ride a vintage steam train along the Connecticut River shoreline, and even board a riverboat for part of the trip. The summer schedule allows you to hop a train at 10:30, 11:45, 1:15, 2:45, 4:15 or 5:30. All but the last connect at Deep River with an optional one-hour boat cruise. Train rides take 55 minutes; the combined trip a little over two hours. Kids love these rides and, we confess, so do we. Santa is aboard special trips running from Thanksgiving to Christmas. Train rides, adults $7.95; children $3.95; train-boat combination, $12.95 and $5.95. Daily in summer, limited schedule in spring and fall.

The **Chester-Hadlyme ferry** operates between the towns of Chester and Hadlyme. The small ferry takes about four cars plus a few passengers for the five-minute trip and operates "on demand" April-November. Car and driver, 75 cents; each additional, 25 cents.

Near the River

Goodspeed Opera House, Goodspeed Landing, East Haddam, 873-8664 (box office, 873-8668). The landmark white Victorian confection that sits high on the banks of the river in the tiny town of East Haddam was built in 1876 by William H. Goodspeed, who had shipping, banking and other mercantile interests in the community but who also had a great love for opera and theater. The building was saved from demolition by preservationists and rededicated in 1963, when it began its second — and very active — life (that alone is reason enough to visit this area). Since then three musicals — revivals and new tryouts — each running for about three months have been produced each season; among the twelve that have gone on to Broadway are "Man of La Mancha," "Shenandoah" and "Annie." People travel from across the state for "an evening at Goodspeed," which can include dinner in the area and the show. At intermission, the audience loves to munch popcorn from the old-fashioned machine or sip champagne from the Victorian-style bar and stand on the open-air porch overlooking the river. There's usually a breeze, and it's fun to see the lights on the water as well as the structure of the old bridge crossing the river. Shows are Wednesday-Friday at 8, Saturday at 5 and 9 and Sunday at 2 and 6. Productions April-December.

Goodspeed-at-Chester, the Norma Terris Theater, North Main Street, Chester. This "second stage" for new musicals is connected with the Goodspeed Opera House. Works of new (and often young) playwrights are produced in an attractive theater in an old factory building. Tickets are available through the Goodspeed box office.

Gillette Castle State Park, Route 148, Hadlyme, 526-2336. Here is one of the most interesting state parks anywhere. William Gillette, a Hartford native and well-known actor early in the century, built the house of his dreams on the last of a series of hills known as the Seven Sisters above the river. Since his parcel of land included the southernmost hill, he called his house "The Seventh Sister." He never called it a castle, but that's what it is, a massive stone building that came from Gillette's own inventive mind. He drew all the architectural plans for the 24-room castle and then designed all of the furniture for it, too. Most of it is heavy, hand-hewn oak. The dining room table moves on metal tracks on the floor. Some bedroom furniture is built into the structure of the castle itself. Stout oak doors are fastened by intricate wooden locks and there are intriguing stone terraces and fireplaces. The actor-architect, who was in his 60s at the time, had the most fun, it seems, designing himself a railroad. A small train ran around the castle grounds on a three-mile-long track, from "Grand Central Station," a depot that survives as a picnic spot in today's park, through a forested glen, to "125th Street Station" and back to Grand Central. Gillette was usually at the throttle, and we're told he was no overly cautious engineer. The train has been moved to the Hershey Lake Compounce amusement park and most of the tracks have been dismantled, but it's interesting to hear stories about it on your tour. A guided walk through the building takes about a half hour, after which you can enjoy trails along the river, gorgeous views of the water below, and picnicking at tables scattered throughout the park. The park is free. Castle tours, adults $1, children 50 cents. Open daily 11 to 5, mid-May to Columbus Day; sometimes, weekends from Columbus Day to Christmas.

Connecticut River Museum, Foot of Main Street, Essex, 767-8269. This small museum is located in an old warehouse with a graceful cupola and porch overlooking the river; outside you can walk on docks and view the passing parade of boats. Inside, a collection of artifacts reflects the river's history. Besides an exhibit of shipbuilding tools, there are half-models and full-rigged models of ships that sailed on the Connecticut, plus a life-size reproduction of David Bushnell's American Turtle, the first submarine. Models, prints, paintings and broadsides with a connection to the Golden Age of Steamboating form a nice collection; the warehouse has hoist barrels and sacks of Valley produce. Open Tuesday-Sunday 10 to 5, April-December. Adults, $2.50.

Pratt House, 20 West Ave., Essex, 767-8987. There is a sweet herb garden behind this center-chimney Colonial, which contains an outstanding collection of American furnishings of the 17th, 18th and 19th centuries, including Connecticut redware and Chinese courting mirrors. Open Thursday, Saturday and Sunday 1 to 5, June-September.

Nathan Hale Schoolhouse, Main Street (Route 149), East Haddam, 873-8529. The patriot taught in this one-room school from 1773-1774; it displays local history and Nathan Hale possessions. Open weekends 2 to 4, Memorial Day to Labor Day. Donation.

The Stone House, South Main Street, Deep River, 526-2609. The 1840 house is a museum of 19th-century furnishings and local history. It contains a Charter Oak piano, marine room, locally-made cut glass and Indian artifacts. Open Tuesday, Thursday and Sunday 2 to 4, July and August. Donation.

SHOPPING. Essex is the first place to stop if you're a shopper (and perhaps the last, if you want to have any money to spare). Its fine stores offer pricey and preppy men's and women's fashions (**The Talbots, Bermuda Shop, Silkworm**); great children's clothes (**The Red Balloon** is about our favorite such store in Connecticut); nautical items (the **Boat House** at Dauntless Boat Yard); jewelry (nice Greek necklaces at **Aegean Treasures**), and gifts. The **Clipper Ship** bookshop has a good nautical collection.

Chester is another great shopping town. The **Connecticut River Artisans Cooperative** has wonderful handmade items, from clothing to furniture to fantastic jewelry. The **Chester Book Company** is tranquil and lovely. The **Red Pepper** is a pretty little shop with kitchen items, many of them European. We liked some hand-decorated Portuguese eggcups the last time we stopped. **Ceramica** is an importer of Italian and other European pottery; it is lush and lovely. There's also a shop in town where custom-designed, old-fashioned chandeliers are made.

In East Haddam, both the **Seraph** and **Arden & Fox** are gift shops worth poking your head into. The Seraph is in a Victorian mansion and has kitchen items, fashions, Crabtree & Evelyn soaps, and fun travel specialties. Up the hill (take Route 82 past the junction with Route 151) is a red antiques shop run by Gerry Miller with a good selection of used clothing, including furs (mostly Persian lamb when we visited).

If you cannot pass up a Christmas shop, try one of the best and biggest we've seen — the **Holly Loft** on Route 81 south of Chester. The antiques shop, **Never Say Goodbye,** on Route 81 in Killingworth is also highly recommended for costume jewelry and vintage clothes.

The **Sundial Herb Garden** off Breault Road (which is off Route 81) in Higganum is an interesting stop. This is a formal herb garden designed by Ragna Tischler Goddard and visitors can see the knot garden, the main garden and the topiary garden. The gift shop has all kinds of herb-inspired paraphernalia and Ragna's husband, Tom Goddard, bakes the wonderful cakes and pastries for occasional teas. The gardens are open weekends only.

Where to Eat

Fine Bouche, Main Street, Centerbrook. (203) 767-1277. Since 1979, Steve Wilkinson, chef-owner of this restaurant in a small house in the center of town, has provided exceptional meals in an area known for good dining. Outside the house both French and American flags are flying; you walk past two small patisserie cases to three dining areas seating a total of 50. Our fireplaced room with off-white walls, white tablecloths and Queen Anne chairs with deep rose seats was tranquil and appealing for a winter dinner. The enclosed wraparound porch with latticework and rattan chairs with chintz-covered seats also is inviting. Dinner may be ordered prix-fixe ($38) or a la carte (entrees, $18 to $25). The menu offers appetizers such as smoked duck with curly and Belgian endive, and goat cheese in a blueberry vinaigrette with fresh chervil; a terrine of duck foie gras with port-flavored aspic, and a salad of celery root, beets, baby carrots and radicchio served with a light pommery mustard vinaigrette. For entrees, try rack of lamb roasted with a breadcrumb, parsley and garlic coating, or sliced veal filet with fresh noodles and a julienne of fennel and cream. Other choices might be bay scallops and scallop-filled ravioli in a light white wine sauce, veal sweetbreads and mushrooms in a cream and sauternes sauce, quail stuffed with a chicken and truffle mousse, and New York strip steak with a celery root mousse and zinfandel sauce. Entrees are preceded by simple green salads. Crusty, warm rolls are served and replenished by accommodating waiters. An extensive wine list offers a wide range of prices. Desserts are creative; the night we visited a pumpkin cheesecake, carrot cake and the house specialty, marjolaine, described by our waiter as "a chocolate confection of unsurpassed wonder," were available. Service is nicely paced and the menu changes every two weeks, bringing diners back again and again. Dinner, Tuesday-Sunday from 5:30.

Restaurant du Village, 59 Main St., Chester. (203) 526-5301. This restaurant is reminiscent of one in a French village. Its blue facade, with ivy geraniums spilling out of window boxes and the bottom half of the large windows curtained in a sheer white fabric, is on the main street of tiny Chester. Sold in 1989 to Alsace-born chef, Michel Keller, and his American wife Cynthia, it has maintained its exceptionally high standards and is, in fact, better than ever. Keller was trained as a pastry chef and admits he handles all the desserts. Cynthia's strengths are particularly in soups and fish dishes, and both of them spend time in the kitchen, although Cynthia also welcomes guests in the evenings. One enters the restaurant through a brick-lined courtyard beside the building into a cozy taproom area and then into the dining room. The decor is simple with white tablecloths and napkins and simple fresh flower arrangements, a perfect backdrop for the culinary expertise that is to follow. The crusty and chewy French bread is appropriately praised, for it is excellent. The changing dinner menu includes six or eight appetizers ($6 to $8), which might be baked chevre served on herbed salad greens with hazelnut vinaigrette or gateau aubergine, an eggplant cake with roasted red pepper and spinach, served with fresh tomato. Possible entrees ($20 to $26) are rosemary-accented leg of lamb, half a roasted duckling with a mild papaya chutney and a mixture of rice and wild rice, and a sauteed salmon filet with braised green lentils in a sherry vinegar sauce. Sauteed veal medallions with assorted mushrooms might include some retrieved from the woods nearby; the Kellers work with a local supplier to obtain wild mushrooms. The wine list is well-balanced with many choices from Alsace. Dinner, Tuesday-Sunday 5:30 to 10. Closed Tuesday in winter.

Copper Beech Inn, Main Street, Ivoryton. (203) 767-0330. Sally and Eldon Senner pride themselves on the reputation of their restaurant at this elegant inn. They are the third innkeepers since the building was saved from demolition in the early 1970s and turned into a dining spot of note by Jo and Robert McKenzie. The inn's three elegant dining rooms are quite formal, but each has a different feeling. The blue Copper Beech Room with Empire chairs has blue oriental carpeting; the main Ivoryton Room with Queen Anne chairs is the most feminine (and most popular) with rose carpet and flowered wallpaper, and the Comstock Room, with its Chippendale furniture and paneled walls, has a decidedly masculine feel. The menu is country French with some classic dishes, such as beef wellington with a truffle sauce. Recently a salmon dish coated with a crisp potato crust was pronounced exceptional as was braised breast of pheasant with vegetables. Hors d'oeuvres range from $8.75 for wild mushrooms with dijon mustard baked in puff pastry to $29.50 for caviar served with warm blinis, sour cream, sieved egg and diced onion. Lobster bisque is often available. Entrees ($22.50 to $27) might include sea scallops roasted with sweet garlic and mushrooms, bouillabaisse or veal sweetbreads coated with minced mushrooms, leeks and carrots, wrapped in leaf spinach and served with a sauce of madeira and veal stock. Entree prices include a house salad and vegetables; lyonnaise potatoes are a favorite accompaniment. Among desserts ($5 to $7) are individual trifle, a terrine of dark chocolate and hazelnuts served with hazelnut meringue and mocha sauce, and chocolate crepes filled with chocolate mousse. Dinner, Tuesday-Saturday 5:30 to 9, Sunday 1 to 7.

Fiddlers Seafood Restaurant, 4 Water St., Chester. (203) 526-3210. An attractive, small restaurant getting good marks for its consistent and interesting food, Fiddlers is located in a wood-frame building and offers a cheerful cafe atmosphere. The curtains are blue and white checked, there are cane and bentwood chairs, and pictures of sailing ships add a nautical touch. The lunch menu lists three soups: cream-style crab, Rhode Island clam chowder, and soup of the day. There's also mesquite-grilled, poached or pan-sauteed fresh fish in season — usually priced about $7 — plus specials such as baked brie with almonds, mussels in puff pastry and pasta primavera. At dinner, along with the soups and fresh fish, add such entrees ($11.95 to $15.95) as baked stuffed sole, oysters imperial, lobster au peche (with peaches, shallots, mushrooms, peach brandy and cream sauce) and — for the landlubber— chicken parmesan and New York sirloin. But this is a place for seafood and we would stick to it. Lunch, Tuesday-Saturday 11:30 to 2; dinner, 5:30 to 9 or 10, 4 to 9 on Sunday.

8 Westbrook, 8 Westbrook Road, Centerbrook. (203) 767-7085. Polly and George Tilghman opened this restaurant in a small and cozy red house in 1989 and quickly got good reviews. George, who spent more than a dozen years in the restaurant business before trying his own, turns out some Maryland crab cakes with lemon butter that are excellent. Dining is in two small rooms, one upstairs across from the kitchen and another downstairs with just three tables. The menu changes every so often but on a recent visit, four appetizers ranged from $4.95 for artichoke fritters with tarragon mayonnaise to $7.25 for Thai shrimp. Pastas, made here, included a spinach fettuccine with gorgonzola and walnuts and capellini with clams, capers and garlic. Entrees ($12.95 to $19.95) included salmon with shiitake mushrooms and a sherry sauce, calf's liver with a cranberry port sauce, filet mignon with a zinfandel ginger sauce, and veal and mushrooms in puff pastry. Salads are a la carte and might be caesar, hearts of palm and radish with a basil-mustard vinaigrette or watercress, endive and beet with orange-caraway vinaigrette. Dinner, Monday-Saturday 6 to 9 or 10.

Black Seal, 29 Main St., Essex. (203) 767-0233. The legendary Tumbledown's Cafe turned in 1988 into the Black Seal, a casual and appealingly nautical spot. All the decorative items along the walls and hanging from the ceilings might distract you from the food, but the dining room always seems to be mobbed. Similar fare is offered at lunch and dinner, although cold sandwiches are only offered at midday and entrees increase in number and price at night. For starters, choose from several versions of nachos, Buffalo wings or potato skins stuffed with chili, shrimp cocktail and cajun shrimp. Salads include house, spinach, chef's, cobb and hunter's — the last, smoked turkey, broccoli, mushrooms, sliced tomato and sprouts on a bed of greens. Quite a few kinds of burgers come from the grill and several different fish dishes from the fryer. Dinner entrees ($11.50 to $16.95) include broiled filet of sole, baked stuffed shrimp, chicken parmesan and steak au poivre. Hot sandwiches (about $7) include the gobbler, sliced turkey with bacon and tomato and melted Swiss cheese, served with Russian dressing, and the balboa, thinly sliced roast beef topped with melted Swiss and served on garlic bread. Sunday brunch includes corned beef hash, french toast, buttermilk pancakes and several egg dishes, all $6.95. Lunch daily, 11:30 to 3:30; dinner, 5 to 10 or 11; Sunday brunch, 11:30 to 2.

The Chart House, West Main Street, Chester. (203) 526-9898. This attractive salmon building with cream trim overlooking the Pattaconk River was once the Rogers & Champion Brushworks factory. Remnants of the water-powered factory remain: old mill works are still seen overhead in one of the large dining rooms on the second floor. Customers enter via a wooden footbridge across the river, from which you can see and hear a waterfall. The main floor is devoted to the fireplaced bar and lounge; an outdoor dining terrace overlooks the river. One upstairs dining room in an addition sticks right out over the water, affording the best views. Tabletops are nautical charts under polyurethane edged in wood. All in all it's a rather rustic and pleasant country atmosphere. As in others in the chain, the emphasis here is on steaks and seafoods. The menu offers four appetizers ($4.25 to $7): clam chowder, lobster bisque, shrimp cocktail and smoked fish ($4.25 to $7). The most popular entree is the prime rib, $17.95 to $22.95, depending on the size. Among other choices ($16 to $23) are rack of lamb, teriyaki chicken, baked scallops, shrimp scampi, New England lobster and filet mignon. Mud pie and cheesecake are favorite desserts. Dinner, Monday-Thursday 5:30 to 9, Friday and Saturday to 11, Sunday 4 to 9.

The Griswold Inn, Main Street, Essex. (203) 767-1776. The dining rooms at this inn, the oldest in Connecticut, are very atmospheric. Currier and Ives prints, ships, brass nautical items and lots of wood all lend charm. There are several dining rooms, and gas-fired fireplaces are inviting in winter or on chilly summer evenings. The lunch menu offers sandwiches, fish dishes and — a specialty — several sausage dishes. The Monte Cristo sandwich is a favorite; omelets, shirred eggs, fried shrimp, oysters, clams and scallops are available from $6 to $12. For dinner, start with New England clam chowder or oyster stew or an appetizer like potato pancakes, stuffed mushrooms with crabmeat and bell pepper, or smoked Scottish salmon with a dill sauce ($4.50 to $7.50). Entrees ($15 to $23) include salmon in parchment served with julienned vegetables, poached sole florentine, New England chicken pie and roast duckling with baked apple and red cabbage. The Gris prides itself on its buffet-style Hunt Breakfast, served Sunday from 11 to 2:30. Lunch daily, noon to 2:30; dinner, 5:30 to 9 or 10.

Zinger's, Plains Road, Essex. (203) 767-1510. Zinger's is a fun spot in Essex with movies Sunday through Wednesday evenings, plus Saturday and Sunday afternoons in a small movie house on the premises. The theme carries over onto the all-day menu: "Bogie's Hoagie" is sliced roast beef with fried onions and Swiss cheese on a hoagie roll. Burgers are big (in size and popularity) and come in a basket with a bunch of fries. Entrees ($7.95 to $14.95) include veal marsala and veal scaloppini. The gray, red and black decor is crisp and contemporary. Lunch daily, 11:30 to 3; dinner, 5 to 9; Sunday brunch, 11 to 3.

Pat's Kountry Kitchen, Route 154 at Mill Rock Road, Old Saybrook. (203) 388-4784. Known for its breakfasts, this casual family place is mobbed most of the time. With a counter plus lots of tables, it has a New England country atmosphere and calico-clad waitresses. Expect to pay $7 to $15 for entrees like chicken in biscuit with salad or charbroiled tuna. You can get beef stew for $6.95. Pat's clam hash at breakfast is famous far and wide. Open daily, 6 a.m. to 9 p.m.

FOR MORE INFORMATION: Connecticut Valley Tourism Commission, 70 College St., Middletown, Conn. 06457. (203) 347-6924.

Last whaleship is focal point of Mystic Seaport.

Mystic, Conn.

Think of Mystic and the word "seaport" comes to mind. It should, for this is the home of famed Mystic Seaport, the nation's premier maritime museum. Think some more and you might add shipbuilding, whaling, fishing, clipper ships and sea captains' homes. You might even think of tourism, now the area's biggest business.

Although Mystic is a mere village and a post-office address straddling the Mystic River — a political nonentity enveloped in the larger towns of Groton and Stonington — it is important beyond its size.

Historically, the Mystic River has been a site for shipbuilding since the 17th century. In the mid-1800s, the village of 1,500 owned eighteen whalers and the boatyards produced 22 clippers, some of which set sailing records that have never been equaled. Later, many of the nation's fastest sailing yachts and schooners were built here, and submarines still are made along the banks of the Thames River on the western side of Groton.

Today, Mystic thrives on its legacy of having produced more than 1,000 sailing vessels, more noted captains and more important sailing records than any place of its size in the world.

Its quaint neighbor to the southwest, Noank, reflects its heritage as both a home of shipbuilders and a lobster fishing port. To the southeast, the tiny borough of Stonington — as upscale an historic seaside village as you'll find along the East Coast — is the home port for about 30 draggers and lobster boats, Connecticut's only surviving commercial fishing fleet.

With a notable maritime tradition chronicled by Mystic Seaport, it's no wonder that Mystic has become the state's largest tourist destination. In addition to the Seaport, visitors are drawn to the Mystic Marinelife Aquarium, the submarine Nautilus and the U.S. Naval Submarine Base in Groton, and the U.S. Coast Guard Academy across the Thames River in New London. The result is a heady melange of motels and B&Bs, seafood restaurants and fast-food eateries, eclectic boutiques and souvenir shops, and other attractions that bring still more tourists.

In the midst of it all is busy downtown Mystic, the only place we know of where U.S. Route 1 traffic is stopped hourly while the rare bascule bridge over the Mystic River is opened to let sailboats pass. But then, Mystic is also one of the few places we know where motorists stop all along Main Street for pedestrians — tourists, most of them — to cross.

Getting There

About 50 miles east of New Haven, the Mystic area stretches along Long Island Sound in southeastern Connecticut from New London to the Rhode Island border. U.S. Route 1 meanders through the heart of Mystic, while Interstate 95 crosses its northern edge. State Route 27 links the two. Regular train service is provided by Amtrak, whose shoreline route between Noank and Stonington is one of the more scenic around.

Where to Stay⁓⁓⁓⁓

Accommodations in Mystic are numerous and vary widely in size, type and quality. Except where noted, they are open year-round. Rates vary from weekday to weekend as well as by season.

Tops for Luxury

The Inn at Mystic, Route 1, Mystic 06355. (203) 536-9604 or (800) 237-2415. Even when this was merely the Mystic Motor Inn, we thought it the nicest accommodation in town, with its superb location atop a hill beside Pequotsepos Cove and its appropriately weathered, shingled look. Now that it has been rechristened the Inn at Mystic, and upgraded to boot, it is even more appealing. Sisters Jody Dyer and Nancy Gray, whose father started this as Mystic's first motor inn of size in 1963, most recently have revamped the twelve rooms in the East Wing, all with Federal-style furniture, queensize canopy beds, wing chairs and fireplaces, plus balconies or patios with views of the water. Six rooms here have huge jacuzzis in the bathrooms with mirrors all around; these are booked far in advance for romantic getaways. In the inn's 1904 pillared mansion atop the hill are five large and antiques-decorated guest rooms, some with fireplaces and all with whirlpools. In summer on a wicker rocker on the inn's spacious veranda, gazing out over English gardens, orchards and the water, or in winter sitting deep in a chintz-covered sofa by a fire in the drawing room with its 17th-century pin pine paneling, you may feel like a country squire. Behind the inn, the guest rooms in the secluded Gatehouse have also been redone in a country look, with Ralph Lauren sheets and coverlets. The 38 rooms in the original two-story motor inn are handsomely furnished as well. In yet another building on the hilly twelve-acre property, the inn's Floodtide Restaurant (see Where to Eat) is well regarded. A tennis court, a small pool and rental rowboats are other pluses at this ever-changing complex (as if this weren't enough to keep them busy, the sisters have also added 50 rooms to their elegant B&B (now a small hotel) called the Harraseeket Inn in Freeport, Maine). Doubles, $100 to $135 in motor inn, $170 to $195 in inn and East Wing, $155 to $185 in Gatehouse.

The Mystic Hilton, Coogan Boulevard, Mystic 06355. (203) 572-0731 or (800) 457-5425. Opened in 1986 to the tune of $15 million, this is not your typical Hilton in terms of head-on, high-rise architecture. Across from the Mystic Marinelife Aquarium, its low red-brick exterior and peaked roofs emulate the look of 19th-century mills and warehouses. Inside, all is luxurious, from the acclaimed Mooring restaurant (see Where to Eat) to the grand piano in the fireplaced lobby with intimate sitting areas next to an open courtyard in which a dolphin sculpture resides. The 187 standard and kingsize guest rooms are decorated in rose and green, each bearing two large prints of Mystic Seaport scenes commissioned from artist Sally Caldwell Fisher. Five deluxe rooms have queen beds and a sitting area plus big jacuzzi tubs in the extra-large bathrooms; they also have separate vanities and enormous closets. The meandering, angled layout puts some rooms an inordinate distance from the elevators but also contributes to peace and quiet; we walked the equivalent of a couple of blocks to our corner room, but never heard a sound all night. Facilities include a small and shallow indoor-outdoor pool and a fitness center. Doubles, $109 to $169.

Red Brook Inn, 10 Welles Road, Box 237, Old Mystic 06372. (203) 572-0349. Take a 1768 stagecoach-stop tavern in Groton, dismantle it, move it to Old Mystic and reassemble it piece by piece. The result is the large new-old building at the expanded Red Brook Inn, as fascinating an historic inn structure as we've seen. After a year's painstaking restoration, innkeeper Ruth Keyes, a transplanted Californian, added the Haley Tavern in 1986 up the hill behind the original red 1770 Creary homestead she opened as a B&B in 1983. Interestingly, Nancy Creary, who was born in the homestead, married the son of Elija Haley, "so we brought the tavern back into the same family," Ruth says. The tavern structure has seven luxurious guest rooms, all with private baths (one with a jacuzzi), and three with working fireplaces. Each is handsomely appointed with period antiques, color-coordinated stenciling and fresh flowers. Most have canopy beds, two of them queensize. The Ross Haley Room has a 200-year-old Shaker chest that still opens as easily as ever. The several downstairs common rooms are furnished with Ruth's fine collection of old lamps, hand-blown glass, pewter and such. Although this could almost be a house museum, it's comfortably lived in. Ruth offers afternoon tea and after-dinner brandies, and converted the original taproom into a game room. Full breakfasts of fresh fruits and walnut waffles or apple pancakes are served in the keeping room. Here, in the enormous open hearth, breads and pies are baked for Saturday night candlelight Colonial dinners available to houseguests by reservation in November and December. The original Creary homestead has four large guest rooms with working fireplaces and private baths. Doubles, $95 to $175. No smoking.

The Palmer Inn, 25 Church St., Noank 06340. (203) 572-9000. The imposing sixteen-room mansion built in 1907 in pillared Southern plantation style for Robert Palmer Jr., when the Palmer Shipyards were among New England's largest, was restored in 1984 as a B&B by Patricia White Cornish. Guests play checkers in the library or gather for afternoon tea in the parlor, where Patti has put out a variety of guides to the house and the area. In the dining room she serves a continental-plus breakfast of fresh fruit salad, homemade granola, breads and muffins. From the impressive main hall with its thirteen-foot-high ceilings, a mahogany staircase leads past one of many stained-glass windows to the six second-floor and third-floor guest rooms, all with private baths. The huge Master Suite has a large fireplace, a rare rocker, a fancy satin bedspread and a canvas ceiling, while the white and blue Wicker Room has a private sitting area. Step up to the balconies off a couple of front rooms for a good view of Long Island Sound. Patti offers winter theme weekends and arranges for lobster bakes on a sailboat, picnic cruises and the like. Doubles, $105 to $175.

Steamboat Inn, 73 Steamboat Wharf, Mystic 06355. (203) 536-8300. Some of the most luxurious new guest rooms we've seen in a long time opened in 1990 in this small inn transformed from a defunct restaurant on the Mystic River. Named after ships built in Mystic, all six guest rooms have jacuzzi baths, fireplaced sitting areas facing the river, telephones and televisions hidden in cupboards or armoires. Local decorator Victoria Cooke outfitted them in lavish style: mounds of pillows and designer sheets on the queensize canopy or twin beds, loveseats or sofas and a plush arm chair in front of the fireplace, mantels and cabinet work that make these rooms look at home rather than in a hotel. We like best the rooms at either end, brighter and airier with bigger windows onto the water and a couple with half-cathedral ceilings. The two rooms in the middle are darker in both decor and daylight. Each room is distinctively different and has its own merits; "one couple stayed here four times in the first month and worked their way around the inn, staying in different rooms," reports co-owner John McGee, a local developer who originally built the place as the Landing restaurant. Guests have little reason to leave their rooms, but there's a common room with all the right magazines and three glass tables for continental breakfast. Resident innkeeper Kitty Saletnik puts out homemade breads and muffins each morning. Doubles, $150.

Moderate Range

Taber Motor Inn and Guest House, Route 1, Mystic 06355. (203) 536-4904. Located in a quasi-residential area, this has 28 rooms in a basic motel, a restored 1829 guest house, a remodeled farmhouse and even a private two-bedroom guest house. New in 1989 were eight townhouse suites out back, each with two balconies overlooking the Mystic River. Two suites have one bedroom and six have two. Each has a fireplaced living room, wet bar and a jacuzzi, with one and one-half or two and one-half bathrooms. Although the owner said Mystic was "over-roomed," his new suites have been booked far in advance. Doubles, $75 to $140; suites, $180 and to $240 all year.

Harbour Inne & Cottage, Edgemont Street, RFD 1, Box 398, Mystic 06355. (203) 572-9253. In an area in which few public accommodations are near the water, here's one that is — although the harbor is cluttered with moored boats and the property with lobster traps and fishing paraphernalia. Bearded commercial fisherman Charles LeCouras (Charley to the guests who have filled his scrapbook with fan letters) runs this small, quirky place. The main house contains four paneled guest rooms with small private baths, cable TV and air-conditioning (one room even has a stereo system). Facilities for guests include a small living room with a wood stove next to an open kitchen where they have kitchen privileges, and a prominently displayed washer and dryer. An adjacent quonset-type cottage finished in cedar has a bedroom with two double beds, a sofabed in the living room, a kitchen and a deck with redwood furniture. Outside are picnic tables beside the water, canoes and rowboats. Doubles, $35 to $75; cottage, $85 to $170.

Days Inn, Route 27, Mystic 06355. (203) 572-0574. As far as Days Inns go, this is a cut above, and so are its prices. Part of the motel row near Exit 90 off I-95, it's located well back from the highway and 122 rooms are off central corridors on two floors. Rooms in the motel have been refurbished in beige, brown and orange; they're rather small, but have either two double beds or a kingsize bed with a sofabed and a desk. Besides an outdoor pool, the motel has a restaurant serving three meals a day. Doubles, $75 to $92.

Seaport Motor Inn, Coogan Boulevard, Box 135, Mystic 06355. (203) 536-2621. Its location back from the highway and high atop a hill overlooking the Olde Mistick Village shopping complex sets this 118-room motel apart from others along motel row. The rooms are pleasant enough (five are two-bedroom suites good for families), the outdoor pool is large, the fireplaced lounge cozy, and Jamm's restaurant serves lunch and dinner daily. Doubles, $68 to $88.

167

Comfort Inn, 132 Greenmanville Ave., Mystic 06355. (203) 572-8531. The newest of the chain motels proliferating around Mystic's main I-95 interchange is this brick structure with gabled windows, cupola and porte cochere. Most of the 120 rooms are on the small side, but pleasantly decorated in mauves and blues. Windows are few (entry is from inside corridors). The basic room with two double beds has two chairs around a table and a free-standing armoire in the modern idiom; the kingsize room has a loveseat. Deluxe suites offer whirlpool tubs. The inn has an indoor exercise facility and an outdoor pool. A complimentary continental breakfast is available. Doubles, $77 to $100.

Other Choices

Whaler's Inn & Motor Lodge, 20 East Main St., Mystic 06355. (203) 536-1506. For those who want to be in the thick of the action in downtown Mystic, this is the place. There are 40 rooms in the old main building and two newer motel buildings surrounding a courtyard. Rooms and rates vary widely. The Macbeth family also owns the Binnacle Restaurant, the outdoor Flying Bridge dining patio and the Ship's Hold gift shop, all part of the complex just east of the Mystic drawbridge. Doubles, $45 to $110.

Cove Ledge Motel, 368 Stonington Road (Route 1), Pawcatuck 06379. (203) 599-4130. Sixteen basic motel and efficiency units are offered at this older motel with a cove view, a 50-foot swimming pool, boat dock and picnic tables. Doubles, $45 to $55; efficiencies, $45 to $75. Open May-October.

Farnan House, 10 McGrath Court, Stonington 06378. (203) 535-0634. Ann Farnan runs a five-room B&B (one with private bath and another with a half bath) in the 1906 home built by her late husband's father. She serves muffins or sweet rolls for breakfast beside the big wood stove in the kitchen. The upper rear porch affords a view of the water. Doubles, $65 to $68.

CAMPING. Seaport Campgrounds, Route 184, Box 104, Old Mystic 06372, (203) 536-4461, is a 130-site campground with hookups and separate tenting area two miles north of I-95. Attractions include a swimming pool, pond fishing, rec room, playground and miniature golf. Closer to the highway is **Highland Orchards Resort Park,** Route 49, North Stonington 06359, (203) 599-5101, a large RV area with pool, fishing pond, playground, basketball court, fireplace lounge, wooded tent sites and more.

RENTALS. Among the many real-estate brokers in the area, several specialize in summer rentals, including Mary J. Meader Real Estate, 22 East Main St., Mystic 06355, (203) 536-3417, and Mammon Realty, 18 Crescent St., Groton Long Point 06340, (203) 536-1183.

Seeing and Doing _____ 〰〰〰

Fish and Ships

Mystic Seaport Museum, Route 27, Mystic. (203) 572-0711. From a local marine historical museum with one building in the old Greenman family shipyard in 1929, Mystic Seaport has evolved into the nation's largest maritime museum, an impressive testament to the lure, the lore and the life of the sea. The seventeen-acre site along the Mystic River contains more than 60 historic buildings, 300 boats, a planetarium and significant collections of maritime artifacts. Together they create a mix of a working seaport village, a museum of massive proportions and a must-visit attraction for any sailor worth his salt.

Landlubbers among the 500,000 annual visitors like the re-creation of a 19th-century seafaring community. Trades of the era are demonstrated in the cooperage and shipsmith, shipcarver and model shops. You can poke through the Mystic Bank and shipping office (the second oldest bank in Connecticut), see handbills being published in the Mystic Press print shop, and visit the hardware store, schoolhouse, the drugstore and doctor's office, and the delightful Fishtown Chapel. Guides cook on the open hearth of the Buckingham House kitchen, sing chanteys and demonstrate sail-setting, whaleboat rowing and fish salting.

Everyone likes to climb aboard the Charles W. Morgan (1841), the last of America's wooden whaleships and a remarkable example of the seaport's ship restoration efforts; the full-rigged training ship Joseph Conrad (1882), and the 1921 fishing schooner L.A. Dunton. About 300 small craft, the largest such collection in the country, are on display in the Small Boat Exhibit and North Boat Shed. Others are afloat along the seaport's docks or can be seen from a visitors' gallery as they undergo repairs in the Henry B. duPont Preservation Shipyard.

Sailors, historians, collectors and those with an interest in things nautical cherish the three-story Stillman Building, which houses ship models, scrimshaw, paintings and an informative exhibit called "New England and the Sea," which traces the region's maritime past. The shipping and shipbuilding businesses are explained in the Mallory Building, and other collections are displayed in more buildings than you can possibly comprehend in a day.

Don't miss the wonderful scale model of Mystic as it appeared in the mid-19th century. Take a ride on the steamboat Sabino (see below), and visit the excellent Museum Store, which offers all kinds of nautical items, an art gallery and one of the best maritime bookstores anywhere.

Among special events are a May lobster fest, a horse and carriage weekend and an antique and classic boat rendezvous in July, an October chowder fest, and daily Yuletide and evening Lantern Light tours in December. The last are particularly charming as guides with lanterns lead tours to selected exhibit areas and ships, where costumed staff portray Christmases past.

Museum open daily except Christmas, April-October 9 to 5 and November-March 9 to 4. Adults $14, children $7.75.

Mystic Marinelife Aquarium, Coogan Boulevard, Mystic. (203) 536-3323. Two Steller's sea lions cavort in an outdoor pool at the entrance to the stark gray building a gull's glide from I-95. Inside are 48 aquariums of various sizes containing 6,000 specimens, themed according to adaptation methods and aquatic communities (New England, tropical and Pacific coast waters). Each is well labeled and highly instructive, and the inhabitants get bigger as you move on, finally reaching the belukha whales and dolphins.

Guides lead periodic tours of the outdoor Seal Island complex, which occupies 2.5 acres of land right beside the interstate (the five species of seals and sea lions seem oblivious to the roar of passing traffic). A marsh pond between the aquarium and Seal Island features a variety of waterfowl, including some colorful redhead ducks. The new Penguin Pavilion is the outdoor home of adorable African black-footed penguins. Beyond is the site of the aquarium's planned $4.3 million Whale Study Center, the first of its kind in the world.

Alone worth the price of the admission is the hourly demonstration in the 1,400-seat Marine Theater upstairs. Aquarium officials call it a training demonstration; the audience calls it quite a show. In one segment, Skipper, a 500-pound sea lion, twirled a ball on his nose, applauded and balanced his entire weight on one flipper; then he bounced a ball as he turned, rolled and slid, finally saying "oh yeah" on command. One of the performing dolphins cleared a hurdle held over the trainer's head, soared through a hoop, tossed a ball and did both a front flip and a one-and-one-half laid-out back flip. As visitors leave the theater, the performers are on view in the tanks downstairs. From that vantage point, little would one suspect how well trained they are.

Open daily, 9 to 5:30 in summer, 9 to 4:30 rest of year; closed Thanksgiving, Christmas and Jan. 1. Adults $7.50, children $4.50.

The USS Nautilus Memorial/Submarine Force Library and Museum, Naval Submarine Base-New London, Route 12, Groton. (203) 449-3174. The storied Nautilus, the world's first nuclear-powered submarine, was built at Groton's General Dynamics Electric Boat Division shipyard in 1954. Returned to its birthplace, it has been opened to visitors after cruising faster, deeper, farther and longer than any craft in history. The submarine museum traces the history of underwater navigation, showing a submarine control room, working periscopes and models depicting submarine style and development. Films of submarines past and present are shown in two mini-theaters, and four mini-subs are available for inspection outside. The highlight for most is a short tour of portions of the 519-foot-long Nautilus. The lines may be long, but you get to see the operations deck, torpedo room, dining quarters and berth areas. Open daily except Tuesday 9 to 5, April 15 through mid-October; rest of year, 9 to 3:30; closed every Tuesday and the third full weeks of March and September, the first full week of June and the second full week of December, plus Thanksgiving, Christmas and New Year's Day. Free.

Boat Tours

S.S. Sabino, South Gate, Mystic Seaport, 572-0711. The 57-foot, two-deck Sabino is the last coal-fired passenger steamboat operating in the country. Built in 1908 and long used on Maine's Casco Bay, it was acquired in 1974 by Mystic Seaport for passenger excursions. Half-hour river cruises are available to 100 Seaport visitors hourly from 11 to 4; adults $2.50, children $1.75. The Sabino is at its best after hours when it gives 90-minute evening cruises down the Mystic River past Noank and Masons Island to Fishers Island Sound. It's at its *very* best during the summer musical cruises: Dixieland jazz on Sundays, banjo nights on Tuesdays and jazz nights on Thursdays. Regular cruises, daily at 5, mid-May to mid-October, also at 7 late June through Labor Day. Adults $7.50, children $6. Musical cruises, $7.50 to $11.

Out O' Mystic Schooner Cruises, 7 Holmes St., Box 487, Mystic, 536-4218. (800) 243-0416. The Mystic windjammer fleet is known for the **Mystic Clipper** and the **Mystic Whaler,** which offer popular seagoing vacations on board. The newer, 125-foot-long Mystic Clipper carries 125 day passengers and can house 56 overnight in private and coed quarters. Trips of one, three or five days may go to Newport, Block Island, Sag Harbor or Greenport. Rates run from $45 for one-day sneak-away cruises and $59 for overnights to $385 to $525 for five-day cruises. Those with less time enjoy three-hour quarterdeck dinner cruises on the Whaler and Clipper Fridays, Saturdays and Sundays at 5. Full dinners with wine cost $45. The Mystic Clipper sails Chesapeake Bay out of Annapolis, Md., in spring and fall. Operating season in Mystic, early May to late October.

Voyager Cruises, Steamboat Wharf, Mystic, 536-0416 or (800) 243-0882. Designed and built by owner-captain Frank Fulchiero, the replica of a 19th-century packet schooner gives day sails to Stonington and cruises of two to three days. The Voyager has ten private cabins (with running water and hot-water showers) and a chef known for his clam chowder and lobster bakes. The Voyager's gaff-rigged schooner **Argia** gives half-day sails daily except Saturday at 10 and 2, as well as two-hour sunset cruises at 6 and a full-day luncheon sail Saturday from 10 to 4. Voyager day cruises, $45; two-day cruises, $199 to $289; three-day cruises, $309 to $359. Argia half-day and sunset cruises, $25 to $29; full day, $45 to $55. Operates June-October.

Mystic River Queen, Cottrell Street next to drawbridge, Mystic. 536-0942. The River Queen enterprise out of Groton (see below) started running narrated sightseeing cruises in Mystic in 1990. Hour-long cruises, leaving roughly on the hour from 10 to 5:15 daily, go down the river and through the harbor into Long Island Sound; adults $8, children $4. Ninety-minute sunset cruises are offered nightly at 6:30, occasionally with music; adults $12 to $16.

River Queen, 193 Thames St., Groton. 445-9516. "See Submarines by Boat" is the pitch for the new River Queen II. It plies the Thames River as it passes the USS Nautilus nuclear sub, the U.S. Coast Guard Academy and the U.S. Naval Submarine Base, and you may see Trident subs under construction at the Electric Boat Division of General Dynamics. It's billed as a friendly one-hour harbor tour, but all the subs and Navy ships look rather unfriendly. Tours daily in summer at 10, 11:15, 12:30, 1:45 and 3, weekends in spring and fall. Adults $7, children $4. The River Queen II has two-hour Dixieland jazz cruises Saturday evenings at 7.

Hel-Cat II, 181 Thames St., Groton, 535-2066, bills itself as the largest steel party fishing boat in New England. No reservations are needed for full-day fishing trips from 6 to 3:30 or 4:30. Daily mid-June through October; weekends and holidays, rest of year. Adults $35, children $17.50.

Captain John's Sport Fishing Center, 15 First St., Waterford, 443-7259, offers Connecticut's first whale-watching boat, Sunday and Thursday from 9 to 3; adults $30, children $20. The center also has numerous party and charter fishing excursions, catching everything from flounder and blues to tuna and sharks.

Mystic Marine Basin, Route 27, Mystic, 572-7547, rents paddleboats, canoes and kayaks by the hour or day from its site along the river, one-half mile north of I-95 on Route 27.

Land Tours

Auto Tape Tours of the Mystic area are available on cassette. Tapes may be obtained for $11.95 at the Mystic Information Center in Olde Mistick Village and at tourist attractions and stores.

Mystic Walking Tour. A guide to the historic homes along Gravel, Clift and High Streets on the west bank of the Mystic River is available from the Chamber of Commerce's depot office. Many of the large white homes with dark shutters are visible from the other side of the river or from Mystic Seaport. For an up-close look, a leisurely walking tour takes about one hour and points out what the guide calls "the little differences of each house."

STONINGTON. There's no tour as such, but a stroll along Water and Main streets and cross streets is a must; at our latest visit, we saw posted good new maps of downtown shops and attractions, but were unable to find any to take. The Stonington Historical Society has marked with signs many 18th and 19th century structures, including the home where the mother of artist James Whistler and later poet Stephen Vincent Benet lived and the birthplace of Capt. Nathaniel Brown Palmer, discoverer of Antarctica. The borough is full of large homes crowding their lots right up to the sidewalks; the architecture is an intriguing mix of gambrel roofs, old Cape Cod and pillared Greek Revival. At the end of Water Street is the **Old Lighthouse Museum,** the first government lighthouse in Connecticut. It houses the Stonington Historical Society's collection of whaling and fishing gear, articles from the Orient trade and an exquisite dollhouse. Today, Stonington is home to a number of celebrities who cherish its quiet charm, which you can best appreciate by walking its streets.

Other Attractions

SWIMMING. Most of the shorefront in this area is privately owned, and beaches are few. For surf swimming, head across the Rhode Island state line to Watch Hill and Misquamicut, which face the open ocean. A protected beach called **Esker Point** at Groton Long Point has picnic tables in the trees; there's no surf, but it's uncrowded and open to the public.

WINERIES. Southeastern Connecticut's mild climate and its proximity to water have spawned a couple of boutique wineries. **Stonington Vineyards,** Taugwonk Road, Stonington, offers wine tastings and sales daily from 11 to 5 and tours by appointment. **Crosswoods Vineyards,** Chester Maine Road, is known for excellent chardonnays among its California-style viniferas and is open weekends from noon to 4:30 (tours by appointment).

ART. The **Mystic Art Association Gallery** off Water Street beside the river features changing exhibitions and special events in the summer. The **Mystic Seaport Museum Store** has an art gallery and a variety of nautical arts and crafts. **Framers of the Lost Art** at 48 West Main St. is one of several galleries. Mystic hosts the annual **Mystic Outdoor Art Festival,** scheduled the second weekend in August and considered one of the largest and best in the East.

SHOPPING. Mystic is one tourist area without a shopping plaza or mall as such, and yet it has an uncommon concentration of good stores.

Olde Mistick Village, Route 27 at I-95, has 60 shops in a nicely landscaped, built-to-look-old complex. Here is a catch-all of boutiques, gift shops and such to appeal to tourists, and catch them all they do. It's a sightseeing attraction in itself, the carillon music from its Anglican chapel lending a happy air and the ducks in a pond beside the water wheel keeping youngsters amused.

Across Coogan Boulevard are the new **Clockworks Factory Outlets,** where Manhattan, Van Heusen, Swank, Quoddy and Bali-L'Eggs-Hanes are among those represented. Nearby on Route 27 is **Seaport Fabric & Gifts,** full of designer fabrics for draperies and upholstery (seconds and overruns), most from $5.95 to $14.95 a yard. Many of our Hartford friends do their fabric shopping here.

DOWNTOWN MYSTIC. Stores here are increasingly upscale and of appeal to residents as well as visitors. **Whyevernot** has unique things, from jewelry to fabrics, and we picked up a few gifts at **Peppergrass & Tulip,** which stocks a choice selection of McBeeton's preserves, wood carvings, lacy pillows and baskets. The **Company of Craftsmen** offers contemporary American crafts. **Everything But the Stamp** purveys a large selection of paper goods, and we chuckled over Humphrey Beargart and Lauren Bearcall, dressed-up bears in the window of **Good-Hearted Bears.** Don't like bears? Then how about **Cat: A Tonic,** gifts with a feline theme. **Mystical Toys** lives up to its name. **Mc-Monogram** has nice bags, purses and totes. **The Bermuda Shop, William Bendett, Pentangle Fashion Boutique** and **Waves Fashions** offer elegant to trendy clothing. **Nantucket Mills** stocks wool and cotton sweaters at discounted prices. **World Traders Limited** has broadened its horizons from its original Irish Currach, which started with everything Irish from tea to over-coats.

Water Street, just off Main Street, has small shops in the restored **Factory Square** buildings, including **Puffins,** a year-round offshoot of a Watch Hill enterprise featuring American crafts, from paperweights to blown glass. Across the street, the **Emporium** has three floors of zany items. Its shopping bag proclaims "Shop Until You Drop," and you just might as you open some of the more offbeat (and offcolor) cards.

In Stonington, more antiques shops pop up every time we visit. **Grand & Water** is one of the best. **Deja Vu** specializes in antiques and interiors, and **Orkney & Yost** adds oriental rugs. We're partial to the **Hungry Palette,** whose screened fabrics are turned into beautiful skirts that match the wall hangings displayed in the window; we coveted some of the corduroy ones for winter. **Quimper Faience** has firsts and seconds of the popular handpainted French china, while **Sugar and Spice** doles out everything from vinegars and coffee beans to English bangers and Portuguese bread. Fabrics cover the high ceiling of the **Painted Surface,** a decorative arts studio at 11 Grand St. The new **Anguilla Gallery** has two floors of paintings and sculptures.

Where to Eat ⎯⎯⎯⎯⎯⎯⎯⎯⎯⎯⎯⎯⎯ _ᏯᏯᏯ_

Fancy Dining

The Harborview, Water Street at Cannon Square, Stonington. (203) 535-2720. Southeastern Connecticut's first restaurant of distinction is still going strong in its second decade, better than ever lately under new owner Terrence McTeague. It's French, has a good view of the water and a convivial spirit, especially in its popular tavern. The large, dark-paneled main dining room with blue linens, pink napkins and fresh flowers is the setting for fine food. Dinners run from $14.75 for breast of chicken with lobster, asparagus tips and sherry sauce to $19.75 for tournedos au poivre. The classic bouillabaisse is a house specialty of long standing. The veal sweetbreads with crayfish tails in a vol-au-vent pastry are superb, as are the curried shrimp, the lobster baked with curried cream and mango chutney, and the veal with wild mushrooms, Smithfield ham and brandied cream. Many dinner items are available at lunch (entrees $6.95 to $9.95), and the rustic bar offers daily specials and lower-priced entrees. We like the lavish Sunday brunch buffet ($14.95), which has interesting hot dishes (wonderful omelets full of fresh crabmeat, seafood en croute) and enough food to keep us happy for a couple of days. Lunch daily, 11:30 to 3; dinner 5 to 10; Sunday brunch, 11 to 3; closed Tuesday in winter.

J.P. Daniels, Route 181, Old Mystic. (203) 572-9564. Flawless service and consistently good continental cuisine are the hallmarks of this off-the-beaten-path restaurant, a favorite with locals who like the candlelit elegance of the converted dairy barn. Some find its high ceilings a bit cavernous; others pay more attention to the white-linened tables and what's on the plate, and everyone appreciates the light fare offered in the lounge nightly except Saturday. Dinner entrees in the $12.95 to $18.95 range include shrimp scampi, broiled scallops and boneless duck stuffed with seasonal fruits and sauced with apricot brandy. We hear the curried shrimp, veal oscar and several filet mignon presentations are especially good, and the wines are moderately priced. A wonderful brunch ($12.95) offers many of the same appetizers and entrees from the dinner menu. Lunch, Monday-Friday 11:30 to 2; dinner nightly, 5 to 9:30 or 10; Sunday brunch, 11 to 2.

Flood Tide, Route 1, Mystic. (203) 536-8140. A porte cochere and lobby lead into this popular restaurant at the Inn at Mystic. Past the airy lounge with its leather chairs is the spacious two-level dining room with handsome patterned wallpaper, brass chandeliers, sturdy captain's chairs and large windows through which to view Pequotsepos Cove. Tables are appointed with white linens, a single rose in a small vase, etched-glass lamps and hammered silverware. We were impressed with the $10.95 luncheon buffet, which had everything from seviche, caviar, seafood salad, eggs benedict, seafood crepes and beef bourguignon to bread pudding and kiwi tarts. Dinner is where chef Robert Tripp excels, with appetizers ($5.25 to $8.95) like the house pate in aspic, a crepe filled with lobster madeira or herbed mushroom soup diana. Shrimp rolled in coconut, chicken in phyllo with sundried tomatoes, veal florentine mornay, and duckling with peach glaze are some of the entrees, priced from $13.95 for a vegetarian fiesta to $24 each for beef wellington or rack of lamb for two. From a large dessert menu you may choose things like pecan pie, chocolate hazelnut torte, praline ice cream cake and flaming desserts as in bananas foster or cherries jubilee for two. An outdoor patio is popular in season. Lunch, Monday-Saturday, 11:30 to 3; dinner nightly, 5:30 to 9:30 or 10; Sunday brunch, 11 to 3.

The Mooring, Mystic Hilton Hotel, Coogan Boulevard, Mystic. (203) 572-0731. A comfortable, three-level dining room with armchairs and banquettes in deep blue looks onto an outdoor courtyard centered with a sculpture of a dolphin. On the main wall is a striking sculptural relief of overlapping oars. The fare has been highly rated, but the menu has been toned down a bit lately in concept, if not in execution. Some townspeople complain that the portions leave them hungry, but we were satisfied after our dinners of roast rack of lamb — four pink little chops accompanied by new potatoes, pieces of grilled yellow squash, zucchini and eggplant, and half a broiled tomato — and medallions of venison with a sauce of port wine, sage and chanterelles, plus green beans and carrots. Good crunchy French bread and salads of mixed greens and radicchio preceded. For dessert, the almond lace cookie filled with chocolate mousse laced with liqueur was enough for two. Dinner entrees are priced from $17.25 for roast chicken to $22.75 for steamed lobster. The steamed blackfish comes with romaine and tomato coulis; the breast of duck with ginger-port wine sauce. The primarily American wine list is priced from $15 to $100. At our latest visit, the express lunch ($4.95) brought fish chowder and a ham salad sandwich with roasted peppers and black olives. Lunch, Monday-Saturday 11:30 to 2; dinner, 6 to 10.

Other Choices

Seamen's Inne, Route 27, Mystic. (203) 536-9649. Adjacent to Mystic Seaport is this large and well-regarded establishment, taken over in 1990 by Charles Baxter and three partners from the Griswold Inn at Essex. The Gris connection explains some of the changes and the menu, which has gone from the traditional seafood of yore to an eclectic — some might say odd — meld from filet of catfish with hush puppies and coleslaw to Irish lamb stew. The mixed-bag dinner menu ($12.95 to $18.95) offers mixed grill of sausages, chicken pot pie, red beans and rice with smoked ham hocks and corn bread, carpetbagger steak, shrimp Creole, and shrimp and oyster pasta with spicy Cajun cream sauce. Think you've departed Yankee-land for the South? Well, you can get seafood pot pie, fried seafood platter, broiled salmon, Yankee pot roast and lobster. The grill room is a particularly fetching place for lunch or supper. It's properly time-worn with a pressed-tin ceiling, bare wood floors and tables, rich red velvet-cushioned bentwood chairs and a greenhouse window filled with plants. We thoroughly enjoyed a lunch of clam chowder (thick and delicious for $3.50 a bowl) and two appetizers, poached mussels with salsa and nachos Atlantic, the latter such an enormous portion of tasty shrimp, scallops, cheese and crisp tortilla chips that we couldn't even think of the pecan pie or hot fudge sundae for dessert. The main dining rooms are a tad more formal with ladderback chairs, carpeting and white tablecloths, just the place for tourists seeking the $9.95 sunset special, weekdays from 4:30 to 6:30. Lunch daily, 11:30 to 2:30; dinner, 5:30 to 9. Sunday, dixieland country breakfast, 11 to 2.

The Fisherman, 937 Groton Long Point Road, Noank. (203) 536-1717. A great view of the water and an elegant nautical decor are offered by Tom Tsagarakis, who took over this traditional establishment in 1990 after eight years in management at Dave & Eddie's in Newport. About 150 diners can be seated at widely spaced tables in three dining rooms, the side room with the best view handsomely outfitted in blue, the larger rooms to the rear in gray and maroon. Once you sit in the unusual cushioned chairs that swivel and rock, you may never want to get up. Tom toned down the menu in concept and price, offering dinner entrees from $8.95 for fish and chips to $19.95 for surf and turf. An acclaimed seafood kabob, baked stuffed shrimp, lobster madeira, bouillabaisse, veal marcaise, chicken cordon bleu and filet mignon are among the possibilities. Salad, vegetables and starch come with, and no one leaves hungry. The lounge menu, offered from 3 to closing, offers bargains like baked bluefish, grilled tuna teriyaki and shrimp Creole over pasta, $4.95 to $6.50. Lunch, Monday-Saturday 11:30 to 3; dinner nightly, 5 to 9:30 or 10; Sunday, dinner and lounge menu, noon to 9.

Captain Daniel Packer Inne, 32 Water St., Mystic. (203) 536-3555. Once a stagecoach stop on the New York to Boston route, this restored 1756 inn receives mixed reviews, but you can't fault the historic atmosphere recreated by owner Richard Kiley. Everyone likes the crowded tavern downstairs, where a light pub menu is served amid the original walls of brick and stone. The main floor has a couple of handsome dining rooms with working fireplaces and bare tables topped by formal mats portraying sailing ships. The dinner menu, with entrees from $13.95 to $18.95, contains some surprises: Thai scallops over pasta, four-peppercorn chicken, sauteed veal tenderloin with roasted shallots, pepper steak glazed with Jack Daniels. Bailey's cream cheese cheesecake, turtle pie, double chocolate mousse and gelatos are favored desserts. Lunch, Monday-Friday 11:30 to 2, weekends in pub; dinner, 5 to 10 or 10:30, Sunday 4 to 9.

One South, 201 North Main St., Stonington. (203) 535-0418. Interesting regional and international cuisine and an intimate Victorian atmosphere are the hallmarks of this popular cafe, which moved in 1989 from a shopping plaza in Pawcatuck into the old Village Pub beneath the viaduct. It gained larger quarters and shortened its name from One South Broad Cafe in the processs. Owner Tricia Shipman decorated her new place in pink, from glass-covered tablecloths to the ceiling, but dark wood wainscoting and a lively bar keep it from looking overly feminine. Nachos, grilled mussels, salads, sandwiches and burgers are featured all day. Dinnertime brings such entrees ($10.95 to $17.95) as scallops florentine, Mediterranean scrod, pasta puttanesca, hazelnut chicken, grilled duck, mixed grill or seafood fettuccine over black pasta. Peanut butter pie, white chocolate macaroon cheesecake, pear sorbet and vanilla bean ice cream might be on the docket for dessert. Lunch, Monday-Saturday 11:30 to 3; dinner, 5 to 9:30 or 10.

Noah's, 113 Water St., Stonington. (203) 535-3925. Small and homey, the two dining rooms here are usually packed with regulars who appreciate good food at refreshing prices. Regional or ethnic specialties are posted nightly to complement dinners on the order of broiled flounder, cod Portuguese, pork chop, pasta and breast of chicken, with everything except the filet mignon ($12.75) priced under $11. Lest we mislead: the fare is interesting, from the house chicken liver pate with sherry and pistachios to the Greek country or farmer's chop suey salads at lunch. A bowl of clam chowder with half a BLT and a bacon-gouda quiche with side salad made a fine lunch for two for less than $10. Save room for the scrumptious homemade desserts. Noah's is fully licensed, offering most wines in the low teens. Breakfasts are a bargain as well, the thick wedges of french toast made from challah bread going for about $3. Breakfast, 7 to 11; lunch, 11:15 to 2:30; dinner 6 to 9 or 9:30. Closed Monday and month of February.

Skipper's Dock, 66 Water St., Stonington. (203) 535-2000. You'll be hard-pressed to find a better waterside location than the outdoor deck at this casual restaurant operated by the Harborview. That the food is so appealing and reasonably priced is a bonus. On a sunny November day we sat beside the water (the plastic sides on the canopy-covered deck were down to cut any chill) and enjoyed a lunch of Portuguese seafood stew ($7.25) and a tasty linguini with shrimps and clams, studded with black olives, red pimentos, artichokes and capers ($7.95). The bloody mary was enormous, the bread so good we asked for seconds and the main portions so ample we didn't want dessert. The lunch menu is a smaller version of the dinner, when entrees are in the $12.95 to $15.95 range and specials might be poached salmon with pineapple and ginger cream or grilled tuna with honey-almond butter. The name and much of the nautical-historical motif came from the original Skipper's Dock in Noank; a rainbow of colorful buoys hangs from the exterior. Lunch daily 11:30 to 4, dinner 4 to 10. Open Wednesday-Sunday in spring and after Columbus Day. Closed January and February.

Just the Basics

Abbott's Lobster in the Rough, 117 Pearl St., Noank. (203) 536-7719. It's altogether fitting that this old lobstering town would be the home for 40 years of a lobster pound like those you dream of (and occasionally find) in Maine. Right beside the Mystic River as it opens into Fishers Island Sound and casual as can be with picnic tables of assorted colors resting on mashed-up clam shells, this is the place for lobster — as well as steamers, mussels, clam chowder, crab rolls and the like. You line up to place your order inside, then take a seat and sip a drink or wine (BYOB) as you await the freshest seafood around. It's not inexpensive (a complete seafood dinner, last we knew, was $17.95), but we always find the experience worth it, and Abbott's mail-order sales of specialties like clam chowder testify to its success. Open daily, noon to 9, May-September. No credit cards.

Seahorse Restaurant, 65 Marsh Road, Noank. (203) 536-1670. You'll likely mix with yachtsmen and fishermen at this out-of-the-way establishment that looks like a gin mill but serves up good steaks and seafood. The lively bar is filled with locals, but at tables or booths in the two-level dining room you can order anything from sandwiches and cold seafood plates to sirloin steaks or shrimp florentine (both $11.95). The setting is basic and so is the food, but the entire menu is available all day. When did you last see a steak or cold roast beef sandwich for $1.95, or a cold seafood plate with lobster and crab for $5.50? Two favorites of the locals are canned spinach and the cheeseburger plate ($3.50). Open Tuesday-Sunday, 11 to 10 or 10:30, Monday 5 to 10.

The Boatyard Cafe, 194 Water St., Stonington. (203) 535-1381. You'd never know it from the front, but there's a lovely deck over the water at the back of this new cafe in the Dodson Boatyard. At lunch, you might find specials like a boboli pizza, a two-inch-thick vegetable quiche, linguini with basil-walnut pesto or grilled chicken with a medley of squash, supplementing salads and sandwiches in the $4 to $7 range. Breakfast sandwiches are featured on the breakfast menu. When we were there, the "big breakfast" was apple-walnut pancakes, choice of meat, juice and coffee for $5.95. A couple of small dining rooms offered tables with white and blue checked cloths, but on a nice day, try to eat on the deck. Open Wednesday-Monday, 7 to 2:30. Closed January. BYOB.

Sailor Ed's, Old Stonington Road, Mystic. (203) 572-9524. Billed as Mystic's oldest seafood restaurant (1924), this large place near the Cove Fish Market is popular with families. They like the touristy-nautical decor and the fresh-off-the-boat seafood, much of it priced under $10. When we stopped, a shore dinner with chowder, boiled lobster, corn on the cob and Indian pudding was going for $12.95, the fisherman's platter for $14.95, and the prime rib came in two sizes, $11.95 and $16.95. "Howard's outrageous onion rings" are a specialty. The five complete dinners for senior citizens ($7.50) offered daily from 1:30 to 6 draw the crowds, and you're apt to find a tour bus or two in the parking lot. Open daily from 11:30 to 9 or 10; Sunday brunch, 11 to 3.

Cove Fish Market Takeout, Old Stonington Road, Mystic. (203) 536-0061. There's no atmosphere or view — just a lineup of picnic tables beside Route 1 — but the prices are right at this takeout stand that's an adjunct to a fish market. You can get a crab pattie burger for $2.70, fish and chips for $5.49, fried clams for $6.79, splurge for a single lobster ($7.75) or twin lobsters ($13.75). Open daily, 11 to 8, May-September. BYOB.

Seaview Snack Bar, Route 27, Mystic. There are picnic tables under a pavilion beside the Mystic River at this seasonal place, where you can get a hamburger, three kinds of "dogs," a flounder sandwich or a lobster roll ($7.95). Three dinners, with french fries and coleslaw, go from $6.45 for flounder to $9.45 for whole fried clams. Open daily, 10 to 8, April through mid-November.

Kitchen Little, Route 27, Mystic. (203) 536-2122. Last but not least is this tiny gem, where people line up to get in for breakfast on hottest summer or coldest winter days. We waited our turn in the January chill for a memorable breakfast of scrambled eggs with crabmeat and cream cheese ($3.95), served with raisin toast, and a spicy scrambled egg dish with jalapeno cheese on grilled corned beef hash ($3.65), accompanied by toasted dill rye. Everything was absolutely yummy — and we could barely eat lunch. The coffee flowed into the red mugs, the folks occupying the nine tables and five seats at the counter were jovial, and two window tables even look onto the Mystic River. You can eat outside at a few picnic tables in season. Florence Brochu's open kitchen indeed is little , but what creations she puts out, all under $4.50. She added lunches a couple of years ago, and in 1990 opened a second **Kitchen Little in the Village** at 142 Main St., Stonington: same great food and prices, more stylish decor. Open Monday-Friday 6:30 to 2; Saturday and Sunday, 6:30 to 1.

FOR MORE INFORMATION: Mystic Chamber of Commerce, Railroad Depot, Route 1 at Broadway, Box 143, Mystic, Conn. 06355. (203) 536-8559. The large Mystic and Shoreline Visitor Information Center, Old Mystick Village, 536-1641, has materials for Mystic as well as for much of Southern New England.

Block Island cove is tranquil shortly before sunset.

Block Island, R.I.

A friend says, "Just give me an island — *any* island." She says that as soon as she boards a ferry, the mantle of quotidian obligations falls away and she downshifts to first. Guaranteed.

For us, it's not quite that universal, although we do love many islands. And Block Island continues to hold our heart. This glorious piece of real estate, thirteen miles out at sea off the coast of Rhode Island, is, to our mind, the Ocean State's crown jewel.

It is an idyllic place to spend a weekend. Block Island's diminutive size, just three by seven miles, makes it explorable. Its access, by a short ferry trip of an hour or two, gives the feeling of distance from your real life. And it's so casual, it's comforting.

The island was settled in 1661 (the name of one small hotel, The 1661 Inn, commemorates that) after having been sighted by the Dutch navigator, Adrian Block, who gave it his name. The sixteen original settlers found ample fresh water in natural ponds, trees for building houses and an ocean full of fish.

Block Islanders are a hardy bunch who have managed to eke from the treeless soil and the blustery winds a way to survive. But as self-reliant as they are, they are usually outgoing and friendly, accepting an annual influx of tourists with equanimity, even enthusiasm. Aside from a few grumblings about "daytrippers," they are economic realists who know how important tourism is.

Given the natural features of the island — a long shoreline of good beaches, one of the best harbors in the Northeast, gently rolling hills and flower-strewn meadows, and such reliable breezes that air-conditioning, even on hot days, is superfluous — it's no wonder that resort status was early and eagerly bestowed.

The Victorian era saw the heyday of island tourism and a few large old hotels testify to the tradition. They're visible, peaked and gabled and gingerbreaded, from the ferry that travels in an hour from Galilee, R.I. to Old Harbor, the one and only town.

Here is a cozy concentration of markets, shops, churches and houses, plus those large hotels that have put their stamp on the place. Although several have been jazzed up in recent years, not one fast-food restaurant has established itself, nor has a Holiday Inn or other motel chain.

Much of the island's charm lies outside town, causing it to be likened to Bermuda or Ireland. Ireland, perhaps. Block Island's rolling green hills, dotted with farmhouses and freshwater ponds and divided by old stone walls, plus the vistas of sea in the distance, may be reminiscent of the Irish isle. Breathe deeply and enjoy the scents of salt air and wild flowers. The wild roses in June are intoxicating, but all summer long the place smells good.

Two-acre zoning on much of the island, plus an active and alert nature conservancy, have protected the unspoiled openness. Yes, Block Island does have a professional town manager now and one hotel tried to condominiumize a couple of years ago (it didn't succeed), but overall, the place is not going to wrack and ruin. It's one of the best spots to spend some time by the water that we know.

It is, however, getting pricey. Lately inns and hotels have upgraded their rooms and are charging accordingly. The same is true for restaurants. In their defense can be cited the shortness of the season; most must make their money during the three months of summer.

Getting There

Off the south coast of Rhode Island, Block Island is accessible by boat or air.

Interstate Navigation Co. runs ferries year-round from Galilee State Pier at Point Judith, (401) 783-4613. The trip to Old Harbor takes a little over an hour. Passengers pay $6.10 each way and automobiles, $20.50. Car reservations should be made well in advance. If you're simply spending a couple of days on the island, you can get by without a car. Bikes and mopeds are easily rented.

From New London, Conn., the Nelseco Navigation Co., (203) 442-7891, runs a two-hour ferry trip daily at 10 a.m. from mid-June to mid-September. It leaves the island at 4 p.m. weekdays and at 4:30 weekends. For a one-day round-trip ticket, passengers pay $16; to leave one day and return another, pay $12 each way. This ferry also accommodates cars.

You can fly to Block Island from Westerly, R.I., via New England Airways, (401) 466-5959 or (800) 243-2460. Round-trip fares are $49; one way, $28.

Passenger ferries also travel between Block Island and Montauk, L.I.

Where to Stay⸻⸻⸻⸻⸻⸻⸻⸻⸻⸻⸻⸻_ʃʊʊʟ_

Block Island offers a good range of guest houses, B&Bs and hotels, most in the Victorian mode. To write for accommodations, simply address the place as listed in care of Block Island, R.I. 02807.

1661 Inn and Guest House, Spring Street, Old Harbor. (401) 466-2421 or 466-2063. The Abrams family of Providence spotted the building that is now the 1661 Inn in 1969 while on a sailing trip to the island. That started a venture that includes the Guest House next door, the Manisses Hotel down the street and, soon, the old St. Ann's Episcopal Church, which is being reconstructed nearby to accommodate more guests. These are innkeepers par excellence and several members of the family, including sons and daughters-in-law, now are into the act. During the winter of 1989, the 1661 Inn was completely remodeled and accommodations were turned into the most exquisite luxury rooms and suites on the island. Four rooms on the first floor and five on the second are individually decorated in the Victorian style with all sorts of interesting touches.

Edwards, a second-floor suite, has a jacuzzi in a loft reached by an attractive wooden staircase, a shower and bathtub in a large bathroom, wall-to-wall carpeting and a deck overlooking the ocean; it rents for $300 a night. Rathbone features twin beds and a deep shelf above the room on which are arranged Victorian accessories: ship's models, a trunk, a globe. And so it goes, with rooms renting for upwards of $200 per night in season.

The Guest House next door is less expensive. Four rooms in the house share two baths and a wicker-filled living room (doubles, about $100). Downstairs in a renovated area are four queen-bedded rooms with private tiled baths. Outdoors is a lovely lawn with distant view of the water where guests sun in comfortable chaise lounges. Guests at both establishments breakfast under an awning on the attractive terrace of the 1661 Inn. Here, pink clothed tables and fresh flowers make for a good start to the day. A buffet breakfast includes fish, pancakes, hash-brown potatoes, sausages or ham, perhaps eggs, and a good selection of breads. Waitresses and chambermaids in period dress add to the charm. Doubles, $100 to $200; suites, to $300. Open April-October.

Hotel Manisses, Spring Street, Old Town. (401) 466-2421 or 466-2063. Those who remember the decrepit hulk of this structure before the Abramses saved it from destruction by the town in the early 1970s marvel at the lovely job they have done. Now a pretty Victorian hotel with eighteen guest rooms, the Manisses is also renowned for its dining room. From the moment you step into the lobby and public rooms on the main floor, wallpapered attractively in blue with large pinkish flowers and with a blue-green carpet and a marble reception desk, you feel you are in a spot where no detail has been overlooked. The hotel, which formerly closed in the dead of winter, remained open year-round in 1991, proof of its increasing popularity. Guest rooms are individually decorated with turn-of-the-century furniture and have double, queen and kingsize beds. Some have jacuzzis; all have telephones. Enjoy tea in the afternoon and all kinds of interesting flaming coffees and desserts in the evening in the **Top Shelf Bar** with its stained-glass windows. There are places to sit outdoors and enjoy especially nice flower beds; you can walk through town to a good beach. Breakfast is included in room rates. Doubles, $130 to $200.

Old Town Inn, Old Town Road, Block Island. (401) 466-5958. This is the most authentic B&B on the island, within good biking distance of the towns and the airport, but a bit far to walk otherwise — one good reason to bring a car, we guess. Eight of the ten rooms have private baths, most located in a newish addition with a large and attractive public area. Innkeepers Monica and Ralph Gunter and son David of Wellesley, Mass., have learned over more than twenty years how to make their guests comfortable. The flowers are gorgoues outdoors and there is a great sundeck out back. Particularly appealing are the breakfast rooms, where tables are topped with pink cloths and placemats and where scrumptious blueberry muffins are always on the menu with a choice of breakfast items — enough to set you up for a full day of sightseeing or beaching. Doubles, $65 to $100. Open Memorial Day through September.

The Barrington Inn, Beach and Ocean Avenue, New Harbor. (401) 466-5958. Howard and Joan Ballard of Pennsylvania operate this redecorated B&B high on a hill near New Harbor and the beach. The location is excellent, for it's a convenient walk into Old Harbor as well. All six rooms have private baths and some have decks. We especially liked those on the second floor. Room 4 weaves around toward the back of the house and offers a good view of New Harbor from its deck. Guests enjoy a main-floor parlor and a small sitting area on the third floor. Lots of pinks and blues are used in the decorating scheme. A couple of rooms have queensize beds, but most have doubles. A continental buffet breakfast is served, hot blueberry-zucchini muffins being among the possibilities. Doubles, $85 to $120. Open April-November.

Rose Farm Inn, off High Street, Old Harbor. (401) 466-2021. We have loved staying at this pretty B&B high on a knoll with a view of the island and distant ocean from a large communal deck. Most of the ten rooms have private baths and some have four-poster or canopy beds. Two rooms with a shared bath are ideal for families or couples vacationing together. All rooms are decorated individually with old-fashioned wallpapers and antiques. In the Victorian parlor are a wet bar and refrigerator for guests to use. A continental-plus breakfast of fresh fruits, yogurt, granola and homemade muffins and breads is served in a circular, windowed dining room. Doubles, $85 to $140. Open April-October.

The National Hotel, Water Street, Old Harbor. (401) 466-2901. Overlooking the action of town, including the arrival of ferries and such, the National's 43 rooms have private baths and have been recently renovated. Rooms have restored antique furnishings like hat stands and dressers with oddly shaped mirrors. But modern amenities are here as well: telephones, color televisions and radios in all rooms. Those in front have ocean views. A continental breakfast is served guests in a pretty dining room with windsor chairs or out on the broad front porch. That porch becomes one of the island's action spots in late afternoon as people gather for happy hour and to figure out what's doing in the evening. Doubles, $165 to $210. Open March-November.

The Narragansett Inn, New Harbor. (401) 466-2626. Operated by the Mott family since 1910, this is an old-fashioned summer hotel, about as authentic as you will find on the island. Corridors are wide and breezy, floors are bare wood with runners and bedrooms, while neat and clean, have not been updated in a long time. Sharing a bath means sharing with several other rooms — possibly about a half dozen — and this was something of an inconvenience, we found. A full breakfast is served in the old-fashioned dining room with dark wicker chairs, white tablecloths, blue walls and floral draperies at the windows; it has looked that way since the mid-1970s and probably for a good while before that. Some rooms have excellent views of the busy harbor and there are dining spots nearby; the beach is not far, either. But we find it a bit pricey for what you get. Doubles, $90 to $100. Open June-September.

The Surf Hotel, Dodge Street, Old Harbor. (401) 466-2241 or 466-5990. This weathered gray and gabled hotel, owned and operated by the Cyr family for 35 years, is very much a part of the Block Island scene. The hotel's location is ideal: right at the end of Water Street where it turns into Dodge and at one end of the great State Beach, which stretches for miles from here. A long front porch with classic rockers is the place to watch the world go by. And the deep red Victorian lobby with the huge oversize chess set is a favorite spot. Rooms have sinks but share baths; some have wonderful water views that a friend described as "powerful." Out back in the Surfside Cottage are a few rooms with private baths. Breakfasts at the Surf Hotel's dining room are famous, served daily from 7:30 to 11 for $6.50 ($6 for hotel guests). The menus are printed on fans and you can get virtually anything you'd like; for the kids, the pancakes come with smiles. Doubles, $75; cottage rooms, $110. Minimum stay up to six nights in summer. Open Memorial Day to Columbus Day.

Gables Inn and Gables II, Dodge Street, Old Harbor. (401) 466-2213. Barbara and Stanley Nyzio have been running these guest houses, with apartments, for several years. They represent one of the best values on the island, for they are clean, convenient to town and the beach (which is right across the street) and well-priced. Some rooms have been remodeled with wall-to-wall carpeting and private baths. Various public sitting rooms and a shaded porch are available, as are a refrigerator, barbecues and picnic tables. Apartments are located on the ground floor of the Gables II building and a cottage is adjacent to the Gables Inn. Doubles, $66 to $90. Open May-November.

The Inn at Old Harbour, Old Harbor. (401) 466-2212. Located right in the middle of the historic district, on the water side but across from the retail stores, this is attractive and convenient. It is run by two couples, Kevin and Barbara Butler and Colleen and Dick Langeloh, and the ten newly renovated rooms are located on the second and third floors of the building, which dates from 1882. Most have private baths. Continental breakfast is available. Doubles, $85 to $140. Open Memorial Day to Columbus Day.

The Seacrest Inn, High Street, Old Harbor. (401) 466-2882. A one-floor, motel-like structure close to town, this is also refurbished and well located. Doubles, $85 to $105, EP. Open May-October.

The Atlantic Inn, High Street, Old Harbor. (401) 466-5883. High on a hill overlooking the island, this renovated Victorian hotel has undergone a few changes of management, which always makes us cautious. But the 21 refurbished guest rooms are quite charming and the dining room has usually been well-rated (it opened late in 1990 and we were unable to review it personally). Doubles, $100 to $165.

Seeing and Doing _____ ♪♪♪

Block Island is a laid-back place. Biking, beaching, boating and fishing are favored pursuits. People spend all day at the beach or circling the island on their bikes or mopeds, then take a long time over dinner in the evening.

There are a few other diversions: a playhouse at Champlin's Marina presents theatrical shows and films, bingo games are run at the fire station, live entertainment and dancing are available at a couple of spots. During the day, there are trails to hike, shops to explore and kites to fly.

The best approach to finding what's on is to pick up a free copy of the biweekly Block Island Times, which is quite comprehensive. Stop at the kiosk by the ferry dock run by the local Chamber of Commerce. Watch the bulletin boards, where events are posted, at places like Millea's Book Nook.

BIKING is the preferred mode of transportation — certainly preferred by the islanders, who have not very nice things to say about mopeds. Moped accidents have caused consternation on the island, especially since there is no local hospital (only a clinic), a situation requiring seriously injured people to be flown to the Rhode Island mainland. Bikes can be brought over on the ferry or rented locally for $5 to $10 a day. There are rental places right at the ferry dock area, or behind the Surf Hotel where **Cyr's Cycles** has single-speed bikes available for $5, five-speed bikes for $7. Mopeds cost about $50 a day and are available at about five locations. Pick up a good map of the island and you're in business.

One favored destination of bikers is **North Light** at the end of Corn Neck Road (the Indians used to grow their corn here). You can picnic once you get there. Here you'll also find **Settlers Rock** with the names of the sixteen souls who first settled on the island.

Hardy cyclists — but you don't have to be too hardy — like to make a circuit of the island. Begin in Old Harbor and travel north along the shore to the intersection with Beach Avenue, then west past New Harbor with its marinas, the island cemetery and onto West Side Road. From West Side Road you can take any number of dirt roads to the water; we like Cooneymus Road to reach a wild, wonderful stretch of beach, often deserted. From there take Cherry Hill Drive to Lakeside Drive and Mohegan Trail, which leads to the Mohegan Bluffs area.

You'll want to stop here to look out over the wild Atlantic from atop these bluffs; often visible is Montauk, Long Island, twenty miles distant. A new staircase leads to the beach below, where you can take a break for a swim and some sunning.

Next to Mohegan Bluffs is the **Southeast Light,** 201 feet above the sea. A new automated light was installed in 1990, ending the age of lighthouse keepers on "the Block." The Block Island Historical Society operates a small but interesting museum at the lighthouse. Rooms detail the history of the island in appropriately low-key style, stressing its early families, resort status and antique artifacts. You can watch a couple of videos, one called "A Beacon on the Bluff," and get some idea of the erosion that chips away at the island's edges. In this instance it will mean moving the lighthouse back from the sea before too long. Open daily in summer, 10 to 4. Admission: $2.50.

BEACHING is best along the island's east coast — and good beaches are a short walk from the town of Old Harbor. There are several names for what is essentially the same strand, from Surfer's Beach to State Beach to Scotch Beach (which is said by some to be the best) and ultimately to Mansion Beach. The whole area is sometimes referred to as Crescent Beach. A new pavilion with changing facilities, showers and a concession was finally opened in 1990 at State Beach. The water here is clear and there's always a breeze on the beach; sometimes it's too breezy and we have seen beach umbrellas fly across the sand.

BOATING is big on the Block and sailboats make it a regular stopover as they ply the coast of New England. You can rent rowboats from the **Twin Maples** on Beach Avenue, New Harbor, 466-5547, for poking around the Great Salt Pond. You can rent sailboards or surfboards at various locations. Boat charters and deep-sea fishing boats go out from New Harbor or Old Harbor. Capt. Bill Gould, 466-5151, takes visitors on the G. Willie Makit for half-day and full-day sportfishing trips.

WALKING is a particular pleasure on Block Island, for it's a compact place. Mosey through the town of Old Harbor, where you can browse in the shops (see Shopping), watch the ferry come in, or visit cultural attractions. The **Block Island Historical Society** at Old Town Road and Ocean Avenue is open daily in summer from 11 to 4. Inside this rambling old house are a Block Island double-ender boat, early tools and implements, costumes and antique furniture. The **Island Free Library** on Dodge Street is surprising for its contemporary design and is a beehive of activity. Leave a deposit and borrow a book. Flyers advertising island events are usually posted here.

Out on the island, a new series of walking trails called **The Greenway,** some five miles in all, were dedicated in 1990. Put together by the Block Island Conservancy, they link the island's highest point, Beacon Hill, with some of its lowest, like Rodman's Hollow. This exciting trail network, which includes donated rights-of-way across private property, is being watched by conservationists across the country as a model.

Rodman's Hollow is a wild and beautiful cleft in the rolling southwestern terrain. It has been preserved by the Block Island Conservancy, which purchased it in the 1960s to keep it from development.

The **Island Cemetery** on Center Road is an interesting place to explore, and some of the tombstones bear unusual legends.

Guided nature tours around the island are offered in summer by the Rhode Island Department of Environmental Management. These are usually announced in the Block Island Times.

SHOPPING. Since we began visiting Block Island in the mid-1970s, shopping has improved markedly. Most of it is in Old Harbor. Art galleries and crafts shops have opened and some fine quality work is for sale.

Don't miss **The Barn** cooperative across from the Manisses Hotel on Spring Street, where many island artists and crafters display their wares. We especially liked the work of Jean Valentine, a local artist who had been working in serigraphs and turned to watercolors in 1990 with a very deft hand.

Check out **Star's Department Store** on Water Street for its T-shirts — a recent one was "Rolling Block," a takeoff on the Rolling Rock beer label, plus postcards, key rings, Bermuda shorts, sun dresses and beach paraphernalia. The second-floor **Ragged Sailor** gallery shows quality paintings and crafts. On the street level is one of two branches of **O Shoreline!** It's one of our favorite sports apparel stores selling Patagonia togs plus other casual clothing for men and women. **Esta's** is another comprehensive store for buying souvenirs, taffy and T-shirts; across the street is Esta's postage-stamp park with benches for looking out to sea. **Millea's Book Nook** carries paperbacks, periodicals and postcards; you can reserve Sunday newspapers here as well. **Island House,** an eclectic shop full of beautiful things from Ireland, is in the arcade of shops just below the National Hotel. **The Scarlet Begonia** on Dodge Street houses an interesting and unusual collection of items for the home, including handwoven and dyed baskets. **The Boat Works** on Corn Neck Road across from the beach sells kites for $8 to $200, clothing, small boats and so forth. Look for the bright kites flying outside.

Where to Eat

The fortunes of restaurants on an island like The Block change from year to year. They depend a great deal on the chef, or on the current nutritional craze, or on the mood of the visitor. Ask around when you arrive. Here are our recent favorites:

Hotel Manisses, Spring Street, Old Harbor. (401) 466-2836. The dining room at the Manisses is well regarded. There are three areas to choose from: an inner room with rattan chairs and circular floral placemats on the tables, inclined to be quieter; an outer room with lots of glass, and a deck overlooking the back yard. Vegetables and herbs from the hotel garden show up in the inventive soups and in many of the dishes. Pizzas ($9.50) and pastas (around $15) are usually on the menu under light fare, as are a cold plate (perhaps a medley of seafood and grilled vegetables served with curried rice) and mussels cataplana (steamed with onion, linguica and green peppers in a wine broth and served with a salad). Appetizers ($5.50 to $7.50) might be clams casino, fish quenelles with a pesto sauce or baked herb polenta. Dinners ($15 to $27) include broiled swordfish (a Block Island specialty), grilled tuna with red pepper coulis, roasted duck, tournedos served on grilled eggplant croutons with a mustard sauce, and rack of lamb with a mustard-garlic bread coating and a rosemary-bordelaise sauce. Lunches include such options as a cold lobster plate, salads and sandwich specials like Mexican delight (guacamole and melted muenster cheese on pita bread). Lunch daily in summer; dinner nightly, 6 to 10, weekends rest of year.

The Spring House, Spring Street, Old Harbor. (401) 466-5844. The dining room was rated among the best on the island in 1990 at this old summer hotel, which had been "upgraded" into a time-share resort and at last check was being run as a hotel while financial backers were trying to reorganize it. Young chef Jack Chiaro was turning out inventive cuisine. The dining room had been set up in what was once the hotel's mammoth lobby, the tables covered with peach tablecloths and set with white chairs for a breezy, summer feeling. Appetizers ($3.50 to $7.95) included smoked seafood pate, oysters or littlenecks on the half shell, artichoke hearts au gratin and escargots bourguignonne. Among dinner entrees ($13.50 to $18) were breast of chicken pecan, baked stuffed shrimp alana, finnan haddie a la Spring House (smoked cod filet, poached and served with a spicy blue cheese cream sauce) and native lobster. Dinner nightly in season.

Winfield's, Corn Neck Road, Old Harbor. (401) 466-5856. This intimate, pretty restaurant has an English Tudor look with dark beamed walls and ceiling and soft lighting. Flowers float in bowls on white linened tables. Chef Gene Hemingway provides creative cuisine in this romantic atmosphere. Appetizers ($5 to $7) might be satay with a spicy peanut sauce, baked montrachet chevre in phyllo pastry, or shrimp and avocado salad with a kiwi-pear vinaigrette. A salad offering was spinach with bacon in a balsamic dijon vinaigrette. Entrees ($13 to $20) could be littleneck clams over fresh red pepper linguini, rigatoni al forno (ground hot Italian sausage tossed with heavy cream, fennel and pecorino), fresh local blackfish baked in a hazelnut crust and topped with a banana-mango chutney, and pan-fried flounder with peach beurre blanc. After dinner, you can go next door to **McGovern's Yellow Kittens,** a nightspot with dancing, usually patronized by a youngish beach crowd. Dinner nightly in season, 6 to 10.

Dead Eye Dick's, Payne's Dock, New Harbor. (401) 466-2654. Boaters particularly favor this one-story, white clapboard building near the Great Salt Pond. Seafood is stressed on the menu. Appetizers ($4.50 to $7) include fried calamari in cocktail sauce, baked oysters cajun, scallops wrapped in bacon and jumbo shrimp cocktail. New England clam chowder is always available. Entrees ($12.95 to $18.95) might be broiled or fried sea scallops, shrimp and broccoli pasta served with sundried tomatoes and sweet red peppers, blackened swordfish with jalapeno jelly or grilled pork chops with roasted garlic butter and tomatillo salsa. For dessert, try mocha cheesecake, apple crisp or Maine raspberry cake. Lunch daily, 11 to 5; dinner nightly, 5 to 11. Open Memorial Day to mid-September.

Harborside Inn, Water Street, Old Harbor. (401) 466-5504. This is a favorite gathering spot, what with being directly across from the ferry dock and having a great outdoor dining area. On a warm night, you cannot beat the atmosphere, and we have had very respectable dinners here, too. A huge bar crowd gathers indoors in the late afternoon, and nearby is another type of bar — the salad bar, which is ample and an attraction since there are not many on the island. Our blackened tuna was a huge portion, moist and beautifully done. Swordfish, lobster, flounder and scrod are also often on the menu (entrees, $15 to $22), usually grilled or blackened and served with potato or salad bar. You can sit here and watch most of Block Island walk by. Lunch and dinner daily in season.

Finn's, Water Street, Old Harbor. (401) 466-2473. You can't beat the freshness of the fish nor the prices at Finn's. The regular restaurant on the lower level is reached directly from the ferry docking parking lot. Upstairs is a raw bar where you can feast on clams, oysters or shrimp, sip a drink, and enjoy the view of ferry comings and goings. Everything is prepared fresh and is not fancy, but this is one of the island's most popular places. Dinners are affordably priced, usually $10 to $16, and you can get lobsters in many different sizes. Open daily for lunch and dinner.

Ballards, Water Street, Old Harbor. You haven't been to Block Island if you haven't been to Ballard's. That's the old saying and this place, at the very edge of Old Harbor, is unbelievable. Rebuilt after a fire in the mid-1980s, the restaurant is in a cavernous hall where long tables and bentwood chairs accommodate hundreds. Overhead hang the flags of every nation in the world, we're told. Outside on two sides are redwood chairs and tables where people like to dine in nice weather. A twin lobster special, served with corn on the cob and baked potato plus coleslaw, was $18.95 at our latest visit. Almost everything from hamburgers to shrimp is available. The enormous bar is always well-attended and, for some, is what counts. By late afternoon the place is sometimes so packed that people are standing three to four deep. The boaters, the daytrippers, the locals, the college workers, the weekenders, they're all at Ballard's and they're having fun already. Later a band will strike up and they may even do a little dancing. Who can tell?. Open daily for dining, 11 to 11.

The Atlantic Inn, High Street, Old Harbor. (401) 466-5883. This is such a gorgeous room, with a nice view over the interior of the island, that it is a favored place to have dinner. It has often been very good, but who's to know with a change in management? In 1990, seafood and pasta were being stressed, with entrees in the $11 to $15 range. Dinner nightly, 6 to 9 or 10.

Sunset sipping. The best view of the sunset may be from **Trader Vic's** at the end of the dock at Champlin's Marina. Here you sip tropical drinks and watch the sun sink into the ocean. It's a fun way to start an evening.

FOR MORE INFORMATION: Block Island Chamber of Commerce, Drawer D, Block Island, R.I. 02807. (401) 466-2982.

The Breakers is largest mansion along Cliff Walk.

Newport, R.I.

As America's yachting capital, an historic seaport and the birthplace of the U.S. Navy, Newport is a nautical city like no other.

After its founding in 1639 at the tip of Aquidneck Island as a religious refuge (the first Quakers and Jews in the New World settled here), Newport was one of the nation's leading ports in the 17th and 18th centuries. The first Navy boats sailed from its harbor into Narragansett Bay and the Atlantic. In the 1800s, the Vanderbilts, the Astors, the Morgans and others of America's 400 created a seaside summer resort unmatched in opulence. In the 1900s, the Navy increased its Newport presence to the point where it has become the area's largest employer, with 10,000 military and civilian personnel at 32 commands and installations.

The Newport-to-Bermuda races, the Tall Ships and the America's Cup extravaganzas solidified Newport's place on the international maritime map.

The nautical presence is all-pervasive. You sense it amidst all the wharves — both old and quaint, and rebuilt and trendy —along Thames Street. It's glittering and glamorous along the Cliff Walk behind the Bellevue Avenue mansions, where the 400 summered. It's more rugged along the ten-mile Ocean Drive around the peninsula where today's 400 live. There are sailboats everywhere and regattas all season. The beaches are fine for swimming and surfing. The new Museum of Yachting has opened; the Newport Yachting Center and Sail Newport promote things nautical.

187

The phone book's Yellow Pages devote nearly four pages to boating, from building to rentals. Restaurants and stores take up the theme in their names: The Mooring, the Pier, the Ark and Rhumb Line, the Armchair Sailor Bookstore, Cast Offs and JT's Ship Chandlery.

Myriad pleasures are to be found by anyone interested in the water, history, sports, good living, shopping, fine dining and the like — some might ask, what else would anybody want? The summer playground of the Astors and Vanderbilts has become a year-round vacation escape for the multitudes, as well as a place for investors to park their dollars in all the condominiums and time-sharing resorts popping up around town.

Much as we like Newport, there are times — especially on summer weekends — when it overwhelms. That's when we'd don the T-shirt we found in a Newport shop: "Frankly, Scallop, I don't give a clam."

Getting There

Newport occupies the southwest tip of Aquidneck Island, the point where Narragansett Bay meets Rhode Island Sound. Some 40 roundabout miles south of Providence, it's reached via Routes 114 or 138 from the north and east; via I-95 or Route 1 and Route 138 across the Jamestown-Newport Bridge (toll $2) from the west.

Where to Stay⎯⎯⎯⎯⎯⎯⎯⎯⎯⎯⎯⎯⎯⎯⎯⎯⎯⎯⎯⎯⎯⎯⎯⎯⎯⎯ ✺✺✺

Newport has an incredible range and number of accommodations, from some two dozen hotels and motels to 115 inns and B&Bs at last count. Rates vary by season (highest in summer, which in some cases runs from mid-May to mid-October), and weekend rates may be higher than weekdays. Most facilities are open year-round.

Hotels-Motels

Sheraton Islander Inn & Conference Center, Goat Island, Newport 02840. (401) 849-2600. This is Newport's all-around resort hotel, from its banquet room, conference center and underground garage to its indoor and outdoor pools and tennis courts. That it happens to be on a narrow island between the Jamestown-Newport Bridge and Newport Harbor and surrounded by water on three sides (the other end of the island has marinas and new condominiums) is an advantage. A disadvantage is that you have to use your car or walk a distance to visit the rest of Newport. Most of the 253 rooms on six floors have views of the water. Ours didn't, unless you consider the indoor pool a water view. That huge pool area is light and airy with high arched-glass roof and a busy cocktail area where imbibers can watch the swimmers. There's also an outdoor saltwater pool beside the tennis courts. The seventh-floor **Rodger's Roost** is a great place for drinks and harbor-watching. The **Cafe Regatta** coffee shop is open all day for meals and snacks, and the **Windward Grille,** which has a greenhouse terrace beside the water, is well regarded locally for contemporary cuisine. Dinner entrees run from $13.50 for roasted chicken with cranberries and peppercorns to $21.95 for mixed grill of beef, lamb chop and smoked duck sausage. Bouillabaisse and veal tournedos au poivre are house specialties. Doubles, $150 to $210.

Newport Marriott, 25 America's Cup Ave., Newport 02840. (401) 849-1000. Newport's biggest hotel opened in 1988 on Long Wharf, next to the new Gateway Center transportation and information complex and with the harbor across the street. Billed as one of the Marriott chain's top ten resort hotels, it has 317 guest rooms arranged around a five-story atrium. Best are those with harbor or city views; others look at the atrium or the parking garage. The top floor is a deluxe concierge level. Facilities include an indoor pool, sauna, whirlpool, fitness center and raquetball courts. There are two bars, the **Atrium Lobby Bar** and the lively **Tickets Lounge.** Dine casually in **J.W.'s Sea Grill and Oyster Bar,** a sprawl of a place with glass, wood, brass and plants, featuring seafood. Northern Italian fare is found in the more formal **Cafe del Mare,** where entrees range from $12.50 for chicken with basil and garlic to $19 for veal chop stuffed with fontina cheese. Doubles, $179 to $219.

Inn on Long Wharf, 142 Long Wharf, Newport 02840. (401) 847-7800 or (800) 225-3522. Blessed with a superb waterfront location, all 40 suites in this time-sharing resort built in 1985 face directly onto the harbor. In fact, if you open the sliding glass doors, only a railing separates you from a spill into the drink. All rooms on four floors open off a corridor into the bedroom; beyond are a bathroom opposite a small kitchenette equipped with refrigerator and microwave, and beyond that a comfortable living room decorated in earth tones with a grape-colored sofabed, chair, TV and that sliding door opening onto the water. The view couldn't be better, unless it's the one from the second-floor **Smuggler's Landing,** a restaurant offering an exotic Polynesian-island menu for lunch and dinner. Entrees are $10 to $18 for items like Szechuan shrimp in hot chile pepper-garlic sauce, Sri Lanka curried chicken and medallions of beef with Japanese dipping sauces. Here, at tables beside the windows, you're perched right over the water. Although the suites lack outdoor balconies, there's a sundeck on the roof. Doubles, $155 to $220.

Inn on the Harbor, 359 Thames St., Newport 02840. (401) 849-6789 or (800) 225-3522. Built in 1982, this older sister to the Inn on Long Wharf has been totally renovated — apparently, time-sharing and transient guests take their toll. The new furnishings are like those at the Inn on Long Wharf, and so are the layouts of the 58 suites on five floors above a parking deck. (Both are among five all-suite waterfront hotels run by Inn Group Hotels here and across Narragansett Bay in Jamestown.) All Newport is on view from the sixth-floor sundeck. Each room has sliding glass doors that open onto a railing with moored boats and harbor beyond, but you don't feel as close to the water as at the Long Wharf. There's a health club on the third floor. Doubles, $130 to $220.

Newport Bay Club and Hotel, America's Cup Avenue and Thames Street, Box 1440, Newport 02840. (401) 849-8600. This is another of the time-sharing resorts whose pitches are varied (discounted visits for some, perhaps a free meal if you tour the facility). Although it doesn't face the harbor head-on like its aforementioned peers, it has 36 larger and more luxurious units, ranging from one-bedroom suites to two-bedroom townhouses. The fourth-floor townhouses have balconies upstairs and down, with side views of the harbor. Fashioned from an old General Electric mill and listed on the National Register of Historic Places, the building retains high wood ceilings and paneling. Each con-dominium-style suite has a complete kitchen including dishwasher, large living room with a sectional pullout sofabed plus a dining area, a marble bathroom with jacuzzi and a queensize bedroom. There's nightly turndown service, and continental breakfast is served. The Perry Mill Market shops are on the ground floor and downstairs is **Gatsby's,** a restaurant and nightclub. One-bedroom suites, $145 to $245; two-bedroom suites and townhouses, $195 to $375.

Sea View Motel, Route 138A, Box 392, Newport 02840. (401) 847-0110. A good view of Easton's Pond and the ocean from a hilltop away from the road commends this older motel of 1950s vintage. In fact, it's the only one of Newport's many standard motels that's close to the ocean; others farther out Routes 138 or 114 in Middletown could be Anytown, but the prices are lower than in Newport proper. This has 40 rooms on two floors, all with balconies or motel-style patios to enjoy the view. Rooms have paneled walls, two double beds, color TV and a couple of wood and leather motel chairs. A coffee shop serves breakfast only. Doubles, $75 to $85.

Inns-Guest Houses

Harborside Inn, Christie's Landing, Newport 02840. (401) 846-6600. If you want to be on the water, you can't get much closer than this, right in the heart of the wharf area off downtown Thames Street. Ten suites and four rooms overlook the water or the landing; be sure to specify. Best are the waterside suites that have balconies, queensize beds, sitting areas with two modern upholstered chairs and an ottoman, and another queensize bed in an upstairs loft reached by climbing almost straight up a ladder. The Harbor Room has windows on three sides with deck chairs for lounging and tables for continental breakfast. Doubles, $115 to $130; suites, $175 to $190.

The Francis Malbone House, 392 Thames St., Newport 02840. (401) 846-0392. Good harbor views across the street, a large lawn, commodious common rooms and elegant guest rooms make this a good B&B bet in downtown Newport. It opened in 1990 in a former physician's residence, converted from a nursing home, converted from a shipping merchant's home dating to 1860. There are eight rooms and a main-floor suite, all with private baths and six with fireplaces. Upstairs off a center hall are eight corner rooms on two floors. The front rooms are bigger and have harbor views. Each is nicely furnished with antique beds covered by monogrammed duvet comforters. Guests spread out in a couple of high-ceilinged front parlors and a library with TV. Innkeeper Jim Maher prepares a continental-plus breakfast, taken buffet-style at a long, linened table in a fireplaced dining room. The spacious back yard includes gardens and a flagstone courtyard, where guests enjoy breakfast in summer. Doubles, $125 to $155; suite, $225.

Admiral Fitzroy Inn, 398 Thames St., Newport 02840. (401) 847-4459 or (800) 343-2863. This is the newest and most luxurious of Jane and Bruce Berriman's three Admiral inns in Newport. It was opened in 1986 in the former St. Mary's Church convent, which was moved to the site to be saved from demolition. Its shingled square facade is so unassuming that people might hesitate to venture in; those who do find a luxurious restoration that the nuns would not recognize. They also wouldn't recognize the state-of-the-art elevator or the rooftop sundeck. Eighteen air-conditioned rooms of different shapes on three floors have hand-painted decorative touches worthy of a gallery. They are nicely furnished with antique queensize or twin beds, upholstered or wicker loveseats and chairs, thick carpeting and duvet comforters. All have private baths, TVs and telephones. We particularly liked a third-floor room with skylights, a view of the harbor, wicker chairs and a private deck. A full breakfast is served in a small front room with walls highlighted by hand-painted garlands of flowers. Tea and crackers are set out in the afternoon. Doubles, $125 to $145.

Sanford-Covell Villa Marina, 72 Washington St., Newport 02840. (401) 847-0206. This Victorian mansion has a wide piazza on three sides from which to take in the view of the water. An old-fashioned glider hangs on chains from the ceiling of the rear porch. Beyond is a small lawn with a saltwater pool and a jacuzzi, and beyond that a dock stretching into the harbor. That's enough for us, but the inside is an architectural dream — shortly after it was completed in 1870 by Boston architect William Ralph Emerson (cousin of Ralph Waldo Emerson), a Boston newspaper called it "the most elegantly finished house ever built in Newport." The four-story tower entry hall rises 35 feet to the ceiling above the fourth floor; small balconies project at several levels, and the stenciling is incredible. The original woods remain, as do many of the furnishings, including a dining set once owned by the founder of the U.S. Naval Academy at Annapolis. One guest room and a two-bedroom walk-out basement apartment have private baths; three rooms on the second floor share an enormous bath, though one room has a half-bath. A continental breakfast is served in the dining room beneath a ceiling with silver stars. Both guest rooms and public rooms are richly furnished by California owners Anne and Richard Cuvelier, descendants of an early owner. Doubles, $95 to $225; apartment, $300.

The Inn at Castle Hill, Ocean Drive, Newport 02840. (401) 849-3800. An out-of-the-way location atop a hill overlooking Narragansett Bay gives a sense of seclusion to this local institution that calls itself "a country inn by the sea." Innkeepers Paul and Betty McEnroe have decorated their fine Victorian inn with flair and sophistication, including well-aged oriental rugs, paintings by Newport artist Helena Sturdevant, and splashy coordinated prints on the wallpaper, draperies and almost everything else in the guest rooms. Seven of the ten rooms have private baths; most rooms are huge and have sitting areas with views of the bay. A continental breakfast is served in a lovely breakfast room. Guests (and the public) enjoy a stunning corner bar, whose tall windows take in a grand view of the bay, and the three-sided dining porch that juts out toward the water (there are two other dining rooms as well). The continental menu with a touch of nouvelle is priced from $22 to $28 for such entrees as dover sole and mallard duck with peppercorn sauce. Jackets are required for dinner. Lunch also is served in summer, and a Sunday jazz brunch on the lawn is popular. In summer, six motel-like units are available in the adjacent Harbor House. Eighteen barebone beach cottages, right on the water, are available by the week and rented a year in advance. Doubles, $80 to $180; suite, $225.

The Inntowne, 6 Mary St., Newport 02840. (401) 846-9200. Paul and Betty McEnroe's in-town version of their Inn at Castle Hill is centrally located at Thames and Mary streets. It, too, has a rooftop sundeck like those of so many downtown Newport inns. There are no elevators nor TVs in the 26 rooms, but there are telephones. All are ever-so-decorated in colorful matching fabrics, canopy beds, upholstered wing chairs and wicker furniture. Side rooms facing busy Thames Street and those on the third and fourth floors catch a glimpse of the harbor. The inn's nearby Restoration House at 20 Mary St. has a basement apartment and six upstairs rooms and suites. A continental breakfast of croissants and muffins is served amid antiques and oriental rugs in the inn's small dining room; tea and cookies are available in the afternoon. Doubles, $95 to $130; suites and apartments, $120 to $160.

The Pilgrim House, 123 Spring St., Newport 02840. (401) 846-0040. A panoramic view of the harbor is afforded from the large rear rooftop deck off the third floor of this Victorian B&B, owned by Pam and Bruce Bayuk. All but two of the eleven air-conditioned guest rooms have private baths — most of them small, in what used to be closets. Guest enjoy books and magazines in a pleasant living room with a fireplace. Continentnal breakfast is served at small tables in the third-floor hallway leading to the rooftop deck or on the deck itself. Doubles, $85 to $125. No smoking.

RENTALS. Rooms, condos, time-sharing units, waterfront houses and others are listed by Public Relations of Newport, 169 Broadway, 849-5325. Private Properties, 174 Bellevue Ave., 847-1331, also deals in rentals. Among seven reservations services are Access to Accommodations, 9 Broadway, 846-9443, and Newport Reservation Service, Box 518, 847-8878.

Seeing and Doing ⟋ᴖᴖ⟍

On or Near the Water

America's Cup Avenue and Thames Street are a sea of humanity in summer, as boat people and tourists jam the streets and the wharves that jut into the harbor at every opportunity. The harbor and Narragansett Bay are filled with powerboats and sailboats. Regattas are scheduled every summer weekend and sometimes during the week. The Newport Yachting Center off America's Cup Avenue is the scene of occasional boat shows and special events.

HARBOR CRUISES. Viking Tours, Goat Island Marina, 847-6921, offers one-hour sightseeing tours on its 48-passenger Viking Princess or its 140-passenger Viking Queen. Summer cruises leave daily at 10, 11:30, 1, 2:30, 4 and 5:15; fewer cruises off-season from mid-May to mid-October. Adults $6, children $3. The **M/V Amazing Grace,** Oldport Marine, America's Cup Avenue, 849-2111, gives one-hour narrated cruises of Newport from a marina adjacent to the Mooring restaurant daily in summer at 10:30, noon, 1:30, 3, 4:30, 6 and 7:30 (limited schedule in spring and fall). Adults $6, children $3. Billed as Newport's most luxurious excursion vessel, the **M/V Spirit of Newport,** 49 America's Cup Ave., 849-3575, sails from the former Treadway Inn marina at 11, 12:30, 2, 3:30, 5 and 6:30 in summer, reduced hours in spring and fall. Adults $6, children $3. **Newport International Sailing School and Cruises,** Goat Island, 683-2738, offers two-hour sailing cruises daily at 10, noon, 2, 4 and 6 for $20 per person; half-day sails are $40. The 42-foot sailing yacht **Copasetic,** Bowens Wharf, 846-0565, gives day sails for up to six people, $300 for a half day and $450 for a full day.

The Museum of Yachting, Fort Adams, Newport. (401) 847-1018. A special place for yachtsmen is this emerging museum that opened in 1985 in a 19th-century granite building on a point at the end of Fort Adams. The goal is to have a center of yachting, says retired marine historian Edward B. Smith, uncle of executive director Tom Benson; "in fact, as you look over the harbor in the summer, this is the center of yachting." Yachting costumes, memorabilia, photos, paintings and models trace the history of sailing inside what was once an Army mule barn. The fascinating photo exhibit called "The Mansions and the Yachts" focuses on the sailing roles of the Vanderbilts, Astors and Morgans ("while the women were here for the social life, this is what the men did," Ed Smith explained). The Hall of Ships displays old wooden boats beneath a model of the boat that won the first America's Cup perched near the ceiling. Upstairs is a Hall of Fame for Singlehanded Sailing and a library detailing ocean voyages. In the harbor is the the prized Shamrock V, captained by Sir Thomas Lipton as the 1930 America's Cup entry; called the last of the famed J-boats, it's considered the largest floating ship of its kind in the world. The museum sponsors the annual Classic Yacht Regatta on Labor Day weekend for older boats. The museum is small, but it's designed to appeal to laymen as well as sailors. Even if you're not into sailing, you'll get a feel for part of Newport's heritage and the hilly waterside site is spectacular. Open daily 10 to 5, mid-May through October. Adults, $2; family, $5. The museum has a new tour office in a rich wooden ship's cabin on Bannister's Wharf, selling tickets for a combination harbor launch trip with a museum admission for $5.

Fort Adams State Park, Fort Adams Road off Harrison Avenue, 847-2400. One of the largest seacoast forts in the nation and guardian of the head of Narragansett Bay from 1799 to 1945 is open to the public for picnicking, fishing, swimming and guided tours. Named for President John Quincy Adams, the fort was designed to accommodate 2,400 soldiers and 463 mounted cannons, and the fortifications can still be seen. The hilly point juts into the bay and provides as good a vantage point today for yacht-watching and the Newport skyline as it did for soldiers defending their country. Tours and garrison drills are given at times. Open daily during daylight hours; parking, $2.

Naval War College Museum, Coasters Harbor Island, Gate 1, Naval Education and Training Center, 841-4052. The U.S. Navy is such a presence here that Newport has come to be called "the campus of the Navy." So, of course, the first museum of its kind would be located here in Founders Hall (1820, first site of the Naval War College), a national historic landmark. Exhibits on the history of naval warfare and of the Navy in the Newport area are featured. Open June-September, weekdays 10 to 4, weekends noon to 4. Free.

Brenton Point State Park, Ocean Avenue. Benches are placed strategically all along a bluff for contemplating the ocean in this scenic prize of a park. Stairs lead down to the rocks, an area popular with fishermen, sunbathers and divers. The grounds along the shore contain parking lots, picnic areas with grills and restrooms, and on good days, kite-fliers are out in droves.

Ocean Drive. The ten-mile Ocean Drive is the East Coast's version of California's Seventeen-Mile Drive in Carmel. It meanders past rocky points with crashing surf, spectacular scenery that provides an awesome setting for equally spectacular mansions and contemporary homes, and a couple of beach clubs including the fabled Bailey's Beach where the 400 sun, swim and socialize.

The Cliff Walk. For an intimate look at the ocean and the backs of the mansions, the 3.5-mile Cliff Walk is a must. Although you can get onto the walk at several points, we prefer to start at the foot of Narragansett Avenue, where you walk down to the ocean on the Forty Steps, recently renovated by a new preservation group that also plans to offer guided walks. The first couple of miles are well-maintained and quite easy; the last part near Bailey's Beach requires good shoes and a stout heart since the path disappears and the going is rocky (we paid for our perseverance with torn stockings). You also must pass through a couple of dark, wet tunnels, and you may be greeted outside the fenced-in Doris Duke estate by a surly guard and the fiercest watchdogs ever. The faint-hearted might better take the first half of the walk and retrace their steps.

BEACHES. Most of the Ocean Drive beaches are private, but you can sunbathe in Brenton Point State Park. Those in the know also go to **Gooseberry Beach,** a private-public beach on Ocean Drive just west of Bailey's Beach; this family-oriented place with little surf charges $5 for parking on weekdays, $10 on weekends. For surf swimming, head for **Easton's Beach** (also known as First Beach), a wide and sandy three-quarter-mile strand from the Cliff Walk to the Middletown line. There's an amusement rotunda, and bathhouses may be rented. Parking costs $10. Beyond Easton's Beach in Middletown are **Second Beach** (where surfing is permitted) and **Third Beach** (parking, $5 to $10 a

193

day). **King Park** along Wellington Avenue in Newport is on a sheltered harbor with pleasant lawns, a pier, a good supervised beach for children, a raft with slides and a free bathhouse. **Fort Adams State Park** has a small roped-off area for swimming; parking $2. At all beaches, lifeguards work weekends starting Memorial Day, and daily from mid-June to Labor Day.

Other Attractions

Guided Tours. Viking Tours, Gateway Visitor Center, 847-6921, offers three different tours daily April-October, ranging from a 90-minute scenic tour past 150 points of interest (adults $10.50, children $7.50) to a deluxe four-hour mansion tour (adults $19.50, children $13). **Auto Tape Tours** of historic Newport can be rented for $10.50 at the Gateway Center. Art's Island Tours has auto tour tapes for $7, also available at Gateway Center.

Walking Tours. Newport is "a small town and if you really want to see it, get out of your car and walk," says the narrator in an audio-visual presentation at the Gateway Visitor Center. The Newport Historical Society, 82 Touro St., 846-0813, guides walkers through Colonial Newport, with visits to its **Wanton-Lyman-Hazard House** (1675), the oldest surviving house in Newport, and the 1699 **Friends Meeting House,** Newport's oldest religious structure. Tours leave Friday and Saturday at 10 in summer. Adults $4, children free.

Mansion Tours. The Preservation Society of Newport County, 118 Mill St., 847-1000, offers guided tours of its seven mansions and a topiary garden. The most visited is the 72-room **Breakers,** the summer home of Cornelius Vanderbilt and the most opulent of Newport's "cottages." It resembles a northern Italian palace and its vast lawn stretches down to the Cliff Walk. From its upper loggias, you can see the Elizabeth Islands far out to sea on a clear day, and you get to tour the kitchens and butler's pantry — an area larger than most houses.

Other choices are romantic **Rosecliff** of "The Great Gatsby" fame, whose living room doubled as a ballroom; William K. Vanderbilt's **Marble House,** where the hostess once gave a ten-course dinner party for 100 of her friends' dogs, and the museum-like **Elms,** with the finest of Newport's grounds. Also open are the 1852 **Chateau-Sur-Mer,** the 1748 **Hunter House,** and **Green Animals** in nearby Portsmouth, considered the best topiary garden in the country. If you've seen the grander mansions, you may like best the 1839 **Kingscote,** a charming Victorian which looks lived in and livable.

Mansion schedules vary: daily 10 to 5, May-September; limited schedules in April and October. Marble House, the Elms and Chateau-Sur-Mer open weekends from 10 to 4 in winter. Admission: Breakers, adults $7.50, children $3.50; other mansions, $6 and $3. Combination tickets run from any two ($11 and $4) to all eight ($32 and $10).

Several other mansions are open under private ownership. **Astor's Beechwood,** 580 Bellevue Ave., is perhaps the most extravagant. It's an 1851 Italian-style seaside villa that was home to the woman who coined the term "400" for the number her New York ballroom would hold. Mrs. Astor had 281 diamonds in her stomacher and looked like a walking chandelier, according to our guide. Open daily 10 to 5 June-December, weekends January-May; adults $5.50, children $4.25. **Belcourt Castle** (south end of Bellevue Avenue), now the home of the Tinney family, is shown by costumed guides and visitors may stay for tea. Open daily 9 to 5 or 10 to 4; closed Jan. 2-25; adults $5, children $2.

Hammersmith Farm, Ocean Drive, 846-0420. The 28-room Auchincloss mansion is where Jacqueline Bouvier Kennedy spent her summers and President Kennedy used one of the second-floor rooms as his Summer Oval Office. The home has more of a seaside country feeling than most Newport mansions and one of the nicer settings — across the island from Bellevue Avenue, overlooking a meadow to Narragansett Bay. We like the beautiful tiled fireplaces in almost every room, the lavish flower arrangements and the huge deck room, where a crowd of grownups and children could find their own niches. The grounds are worth a stroll, and there's a small gift shop in the old children's playhouse. Open daily 10 to 5, April-Nov. 11; 10 to 7, June-August; weekends in March and November. Adults $5.50, children $2.50.

International Tennis Hall of Fame, 194 Bellevue Ave., 849-3990. The stately Newport Casino, a masterpiece designed by Stanford White, was the home of the U.S. lawn tennis championships before they were moved to Forest Hills. Now it's the site of the world's largest tennis museum, housing displays and memorabilia covering more than a century of tennis history. Visitors can watch occasional tennis tournaments, see court tennis as played by Europeans in the 13th century, and play on one of the dozen well-maintained grass courts for a fee. Open daily 10 to 5, May-September; 11 to 4, rest of year. Adults $4, children $2.

Historic Sites. Newport has more than 400 structures dating from the Colonial era on Historic Hill and the Point. Among them: the 1763 **Touro Synagogue,** the oldest house of Jewish worship in the country; the Christopher Wren-inspired **Trinity Church** (1726), which has the second oldest organ in the country; the 1739 **Old Colony House,** locally believed to be the real Independence Hall (Rhode Island was the first colony to separate from Britain and the Declaration of Independence was read from its balcony); the 1748 **Redwood Library,** oldest in the country; the **Old Stone Mill** that some believe was built by Norsemen in the 11th century in Touro Park; the 1772 **Brick Market,** and the 1741 **Newport Artillery Company Armory and Museum,** headquarters of the oldest militia organization in America.

SHOPPING. With all its other attractions, one might not expect to find so many shopping opportunities, but Newport does not disappoint. The main shopping area is along Thames Street, Brick Market Place, and Bowen's and Bannister's wharves. Lately, the hot spots are along lower Thames Street, where shops are burgeoning out to the new Wellington Square and beyond, and Spring Street, home of some exotic galleries and boutiques. Bellevue Avenue near Memorial Boulevard is where the 400 used to shop and still do.

We enjoy browsing in the shops along the wharves: — **Marblehead Handprints, Spring Pottery, Laura Ashley, Crabtree & Evelyn, Sarah Elizabeth** (where cute country things are displayed amidst a wonderful spicy aroma), **Operculum** (a trove of shells, with seahorses and mermaids in the window), **Frillz** and **Mykonos** for Greek clothes and gifts. Pick up a T-shirt or sweatshirt, most with Newport insignia, at **Newport Breeze.** Facing each other across the plaza at Brick Market Place are **Resort Works** and **Beach Party,** both resort wear shops; farther along are **Davison's of Bermuda, Born in America** (contemporary crafts) and the **Book Bay.** Lower Thames is now worth a stroll, too, with lots of new (and ever-changing) shops. We liked the glazed tiles and unusual jewelry at **Tropea-Puerini.**

Along Spring Street, we were taken by **Lily's of the Alley** (a "fragrance factory"), the **Liberty Tree** for contemporary folk art, and the **Native American Trading Co.**

Where to Eat ⟋⟋⟋⟋⟋

Newport's concentration of yachtsmen, big-spenders, high society and tourists has spawned an enormous range and number of restaurants, with new ones popping up every year. Again we concentrate on those near the water.

Fine Dining

The Black Pearl, Bannister's Wharf. (401) 846-5264. The Commodore Room, whose small-paned windows overlook the water, dispenses contemporary cuisine (entrees from $16.50 for paillard of chicken with beurre blanc to $26 for entrecote au poivre or rack of lamb with roasted garlic and rosemary). More casual is the cozy and noisy **Tavern,** where people line up for the great clam chowder ($2.50 a bowl, and seemingly better every time we order it), crab benedict, a tarragon chicken salad and the famous pearl burger in pita bread with mint salad ($5.50). Most popular in summer is the outdoor patio, where you sit under colorful umbrellas and watch the world go by. You can get most of the tavern fare outside, with heartier entrees (Cape scallops, mandarin swordfish, calves liver and tenderloin bearnaise, $12.50 to $18.50) available inside at both lunch and dinner. Desserts are few but scrumptious. Although the service may be so fast as to make you feel rushed (the world's smallest kitchen serves up to 1,500 meals a day in summer), we've never been disappointed by the fare. Tavern and outdoor cafe open daily from 11; dinner in Commodore Room from 6. Closed early January to early February.

Le Bistro, Bowen's Wharf. (401) 849-7778. Regional American cuisine and an airy, elegant decor in the second-floor and third-floor dining rooms with windows toward the water make this fancier than the usual French bistro. We've enjoyed a fine salad nicoise ($7.25) and a classic bouillabaisse ($13.95) from a luncheon menu on which everything looks good. At night, the changing fare is among Newport's most interesting, priced from $9.95 for Burgundian sausages with hot potato salad to $22.95 for rack of lamb. Start perhaps with hot oysters and golden caviar ($6.95) and finish with Creole bread pudding or Ivory Coast chocolate rum cake. At our latest visit, a new French bistro menu had been introduced, featuring such specialties as cassoulet and pot au feu, $9.95 to $11.95. Lunch daily, 11:30 to 2; dinner, 6 to 11; bar menu, 11:30 to 11.

Clarke Cooke House, Bannister's Wharf. (401) 849-2900. Long considered one of Newport's finest and fanciest, the Clarke Cooke converted its main-floor dining room in 1990 into a bistro and lounge, yielding more space for casual fare at affordable prices. The stylish **Bistro** joins the existing downstairs **Candy Store Cafe,** more casual with marble-top tables and bentwood chairs. Both serve the same menu: things like burgers and black pepper fettuccine with shrimp and scallops, $5.75 to $12.95 at lunch; lamb stew and medallions of pork with cider gravy, $9.95 to $15.95 at night. Upstairs is a formal dining room called the **Skybar,** colorful in white and green, with banquettes awash with pillows beneath a beamed ceiling. In summer it opens to a breezy but elegant canopied upper deck with a great view of the waterfront. Entrees are priced from $21.95 for sauteed duck with pumpkin confit to $25.50 for rack of lamb with onion confit. Terrine of pheasant with foie gras and pistachios is one of the appetizers. Dessert might be cinnamon bread pudding with whiskey sauce or bittersweet chocolate torte with espresso cream. Bistro and cafe, 11:30 to 10 or 11 in season; off-season, lunch on weekends, dinner Wednesday-Sunday. Skybar, dinner nightly in season, 6 to 10 or 10:30, weekends in winter.

196

The White Horse Tavern, corner of Marlborough and Farewell Streets. (401) 849-3600. This is the oldest operating tavern in the United States (1673), beautifully restored by the Newport Preservation Society and now run as a fancy restaurant by Texas owners with sailing interests. Although our Colonial ancestors would be appalled by the prices, the warm and historic atmosphere captivates, particularly on chilly days or in winter. We've enjoyed lunch and dinner splurges here, but be forewarned, dinner entrees start at $21 for roasted chicken stuffed with prosciutto, mozzarella and spinach and rise into the high twenties for grilled barbarie duck, baked halibut with pistachios, roast loin of veal and beef wellington. The mixed green salad with goat cheese is $5, and the cheapest appetizers (roasted red pepper terrine or squash trilogy) are $7. At lunch, the shrimp tempura was $13 and tasty; the curried chicken salad was $8 and bland. Lunch, daily noon to 3; dinner, 6 to 10 (jackets and reservations required); Sunday brunch, noon to 3. Closed Tuesday in winter.

Seafood by the Water

The Mooring, Sayer's Wharf. (401) 846-2260. Ensconced in a building that once served as the New York Yacht Club, this has one of the best waterfront locations in town. The brick patio with blue umbrellas and an upper deck covered by a green and blue canopy take full advantage. If the weather's bad, sit inside by the windows or in a cozy area with a huge fireplace opposite the famed oak bar; beware, though, the curved-back chairs that rub you in all the wrong places are uncomfortable. A very spicy bloody mary served in a pilsener glass may help; the all-day menu, while extensive, may not excite you. For a late lunch on a summer Saturday, we only had to wait ten minutes for a table on the breezy patio as we eyed the abundant seafod salads and a monstrous one called simply "The Salad" ($5.50, to feed one to four) passing by. Our party of four sampled said salad, plus the seafood quiche with coleslaw, steamed mussels with garlic bread, half a dozen littlenecks, and a terrific scallop chowder we deem even better than the award-winning clam chowder. Inside, the dark tables are bare (without even a mat), the decor is nautical with old photographs and prints, and the Mooring is obviously popular. At our 1991 visit, the Mooring had acquired an adjacent property for use as a deli and chowder house. Lunch and dinner daily, 11:30 to 10 or 11. Closed in January.

The Deck, 1 Waites Wharf. (401) 847-2211. An island feeling is afforded by this relatively new establishment with a tropical plant-filled tent, its flaps up to let in the harbor breeze. It draws an avant-garde crowd to feast on things like tuna tempanade, grilled salmon with citrus sauce, chicken azteca and roasted duck with cranberry-orange sauce. The grill menu changes weekly, entrees starting at $7.25 for a vegetable platter and topping off at $14 for medallions of filet mignon with mushroom sauce. Appetizers run from $3.75 for pate to $5.75 for smoked salmon. With prices like these and a festive atmosphere, it's little wonder that this is the hottest place in town on a summer's evening. Dinner nightly in summer.

Dave & Eddie's, Brick Market Place. (401) 849-5241. This contemporary seafood grill and raw bar owned by a Mystic (Conn.) restauranteur purveys the freshest of seafood. It's fairly large, with a lounge, two dining rooms on several levels and an outdoor sidewalk cafe in the thick of things, though not by the water. For dinner, votive candles flickered on white tablecloths as we sampled a shrimp dish chosen for its proferred ginger (which we couldn't find a trace of) and a special of baked sole stuffed with crabmeat and artichokes that sounded more interesting than it tasted. Steamed new potatoes or rice and a fine winter medley of sauteed zucchini, snow peas, carrots and summer squash accompanied. The fresh fish specials (their origin is listed on the blackboard) are best; regular dinner entrees run from $13.95 for chicken picasso to $19.95 for lobster thermidor or broiled tenderloin with lobster meat and bearnaise. The seafood selection is extensive, from fried calamari to bouillabaisse (the seafood nachos are something different), and the wine list has some unusual offerings at appealing prices. Lunch daily from 11:30 to 4; dinner from 4 to 9:30 or 10:30. Closed Tuesday in winter.

Christie's of Newport, Christie's Landing, Thames Street. (401) 847-5400. This is Newport's oldest waterfront restaurant, evolving out of a fish market in 1941. The hostess said 450 people can be seated comfortably in the main red and white dining room, a tiered upstairs dining room, on the large outdoor deck or at picnic tables beside two shacks containing a raw bar and a cocktail bar on the pier. Pictures of famous visitors grace the walls, and Navy chaplains used to sit beneath a stained-glass window in the chaplain's corner. Dinner fare is standard steak and seafood, priced from $12.50 for chicken chasseur to $28 for the lobsterman's special (split and stuffed with scallops). Broiled swordfish, seafood pie and a clamboil are house specialties. Prices are relatively high (most lunch items are $5.50 to $11), but the tourist trade doesn't seem to mind. Lunch daily, 11:30 to 3:30; dinner 5 to 10 or 11.

Shore Dinner Hall, Waites Wharf. (401) 848-5058. Newport finally has a casual, inexpensive family seafood place to eat beside the water. Huge garage doors open onto the harbor at the rear of this cavernous room, connected to **Anthony's Seafood** market next door. You know the fish has to be fresh, and indeed it is — nothing fancy, but pleasantly priced by Newport standards. Lobster is featured: a lobster roll is $8.75, a 1 1/2-pound boiled lobster with clam cakes and corn on the cob is $12.75, and a full-blown lobster boil is $14.95. Also available are chowders, a raw bar, fried clams, fish and chips, hot dogs and fried chicken. Place your order at the front counter, pick a spot at the communal picnic tables, and sip a beer or glass of wine as you wait. This is Newport's version of the shore as it should be. Open daily, 11 to 10 or 11, April-October.

Other Choices

Scales & Shells, 527 Lower Thames St. (401) 846-3474. Retired sea captain Andy Ackerman cooks up a storm in an open kitchen near the door of this casual restaurant, almost as fast as his seafood can be unloaded from the docks out back. An enormous blackboard menu lists basic and exotic seafood in many guises. You'll find salmon, swordfish and shrimp grilled over mesquite, monkfish piccata, linguini with seafood in garlicky tomato sauce, and lobster fra diavolo (entrees, $9 to $16.50). Starters range from calamari salad to grilled clam pizza. Black and white-striped cloths cover the tables, and there's a raw bar. Dinner, Monday-Saturday 5 to 9 or 10, Sunday 4 to 9.

Amsterdam's Bar & Rotisserie, 509 Thames St. (401) 847-0550. A branch of the two Amsterdam's Rotisseries in New York City, this trendy place opened in a small storefront and quickly needed more space, moving in 1988 to the quarters formerly occupied by The Southern Cross. A casual place with red and white woven cloths and black lacquered chairs, it offers a new clubby lounge upstairs. Start with duck liver mousse with lingonberry sauce ($4.95) or smoked brook trout with freshwater caviar sauce ($5.50). Entrees ($8.95 to $15.95) include a roasted half chicken with fresh green herb sauce, grilled salmon with lobster-tarragon sauce, filet sandwich on toast, or Amsterdam's "grand salad" with zucchini, carrots, roasted peppers and roasted meats. Entrees come with a three-greens salad and fried potatoes. Desserts include mud cake and key lime pie. Egg dishes are added for the popular Sunday brunch ($11.95). Lunch daily, noon to 4:30 (Saturday only in winter); dinner, 5 to 11; Sunday brunch, 11:30 to 4.

Puerini's, 24 Memorial Blvd. West. (401) 847-5506. Chef-owner Dan Puerini's cafe-like restaurant packs in the crowds at twenty tables in two small tiled-floor dining rooms with lacy white cafe curtains. The Italian menu seldom changes. Pasta dishes are a gentle $8.95 to $9.95; chicken and shrimp dishes go up to $12.95. Linguini with pesto (voted best in the state), spinach fettuccine with boneless breast of chicken and artichoke hearts, and sole rolled and stuffed with pesto and crabmeat are some yummy entrees. Desserts include tartuffo, gelato and apple strudel. There's no liquor license but you may bring your own wine; espresso and cappuccino are available. Dinner nightly, 4 to 10 or 11. No credit cards.

The Rhumbline, 62 Bridge St. (401) 849-6950. For casual fare in informal surroundings, this bistro-like place with the nicely nautical name is a favorite with locals. Located away from the water in the historic Point section, it's off the tourist path. Oriental rugs on the wide-plank floors, old-fashioned lamps, woven tablecloths, and a wood stove in one corner and an old piano in another lend a cozy feeling. Entrees like curried chicken, baked sole with a chilled spinach remoulade, scallops provencale, wiener schnitzel and mixed grill are priced from $12.95 to $17.95. Burgers, sandwiches and salads are available on the tavern menu. Lunch, Monday-Friday 11:30 to 2, Saturday and Sunday to 5; dinner, 5 to 10 or 11.

Wave Cafe, 580 Thames St. (401) 846-6060. This small cafe and bakery is also the home of Ocean Coffee Roasters, with a large selection of beans and all the coffee accoutrements. The cafe is basically a takeout place but there are a few tables. Among the offerings are handmade bagels, a vegetable cheddar board, spinach ricotta pie, hummus, three-cheese calzone, pizzas, pesto bread and desserts so good they're supplied to other restaurants. Open for breakfast and lunch.

The Newport Star Clipper, 19 America's Cup Ave. (401) 849-7550 or (800) 462-7452. The backs of historic Newport structures and sections of Narragansett Bay can be glimpsed from this dinner train, which takes diners on a leisurely, three-hour ride up to Portsmouth and back. The trip brings back memories of the old days when meals on dining cars were the highlight of a train ride. The food is quite good (choice of Iowa prime rib, broiled swordfish or cornish game hen — plus soup, salad and dessert, when we dined). High beverage prices, tax and gratuity add considerably to the basic $42.50 tab. But the outing is fun — once. Reservations required. Departures nightly at 7, Sunday at 6.

FOR MORE INFORMATION: Newport County Convention & Visitor's Bureau, Gateway Center, 23 America's Cup Ave., Newport, R.I. 02840. (401) 849-8408 or (800) 458-4843.

Old drawbridge allows sailboat through and stops traffic in Woods Hole.

Falmouth-Woods Hole, Mass.

Falmouth is one of Cape Cod's largest towns, 44.5 square miles to be exact, with ten villages and 1,500 acres of saltwater bays. But it is the coastline that really impresses: 68 miles in all, much of it accessible, most of it picturesque.

Woods Hole is one of Falmouth's villages, seemingly an independent town in this southwest corner of the Cape, with its own style and substance. It is from Woods Hole that ferries embark for the island of Martha's Vineyard. It is in Woods Hole that marine science reigns: both the Woods Hole Oceanographic Institution and the Marine Biological Laboratories are headquartered here.

When one of us was a waitress in Woods Hole one summer during her college years, she referred to the area as "the armpit" of the Cape. For if Provincetown is the fist and Chatham the elbow, then Woods Hole and Falmouth are, well, the underarm.

The "pit" we would say or, about *our* town, the "hole." But even then, underneath all that youthful bravado and cynicism, we recognized its charms.

In the center of Woods Hole is Eel Pond, a picturesque saltwater harbor filled with sleek sailboats, small skiffs, wooden rowboats and a few honest-to-goodness lobstermen's vessels. In order for all but the tiniest of them to get out onto Vineyard Sound, they must wait for the hand-operated drawbridge that stops traffic on Water Street, the main drag, as they sail through — sometimes to the cheers or hoots of those who are waiting.

Water Street is a great place to find good restaurants and gourmet ice cream cones, handcrafted pottery and silkscreened T-shirts, and souvenirs of the oceanographic institution or the MBL, which dominate the town.

Their large brick and concrete buildings overshadow the rest of the gray clapboard Cape Cod architecture. It must be the Oceanographic's influence that makes Woods Hole seem, curiously, like an open-air college student center of the 1960s. Everywhere you go you find bulletin boards advertising rides, rents or relationships, hatha yoga classes and folk festivals.

All the women seem to wear wraparound Indian print cotton skirts and heavy leather sandals, long hair and dangling earrings. You can find the garb in a good local shop called From Far Corners.

Up in Falmouth proper things are more sedate. Here are splendid B&Bs and first-class restaurants. There are miles of roads to drive, many of them along the waterfront, with good vistas of Vineyard Sound and Buzzards Bay. There's an active harbor with daytripping boats to the Vineyard. Or you can take a sail around the Elizabeth Islands.

The beaches are good and quite accessible. You can tour historic houses, visit art galleries, and shop in one-of-a-kind stores. The variety alone makes the Falmouth-Woods Hole area so desirable.

Getting There

From Routes 3, 6, 25 or I-195, take the Bourne Bridge onto the Cape and follow Route 28 south to Falmouth and Woods Hole.

Where to Stay

The options are excellent. You can stay in a motel with a view of a tiny harbor in Woods Hole, in a glorious B&B on the green in Falmouth, or at a beach resort on Old Silver Beach. Try a Victorian B&B on the beach in Falmouth Heights or the venerable inn, the Coonamesset, in town. You can't go wrong.

Coonamessett Inn, Jones Road and Gifford Street, Falmouth 02541. (508) 548-2300. In 1796, in a rolling field that sloped toward a pond, Thomas Jones, a leading figure in Falmouth, constructed the original house and barn that were to become Coonamessett Inn. (The name is Indian: it means the place of the large fish.) During the 19th and 20th centuries, the place passed from one family to another until 1953 when Edna Harris purchased the property as the site for her famous Coonamessett Inn. The lady had style, and she imparted it to this comfortable and gracious spot. Now owned by the Josiah K. Lilly family, the red inn with white trim is situated on six acres of lush lawns and gardens overlooking scenic Jones Pond. The public rooms are particularly inviting with Colonial furnishings and colors, and the three dining rooms are highly rated (see Where to Eat). The 25 guest suites are comfortably furnished and kept up-to-date. On the premises is a tony clothing shop, **Marty Sullivan's,** with fashions for men and women with a New England weekend country look. A clambake buffet on Tuesday nights in winter is popular and you can enjoy drinks on an outdoor patio in warm weather. Doubles, $115 to $140.

Grafton Inn, 261 Grand Ave. South, Falmouth Heights 02540. (508) 540-8688. This oceanfront B&B is across the street from a good beach and has fine water views from many rooms. Liz and Rudy Cvitan take charge, Liz overseeing the day-to-day operations and Rudy on tap for repairs and renovations as needed. The result is an inviting, well-kept and creatively decorated spot, cooled by ocean breezes on even the hottest days. Wonderful breakfasts are served on the large enclosed front porch. Specialties of the house include Hawaiian french toast and blueberry pancakes. Most of the eleven airy rooms are on the second and third floors and all have private baths. Three turret rooms have especially interesting angles and good views; the Peach Cloud Turret on the top floor says it all. We also like Uncle Wallace's Room with its family touches and a portrait of Uncle Wallace on the wall. Extra pillows, English soaps and shampoos, and homemade chocolates at bedside before you turn in for the night are among Liz's special touches. Doubles, $65 to $90.

Peacock's Inn on the Sound, 313 Grand Ave., Falmouth Heights 02540. (508) 457-9666. Phyllis and Bud Peacock prepared to be innkeepers by managing several facilities around town. By 1989, when they converted a boarding house into this charming oceanfront B&B, they knew what they wanted and how to accomplish it. The living room provides an ocean view, a huge stone fireplace, color TV and seating areas for relaxing, conversing and taking breakfast. The front deck is great for sunny days and the ten guest rooms, all with private baths and two with fireplaces, are attractively decorated. All rooms have queen beds; some have an extra daybed as well. Almost all is blue and white in the public rooms; lots of blue and green with white shows up in the guest rooms as well, giving a cool, seaside feeling. A continental-plus breakfast includes fresh pastries made on the premises — perhaps muffins or cinnamon rolls or a specialty, Canadian bacon, spinach and eggs in a bread roll. Doubles, $75 to $98.

Sands of Time Motor Inn, Woods Hole Road, Woods Hole 02543. (508) 548-6300. One of the nicest motels we've seen, this has balconies or patios for all 33 units, a view from most rooms of an enchanting little harbor and a pool out back with lovely flowers all around. The large, rambling Harbor House to the rear, with weathered shakes and nine guest rooms, all with fireplaces, also offers great views. Some rooms have kingsize beds and some have kitchenettes for longer stays. All have TVs, telephones, private baths and air-conditioning. Innkeeper Susan Veeder offers complimentary coffee in the lobby to start your day. Doubles, $95 to $105. Motel open April-October, Harbor House year-round.

Palmer House Inn, 81 Palmer Ave., Falmouth 02540. (508) 540-8688. This Victorian B&B, located just off the green in the center of Falmouth, was taken over by Ken and Joanne Baker in 1990. The weathered brown house with white trim and red shutters and a large porch across the front offers eight guest rooms, all with private baths. They are inventively furnished and decorated, some with overhead paddle fans, and with ruffled curtains, floral designs, antique wicker and perhaps a brass or a four-poster bed. The original woodwork is gorgeous. "Breakfasts are our signature," says Joanne, a former accountant, who loves to cook. Guests dine at a large table in a lace-curtained dining room, perhaps on something as decadent as chocolate-stuffed french toast with vanilla sauce. Other possibilities include Finnish pancakes with strawberry soup and poached eggs on English muffins with a cheese and dill sauce. Doubles, $90.

Village Green Inn, 40 West Main St., Falmouth 02540. (508) 548-5621. Don and Linda Long have been providing hospitality at this large white inn with green shutters for half a dozen years. Located on one leg of the triangle-shaped village green, the inn has five guest rooms, including a two-room suite. All have large private baths and interesting fireplaces. The public rooms are soft and gracious and the wicker-filled porches are perfect for watching the world go by. Breakfasts are taken seriously by the Longs, who provide entrees like pecan pancakes, peach french toast and eggs benedict with cheese served on croissants. Don is a retired schoolteacher who grew up in the area and can help you find your way around. Doubles, $80 to $95.

Red Horse Inn Motel, 28 Falmouth Heights Road, Falmouth 02540. (508) 548-0053 or (800) 628-3811. This in-town motel is right across from the dock, a bonus for daytrippers to Martha's Vineyard. Grace and Bob Cashman took over an old inn some ten years ago and turned it into this well-run establishment. The 22 units are located in a two-story motel building or in the main building, which was renovated from the original inn. Six rooms have two queensize beds; the rest have a single queen and all have air-conditioning, color TVs, private baths and small refrigerators. There's a pleasant pool out back, and the flowers and plantings are stunning. The Cashmans offer parking permits granting access to some of Falmouth's nicest beaches. And, a special feature, guests can park free on their day of checkout and take off for a day on the Vineyard. Doubles, $86 to $94. Open April 15 to Nov. 15.

Sjoholm Bed and Breakfast Inn, 17 Chase Road, West Falmouth 02574. (508) 540-5706. Barbara Eck Menning left a nursing career in the mid-1980s to take over this fifteen-room inn. There are five rooms with private baths, six with semi-private, and four rooms in a separate building, the Sail Loft, which she describes as "one step up from camping." While she didn't give the inn its Swedish name, she is half-Swedish and plays out the theme. In a pretty dining room she serves a buffet breakfast that occasionally includes Swedish pancakes and might have quiches, muffins and other baked goods. She makes her own granola. The porch and living room serve as common areas. Maple chairs and tables and cozy seating groups lend a country feeling. Chapaquoit and Old Silver beaches are nearby. Doubles, $65 to $80, $45 in the Sail Loft.

Old Silver Beach B&B, 3 Cliffwood Lane, West Falmouth 02574. (508) 540-5446. Jack Kane is a schoolteacher; his wife, Beverly is the innkeeper for this small and personal B&B in the Old Silver Beach area (but not on the water). Located in a development of newish homes, the house offers three charmingly decorated guest rooms, along with a smashing glassed-in, wicker-filled room out back where a continental-plus breakfast of cereals, fresh fruit and homemade breads and muffins is served. Two upstairs bedrooms share one bath; one is twin-bedded and the other has an antique spool bed. A third room on the main floor is decorated with Laura Ashley fabrics and has a private bath. Doubles, $55 to $65.

Sea Crest, 350 Quaker Road, North Falmouth 02556. (508) 540-9400 or (800) 352-7175. Old Silver Beach, a glorious beach, is the major attraction at this resort, which has a long and interesting history. Television journalist Barbara Walters played on the sands here as a child when her father, Lou Walters, opened it as "The Latin Quarter" nightclub. Before that it was a summer theater. Recently this magnificent piece of real estate has been turned into a first-class resort with indoor and outdoor pools, a putting green, shuffleboard, day camp for kiddies, two lounges and entertainment, often in the form of Irish comedians. Meals are available in the dining room, but we'd choose European Plan to sample the area's many wonderful restaurants. The gorgeous beach and boardwalk are the real draws, and chaise lounges are lined up, waiting for the sunning hours.

The water is that of Buzzards Bay, but it often has such waves that surfers come here. The 266 rooms range in amenities but some are oceanfront; others have ocean views, several have fireplaces, and most have patios or sundecks. Light pine furniture and airy florals make the rooms seem country and cool. Doubles, $154 to $239 EP, add about $50 for MAP.

Seeing and Doing
Falmouth and Woods Hole are busy in summer. In addition to the options listed below, there are frequent antiques shows and flea markets, church suppers, bazaars, concerts, lectures and other special events.

Activities
BEACHES. Public beaches with parking available at a nominal fee are Menauhant Beach, East Falmouth; Old Silver Beach, North Falmouth; Surf Drive Beach, Falmouth, and Grew's Pond (freshwater) in Goodwill Park, Falmouth. Falmouth Heights Beach in Falmouth is open to the public but parking is by beach sticker only. Bathhouse facilities are available at Surf Drive and Old Silver beaches. In some cases, innkeepers can help with beach access.

Windsurfing is allowed on beaches only before 9 and after 5 for public safety. For information call the town beach committee at 548-8623.

BOATING. Falmouth Harbor is the embarkation point for frequent day sails to Martha's Vineyard. **The Island Queen,** 548-4800, ferries passengers only to Oak Bluffs in about a half hour and you can spend the day on the island. Round-trip fares: adults $8, children $4, bicycles $5.

Steamship Authority ferries, 540-2022, leave Woods Hole for 45-minute rides to Vineyard Haven in Martha's Vineyard. Round-trip fares: adults $8, children $4, bicycles $5.50.

Patriot Party Boats, 548-2626, offer several boat trips for fishing or scenic cruising from Falmouth Harbor. Particularly recommended are two-hour cruises to the Elizabeth Islands, which are strewn like pebbles offshore. These trips leave Monday-Friday at 2 and 4 and daily at 6 in midsummer. A sunset cruise at 6 runs from late spring into the fall. Adults $8, children $4. Talk to these people about the schooner day sails aboard the Liberte (three-hour trips cost $18 for adults, $12 for children), deep-sea and sport-fishing trips.

BIKING. One of the most glorious bike paths we've seen is the 3.6-mile paved Shining Sea Trail that runs from Locust Street and Mill Road in downtown Falmouth to Railroad Avenue in Woods Hole, with a couple of access points en route. Winding by breaking surf and quiet woodlands, this is a scenic and well-maintained route and bikers love it. There are connections with routes heading north and east as well.

Places of Interest
Falmouth's **Village Green** is a picturesque, triangular-shaped parcel on which the militia trained in 1749. The houses surrounding it are pretty and in the Congregational Church is a Paul Revere bronzed bell.

The **Falmouth Historical Society,** Palmer Avenue, 548-4857, opens two 18th-century restored houses on the village green for guided tours. The **Julia Woods House** is a dignified Colonial house built in 1790 by Falmouth's famous early physician, Dr. Francis Wicks, who served as a medical corpsman in the

Revolutionary War. The house has one of the town's few remaining widow's walks. Interesting exhibits include original 18th-century scenic wallpaper brought from Paris, period furniture, antique hooked rugs, an extensive handmade quilt collection, toys and dolls, and a restored kitchen with fireplace and early utensils. The **Conant House Museum** has mementos of whaling days, a military exhibit, a shell collection and a large collection of china, silver and glass. The Katharine Lee Bates room contains the society's collection of books and pictures pertaining to the writer of the song, "America the Beautiful." (The house Katharine Lee Bates lived in is near the village green but is occupied by private owners; a placard identifies it.) The Hallett Barn out back displays early tools and farm implements and houses the society's gift shop. Open Monday-Friday 2 to 5 in summer; Wednesday 9 to 11:30 and Friday 9 to 4, rest of year. Donation.

Hiking and Nature Trails. Wooded trails excellent for short walks or day-long hikes and picnicking wind through the villages of Falmouth. Some of the most popular include Beebe Woods, Washburn Island, Salt Pond Sanctuary, Crane Wildlife Reserve and Goodwill Park. The **Ashumet Holly and Wildlife Sanctuary** on Ashumet Road near the intersection with Currier Road (close to Route 151) is a 45-acre site operated by the Massachusetts Audubon Society. It is renowned for the holly collection assembled by the late Wilfred Wheeler, the first state agriculture commissioner early in this century. The reservation has several easy-to-travel nature trails that lead through groves of ornamental and native trees. The area is also known for its large colony of barn swallows, observable in summer.

Band concerts are offered free on Thursday evenings in July and August at the Harbor Band Shell in Falmouth.

WOODS HOLE. A small waterfront park in Woods Hole has benches and is a good place to relax by the water and maybe eat an ice cream cone. You can watch the harbor activity and sometimes see vendors painting on T-shirts.

Wander around to watch the drawbridge and boat traffic, view Eel Pond, browse through the shops and participate in special events mounted because of the large scientific community here (the Oceanographic Institution and Marine Biological Laboratory have more than 1,000 employees). The **Church of the Messiah** on Church Street is the setting for many evening concerts, usually free or by donation; we heard two classical guitarists at one such event. A guided walk for illuminating Woods Hole history is conducted weekly during July and August by the Woods Hole Historical Collection, 548-7270. The Woods Hole Oceanographic Institution maintains a small museum in the village.

National Marine Fisheries Service Aquarium, Water and Albatross Streets, 548-7684. Two frisky seals, Cecil and Skeezix, splash in their own pool outside this interesting research/information/education aquarium at the west end of Water Street. Inside you can view various fish species in their water tanks. Even more interesting is the "Behind the Scenes" area out back, where you can see an enormous blue lobster, look at a starfish under a microscope and touch all sorts of sea life, including hermit crabs and horseshoe crabs. Open daily in summer, 10 to 4:30; rest of year, Monday-Friday 9 to 4. Free.

SHOPPING. They do their own silk screening on T-shirts at **Howlingbird** on Palmer Avenue in Falmouth and the designs are especially nice. Check this shop for unusual women's sportswear as well. Across the street is **The Bird Store**, a good place to buy decoys, feeders, wild bird food and gifts for ornithologists. At the corner of Route 28 and Palmer Avenue is the **Cape Gallery of Contemporary Art** with work by artists from across the Cape.

In the center of Falmouth check out **Marshmallow,** especially its kitchenware shop where a great collection of cookbooks, neat napkin rings, fun refrigerator magnets and sophisticated crockery are to be found. **Soft as a Grape** has fancy T-shirts, some hand-painted, and you can get your Geiger wear at **Cynthia Gardner.** Sophisticated women's clothing is also found at **Panache,** while men gravitate next door to **Maxwell & Co.**

Check out **Marty Sullivan's** at the Coonamessett Inn. It's the place to get those preppy pants with the embroidered whales.

In Woods Hole, **Handworks** — a cooperative gallery of fine arts — has tasteful handmade items of all sorts. We especially liked the fish design platters by Pat Warwick. **Liberty House** sells terrific contemporary women's clothing. The **Market Bookshop,** a branch of a Falmouth establishment, is downstairs from **Under the Sun,** and next door to **From Far Corners,** both with good jewelry and that Indian cotton stuff, from skirts to bedspreads. Mosey along Route 28A for more shopping and antiquing.

Where to Eat _____ ⚭⚭⚭

The range of dining is broad, from a little clam shack where you can eat fried fish to a couple of restaurants that rank among the best restaurants on the entire Cape. There are places to get luscious ice cream cones and frozen yogurt or breakfast with homemade breads and a gourmet deli.

Falmouth

Domingo's Olde Restaurant, Route 28A, West Falmouth. (508) 540-0575. Domingo Pena, a Cape Verdean who came to the States when he was young, has established a wonderful restaurant in this pretty section of town. The two-story, dark wood frame house used to belong to his grandfather; in it are three attractive dining rooms with bare wood floors, blue tablecloths, fresh flowers on the tables and white stucco walls. The room on the second floor tucked under the rafters seems especially popular; early diners gravitated there first one Saturday evening in summer. Cape Cod Life magazine called Domingo one of the eleven best chefs on the Cape in 1989. Diners can start with oysters or cherrystone clams on the half shell, escargots provencale or mussels baked in white wine ($1.50 to $6.50) or a cup of the signature clam chowder. Seafood is emphasized; among the most popular dishes are the fish and chips fried in a seafood batter at $9.50 and the bouillabaisse, prepared to order, at $17.25. Fresh haddock Portuguese, Domingo's specialty, is prepared with celery, tomatoes, green peppers, herbs and white wine. On the back of the menu are the non-seafood items: veal marsala, veal piccata, chicken francais, New York steaks and a vegetable plate. There is also a children's menu. Finish your meal with mud pie, sabayon cake or natural ice cream and waddle home. Dinner nightly, 4 to 11.

The Regatta of Falmouth, end of Scranton Avenue, Falmouth. (508) 548-5400. Located right on the water in what looks like a low, weathered yacht club building with jaunty striped awnings, this is one of two Regattas (the other is in Cotuit) with the same owners and seriousness of purpose. This is Wendy and Brantz Bryan's original and has gained a reputation for being one of the very best on the Cape. Its harborfront location allows you to have a pleasant walk to look at some of the boats before or after dinner, and once inside the simple but sophisticated pink and white dining room, you'll probably have a water view from your table. Among appetizers ($4 to $8.50), you might start with fried calamari in a lemon verbena mayonnaise or grilled shrimp with a relish of cucumber, coriander and red pepper. Entrees ($14 to $25) might involve such choices as veal fettuccine with veal and shiitake mushrooms in a madeira cream sauce, seared Norwegian salmon with Cotuit Bay oysters in a leek and chardonnay sauce, or oven-roasted monkfish in a rosemary and juniper berry vinaigrette. Dinner nightly from 5:30. Open May-September.

Coonamessett Inn, Jones Road and Gifford Street, Falmouth. (508) 548-2300. The Coonamessett has three dining rooms: the main Cahoon Room, known for its Ralph Cahoon whimsical mermaid paintings on the walls; the Garden Room, trellised and summery, used for lunch and Sunday brunch, and Eli's, an informal dining area for lunch and dinner near the bar. The Vineyard Room, with a fireplace and a cozy feeling, is part of the main dining room and is especially inviting on a cool evening. The chicken pot pie is a house specialty, available at lunch and in Eli's. Dinner in the Cahoon Room might start with Cape Cod lobster cake, served with creole mayonnaise and roasted red pepper sauce, or sliced breast of smoked duck with raspberry vinaigrette (appetizers are in the $7.50 range). Or sample the chilled vichyssoise or the award-winning lobster bisque. Entrees ($15 to $20) include grilled native sea scallops, sauteed chicken with chardonnay-lemon-basil sauce, seafood newburg and roast rack of lamb with roasted garlic, shallots and a port wine sauce. Lighter fare in **Eli's** ($10 to $15) includes barbecued baby back ribs, lobster pot pie, open-face steak sandwich and pasta of the day; sandwiches and burgers are served from 11:30 a.m. to closing. Lunch daily, 11:30 to 2:30; dinner, 5:30 to 9:30.

Lawrence's, Nantucket Avenue, Falmouth Heights. (508) 548-4441. Falmouth's oldest restaurant has been in business for nearly 100 years in this stone building with huge brick fireplaces, hand-hewn timbers and a delightful outdoor patio enclosed by high stone and stucco walls. Now owned by Gayle and Jim Carroll and their family, the restaurant is set back one block from the beach and has a dark, cool, end-of-the-day feeling for dinner, the only meal served. Select from a host of seafood starters ($2 to $7): stuffed quahogs, quahog chowder, cherrystone clams on the half shell, shrimp cocktail and clams casino. Try pasta as an appetizer or an entree, including pasta primavera or linguini with clam sauce ($9 to $10 for the larger portion). Among entrees ($11 to $19) are surf and turf (petite filet mignon accompanied by twin baked stuffed shrimps), roast duckling with a spiced fruit sauce, scrod newburg, shrimp scampi or a lobster fest (lobster on a bed of steamers). Dinners include a trip to the salad bar, homemade rolls, and a starch or vegetable. Dinner nightly, 6 to 10, May-October.

The Golden Swan, 323 Main St., Falmouth. (508) 540-6580. Innkeepers say their guests rave about this restaurant in the heart of the retail district. Though it sounds as if it might be Chinese, it offers continental fare at competitive prices. Ingrid Mruseh opened the restaurant about ten years ago. Pink dominates the color scheme, but subtly: tablecloths are deep pink and a carpet is patterned in black and pink. The captain's chairs are sturdy and entrees have proved their staying power. Veal is considered the house specialty and veal Golden Swan (medallions sauteed with finely chopped mushrooms and shallots and glazed with mozzarella) is popular. Other options include veal marsala or St. Peter, the latter sauteed with scallops, mushrooms and shallots, and finished with a madeira brown sauce. Chicken with dill sauce, wiener schnitzel, broiled scallops and seafood medley are among the possibilities in the $12 to $17 range. Fettuccine alfredo is offered as an appetizer or entree. Other appetizers ($2 to

$4.50) include onion soup au gratin, marinated herring and New England clam chowder. Sacher torte is one of the dessert favorites. Dinner nightly, 5 to 10.

The Wharf, Grand Avenue, Falmouth Heights. (508) 548-0777. Advertised as "Falmouth's only oceanfront dining on the beach," this popular and casual place is right at Falmouth Heights beach. The rambling white wooden building with green awnings is very atmospheric, a real down-by-the-sea kind of spot where the bar dominates the dining room and all sorts of memorabilia — from lobster buoys to driftwood — constitute the decor. The large, well-patronized bar is enclosed in what looks to be a lobster shanty and nautical charts are varnished onto the tabletops in the dining room. We're not sure what the moose head is doing here, unless it's to advertise the ale. There's an outdoor deck right above the water and many of the inside tables have water views. At lunch you can have steamers, chicken wings, shrimp cocktail or stuffed quahog to start ($2 to $7). The Wharf chowder, served in a crock, is particularly thick and quite filling along with the house salad, a mediocre but passable bowl of greens. French fries and coleslaw come with the meals: fish and chips, fish filet, barbecued pork ribs and lobster salad roll in the $4 to $6 range. At night, prices are $9 to $15 for the likes of shrimp scampi, fried clams, seafood pot pie, fisherman's platter and pasta of the day. Chocolate truffle mousse and chocolate chocolate mousse are among the rich desserts. Lunch daily, 11:30 to 4; dinner from 5.

Laureen's, 205 Worcester Court, Falmouth. (508) 540-9104. When you feel like a little something different, consider lunch or teatime here. Located in a strip shopping center in the middle of town, this is both a gourmet shop and a restaurant. For lunch ($5 to $7), Laureen Palanza offers daily specials like fresh vegetable and pasta stir-fry with hummus and flatbread, Vermont country lamb pate with French bread and sweet pickles, or a crab and red pepper mousse served with a salad and French bread. Sandwiches can be smoked turkey or ham on a variety of breads and there are pizzas, too. Homemade brownies, fresh blueberry pie or a sour cream pound cake with berries and whipped cream might finish the meal. For afternoon tea, Laureen's serves freshly baked scones with cream and preserves, assorted finger sandwiches and desserts with a choice of teas. Lunch, Monday-Saturday 11:30 to 2:30; tea, 3 to 5. Closed Sunday.

The **Clam Shack** at Falmouth Harbour is perfect for clam, lobster and shrimp rolls, french fries and the like, eaten outdoors at picnic tables on a tiny grassy plot or inside at simple wooden booths. The **Hearth and Kettle** is a family restaurant considered consistently good and affordable.

Woods Hole

Fishmonger's Cafe, 50 Water St., Woods Hole. (508) 548-9148. This natural-foods restaurant established in the mid-1970s is ensconced in a weathered gray building overlooking the harbor and drawbridge activity. Some seats have quite interesting views of the water. Bare, polyurethaned wood tables with fresh flowers, candles in hurricane lamps and simple wood chairs offer an informal environment for some very good food. A blackboard menu lists daily specials, such as a cold chicken and noodle luncheon plate, which was outstanding, or a Middle Eastern plate with hummus, tabouli and Syrian bread — a house favorite. Among other lunchtime specials ($6 to $7.50) were a Bombay tuna salad made with walnuts, raisins, apples, onions and celery; grilled marinated chicken salad, and fresh berry fritters. For dinner, you might start with blue and white corn chips and salsa, clam chowder, gazpacho or a half dozen fresh shucked oysters ($3 to $7). The salad can be dressed with lemon tahini, blue cheese, creamy garlic or vinaigrette, all homemade. Vegetarian entrees ($6.50 to $8) include avocado tostada, rice and refried beans, and tofu and vegetables. Other entrees ($9 to $15) might be fisherman's stew in an herbal tomato broth, chicken California (fried breast covered with guacamole, melted muenster cheese, tomatoes, sour cream and sprouts) and fish and chips. Desserts are ample: hot fudge sundae, a smoothie (fresh fruit and frozen yogurt blended with your choice of juice) and homemade pies and cakes. Open daily in season, 11:30 to 10.

The Captain Kidd Waterfront Dining Room, 77 Water St., Woods Hole. (508) 548-8563. With blue tablecloths on the tables, windsor chairs, barnboard walls, wood floors and large doors opening out onto Eel Pond, this is a cool and inviting environment for upscale dining. Head chef Jim Murray gets good marks for the food, which is a bit pricey, but this is one of those places for a big night out. Appetizers ($6 to $9) might be wild mushroom strudel, steamed clams, tortellini with pesto and cream, and smoked seafood plate. Entrees ($11 to $26) include pasta and scallops provencale, broiled seafood kabob, bluefish oriental, rack of lamb and grilled duck breast. Dinner nightly, 6 to 11; reservations taken after 5:30.

Shuckers World Famous Raw Bar, 91A Water St., Woods Hole. (508) 540-3850. Walk down a driveway to get to this popular spot at the edge of Eel Pond with tables indoors and out. In addition to an all-day menu, certain entrees are served after 6. You can get sandwiches and salads any time, as well as raw-bar items sold by the piece (80 cents each for clams and oysters). Seafood chowder and seafood gumbo are on the menu, as are grilled shrimp and shrimp scampi (all daytime items in the $5 to $7.50 range). In the evening, try things from the mesquite grill (such as chicken lemon pepper, sirloin steak, barbecued ribs and yellowfin tuna, $11 to $14) or such entrees ($11 to $15) as seafood newburg, cioppino naturale and haddock au gratin. On Tuesday evenings, twin boiled lobsters with mussels, steamers and corn are the special. Open daily, noon to 10.

Landfall, 2 Water St., Woods Hole. (508) 548-1758. The location close to the ferry terminal could not be better and this restaurant, run by the sons of founder David Estes, has been thriving for nearly 50 years. The building has not changed in at least 30. Here are your wood tables and captain's chairs, wood floors, a bar made from a dory, beams taken from a Gloucester dock, lobster pots and lamps hanging from the ceiling, and french doors across the front opening directly onto the water. When one of us was a waitress here in the 1960s, the place was jumping with high turnover and good tips. That feeling remains and while the food may not be gourmet, it is solid, predictable and apparently what a lot of people want. For lunch you can have jumbo sandwiches (from $3.50 for grilled cheese and tomato to $10 for lobster salad) or fried foods like chicken fingers, seafood platter, fried chicken in a basket, fried clams or scallops, all priced around $5 to $6.50. Naturally Cape Cod clam chowder is on the menu. In the evening, entrees ($13 to $19) include baked stuffed shrimp, broiled scallops, broiled scrod, barbecued baby back ribs and "land and sea" (ten ounces of prime sirloin steak plus twin stuffed shrimp). Open daily, 11 to 10, late May to mid-September.

FOR MORE INFORMATION: Falmouth Chamber of Commerce, Academy Lane, Falmouth, Mass. 02541. (508) 548-8500 or (800) 526-8532.

Sea captains' homes are on view from observation deck at Edgartown harbor.

Martha's Vineyard, Mass.

We have come to the Vineyard in the sun and in the rain, in fog and in storms, in summer and autumn and in the late spring (never, yet, in winter).

Each time, it has presented a different face. Once, we arrived on the ferry to Oak Bluffs in pea-soup fog, a few hours before a hurricane was scheduled to hit. Later in the day the rain and the wind pounded the island and at night we joined others at South Beach to watch the storm's fury. Another time we took the ferry across Vineyard Sound at noon on such a hot day that we were sunburned in the 45 minutes it took to cross.

The first trip to the island for one of us was during a summer in college, when we'd lined up a job as a waitress at an Edgartown hotel (now a posh resort). Between serving three meals a day, there was time for swimming and sunning at Lighthouse Beach across the road. At night there were bonfires and beach parties and the Firemen's Ball. There were afternoons spent at the Gay Head cliffs, and evenings spent rowing around Edgartown Harbor. There was Illumination Night in Oak Bluffs. In September, back at college, it all seemed magical and a little unreal.

It is those feelings of magic and unreality that have consistently drawn visitors to Martha's Vineyard. Its variety alone, from the beautiful old whaling homes and brick sidewalks of Edgartown to the wildly colored gingerbread cottages and honky-tonk of Oak Bluffs, suits many moods. There is busy, bustling Vineyard Haven (so busy on a rainy summer day that you might as well forget it) and charming, picture-perfect Menemsha, the only true fishing village on the island. There are those gorgeous, high clay cliffs at Gay Head, a town in which many residents are of Indian descent, and there are surprisingly agricultural Tisbury and Chilmark. There are fabulous beaches, fine restaurants, scores of guest houses and inns, paved bikeways, wonderful shops and good harbors. And everywhere, there is the sea.

Because of all it has to offer, Martha's Vineyard has been discovered. The rich and the famous — Jackie Onassis, Mike Wallace, Art Buchwald and Patricia

Neal among them — own summer homes. Condominiums crowd close to South Beach, where once there were just dunes and beach grass. Summer rentals are sky high and accommodations and dining are not cheap. The cars and the clothes attest to the affluence of the visitors.

If you want a summer vacation away from it all, you'll be hard-put to find it on the Vineyard in season; wait until the fall, which is luscious. But if you don't mind crowds and having to make ferry reservations for your car months in advance, if you're willing to share your sidewalk when you shop and your beach when you swim, then you will love the Vineyard in summer.

Move beyond the annoyance of the masses and focus on what brought you here in the first place. You will enjoy the sunning and the surfing, the gorgeous views and the wonderful walks. You'll dine well and enjoy sophisticated shopping. You'll sleep deeply and awaken to the scent of the sea. The island will exert its hold on you.

Getting There

The ferry from Woods Hole is the most popular way to reach the island, although it has an airport with scheduled flights from major East Coast cities. There are also ferries from New Bedford, Falmouth and Hyannis (passengers only).

The Woods Hole, Martha's Vineyard and Nantucket Steamship Authority, Box 284, Woods Hole 02543. (508) 540-2022. Approximate costs for cars are $30 each way; for passengers, $4 each way. Reservations for cars must be made far in advance, especially for late June through early September. The trip from Woods Hole to Vineyard Haven takes approximately 45 minutes and departures are frequent. Four boats a day operate between Woods Hole and Oak Bluffs.

From Falmouth, the **Island Queen,** (508) 548-4800, makes several sailings daily to Oak Bluffs; round trip, $9. From Hyannis, the **Hy-Line,** (508) 775-7185, operates a passenger boat to Oak Bluffs three times a day in summer. Adults $10, one-way; children $5.

From Hyannis and New Bedford, planes from Edgartown Air, (508) 627-9631, fly to Martha's Vineyard. You also can take Continental Express, (800) 525-0280, from Boston or New York.

Where to Stay_____/ℭℭℭ_

Larger than most people realize (twenty miles long and nine miles wide), the island is full of delightful B&Bs and inns. Your lodging choice will depend on location and style. Many visitors like to stay in Edgartown because of the charming old whaling homes, colorful harbor and good shopping; if you don't have a car, that's a good choice because there's so much to do on foot. Be advised, however, that the beach is a bit of a hike; you'll have to take the shuttle bus, which runs frequently, or perhaps a bike or moped.

Oak Bluffs, the first real resort town of the island, was given that status because of the religious enthusiasts who developed a Methodist Camp Meeting. The ornate, colorful gingerbread cottages near the present-day Tabernacle are a must for the sightseer. Oak Bluffs has several B&Bs, plus a couple of larger summer hotels. There's a nice beach within walking distance (this is the Vineyard Sound side of the island) and a movie theater, merry-go-round and funky shops.

Vineyard Haven is more commercial, but in recent years tony shops and restaurants have found their way onto its main street. Most of the ferries land here, which makes it a convenient location. You'll have to ask about the small beaches nearby, or take a longish drive to the island's south-side ocean beaches, which are favored by most visitors. There are some fine places to stay.

Menemsha is charming and small. There's a beach in town and if you're staying in a local inn, you'll probably be given a beach pass to the wonderful Lucy Vincent Beach.

Vineyard Haven

Thorncroft Inn, Main Street, Box 1022, Vineyard Haven 02568. (508) 693-3333 or (800) 332-1236. Lynn and Karl Buder, formerly of Simsbury, Conn., said goodbye to the corporate life and opened this fine inn just a mile up Main Street, toward West Chop. Previously the Haven Guest House, the name was changed in 1986 to reflect the inn's origin as part of the Thorncroft Estate owned by a Chicago grain merchant in the early part of the century. This house, which was used to accommodate relatives and dignitaries visiting Thorncroft, was built in 1918 and is described as a classic craftsman bungalow. In recent years, Thorncroft has been expanded and upgraded to include the five-room Carriage House out back plus the Greenwood House buildings — two structures a short distance away. Now there are twenty guest rooms in four buildings with gorgeous appointments: wood-burning fireplaces in many rooms (for use only between September and June), jacuzzis (some for two people), Louis Nicole wallpapers and canopied beds, turndown service and thirsty beach towels. The Boston Globe is delivered to your room daily and all rooms are non-smoking to preserve their freshness. From the moment you step into the parlor of the main inn, with its dark wicker furniture, rose carpeting and small flowered rug in front of the fireplace, you'll know you are someplace special. Thorncroft is one of the few Vineyard inns to serve a full breakfast and Karl is proud of theirs: almond french toast, quiche lorraine and unusual egg dishes are on the menu. New in 1990 was dinner for inn guests only, prepared and served by Cindy and Jeff Medeiros, she a graduate of the Culinary Institute of America. Among entrees were blue diamond sole, coated with nuts and served with a lemon-ginger sauce, and veal with wild mushrooms, peppers and brandy. There was some thought that eventually meals might be made available to the public by reservation. Until then, only house guests get to enjoy all this indulgence and pampering. Doubles, $159 to $249. No smoking.

The Tisbury Inn, Main Street, Vineyard Haven 02568. (508) 693-2200. This is the place to stay if you want to be smack dab in the middle of things. The 29 rooms located on the second and third floors of the inn are decorated in pastel colors such as yellow, lilac and peach, with bright quilted spreads on the mostly queensize beds. Rooms have been upgraded by owner Sherman Goldstein and all have private baths and cable TVs. There's a 42-by-22-foot indoor pool and health center. A complimentary continental breakfast, with pastries and muffins, is set out for guests each morning. Step out the door and you're on Vineyard Haven's busy Main Street, a short walk from the ferry and accessible to almost everything. You can rent a beach towel for a dollar. This is not a fancy place, but it's clean and central. The cafe that adjoins serves breakfast, lunch and dinner — an added convenience. Doubles, $85 to $105.

Hanover House, 10 Edgartown Road, Box 2107, Vineyard Haven 02568. (508) 693-1066. Mark Hanover — with help from his accommodating mother — runs this pleasant inn, located a bit out of town. Since opening in 1979, he has renovated twice and now has fifteen rooms, including five housekeeping units. A wicker-filled front sun porch, decorated in shades of blue and peach, is where a continental breakfast is served to guests. Several rooms in the main house, plus a few units in another building separated by a terrace, are decorated mostly in earth tones. All accommodations feature private baths and color TVs; guests also can use picnic tables and barbecue grills outside. Doubles, $103 to $114; efficiencies, $130 for two, $145 for four.

North Tisbury

The Bayberry, Old Courthouse Road, North Tisbury (address: RD 1, Box 546, Vineyard Haven 02568). (508) 693-1984. Rosalie Powell, an island native and descendant of Thomas Mayhew, the first settler, runs this exceptional B&B located in a charming Cape Cod house that looks antique but is not. A former home economist, Rosalie opened the Bayberry in the early 1980s. When we visited one summer morning, she was ironing linens in front of the huge fireplace in her keeping room-kitchen. Guests are served a full breakfast there or on the brick terrace outside. Rosalie had just made a favorite, "Dream Boats," puffy pancakes filled with fresh fruit and yogurt. Other breakfasts might be blueberry waffles, omelets or souffles. She also sees that all rooms have fresh flowers. Three of the five guest rooms have a private bath and two have semi-private. Upstairs, a blue and pink room with private bath, a kingsize bed and heart-shaped, lace-edged pillows is perfect for honeymooners. The setting is bucolic — there's a horse in the pasture next door. Doubles, $90 to $130.

The Farmhouse,, State Road, North Tisbury (address: Box 531, RFD, Vineyard Haven 02568). (508) 693-5354. Kathleen Hold, who is a school teacher in Cold Spring, N.Y., spends summers as the proprietor of this attractive and homey B&B. Five double rooms include one queen-bedded room with private bath and four rooms sharing two baths. The guest living room, with its wide floor boards, has a table where a family-style breakfast is served — usually homemade muffins, juices, fresh fruits and tea and coffee. A private outdoor shower with hot water is appreciated by returning beach bums. Next door is **The Roadhouse,** a quite good restaurant. Doubles, $55 to $75. Open June-September.

Chilmark

Breakfast at Tiasquam, off Middle Road, Chilmark 02535. (508) 645-3685. Ron Crowe, a former food-service manager at Bowdoin College in Maine, now does his own food service (ample breakfasts) at this large new house set back a quarter mile into the woods in the western part of the island. Corn and blueberry pancakes or cinnamon french toast might be on the menu for guests who occupy six guest rooms, two with private baths. Fancy tilework in bathrooms, cherry wood trim, and skylights and decks make this a somewhat contemporary experience in a house that looks, from the outside, quite traditional. Hammocks and swings add to the restful environment and it would be easy to imagine spending most of your vacation right here. A loft accommodating four children allows for parental privacy. Doubles, $95 to $150. Two-night minimum in season. No smoking.

Menemsha

Menemsha Inn and Cottages, Box 38, Menemsha 02552. (508) 645-2521. Twelve cottages, a new nine-room inn and six luxury suites in a recently added Carriage House form an attractive complex on eleven acres. They're set back from the road, approached by a dirt driveway, above the fishing village of

Menemsha. Richard and Nancy Steves run a homey operation at a place that has been welcoming visitors for about 50 years (Alfred Eisenstadt, the Time-Life photographer, has been coming for most of them). People rent cottages for a week at a time; inn rooms may be available for shorter periods, along with the smashing new suites that have sitting areas and beautiful private decks. Almost all have distant water views. The complex spreads over the hillside in a treed meadow, down toward a beach. All but two cottages have water views; only two inn rooms do. While there is a rustic, camplike quality to the cottage setting, the cottages themselves are bright and attractive with floral bedspreads, crisp curtains and scatter rugs. All have screened porches, grills, picnic tables and kitchenettes. There are nine studios, two one-bedroom and two two-bedroom cottages. All inn rooms have private baths and a bright common area is the setting for continental breakfast for inn guests and those in the Carriage House. Doubles, $95 to $110 in inn; suites, $150. Cottages, $675 to $875 weekly. Open May-October.

Oak Bluffs

The Oak House, Seaview Avenue, Box 299, Oak Bluffs 02557. (508) 693-4187. This marvelous, sprawling 19th-century summer home is located directly across from the ocean and most of the ten rooms and suites with private baths have water views. They also have some of the most elaborate woodwork we've seen. Our family of four was cozily ensconced on the third floor in a huge suite with walls and ceilings covered in beautiful oak paneling with great detail. A tiny private balcony afforded a view of the shoreline. Public rooms on the main floor have elaborate oak paneling and Victorian-style furnishings. There are a huge front parlor and a formal dining room (where guests breakfast, unless they want to carry their coffee to the front porch). Innkeeper Betsi Convery-Luce includes continental breakfast and Victorian tea in the rates. Doubles, $95 to $140; family of four, $190. Three-night minimum. Open May-September.

The Beach House, Seaview Avenue, Box 417, Oak Bluffs 02557. (508) 693-3955. Perfectly named, this inn has a beachy feeling and a nice beach is across the street. Of the same vintage, but with not quite the elaborate wood-work of the Oak House, it features a cozy alcove with pink patterned window-seat cushions and a large open front porch with a telescope for viewing distant ships. All nine rooms have private baths, wall-to-wall carpeting and queensize beds, a recent upgrade. Some rooms are paneled and others are painted white. Innkeepers Pamela and Calvin Zaiko offer include items like bagels with cream cheese and muffins in the continental breakfast. The location of this and the Oak House are super for those without wheels; the ferry dock is just a five-minute walk. Doubles, $90 to $125. Open mid-May to Columbus Day.

The Wesley Hotel, Lake Avenue, Oak Bluffs 02557. (508) 693-6611. A landmark for years, the Wesley was refurbished and renovated in 1985 by Peter Martell, who also owned the Pequot Hotel in Oak Bluffs and was part-owner of the Colonial in Edgartown. The hotel has 58 rooms in the main building, which overlooks the Oak Bluffs harbor, and a wide front porch with rockers. The Wesley Arms building out back has twenty more simply furnished rooms that share baths. Rooms in the main building have wall-to-wall carpeting, one or two double beds, and fresh quilts and curtains. The main lobby is done in Victorian style with a red velvet sofa and chairs in a conversation grouping amid marble-topped tables, oriental rugs on bare floors, and elaborate light fixtures suspended from colorful ceiling medallions. A raised-platform breakfast area overlooks the lobby. This is a busy hotel with lots of coming and going through the lobby; the activity of the harbor is also a draw. Doubles, $100 to $135 in hotel, $50 in Wesley Arms building. Open mid-May through September.

Edgartown

The Charlotte Inn, South Summer Street, Edgartown 02539. (508) 627-4751. A very elegant and special place to stay on Martha's Vineyard, the main inn, white clapboard with black shutters, was a sea captain's home and dates from the mid-1800s. From the moment you walk up to the front door, you know you're in for something wonderful. The two front rooms inside are an art gallery; fine art also hangs in hallways and some of the rooms. Rooms here are decorated with French and English antiques and fine reproductions, and have four-poster beds, candlewick bedspreads and fresh flowers. Most rooms have an attractive sofa-sitting area. Rooms are slightly less formal in the other buildings, the Carriage House (with cathedral ceilings and French doors), the Garden and Summer houses. All rooms in the Garden House have brass beds, and a first-floor bedroom with its own porch looks out on a colorful garden. Suites with fireplaces are coveted in fall and winter. Innkeepers Gery and Paula Conover run their 24-room inn with great attention to detail. Continental breakfast is taken in the airy conservatory dining room, the site of a fine classic restaurant, **L'Etoile,** which serves dinner in season. Doubles, $175 to $295; suites with fireplaces, $245 to $350.

Point Way Inn, Main Street at Pease's Point Way, Box 128, Edgartown 02539. (508) 627-8633. Through the white swinging gate on the corner and past the shrubbed and flowered yard, you walk up to this lovely old sea captain's house-turned-inn. Although there's no view of the water, things are very nautical inside — no doubt related to the interest of innkeepers Linda and Ben Smith in the sailing life (they'd just sailed into Edgartown harbor after a 4,000-mile, year-and-a-half cruise, when they found the house in 1979 and decided to make it over). Point Way has twelve rooms plus two suites in various configurations; all have their own baths, eleven haveoriginal fireplaces and some have canopied four-poster beds. A two-room fireplaced suite has an outdoor deck. Continental breakfast is served in a cheery yellow room with ladderback chairs and there's a living room-library with a large fireplace where guests can relax or have a drink. The Smiths used to host sailing trips in the Caribbean in the winter, but they now devote full attention to the inn. Croquet is played on the lawns and lemonade and cookies are served in the gazebo in summer. Doubles, $125 to $205.

The Harbor View Hotel, Starbuck's Neck, Edgartown 02539. (508) 627-4333. Two large gray-shingled structures with an unimpeded view of the Edgartown Light and the entrance to the harbor are the signature buildings of this resort complex. With seven large "cottages" and a lanai with motel-type rooms surrounding the pool, the hotel provides a total of 127 rooms. Built in 1891 and updated in 1984 and again in 1989, the Harbor View has a commanding position on Starbuck's Neck, a prime piece of Edgartown property. The location — and the amenities of a full-service resort — bring guests back. Rattan furniture in the lobby gives a light summery mood and rooms are furnished in soft tones of gray, beige and taupe. Many of the beds have iron headboards and TVs are in armoires. Ask for a room in front for a view of the lighthouse and the water traffic. A path leads to a private beach by the lighthouse, a short walk from the hotel. **Starbuck's,** a large, gracious dining room, is decorated classically with white linens and formal Duncan Phyfe chairs. Its view of the lighthouse and the water is stunning. The Harbor View is now one of the

Winthrop Hotels & Resorts. Among the extras are two tennis courts, and a large pool with flower edged terrace out back. Doubles, $165 to $495, EP. Open May to late fall.

The Colonial Inn, North Water Street, Edgartown 02539. (508) 627-4711. The location of the Colonial is splendid if you want to be in the middle of the action. Situated on prestigious North Water Street — a street of stately white whaling homes — and just a few steps from shops, restaurants and the waterfront, this large summer hotel with broad porch and window boxes filled with petunias and geraniums is a classic. It has now been upgraded, with little shops added to the front lobby area and a massive set of brick stairs that detract a bit from the simplicity of former years. However, the newly decorated rooms have private baths and air-conditioning (which we needed during a very hot August spell). Puffy quilts, matching draperies, carpeting and snazzy bathrooms add to the comfort, and the towels are thick and luxurious. A continental breakfast of juice, coffee and muffins from a cart is provided in the lobby. Doubles, $100 to $195. Open April-December.

The Daggett House, 59 North Water St., Edgartown 02539. (508) 627-4600. Because the Daggett House was built as an inn in 1750, it exudes a charm that eludes many other hostelries. Also, because it has been run for nearly 40 years by the Chirgwin family, it has a settled, comfortable feeling. The main building is square and shingled with seven guest rooms, all of which have low ceilings, wainscoting, mini-print wallpaper and appropriate furnishings. A period parlor on the entry level is for the use of guests; downstairs is a mammoth brick fireplace in the Chimney Room, which opens into the back yard leading directly to Edgartown Harbor. Antique artifacts adorn this room, where a full country breakfast is served guests. Also part of the complex are the fourteen-room Capt. Warren House, which includes efficiency units good for families, and a three-bedroom garden cottage. The long, narrow back yard of the Daggett House leads to a postage-stamp beach. Lounge chairs are available for guests, and from here you get the best possible view of the On-Time ferry, which runs across the channel to Chappaquiddick Island. In fact, the traffic lines up along the street at the side of the Daggett House. Doubles, $110 to $150. Main inn open year-round.

The Edgartown Inn, 56 North Water St., Edgartown 02539. (508) 627-4794. A variety of accommodations is available here, from the eleven antiques-decorated rooms with private baths in the main inn to the more simply decorated rooms with shared baths in the Captain's Quarters and Barn beyond a terrace out back. Built in 1798 as a sea captain's residence, the house became an inn in the early 1800s. Among its distinguished guests have been Daniel Webster, Nathaniel Hawthorne and John F. Kennedy. An optional breakfast is served guests in a cozy rear room or on the terrace. A porch out front is a good place to sit and watch the North Water Street traffic. Henry, the maitre 'd, has been here since 1945 — talk about length of service! Doubles, $80 to $145 in inn, $60 to $100 in Barn, $55 in Captain's Quarters. Open April-October.

Mattakesett of Edgartown, South Beach (address: 252 Main St., Hyannis 02601). (508) 778-1101. Here's a place to rent a condominium or home right at the best public beach on the island. Altogether 91 units with tennis courts and pool form what is like a private tennis club for the renters. The condos and homes, which have attractive gray-shingled exteriors with white trim, come with linens, blankets, towels, kitchen utensils and housecleaning service (both prior to and after the week of rental). The beach is just a few steps away. All homes have three bedrooms, each with private bath. Condos have three bedrooms and two baths. Rents, $2,700 to $4,100 weekly in season.

Camping

Webb's Camping Area, RD 2, Box 100, Vineyard Haven 02568. (508) 693-0233. Located off Barnes Road, in roughly the center of the island, Webb's has 131 wooded sites, 25 trailer hook-ups and a separate area for cyclists and backpackers. Each site has a picnic table and natural stone fireplace, and bikes can be rented. A few sites have views of Lagoon Pond, where there's a small public saltwater beach. Open May 15 to Sept. 20.

Martha's Vineyard Family Campground, Box 1557, Edgartown Road, Vineyard Haven 02568. (508) 693-3772. This campground is located off the Edgartown-Vineyard Haven road, closer to Vineyard Haven.

Seeing and Doing _____ _ꓚꓣꓚ_

Martha's Vineyard has much to offer. Each of the major towns has its own identity and spirit and deserves to be explored. The beaches are wonderful. Sailboats and sailboards, rowboats and motor boats can be rented. A ferry goes to Chappaquiddick, which has a very good beach at the far end. Shopping is interesting. Historical homes and sites can be visited. There are movies and artistic performances. Art galleries are especially good. The twice-weekly newspaper, The Vineyard Gazette, is excellent and you should pick one up — not just to find out what's doing but to get the flavor of the island. Enjoy!

Getting Around

A car is useful, but hundreds of visitors come just with bicycles; 25 miles of bike paths are well-maintained. Bike rentals, widely available, average $10 a day for a three-speed; $12 to $15 for a ten-speed.

Mopeds have hit the island and big. Just up the street from the ferry in Oak Bluffs are two rental places. Others are available in Vineyard Haven.

Buses, operating hourly, connect Vineyard Haven, Oak Bluffs and Edgartown from mid-May to mid-October. They run at least twice an hour from mid-June to Labor Day. Buses stop on Union Street in Vineyard Haven (straight ahead from the steamship wharf), at the traffic circle in Oak Bluffs and at the police station in Edgartown. Shuttle buses between Edgartown and South Beach operate frequently during the summer. In July and August, a shuttle leaves Church Street in Edgartown for Gay Head with stops at the airport, West Tisbury and Chilmark. Taxis meet incoming ferries at Vineyard Haven and Oak Bluffs and pick up passengers anywhere on the island.

Sightseeing buses leave the ferry terminal areas in Vineyard Haven and Oak Bluffs almost hourly during the summer and cover the island.

The Beaches

Most people love the Vineyard best for its beaches. Waters off the shore are relatively shallow, and the Gulf Stream and protection from Cape Cod assure comfortable temperatures for seasonal swimming. Several beaches are open to the public. Others are reserved for town and summer residents and a sticker is required. Among the best:

Oak Bluffs Town Beach is a calm, shallow and supervised beach on the Vineyard Sound side of the island and is open to all; it stretches from the ferry terminal to the first jetty heading toward Edgartown. **Joseph Sylvia State Beach** is two miles of a clear, mild beach between Oak Bluffs and Edgartown. **Lighthouse Beach,** the small harbor beach at Starbuck's Neck in Edgartown, is reached via a paved path from North Water Street.

Katama Beach (more familiarly known as **South Beach**), three miles of public barrier beach on the south shore at Edgartown, has fine ocean surf on one side, plus a protected salt pond. **Menemsha Public Beach** is a gentle beach with clear, bright water typical of the North Shore.

Several other beaches, including Lambert's Cove Beach, Lucy Vincent Beach, Squibnocket, Lobsterville and Gay Head Town Beach, are open only to town residents.

The **Cape Pogue Wildlife Refuge and Wasque Reservation (East Beach)** at the tip of Chappaquiddick is considered one of the best. It's open subject to regulations of the Trustees of Reservations.

Boating

Learn to sail or rent a sailboat yourself at the Harborside Inn in Edgartown Harbor, 627-4321. **Sailboat charters** are available through Tesoro Charters on Lower Main Street, Edgartown, (627-7245) or Ayuthia Charters, Beach Road Extension, Vineyard Haven (693-7245).

Windsurfing rentals, lessons and sales are available through Precision Water Sports on Beach Road, Vineyard Haven, 693-4221.

Sailing aboard the classic wooden 54-foot ketch, the Laissez Faire, is offered through John and Mary Clarke at the Lothrop Merry House in Vineyard Haven, 693-1646. They have full and half day sails, evening harbor sunset sails and overnight charters.

Fishing charters are widely available, among them: Sportfishing on the Misa with Capt. Charlie Blair at 627-4219; the Scrimshaw with Captain Flip of West Tisbury at 645-9049; shark, tuna, bass and blues fishing aboard the Banjo with Capt. Robert Plante, 693-3154. Get your gear from Larry's Tackle Shop on Dock Street in Edgartown, 627-5088.

Jetboats are the latest rage. You can rent them from Vineyard Boat Rentals in Oak Bluffs Harbor, 693-8476.

Sightseeing

WALKING TOURS. In **Edgartown,** be sure to see the Vincent House, built in 1675 and now operated as a museum; the Old Whaling Church on Main Street; the Dukes County Historical Society, a Colonial home decorated with period furniture, and the giant pagoda tree on South Water Street (brought as a seedling from China and planted in the mid-1800s). Climb to the observation deck at the Town Wharf for a good view of the harbor. See the Old Sculpin Gallery, housed in an old boat shop. St. Andrew's Church on North Summer Street has stained-glass windows designed by Louis Comfort Tiffany and its pulpit is the bow of a boat. Ogle all the beautiful whaling homes; we especially like to stroll up North Water Street to Starbuck's Neck from the center of town.

In **Oak Bluffs,** the many gingerbread cottages painted in vivid colors are a delight to see; just wander the streets as you will. Don't miss the Tabernacle at Trinity Park. Originally designed for wood, the open-air auditorium was built of wrought iron and replaced a one-ton tent. Check out Ocean Park with its gazebo and the Civil War statue on Seaview Avenue. The Oak Bluffs harbor is busy and colorful. Take a ride on the Flying Horses, one of the oldest carousels in the country. And don't miss Circuit Avenue with its shops and its fudge stands.

A SPECIAL EVENT. Probably the most distinctive and exciting night on the island is **Illumination Night** in Oak Bluffs. It's hard to predict when it will be except an evening in mid-August. The announcement appears in the newspaper only a few days ahead and while tourists are not discouraged from attending, this is an event that islanders revere as their own.

The tradition goes back about 100 years in the campground area in Oak Bluffs. Today, the evening begins in the Tabernacle with about an hour's sing-a-long of favorite old and patriotic tunes. As the sky darkens, the tension and excitement grow. Finally, a respected member of the island community is asked to light the first lantern. The Tabernacle is completely darkened and the designee lights a paper oriental lantern, which he or she carries to the edge of the open-air building for all to see. Residents in the colorful gingerbread houses in the campground take this as the signal to light their own colorful lanterns, most of which are massed on the porches and fronts of the cottages. The crowd then walks up and down the narrow streets in the area, oohing and aahing over the beautiful lanterns. A few of the inhabitants of the cottages even offer refreshments: cookies or gingerbread, for example.

There is a magic, ethereal quality to Illumination Night. It is a family event and everyone loves it.

Other Attractions

ART GALLERIES. Many on the island are of quite high quality. **John Stobart,** the marine painter, maintains a gallery in Edgartown. The **Old Sculpin Gallery** in Edgartown represents several island artists. The **Granary Gallery** in West Tisbury shows many local artists and photographers. There are many more.

ANTIQUING. A brochure, "Antique Shops on Martha's Vineyard," lists no fewer than seventeen, most of them in Edgartown.

SHOPPING. The stores are almost irresistible. Boutiques and pricey clothing shops are concentrated in Edgartown, though they're making appearances in Vineyard Haven as well. Funky clothes and T-shirt shops are located in Oak Bluffs. The **Bunch of Grapes Bookstore** in Vineyard Haven is where everyone goes, and on a rainy day you'll be hard put to shoehorn your way in or out. Sweaters are to be found at **Northern Isles** in the Tisbury Inn in Vineyard Haven. Basics — raingear, Jams, jeans, shoes and such — are available at **Brickman's** in Vineyard Haven and Edgartown.

The Vineyard has a vineyard, **Chicama Vineyards** in West Tisbury, where you can tour and buy wine, as well as specially flavored vinegars. **Lorraine Parish,** a designer of interesting women's clothing, has her own shop "up island" in Chilmark (next door to the restaurant, Feasts).

In Edgartown, **Chica** has clothing, jewelry and art and we think **Petunia's** has great clothes. **A Gift of Love** on North Water Street, a shop for hostess items, games and gifts, has stock of impeccable taste. **Rags** is another place to check out for clothes, and the **Fligors'** with its many rooms and levels is almost a department store. You can spend a half day browsing on Main and Water streets, but don't forget your wallet.

In Oak Bluffs, we love Circuit Avenue. Walk past **Murdick's** at the lower end and go all the way to the top of the street to **Hilliard's Kitch-in-vue** store where they roll out caramel, "paint" it with chocolate, and sprinkle nuts on top to make butter crunch; fudge is great here, too. Part of a three-store candy chain, this has the original family firmly in charge. Other shops on Circuit Avenue include a terrific Army surplus store, a vintage clothing store, a children's store and T-shirt emporiums. If you have teenagers, drop them off here for a few hours.

Where to Eat _____ ⟋⟍⟍⟍⟍

More and more trendy, pricey restaurants are dotting the island and are very popular; reserve a table well in advance. There are also casual spots, and one of New England's great pizza places. Liquor is served in restaurants in Oak Bluffs and Edgartown only; other towns are BYOB.

Fancy Dining

Savoir Faire, Post Office Square, Edgartown. (508) 627-9864.

Inside, all is black and white and sophisticated. That feeling is carried through to the outdoor deck, which has a tree growing through it. There's no view except the gift shop across the way and the side of Warriner's, another restaurant, but it is green and cool and no one seems to mind. The ficus trees bear little white lights and a candle in a glass cup flickers on each table. A starched white napkin, tucked into a wine glass, sets the tone for serious dining. Our waitress was a young Englishwoman who interrupted a career in London to enjoy a summer on an island. A limited menu at dinner offers a choice of entrees ($17 to $25) such as cold poached salmon with a ginger-basil creme fraiche and glazed pearl onions, cioppino (which seemed to be ordered by many diners) or ziti with grilled duck breast, tomato coulis, grilled eggplant, fresh herbs and goat cheese. For starters ($7 to $9) you might try scallops ceviche with kiwi and lime vinaigrette or smoked poussin salad with snap peas, pinenuts, yellow pear tomatoes and baby beets in a raspberry vinaigrette. With our entrees came a small green bean salad and new potatoes, perfectly cooked. The hazelnut decaffeinated coffee to finish was out of this world. At lunchtime, sample the curried chicken salad, a lobster with grapefruit salad or bow tie pasta salad with julienned prosciutto ($6.50 to $9). Reservations are essential. Lunch, Monday-Saturday 11 to 3; dinner nightly, 6 to 10. Closed midwinter.

Warriner's, Post Office Square, Edgartown. (508) 627-4488. Bookcases filled with books, dark paneled walls, Queen Anne chairs with green seats, white tablecloths and tiny bouquets of fresh flowers on the tables create the aura of an Englishmen's clubroom. Tables are set with striking Dudson china from England; small brass lamps with pleated shades add a homey touch. Sam Warriner, who once ran the Dunes restaurant at the Katama Shores Inn, rocketed to the apex of the island restaurant scene after opening this in 1984. The location is a small white house, and dining is in several intimate rooms with a total seating capacity of 60. One of the rooms has been renamed **Sam's** and offers lighter, less expensive fare. Entrees at Warriner's ($20 to $25) range from sole amandine to tenderloin of veal with pignoli and spinach. Also offered are black bass grenobloise, stuffed shrimp, medallions of lamb provencale, and duck steak with a plum and ginger sauce. They come with a mixed salad, vegetable and potato. Warriner's also offers an exceptional wine list. For dessert, try chocolate mousse with raspberry sauce, apricot ice cream with a cinnamon-ginger sauce, papaya with lime-rum sabayon or chocolate truffles. Dinner nightly, 6 to 9.

Lambert's Cove Country Inn, Lambert's Cove Road, West Tisbury. (508) 693-2298. It sounds as if you should have a view of the water here. You don't. This is a real country inn, the kind you'd drive to for Sunday dinner, set among trees. New innkeepers Ron and Kay Nelson took over in 1990. The dining room gives you that old-fashioned feeling, but the food is anything but. A typical dinner menu might offer rack of lamb with lavender and ginger hollandaise sauce, veal scaloppini and shrimp with champagne and a garlic sauce, half a lobster broiled and served with garlic-lemon butter, or sauteed chicken breast with a green peppercorn and sweet vermouth sauce ($18 to $21). Start your meal with lobster bisque, chilled gazpacho or fresh fruit salad in liqueur juices ($6 to $7). Desserts are homemade. One evening they included a chocolate-cognac mousse, Norwegian chocolate cake, key lime or apple crumb pie and a french nut torte. The famed Sunday brunch offers a menu of choices (not buffet, thank goodness) such as sauteed chicken francais, eggs benedict, blueberry buttermilk pancakes and sliced steak with scrambled eggs. Prices are $9 to $15. Dinner nightly; Sunday brunch. Closed in January.

Martha's, 71 Main St., Edgartown. (508) 627-8316. This is an unusually pretty restaurant with both a first-floor and a second-floor dining room and a tiny porch upstairs overlooking Edgartown's busy main street. New Yorkers Bart Fleishman and Gerald Ottinger began this successful venture in the early 1980s. They serve the crowds of Edgartown virtually all day long. Flowered tablecloths and peach walls make for a very feminine street-floor dining room. There's no view of the water except for that which flows down the mirror in the second-floor bar. Typical dinner entrees are bouillabaisse, roasted Long Island duckling, veal loin baked with avocado, monterey jack cheese and a light tomato sauce, and twin filet mignon, pan-roasted with white wine, cream, wild mushrooms and in a brown mustard sauce. Sushi is also available, as are pastas and salads including a grilled quail salad. Entrees are priced from $18 to $28; appetizers from $7 to $40 (for caviar). Breakfast and lunch are available from 10:30 to 3; dinner, 6 to 10; Sunday brunch, 10:30 to 3:30. Open April-November.

Le Grenier, Main Street, Vineyard Haven. (508) 693-4906. The classic French restaurant above La Patisserie Francaise is run by French chef Jean Dupon of Lyon and his partner, Robin Salisbury. The small porch overlooking the street is the place to dine if you can. Dress is a step up from casual, but no jacket or tie is required. Among the hors d'oeuvres are escargots bourguignonne, onion soup gratinee, French mussels steamed in white wine and oysters rockefeller ($6 to $8). Entrees ($15.95 to $26.95) include steak au poivre, frog's legs provencale, pasta primavera, vegetarian wellington and shrimp pernod. Desserts, some of which are special pastries from the bakery downstairs, include peaches in raspberry sauce on meringue, creme caramel and chocolate mousse cake. Dinner nightly from 6. Open mid-March to mid-October. BYOB.

The Oyster Bar, Circuit Avenue, Oak Bluffs. (508) 693-3300. Formerly The Brass Bass, this restaurant is mobbed by the sophisticates who come to Martha's Vineyard but like to think they are still in New York. It's usually crowded and even arriving at 6 on a Tuesday evening in summer, we were told we'd have to wait more than an hour for a table. People are dressed up and so are the prices. Entrees ($20 to $24) include marinated quail and polenta, charred rack of lamb with Chinese glaze, lacquered peppered duck breast with pinot noir sauce and Chinese red-cooked snapper. You might start with escargots and brie ravioli or duck and wild mushroom ravioli. It is all too-too. Dinner nightly from 5.

More Casual Choices

The Home Port, North Road, Menemsha. (508) 645-2679. Overlooking the water in the quaint fishing village of Menemsha, the incredibly popular Home Port offers the best seafood platters on the island and prepares its food simply and honestly. Owner Will Holtham has not deviated from his original concept since he opened fifteen years ago. In the last two weeks of August it is not unusual, we're told, for the restaurant to turn away 200 would-be diners a day. The place is simple: bare wooden floors, captain's chairs, seating for 135. There is a small waiting area with a raw bar outside where you can have drinks if you've brought your own. The blue and white menu is not elaborate but it covers the basics. Lobsters come in eight variations and a shore dinner (one-pound lobster, corn, stuffed quahog, steamed clams or mussels) is $24. A fish platter of fried shrimp, fish, scallops and oysters plus a boiled lobster and a stuffed quahog goes for $26. Other specialties ($15 to $26) are baked stuffed shrimp, broiled bluefish and broiled Menemsha swordfish. Baked or french-fried potatoes come with the entree, as does an appetizer (quahog chowder, steamed mussels, fruit cup, cranberry juice) and a tossed salad or coleslaw. Desserts include homemade pies and ice cream. Dinner nightly, 4:30 to 10. Open May to mid-October. Reservations required.

The Square Rigger, at the Triangle, Edgartown. (508) 627-9968. Building on his success with the Home Port, Will Holtham opened this restaurant in an old house in Edgartown in 1986. It has a quite different atmosphere — and the food is prepared differently — but we found it very cozy and pleasant. The larger of two dining rooms has tables arranged around an open brick hearth where the cooking is done; the tiny, four-table room at the rear is Colonial with mini-print wallpaper and candles on the tables. In 1990 the menu was changed here to reflect the economic times; you could get entrees priced from $13 to $19 when previously you had to order a complete dinner at a higher price. Items tend to be simple and straightforward: broiled Vineyard scallops, charbroiled chicken breast or lamb chops, prime rib ($18) and fresh pasta in an alfredo sauce with shrimp. Cheesecake is always one of the dessert offerings, but there is usually a special or two. Dinner nightly from 5:30.

The Roadhouse Restaurant, State Road, West Tisbury. (508) 693-9599. This roadside restaurant gained extreme popularity in the late 1980s for its simple, straightforward presentation of food and its excellent prices. It's a takeout place where you can get a hamburger or hot dog or chili, but it's also a nifty little restaurant where everyone from tourists to telephone workers stops for lunch and sometimes dinner. At lunchtime you're able to order the regular Roadhouse chili or vegetarian chili ($4 a bowl); a watercress and tomato salad, different varieties of burgers, and barbecued chicken and ribs, the latter priced at $7 to $9. In the evening prices go up a notch: $10.75 for the quarter barbecued chicken, $12.75 for the half, $14.50 for New York strip steak and $10.50 for mixed grilled vegetables. Open Monday-Saturday for lunch and dinner. BYOB.

The Aquinnah, at the Cliffs, Gay Head. (508) 645-9654. The spectacular location of this restaurant/gift shop is almost all you need, but it has good food, too. Perched atop the cliffs with an exceptional view of the open ocean to the west, its two outdoor decks are especially popular. We love to have breakfast here: things like blue corn pancakes and real maple syrup, mugs of hot coffee, and nobody pressuring you to get on with the day. The breeze is blowing just enough and there's a mix of regulars and once-in-a-whilers. French toast made with Portuguese sweet bread and homemade fish cakes and eggs with toast ($5 to $6 range) are excellent. For dinner you can have linguini with clam sauce for $11 or lobster for about $20 and lots in between. You want atmosphere? This is it. And pick up a couple of Aquinnah T-shirts while you're at it. Open for breakfast, lunch and dinner. Seasonal.

Louis' Tisbury Cafe and Take-Out, 102 State Road, Vineyard Haven. (508) 693-3255. This is a low-key hit; the dining room is in the back with red and white checked tablecloths on as many tables as can be crowded in. Out front is a takeout counter offering homemade pasta dishes, pizza, barbecued chicken and ribs, gazpacho, subs, clam chowder and so on. Dinner specials ($10.95 to $16.95) include barbecued half chicken, chargrilled shrimp and pastas (the one with seafood is popular with the locals). You can get a chargrilled rack of lamb, too. Dinner nightly, lunch in season. No credit cards. BYOB.

Papa John's on Circuit Avenue in Oak Bluffs has the best pizza on the island, we think, and it's a cut above many places on the mainland. Patrons sit at long tables, drink from pitchers of beer, and order pizzas with almost anything on them (including pineapple). This is a favorite spot of teenagers and college students.

Good ice cream can be found at any of the several **Mad Martha's** establishments around the island. "Oreo cookie nookie" comes with hot fudge and marshmallow sauce, topped with whipped cream and a Hershey kiss. The Vineyard Surprise is orange-pineapple ice cream laced with tequila. And for the big eater, there's "Pig's Delight," one dozen scoops of ice cream with toppings, "hosed down with whipped cream." Order by saying "oink."

The **Scottish Bakehouse** on State Road, going up-island about 1.5 miles from Vineyard Haven, is a wondrous little spot. Breads, scones, shortbread, steak and kidney pies, Scottish meat pies, sausage rolls, and cakes and pastries all taste as if they've just been taken out of the oven in Edinburgh, my lads! Makes for a good picnic lunch.

Among the Flowers Cafe on Mayhew Lane in Edgartown has homemade waffle cones and ice cream and good light lunches. You can sit indoors or outside on a pleasant little terrace.

Happy Hour and Later

The **Wharf Pub** in Edgartown, on lower Main Street, is the place to rub knees and elbows with just about anybody who can push his way in. The place has piano music nightly.

David's Island House on Circuit Avenue in Oak Bluffs should not be missed. Small bare wooden tables, Tiffany-style lamps and bentwood chairs provide the atmosphere at the bar and restaurant owned by David Crohan, the well-known blind pianist. David tickles the ivories nightly and everyone comes to listen and sip.

Hot Tin Roof, Carly Simon's night spot at the airport, brings in a variety of entertainment. Call 693-1137 to find out what's on.

FOR MORE INFORMATION: Chamber of Commerce, Beach Road, Box 1698, Vineyard Haven, Mass. 02568. (508) 693-0085.

Pavilion facing ocean awaits swimmers at Cliffside Beach Club.

Nantucket, Mass.

Everything about Nantucket epitomizes an island at sea.

No point on the fourteen-mile-long island is more than a mile or two from the ocean. From historic Nantucket Town to beachy Surfside across island, from quaint Siasconset on the east to remote Madaket on the west, you can feel the breeze and smell the salt air (and almost touch it in times of pea-soup fog). Nearly everywhere you see the dunes, moors and heathlands honed by time, and hear the sounds of the sea.

Here is an island of history and romance some 30 miles off Cape Cod, with no land visible on the horizon. Historically it has been known as the "Little Gray Lady of the Sea," but we think of Nantucket in the preppy pink and green of its more contemporary veneer, as well as in the azure blue of its waters and the gold of its sandy beaches.

Nantucket was settled in the early 1600s, harbored fortunes as a whaling port in the 19th century, and today carries well its history and affluence. That's partly due to its relative isolation and an inherent sense of preservation, and partly due to the resources of Walter Beinecke Jr. of the S&H Green Stamps family.

Variously considered Nantucket's visionary or villain, he started in the early 1960s to turn the town around to face the waterfront that had been abandoned over the years. When he sold his holdings to First Winthrop Corp. of Boston a quarter century later, he had built or restored three leading lodging establishments, the Nantucket Boat Basin, 40 cottages on the wharf and 36 retail buildings in the downtown area. He was a principal force behind the Nantucket Historical Trust and the Nantucket Conservation Foundation, which set the twin themes for the preservation of Nantucket.

Seldom has one man so greatly influenced the look, feel, fate and fortune of a place as Bud Beinecke has for Nantucket, in the opinion of Yesterday's Island newspaper. Recognizing the small size of the island and its finite quantities, he managed its growth by limiting access. Nantucket became an upscale, year-round community, not a seasonal carnival midway.

The season has been extended, starting with the annual Daffodil Festival in late April and ending with the famed Christmas Stroll the second weekend in December, two events that attract visitors by the score.

Daytrippers do come to Nantucket — for a price. But they return on the late-afternoon ferry to their tour buses in Hyannis, leaving the island for those who are willing and able to pay up to $150 for dinner for two and often an equal or higher amount for overnight lodging.

For the good life that Nantucket offers, you may think the price is worth it. Whether you're into beaching or boating, luxury lodging or fine dining, the arts, history or nature, Nantucket is one island that has it all.

Getting There

Nantucket is reached by ferries or airplanes.

Woods Hole, Martha's Vineyard & Nantucket Steamboat Authority, Box 284, Woods Hole 02543. (508) 540-2022. Called simply the Authority (in more ways than one), it has six trips a day in summer between Hyannis and Nantucket (about 2 1/2 hours) and occasional connecting service from Woods Hole via Martha's Vineyard (3 1/2 hours). One-way costs are $71 for cars and $9 for adults, $4.50 for children. Auto reservations are imperative, far in advance.

Hy-Line, Ocean Street Dock, Hyannis 02601. (508) 778-2600 (information) and 778-2602 (reservations). Faster crossings (just under two hours, without vehicles) for passengers are provided by the smaller Hy-Line ferries, which have six sailings daily in summer, three in early June and mid-September, and one in May, late September and October. One-way, adults $10, children $5.

Nantucket's airport, we're told, has become the second busiest in Massachusetts, serving commercial jets from New York, Boston and Hartford, smaller airlines from Hyannis and New Bedford, and an inordinate number of private planes.

Where to Stay

Near the Water, In Town

Cliffside Beach Club, Jefferson Avenue, Box 449, Nantucket 02554. (508) 228-0618. Nantucket's niftiest waterfront accommodations, we think, are in the fourteen new "hotel" rooms at the old Cliffside Beach Club, dating to 1924. Here on a glorious 400-foot strand, members waited years to reserve one of the prime sections of the west beach, and the same umbrellas and chairs are still in the same spots, according to general manager Robert F. Currie. Some of the old-fashioned changing rooms have been transformed into fourteen airy, contemporary guest quarters with cathedral ceilings and modern baths. All the beds, tables, vanities, doors and even the pegs for the beach towels were built by Nantucket craftsmen; angled wainscoting serves as the headboards for the built-in queensize beds. The woodwork from the old bathhouses is handsomely accented by dark green colors and prints by local artists. Seven rooms have decks facing the beach head-on (the rest are angled), and all have cable TV, phones and mini-refrigerators. Also facing the beach are four of the nine air-conditioned studio apartments (dubbed the Gold Coast by the irreverent), away from the main hotel beyond the Galley, the beach club's appealing waterfront restaurant (see Where to Eat). Two new suites as well as a health club with Nautilus equipment opened in 1990. Continental breakfast is served in the spectacular lobby, full of smart wicker furniture and planters, and topped by quilts suspended from the beamed cathedral ceiling. Doubles, $220 to $335. Open Memorial Day to Columbus Day.

The White Elephant, Easton Street, Box 359, Nantucket 02554. (508) 228-2500 or (800) 475-2637. Big bucks have been invested in the upgrading of this old-timer, which no longer more lives up to its name, acquired years ago based on the small size of its 22 main-hotel bedrooms and the lofty level of its prices. Even the skeptics concede the charm of the fifteen rose-covered cottages scattered about the property, and are impressed with the 26 magnificently refurbished rooms in the Breakers annex. A major renovation in 1990 resulted in air-conditioned and redecorated hotel rooms, relocation of the pool so it no longer blocks the harbor view from the dining room, expansion of the outdoor dining terrace, and refurbishing of the restaurant and lounge. A superb harborfront location offers lush lawns, fancy walkways lined with hedges, and plantings that focus on a white elephant statue in the middle, two nine-hole putting greens and a pleasant pool to the side of the outdoor terrace and restaurant. Who wouldn't adore the cozy weathered-shingled Spindrift cottages done up in wicker, their living rooms with bay windows overlooking the water? Who wouldn't want to indulge in the sumptuousness of the ne plus ultra **Breakers,** a nearby facility outfitted in Ethan Allen furniture and modern baths with twin sinks? Here, complimentary wine and cheese are served in the lounge, as is continental breakfast, and your refrigerator is stocked with champagne and mixers. You even receive Breakers canvas tote bags to remember them by. Third-floor rooms have patios and decks, but some rooms here and many of the cottages do not have water views — be sure to specify. Although we're partial to the corner room in the hotel with windows onto Children's Beach, some find it too public and cherish the privacy of the interior. Doubles, hotel, $230 to $270; cottages with one to three bedrooms, $145 to $575; Breakers, $295 to $395. Open Memorial Day to late September.

Westmoor Inn, Cliff Road, Nantucket 02554. (508) 228-0877. A distant ocean view from a hilltop is afforded by this striking yellow 1917 Vanderbilt mansion, which was renovated and expanded by five investors in 1988 and turned into probably Nantucket's most choice B&B. Up a grand staircase on the second and third floors are fourteen rooms and suites, all with private baths. They vary widely in size, but each is handsomely appointed with a mix of antique and more modern furnishings — a canopied four-poster and a peach-colored chaise longue in one, a king bed with a working fireplace in another. A deluxe suite has a sitting area and a jacuzzi, and resident innkeeper Nancy Drahzal said they hoped to have three cottages with kitchens ready for 1991. The formal living room is where wine and hors d'oeuvres are served early in the evening. A small library, furnished in antique white wicker, has books, cable TV and VCR. A solarium porch is the scene of abundant buffet breakfasts, supplemented in summer by a choice of eggs, pancakes, french toast and the like. Outside, guests enjoy two acres of grounds, including a back garden full of birdbaths; there's garden furniture for taking in the view, and all-terrain bikes are available. Doubles, $140 to $250. Open May-September.

Cliff Lodge, 9 Cliff Road, Nantucket 02554. (508) 228-9480. A harbor view from three of the eleven crisp guest rooms (plus an apartment), five common rooms on three floors, two patios and a rooftop deck are attributes of this appealing guest house, which opened in 1986. Built in 1771 on a hillside overlooking the harbor, the onetime whaling master's mansion is notable now for paint-speckled floors and Laura Ashley wallpapers. All rooms have private baths and TVs hidden in cabinets, and many have kingsize beds and fireplaces. But the sitting rooms, reading porches and well-furnished patios set Cliff Lodge apart. "People don't want to be cooped up in their bedrooms all the time," avows manager Gerrie Miller, "so we provide lots of common rooms and mixing areas." A complimentary breakfast of granola, cereal, fresh fruit, homemade muffins and bagels is served. Tea and cocktail snacks are offered in the afternoon. Cliff Lodge is owned by Nantucket Roosts, which also rents five kitchenette cottages known as **Still Dock Apartments** on old North Wharf, $150 to $225 a night, $1,150 to $1,400 a week. Doubles in lodge, $90 to $150.

Nantucket Landfall, 4 Harbor View Way, Nantucket 02554. (508) 228-0500. Nantucket's only B&B located across from the water was opened in 1985 by Gail and David More in an old house with a great front porch furnished in white and navy wicker and nicely expanded in 1990 with two larger front rooms on the main floor — one with a king bed and the other with a queen canopy — facing the water. All seven guest rooms have private baths, a couple of them ingeniously tucked into cubicles "because this is a small house and we had to use every inch," Gail relates. She made up for lack of space with interesting decor and colorful comforters. Two second-floor rooms have sitting areas overlooking the harbor, and a downstairs room has its own patio. The living room contains a fireplace and library, where Gail has put together a good scrapbook on the area's offerings. There's a small kitchen for guests to use. From it comes a continental-plus breakfast of fresh fruit, local bakery breads and occasionally extras like hard-boiled eggs, pineapple-blueberry cobbler and baked apples ("we don't put out cold watermelon when the fog horn is going," says Gail). Doubles, $85 to $130.

Brass Lantern Inn, 11 North Water St., Nantucket 02554. (508) 228-4064. The large contemporary rooms are best at this in-town B&B, which is closest to the ferry docks — a consideration for baggage-toting visitors without cars. Redone in 1990, the ten older guest rooms in the front of the 1846 Greek Revival house vary in size, and all but two share baths. We prefer the eight luxury rooms built by the contractor-son of the former innkeeper — especially the two extra-large rooms with cathedral ceiling, queensize bed, and sitting area with two white wicker chairs, a skirted table and a sofabed. Guests have access to a living room with TV and books. A light continental breakfast (very light — one of us had to have another at the Morning Glory Cafe to last the morning) is delivered to the rooms, or can be taken at a table on the small side lawn. The new owners also have **Fair Gardens Guest House** and **Great Harbor Inn** elsewhere in town. Doubles, $85 to $140.

Cobblestone Inn, 5 Ash St., Nantucket. (508) 228-1987. There's a harbor view from the the third-floor bedroom, all white and pink with a fancy brass and iron headboard and teal spatter-painted floors. Some of the five rooms, all with private baths, have fireplaces and queen canopy beds, and all are nicely furnished with period pieces. A collection of wooden lighthouses lines the stairs, typical of the thoughtful touches offered by Robin Hammer-Yankow, the young innkeeper whose husband is a local attorney. Guests gather for a continental breakfast, including cereal, fruit and homemade muffins, at a long table in the dining room. They also enjoy a large fireplaced living room with cable TV, a sunporch with wicker furniture and a guest refrigerator, and a brick patio overlooking the garden. Doubles, $90 to $130. No smoking.

The Wharf Cottages, New Whale Street, Box 1139, Nantucket 02554. (508) 228-4620 or (800) 228-4620. Twenty-five harborfront cottages on Swain's and South wharfs were refurbished by Sherburne Associates, the Walter Beinecke-inspired company that also owned the White Elephant and the Harbor House and now is an affiliate of the First Winthrop Corporation. Celebrities often rent them by the month or season and three-night minimums are required in season,

227

but single nights may be available (by chance and without reservations). Some transformed from old fishermen's shacks, the cottages vary from studios to three bedrooms, and are right on the water amidst all the yachts. Each has a kitchen, telephone and cable TV, and some have pleasant touches like skylights in the kitchen, living rooms with decks over the water, and brick patios. As the brochure says, "you're part of the scene, right on the harbor," with boats and boatpeople traipsing by, for better or worse. Cottages, $210 to $395 daily; ten percent less by month, twenty percent less by season. Maid service is included. Some cottages open through December.

Tuckernuck Inn, 60 Union St., Nantucket 02554. (508) 228-4886 or (800) 228-4886. The old Center for Elderly Affairs was gutted and turned into a motel-like inn with sixteen guest rooms and a two-bedroom suite, a main-floor breakfast room that innkeeper Ken Parker hoped would become a restaurant, a third-floor library-common room and a rooftop deck with a wide-angle harbor view beyond the adjacent shipyard. Rooms that smell of newness have comfortable furnishings, cable TV and private baths, and queen or twin beds. Ken and his wife Barbara, who formerly owned the Parker Guest House at 4 East Chestnut St., serve a continental breakfast in the oak post and beam dining room. Doubles, $120 to $130.

On the Water, Out of Town

The Wauwinet, Wauwinet Road, Nantucket 02584. (508) 228-0145 or (800) 426-8718. "An inn by the sea" is how this beautifully restored hostelry promotes itself. That it is, but that's not the half of it. The 28 guest rooms in the three-story inn plus twelve more in five cottages across the street are the ultimate in taste and luxury, though some seem a bit small for the price. All are furnished in wicker with TVs in painted armoires and trunks with hat boxes (one of the inn's decorating signatures, along with the striking stenciled borders that sometimes turn up in curious places), interesting artworks and sculptures, and modern bathrooms with baskets of Crabtree & Evelyn amenities. The rooms are almost upstaged by the inn's location, on a residential-parkland strip between Nantucket Bay and the Atlantic. The back lawn has sculptures and chairs spotted strategically for taking in the view or enjoying a drink from the beachside grill. There's swimming off the dock, but most prefer to walk across the road and through the dunes to the gorgeous ocean beach. Sailboats, sculls and tennis are available, and a 21-foot Mako runabout (plus jitneys and vans) takes guests to and from town. A hearty continental breakfast which can be served in your room is included in the rates, and excellent meals (see Where to Eat) are served in Topper's and on the outdoor terrace facing the bay. For those with deep pockets and social inclinations, the Wauwinet is Nantucket's ultimate water escape. Doubles, $290 to $500. Open mid-April to early December.

The Summer House, Ocean Avenue, Box 313, Siasconset 02564. (508) 257-9976. Eight romantic, rose-covered cottages of the old school have been delightfully upgraded by new owner Peter Karlson and present an idyllic oceanfront scene straight out of Bermuda on the south side of 'Sconset, as the islanders call it. The complex includes a heated pool halfway down the bluff across the road, beside the dunes leading to the open Atlantic, and a good restaurant (see Where to Eat) in the veranda-fronted main house. Continental breakfast is served to overnight guests. Under a canopy of trees and ivy, the cottages have been sweetly redecorated with English antiques, colorful wallpapers, eyelet-embroidered pillows, lace curtains and such. Interesting roof lines, painted floors and chests, stained glass, leaded windows, stenciling, and little nooks and crannies add to the charm. Contemporary as can be are the newly remodeled bathrooms, all with marble jacuzzis. The Jimmy Cagney cottage, where the actor frequently was ensconced, offers two bedrooms, one with a kingsize bed with real ivy growing over it, and another smaller room with a queen bed. Cottages have one or two bedrooms, two have kitchens, one has a sitting room and another a fireplace. Ours had no good place to sit except on the front patio, where we felt on display as dinner guests paraded up the path to the main house. Cottages, $275 to $365. Open mid-May to mid-October.

The Wade Cottages, Sankaty Avenue, Siasconset 02564. (508) 257-6308. Eight guest rooms, five apartments and three cottages are offered in this venerable, family-run summer compound atop the 'Sconset bluff, with a private beach below. Old-fashioned chairs on the spacious lawn, typical of the 'Sconset tradition, afford magnificent ocean views. Room guests are served continental breakfast in the Card Room of the beautiful main house, much of it still occupied by the Wade family. Accommodations range from guest rooms with private or shared baths to apartments (one with the tiniest kitchen ever) and housekeeping cottages with three to five bedrooms. Doubles, $80 to $155; apartments and cottages weekly, $1,300 to $2,000. Open May-October.

Star of the Sea Youth Hostel, Surfside, Nantucket 02554. (508) 228-0433. The 1873 Surfside Life Saving Station, one of the few remaining in the United States, is listed on the National Register of Historic Places. Today it serves as a hostel, offering 72 beds in single-sex dorms for up to three consecutive nights. Accommodations are open to American Youth Hostel members or to travelers who purchase a temporary guest membership card. The hostel rents sheet sacks and provides blankets, mattress and pillow and usually a stash of free food left by fellow travelers. Open late April to mid-October.

Away from the Water

Jared Coffin House, 29 Broad St., Nantucket 02554. (508) 228-2405. One of New England's grand old inns, the Jared Coffin House has 60 rooms in a complex of six historic homes at the edge of downtown. All have private baths and most have television; most deluxe are the queensize canopy rooms in the Swain, Coffin and Grey houses. The public rooms are a sight to behold, furnished in priceless Chippendale and Sheraton antiques. Formal dining is offered at **Jared's.** The downstairs **Tap Room** and outdoor patio are popular for good food at reasonable prices. Doubles, $110 to $175.

Harbor House, South Beach Street, Box 1048, Nantucket 02554. (508) 228-5500 or (800) 228-7197. Local purists are not partial to this luxury motor lodge and time-sharing resort put up by the Beinecke interests, but visitors who appreciate their creature comforts are. Amid some fancy landscaping are a total of 54 guest rooms with phones and cable TV in the motor lodge, Garden Cottage or Springfield House. Most coveted are the newer 57 rooms in six townhouses, built to resemble early Nantucket homes (surely the sea captains would wonder at today's amenities). The Harbor House has a heated pool, putting green, conference facilities and restaurant. Doubles, $185 to $225.

Dozens of other guest houses and cottages are available on the island. The only real motel is the **Beachside** (not on the water) on North Beach Street, (508) 228-2241, 88 units from $135 to $175, unless you include the Harbor House or the large new **Nantucket Inn at Nobadeer,** a Koala enterprise with indoor and outdoor pools, a fitness center and a rooftop restaurant beside the airport at 27 Macy's Lane, (508) 225-6900, doubles $140 to $195.

229

A central source for details is **Nantucket Accommodations,** 6 Ash Lane, Box 217, (508) 228-9559.

RENTALS. The pages of the Inquirer and Mirror, Nantucket's weekly newspaper, are filled with real-estate advertisements for properties generally priced from $250,000 to more than $1 million. At our last visit, we were told that 900 properties — ten percent of the total stock — were on the market. Rentals are fewer, and range from $700 to $3,000 a week; the prevailing rate is $1,000 to $1,500 a week. We saw classified ads asking $4,000 a month and $13,000 a season. Among the score or more of Nantucket realtors with rental listings are Nantucket Vacation Rentals, 6 Ash Lane, 228-3131; Coffin Real Estate, 51 Main St., 228-1138, and Congdon & Coleman, 57 Main St., 228-0344. Tristram's Group, 228-0359, bills itself as Nantucket's largest property manager for rentals of one week or longer.

Seeing and Doing

What you do in Nantucket depends somewhat on where and how long you're staying. Daytrippers and weekenders probably will remain close to Nantucket town. Those staying longer and those with cars can explore the island. Here are a sampling of its attractions.

Touring

Getting Around. If you have a car, it's easy to see the island, though the heart of town is congested, some streets are one way and confusing, and parking is limited. Bring your car by ferry — be sure to reserve well ahead — or rent a car from Island Rentals (228-4316), Barrett's (228-0174) or Affordable Rentals (228-3501). On our latest two-night trip, we rented a clunker (and we do mean a clunker) for 48 hours (noon to noon) for $60 from Barrett's, which gave the best deal, and covered all the island that we didn't walk or bike. There are taxis and bus services, and more bicycles and mopeds than you can honk your horn at.

Sightseeing Tours. Barrett's, 20 Federal St., 228-0174, offers three 90-minute bus tours daily, with a stop in Siasconset. Bus service is also provided six times a day to Surfside and Jetties beaches and 'Sconset village. The service has been operated for more than 60 years by descendants of Nantucket whaling captains. Tour prices are $9 for adults, $5 for children. **Island Tours,** Straight Wharf, 228-0334, has six one-and-one-quarter-hour tours of Nantucket town and the east side of the island out to 'Sconset, adults $9.

BICYCLING. Bikes or mopeds are the best way to see the outskirts of Nantucket town (the cobblestone streets of downtown present a problem there), as well as a good way to get out to Surfside Beach. The ride is flat, on a path bordering the roadway. The most popular trip is out the bike path bordering the road to Siasconset, an easy (make that boring) eight-mile straightaway past the airport with the wind generally from behind. The beguiling east-end village perched on a rose-dotted bluff is a world away from busy Nantucket town. The sand dunes, the azure-blue ocean, the golf courses and the birds a-twitter between vine-covered cottages present "a magical setting like that of Bermuda," as a Summer House manager reminded us. Instead of retracing your path, return via the winding, sometimes up-and-down loop road past Sankaty Light, Quidnet and Polpis. Here you'll see cranberry bogs and ponds, striking homes and rolling moors, and you'll get a feel for the real island. The real island is also sensed from the bike path out to Madaket and you get the same kind of ups and downs and arounds on the pleasant, paved path beside the road — rather than being in the road, as on the Polpis loop.

Bike and Moped Rentals. Young's Bicycle Shop, Steamboat Wharf, 228-1151, is in one of the first buildings one passes upon leaving the Steamship Authority ferry. Rent wheels, grab your bag and you're on your way. No prices were posted at any bike shop when we last were there, but we were quoted rates of $12 a day for a three-speed and $16 for an all-terrain bike. Young's also has mopeds, as do **Nantucket Bike Shop** and **Cook's Cycles.**

Walking Tour by Roger A. Young, 28 Easy St. (508) 228-1062. A number of self-guided tours of Nantucket town are available — or just meander in any direction, and you won't be disappointed. Best for local color is the tour sponsored by the Nantucket Historical Association and led by Roger Young (of the Young Bicycle Shop family). By appointment, the energetic semi-retiree gives two-hour tours after which participants receive little blue cards saying the bearer "has successfully completed the leisurely walking tour through some of the lanes and byways of Nantucket town." You arrange to meet under the tree at the Foulger Museum. Roger won't be in Nantucket pinks ("those are for the summer folk," his wife advised), but you'll recognize him by his MAA (Madaket Admiralty Assocation) cap and the walking cane he uses as a pointer. A former town selectman and a civic leader, he knows everyone in town and everyone knows him, which makes the tour that much more interesting as he waves to the bank president and jokes with a young shopkeeper. "I go where the buses don't," he said as he led our group of seven down a two-foot-wide walkway beside the newly restored 1809 South Church (Unitarian-Universalist), where he arranged for a special viewing of the interior, in which the 1843 trompe l'oeil painting is quite a sight. He relates the inside scoop on all the history and personalities of Nantucket, from the mother of Ben Franklin to the Macy who founded the department-store chain. Barely slowed after two hip operations, he nevertheless has curtailed his schedule from two trips to one a day (at 9:30 or 1:30 — the first caller sets the time). Adults, $10.

On or Near the Water

Nantucket Harbor Cruises, Straight Wharf, 228-1444. If you've already arrived by ferry, this may seem redundant, but at least you find out what you were looking at. Ice-cream cruises depart daily at 1, 2 and 3; adults $12.50, children $10, less $2.50 without ice cream). Longer cruises go out before dinner, before sunset and by moonlight ($12.50 to $20). A lobster fishing cruise among the traps is offered daily except Sunday at 10:30.

Fair Tide Charters, Slip 18, Straight Wharf, 228-4844. Capt. Lee Groth and crew sail out of Fort Lauderdale in winter but say they like Nantucket better — the island provides a shelter for Nantucket Sound that the coast lacks, giving "a strange combination of flat ocean but a lot of wind." Sailors know that, but landlubbers enjoy a short cruise on their 43-foot oceangoing yacht. "After you've been to so many restaurants and clubs, you get restauranted out and this becomes a nice afternoon off," said a crewman. The main two-hour sail departs daily for Great Point or Madaket at 10, 1, 3:30 and 6:30 (sunset), $25 a person.

Harbor Sails & Rentals, Slip 15, Straight Wharf, 228-5585. Capt. James Genthner offers a variety of cruises on his 31-foot Friendship sloop **Endeavor.** One or one-and-a-half-hour sails cost $15 to $20 per person. A three-hour beachcomber cruise to Coatue, where you're rowed ashore for swimming or shell-collecting, costs $320 for one to ten people.

Fishing Charters. The Flicka, Straight Wharf, 228-9224, is Nantucket's longesr-running sportfishing charter. It takes one to six people for $70 an hour, supplying everything but the food. "We're fishing ten minutes after we leave the dock," Capt. Gibby Nickerson said. **The Albacore,** Straight Wharf, 228-1439, has been involved in the catching of three world-record bluefish. Several surfcasting charters are offered for the more adventurous.

Windsurfing. The lack of choppy seas that sailors enjoy also is attractive to windsurfers on Nantucket's north shore, particularly around Jetties Beach. **Indian Summer Sports** on Steamboat Dock and at Jetties Beach, 228-6086, rents windsurfers, surfboards and sunfish, and offers instruction. Madaket Harbor, Dionis and Pocomo Point are also popular with windsurfers. We're told that several have windsurfed all the way to Martha's Vineyard, some 30 miles away. For surfing, the south shore around Surfside is challenging — big waves but strong rip currents going the other way.

BEACHES. Despite the allure of great restaurants, inns, shops, history and such, the beaches are what entice many to Nantucket. And there's quite a choice. The north shore beaches facing Nantucket Sound tend to be calmer and more tranquil than those facing the open ocean. On the south shore, the waters are warmer (up to 75 degrees in summer), the ocean bottom slopes more gently and the beaches are wider. Just north of town is **Jetties Beach,** the best all-around for calm waters and named for the jetties that jut out into the ocean from its sandy shore. Bathhouses, lifeguards and a snack bar are available. **Children's Beach,** closer to the center off Harbor View Way, lives up to its name and has a playground. More secluded and harder to reach on the north shore is **Dionis,** a harbor beach favored by snorkelers. On the south shore, our favorite all-around is **Surfside,** four miles south of town. It has lifeguards, a food concession, bike racks, changing areas and an impressive surf — the beach is most expansive, of course, at low tide. Less crowded and more private is **Siasconset Beach,** a pleasant strand along the east shore. The beaches at **Great Point, Coskata** and **Coatue** are popular with those who can get to them, either by boat or jeep. At the island's west end is **Madaket,** a great place for sunset-watching and isolated beaching; here the water deepens rapidly.

Wildlife Refuges. Twenty-one miles of ocean, harbor and sound shoreline are protected by the Coatue, Coskata-Coatue and Great Point-Nantucket National wildlife refuges. Mainly barrier beaches, marshes and dunes, they harbor a variety of birds, shellfish and even jack rabbits. Visitors are welcome, but are warned that swimming may be dangerous. Coatue is part of the Nantucket Conservation Foundation, which has protected more than 6,100 acres of the island. Great Point is a remote and desolate stretch, reached by jeep or foot. On the way out, you'll see clamming and oyster ponds, eagle and tern nesting grounds, and bayberry forests as you cross the dunes to the ruins of America's oldest working lighthouse, now being restored.

Church Tower Tour, First Congregational Church and Old North Vestry, 62 Centre St., is billed as Nantucket's "most unique tour." Church officials say that you get a bird's-eye view of town and can see the entire island from the church tower atop Beacon Hill. Open weekdays 10 to 4, June-September.

Historic Sites and Museums

Historic Nantucket. Dating to 1659 when Thomas Macy arrived as the first settler, Nantucket town has more than 400 pre-1840 structures, the greatest concentration in the country. Walk up Main Street for a look at the Three Bricks,

Georgian mansions built by whaling merchant Joseph Starbuck. Twelve buildings of special significance are open to the public by the Nantucket Historical Association, headquartered in the Thomas Macy Warehouse museum, Straight Wharf, 228-1894. Tickets may be obtained individually or in combination. On the outskirts, don't miss the Oldest House (1686) on Sunset Hill, the Old Mill (1746) and the Old Gaol (1805). Five period houses of different eras and two museums (see below) are opened by the association as well. Combination visitor pass to all buildings: adults $6, children $2.50.

Nantucket Whaling Museum, Broad Street. The single largest attraction in town is the Whaling Museum, as befits a community that was a major whaling port. The story of Nantucket whaling is detailed in the inviting red-brick building just off Steamboat Wharf. The museum opened in 1930 as an outgrowth of the private collection of summer resident Edward F. Sanderson and has expanded since. The extensive exhibit includes a 43-foot finback whale that washed onto the north shore in 1967, an eighteen-foot whale jaw, what's said to be the only candle press in existence, the original lens from the Sankaty lighthouse, a room full of scrimshaw, whalecraft shops, whaling implements and whalers' finds, along with portraits and memorabilia of those who made Nantucket the third largest port in the United States at the time. You leave the rambling structure via an outstanding museum shop. Open daily 10 to 5, Memorial Day to mid-October; weekends in fall and spring. Adults $3, children $1, or combination visitor pass.

Fair Street Museum, Fair Street. Located next to the 1838 Quaker Meeting House, this 1904 structure was built to house the Nantucket Historical Association collections, which since have been dispersed throughout its properties. It is now the town's art museum, hosting exhibits of local cultural heritage and decorative arts. Open daily 10 to 5. Adults $1, children 50 cents, or visitor pass.

Maria Mitchell Science Center, 1 Vestal St., 228-2896. The birthplace of America's first woman astronomer, who discovered the Mitchell comet, remains as it was in 1818 and offers herb and wildflower gardens. Next door is a memorial observatory open Wednesday evenings. The center also has an aquarium at 29 Washington St. Open Tuesday-Saturday in summer, 10 to 4. Adults $3.

The **Nantucket Life Saving Museum,** Polpis Road, is said to be the only one of its kind in the world. The new museum building is a re-creation of the original Surfside Station, built by the U.S. Life Saving Service in 1874. The drama of rescue at sea is presented through photos, original boats and life saving equipment, quarterboards of vessels wrecked around Nantucket and more. Open Tuesday-Sunday 10 to 5, mid-June to mid-September. Adults, $1.50.

SHOPPING. Nantucket is a paradise for shoppers, and every year new stores open (residents bemoaned the arrival of Benetton, the first mainland chain store other than the Country Store of Concord and Crabtree & Evelyn, both of which pass muster (as does the vital A&P supermarket on the wharf). Fine small shops, boutiques and galleries are scattered along the wharves, Main Street and side streets. Among standouts are **Erica Wilson Needle Works, Kenneth Taylor Gallery, Zero Main** for suave women's clothing, the **British Boys Club** for men's clothing, the **Forager House Collection** of folk art and accessories, and **Nantucket Looms,** with beautiful, whimsical woven items and a sweater in the window for $750. Good for arts and crafts are the **Artisans Cooperative** (from quilts and sweaters to toys and cards) and **The Spectrum. The Lion's Paw,** one of the nicest shops we've seen, is too elegant for words; we especially like their lines of pottery.

Almost everything is fishy, from T-shirts to expensive jewelery, at **Go Fish.** At **Porthole Gift Shop,** a Nantucket scallop filled with potpourri ($8) makes a good island souvenir. **Petticoat Row** has incredible hand-painted bird houses (one at $5,000 comes with two live zebra finches in it) among other wonderful gifts. Out of town, don't miss the **Studio Gallery** in Siasconset; it's the place to pick up a painting of a dear little 'Sconset cottage with its picture-perfect garden.

The Hub newsstand and sundry store is a local institution. Other local institutions are Nantucket faded pink pants worn by men, while women tote Nantucket's famed lightship baskets on their tanned arms. The baskets come in assorted shapes and sizes, and are carried in many shops. At Michael Kane's **Carvers Guild** shop, we looked at a small $800 number without the ivory and decided to pass. Instead, we picked up a couple of nice-looking sweaters at a good discount at **Nantucket Mills.**

Where to Eat _____ ⟋ℭℭℭ

For an island with a year-round population of 7,000 (augmented by up to 40,000 high-livers and free-spenders in the summer), Nantucket has an uncommon concentration of uncommonly good restaurants. Even the summer-long vacationer would be hard-pressed to visit them all — and might go broke in the process. But most visitors, whether staying in an in-town inn or a Surfside cottage, make a point of dining out at least once. Most of the top restaurants require or advise reservations; a few don't take them.

Here we concentrate on those near the water, or those with a particularly summery air.

On or Near the Water

The Chantecleer, New Street, Siasconset. (508) 257-6231. Renowned across the world for world-class dining, this elegant French restaurant on two floors of a large 'Sconset cottage has been considered tops since Jean-Charles Berruet acquired it in 1969. A la carte lunch (entrees $15 to $20) in the outdoor garden, at tables beneath trellised canopies of roses and beside impeccably trimmed hedges, is a 'Sconset tradition, as is an after-dinner drink accompanied by piano music in the beamed and nautical **Grill,** formerly the Chanty Bar. Amidst heavy silver and pretty floral china, dinner is served in the lovely fireplaced dining room opening onto a greenhouse, in the Grill or upstairs in a pristine peach and white room. Although you can order a la carte, prix-fixe dinners are $50 "and worth every cent," townspeople informed us, although we and some other writers have been a tad disappointed lately, perhaps because of such high expectations. Regulars put themselves in the hands of a knowledgeable staff to steer them to the right choices on an ambitious and complex menu. Feast, perhaps, on a mousse of duck liver and foie gras served with a sweet and sour sauce garnished with crayfish tails, cassoulet with roasted monkfish and lobster sausage or saddle of rabbit with fried polenta, salad and cheese, and a grand marnier souffle. The possibilities are limited only by chef Jean Charles's imagination and the sensibilities of his kitchen staff of eleven. Recent additions to the Chantecleer are a healthful, light-cuisine menu and a bar and grill menu. The award-winning wine cellar contains 1,000 selections, with good values at the high end. Lunch, noon to 2 in summer; dinner, 6:30 to 10; closed Mondays. Open late May to mid-October. Reservations and jackets required.

Topper's at the Wauwinet, Wauwinet Road, Nantucket. (508) 228-0145. Lunching on the outdoor terrace or dining in the light and airy dining room at the sun sets over Nantucket Bay is an occasion. The setting is summery as can be; that the food is so good is a bonus. Chef Keith Mahoney's menu is creative and ever-changing. We liked the grilled quail on a toasted brioche and the mustardy lobster and crab cakes for starters. Among main courses ($22 to $31), the sauteed veal with wild mushrooms and risotto and the grilled rack and leg of lamb with a tomato-eggplant timbale were standouts. After a meal like this, the homemade ice creams and sorbets appeal to us more than the richer pastries that catch many an eye. Service is friendly, the water comes with a lemon slice, the bread is crusty, and everything's just right. Could be that the location puts one in the proper frame of mind. Be advised, however, that many tables in the two side-by-side dining rooms don't get water views. For that, you may just have to return for lunch on the terrace another day. Lunch daily, noon to 2; dinner, 6 to 9:30.

The Summer House, Ocean Avenue, Siasconset. (508) 257-9956. The main house behind the wide veranda is summery as can be with beachy furniture and an idyllic, Caribbean-style decor of white, pink and dark green. Hanging baskets of flowers, flickering candles and a display of desserts and cognacs add to the romance. With pianist Sal Gioe playing in the background, dining by candlelight on the veranda as the moon rises over the ocean is magical. New chef Charles Salliou, who trained with Paul Bocuse, is winning accolades with entrees like filet of salmon souffle with scallop mousse, grilled lobster with coral butter, and mignonettes of beef with truffle and port sauce, priced from $20 to $31. Appetizers could be smoked pheasant with endive and watercress and sauteed barbarie duck foie gras with mangoes. For dessert, how about a fruit compote with ginger or a palette of sorbets with berry coulis? Lunch on the expanded terrace at poolside is summery as well. Inexplicably, the menu lists the burger at $8 under entrees and salad nicoise with yellowfin tuna at $13 under lighter fare. We'd get turned around, too, after a pina colada or two above one of the alltime great beaches. You can refresh with a dip in the pool ($15, free for lunch guests). Owner Peter Karlson was planning to inaugurate light, casual dinners at poolside in 1991. Lunch daily, 11:30 to 4; dinner, 6 to 10.

Straight Wharf Restaurant, Straight Wharf, Nantucket. (508) 228-4499. A few years ago, Marian Morash of television and cookbook fame was the force behind this seasonal restaurant on the waterfront, specializing in fresh seafood and produce. Her tradition continues, and the crowds waiting in line for a table in The Bar attest to its success. We wish that the June night we dined had been warm enough to eat outside on the canopied, rib-lighted deck beside the water, that the service had been more prompt and that the acclaimed vegetables were more exciting and seasonal than broccoli and carrots. But the complimentary bluefish pate, the grilled salmon and the lobster crepes were first-rate, the peach bavarian laden with raspberry sauce excellent, and the elaborately written bill was served with two chocolate shells. The shiny parquet floors and the soaring, shingled interior walls topped with billowing canvas create a summery feeling. With candles in hurricane lamps and classical music in the background, dining here is a real treat. Entrees on the mostly seafood menu run from $23 to $28. Grill items in the bar are about half the price; no wonder it's packed all the time. Dinner nightly except Monday, 6:45 to 9:30. Open mid-June to late September.

The Second Story, 1 South Beach St., Nantucket. (508) 228-3471. The pink and green decor (including a pink-spattered, green-painted floor), enormous hurricane lamps and a harborview-window alcove awash with pillows are all very striking and glamorous. At night, candles are the only illumination. The dinner fare, changing nightly, is a mix of regional cuisines from around the world, from Thai to European to Brazilian to American. We enjoyed the good hot monkey bread, and a thick slab of country pate that was piping hot and bathed in a creamy green peppercorn sauce. Among entrees ($18 to $28), the Thai shrimp with black bean and coriander sauce was super spicy, and the scallops au gratin so ample that we needed neither salad (extra, as in many Nantucket restaurants) nor appetizer. Our amaretto souffle had barely a hint of amaretto and tasted more like a mousse; pears in puff pastry with caramel sauce might have been a better choice. Dinner nightly, seatings at 7 and 9:15; lunch in off-season. Open April-December.

The Galley on Cliffside Beach, Jefferson Avenue, Nantucket. (508) 228-9641. Nantucket has no better waterfront setting for a restaurant than this canopied, flower-lined deck right on the beach beside the ocean. Rimmed with red geraniums and hanging plants, the blue wicker chairs and white tablecloths make an enticing setting against a background of azure water and fine sand. Regional American cuisine is featured, from $19 for steamed mussels to $27 for Catalan fish stew. Scampi with a spinach timbale, marinated lamb brochette and roasted chicken with lentils and summer greens are among the choices. At midday, take a break from the beach for a lunch of cold lobster salad with roasted peppers and asparagus, deep-fried calamari with orange aioli and coriander salsa, or sauteed sea scallops over watercress, finishing with the chef's special homemade cognac ice cream. Lunch daily, noon to 2:30; dinner, 6:30 to 10. Open mid-June through mid-September.

The Regatta at the White Elephant, Easton Street, Nantucket. (508) 228-2500. A large harborfront terrace beside the pool — with a feeling rather like that of a yacht club — makes this another good bet for lunch, though we thought our interesting seafood and chicken salads were paltry for the price and we had to ask for seconds on rolls. The caesar salad with shrimp, scallops and crabmeat and the smoked chicken and grilled vegetables with chipolte mayonnaise, both $8.95, appealed at our latest visit. The dinner menu gets fancier in the lately redecorated, elegant white and hunter green dining room on several levels, some with water views. All is serene and lovely amid exotic porcelain flowers, column dividers, draped niches, chandeliers and tiny lamps. The dinner menu runs from $17.50 for griled tuna in ginger and soy or pan-roasted breast of duck to $24.50 for herbed rack of lamb with minted apple chutney. For dessert, take a fresh pastry with coffee and a cognac in the pretty peach and wicker lounge, where there's live music in season — before dinner, during and after. Lunch daily, noon to 2:30; dinner, 6 to 10. Open Memorial Day to late September.

The Westender, Madaket Road, Madaket. (508) 228-5197. If you find yourself near the west end of the island, at the beach or simply OD'ed on high prices, consider this lively establishment run by scallop fisherman Peter Dooley and his wife Annie. At our latest visit, the rustic house they started in a decade earlier had been gutted and a two-story contemporary structure had taken its place. The bar and takeout window occupy the first floor. Upstairs, large windows yield views of distant water on three sides, and the setting is casual with polyurethaned tables and windsor chairs beneath a cathedral ceiling. Track lights illuminate the local paintings, which are for sale. Regulars like to start with a Madaket mystery, a secret $4 drink blending rums and fruit punches. The lunch menu offers everything from vegetarian nachos to burgers to popcorn shrimp ($5.50 to $9.95). The dinner menu is one of the island's more extensive, with twenty entrees priced from $12 for mussels marinara to $23 for rack of lamb. Seafood stew, lobster linguini alfredo and grilled swordfish, salmon and yellowfin tuna are listed. Chocolate madness cake is the favored dessert. Lunch daily, 11:30 to 4; dinner 6 to 10. Open mid-June through October.

The Rope Walk, Straight Wharf, Nantucket. (508) 228-8886. A serious restaurant or a singles bar? This establishment can't seem to make up its mind, or the customers can't. But there's no denying the water view from the small outdoor patio and the two interior dining rooms, where management says they serve 200 daily for both lunch and dinner in season. No reservations are taken, and the scene can get crowded. If you can get in, and if it's not too noisy, folks say you'll like the grilled seafood and meats, with some occasional creative twists. Entrees range from $14 to $18, and lunches run about half that. Lunch daily, 11:30 to 3; dinner, 5:30 to 10. Open May to Columbus Day.

Other Choices

More options, from elegant to casual:

Le Languedoc, 24 Broad St., Nantucket. (508) 228-2552. Three serene candlelit dining rooms upstairs and a more casual cafe downstairs room are the setting for what some consider the town's most consistently fine meals. The limited menu is supplemented by nightly seafood specials. Of the entrees ($19.75 to $26), we liked the noisettes of lamb with artichokes in a rosemary sauce and the sauteed sweetbreads with lobster in puff pastry, finished off with a chocolate hazelnut torte spiked with grand marnier. Lunch in season, noon to 2; dinner nightly, 6:30 to 10.

21 Federal, 21 Federal St., Nantucket. (508) 228-2121. New in 1985, this expanded onto the mainland with a "branch" by the same name in Washington, D.C., and has slipped a bit from its lofty heights, according to local raters. Nonetheless, we enjoyed a mighty fine lunch on the terrace. The menu changes daily. A typical one runs from $18 for sauteed chicken breast with tomatoes, rosemary and polenta to $26 for grilled tenderloin with roquefort sauce or walnut-crusted lamb in sweet garlic sauce. Lunch, 11:30 to 2:30; dinner 6 to 10. Open April-December.

American Seasons, 80 Centre St., Nantucket. (508) 228-7111. Southwest decor/Nantucket style, and a fresh, seasonal menu are the hallmarks of this new eatery, along with refreshing prices. Brothers Stuart and Everett Reid, the chef-owners, put out wonderful meals. We can vouch for appetizers of chilled tomato and leek soup topped with goat cheese, corn tortilla flutes with shredded pork and a spicy black bean sauce, a special salad of wild greens with a potato cake topped with crabmeat and smoked chedder, and a main dish of assertive smoked tomato pasta with grilled scallops, mussels and a watercress pesto. Entrees run from $14 for roast chicken with creole remoulade to $22 for grilled swordfish with fresh rock shrimp etouffee. The presentations are remarkable, especially the garnishes and decorations adorning the dessert plates. Dinner nightly, 6:30 to 10.

The Boarding House, 12 Federal St., Nantucket. (508) 228-9622. The shady outdoor patio and a cathedral-ceilinged Victorian bar with slate floor and small marble tables are perfect for lunch or drinks. And the sunken dining room in pink with a Mediterranean feeling is the setting for good food. Starters might be duck and pancetta ravioli or grilled lamb salad; main courses, swordfish steak or grilled filet mignon. Entrees are priced from $19 (for the daily duck presentation) to $22. On a warm night, the outdoor patio is great for people-watching as you nurse an after-dinner drink. Lunch, Monday-Friday 11:30 to 2:30; dinner Monday-Saturday 6:30 to 10.

The Beach Plum Cafe and Bakery, 11 West Creek Road, Nantucket. (508) 228-8893. The decor is minimal, but that's not why you go here. You go here for breakfast, for excellent pastries (this is the bakery for the Straight Wharf restaurant enterprises), super pancakes and create-your-own omelets. You go here for dinner, for some fantastic cooking at off-island prices (entrees, $9.75 for homemade fettuccine with summer vegetables to $12.95 for pan-seared loin of lamb — that's right, lamb — at half Nantucket's usual price). To start, go for the fresh ravioli of the evening. Could it possibly be as good as ours with feta cheese, sweet peppers and a fabulous cream sauce? Breakfast, Monday-Saturday 7 to 11:30; dinner nightly, 6 to 9; lunch in off-season, Sunday brunch.

The Morning Glory Cafe, Old South Wharf, Nantucket. (508) 228-2212. The quaintness of the wharf patio is exceeded only by the uniqueness of the small inner dining room with striking murals painted on the walls by an artist neighbor of owner Liz Gracia. The patio is where everyone who is anyone in town seems to congregate at breakfast to exchange gossip of the goings-on the night before. Breakfasts of Morning Glory muffins (which include everything but the kitchen sink) and omelets are memorable, and at night you can BYOB to enjoy with such eclectic fare as Chinese egg rolls, monkfish, Szechuan shrimp or lamb chops parmesan, priced from $7.25 to $10.50. Breakfast, 7:30 to 11:30; lunch, noon to 3; cafe supper, 6 to 10. Seasonal.

Sconset Cafe, Post Office Square, Siasconset. (508) 257-4008. Pam McKinstry, founder of the Morning Glory Cafe, moved to the Sconset Cafe, packing her followers in at eight tables for lunches of fajitas salad in a tortilla shell, boboli (a pizza-like creation with pesto and artichoke hearts), and interesting soups and sandwiches. At dinner you might order fresh tuna with a potato, garlic and chive puree or filet mignon with cabernet sauce ($15 to $21). For dessert, try the frozen key lime pie or a grand marnier brioche pudding. The summery decor is minimal, but the food isn't. Many of the recipes are detailed in the three Sconset Cafe cookbooks sold across the island. Three meals daily from 8 a.m. to 10 p.m., May-September. BYOB.

Claudette's on the Porch, Post Office Square, Siasconset. (508) 257-6622. If you don't want to sit down to lunch, visit the seasonal little place beside the cafe to pick up a box lunch for the beach ($5.75 for a sandwich, veggie sticks and brownies or lemon cake) or to eat on a shady outdoor deck facing the square. You can get seafood salad, sandwiches or a piece of the celebrated lemon cake. Iced coffee and tea are available for overheated bikers. Open daily in summer, 9 to 5.

Something Natural, 50 Cliff Road, Nantucket. (508) 228-0504. If you are out for a walk or a bike ride, stop here to pick up a great sandwich (a choice of thirteen, from $4.50 for cream cheese and olive to $5.75 for seafood salad, also available in half sizes), or a salad. Sandwich garnishes, 25 cents each, range from sliced egg to chutney, and the seven breads, available by the loaf as well, are sensational. The muffins are good, too, and there's carrot cake, Scotch-Irish cake and fresh lemonade. Open daily in summer, 9 to 6, to 3 in spring and fall.

FOR MORE INFORMATION: Nantucket Island Chamber of Commerce, Pacific Club Building at foot of Main Street, Nantucket, Mass. 02554. (508) 228-1700. We have not found the Information Bureau at 25 Federal St. particularly helpful on any of our visits.

Cahoon's Hollow is one of four ocean beaches in Wellfleet.

Wellfleet-Truro/Cape Cod, Mass.

You're driving up Route 6, the Mid-Cape Highway, toward Provincetown. The traffic is horrendous and the landscape isn't great either: motels, pancake houses, fast-food restaurants, flea markets. You've come to Cape Cod to cool off, relax, put your feet up, find a little space — and you think you've made a mistake.

Then you turn left, following the signs to Wellfleet Center. Immediately, the traffic eases. The road becomes charming, meandering past handsome old clapboard houses and dipping down to the Town Pier. There are authentic fishing boats, plus sailboats and yachts bobbing on the waters of Wellfleet Harbor. You get a cool drink and sit on the dock. You watch a few sailboarders out on Cape Cod Bay. The breeze is cool and fresh.

This is just the beginning. In the center of town, the shops are small and select. A variety of restaurants — from seafood by the pier to gourmet cuisine in a house-cum-art-gallery — are available. Several good art galleries offer water-colors, oils, Salt Marsh pottery and Wellfleet brownware.

The ocean side of town is no less attractive. Five gorgeous beaches, including one that is part of the Cape Cod National Seashore, beckon. Better still, you can find a parking place and a spot on the sand. This is the Cape as you'd hoped it would be.

Wellfleet has managed to retain the character of the Cape and to reject its blatant commercialism. Located next door to Eastham, and the main visitors' center for the Cape Cod National Seashore, the town has much to offer in the way of sun and sand and surf. And the fishing is fine. The next town to the north is Truro and there's more to be found here.

Accommodations such as rental cottages, campsites, a couple of inns and a few motels on the highway suffice. There is no Ramada or Sheraton, no McDonald's or Burger King. You will not be in bumper-to-bumper traffic every time you drive on one of the town roads. The contrast becomes particularly apparent when you pull out onto Route 6 to get to another location. Even early on a Saturday morning — when we needed to take a sick child to a medical-care center further up the Cape — the traffic was impossible. By the time we returned to our inn in Wellfleet, we were doubly appreciative of the difference.

Of course, you'll want to drive to Provincetown for a day or an evening. You will spend time at the National Seashore. You may even visit a shopping mall in Hyannis on a rainy day. But if you want to experience the best the Cape has to offer, you will find much of it here. The pace is more relaxed, the dress more casual, the welcome warmer. We wish you a good holiday in Wellfleet and Truro.

Getting There

Wellfleet and Truro are located on the outer or lower Cape between Provincetown and Eastham. If Provincetown is the "fist," this is the "forearm." From the Bourne or Sagamore bridges take Route 6, the mid-Cape Highway, until you see signs for Wellfleet Center. Continue up Route 6 until you can take off for Route 6A and Truro. Bus service is available from Boston to Wellfleet.

Where to Stay_____ *CCC*

The Inn at Duck Creeke, East Main Street, Wellfleet 02667. (508) 349-9333. Two energetic innkeepers, Bob Morrill and Judy Pihl, have put together a most interesting complex: a main inn that was once a sea captain's house built in the 1800s, several smaller buildings, a duck pond, salt marshes, a fine restaurant called Sweet Seasons (see Where to Eat) and a cozy tavern. Popular and appealing, it's wonderfully located — near Route 6 but far enough apart to be quiet and relaxed. The 25 guest rooms are decorated individually with spool beds, Boston rockers, cane-bottom chairs and painted furniture. Many have mini-print wallpaper and some, like our large family room on the third floor (the old attic), have exposed beams, dormer windows and wall-to-wall carpeting. The front parlor is outfitted with wing chairs and period furniture. A small breakfast room to one side with several tables is where you'll get continental breakfast with coffee cake and muffins set out buffet style, along with coffee and tea. Five rooms are in a building out back and two more in a smaller building to the side of the main inn. Most rooms have private baths with showers. Doubles, $55 to $80. Open mid-May to mid-October.

The Holden Inn, Commercial Street, Wellfleet 02667. (508) 349-3450. Operated since 1969 by the Fricker family, this complex has three buildings: the main white clapboard, black-shuttered inn, a cottage next door, and the Lodge out back with some wonderful views of Cape Cod Bay, especially from a screened porch. Rockers are set along the front porch of the main inn on Commercial Street and guests also relax in a wicker-filled public room. All rooms in the inn and cottage have private baths; those in the lodge share. The Holden Inn can accommodate 50. Room 3 in the main building, on the front, has a double bed with brass headboard and pink printed spread, and wide floorboards indicating the age of the house. No meals are served. Doubles, $50; two-bedroom suite, $100. Open April to Columbus Day.

The Moorings, Commercial Street, Wellfleet 02667. (508) 349-3379. Innkeeper Sally Scribner comes to the Cape each summer from Syracuse, N.Y., to operate this attractive small complex with two cottages and two smaller cabins out back, plus one three-room suite with private bath in the white house with black shutters. Duck Creeke runs behind the property; it is now mostly marshland, but the harbor and the Town Pier are just a short walk down the street. The main house dates from 1850 and has a welcoming feel to it; coffee and tea are offered to guests mornings in the dining room. The three-room suite with private entrance features a twin-bedded bedroom, a sitting room, and a bathroom with an old-fashioned tub. It rents for $65 a night; the fully furnished three-bedroom cottage with kitchen is $490 per week; the two-bedroom cottage is $460. Two cabins each have a double-bedded bedroom and a private W/C, but share a shower. They are $40 nightly or $240 by the week. Open summer only.

Wellfleet Motel and Lodge, Route 6, Box 606, South Wellfleet 02663. (508) 349-3535 or (800) 852-2900. Located across busy Route 6 from the active Audubon Society grounds, this motel and lodge have been operated for twenty years by Bob and Helen Wilson. The 25-unit motel is the older building; it has pine-paneled rooms (fifteen of them family size) with refrigerators, color TVs, coffee-makers and air-conditioning, The two-story, 40-unit lodge, built in 1984, is more contemporary and has several two-room suites in two buildings. Attractions here are both an indoor and an outdoor pool, a hot tub, coffee shop, bar, picnic tables and a barbecue grill. The grounds include about twelve acres, many of them wooded. Doubles in lodge, $68 to $98; two-room suites accommodating up to four persons, $90 to $130. Doubles in motel, $65 to $94.

The Mainstay Motor Inn, Route 6, Wellfleet 02663. (508) 349-2350. Located on busy Route 6, but set back from the road a bit, this two-story, L-shaped motel has twenty pleasant units. Simply furnished, they feature two double beds, television and air-conditioning. The second-floor units have balconies. Continental breakfast is served in season in a small breakfast area. A plus for beachgoers is an outdoor shower. A large outdoor pool is also appealing. Doubles, $70.

Topmast, Route 6A, Box 44, North Truro 02652. (508) 487-1189. Located directly on the beach on Cape Cod Bay and run with great attention to detail for nineteen years by Nancy and Al Silva, Topmast is very popular and we can understand why. There's a 650-foot private beach with chairs and lounges, plus a large outdoor pool. The motel has two buildings, one directly on the beach, the other across the street with the pool. The **Harbor Lights** restaurant, also a part of the complex, is a good spot to have lunch or dinner. Rooms feature two double beds, balconies and pine paneling. Guests can use picnic tables and charcoal grills on the beach. Rooms on the bay rent usually by the week in July and August; those on the poolside are available for a couple of days. Some are efficiencies. Beachfront efficiencies are $550 to $725 a week in season. Doubles, $60 in poolside motel; beachfront motel, $500 weekly. Open May-October.

Brownie's Cabins, Route 6, South Wellfleet 02663. (508) 349-6881. One of the original, old-fashioned cottage colonies (there are many in the area), Brownie's consists of eleven cabins clustered in a pine grove just off Route 6. Operated by the Marshall family of West Springfield, Mass., the cabins come in three configurations: two bedrooms, one-bedroom efficiencies and one-bedroom overnights without kitchen facilities. The two-bedroom cabins have one double bed and two twins and fully equipped kitchens; they rent for $395 weekly. One-bedroom efficiencies; $330 weekly; overnight cabins, $310 weekly. Open Memorial Day to Columbus Day.

The Summer House, Pond Road, Box 778, North Truro 02655. (508) 487-2077. Steep granite steps lead up to this charming older house now turned into a B&B in North Truro. Five guest rooms share one bath and an outside shower. Two rooms are on the first floor and three on the second. Breakfast is served on a sun porch. It is two miles to the ocean from here. Doubles, $60.

CAMPING. The Cape Cod National Seashore does not operate a campground. Private campgrounds in the area include the **North Truro Camping Area** on

Highland Road, North Truro, (508) 487-1847, with 350 sites in a pine woods and **North of Highland Camping Area** on Head of Meadow Road, North Truro, (508) 487-1191, with 237 sites.

Seeing and Doing _____ ©©©

The beaches are the main draw in Wellfleet and Truro. Roads are good for bicycling, and the bay is fine for windsurfing, sailing and boating. Fishing is great. Rainy-day possibilities include splendid art galleries, interesting shops and historical society buildings. Just relaxing on the town pier to watch the goings-on deserves some time, too.

Cape Cod National Seashore. Start at the Salt Pond Visitors Center, Route 6, Eastham, where you can view dioramas and get a feeling for these 27,000 acres, including some of the best beaches on the East Coast. In Wellfleet, **Marconi Beach** is part of the National Seashore; it has lifeguards and changing facilities. An extraordinary resource, the national seashore offers more than fine beaches. A full range of guided nature walks, talks and evening programs is run by park rangers; a schedule may be obtained at the visitors' center. Three of the self-guided trails are designated for horseback riding; horses can be rented at nearby stables. Bikers especially like riding through the seashore; pick up the folder, "Bicycle Trails of Cape Cod National Seashore," so you'll know where you're headed. Surf-fishing does not require a license and you can try your luck at any of the beaches as long as you're not in the lifeguard-protected areas. Open fires are allowed only with a permit, available at visitor centers. Centers are open daily from late spring through fall.

Among the walks recommended in the Wellfleet area is that around **Great Island.** This six-mile round trip will take three to four hours — much of it is in deep sand and is challenging. Pick up the National Park Service's mimeographed map at the trailhead in the parking lot before you set out (maps are kept in a box beside the large metal display map). You should carry your own water. The trail is one of the most primitive in the National Seashore area. Because no vehicles are permitted on Great Island, the only sounds are those of the birds and the surf — lovely.

Wellfleet Bay Wildlife Sanctuary, off Route 6, South Wellfleet, 349-2615. Operated by the Massachusetts Audubon Society, this is a treat. There are five miles of trails through a salt marsh, moor field and pine woods. Activities include family and sunset hikes, shorebird walks, early bird walks, night hikes, bird-banding demonstrations and birding programs for beginners.

Swimming and Boating

In addition to Marconi Beach, which is overseen by park rangers from the National Seashore, four other ocean beaches are within the Town of Wellfleet. **White Crest** and **Cahoon's Hollow** are open to the public for a $10 daily parking fee. If you're staying in town for at least a week, buy a $25 beach sticker that allows you to park at all town beaches. On Cape Cod Bay, two popular beaches are **Sunset View,** which is next to town, and **Duck Harbor.** But we prefer the ocean beaches and particularly like Cahoon's Hollow, which is reached after hiking over a dune.

In Truro, $4 daily parking fees are charged at **Head of the Meadow Beach** on the ocean and **Corn Hill Beach** on the bay.

Swimming is easier in the bay than the ocean. In fact, the ocean's high waves and rip tides at this part of the Cape can be awesome and frightening. A lovely place to swim is the freshwater pond, **Great Pond,** located off Cahoon Hollow Road. A rough-hewn set of wooden stairs leads down to the water, which is clear and turquoise like the Caribbean. **Gull Pond** is another nice freshwater pond; a large parking area is next to it, off Gull Pond Road from Route 6.

If you've brought your own boat, you can launch it at the Town Pier at the end of Commercial Street in Wellfleet for a small fee. Ample parking is available. Very small boats also can be launched at the Indian Neck parking lot at the foot of the breakwater, but any boat with a trailer is best handled at the pier.

You can rent paddleboats, sunfish, sailboards, canoes and Hobie catamarans from **Jack's Rentals** on Gull Pond, 349-9808. **Bay Sails Marine** at the Town Pier in Wellfleet, 349-3840, rents power and sailboats.

Sport fishing. The Naviator, 349-6003, runs trips to fish for porgies, flounder and blackfish from the Wellfleet Town Pier. Morning trips leave at 9 and return at 1; afternoon trips are from 2 to 6. Sunset sightseeing trips are offered Tuesday and Friday nights in July and August.

WHALE-WATCHING. Trips leave from Provincetown on regular schedules. The **Dolphin Fleet,** 255-3857, operates some fifteen trips daily on several boats. All leave from the Provincetown Pier and most are four hours in length, beginning at 8. Plans were being made to run two all-day whale-watch trips on weekends. **The Ranger V,** 487-3322, is another whale-watch boat, with trips leaving in the morning, afternoon and at sunset. **The Portuguese Princess,** yet another, can be reached at 487-2651. Often you must book ahead.

Other Activities

The **Wellfleet Historical Society** operates a museum on Main Street and the Samuel Rider House on Gull Pond Road. The society's collection of old photographs, maps, documents, marine artifacts, period clothing and household and agricultural items are on exhibit at both places. Several unusual gift items are sold at both. Combination fee, $2. Open Tuesday-Saturday, 2 to 5 in summer.

The **Highland House** operated by the Truro Historical Society on Lighthouse Road in North Truro is worth a stop. Once a resort hotel, the building is located near Highland Light, the first lighthouse on Cape Cod, which was built in 1798. Here you will find a potpourri of memorabilia: cooking utensils, lithographs by local artist Edward Wilson, listings of the old Portuguese families of Truro, old postcards, an exhibit of photographs of people who have meant a lot to the town, and the like. Open daily 10 to 5, mid-June to mid-September. Adults, $2.

Out at the **Highland Light,** an informal but informative talk is given visitors "on demand" by Joe Manning, a retired summer resident whose deep tan attests to his taking off in the afternoon for the beach. If you get there before 1 p.m. you stand a good chance of finding him and learning a bit about this part of the Cape.

BICYCLING. The Wellfleet Chamber of Commerce issues a map of the town with many bicycle routes indicated. Although fairly hilly, it's quite pleasant to ride from the Town Pier all the way across town to the Atlantic, and then to traverse several trails through the Cape Cod National Seashore. Wellfleet Cycles on East Commercial Street, 349-9322, and Black Duck Sport Shop, 349-9801, rent bikes.

ART GALLERIES. Wellfleet has more than a dozen art galleries, most offering a fine range of work. We particularly like **Left Bank Gallery** on Commercial Street, a spacious place with paintings out front and an exceptionally good pottery room in back. **Salt Marsh Pottery** on East Main Street displays wheel-thrown earthenware and stoneware at attractive prices. **Wellfleet Pottery** on Commercial Street sells a vitrified, chip-resistant lead-free country china, charmingly decorated with wild grasses and flowers and known as Wellfleet Brownware. We coveted a four-cup teapot with floral decoration for $70. **Truro Crafters** at the corner of South Highland Road and Moses Way in North Truro is the home of Jobi Pottery, which is made in the studio.

SHOPPING. You shouldn't overlook the **Bookstore & Restaurant** on Kendrick Avenue, not far from Wellfleet Harbor. We're more interested in the food for thought here; the oceans of used books out back behind the restaurant are extraordinary. We saw comic books for as much as $150 and other collectors' items. The **Higgins House** shops located in a white clapboard house with blue shutters in the center of Wellfleet include sportswear shops as well as a candy store. **Bank Square** is another house that's been turned into a group of nifty shops. The **Country Store** at the Whitman House restaurant in North Truro has a large selection of handmade Amish and Mennonite quilts in addition to all sorts of gift items.

Up for a movie? The Wellfleet Drive-in on Route 6 at the Wellfleet-Eastham line has a different movie every night in summer. The box office opens at 7 and the movie begins at 8. This is also the site of busy **flea markets** on Wednesdays, Thursdays, Saturdays and Sundays. The mix of old and new attracts shoppers from miles around.

Where to Eat

The dining emphasis is on seafood, of course. You can get it in every way from clambakes-to-go and fried clams on paper plates to rather formal fare in elegant restaurants.

Sweet Seasons, the Inn at Duck Creeke, East Main Street, Wellfleet. (508) 349-6535. When you make a reservation for a room at the inn, you can, as we did, also ask that a table be reserved in its attractive restaurant. Entered off the main driveway through a screened porch and then a broad lobby wallpapered in a pink Colonial print, the dining room is simple with bare wood tables and floors, a few plants, dark brown placemats and napkins and pale gray walls on which paintings are shown to good advantage. Lace curtains and mauve draperies add a touch of sophistication. Fresh table flowers are set in white milk glass vases. On weekend nights there is a musician; the evening we dined, a guitarist strummed pleasantly in the background. Often a harpist is featured. A small loaf of bread on a board was brought to the table and promptly replenished after two teenagers had decimated it. Appetizers ($3.50 to $6) include lobster bisque, caponata (a chilled medley of eggplant, zucchini, capers and olives served with crackers), stuffed grape leaves and shrimp cocktail. The house salad ($2.75) is a nice selection of greens tossed with colorful vegetables and dressed with a vinaigrette. Entrees range from $13.50 for chicken valencia, a boneless breast prepared with fresh basil, sundried tomatoes, white wine and essence of orange sauce, to $18 for beef tenderloin glazed with brandy butter. Other possibilities include salmon broiled with sake, fresh ginger and scallions or twin lamb chops with roasted garlic and fresh garden chutney. Next door is the inn's **Tavern Room,** 349-7369, which features lighter fare, more casual atmosphere (exposed beams, a fireplace) and entertainment nightly. Appetizers are served until midnight and include mini-pizzas, cajun chicken wings, steamed mussels and stuffed quahogs in the $5 to $6 range. Entrees here ($11.50 to $15) might be lasagna, Brazilian chicken, Mexican mussels, seafood gumbo and broiled scallops. Desserts and specialty coffees, plus a complete wine list, are available at both restaurants. Sweet Seasons, open nightly 6 to 10 in season; tavern, open nightly except Monday.

Cielo, East Main Street, Wellfleet. (508) 349-2108. The name means "heaven" and young chef John Burns provides that for appreciative diners in this combination of cafe and art gallery in a small house. The prix-fixe ($39.50), five-course meal changes nightly. A sample dinner might start with fettuccine with smoked scallops and puttanesca, followed by yellow squash and basil soup. The main course could be salmon in puff pastry with spinach. A salad of mixed greens with beets and gorgonzola precedes the dessert, perhaps a peach tart with homemade whipped cream. Up to twenty patrons dine at a single seating on an enclosed rear porch, which has a pleasant view looking over a tidal marsh. Diners generally come early to browse and look at the artworks in the front gallery, photos on the walls and pottery all around. The short lunch menu might include carrot-ginger soup or curried orange gazpacho, salad nicoise, a couple of pastas, and five fancy sandwiches served with potato salad and marinated vegetables, priced in the $5.95 to $7.25 range. Lunch, 11:30 to 2; dinner at 8 by reservation. Open Memorial Day to Columbus Day. BYOB.

The Wellfleet Oyster House, East Main Street, Wellfleet. (508) 349-2134. This mainstay on the Cape was opened nearly twenty years ago by Tony Costello, who spent the 29 previous years managing a restaurant on Fulton Street in New York City. His restaurant is equally popular with locals and visitors, often a difficult feat to pull off. The white-trimmed, blue house, with large white letters announcing the name, dates from the 18th century. It is simply furnished inside with tables covered in gold cloths and red napkins. An upstairs dining room is used for overflow or private parties. Wellfleet oysters top the menu, of course, and oyster stew is made on request. Salad, potato or rice and garlic toast accompany all entrees. According to Tony, the most popular entree is the Spanish paella at $16.95. Also in demand is Poor Richard's Platter, which includes saffron rice, two oysters, scallops, shrimp and crabmeat for $15.95. Steaks and prime rib are available. The Jamaica mystery cake for dessert ($4.25), the owner's specialty, contains bananas, walnuts and kahlua. Other desserts include midnight chocolate cake and a fruit fondue with chocolate brandy sauce for dipping, $12.95 for two. "You should try the cappuccino!" says Tony. It is made with Spanish brandy and kahlua and topped with homemade whipped cream. Dinner nightly, 6 to 10 in season; fewer nights rest of year.

Aesop's Tables, Main Street, Wellfleet Center. (508) 349-6450. This restaurant, ensconced in an 1805 house in the center of town, features highly regarded new American cuisine. Owner Brian Dunne has created an elegant looking spot with several dining rooms decorated individually and a porch with pink director's chairs and mauve tables. The fantastic paper constructions of his wife, Kim Victoria Kettler, are displayed on the walls. The menu is slightly pricier than most in the area, with appetizers ranging from $5.25 to $7.25 for the likes of mussels anise, lobster boudin (a mousse of scallops and lobster meat) and duck salad. Aesop's oysters, chilled or hot, are always an excellent choice; they may come in a sauce of soy and balsamic vinegar, topped with all kinds and colors of peppers including jalapeno. Entrees ($14.25 to $19.75) include scallops sauteed with sundried tomatoes and vidalia onions, herb-roasted duck from Wisconsin, broiled filet mignon and grilled paillards of veal with a pignoli and pancetta duxelle. Desserts could include hazelnut fruit torte or white chocolate mousse on strawberry puree. Summer brunch features Aesop's strada, a baked egg custard specialty with fresh fruit or vegetables, and huevos rancheros. Dinner, nightly from 6; Sunday brunch, 9:30 to 1. Open mid-May to mid-October.

Adrian's, Route 6A, North Truro. (508) 487-4360. In this small weathered Cape Cod house with bare wood tables and simple surroundings, Adrian Cyr has been developing a following for at least a half dozen years. Chef-owner Cyr describes his food as "regional Italian." A large pasta menu includes both small ($7 to $8) and large ($11 to $13) plates of such specialties as spaghetti aglio e olio, made with garlic, olive oil and fresh parsley; pasta valerio, with a sauce of tomatoes, pancetta and hot pepper and tossed in pecorino sardo cheese, served on penne, and fettuccine al gamberi, a classic combination of shrimp, garlic, olive oil and lemon. Some fifteen varieties of pizza include pizza bianco, made with ricotta, romano and mozzarella cheeses without tomato sauce; pizza al tonno e cappero, imported Italian tuna, capers, tomato sauce and mozzarella, and pizza melanzane, slices of marinated grilled eggplant, pecorino romano cheese, mozzarella and tomato sauce on grilled dough, served "individual size" only for $8 to $9. A good variety of salads and antipasti complete the menu. Breakfast daily, 8 to 11; dinner nightly, 5:30 to 10. Open May-October.

J.P.'s Flying Fish Dinner Cafe, Briar Lane, Wellfleet. (508) 349-3100. Creative cooking is offered at three meals daily in this place that opened in 1990 at the edge of downtown Wellfleet. For breakfast, try the sunrise special (two eggs, toast and homefries, $1.99) or the Flying Fish omelet with cream cheese, bacon and guacamole ($4.95). Lunch runs from a BLT ($3.75) to salad plates of chicken, tuna or smoked turkey ($6.75). Candlelight and linens take over at dinner time, when a short menu might list grilled swordfish with green olive relish or sauteed medallions of pork with apples and goat cheese in the $11.95 to $13.95 range. The yummy desserts come from from the bakery that's part of the same operation in the front of the building. Breakfast, 7 to noon; lunch, noon to 3; dinner, 5 to 10. Open Memorial Day to Columbus Day. BYOB.

Captain Higgins Seafood Restaurant, Town Pier, Wellfleet. (508) 349-6027. So you want to sit outside on a deck with a view of the harbor? This is the place to do it. For more than twenty summers Betty and John Balch and their family have run this establishment, which seats 160 at plain wood barroom-style chairs and tables indoors and another 40 at umbrellaed tables on the deck. We had reserved an outdoor table, but when evening arrived with a chill wind, we were happy to be accommodated at a window table inside. The food emphasis is on New England seafood favorites, including deep-fried seafood platters ranging from $11 for flounder filet to $13.95 for the fisherman's with scallops, shrimp, clams and a fresh fish in season. Fish may be ordered broiled as well. Other entrees include baked stuffed shrimp, hot steamed shrimp served in the shell New Orleans style, crabmeat in casserole or au gratin and, for the meat eater, broiled sirloin and southern fried chicken. Baskets of warm rolls come to the table, as do tossed salads and decanters of two dressings, caesar with cheese and creamy cucumber. Entrees also include baked or french-fried potatoes or rice. The house wine is Sebastiani and strawberry margaritas are popular. For lunch, an open seafood sandwich au gratin served hot on an English muffin is $8.95. Lobster, crabmeat and shrimp salads range from $8.95 to $10.50. Open daily for lunch and dinner, mid-June to early September.

Whitman House, Route 6, North Truro. (508) 487-1740. This very Colonial-looking restaurant has several dining rooms, one with a slate floor, and fireplaces with cheering blazes on cool nights. A favorite appetizer is the Whitman House Sampler ($12.95 for two), with shrimp, sea scallops and swordfish pieces slightly blackened and served with a bearnaise sauce. Other choices ($3.50 to $5) include stuffed mushrooms, broiled scallops with bacon, french onion soup and baked Portuguese oysters. Entrees (generally $12 to $18) range from prime rib in three sizes to seafood newburg and fisherman's catch. Steak teriyaki, chopped sirloin lyonnaise and chicken cordon bleu are also on the largish menu. Cheese and crackers, tossed salad, bread and rice pilaf or baked potato come with. A children's menu is available. Dinner nightly from 5; Sunday brunch, 11 to 2. Open April-December.

Serena's, Route 6, South Wellfleet. (508) 349-9370. Two ambitious young couples and their kids joined forces fourteen years ago to create this favorite restaurant right off the busy highway. Paul Johnson and Ed Simpson, who were college roommates, and their wives leased a spot for five years in Yarmouth before being able to build their own place. The decor is simple: wood tables and chairs and booths. Paul invents the cuisine, Ed manages the bar, Linda Johnson manages the front of the house, and Jane is back in the kitchen, presiding over salads and soups. The menu changes with Paul's whims and included many cajun specialties when we visited, but the emphasis is always an emphasis on seafood. The house favorite is seafood fra diavolo, with mussels, littlenecks, oysters, scrod, scallops and shrimp in a light wine and marinara sauce for $15.95. Among other dinner choices ($12.95 to $14.75) are broiled haddock in a wine-butter sauce, shrimp scampi and grilled shrimp with chicken, served with a mustard butter. Veal parmigiana amd veal milanese are among the "Butcher's Block" entrees; pasta selections ($9 to $10) include ziti or spaghettini with red or white clam sauce or with sausages or meatballs. Portuguese bread from Provincetown is a fine accompaniment to most meals. Be prepared for long waiting lines in season. Dinner nightly, 4:30 to 10:30, Sunday from noon; the schedule is pared back slightly in late spring and until mid-November.

Moby Dick's, Route 6, Wellfleet. (508) 349-9795. Three peaked gray buildings set back from the highway with a crushed clam-shell parking lot and lots of nautical memorabilia are the place to get real New England "chowdah," lobster in the rough, and all those other goodies that you must have on a trip to the Cape. Affable Todd Barry, who has a graduate degree in hotel management from the University of Massachusetts, has been running the place for the past eight years. The atmosphere is just right: blue and white or red and white checked tablecloths on picnic tables in three dining rooms plus a screened porch. Rough wood walls are decorated with nautical charts, lobster buoys and so on. You order at the counter and leave your name; the food is delivered to your table by pleasant young waiters and waitresses. The simplicity of the plastic implements, paper cups and plates, and baskets (for some sandwiches) emphasizes the freshness of the food. The chowder is creamy and full of clams, $2.10 for a cup, $2.50 a bowl. A fried clam plate is $7.95, broiled scallops or shrimp, $9.25, and lobster priced at market rates, but a good value. Hamburgers and chicken are also on the menu and you can get an ice cream cone for dessert. There's a salad bar at night. Open daily, 11:30 to 10 in season. BYOB.

Paparazzi, Beach Point, Route 6A, North Truro. (508) 487-2658. This small weathered gray restaurant right on the water as the road bends and heads for Provincetown is very popular. Now in its second decade, it features mostly Italian food and the largest list of appetizers we've seen in this area. They are priced from $2.50 to $7 and include onion rings, fried clam strips, hot chicken wings, pizza skins (potato skins with pizza sauce and cheese), calamari and shrimp scampi. Among dinner choices ($12 to $18) are fried clams, scallops, shrimp, sole and cod; shrimp scampi, baked bluefish, and something called first-prize chicken — a blending of garlic butter, artichoke hearts, broccoli and melted cheese in a casserole with chicken. Italian specials like lasagna, baked shells and various pastas are priced from $9 to $13. All entrees include soup and a salad bar. Dinner nightly 10.

The Blacksmith Shop Restaurant, Truro Center. (508) 349-6554. You can't miss this spot, with its unpretentious barn red exterior, as you drive down into Truro Center. There are three dining rooms, one with ladderback chairs at the tables, while the lounge has church pews. Once a real blacksmith shop and a restaurant since 1946, it burned down in 1983 but was duplicated. Owner since 1973 is Al Tinker, a Cornell hotel school grad with Hilton experience. Steak polonaise is featured on weekends and a classic dessert is the apricot souffle. According to Tinker, whose brother Marty is a force in the kitchen, the chicken milanese and veal oscar are highly rated. The menu offers a good range, including such dinner entrees ($13 to $20) as filet of sole mornay, frog's legs provencale, steak bearnaise and rack of lamb. Among appetizers ($6 to $7) are baked stuffed clams and mushrooms stuffed with lobster and crabmeat. A new patio and a fireplace were promised for 1991. This is a favorite haunt of locals and is open year-round. Dinner nightly, from 5:30.

The Lighthouse, Main Street, Wellfleet Center. (508) 349-3681. Everyone stops here at some time, it seems. The little center-of-town restaurant with the lighthouse above the door serves three meals a day in summer. Pictures of lighthouses line the walls and bare wood tables contain ketchup and mustard bottles; a few more tables are set on a side porch. Soft rock music plays in the background and you can get anything for lunch from a peanut butter and jelly sandwich for $1.95 to a tuna salad plate for $6.95. Dinner items ($8 to $12) include drunken mussels on a bed of rice pilaf and scallops parmesan. You also can get a hamburger, cheeseburger or reuben. Mexican Night is on Thursdays when margaritas and sangria are offered along with enchiladas, burritos, tostadas and tacos in the $7 to $9 range. Breakfast is predictable, with homemade blueberry muffins and blueberry pancakes as well as raisin french toast and a Wellfleetian omelet with Portuguese linguica, cheese and green pepper for $4.95. Open daily for breakfast, lunch and dinner in season.

Bayside Lobster Hutt, Commercial Street, Wellfleet. (508) 349-6333. In an old white-shingled oyster shack on the road to Wellfleet Harbor (look for the dory on the roof), people dine on lobsters amidst tanks marked "see 'em swim." The clambake, which includes a one-pound lobster, steamed clams and corn on the cob, is $15.95; a bowl of chowder goes for $3.50 and you can get steamed clams for $7.95. The fisherman's platter is $12.95. The Hutt's a favorite with families. Lunch daily, noon to 5; dinner, 4 to 10:30, late June to Labor Day. Dinner only in off-season. Open mid-May through September. BYOB.

The Harbor Freeze at the Town Pier is good for soft ice cream, or a delicious ice cream and orange juice mixture, hot dogs, hamburgers and clam rolls. For us, unfortunately, service was as slow as molasses in winter. **Just Desserts** at Depot Square, with a porch overlooking a tidal marsh, serves ice cream in various guises daily from 4 to 10:30. **The Beachcomber** at Cahoon Hollow Beach is reminiscent of California; surfboards tied to tops of cars, guys in wet suits wandering around, rock music blaring, and hamburgers and beer being enjoyed. There's a small deck out front for daytime, sunny dining or after-the-beach drinking; rock bands set up indoors at night and all the kids come.

FOR MORE INFORMATION: Wellfleet Chamber of Commerce, Box 571, Wellfleet, Mass. 02667. (508) 349-2510. Truro Chamber of Commerce, Box 26, North Truro, Mass. 02652. (508) 487-1288.

Swimming is fine at Rockport's Front Beach.

Cape Ann, Mass.

Nowhere does the marriage of sea and land seem more felicitous than on Cape Ann. This chunk of land, which juts into the Atlantic north of Boston, offers a rich melange of seascapes and land views, of working and leisure classes, of dockside activity and sandy strands. We have loved it since we first set foot here years ago and are drawn back again and again. So are thousands of others.

Who can blame them? Cape Ann is split between two markedly different but complementary towns, Rockport and Gloucester. Rockport is a charming, picket-fenced village by the sea, with a colorful harbor, several small beaches, boutiques and restaurants. It is so picturesque that it has drawn artists since the turn of the century and art galleries abound. Motif No. 1, the red fish warehouse in the harbor, is said to be the most painted and photographed waterfront locale in New England.

Gloucester is characterized by the huge bronze statue of the fisherman in foul-weather gear at the wheel along State Route 127. Fishing boats crowd this working harbor and "men that go down to the sea in ships" still sail in great numbers to the rich fishing grounds of Georges Bank. Stores along the city's main street cater to locals, rather than tourists. Rocky Neck, an artists' community in East Gloucester, has colorful galleries and fun restaurants, many with dining overlooking the harbor. Eastern Point embraces the priciest real estate on Cape Ann and one of its mansions, Beauport, is open to the public as a museum.

Visitors have been coming to Cape Ann for years and so guest houses, inns and B&Bs abound, especially in Rockport. Several attractive motels overlook the ocean in the Bass Rocks section of Gloucester. Dining is dominated by seafood restaurants.

There is much to see and do. Art-gallery browsing and strolling among the boutiques on Rockport's Bearskin Neck take the better part of a day. Gloucester's Good Harbor Beach is one of our favorites for sunning and swimming anywhere. Whale-watch trips are numerous and there are historic homes to visit. Just driving around the Cape and poking through the charming villages of Annisquam and Lanesville and the section of Rockport known as Pigeon Cove are rewarding. You can walk out to Halibut Point and picnic on a flat rock at sunset.

249

Winslow Homer found inspiration on Cape Ann (he lived for a while in Gloucester), as did T.S. Eliot. Surely you will, too.

Getting There

Cape Ann is located 35 miles northeast of Boston. By car, Route 128 and Route 133 lead to the Cape from Route 1 and Interstate 95. Trains run from Boston to Rockport, one of the few shore towns that still has train service.

Where to Stay⎯⎯⎯⎯⎯⎯⎯⎯⎯⎯⎯⎯⎯⎯ ⟋⟋⟋

By the Sea

Rocky Shores Inn and Cottages, Eden Road, Rockport 01966. (508) 546-2823. Because we first fell in love with Rockport when we stayed here, this seaside inn has a special place in our hearts. Now owned and operated by a warm and friendly German couple, Renate and Gunter Kostka, the inn is almost an anachronism in today's rushed world. A gracious but old-fashioned lobby welcomes guests; soft classical music plays somewhere in the distance, and the breezy salt air blows the light curtains at the windows. All ten inn rooms have private baths and TV; there also are twelve housekeeping cottages, eight behind the inn with two bedrooms and four in front with three bedrooms. From a large porch across the front of the inn, guests can look down sweeping green lawns toward the Atlantic and the twin lighthouses on Thachers Island. While you can walk along the ocean across the road, you really need to drive to the beaches (the closest are Cape Hedge and Pebble Beach). Breakfast is buffet style: English muffins, coffee cake, soft-boiled eggs and cold cereals when last we dined here in the old-fashioned dining room. The outstanding dark woodwork in the main house, the impeccable housekeeping and the great location appeal. Doubles, $76 to $95 in inn; cottages weekly, $635 for two bedrooms and $775 for three. Open mid-April through October.

Seaward Inn, Marmion Way, Rockport 01966. (508) 546-3471. Once a private home, the main house became an inn in 1945 when it was acquired by Anne and Roger Cameron, who are still the innkeepers. After changes and additions, including a few separate cottages, the complex is comfortably complete, with beautifully tended flower beds, lush lawns and pretty paths. The view from the inn's property and front porch is stunning: the ocean breaking on boulders across the street. It's easy to walk along the oceanfront, too, on this street. Altogether, 38 rooms are spread among the various buildings and most of those who stay take Modified American Plan, which includes breakfast and dinner in the charming dining room. A B&B rate is also offered. The glass-enclosed garden terrace across the front of the inn, with its flagstone floor, is a beautiful room. Doubles, $85 to $105 B&B, $140 to $170 MAP. Open mid-May to mid-October.

Eden Pines Inn, Eden Road, Rockport 01966. (508) 546-2505. Here is a former summer home set so close to the ocean that you're literally perched above the rocks and crashing waves when you sit on the brick deck out back. A knotty-pine living room with fieldstone fireplace is cozy; from it you walk into the breezy, California-style side porch and breakfast room, where a buffet-style continental breakfast of homemade pastries is put out for guests. Out back is a porch above the brick terrace, a great place for tea or cocktails. All six large upstairs guest rooms have private baths; most have two double beds (Room 6 has an enchanting canopied bed) and a private balcony over the water. Innkeeper Inge Sullivan's fondness for marble and California fabrics shows. She is

250

a warm and energetic hostess who's been at it for almost 25 years now. Doubles, $95 to $115. Open May-November.

Seacrest Manor, 131 Marmion Way, Rockport 01966. (508) 546-2211. Although this weathered-gray mansion is not at the water's edge, sea views are possible from the second-floor deck above the living room. (The deck is divided into thirds; two rooms each have their own section and the rest of the guests share the other section). The lawns and flowers are gorgeous, and guests love to sit and read in the garden. Innkeepers Dwight B. MacCormack Jr. and Leighton T. Saville make you feel as if you're treating yourself very well when you visit — and why not? The intimate breakfast room, warm with red tablecloths and a red brick-look floor, is the site for a full morning meal that *Town & Country* magazine called one of the 50 best breakfasts in America. It begins with fresh fruit cup, includes oatmeal, bacon and eggs, and ends with a specialty such as blueberry pancakes or corn fritters. A large living room is where afternoon tea is served; there's also a library on the main floor. Six of the eight guest rooms have private baths. All are decorated comfortably and have color TVs. Doubles, $76 to $98. Open mid-February to Christmas Eve.

Yankee Clipper Inn, Route 127, Rockport 01966. (617) 546-3407. This has remained a favorite place of visitors to Rockport for good reasons: location, location, location. The 28-room inn is composed of three spacious buildings, two perched close to the rocky shore and the Bulfinch House just across the road. The Wemyss family has been in charge for more than 40 years; their daughter and son-in-law, Barbara and Bob Ellis, now manage the place. Both the main inn and the Quarterdeck (the most modern building) have water views, plus lots of space for lounging in lawn chairs. A saltwater pool is tucked artistically into the landscape. Lately, the dining room has been open to the public as well as inn guests. Located on a wraparound porch, the blue and rose room with garden chairs offers wonderful water views. Entrees ($14 to $20) include seafood, veal and chops as well as dishes like chicken sauteed with artichoke hearts. Houseguests in the inn and Quarterdeck enjoy particularly attractive accommodations, most with ocean views, and some with four-poster beds. The Bulfinch House on the other side of the street has smaller, but still pleasant rooms. Doubles, $98 to $108 in Bulfinch House; $131 to $169 on the water.

Motel Peg Leg, 10 Beach St., Rockport 01966. (508) 546-6945. Built by the Erwin family, who still run it, this motel has an exceptional location, across the street from Front Beach, and a very short walk into town to the shops. Park your car, and you may not have to move it for the entire stay. Each of the fifteen rooms is done in an Ethan Allen style and all have cable TVs plus ceramic tile baths with tubs and showers. You can find breakfast at several places nearby. Doubles, $95 to $105. Open May-October.

The Atlantis Motor Inn, 125 Atlantic Road, Gloucester 01930. (508) 283-5807. Highly regarded, this motel is in the Bass Rocks section of Gloucester. Picture windows in the 41 motel rooms look out at the rocky shorefront where waves crash and churn; the coffee shop, furnished in rattan, has fabulous views as well. Rooms are furnished in Danish modern for the most part. There's a pool, and guests can walk across the street and sun on the rocks at water's edge. Doubles, $95 to $100. Open April-October.

Bass Rocks Motor Inn, 119 Atlantic Road, Gloucester 01930. (508) 283-7600. This large brick motor inn with columned facade promises an ocean view from every room. Located next to the Atlantis, it has 48 well-furnished and comfortable units plus a heated swimming pool. Views of the rockbound coast are stunning and the decks in front of each room offer a place to watch the sunrise. Doubles, $105 to $120. Open April-November.

The Williams Guest House, 136 Bass Ave., Gloucester 01930. (508) 283-4931. This friendly B&B proves to be a bargain, for it is virtually on Good Harbor Beach (just take the footbridge) and prices are unusually reasonable. The carpeted parlor is warm and inviting; the nearby dining room is where a light breakfast is served. There are four rooms with private and shared baths and three apartment units (one of these is its own little cottage out back). The Williamses make you feel right at home. Doubles, $45 to $55. Open May-October.

On the Beach

Chicataubut Inn, Long Beach, Rockport 01966. (508) 546-3342. So you want to be right on the beach, roll out of bed and hit the sand? This is the only lodging place on Cape Ann where you can do that. The sprawling white beach house is set in the midst of a cottage colony at Long Beach (one of the best, and sandiest, beaches on Cape Ann). Run by the same family for fifteen years, the inn has basic but adequate accommodations and great views. All ten rooms have private baths; there are five efficiency apartments as well. Most rooms have three single beds and are very simply furnished — the kind you can sweep the sand out of. A fireplace warms the lobby on chilly mornings and evenings. Out front is a terrace with lounge chairs. A small refrigerator is in each room and complimentary coffee is served to guests. Doubles, $80 to $100. Open mid-May to mid-October.

Other Choices

Sally Webster Inn, 34 Mount Pleasant St., Rockport 01966. (508) 546-9251. Opened in 1985 by the Webster family (no relationship to Sally), this in-town inn is a winner. Affable Janet — a former Gloucester school teacher — loves to tell guests the fascinating history of the old white house with red shutters. Sally was the daughter of William Choate, who built the house in 1832. Her picture in the front parlor, known as "Sally's Share" because that was the part of the house she inherited, shows a woman of stern demeanor. There is nothing stern about Sally's inn, however. Rooms have been renovated and made charming by Janet. A small deck off a couple of rear rooms looks onto the spacious (for Rockport) back yard. The dining room with mahogany table and period chairs is gracious; Janet does her own baking for the buffet breakfast that's set out for guests. All six bedrooms have private baths. The inn is one-fifth of a mile from the center of Rockport, which tends to be teeming with humanity and short on parking spaces on weekends. The closest beach is Old Garden Beach, a five-minute walk. What this inn lacks in water views, it makes up for in charm and convenience. Doubles, $65 to $75. Open February-November.

Old Farm Inn, 291 Granite St., Rockport 01966. (508) 546-3237. Until 1986 one of the most popular eating places on Cape Ann, the Old Farm Inn is now being run sans dining room to the everlasting regret of anyone who ever ate there. One of the dining rooms, in fact, has been turned into a parlor with wing chairs and sofas and a wonderful, warming fireplace, used on chilly days. Of the eight guest rooms, four are located in the main 1799 house and four in the adjoining Barn Annex. All have private baths and TVs. Two upstairs rooms have fireplaces and are offered as a suite with a sitting room sharing a bath. Its quiet, peaceful location in the Pigeon Cove section near Halibut Point State Park and Folly Cove make the inn especially appealing, as do its spacious grounds. The

252

Balzarini family is still in charge. Breakfast is served in a bright breakfast room overlooking the lawns and trees. Doubles, $75 to $88.

The Linden Tree Inn, 26 King St., Rockport 01966. (508) 546-2494. Only the cupola atop this huge old Victorian-style home has a view of the ocean, and you have to hike up two steep flights of stairs to get there, but there are other assets. Penny and Larry Olson and children run this large inn, which has eighteen guest rooms, most furnished with period pieces; one has twin beds with pineapple posts. All rooms in the main inn have private baths; two in the annex share. The Carriage House has four large modern rooms, each with a double and twin bed and a deck. An ample continental breakfast is served in the dining room, where the stencil design near the ceiling is a reproduction of that originally found in the house. Guests rave about the lemon nut bread and sour-cream chocolate chip cake that Penny serves on Sundays. The inn is located a couple of blocks from Front Beach and the shops of Rockport. Doubles, $70 to $75 in inn, $60 in annex, $85 in carriage house.

Pleasant Street Inn, 17 Pleasant St., Rockport 01966. (508) 546-3915. This white Victorian inn, situated on a knoll overlooking the village of Rockport, is operated by the Norris family, originally from western Pennsylvania although husband Roger grew up in nearby Newburyport. The seven rooms have private baths, and are located on the second and third floors. Be ready for a steepish climb up the staircase; you'll be rewarded with quite special rooms once you arrive, especially Room 7 with its turret and futon. Room 6 is the one we like, with a window seat from which you can look out on all of Rockport. Three generations are at work here and it's a pleasant experience. A continental breakfast with homemade muffins or coffee cake is served in the dining room. Doubles, $76 to $88.

Seeing and Doing _____ ⟋ᑕᑕᑕ_

On or Near the Water

WHALE-WATCHING. Gloucester touts itself as the whale-watching capital of the world and has good statistics to back the claim. Half a dozen boat companies take visitors out in the Atlantic toward the whale-feeding grounds, Jeffrey's Ledge and Stellwagen Bank, where more than 500 whales are said to go annually. The area, some ten to twelve miles offshore, hosts finback, humpback, right and minke whales. Midsummer trips are often filled and reservations are advised, especially for weekends. Most trips take about four hours; adults pay about $20 and children $12. Among the choices:

Cape Ann Whale Watch, 283-5110, leaves from Rose's Wharf in Gloucester daily at 8:30 and 1:30, May-October. **Capt. Bill & Sons,** 283-6995, departs from Rose's Wharf, Gloucester, at 9 and 2. **Yankee Whale Watch,** 283-0313, leaves from the Cape Ann Marina at 8:30 and 1:30 daily.

FISHING AND BOATING. The Yankee Fleet, Cape Ann Marina, 75 Essex Ave. (Route 133), Gloucester, 283-0313, offers deep-sea fishing excursions. They include all-day trips for haddock, pollock, cod and halibut. Evening bluefishing trips from 7 to 1 are offered nightly except Sundays. Distant trips include haddock specials, marathons and two or three-day Georges Bank trips with a Nantucket layover. Priced from $49 to $329, they are offered on varying days.

The **Lady Dianne** leaves from the T Wharf in Rockport Harbor for five-hour deep-sea fishing trips daily at 7:15 from late June through Labor Day. The $18 cost includes bait and tackle.

Sail around Cape Ann on the 56-foot schooner, the **Appledore,** 546-9876. Ninety-minute sails from the Tuna Wharf at Bearskin Neck in Gloucester leave daily at 9, 11, 1, 3, 5 and 7. Passengers pay $18.

The **Cape Ann Island Cruise,** Rose's Wharf, Gloucester, 283-5110, gets you out onto the water for a 2 1/2 hour cruise that is really fun. Ours lasted more than three hours, partly due to the incredible traffic on the Annisquam River as we were returning to Gloucester Harbor. The narrated cruise leaves at 11 and 2 on weekends. Adults, $10.

THE BEACHES. We like best the **Good Harbor Beach** on Thatcher Road, Gloucester (close to the Rockport line). This half-mile barrier beach is protected by sand dunes and has a bathhouse and a snack bar. Parking fees are in the $5 to $6 range.

Rockport's beaches are sometimes hard to find, especially **Cape Hedge, Pebble** and **Old Garden** beaches, which are small but pleasant. These do not have changing rooms or snack bars. Find those facilities at **Front Beach** and **Back Beach** on Beach Street in downtown Rockport.

Wingaersheek Beach on Atlantic Street in Gloucester is a bit removed from the itineraries of most visitors to Cape Ann. This open, wind-swept strand is favored by people from surrounding towns. Parking fees are the same as at Good Harbor Beach.

On Shore

Leave your car behind when exploring in Rockport. Take the trolley that was put into service in 1986. Its two routes involve a continuous circuit of the downtown area or a wider trek known as the "scenic sightseeing tour" to the beaches and inns farther out (as far as Cape Hedge Beach to the south and Folly Cove to the north).

Tour the area on a bicycle. Giles of Gloucester, a sporting goods store at 232 Main St., 283-3603, rents bikes.

Take a Walk. Walking is one of the supreme pleasures on Cape Ann. The center of Rockport, with its old and architecturally interesting houses, its Cape Cod cottages with picket fences, its art galleries and boutiques, the picturesque harbor and **Bearskin Neck** (the narrow piece of land that juts into the ocean and is crammed with shops and eateries) invite strolling. In fact, the center of Rockport is so crowded you have to leave the car and go by foot. East Gloucester's **Rocky Neck,** another art colony with some waterfront restaurants, invites more walking. Hike out to **Halibut Point Reservation** in Rockport for a picnic on the flat rocks or possibly the best sunset ever. Guided tours of the area are offered on Saturday mornings from 9:30 to 11:30, and special tours are scheduled. Sunsets are also said to be spectacular at **Folly Cove, Lane's Cove** and **Plum Cove,** to which you drive, then sit.

Drive around all of Cape Ann on Route 127 and 127A, staying as close to the water as you can to find many scenic spots. Sneak down into the little village of **Annisquam** where, once again, you may want to park and walk. The narrow streets and houses are charming.

THE ARTISTS. Gloucester and Rockport have attracted artists since shortly after the Civil War. They come to sit by the shore, to watch the sea and to paint the ineffable beauty of Cape Ann at all times of day and year. Among their numbers have been Childe Hassam, Winslow Homer and Fitz Hugh Lane. Artists are drawn particularly to Rocky Neck in East Gloucester and Bearskin Neck in Rockport, where their galleries are located.

The **Rockport Art Association** at 12 Main St., 546-6604, is open free year-round. It sponsors Tuesday and Thursday evening art demonstrations in summer, changing exhibitions of paintings, graphics and sculpture, and an annual fair.

The **North Shore Art Association** on Reed's Wharf at 197 Main St. in East Gloucester, 283-1857, is active in the summer with exhibits and art demonstrations.

Watercolors seem to be the predominant medium on Cape Ann and Motif No. 1 the favorite subject. The paintings are for the most part realistic. It is fun to poke around in the galleries, chat with the artists and maybe take a painting home. It's a sure bet that somewhere you'll find an artist and his easel poised at land's edge.

SPECIAL EVENTS. The **Blessing of the Fleet** occurs during the St. Peter's Fiesta on the last weekend of June. The blessing actually takes place on Sunday afternoon. St. Peter is the patron saint of fishermen, and the Portuguese fishing community celebrates this weekend with gusto.

The **Gloucester Waterfront Festival** takes place on an August weekend, with a pancake breakfast on Saturday and a fish fry on Sunday. There are also an arts and crafts show, entertainment and food booths.

SHOPPING. Stores in the center of Rockport and on Bearskin Neck are crammed with sophisticated fashions, giftware and objets d'art, as well as postcards, ceramic lobster ashtrays and beach towels. The emphasis is for the most part upscale, and we often get bogged down by the selections of classic clothing at places like the **Motif**. The **Christmas Dove** has intrigued holiday-minded shoppers for years and the **Toad Hall Bookstore** is a great place to browse. The **Madras Shop** is one of those places you cannot afford to overlook: everything from thongs to sunglasses and at good prices can be found here. For homemade fudge and the best saltwater taffy, there's no place like **Tuck's** (two shops in Rockport).

Historic Attractions

Hammond Castle, Hesperus Avenue, Magnolia. (508) 283-2080. This replica of a medieval castle was built between 1926 and 1929 by John Hays Hammond Jr. to house his classic and medieval art collection. It has an exceptional 8,600-pipe organ in the Great Hall, which is the setting for concerts by famed organists from around the world. The hall has two beautiful stained-glass windows, one designed by Jacques Simone and the other a reproduction of a window from Chartres Cathedral. The dining room is styled after a monastery refectory. The courtyard is intended to depict an ancient French church opening into a town square. The pool in the center and the lush plants give it almost a tropical air. Changing exhibits are mounted in several galleries in the castle. Just offshore is the "Reef of Norman's Woe" made famous by the Longfellow poem. A gift shop features handcrafted items. Open daily 9 to 5, June-October; Thursday, Friday and Sunday 1 to 4, Saturday 10 to 4, rest of year. Adults $4.50, children $2.50.

Beauport, 71 Eastern Point Blvd., Gloucester. (508) 283-0800. The Society for the Preservation of New England Antiquities oversees this remarkable mansion, located on the exquisite Eastern Point Boulevard among the most exclusive homes on Cape Ann. Beauport was the home of Henry Davis Sleeper, a collector of antiques and a leading interior designer of the 1920s and 1930s. The house, begun in 1907, was enlarged continually by Sleeper (in collaboration with Gloucester architect Halfdan Hanson) until his death in 1934. The result is a maze of 40 rooms filled with vast collections of American and European decorative arts. The house was bought by Charles and Helena McCann and given by them as a museum — virtually untouched — in 1942. The museum is closed, maddeningly, on summer weekends. Open weekdays 10 to 4, mid-May to mid-September; 10 to 4 weekdays and 1 to 4 weekends, through Oct. 11. Adults $5, children $2.50.

Sargent-Murray-Gilman-Hough House, 49 Middle St., Gloucester, 281-2432. This 18th-century house serves as an example of shipping and other merchant residences that once lined the street. Exhibits of portraits, antique furniture and furnishings and Georgian architecture are of interest. Open Friday, Saturday and Sunday, 10 to 4. Adults $2, children $1.

The Paper House, 50 Pigeon Hill St., Rockport, 546-2629. A strange little place, this was built nearly 50 years ago of old newspapers especially treated and rolled. The house includes desks, chairs, lamps, tables and other furnishings made entirely of newspapers, and it probably is someplace you'll remember, even though you can see it all quickly. Open 10 to 5 daily in summer. Adults 50 cents, children 25 cents.

Where to Eat ⟋⟋⟋

Rockport is dry; Gloucester is not. Most Rockport eateries allow you to bring wine (purchase it in Gloucester if you haven't brought it from home) and may charge a corkage fee.

On the Water

My Place By-the-Sea, 72 Bearskin Neck, Rockport. (508) 546-9667. You can't argue with this location, at the tip of Bearskin Neck and surrounded, or so it seems, by water. It's also quite a romantic feeling that you get from the pastel color scheme and at sunset the setting is magical for diners on the two flower-lined outdoor decks. Chef Charles Kreis took over the restaurant a couple of years ago, and most Rockporters consistently name it among their favorites. The lobster roll at lunch seemed a bit pricey ($12.50 last time we checked), but it is made daily with all lobster meat. Other noontime possibilities include salads like tuna or shrimp in the $5 range; clam chowder, seafood scampi and a large selection of sandwiches. At dinner, entrees from $11 to $16 include baked scrod in lime butter, seafood scampi, chicken marsala, seafood fettuccine and prime rib. Open Thursday-Tuesday, noon to 9, April-October.

Sea Level Cafe, 14 Bearskin Neck, Rockport. (508) 546-2180. Ever since Peter Amero and Cutty O'Leary opened this tiny, two-level spot (the lower level really is at sea level and there's a great, closeup view of the harbor), the reviews have been mostly raves. Peter's the chef and they will take reservations — probably a good idea since only fifteen can be served upstairs and twenty down. Among the dinner entrees (most $10 to $14), two that are highly recommended are the lobster linguini, cooked in sherry and spices, and the squid with black pasta, made with a sherry sauce. Other possibilities include baked stuffed jumbo shrimp, roast breast of chicken and broiled sirloin tips in a light marinade. A side salad is $2. Homemade desserts are raved about, especially the fudge brownies and chocolate mousse pie. For lunch, the lobster salad roll is $7.25;

sandwiches range from $2.50 for grilled cheese to $8.95 for lobster salad and you also can get quiche of the day, cold boiled lobster, broiled swordfish or haddock. Lunch daily, 11 to 4; dinner, 5:30 to 10. Open April-December.

Boulevard Oceanview Restaurant, 25 Western Ave., Gloucester. (508) 281-2949. Across the street from the waterfront, this small establishment draws praise for the Portuguese specialties cooked up by owners Maria and John Borge and their relatives. Even Sagres beer, favored in Portugal, is served. Among specialties ($10.95 to $12.95) are charcoal salted cod, grilled jumbo shrimp in a butter and lemon sauce, a seafood plate "sao style" (with shrimp, scallops, clams, haddock and squid) and mariscada, made with lobster, shrimp, scallops, littlenecks and mussels. French fries and coleslaw accompany most items. For the less adventurous, there are a sirloin tip dinner and a shrimp roll. The puffy pink curtains, pink venetian blinds and pink tablecloths are a bit surprising, but pleasant. Breakfast weekends, 7 to 11; all-day menu daily from 11 to 9.

The Gull, 75 Essex Ave. (Route 133), Gloucester. (508) 283-6565. This is another restaurant favored by locals. Open at 5 a.m. to feed the fishermen who head down the Annisquam River and into Gloucester Harbor from the Cape Ann Marina where it is located, the Gull is a place where the fish is sure to be fresh. Bare wood tables and captain's chairs look out over the water and the marina, where boats are crammed cheek by jowl and jockeying back and forth to dock. It's an active scene, just the place to enjoy seafood, fish or clam chowder, all of them rich with cream and butter, but not so thick that you wonder if a little Elmer's has been mixed in. This is good New England seashore cooking and a tank near the entrance has some of the largest lobsters we've seen. You can order broiled scallops, haddock or scrod, fried fish of many sorts and lobsters ranging from chicken to large. A specialty is haddock and broccoli scuderi served in a casserole with a homemade cheese sauce. With salad and potato, it's $9.95. Prime rib is served nightly; sandwiches and burgers are also available. Homemade grapenut pudding is one of the down-home desserts. Open for breakfast, lunch and dinner. Closed November-March.

The Rudder, 73 Rocky Neck Ave., Gloucester. (508) 283-7967. Housed in a building that was once a fish cannery, right on the water, the Rudder is enormously popular — and has been for 33 years. The location, smack dab in the middle of the Rocky Neck artist colony, with a back porch that overlooks Gloucester Harbor, is hard to beat. A mixed bag of locals and tourists crowds into the place, even though the food's reputation goes up and down. Service is slow, says the menu (it also says "leisure dining is best"). But everyone has to stop in at least a couple of times a season and we have had enormously enjoyable evenings here. Entrees start at $10.95 and include a good choice, from pasta, to seafood, to prime rib, and even leg of lamb ($24.95). Lunch daily in summer, noon to 3; dinner, 6 to 10; off-season, dinner Wednesday-Sunday and weekend brunch. Open mid-April to mid-November.

Peg Leg, 18 Beach St., Rockport. (508) 546-3038. This prim white clapboard restaurant (with a greenhouse room out back) is considered solid if not innovative, and the faithful return again and again for such seaside favorites as scallop or lobster pie, baked stuffed shrimp, scrod au gratin, lobster newburg and meat items such as baby beef liver or lamb chops. It is an especially nice spot on a Sunday afternoon for dinner and the garden dining room in front seems a perfect place to take Grandma. Entrees at dinner range from $8.95 to $17.95. At lunch you get the same type of food (not sandwiches) from $6.95 to $8.95. Lunch, Wednesday-Monday 11:30 to 2:30; dinner, 5:30 to 9. Open April-October.

The Studio, Rocky Neck, Gloucester. (508) 283-4123. We like the Studio for everything from the artist palette tables and director's chairs in the cocktail lounge to the high-backed booths along the wall to the beautiful view over Gloucester harbor. It's one of our favorite places to stop for a drink. The cocktail lounge has a piano bar and people do get into the mood. Piano bar operates nightly from 8. Open daily for lunch and dinner.

The Lobster Pool overlooking Folly Cove, Rockport, is the place to get your lobster stew with an ocean view or maybe your lobster in the rough, clam roll, lobster rolls (excellent and just $7.95 the last we knew), plus hamburgers and hot dogs. Sit at picnic tables on a patch of green lawn in the sun and enjoy the water view, or there's an indoor dining room. The desserts are very good — things like hot apple crisp, made daily.

If you want a snack, a cool iced tea or a soft drink, and a rest for your weary bones while you view the Rockport Harbor activity, don't overlook the **Deck at the Hannah Jumper** restaurant on Bearskin Neck. We could sit there for hours.

Table for Two, But Alas, No View

The Hungry Wolf, 43 South St., Rockport. (508) 546-2100. One of the best restaurants on Cape Ann, this small spot looks as if it will succeed where others have failed. Charles Wolf is the chef-owner and his credentials include studying with Madeline Kamman when she had her place in Newton, Mass. His wife Laura does the decorating and managing. The dining room is pretty with blue flowered curtains over lace and pink cloths atop flowered cloths, romantic and decidedly un-nautical. In 1990 Charlie was getting into some cajun cooking, offering cajun swordfish and tuna. Shrimp newburg is a favorite item, and other entrees ($11.95 to $14.95) include sirloin teriyaki, sirloin dijon, shrimp scampi and daily lobster specials. Dinner, Monday-Saturday 4:30 to 9:30.

Barish's, 110 Main St., Gloucester. (508) 281-1911. Jane Barish, a graduate of the Culinary Institute of America, opened this narrow, center-of-town restaurant in 1989 and the word was out almost immediately: good, good, good. Having worked at Another Season on Beacon Hill, she knows how to prepare creative food. Here there's a great emphasis on fresh herbs and spices and the entire restaurant is non-smoking. The country Italian and French menu offers such treats as tomato-basil linguini, spinach fettuccine, chicken bouillabaisse with rouille, pork tenderloin giambotte and veal with leek and roquefort sauce among entrees from $9.50 to $18.50. Start with scallop and corn fritters, cheese souffle crepes with tomato coulis or seafood sausage. Beer and wine are available. Since only 23 can be seated in this cozy spot, reservations are essential. Dinner, Tuesday-Saturday in season; fewer days in winter. No credit cards.

The Greenery, 15 Dock Square, Rockport. (508) 546-9593. This casual spot with plants is popular and the surprise is the view of Motif No. 1 across the harbor from a few tables out back. Located in the center of Rockport's busiest area, the Greenery emphasizes salads and seafood but you also can get sandwiches and dinner entrees. A salad, ice cream and pastry bar out front is self-service; to the rear there is table service. Sandwiches include the sprout-wich, with muenster and cheddar cheese, fresh mushrooms, sunflower seeds, sprouts and dressing ($4.50), and the Middle Eastern featuring hummus, muenster, lettuce and tomato. Charbroiled hamburgers and cheeseburgers are available. Entrees range from $7.95 to $15 and include specials like seafood

258

linguini, baked stuffed lobster, stuffed shells and baked scrod. The particularly fine desserts include cheesecake made on the premises, homemade apple pie with a cheddar streusel topping and hot fudge sundaes made with frozen yogurt. Open daily, 9 to 9, May-October.

The Raven, 197 East Main St., East Gloucester. (508) 281-3951. This romantic restaurant has a plant-filled floor-to-ceiling bay window, pink silk flowers hanging from baskets, black lacquered chairs, pink napkins in the glasses and white tablecloths. The wallpaper with a black background is strewn with pink flowers, and tiny white lights twinkle on jade plants in the bay window. It is small, intimate and feels a bit crowded if you're at one of the tables in the center of the room where people have to keep pressing past. The mixed menu offers seafood, veal, beef and poultry dishes. We had one of the more popular items, the Raven stir-fry, with scallops and shrimp sauteed with pea pods, mushrooms, onions, green peppers and light soy sauce and a lobster special with pea pods and huge chunks of lobster. Other entrees ($12.95 to $16.95) include veal chesterfield (veal sauteed with parsley, garlic and tomato sauce, and served in a casserole) and steak au poivre. Among desserts are Bailey's cheesecake, a mousse of the day (ours was lemon, creamy and delicious) and a fresh strawberry tart, which was disappointing. Service was less than perfectly solicitous, but this restaurant patronized more by tourists than residents has great potential. Dinner nightly, 5:30 to 9:30. Closed Monday and Tuesday in winter.

Halibut Point, 289 Main St., Gloucester. (508) 281-1900. Unimposing on the exterior (an old and narrow building built by Howard Blackburn as a tavern in 1900), this restaurant has brick walls, wooden floors and the scrumptious smell of charcoal grilling when you enter. Charbroiled swordfish couldn't be fresher and the charcoal burgers, charcoal chicken breast sandwiches and chargrilled hot dogs are fine. Creamy white clam chowder and Italian fish chowder (a spicy tomato base with vegetables) are specialties. You can get cherrystones or oysters on the half shell from the **Oyster Bar.** Prices range from $2.95 for chowder to $10.95 for a full dinner. Sirloin steak is always on the menu, but ask about the seafood specials. Save room for the low tide pie, a chocolate cookie crumb shell filled with coffee ice cream and topped with fudge. Open daily, 11:30 a.m. to midnight or 1.

Picnicking. Try Halibut Point Reservation off Route 127 north of Rockport. You will have to carry your picnic supplies in from the road. You can tote picnics to most beaches. We have enjoyed ours at the end of Bearskin Neck on the rocks (off-season, we admit).

FOR MORE INFORMATION: Rockport Board of Trade, Box 67, Rockport Mass. 01966, (508) 546-6575. Cape Ann Chamber of Commerce, 128 Main St., Gloucester 01930, (508) 283-1601.

Pier at North Hero House faces Green Mountains across Lake Champlain.

The Champlain Islands, Vt.

Its promoters call this area Vermont's West Coast, an appellation that we find appropriate. Viewed from Interstate 87 above St. Albans, deep green islands, large and small, fill the expanse of blue water beneath a backdrop of towering peaks as far as the eye can see. Every time we pass this breathtaking vista it reminds us of a similar panorama of the San Juan Islands, viewed from the interstate above Washington's Puget Sound.

They call Lake Champlain the inland sea, which is not all that far-fetched. After the Great Lakes, it's America's sixth largest freshwater lake, its cool, crystal-clear waters a canopy between the Adirondacks to the west and the Green Mountains to the east. But for the presence of mountains and the lack of tidal ups and downs, you could close your eyes and imagine yourself near the ocean in Maine's Casco Bay or Nova Scotia's Mahone Bay.

Given the "West Coast" and "inland sea" attributes, it's amazing how undiscovered — and unspoiled — the Champlain Islands are. Although barely fifteen minutes north of Burlington, Vermont's largest city, and an hour's drive south of Montreal, the islands convey a palpable isolation. This 30-mile stretch of rural retreat in the middle of the Northeast's largest lake is a never-never land near the international border, too distant for most Americans and another country for Canadians. Thus it has been spared the onslaught that tarnishes similar waterways within development distance of three million people. Grand Isle County, Vermont's smallest, claims a year-round population of 5,000, tourist accommodations built years ago, summer cottages and campgrounds, rolling farmlands and apple orchards, abundant shoreline, and not much else.

U.S. Route 2 is the main road through the islands, from South Hero through Grand Isle, North Hero and Alburg. The islands, incidentally, were part of a charter granted in 1779 to Ethan Allen, Ira Allen and others of the Green Mountain Boys. The grant was given the name Two Heroes, referring to the Allens, and some people still refer to the area as "The Heroes."

These little-known islands are replete with history and their own identity, as attested by the 470-page history of the Town of Isle La Motte, one of the more remote islands. "There is a certain indefinable spell about it," writes author Allen L. Stratton. "It is a quietness, a sense of peace."

The islands are long and narrow, never more than five miles wide and sometimes, as at the portage point the Indians named Carrying Place, only the width of a road separating lake from bay. They're connected by causeways, bridges and a shared sense of place.

Getting There

The Champlain Islands are in the northern part of Lake Champlain, stretching from about fifteen miles north of Burlington to the Quebec border. From Vermont, they are reached via Route 2 from Interstate 89 near Colchester or Route 78 from Swanton. From New York, take the Champlain exit off Interstate 87 east to Rouses Point and Route 2, or the Grand Isle ferry from Plattsburgh.

Where to Stay

Inns and B&Bs

North Hero House, Route 2, North Hero 05474. (802) 372-8237. The premier place to stay in the Heroes is the waterfront complex around this three-story, mustard-colored frame house, built in 1891 right across the road from the lake. Red rocking chairs are lined up in a row on the hospitable porch. There are six rooms in the main inn, but the coveted ones are in three buildings beside the water, Cove House, Southwind and Homestead. In Cove House, the wallboard was stripped on one wall of each of the six rooms so the original brick and peg beam construction could be seen. Here you can relax on your screened porch right over the water. Downstairs is the old Cobbler's Room, a prized suite with a fireplaced living room, beamed ceilings and private porch. The foundation is Grand Isle granite and the fieldstone walls are three to four feet thick. Of the 23 rooms, only three in the back of the main house do not have water views. All have private baths. Boats moor at the old steamship dock in front, next to one of the lake's few sand-bottom beaches. Big inner tubes and snorkel gear are available, as are a tennis court, sauna and bicycles. There are also two outboards, four sunfish and canoes. A restaurant (see Where to Eat), game room/lounge and the **Linnipin Shop,** with locally made goods, maple products, those neat Vermont cow T-shirts and the like, are in the main inn. Energetic young innkeeper John Apgar, a friend of longtime owners Roger and Caroline Sorg, is carrying on their tradition with his partners, the Sherlocks. This is the kind of place where guests get to know each other and return year after year to the same rooms. Doubles, $41 to $80; suite, $95. Open mid-May to mid-October.

Thomas Mott Homestead, Off Route 78, RD 2, Box 149B, Alburg 05440. (802) 796-3736. Here is one of those rare B&Bs that has everything: a magnificent waterfront location, spacious and comfortable guest rooms with private baths, homey common rooms and porches, gourmet breakfasts and caring touches. Californians Dottie and Pat Schallert, he a retired wine distributor, discovered the Champlain Islands during a visit to Auberge Alburg and decided to settle here. They took an 1838 farmhouse and transformed it into a B&B in 1988. The original beamed walls and a massive collection of cookbooks and wine books flank the stairway. There are four guest rooms, each furnished with antiques and quilts from different states. The twin-bedded Carrie's Room could not be more colorful with hooked rugs, pillows and quilts, even on the walls. Laura's Room has two queen beds, and the downstairs Corner Suite offers a queen bed, day bed, cathedral ceiling and walk-in closet. But the ultimate accommodation is Ransom's Rest, sequestered beneath a cathedral ceiling with a queen bed, Shaker pegs, two comfy chairs in front of an angled fireplace and a balcony onto Ransom's Bay, affording a view to Mount Mansfield. Between the moonlight and the fire, it's heaven on earth, says Pat. The common rooms are a joy as well: a fireplaced living room stocked with books and magazines, TV and games; a big side porch with a combination games and pool table, and two other porches. Antiques fill the expansive dining room, centered by an old Canadian tailor's table and with a piano at one end. Here, the Schallerts serve a hearty breakfast, perhaps quiche, omelets with fresh crab or french toast doused with syrup tapped from the maple trees outside. They arrange for gourmet dinners, catered by Bonnie's Catered Affairs of St. Albans, for $17.50 to $24 a head, in the dining room or on the porch. Other special touches: ten kinds of Ben & Jerry's Ice Cream are always in the freezer ("I spend a lot of my time in the ice cream shop," reports Pat — in fact, that's where he was when we arrived); ice cream glasses are kept cold in the refrigerator, birds are fed at an array of feeders, and there's a canoe for guests' use. Doubles, $50 to $65. No smoking. No credit cards.

Auberge Alburg, South Main Street, RD 1, Box 3, Alburg 05440. (802) 796-3169. This eclectic and rather funky place is a B&B, a continental-style cafe and the host for a series of special events from yoga sessions to theater workshops. What she calls this "little Chautauqua" is run by Gabrielle Tyrnauer, an anthropology professor, and Charles Stastny, a political science professor, both at Concordia University in Montreal. It exudes their tastes — from a downstairs room full of books to the Russian dinners and entertainment occasionally provided by a Russian friend named Alina, who is a regular visitor. Located near the Canadian border, the house is also a haven for refugees on what Charles refers to as "the overground railroad;" at our visit, the pair were planning to write a book on their experiences. Upstairs, two of the three bedrooms each have a double bed and two twins, paneled walls and scatter rugs, and are good for families. In the rear barn, a suite has two rooms, one with a custom-made futon that turns into a double bed, a small refrigerator and a tiny bathroom. The loft hideaway on the barn's third floor has floor-to-ceiling windows, colorful rugs and a private bath; it was pressed into service as an office by a visiting editor at our latest visit. The airy second-floor space used for workshops also has beds available, dormitory-style. Gabrielle officially serves a continental breakfast of croissants, muffins and bagels, but unofficially Kenny, her step-nephew and former professional cook, might offer eggs or pancakes. A rear deck offers a glimpse of the lake, and it's a short walk to a little beach. At **Cafe Etcetera,** on the wraparound screened porch, you may order espresso, cappuccino, croissants and continental pastries, plus occasional light meals. Among pastries are cheesecake with apricot and strawberry glaze, sacher torte with fresh whipped cream, kiwi cake, Black Forest pie and strudels, priced from $1.25 to $2.50. Doubles, $45 to $55; suite, $70 to $85.

Ransom's Bay Inn, Centerbay Road, Box 57, Alburg 05440. (802) 796-3359 or 796-3417. Michael Perry, who runs the Alburg Country Store and Deli, welcomes "stranded folk at all hours" into his stone house, an inn dating to 1810. Made of gray marble quarried on Isle La Motte, it has four antiques-filled guest rooms with brass beds and hardwood floors. They share two baths, one upstairs and one down. Guests have the run of a formal living room, a family room with TV and one of the inn's three fireplaces, and no fewer than three dining rooms

— in one of which, the country room overlooking a marble patio, Michael serves a complimentary breakfast at a table big enough for eighteen people. That breakfast is glorified continental in summer, when he's busy at the store. In winter, he prepares a full breakfast on an old cast-iron cook stove. Guests have access to seventeen acres and a private sand beach. Doubles, $49.

Paradise Bay Bed & Breakfast, Kibbe Point Road, R.R. 1, Box 496-C, South Hero 05486. (802) 372-5393. Here's one beauty of a house, the kind everyone dreams of owning beside a lake. Hard to find and sequestered at the end of a long country road, it's large, new and very much lived in by Rhonda Colvard and Scott Light and their young children. They take guests in two second-floor rooms that have queen beds and share a bath as well as in a skylit, third-floor room that has a queen and a double bed and a private bath on the floor below. Stuffed toys are all around. When we visited, all three rooms could have used more furniture, particularly chairs, since the main-floor living rooms seem to be reserved for family. There's a rear deck with a few chairs for taking in the view. Rhonda serves a full breakfast in her kitchen. Doubles, $60 to $75. No smoking.

Motels and Cottages

Shore Acres Inn & Restaurant, Route 2, R.R. 1, Box 3, North Hero 05474. (802) 372-8722. Although not really an inn, this appealing place situated well away from the highway on the edge of a ledge beside Great East Bay is otherwise appropriately named. Shore Acres rests on lovely lawns amid 50 acres of rolling grounds and has a half-mile of private lakeshore. White with blue trim and blue awnings, it has nineteen lakeview rooms in two motel-type wings on either side of the restaurant. Innkeepers Susan and Mike Tranby have added four newer, queensize rooms in a garden house annex that operates as a B&B in the off-season. Each room has private bath, color TV, maple furniture and pine paneling, plus ceiling fans or air-conditioning. Benches and lawn chairs are scattered about the lawns for viewing the lake and Mount Mansfield beyond. Below are a pebbly beach and a raft. Breakfast and dinner are served in the restaurant (see Where to Eat). Doubles, $63 to $95. Open May to mid-October.

Sandbar Motor Inn, Route 2, South Hero 05486. (802) 372-6911. Located at the west end of the Sandbar causeway, this is the first accommodation you'll find in the Champlain Islands when you're arriving from the south. In fact, the site has been used for lodging since the 1890s, when the Sandbar bridge toll collector took in guests in his toll house and ultimately added an inn. Now the motel has 37 units, facing Great East Bay across the highway and backing up to the edge of what the locals call the broad lake at the rear. The motel rooms are quite small but clean and adequate, with color TVs and modern baths. Six have kitchens and there are two cottages. Owners Cliff and Poe Sheard have put Poe's handmade rag rugs in the bathrooms and her straw hats decorated with flowers in the bedrooms, enhanced the front gardens and cleaned up the back beach, where they offer a hammock for guests. They rent bicycles and boats, and plan to expand their marina. There's good swimming from a private dock and beach, or you can drive across the causeway to Sandbar State Park. Breakfast and dinner are served at the Sandbar restaurant (see Where to Eat). Doubles, $45 to $65; cottage for six, $85. Open May to mid-October.

Ruthcliffe Lodge, Old Quarry Road, Isle La Motte 05463. (802) 928-3200. A long way from anywhere but the lake, this lodge with restaurant and motel is good for those who want to be away from it all. It's a family operation, Mark and Kathy Infante having taken over from his parents who started the lodge in 1951.

Three meals a day are served in the lodge, which has a cathedral ceiling opening to a second-floor loft with five guest rooms. Furnished in lodge style, each has a double bed and a half-bath, and shares one full bath. Seven good-sized rooms in the adjacent motel look out onto the lake; they have two double beds, wall-to-wall carpeting and TV on request. Weekly rentals and American Plan meals are available. Doubles, lodge $50, motel $60. Open May 15 to Sept. 15.

Holiday Harbor Motel, Route 2, North Hero 05474. (802) 372-4077. Twelve motel units are lined up near the road and an office containing a bait and tackle store and small gift shop. By the shore, six housekeeping cottages, rustic and plain, face the lake. All units have color TVs, barbecues and picnic tables. A small beach, playground area and boat rentals are available. Doubles, $37 to $49; housekeeping cottages, $260 to $285 weekly. Seasonal.

Hislop's Landing, Route 2, RD 1, Box 339, Grand Isle 05458. (802) 372-8229 or 372-8309. Down a long hill from the road are ten cottages with decks overlooking the lake. The five on the shore are older; five behind them were built in 1979. All have two bedrooms, a day bed in the living room, shower bath, modern kitchen and front decks with picnic tables; two by the shore have fireplaces. There's a sandy beach, and the protected bay called the Gut is fine for sailing and water skiing. Cottages, $265 to $295 weekly. Seasonal.

RENTALS. Cottages and houses are advertised in the Islander newspaper. Listings may be available from Island Property Management, Box 203, North Hero 05474, (802) 372-5436; Billie Tudhope Realtor, North Hero 05474, (802) 372-6916, or Hill Real Estate, Box 122, South Hero 05486, (802) 372-5777.

Camping

Camping is big in this area. In fact, there are far more campsites than there are guest rooms. Among the best:

Grand Isle State Park, Box 648, Grand Isle 05458. (802) 372-4399. Thirty-one lean-tos are included among the 157 campsites offered in this 226-acre park. Many sites are grouped around a big central lawn. More appealing are the eleven lean-tos on a shoreline ledge, most with views of the lake. The sites have no hookups, but shower and toilet facilities are available. A small playground is beside the beach, and there's a recreation hall. Tent sites, $9; lean-tos, $11.50.

North Hero State Park, North Hero 05474. (802) 372-8727. This 399-acre park has 108 campsites and sixteen lean-tos amid the trees along three well-spaced loop roads — none on the water, although within walking distance of the swimming and boat launch area. Shower and toilet facilities are available, as are boat rentals. A small gravel beach is popular with wind surfers, and there's a nature trail. Tent sites, $7.50; lean-tos, $10.50.

Among many private campgrounds, a location on a peninsula at the entrance to Mallett's Bay, with a panoramic view of the broad lake, is an asset of **Camp Skyland,** South Hero 05486. (802) 372-4200. Thirty-two campsites starting at $12 daily are located on six acres along the lakeshore. Also available are eight single-room cabins and four housekeeping cottages, $175 to $200 a week.

Seeing and Doing _____ ⌒⌒⌒

Water recreation reigns in this area, naturally. Although there are an eighteen-hole golf course at Alburg Country Club, two smaller courses and a few tennis courts, there's not much else. People are always on the lookout for Champ, the Lake Champlain sea monster whose sightings are front-page news in the Islander newspaper ("Champ must be touring the whole island, for just a few days ago 35 people reported seeing the creature off the YMCA Camp in South Hero," the Islander reported after two sightings off Grand Isle one summer). Visitors who get cabin fever can go off to Burlington or Montreal for the day.

On or Near the Water

BOATING. From canoes to luxury yachts, sailboards to schooners, boats ply the sheltered coves and bays around the Champlain Islands. Great East Bay, that part of the lake between the islands and the Vermont mainland, is generally more protected than the "broad lake" to the south and west.

There are no excursion boats touring the Champlain Islands. The closest boat is the **Spirit of Ethan Allen,** 862-9685, which gives 90-minute scenic lake cruises at 10, noon, 2 and 4 daily from Perkins Pier in downtown Burlington (adults $7, children $3.50). Dinner, Sunday brunch, jazz, sunset and moonlight dance cruises also are scheduled. Tour promoters tell visitors to look for Champ. In 1984, 70 passengers aboard the Spirit of Ethan Allen made the largest mass sighting ever of the legendary creature.

Lake Champlain Transportation Co., King Street Dock, Burlington, 864-9804. Another way to see the lake is aboard the Lake Champlain ferries, which connect Vermont and New York on three crossings: Charlotte to Essex, Burlington to Port Kent and Grand Isle to Cumberland Head near Plattsburgh. The Grand Isle crossing leaves from the heart of the Champlain Islands, is the shortest and runs the most frequently, every twenty minutes from 5 a.m. to 1 a.m. in summer. It's also the only ferry to run year-round. The twelve-minute crossing costs $6.50 for car and driver, $1.50 for adults, 50 cents for children, $10.25 maximum per car.

A number of marinas offer boat rentals. One of the largest is **Tudhope Marine** in North Hero, 372-5545, where you can get a six-horsepower or twenty-horsepower motorboat or a 25-horsepower pontoon boat by the day or week. It also has windsurfers, sunfish and a seventeen-foot day sailor. **Tudhope Sailing Center,** at the bridge in Grand Isle, 372-5320, has marina facilities and offers sailing instruction and charter services. The islands have eight public boat launching areas from Keeler's Bay in South Hero to Kelly Bay at the Rouses Point Bridge in Alburg.

FISHING. Cool, clear and up to 400 feet deep, Lake Champlain is said to have as large an assortment of freshwater fish as any lake in the world. The annual **Lake Champlain International Fishing Derby** in mid-June helps raise funds for the lake restoration program, started in 1974 to restore fisheries for landlocked Atlantic salmon and rainbow trout. More than three million salmon and trout have been stocked in the lake and they're growing fast, according to LCI derby sponsors. In one recent derby, 1,099 fish were registered, among them 350 lake trout, 228 walleyed pike, 180 smallmouth bass, 128 northern pike and 46 Atlantic salmon.

SWIMMING. Lake Champlain's water is so pure that people drink it and so refreshing that some swimmers find it chilly. We don't. Our only complaint is the dearth of sand beaches, as opposed to gravel or rock beaches. Often swimming is done from docks or rafts to avoid the stony bottom. Some of the best swimming is available in state parks. **Sand Bar State Park** at the causeway in Colchester is deservedly popular with daytrippers from Burlington; it has a long beach, shady areas with picnic tables, a snack bar and boat rentals. **Knight**

Point State Park at North Hero offers a small, manmade sandy beach, picnic area and shelter, and boat rentals. **North Hero State Park** has a small gravel beach and a few picnic tables for day use. You also can swim off a beach at St. Anne's Shrine.

BIKING. The islands are relatively flat and most of the rural byways little traveled, so biking is popular. Rentals are available from **Champlain Islands Cycling,** Old Quarry Road, Isle La Motte, 928-3202, and **Island Cyclery,** South Hero, 372-6619.

BIRDING. Nearly 300 species of birds have been recorded in the area, which lies on one of the major north-south flyways for migratory birds. Herons, eagles, falcons, ravens, osprey, hawks, snowy egrets, cormorants, ducks, geese and songbirds are among the finds. Birdwatchers say the **South Hero Swamp** and **Mud Creek** in Alburg are particularly good sites. **Sand Bar Wildlife Refuge,** an 800-acre state wildlife management area across from Sand Bar State Park, is known for its duck population.

Other Attractions

Hyde Log Cabin, Route 2, Grand Isle. If Grand Isle has a tourist attraction, this is it, one of the oldest log cabins in the United States. Built in 1783 with an enormous fireplace at one end and an overhead loft, it housed the family of Jedediah Hyde Jr. and his ten children. Members of the Hyde family lived there for nearly 150 years. In 1945 the Vermont Historical Society acquired the cabin and moved it two miles to its present location along Route 2. Inside you see original furnishings, agricultural and household implements, bedspreads, clothes and such. A guide from the Grand Isle Historical Society informed us that more than two-thirds of the artifacts came from the Hyde family or their descendants and the rest from other pioneer families on the island. We felt we were part of an earlier era, listening to birds twittering out back through the open door and watching cows grazing on the next property. Open free Wednesday-Sunday, 9 to 5, July 4 through Labor Day, weekends til Columbus Day.

St. Anne's Shrine, Isle La Motte, 928-3362. Thousands of pilgrims find solace at the Edmundite Fathers' shrine on the site of Fort St. Anne, Vermont's oldest settlement, where the first Mass in the state was celebrated in 1666. In keeping with island tradition, the shrine is rather primitive: a covered, open-air chapel where Eucharistic celebrations are offered daily, an Italian marble statue of St. Anne housed in an A-frame, a grotto and the Way of the Cross, its stations nestled among tall pines beside the lake. A granite statue of Samuel de Champlain, sculpted in the Vermont Pavilion at Expo 67 in Montreal, now occupies the site where he landed in 1609. There are a no-frills cafeteria and picnic tables, and visitors may swim from the beach or simply relax on a lovely, peaceful piece of land. Shrine is open free, May 15 to Oct. 15.

Isle La Motte Historical Society, Isle La Motte. Originally the South District schoolhouse (circa 1797), this small building now holds local artifacts, looms, spinning wheels and other items collected since 1925 by the historical society. The island is noted geologically for having examples of every known geological period and a few specimens are here, according to assistant curator Edith Andrews, who lives in a house occupied by five generations of her family at the four corners. There are examples of the island's famed black marble that graces the U.S. Capitol and Radio City Music Hall, a piece of coral from a nearby farm field and two pages of Champlain's diary written upon his landing here. Open Saturdays from 2 to 4, July and August, or by appointment. Free.

SHOPPING. Stores are basic and the shops few and far between. We always stop at the **Apple Farm Market** in South Hero, where Judy Allen dispenses cider, apples, jams and gifts (many with an apple theme). You can choose from many kinds of apples (Empires are the best for eating), watch cider being made, and pick up a fresh apple pie to take home. Next door is the **Sandwich Shop,** where sandwiches go for $1.75 to $3.95 and you can get a taco salad or a watermelon slice, and the **Ice Cream Shoppe,** dispensing Ben & Jerry's cones for $1.10. A six-foot-tall green frog is in front of **Green Frog Gifts & Clothing,** Route 314, South Hero. Inside is a little bit of everything from moccasins to Vermont food products, T-shirts to books, plus a large selection of frogs. Amid the array is an old refrigerator covered with "I Love Vermont" magnets. In 1982, Frank and Lynda Clark converted an old hen house into the fine **Hooting Owl Gift Shop,** Route 314, Grand Isle. It's an intriguing shop chock full of Vermont handcrafts, kitchenware, jewelry, dolls, Christmas decorations and, of course, owls. Through the rear window is a nice view of the lake. The **Alburg Country Store and Deli** has fine crafts and Vermont products, plus a patio outside on which to eat a sandwich (maple sugar cured ham is $3.10 and one of the five kinds of bread you can have it on is Vermont cheddar) or ice cream obtained inside. Other shops specializing in antiques and collectibles include **The Back Chamber, Vallee's Den of Antiquity** and **Donna's Tinker Barn.**

Where to Eat _____

North Hero House, Route 2, North Hero. (802) 372-8237. A greenhouse dining room decked out in gold and red linens, Villeroy & Boch china and hanging fuschias is not what you'd expect at an historic inn in the Champlain Islands. Nevertheless, it's what you get at the North Hero House unless you're too late, as we were for lunch one afternoon (lunch is served only from noon to 1). We were seated instead in a circular screened outdoor gazebo beside a little fountain in a garden off the lounge and were grateful to be served, there not being many places for lunch in this area. With a glimpse of the lake, we enjoyed a roast beef sandwich on sourdough bread ($4.95) and pie of the day (a shrimp, tomato and brie quiche, $4.45), served with pasta salad and cole slaw. The dinner menu changes nightly with a choice of three entrees priced from $13.95 to $16.95. A typical offering might be cornish game hen with brandied peach sauce, a duo of grilled tuna and swordfish steaks with citrus butter, and twin medallions of beef with bearnaise sauce, accompanied by roasted red potatoes, local swiss chard and baked stuffed tomato and garnished with edible flowers. Appetizers might be chilled pumpkin and ginger bisque, a pate of duck and pork, and mushroom caps stuffed with sausage, sour cream and diced apples. Desserts range from strawberry almond dacquoise to plum puree with blackberry brandy. Fresh whole grain bread and garden salads accompany. Friday night brings a lobster buffet dinner served picnic-style on the steamship dock. Breakfast, 8 to 10; lunch, noon to 1; dinner, 6 to 8. Open mid-May to mid-October.

Shore Acres Inn & Restaurant, Route 2, North Hero. (802) 372-8722. The pine-paneled dining room dressed in blue and white linens and fresh flowers has a stone fireplace and looks out onto Lake Champlain. The limited menu is priced from $8.95 for charbroiled sirloin to $16.95 for New York strip steak. Charbroiled swordfish, scampi, rainbow trout, seafood fettuccine, leg of lamb and smoked pork chop with homemade apple sauce are among the offerings, all served with homebaked bread, salad and seasonal vegetables. Appetizers are not all that interesting (Vermont cheese and crackers, clam chowder); desserts include chocolate and other homemade pies, maple syrup sundae and lemon pudding. At lunch, a new summertime offering in 1990, you could choose among a handful of items like grilled mesquite chicken sandwich with potato salad, grilled swordfish sandwich with steak fries, and deep-fried scallops with steak fries, $5.95 to $7.95. Lunch, 11:30 to 2; dinner, 5 to 9. Open May to mid-October.

Ruthcliffe Lodge, Old Quarry Road, Isle La Motte. (802) 928-3200. Meals are served in a rustic, pine-paneled dining room with a cathedral ceiling or on an adjacent outdoor deck with pipe furniture overlooking the lake. Owner Mark Infante handles the cooking chores. Full dinners, from juice and soup to dessert, are priced from $12.95 for chicken or stuffed sole to $14.95 for shrimp scampi, broiled swordfish or filet mignon. The veal marsala and the veal with three-mustard sauce are particularly well regarded. Homemade desserts include amaretto cheesecake and rice and apple pudding. For breakfast, all you can eat is $4.95. Breakfast daily, 8:30 to 10; dinner, 5 to 9. Open mid-May to mid-September.

Sandbar Restaurant, Route 2, South Hero. (802) 372-6911. This traditional place has been upscaled in food and decor by Cliff and Poe Sheard, who finally have the dining room the way they want it. It's attractive with new curtains, blue linens, and lots of fresh flowers cut from the gardens outside. Candles flicker and the view up the lake is quite magical. To the basic fare like roast turkey and seafood newburg, the Sandbar has added chicken cordon bleu, baked stuffed shrimp, scallops au vin and three steaks including filet mignon ($8.95 to $15.25). The "Green Mountain Surprise," a homemade spicy preserve, is served as an appetizer over Vermont cream cheese with crackers, and sold by the jar for $5.95. Dinners come with assorted breads, crispy vegetables and potato or rice pilaf. Our New York strip steak and filet mignon dinners were so filling we had no room for dessert. Homemade coffee cake and muffins are featured at breakfast, and the Sunday brunch packs in the locals. You might try Vermont hash topped with poached eggs, seafood crepe, boneless trout with eggs any style or stuffed french toast filled with strawberries and nuts, priced from $3.95 to $6.95. Poe was still recovering from a record 300 brunchers the day before our last visit. Breakfast, 8 to 11; dinner, 5 to 9; Sunday brunch, 8 to 1.

Commodore's Table, Route 2 at Route 314, South Hero. (802) 372-4345. Another possibility for breakfast is this nondescript family restaurant and gift shop. Pancakes are $3.25 and omelets $2 to $3.50. Steaks, seafood, turkey, chicken and sandwiches are offered for lunch and dinner. At lunch, try the specials: perhaps a Philly cheesesteak sandwich ($3.99) or fish and chips, $4.25. Complete dinners go from $7.50 for filet of haddock to $9.95 for sirloin steak. Homemade breads and carrot cake are for sale. Sutter Home wines are $2.25 a glass, $7 a bottle. Open daily year-round, 7 a.m. to 9 p.m.

Northern Cafe, Route 2, Alburg. (802) 796-3003. Three meals a day are served at this unprepossessing little roadside restaurant. Dinners go from $5.50 for chicken tenders to $9.75 for ribeye steak; all the others were $6.50 or $6.95. They come with choice of homemade soup, salad or coleslaw, and potato, vegetable, roll and beverage. Lunches are in the $1.50 to $2.95 range, but you can get a grilled cheese sandwich or a hot dog for $1.10, a cheese dog for another dime. Open daily year-round, 7 a.m. to 9 p.m.

Bo's Restaurant and Lounge, Route 2, Alburg. (802) 796-3333. Formerly known as Caldwell's, this started in 1990 and offered a fancy-for-the-area menu. Prices ranged from $8.95 for teriyaki chicken or grilled pork chops smothered with mushroom gravy to $15.95 for a broiled seafood platter. Seafood fettuccine, stuffed sole and fried haddock were other possiblities. Dinner, Wednesday-Sunday, 5 to 9.

Cafe Mooney Bay, Mooney Bay Marina, Point au Roche, N.Y. (518) 563-3328. For contemporary cuisine and a waterfront setting, this stylish place is worth going out of the way for. Hop in your boat for the a short jaunt across the lake, take the Grand Isle Ferry, or drive up and around through Rouse's Point (Exit 40 off I-87). Once you arrive, you'll know why. You can't get much closer to Lake Champlain, and expansive windows in this two-level dining room take full advantage, as does the deck outside. Marina owners Jerry and Dale Everleth created the place a few years back for their son Kevin, a Culinary Institute of America grad, who's the chef and admittedly "trying to offer a new taste" for the area. His menu changes often, but brings a dozen entrees ($15.95 to $24.95). You might find filet of red snapper with mango chile salsa, grilled shrimp and andouille sausage en brochette with ginger-citrus vinaigrette, grilled sliced duckling with black mission fig and port wine sauce, and filet mignon with black beans, mixed peppers and bourbon sauce. Appetizers are equally enticing, but save room for dessert: perhaps raspberry and blackberry shortcake, almond dacquoise with white chocolate mousse and raspberry sauce, or homemade Jack Daniels chocolate ice cream. The chef knows what he's doing, and the decor is sleek in blue and white, with deep blue towels for napkins, silk flowers and a collection of Tiffany-style lamps, many in deep blues and whites. You couldn't get a more nautical feeling unless you were on a boat. Dinner nightly in summer, 6 to 9 or 10, Sunday 5 to 9; Wednesday-Saturday in spring and fall.

The Pier Restaurant, 30 Montgomery St., Rouses Point, N.Y. (518) 297-3434. This casual waterfront eatery beside the Lighthouse Point Marina is also popular with Champlain Islanders. The paper placemat tells some of the history of the site, which was a key rail link between Boston and the Great Lakes. An unassuming place in blue and gray, it has windows onto the marina and two outdoor decks for dining beside a pool. The all-day menu is standard, from pancakes and omelets in the morning to hot meatball subs and burgers for lunch. Heavier eaters can find eighteen entrees ($6.95 to $14.95), including veal parmesan, ham steak, pork chops, fried shrimp and five kinds of steak. Open daily year-round, 7 a.m. to 10 p.m.

St. Anne's Shrine Cafeteria, Isle la Motte. A plain cafeteria serves plain food for pilgrims visiting the shrine, passing tourists or swimmers using the beach. You can get bacon and eggs, juice and coffee for $4; a sandwich for $1.50 to $2.95, and a special like baked ham, potatoes, copper pennies and roll, $3.25. We settled for good turkey noodle soup and a couple of hot dogs, each $1.25. Complete dinners are served Sundays for $5.50. Hours vary, weekdays from 8 to 3 or 4, weekends to 6 or 7.

Church Breakfasts. St. Rose of Lima Church at Keeler Bay alternates with St. Joseph Church of Grand Isle in offering Sunday morning breakfasts from 7 to noon. At St. Rose, you pay a contribution ($5 suggested) at the door of the church basement, go through a very generous buffet line and sit communally at long tables. We got more than filled up on french toast, scrambled eggs, hashed potatoes, ham, sausage, all kinds of muffins and bowls of fresh fruit. Orange juice and coffee are brought to the table. Even the glutton among us didn't have to go back for seconds. One of the women in charge said 400 to 500 people are served every other Sunday, the biggest rush is right after any of the Masses, and proceeds will go to installing an elevator in the church. St. Rose and other churches occasionally serve family suppers as well.

FOR MORE INFORMATION: Lake Champlain Islands Chamber of Commerce, Box 213, North Hero, Vt. 05474. (802) 372-5683.

Sportsmen take to waters of Connecticut River.

Connecticut River/Hanover, N.H.

Ever since our son went to summer camp in this area, we have been enamored of the twenty-mile stretch of the Connecticut River that reaches from Lebanon in the south to Orford in the north. The area includes Hanover, N.H., home of Dartmouth College, and Lakes Morey and Fairlee in Vermont as well as a couple of ponds and waterfalls.

Water may not be its prime attraction, but there is plenty of it, and the river is particularly appealing. It's possible to canoe from inn to inn in one section, to try windsurfing in another. Members of Hanover's Ledyard Canoe Club regularly spend weekends and vacations on the water, kayaking, canoeing, rowing and sailboarding.

While Hanover (and Dartmouth) bring a cultural sophistication to the area — and a fine art museum and performing arts center as well — this is an area for outdoorsmen who dress comfortably and spend their time hiking, biking or engaging in water sports. Canoes tied to the tops of cars are common sights; so are backpacks and hiking boots. The Appalachian Trail runs through Hanover, and the presence of six sports outfitters among the shops in town tells the story.

Accommodations range from country inns to cottage colonies and include a few bed and breakfasts as well. For families, there are bargains — good places for camping, and inexpensive cabin arrangements where the kids will have as much fun as their parents. Dining options are varied, from fine restaurants to low-key sandwich spots, and, except for West Lebanon, there are no golden arches.

The region is very scenic. The river cuts its swath between the mountains of Vermont and New Hampshire and there are breathtaking views from several spots. Come along with us and explore this upper Connecticut River area, which has much to offer the vacationer.

Getting There

Hanover is located at Exit 13 off Interstate 91, just north of the I-89 interchange in White River Junction. Exit 15, two exits to the north, leads to Fairlee, Vt.

270

Where to Stay _____ 〰〰〰

By the River

Stone House Inn, Route 5, North Thetford, Vt. 05054. (802) 333-9124. For nearly fifteen years, Art and Dianne Sharkey have been running this homey B&B, one of our favorites. The large stone house, set at a bend on Route 5 in the sleepy hamlet of North Thetford, is right beside the Connecticut River, and views are wonderful from a grassy back yard and from several rooms. The Sharkeys started the "Canoeing Inn to Inn" program (see below) and theirs is the middle stop of three inns on the trip. School teachers who taught in various countries around the world, they and their two teenagers have put down roots in Vermont. Art teaches at nearby Thetford Academy and Dianne is a font of information about the area. Seven rooms on the second floor share three baths, one with stall shower. The rear, paneled porch bedroom with windows all around has the best view of the river. We also like a front twin-bedded room with pink and navy flowered wallpaper and soft rose bedspreads. The main parlor has a welcoming fireplace and there's a gorgeous screened porch for summer sitting. The porch has two white hanging swings, a few rockers, and pots filled with impatiens. Dianne cooks breads, muffins, scones and other delicious pastries for the ample continental breakfast, which also may include cereal; the basket of breads is always heaping. Breakfast is served in a sunny glassed-in porch out back, next to the kitchen. Doubles, $48.

The Chieftain Motel, Route 10, Hanover, N.H. 03755. (603) 643-2550. This gray wood motel with white trim and yellow doors occupies a choice piece of real estate: a terrace high above the Connecticut River two miles north of town. Most of the 22 pine-paneled rooms have river views; if yours doesn't you can sit out back in a grassy area with chairs and tables and watch the river from there. Trails lead down to the water's edge (although it's a steep hike) and there's a pool for those who want to swim. Each room has two double beds and color TV. There's a simple breakfast room where a continental breakfast (primarily donuts and muffins plus coffee and fruit) is complimentary. Doubles, $68.

The Sunset Motel, Route 10, Hanover Road, West Lebanon, N.H. 03784. (603) 298-8721. This gray-stained board and batten motel also sits high above the Connecticut; in this case it's a few miles south of Hanover. Most rooms have river views; again, the view is great from behind the motel and there are a few chairs for enjoying it. The eighteen rooms feature one or two queensize beds and cable television, and coffee is served mornings in the lobby. Doubles, $65-70.

Lakeside

The Rutledge Inn and Cottages, Lake Morey, Fairlee, Vt. 05045. (802) 333-9722. The Stone family has been operating this rustic inn and cottage complex on the shores of beautiful Lake Fairlee for more than twenty years. The green-shuttered white inn with screened porch stretching the length of the building, a cozy dining room with red placemats and napkins and flowers on the tables, and a warm fireplaced lobby with sofas you can sink into all spell New England hospitality and quintessential summertime Vermont. The cottages, some of them at water's edge and others climbing the hillside past the inn, are basic. Some have working fireplaces and a few have screened porches; from many there are splendid views of the lake. The inn is oriented to lakefront activity; canoes, rowboats, water skiing and swimming are available. Large old white Adirondack chairs, set on the grass beside the water, are a good place to read and sun. You can book your room with or without meals, although full American plan is the traditional way to go. They'll put up a picnic lunch if you want to go off for the day. The dining room is famed for its desserts: more than thirty are on the menu, compared with just four or five entrees. The Rutledge attracts many of the same visitors year after year, most for a week or two, and it is often difficult to find a shorter-term accommodation. Doubles in cottages, AP $110 to $138 nightly, $730 to $900 weekly; doubles with shared bath in inn, $110 daily. Doubles, EP $60 to $76.

Inns and B&Bs

Trumbull House, Etna, N.H. (Box C-29, Hanover 03755). (603) 643-1400. Mink Brook rushes past across the street from this elegant new B&B just three miles from Dartmouth. The beautifully decorated house is named for the man who built it and innkeeper Ann Fuller says the front door was taken from a fraternity house at Dartmouth. Decor is serene and tasteful. A wide central hallway with stenciling on the walls has green carpeting up the stairs and oriental runners. A porch with white wicker and green cushions is a place to enjoy a warm day and the mostly pink living room has a fireplace. A full breakfast is served to guests in the dining room, and includes homemade breads, choices of eggs or perhaps pancakes — enough to hold you for a day of touring. Five guest rooms, three on the second floor and two tucked under the eaves on the third, are wonderfully decorated and all have private baths. We particularly like the two extra-large rooms on the third floor with window seats, angles and pretty floral wallpapers. A twin-bedded room on the second floor is furnished entirely with light Danish furniture. Doubles, $110; suite, $130.

White Goose Inn, Route 10, Orford, N.H. 03777. (603) 353-4812. Karin and Manfred Wolf emigrated from Germany, managed inns in Carmel and Monterey, Calif., and eventually found their own place after what they say was a "wild goose chase" in 1984. The White Goose Inn, set in the riverside town of Orford, is stunningly decorated by Karin, an artist. As we approached the imposing brick house with its wide porch (painted green to match the shutters), classical music was playing on the stereo, and a film crew for a country magazine had just left. The inn is picture-perfect, the result of the Wolfs' painstaking renovation from an apartment house. The 19th-century brick front and 18th-century clapboard back blend beautifully. Karin's stenciling can be seen throughout, and each antiques-filled room has its own charm. Ten guest rooms in the main inn plus five more in the newer Gosling House next door make up the offerings; all but two small rooms in the main inn have private baths. Our favorite, the peach room, has a fireplace. A complete breakfast is served in a sunny room stretching across the back of the new building, with a deck outside. French toast and Dutch baby pancakes are among Manfred's specialties. Guests relax in the inn's two front parlors. Outside is a gorgeous yard with comfortable chairs and a small spring-fed pond for swimming. A fishing rod is available for anglers who want to try their luck; several trout have been snagged, then returned to their happy home. Doubles, $75 to $150. No smoking.

Mann Tavern Inn, Route 10, Orford, N.H. 03777. (603) 353-9071. This inn, just up the road from the White Goose Inn, might be fun — especially if you're traveling with children. Joan Harris, the diminutive wife of the local pediatrician, opens five rooms of this large period home to guests. All but one share baths. The Harrises and their two young daughters have their own rooms among those used by the guests. A full breakfast, cooked by Joan in the large kitchen with its black iron stove, is served in the dining room. An attractive front parlor is available for guests. Three horses out back, a couple of dogs and a small pond on the property add to the intrigue for little ones. The rooms, except for the large one with the private bath, are a bit smaller than average, but the welcome is warm indeed. Doubles, $48 to $68.

Lyme Inn, Route 10, Lyme, N.H. 03768. (603) 795-2222. The white wicker-filled front porch promises tranquil moments at this beautiful country hostelry run by Fred and Judy Siemons. Canopied beds, chaise lounges, clawfoot bathtubs, braided rugs and antique furniture remind visitors of days when the living was simpler. Ten of the fourteen rooms have private baths. Three rooms on the top floor are often booked by families or friends who enjoy the privacy of their own floor and don't mind sharing a bath. Famed chef Hans Wichert (see Where to Eat) provides inventive cuisine in two dining rooms furnished tastefully with bare wood tables, Hitchcock or ladderback chairs, and woven placemats. The fireplaced tavern is especially popular in winter with skiers from Dartmouth College's own ski area nearby. Doubles, $120 to $150 MAP.

The Dowds' Country Inn, On the Common, Lyme, N.H. 03768. (603) 795-4712. This ambitious venture is the creation of Mickey Dowd, who was the founder of the immensely popular pizza spot, Everything But Anchovies (E.B.A. to locals) in Hanover, and his young wife, Tami. The Colonial home, originally built in 1780, has been added onto with a large section to the rear to provide 22 rooms with private baths. Those in the front and older section are named for their style of stenciling, done by hand by Tami; those to the rear are named after Dartmouth dormitories. All beds have comforters or quilts and there's an individuality to most of the rooms, especially the older ones. Afternoon tea is offered in the Old Carriage House section. Rates include a full breakfast and Portuguese french toast is a possibility. There's a pond with a picnic table out back. Doubles, $55 to $135.

The Hanover Inn, Main Street, Hanover, N.H. 03755. (603) 643-4300 or (800) 443-7024. An institution along with Dartmouth College, this 92-room Colonial inn is usually host to a few old grads, and even posts a list of those who are in town. Facing the College Green, with a stone terrace where the early claimants sit in rockers and watch the activity, the inn has rooms decorated with period furniture, handmade lampshades and comforters, but ours — one of the less expensive — was not particularly impressive in its decor. The main Daniel Webster dining room is formal in cream and green; a terrace for dining out front is appealing on nice days and the most popular place in town for the buffet Sunday brunch, and the newly decorated **Ivy Grill** offers a city sophistication with a mixed-bag menu. The front parlor, done in brick red and dark green, features window seats, wing chairs and Chippendale sofas. Doubles, $129 to $144; suites, $189 to $267.

Camping

The Pastures Campground, Route 10, Orford, N.H. 03777. (603) 353-4579. Dot and Tom Parkington run a fine private campground on the banks of the Connecticut River and you can launch a boat at the Orford public boat launch ramp adjoining the site. The sites are mostly sunny, arranged on both sides of the road forming a wide rectangle. In the center is a barnlike building with restrooms and hot showers. Most sites have water and electricity; picnic tables are available and there are large open play areas. Nightly, $12; weekly, $72.

Seeing and Doing _____ _∽∽_

On the River

Canoeing Inn to Inn, c/o Stone House Inn, Route 5, North Thetford, Vt. 05054. (802) 333-9124. Started a few years ago by the Sharkeys of the Stone House Inn, this program offers canoeists a leisurely two-day, thirty-mile paddle down the Connecticut River from Haverhill to Hanover, with a mid-trip stop at the Stone House Inn in North Thetford. Participants may leave on a Monday or a Tuesday, starting at the Ledyard Canoe Club in Hanover. The group is met there and given information about the trip, then shuttled north to the Haverhill Inn for the first night's dinner and lodging. Canoeing begins the next morning with the stretch from Haverhill to North Thetford. After dinner and a night's rest at the Stone House Inn, the final leg of the journey takes canoeists to Hanover, where they are driven to Moose Mountain Lodge for dinner and overnight. Groups have included a wide range of ages and Dianne Sharkey particularly remembers the woman who celebrated her 75th birthday and combined it with a family reunion on the water. They even had T-shirts made up for the venture. All-inclusive cost, $250 per person; canoe rentals extra. Trips offered midweek only, late June to late August.

The Connecticut River Watershed Council also offers canoe trips in the region. These are either one-day outings or overnights, and are good values. Plus, you'll learn about the river and how to use a canoe. Day trips cost around $15 (including canoe rental) or $10 with your own canoe; overnights are $50 with canoe, $40 with your own. Children under 15 pay about half. For information call the CRWC in West Lebanon at (603) 448-2792.

The Ledyard Canoe Club, Hanover, N.H. (603) 646-2753. Located on the banks of the Connecticut River and affiliated with the famed Dartmouth College Outing Club, this club rents canoes and kayaks. It's the oldest and best-known collegiate canoe club in the country. Founded in 1920 by Dartmouth undergraduates, it continues to be managed by students. The white clapboard clubhouse is open daily from 9 to 7 in the summer for rentals — canoes for $25 a day or $5 an hour. On weekends, they'll shuttle you up north and let you drift back down the river for a small extra fee. Kayak instruction is available at $20 an hour.

The Wilder Dam south of Hanover off Route 10, operated by the New England Power Company, welcomes visitors. The tour involves crossing the dam on a special walkway, seeing the control house and viewing a new fish ladder. The fish ladders here and at two other sites along the river have been built to encourage the return of salmon to the river. Picnicking and hiking are permitted in the area. Free.

SWIMMING. Even though the Connecticut River is swimmable, there's no public swimming access in this area. Good swimming is available at Lake Fairlee (Treasure Island), Lake Morey (public beach) and at the Storrs Pond Recreation Area in Hanover.

CYCLING. This section of the Connecticut River is a cyclist's delight, for both Route 5, following the west bank in Vermont, and Route 10, which parallels the eastern shore in New Hampshire, are scenic. Vermont Bicycle Touring of Bristol, (802) 453-4811, organizes weekend to five-day trips, some in the Hanover-Fairlee area.

Touring

Dartmouth College is a must. Founded in 1769 by the Rev. Eleazor Wheelock, Dartmouth dominates the town of Hanover and provides its character. The large Dartmouth College Green opposite the Hanover Inn is a center of activity. Campus tours are offered four times daily Monday-Friday at 9, 11 and 3 from McNutt Hall, which faces the Green, and at 2 from the Information Booth on the Green. On Saturdays, one tour leaves from McNutt Hall at 10.

Hood Museum of Art, connected to the Hopkins Center for the Arts on the south side of the Green, is a fine college museum. As you enter, you see seven ten-foot-high Assyrian reliefs from a palace built between 883 and 859 B.C. On display are representative pieces from many periods, including some splendid contemporary art on the second floor. Open Tuesday-Sunday 11 to 5, Thursdays to 8. Donation.

Orford, N.H., is one of the area's most picturesque villages. One of the original "fort towns" strategically placed by the British to control French and Indian uprisings on the Connecticut, Orford was settled in 1765. The town is known for its architecture, especially the seven so-called Ridge houses set dramatically on a high ridge east of Route 10 in the center of town. These elegant residences were built between 1775 and 1859. The southernmost house (circa 1815) was probably designed by the Boston architect, Asher Benjamin, an associate of Charles Bulfinch. Orford also has a pleasant green with picnic tables.

Take a scenic drive around picturesque **Lake Morey.** The road hugs the lake and the views are lovely.

The Montshire Museum of Science, Norwich, Vt. (802) 649-2200. Directly across the Connecticut River from Hanover, this is in its new, contemporary home and there's lots to see. Several hands-on and participatory exhibits allow visitors to check out optical illusions, see waterlife, launch balls into orbit while tracing their trajectories and see boa constrictors. Also available are a sea shell collection and a dinosaur exhibit. A couple of trails on the property lead down to the river. The gift shop is a good place to buy birthday presents for little ones. Open daily. Adults $4, children $2.

SHOPPING. Hanover is a fun place to shop. The **Dartmouth Bookstore** on Main Street carries an extensive selection of foreign magazines and literary periodicals, plus cards, tapes, textbooks and all types of books. Dartmouth College sweatshirts and other official college gear can be purchased at the **Dartmouth Co-op.** Other shops with interesting wares include **Bare Essentials,** a women's clothing store where very sophisticated styles are to be found, and **The League of New Hampshire Craftsmen,** which maintains a great shop on Lebanon Street. **Rosey Jeke's** on Lebanon Street has some funky stuff for women.

Several antiques dealers and shops are located along both Routes 5 and 10.

The Powerhouse, a newish shopping center in West Lebanon, N.H., is a mill-like expanse of brick built along a rushing river. The shops are tasteful but a bit pricey. **Great Eastern Sports, Mink Country Outfitters, Rapt in Chocolate,** and several women's clothing stores are fun to explore.

Where to Eat ⟋⟍⟍

D'Artagnan, 13 Dartmouth College Hwy. (Route 10), Lyme, N.H. (603) 795-2137. A handsome dining room located in the basement of the Ambrose Publick House in a small complex of restored offices and buildings ten miles north of Hanover is the place for some incredibly creative meals. Peter Gaylor, a French-trained chef, and his wife, Rebecca Cunningham, have established a reputation locally for serving outstanding food. Both trained with noted chef Yannick Cam at Le Pavillon in Washington, D.C., before heading north to found their own country French restaurant in 1981. The restaurant seats 60 at simple tables, some of which overlook the rushing stream outdoors. An especially pleasant setting for cocktails is the outdoor terrace, where you can see and hear the water. The prix-fixe dinner ($35 or $40) includes one or two appetizers, main course, house salad, dessert and beverage. Among appetizers offered at one Saturday evening dinner were cold cantaloupe soup with mint and port and chilled curry of shrimp and scallops with carrot, celery, onion and apple. Entrees involved a choice of poached halibut with mushrooms and tarragon sauce or sauteed medallions of beef tenderloin in a red wine cream sauce. Rebecca's famed desserts include such temptations as white chocolate mousse with almond-hazelnut praline and fresh figs with red wine vanilla bean sauce. Sunday lunch (prix-fixe, $18 or $21) is a special treat. Appetizers might be salad of sauteed chicken breast, green beans, tomato and mushrooms in a tarragon vinaigrette or chilled cucumber soup with fresh herbs and creme fraiche; main-course choices could be sauteed beef sirloin with an aromatic cabernet sauvignon sauce or an omelet with smoked trout and leeks. It is an exceptionally elegant and not-to-be rushed experience. Dinner, Wednesday-Sunday 6 to 10; Sunday lunch, noon to 1:15. Reservations required.

Cafe Buon Gustaio, 72 South Main St., Hanover. (603) 643-5711. Murray Washburn, the dapper owner of Peter Christian's Tavern in Hanover and a man-about-town for some time, opened this new restaurant in 1990. Serving dinner in attractive rooms in a house just south of the town center, the restaurant was getting raves almost immediately. Chef Brad Spavin, a longtime friend of Murray's, used to be at Harvest in Harvard Square. The menu emphasizes "a lot of grilling, a lot of seafood" says Brad, and changes daily. Typical appetizers ($4.50 to $6.50) include duck consomme with egg-fried ravioli, panfried rabbit livers with oregano and port and grilled sea scallops with red pepper aioli and bitter greens. For entrees ($17 to $22), you might have grilled Chilean swordfish or panfried soft-shell crabs, Vermont spring lamb with truffle-green pepper cream or Norwegian salmon. Pastas ($10 to $14) include lasagna with grilled eggplant, red pepper and smoked mozzarella or fettuccine carbonara with cracked black pepper and garlic oil. The freshly baked Tuscan bread costs extra. The dining room is most attractive: deep green walls, white tablecloths and bentwood chairs (black in one room, natural in another) offer a simple backdrop to the culinary creativity. Dinner nightly, 5:30 to 9:30.

Cafe la Fraise, 8 West Wheelock St., Hanover, N.H. (603) 643-8588. This 1823 house just off Hanover's Main Street as you drive into town from I-91 serves dinner in three most attractive small rooms. The country French decor involves polished dark wood or windsor chairs and brass and glass lamps against a dark green wallpaper. Dinner entrees include fresh Idaho rainbow trout baked en papillote and served with a garlic beurre blanc, sauteed chicken breast coated with almond flour and a honey and lemon sauce, and broiled Norwegian salmon with lemon and dill beurre blanc. You could start with escargots bourguignonne or homemade fresh basil fettuccine with imported goat cheese in a balsamic vinegar beurre rouge ($5 to $8). The menu changes every two weeks and sometimes includes homemade ice cream, Turkish apricot having been one of the more exotic choices. Dinner, Monday-Saturday 6 to 9.

Lyme Inn, Route 10, Lyme, N.H. (603) 795-2222. Chef Hans Wichert features German specialties on the menu at this country inn's dining room. Two rooms, the rear one being darker and more atmospheric, have bare wood tables and Hitchcock chairs, wall sconces and the ambience of an old-style tavern. On the menu one Saturday night we were there were such entrees ($12 to $17) as hasenpfeffer and wiener schnitzel as well as red snapper with a shrimp sauce, roast lamb (cooked rather too well done for our taste), and Cape scallops sauteed with butter and sherry. A light supper is always available; in this instance, seafood crepes for $7.95. Dinner nightly except Tuesday, 5:30 to 8:30, Sunday 5 to 8. Closed most of December and April.

Bentley's, 11 South Main St., Hanover, N.H. (603) 643-4075. A masculine feeling, that of an English club or an old library, is quite appropriate for the Dartmouth grads and faculty members who find their way here. The dark wood paneling and mood are relieved by flowered banquettes in the back room and a ficus tree adorned with tiny white lights growing toward a skylight, but the bar and the small room up front beside the street seem clubby. Old books on a shelf in the bar add to the library feel and there are historic photos of Hanover on the dark green walls. Owned by David Creech and Bill Deckelbaum, who have run a sister restaurant since the mid-1970s in Woodstock, Vt., Bentley's attracts a large following. One reason is the menu variety, with light, eclectic fare as well as full meals available at both lunch and dinner. Lately, there's been a Mexican emphasis, but basic burgers, grilled sandwiches and creative options are always available. Among dinner entrees ($11 to $17) are vegetarian stir-fry, boneless chicken breast with a light tomato garlic sauce, chicken satay and scampi portofino. The South of the Border section includes deluxe chicken quesadillas and vegetarian burritos. Burgers come in various guises for about $5 and there are quite a few salad plates. On Friday and Saturday evenings there's entertainment. Open Monday-Saturday, 11:30 to 10 or 11; Sunday brunch.

Five Olde Nugget Alley, 5 Olde Nugget Alley, Hanover, N.H. (603) 643-5081. "The best kept secret in Hanover" is the way chef and co-owner Patty Dodds describes this basement restaurant off South Main Street. Only a solid wooden door and a red canopy proclaim its presence, but Dartmouth students and faculty as well as locals crowd the lounge and 90-seat restaurant for "big drinks and hearty portions." A collection of unusual beer cans is displayed behind the bar, and antique artifacts hang from the walls. The all-day menu changes every now and again, most recently taking a Mexican turn. You'll also find cajun specialties plus the usual varied fare that includes chili con carne and baked onion soup as starters, a full range of nachos including nachos el nugget (beef, tomato, onions, lettuce, melted cheddar, guacamole, sour cream and salsa) for about $5; big burgers (one of them a "rajun' Cajun") and the like. Dinner entrees ($9 to $12) can be sesame chicken with stir-fry vegetables, steak or chicken teriyaki, steak and shrimp scampi, broiled swordfish and Alphonse's baked lasagna. Open daily, 11:30 to 10, weekends to 1, Sunday from 4:30.

Jesse's, Route 120, Hanover, N.H. (603) 643-4111. Steak, seafood and a salad bar bring so many patrons to this log-cabin-style restaurant that you may have to wait for a table as early as 6:30 on a summer Saturday. Hanging plants, Tiffany lamps, stained glass, bare wood tables with mismatched chairs and subdued lighting lend atmosphere to a spot that seems perfect for all ages. Beef, seafood and chicken and ribs are on the dinner menu regularly, but specials such as mesquite-grilled salmon filet with dill hollandaise sauce at $14.75 may be the best choices. Three of us chose the salmon, an ample slab and quite delicious. The fourth enjoyed a steak kabob. The salad bar, set up in a huge wooden sled, includes good warm breads like pumpernickel-raisin and country wheat. Wild and long-grained rice or a baked potato come with the entree. Other dinner choices ($10.75 to $15) might be peppercorn steak, prime rib, barbecued baby back pork ribs or fresh sea scallops and sirloin. Desserts are things like homemade brownie a la mode and deep-dish apple crumb pie. Dinner nightly, 5 to 10 or 11, Sunday 4:30 to 9:30.

Molly's Balloon, 43 Main St., Hanover, N.H. (603) 643-2570. Owned by the same people who run Jesse's, this creative and bright place in the center of Hanover offers a light, interesting all-day menu. A greenhouse out front has a bar in the center and booths with upholstered green backs and slatted wooden seats, all set on a tile floor. Decorated with plants and framed prints and posters, Molly's Balloon is fun and upbeat. Helium-filled balloons are handed out to the kids in the group, which seems to bring hordes of them in on rainy Saturdays. "Mollypops" are frosty drinks like the "Yuppie Puppy," 95-octane vodka and tonic, or the peach-almond shake (peaches, amaretto, vanilla ice cream and cream). Snacky dishes like fritto misto, vegetables fried in tempura batter and served with horseradish mayonnaise or potato skins stuffed with monterey jack cheese and bacon crumbs and served with sour cream and chives are good for lunch. French onion soup or a soup of the day can be ordered with a chef's or neptune salad. Mexican entrees include tortilla fats (a giant tortilla filled with meat, beans, cheese, green chilies and onions and covered with salsa and melted cheese, then served with guacamole, black olives, and lettuce and tomato). Sandwiches, burgers and dinners (available after 5) such as steak and fries for $11 or Molly's marinated sirloin are also on the brightly colored, many-paged menu. It's printed in the style of an aviator's handbook and called the Owner/Operator Manual. Apple crisp is a dessert specialty; other choices are cheesecake and bananas sauteed in kahlua with nuts and raisins, served over ice cream. Open daily, 11 to 11.

Peter Christian's Tavern, 39 South Main St., Hanover, N.H. (603) 643-2345. The tiny, tree-shaded deck with flower-filled window boxes and white bentwood chairs and small tables is especially pleasant on a summer's afternoon. Our gazpacho was chunky and spicy; sandwiches were served on wooden boards or pottery plates and included Peter's Mother's Favorite (ham, turkey, Vermont cheddar and tomatoes at $4.95, or $2.95 for a half) and Peter's Father's Favorite (roast beef, cream cheese, horseradish, sliced onions and tomatoes, at the same prices). Salads, yogurt with fresh fruit and honey, and beef stew are also on the menu. Some evenings there are special foods — usually Mexican favorites plus a few other choices. The early-American tavern, all dark wood and booths, is tucked a couple of steps down from Main Street. More than twenty beers are available. Open daily, 11:30 a.m. to 12:30 p.m., Sundays from 12:30.

Lou's, Main Street, Hanover, N.H. (603) 643-3321. Lou's is one of those storefront restaurants, with booths on one side and a counter on the other, that stay full all day because they are reliable. Actually, Lou's is more than reliable, and the baked goods produced by the bakery associated with the restaurant are really good (try the cheesecake). The all-day menu offers sandwiches, salads, burgers, homemade soup, old favorites like lasagna and a hot turkey sandwich, and "breakfast all day." The ubiquitous coleslaw, better than most, has some red cabbage in it; beers and wines please the college kids. Dinners emphasize Mexican fare (they seem to love it in Hanover) and health food. The buttermilk pancakes in the morning are especially good. Open daily from 5:30 a.m. to midnight, Sunday from 8:30.

FOR MORE INFORMATION: Hanover Chamber of Commerce, Box A-105, 37 South Main St., Hanover, N.H. 03755. (603) 643-3115. The Information Booth is a kiosk on the Dartmouth College Green.

Lake Winnipesaukee is seen through trees from parlor of Pick Point Lodge.

Wolfeboro/Lake Winnipesaukee, N.H.

Wolfeboro has laid claim to being America's oldest summer resort ever since its last English Colonial governor, John Wentworth, built in 1768 the country's first summer home, a palatial mansion on the shore of the lake that bears his name. "Everybody in the country was talking about that house," advised our guide in the Wolfeboro Historical Society museum complex. "He summered here with his hunting and fishing cronies. He was one of those summer people!"

Sequestered between Lake Wentworth and Wolfeboro Bay, the east end of Lake Winnipesaukee, Wolfeboro's year-round population of 2,000. That population triples in the summer, thanks to summer people like Kirk Douglas and David Meredith plus as many tourists as can be accommodated in relatively limited facilities.

Though Wolfeboro is blessed with a magnificent location at the foot of mountains along New England's second largest lake, it maintains a sedate, small-town atmosphere. Brewster Academy opens its beach to the public in summer. Museums attract just enough visitors to make opening worthwhile. The mail-boat delivers mail and passengers out to the islands. Between quick dips, a young swimsuit-clad peddler dispenses hot dogs from a cart next to Cate Park at the town dock. There are benches for relaxation on the dock and along Main Street. Shopkeepers know their customers by name, and everyone on the street seems to know everyone else.

Happily, there's little schlock. Wolfeboro has resisted the honky-tonk that is the norm along other parts of the lake at Alton Bay and Weir's Beach, for instance, or beyond in the Conways and White Mountains. Zoning is strict and shoreline property in such demand that the pressure of residential real estate

279

has blocked commercial development, according to Dick T. Newcomb, vice president of Pick Point Lodge. "What's hurting Wolfeboro is its lack of rooms," he says.

That's just fine with most of the natives, the summer regulars and those transients lucky enough to find accommodations. They enjoy the myriad pleasures of a lovely section of Lake Winnipesaukee, good restaurants and shops, two golf courses, a low-key social life, and the small-town atmosphere of one of New England's more pleasant villages.

Says Alan Pierce, owner of a bookstore and gift shop aptly named Camelot: "People come back to Wolfeboro every year and are so glad to see that it hasn't changed."

Getting There

Wolfeboro is about 45 miles northeast of Concord at the east end of Lake Winnipesaukee. From Interstate 93, take Route 28 directly to Wolfeboro, or take Routes 3 and 11 to Route 28.

Where to Stay⎯⎯⎯⎯⎯⎯⎯⎯⎯⎯⎯⎯⎯⎯⎯ ⋏⋎⋎⋲

By the Lakeshore

Pick Point Lodge & Cottages, Route 109, Box 220A, Mirror Lake 03853. (603) 569-1338. The signs get smaller and smaller and the roads narrower and narrower as you drive more than a mile off the highway north of Wolfeboro through a pine forest to the lakeshore. When we told the manager that we thought we'd never get there, he responded, "that's why we're down here." And once down here, you don't want or have to leave. The Newcomb family-run resort has ten large, well-furnished housekeeping cottages that are more secluded than many summer homes and an impressive main lodge built in 1924 as a private estate with two inn-style guest rooms, a grand sitting room with a fire blazing in the stone hearth and a full-length porch with a spectacular view through the pines of Lake Winnipesaukee. The club-like atmosphere and the 113 acres of grounds with half a mile of shore frontage appeal to many. "The sun stays with us all day on the beach," manager Jeff Newcomb said, showing a sandy beach running between two sides of Pick Point. Beyond are lounge chairs on a 200-foot jetty that he calls a sundeck; it has views down three directions of the lake. Rented weekly in summer, the ten lodge-style cottages vary in size from one to four bedrooms; all are pine-paneled, have new early American-style furniture, brass beds, carpeted bedrooms, full kitchens, color television, porches, decks, outdoor gas grills and daily maid service. Seven have fireplaces, and all have large, comfortable rooms that belie the name "cottage." The two rooms upstairs in the main lodge have queen or king beds and a color TV, and guests here are served complimentary breakfast in the dining room. There are outdoor and indoor tennis courts, a game room, a library, free rowboats, a canoe and sunfish, and a wildlife sanctuary with birdhouses, feeding stations and three miles of trails. The Newcombs host a complimentary Sunday flapjack breakfast and a Monday cocktail party followed by a steak or chicken cookout; otherwise guests are on their own. Except for use of the indoor tennis court and laundromat, there are no extra charges. Asked what to bring, the owners respond "yourself, your food and a good disposition, and we'll give you a good time." Cottages, $1,200 to $2,000 weekly; inn rooms in lodge, $840 weekly, $120 nightly. Cottages rented by day spring and fall, $100 to $200. No credit cards. Open mid-May to mid-October.

The Wolfeboro Inn, 44 North Main St., Wolfeboro 03894. (603) 569-3016 or (800) 451-2389. This venerable inn, built in 1812, was greatly expanded in 1988 to make 43 rooms and suites, five with patios or balconies but, strangely, very few with a water view. The layout is such that most rooms overlook parking lot or village; three end suites and three balconied rooms on the second floor would appeal more to those seeking proximity to the water. The main-floor suite we saw had a large, angled living room, a kingsize four-poster in the bedroom, Lord & Mayfair toiletries and a hair drier in the bathroom, a desk, two phones, TV in the armoire and a door to a small patio outside with a glimpse of the lake beyond a gazebo. Some of the original 1812 bedrooms retain their fireplaces and a sprightly country look. Although situated away from the water, the inn has its own sand beach, docks, windsurfers and rowboats. It also runs the MV Judge David Sewall luncheon excursion boat, which is available for charter. The inn is a popular conference center, and a section of the lobby was given over to an artist's reception the afternoon we visited. Room rates include continental breakfast, and meals are served in a large dining room and the tavern (see Where to Eat). In 1990, innkeeper Leigh Turner and the inn's other two owners acquired the Kineo resort on Maine's remote Moosehead Lake and planned a $1-million-plus investment to create an upscale, year-round operation. Doubles, $89 to $105; suites, $135 to $185.

The Lake Motel, Route 28, Box 887-B, Wolfeboro 03894. (603) 569-1100. Among the area's few motels, this is the best bet, thanks to its location on tiny Crescent Lake. Opened in 1956, it has two entries to each of the 30 rooms, one from an interior corridor and the other from the outside. The rear half face the water. All have two double beds, two upholstered chairs and cable TV. Five more housekeeping apartments are located away from the water. Situated well off the highway on sixteen acres sloping to the lake, the motel has a busy little beach popular with families and 600 feet of lake frontage, a tennis court, lawn games and boats for rent. **Bailey's Restaurant,** open from 8 a.m. to 11 p.m. daily at the entrance to the grounds, serves the most for the money in town, according to motel owners Allan and Julie Bailey, who run their operation more like an inn than most motelkeepers. Doubles, $75 to $85. Open mid-May to mid-October.

Piping Rock Motel & Cottages, North Main Street, Wolfeboro 03894. (603) 569-1915. An eight-unit, two-story motel with balconies and decks overlooks a lawn down to Lake Winnipesaukee. Rooms in the motel are carpeted, have two double beds and TV, and some have kitchens. Thirteen white and aqua housekeeping cottages with water views, two to four bedrooms and decks facing the pine trees are scattered about the nine-acre property. There also are two three-bedroom suites that are considered apartments. By the shore are a sandy beach with raft and boathouse. Doubles in motel, $90 to $110; cottages, $775 to $1,090 weekly. Motel open year-round.

Clearwater Lodges, Route 109, HC 69-Box 604, Wolfeboro 03894. (603) 569-2370. Now in its 44th season, this rustic resort with fifteen housekeeping cottages is on the lakeshore about four miles north of town. The one and two-bedroom cottages have kitchens, fireplaces, shower baths and tiny porches. The cottages are lined up along a road down a hill to the waterfront, where there are rental boats and a recreation hall with television and games. Longtime owners Herb and Anne Vinnicombe also rent a contemporary three-bedroom lodge with panoramic deck overlooking the lake. Cottages, weekly $523 (one-bedroom) to $678 (two-bedroom); lodge, $1,260; daily rates available off-season. Open mid-May to mid-October.

Lakeshore Terrace, Route 28 & 109, Box 18C, Wolfeboro 03894. (603) 569-1701. Three beaches and a boat basin along a point on Lake Wentworth are assets at this cottage colony. So are the rose garden and the well-kept garden and lawn facing one curved beach. Four of the eight cottages have housekeeping facilities. Nicest is the new Sandbox cottage with living room, kitchen-dining room, twin bedroom and deck. Doubles, $35 to $45; housekeeping units, $48 to $70 (usually rented by the week). Open mid-May to mid-October.

Mirror Lake Lodging, Route 109, HC69, Box 674, Wolfeboro 03894. (603) 569-3239. This unusual name involves a three-room efficiency apartment on the main floor of what looks like a house and, underneath, three efficiency motel units facing Mirror Lake. All are available nightly, weekly or monthly year-round. Each motel unit has a kitchenette with a table for two, a double bed and shower bath. There's a volleyball net on the back lawn, and two rowboats are available at the dock. Doubles, $65 to $95.

Away from the Water

The Lakeview Inn, North Main Street, Box 713, Wolfeboro 03894. (603) 569-1335. This establishment's name is a misnomer, for trees now block any lake view and it's more a motor lodge than an inn. Three of the seventeen guest rooms are upstairs in the restored 200-year-old main house, known for a good restaurant (see Where to Eat) and a striking fan doorway with bull's-eye glass. The rest are in a two-story air-conditioned motel annex with patios or balconies overlooking apple trees and a mountain. All have private baths, color TV, thick carpeting and towels, and four have kitchenettes. A continental breakfast is served to guests in the lounge. Doubles, $75 to $85; efficiencies, $82.50.

The Tuc'Me Inn, 68 North Main St., Wolfeboro 03894. (603) 569-5702. Three of the seven guest rooms in this early 1800s village house have private baths, and the other four share two. A spacious living room has big sofas, TV and lots of books. Two bedrooms have access to an upstairs screened porch. An upstairs sitting room has been converted into a seventh bedroom. Irma Limberger, innkeeper with her husband Walter, serves a hearty breakfast, perhaps including apple-sherry pancakes, the apples having been marinated in cream sherry overnight. The meal is taken in a pleasant dining room or outside on a porch that's usable late into the fall. Doubles, $72 to $78.

Allen "A" Resort, 1800 Center St., Box 1810, Wolfeboro 03894. (603) 569-1700. When we first visited the former Allen "A" resort, it was under interim ownership as Wentworth Winds, with a billing as a motel and recreational vehicle resort. New owners have restored the original name, and the billing is that "the tradition continues." Dating to 1932, the resort has seen better days, but it was the only place with a vacancy when we visited one August. The 51 rooms have been renovated; ours in the rear faced a ramshackle lineup of green cabins and a dirt road that led to the beach, four tennis courts and who-knows-where. But they're trying: there's a new swimming pool, 360-seat theater and a bandshell, although the restaurant was closed in 1990. A playground and the prices make it good for families. The 800-foot beach along Lake Wentworth is pleasant, if a bit spooky when deserted, as it was when we were there. Doubles, $50 to $65.

RENTALS. Private houses and cottages are available through individuals or local real-estate agents, including the Turners Inc., South Main Street, Wolfeboro, (603) 569-1442, and Yankee Pedlar Realtors, 8 Main St., Wolfeboro, (603) 569-1000. Summer homes are available for monthly rental through **Brook &**

Bridle Summer Homes, Roberts Cove Road off Route 28, Wolfeboro, (603) 569-2707 or 888-3924. The family-owned resort has ten summer homes with one to four bedrooms spaced through 35 acres of fields and woods beside Lake Winnipesaukee. There are stables, three beaches and a beach house for games. Rentals, $1,700 to $4,400 per month.

Wolfeboro Campgrounds, Haines Hill Road, Wolfeboro, (603) 569-9881 or 569-4029, offers 50 campsites in the pines for tents and trailers. Family rates are $13 daily.

Seeing and Doing

Lake Winnipesaukee, obviously, is the main attraction here. Glacier-formed and spring fed, it is flanked by three mountain ranges and dotted by 274 inhabitable islands. The 26-mile-long lake, New Hampshire's largest and one of the busiest in New England, is more than 60 miles around. Wolfeboro Bay and environs are among the prettiest and quietest sections. Supposedly, more than 15,000 powerboats are registered on the lake, and you see far more of them than sailboats. As we dined by the water one night, we enjoyed the sounds and lights of motorboats after dark — a traditional lake effect we had forgotten after years of vacationing at the ocean.

On the Water

The best way to see this lake and its generally sheltered shoreline away from the road is by boat.

M/S Mount Washington, Weirs Beach, 366-5531. The hulk of this three-level excursion boat is far larger than you'd expect as it cruises ever so carefully up to the Wolfeboro town dock. On board, you're told that the ship was built in 1888 and traversed Lake Champlain from Burlington to Plattsburgh until 1940, when it was moved to Winnipesaukee to replace the original 1872 sidewheeler Mount Washington. In 1982, the ship was cut in half and lengthened to 283 feet, for a capacity of 1,250. The three-hour cruise covers 50 miles and visits Weirs Beach, Wolfeboro and either Center Harbor or Alton Bay, boarding and disembarking passengers at each stop. The narrated cruise takes you through "The Broads," twelve miles long and five miles wide, beneath the Ossipee, Sandwich and Squam mountain ranges on the north, the Belknap Mountain range on the south and the White Mountains in the distance to the northeast. Powerboats come up close to ride the wake; the ship seldom gets close to shore, though you do get a good view of the rocks known as Witches Island and the exclusive Governor's Island community that housed the German Embassy prior to World War I. The sound of the ship's horn reverberates off the mountains as it prepares to dock at busy Weirs Beach, where most of the passengers board. Just before returning to Wolfeboro after a stop at Alton Bay, it crosses the longest section of the lake; you can see twenty miles up to Center Harbor, and across the bay to the lawns and buildings of Brewster Academy, which identify Wolfeboro from afar. If you time it right, you may get a seat in the Flagship Lounge, where two can lunch on a roast beef sandwich, turkey club and a beer each for $18, including tip. Cruise leaves Wolfeboro daily at 11, also 2:15 in summer. Adults $12, children $6.

Blue Ghost, Town Dock, Wolfeboro. Six or eight passengers can join Sandy or Betsy McKenzie on the U.S. mailboat as they deliver mail for residents to docks on 30 islands on eastern Lake Winnipesaukee. The 60-mile, three-hour cruise gets you up close to the shoreline. The boat leaves at 9:50 daily except

Sunday and postal holidays. Adults $14, children $7. Reservations are required through Lakes Region Sports, 569-1114. The powerboat is also available for charter, sunset and foliage tours from early May to late October.

MV Judge David Sewall, Wolfeboro Town Dock, 569-3016. Run by the Wolfeboro Inn, this 60-foot-long boat gives luncheon cruises around the eastern end of Winnipesaukee. Up to 75 passengers embark at 11:45 and return 90 minutes later after sampling a buffet lunch. It's also available for charter. Lunch cruises, Monday-Friday. Adults $12, children $6.95.

BOAT RENTALS. Everybody seems to want to get on this lake, and you can, too. **Wolfeboro Marina,** Bay Street, Back Bay, 569-3200, offers boats from 10 to 90 horsepower, as well as canoes and rowboats. More powerful runabouts are available from **Goodhue Hawkins Navy Yard,** Sewall Road, 569-2371. **Brewster Sailing,** Main Street, 569-1600, offers both lessons and rentals.

CANOEING. Along the lake's 183-mile shoreline are countless coves perfect for fishing, snorkeling and canoeing. The Carroll County Independent newspaper advises canoeists: "Hug the islands and shore for a delightful paddle on the largest lake in the state. Keep out of the Broads, where the wind and big boats will swamp a canoe, and don't chase the loons."

SWIMMING. Most lodging establishments have their own beaches. The public is welcome at **Brewster Beach,** a fine little strand off Clark Road, operated by the town and made availale by Brewster Academy. Another good town operation is **Carry Beach** off Forest Road. **Wentworth Beach** is a small, sandy beach and park on Lake Wentworth, off Route 109 between Wolfeboro and Sanbornville. Swimming and picnicking also are offered at **Wentworth State Park,** six miles east of Wolfeboro.

Other Attractions

Molly the Trolley makes its rounds every 30 minutes in summer, showing off the town and providing transportation to the downtown area from outlying parking lots. Fare, 50 cents.

RECREATION. Cate Park, a pleasant little waterfront park beside the town dock, is the site of concerts, dances and art shows throughout the summer; a highlight is the annual Artists in the Park arts and crafts fair in mid-August. **Back Bay Recreation Area** has a playground and four tennis courts that are lighted until 10 p.m. Golfers are welcome at the eighteen-hole **Kingswood Golf Club,** next to the Windrifter Resort off South Main Street, and at the new **Perry Hollow Golf and Country Club,** Wolfeboro Falls.

Libby Museum, Route 109 North, Wolfeboro. (603) 569-1035. Across the road from the shore of Winnipesaukee stands the town-operated Libby Museum, started in 1912 by retired dentist Henry Forrest Libby to house his natural history collections. His original collection includes an alligator, a human skeleton, mummy hands, old surgeon's equipment and paintings from General Wolfe's campaigns, for whom Wolfeboro was named. Visitors have added to the museum, which now has three main exhibits: nearly 600 animals, birds, fish and reptiles in its natural history collection, and 350 Indian artifacts, among them two dugout canoes found in Rust Pond. More than 800 pieces in the Newcomb collection form the basis of Northern New England country living artifacts, which include farm machinery, household items, pottery and Shaker implements. The museum has changing art exhibits, conducts a Wednesday evening lecture series in summer, and leads nature walks for young children on

Friday mornings. The museum's annual August cocktail fundraiser is considered the social event of Wolfeboro's summer. Museum open Tuesday-Sunday 10 to 4 in summer. Adults $1, children 50 cents.

Wolfeboro Americana Museums, South Main Street at Clark Road, Wolfeboro. Operated by the Wolfeboro Historical Society, this complex of three museums is well worth a visit. The Clark House (1778), a Revolutionary farmhouse, was home to three generations of the family, which donated the house to the society in 1929. Everything in it is more or less original, according to our guide. That includes the first piano in Wolfeboro, an applewood four-poster bed, a dining room table from the Wentworth mansion, outstanding pewter, clocks and kitchenware. The Pleasant Valley Schoolhouse (circa 1820) contains old school paraphernalia plus a replica of the Wentworth mansion (it burned to the ground in 1820, and there's considerable debate over what it was like). A copy of the New York Herald reporting Lincoln's death is at the door. A replica of the 1862 Monitor Engine Co. firehouse museum was erected in 1981 to house an 1872 Amoskeag steam pumper donated by David Bowers of Wolfeboro, plus five pieces of apparatus, leather fire helmets and horse-drawn sleighs. Museums open 10 to 4:30 daily except Sunday, July through Labor Day, or by appointment. Donations accepted.

Hampshire Pewter Co., 9 Mill St., Wolfeboro, 569-4944. Free half-hour factory tours are conducted on the hour Monday-Friday from 9 to 3 in season at this pewter factory and showroom. Started in 1973 as a crafts shop, Hampshire Pewter has grown into a nationally known manufacturer of quality cast (rather than spun) pewter. The owners are proud that their firm has decorated New Hampshire's Christmas tree at the White House. They say President George Bush not only displays but uses his set of six wine goblets, a gift from Wolfeboro. You'll no doubt be impressed, as we were, by the variety of 125 items of handmade pewterware, from Christmas tree ornaments to lamp bases, bells and even a loon. Showroom open Monday-Saturday 9 to 5.

SHOPPING. Wolfeboro is a shopping area of quite good taste along its Main Street, the Wolfeboro Marketplace, the new Back Bay Shops and emerging Mill Street.

The Marketplace has two levels of shops in an attractive brick-walked complex that's nicely landscaped. The **Camelot Book and Gift Shop** across the street sports a huge and colorful nutcracker in front that really livens up the scene — the books, cheeses and gifts are worth a look, and the cheddar cheese spread the owners make themselves is delicious. The **Yum Yum Shop** offers baked goods. Cute children's things are at **Tender Times,** and Southwest jewelry at **The Turquoise Door. John Stewart** is known for fine brass and jewelry. **Black's Paper Store** has paper goods, newspapers and magazines, as well as a gift shop and an interior accessories section upstairs.

Stop at **Cornish Hill Pottery** on Mill Street to see fine stoneware pottery, from lamps to tableware, and you usually can see the potters at work. Be sure to check out the delicious breads, croissants and pastries at **Bread & Roses Bakery,** just across the street from Hampshire Pewter. Big cookies here are a bargain twenty cents.

Where to Eat

One local skeptic said the only really good restaurant around is the William Tell Inn on the south shore at West Alton. And a museum staffer said she and her associates go to the cafeteria at Huggins Hospital for the best and cheapest food in town. Wolfeboro has a growing number of serviceable to good restaurants, however.

Waterside Dining

Rumors Cafe, Main Street, Wolfeboro. (603) 569-1201. Aw shucks — they changed the name of our favorite Aw Shucks to the Oyster Club and then to Rumors, with a change of ownership in 1990. But the first-rate location remained the same. This is a casual place to eat by the water, outside on a deck beside all the boat action or inside in a raftered bar with a long kayak and stuffed animals overhead. The front dining room has paneled and glass dividers in Victorian style, with mooseheads, old skis and canoe paddles on the walls. For a waterside dinner we sampled six oysters on the half shell ($6.95), served with enough hot sauce for 85 oysters but, alas, no crackers. Good salads with creamy dill dressings and a loaf of bread preceded our entrees of blackened swordfish and beer batter shrimp, accompanied by curly french fries. Someone had a field day with names on the new menu, which is too cutesy for words (stool pigeon for chicken cordon bleu, scandalous for shrimp and scallops cooked in tequilla, and speculations, desserts that "change daily — ask your scandal-monger"). Entree prices run from $9.95 to $12.95. Instead of mocha mud pie or cheesecake, we indulged in a couple of liqueurs as we watched the lights of boats darting to and fro after dark. Open daily, 11 to 10.

Back Bay Boat House, Bayside Village, Mill Street, Wolfeboro. (603) 569-2124. At the rear of a gray shingled contemporary structure, a breezy porch right over the waters of Front Bay has round glass and wood tables flanked by ice-cream parlor chairs. Adjacent is an elegant chandeliered dining room with brass wall sconces, ceiling fans and rattan-type chairs. It's unfortunate that to reach these appealing dining areas, you have to pass through a busy bar, and many apparently won't or don't. A fairly extensive menu offers something for every taste, from chicken fingers and potato skins to chicken teriyaki and prime rib ($9.95 to $15.95), plus seven specialties — among them, chicken moutarde, veal marsala and roast duckling. The limited wine list, all imported, states not the vintner but the country of origin (valpolicella, Italy; beaujolais, France). Lunch daily, 11:30 to 2; dinner, 5 to 9 or 10; Sunday brunch.

Bailey's Dockside, Town Dock, Wolfeboro. (603) 569-3612. This established restaurant by the Mount Washington landing is not our kind of place, but it's very popular. The pine-paneled dining room with booths and paper mats was packed in late-afternoon with people enjoying sandwiches, salads, any number of ice cream concoctions and a few entrees like fried clams, fried scallops, fried shrimp (or combinations thereof), fried haddock, fried chicken and baked ham steak ($6.75 to $10.95), most served with coleslaw, tomato on crisp lettuce, rolls and butter. A take-out counter dispenses ice cream cones, fifteen flavors for $1.10 to $1.95. Open daily, 11 to 9, mid-May to October.

Away from the Water

Lakeview Inn, 120 North Main St., Wolfeboro. (603) 569-1335. The Lakeview is locally regarded as the town's best restaurant. Done up in pink, green and burgundy, it's country elegant with wallpaper of flower baskets, swagged curtains, votive candles and fresh flowers from the inn's garden. The lounge has lately been expanded, and the light menu available there as well as in the dining room was packing them in at our visit. Among starters are chef-owner Michelle Gerasin's favorite Portuguese soup from her mother's recipe, escargots en croute and artichokes gratinee ($2.95 to $6.95). Nightly specials augment a rather wide-reaching list of entrees, many of them available in smaller and larger portions. Prices range from $10.95 for filet of sole meuniere, blackened sole or London broil, smaller sizes, to $19.95 for tournedos, snow crab legs and asparagus spears. One diner reported she had the best swordfish ever here. Scampi alla carbonara, roast duckling with choice of sauces, loin lamb chops with tarragon mint sauce and filet boursin wellington are other favorites. Salad, homemade breads and vegetables come with. Desserts might include hot apple crisp, mud pie, chocolate mint torte, ice cream puff and hot Indian pudding. Dinner nightly from 5:30.

Wolfeboro Inn, 44 North Main St., Wolfeboro. (603) 569-3016. Expanded in 1988, this nouveau-elegant dining room is graced with an authentic Rumford fireplace and 230-year-old paneling from Daniel Webster's birthplace. Fine china, burgundy and white linens and vases of freesia dress the nicely spaced tables. Dinner entrees are priced from $11.95 for baked scrod to $18.95 for seafood fettuccine or twin lamb chops with apple-mint jelly. Venison medallions with a wild mushroom sauce is a menu fixture. The night's specials might include Norwegian salmon served on green tomato and red onion relish or braised veal chop with prosciutto and shiitake mushrooms. Start with calamari stuffed with shrimp, scallops and lobster ($6.25) and finish with raspberry linzer torte or tirami su. The cozy **Wolfe's Tavern** embraces three of the inn's oldest common rooms and offers 72 menu items with an English theme (dinner entrees, $5.95 for baked beans with knockwurst to $11.95 for sirloin steak or prime rib). Dinner nightly, 5 to 9:30; tavern, open daily from 11:30.

The Cider Press, 10 Middleton Road, Wolfeboro. (603) 569-2028. There's a cider press at the door, and apple trees are out back. Hence the name for this rustic restaurant that started as an inn and has expanded several times under the aegis of Robert and Denise Earle, a young local couple who met while working at the Wolfeboro Inn and who have acquired a substantial local following. They now seat 165 diners by candlelight in three country-pretty barnwood rooms and a lounge where there are two chairs in front of a three-sided open hearth which, Denise says with a laugh, "people fight over" in winter. Listed on the menu as "the odd couple," baby back ribs and golden fried shrimp are the specialty, says Bob Earle, who oversees the cooking. The dozen straightforward entrees run from $7.95 for chicken parmesan to $15.95 for steak and shrimp. One restaurateur said the best lamb chops he ever ate were served at the Cider Press. Halibut oscar and steak au poivre might be blackboard specials. Most of the desserts are baked on the premises, and the tortes and ice cream crepes are the downfall of many. A few house wines are offered; the spiked hot apple cider is more popular. Dinner, Tuesday-Saturday 5:30 to 9, Sunday 5 to 8.

East of Suez, Route 28 South, Wolfeboro. (603) 569-1648. Although Charles Powell and his family, some from the Philippines, have operated this restaurant for the past 22 summers, it seems to be almost a secret except to devotees of Asian food. Housed in a building that once was part of a camp, it looks the part — an almost rickety house with a big side porch, set in a field south of Wolfeboro. Decor is spare oriental, with paper globe lamps. The kitchen is huge, and out of it comes a parade of interesting food; $16 to $18 will buy you a full dinner of appetizer or soup, salad, entree and dessert, but you may also order a la carte from the short menu. To start, poached scallops with crab in miso sauce and the Philippine egg rolls known as lumpia are standouts, but you could also choose a tempura of shrimp and vegetables, pork and chicken steamed with soy, oyster and brown bean sauce, or a highly seasoned tikka chicken. At our first visit, the day's soup was clam chowder, almost like a New England version, but curiously spicy. About ten entrees are listed and all sound so good that it's hard to choose. The tempura included a wide variety of vegetables and many large shrimp; the batter was perfect. And the Szechuan shrimp and cashews, stir-fried with snow peas, was great. On another visit, we liked the Philippine pancit, curly noodles sauteed with morsels of shrimp and pork with oriental vegetables, and the Philippine national dish, adobo, pork and chicken stewed in soy, vinegar and garlic and then broiled. Everything is served with shiny crackers that come sizzling from a pan. For dessert, the "sans rival," a cashew and meringue torte, is a worthy ending. Portions are enormous. Don't eat lunch the day you come, and do bring your own wine. Dinner, Tuesday-Sunday 6 to 9:30, June through early September. No credit cards. BYOB.

The Bittersweet, Route 28 and Allen Road, Wolfeboro. (603) 569-3636. Chef-owner Garry Warren has put together quite a collection of artifacts and eateries in this rambling yellow farmhouse east of town. The upstairs has an airy barnlike dining room with paper mats on bare tables and an amazing array of mismatched chandeliers, pinkish painted wood chairs and farm implements on the walls, and an interesting menu. There's also the main-floor tavern featuring light fare. Downstairs, **Papa John's Pub** is a family place full of booths, more artifacts and an old jukebox. It features made-from-scratch pizzas, heroes and sandwiches at old-fashioned prices. Upstairs, the chef does interesting things like French onion soup laced with vermouth or almond shrimp flamed with amaretto for appetizers ($2.95 to $5.25), Norwegian salmon with a seafood mousse in puff pastry or lamb and cider pie for entrees ($8.10 to $15.10). The nightly specials are unusual for the area: grouper en papillote, haddock topped with julienned vegetables, halibut with dill butter and bouillabaisse. But the regular menu offers a range from barbecued chicken to beef liver and onions, with lighter fare like fish and chips, broiled cod fillets and veal parmesan ($5.15 to $8.25). Desserts are homemade, and the wine list, though small, is serviceable. Ten hot dishes, including roast beef, are featured at the Sunday brunch buffet for $10.95. Lunch, Monday-Friday noon to 2; dinner, Monday-Saturday 5 to 8:30; Sunday brunch, 11 to 2. Pub, Monday-Saturday 4 to 10. Reduced hours in winter.

West Lake Asian Cuisine, Route 28, Wolfeboro. (603) 569-6700. Occupying the corner of a commercial building on the eastern outskirts of town, this new restaurant offers a surprisingly plush, linened dining room and highly regarded oriental fare. The lengthy menu is by the numbers, with about half the items noted as hot and spicy. Most dishes range from $6.75 to $10.95. The 35 "specialties," including tangerine beef, lamb in two styles, sizzling squid and crispy whole fish covered with wine sauce, go up to $13.95. Lunch daily, 11 to 2:30; dinner from 2:30.

Casual Choices

The Strawberry Patch, 30 North Main St., Wolfeboro. (603) 569-1212. "Have a berry nice day," says the menu at this breakfast and lunch place where you might be strawberried into oblivion. The decor is all strawberries, from stenciling on chairs to toddler's bibs. So is most of the menu, from strawberry omelet (no thanks) to strawberry pancakes (sensational) and strawberry waffles, piled with strawberries and whipped cream, all in the $3 to $5 range. At breakfast, our orange juice came in a glass covered with strawberries and served with a sliced strawberry. Lunch brings homemade soups, sandwiches, salads and

288

quiche, $4.95 to $6.75. Upstairs is a gift shop where, you guessed it, everything is in a strawberry motif. Breakfast, 7:30 to 11; lunch 11 to 2:30; Sunday, breakfast only, 7:30 to 12:30.

Victuals & Drafts, 51 Lehner St., Wolfeboro. (603) 569-6995. This casual, family dining spot has squiggly neon in the window and glass-topped tables with colorful squiggles on the cloths. The food is basic, from a BLT sandwich ($2.50) to broiled sirloin ($12.25). Nachos, spaghetti with meat balls, clam roll, stuffed chicken breast, shrimp scampi — you name it, they probably have it. Lunch and dinner; weekend breakfast.

Adam's Rib, Wolfeboro Marketplace, Wolfeboro. (603) 569-6605. You can eat in or take out at this casual establishment in the marketplace. Pork and chicken ribs come in a variety of styles and combinations. A feast for four is $44.95. Dirty rice, baked beans, coleslaw, potato salad, corn on the cob and cornbread are the accompaniments. Philly cheese steak sandwiches and hot dogs also are available. Open daily, 11:30 to 9.

I Scream on Railroad Avenue has any number of ice creams, from strawberry-chocolate chip and pineapple blend to honey cinnamon and coffee oreo, all made on the premises. You'll also find homemade frozen yogurts, mixed nut and grapenut among them. Cones are priced from $1.40 to $2.50; walk-about sandwiches from $3.75 to $4.75.

The Hot Dog Stand, on the wharf facing Cate Park. The boys manning this cart-stand beneath a Perrier umbrella weren't quite sure what to call it, nor did they seem to be terribly interested between swims in the lake. But we managed to get a hot dog for $1.25 and soda for 50 cents, and learned that the hours are daily, 10:30 to 5.

The Dairy Works, Railroad Avenue at Maple Street, proclaims "not just ice cream." You can order thick frappes or frozen yogurt, plus nachos for $2 and a hot dog for $1.75, as well as ice cream cones, 75 cents to $1.50. There are three umbrellaed tables outside this takeout stand.

FOR MORE INFORMATION: Wolfeboro Chamber of Commerce, Box 547, Wolfeboro, N.H. 03894. (603) 569-2200.

Historic structures and working boats characterize Portsmouth waterfront.

Portsmouth, N.H.

The wide tidal river that flows into the Atlantic forms Portsmouth's great harbor and it's no surprise that this spot became the state's first settlement. The river and the sea have ever since dominated the life of the small city which has grown up here.

English settlers arrived in Portsmouth in 1630. No wonder they were so enamoured: the deep harbor formed by the Piscataqua River gave good anchorage and the settlers even found wild strawberries growing along its banks.

They named the settlement Strawbery Banke. The name lives on in a fine historic restoration in the city's South End, but Portsmouth itself was renamed some 23 years after those first Englishmen set foot on its soil.

In view of Portsmouth's rich history, present-day residents take great pride in the past, and many beautiful old homes are open to the public as historic house museums. One, the John Paul Jones house, was the boarding house where the great Naval hero rented a room while overseeing the building of ships during the Revolutionary War.

The waterfront is important and charming and a great place to prowl. Old warehouses along Ceres Street have been turned into restaurants and gift shops by creative owners, and the three red tugboats that guide ships up the tricky, tidal waters of the Piscataqua dock here. Prescott Park, with its lavish floral plantings, is also beside the river and a good place to stroll and watch the action.

There's not really an oceanfront, and no beaches in Portsmouth proper — you must go south to nearby Rye and Hampton Beach for those — but the city's connection to the sea is strong. For those who like to get out on the water, it's possible. A fascinating boat trip goes to the rocky Isles of Shoals, about ten miles out to sea. These once were a summer resort, but are today much more low key. One serves as a summer conference and retreat center and another as a university's marine biology station.

Not too many years ago, the next-door neighbor to Portsmouth, New Castle, was home to one of the great summer resorts of New England — Wentworth-by-the-Sea. Since its demise in the mid-1980s, the stunning oceanfront property has been suggested for different developments, none of which has yet taken off. There is, so far, only a tony marina and a cafe that overlooks it.

The ocean's presence informs much of what happens here. The great Portsmouth Naval Shipyard, located on the other side of the river in Kittery,

Me., is one of the area's major employers and always has been. Lobstermen leave from here to catch the succulent shellfish for which New England is famed. Barges tote their cargoes inland from the Atlantic by way of the river. And the tang of salt air hangs over the town.

Entrepreneurs seem to flock to Portsmouth to open creative restaurants, attractive B&Bs, boutiques and gift shops. Something about the place — its friendliness and lack of pretension, perhaps — draws people to it; the beauty of the location and its interesting past keep them here.

For visitors, Portsmouth is great fun. There is Strawbery Banke to explore, which will take the best part of a day, and other historic houses as well. There are all the little shops in Portsmouth — plus factory-outlet shopping, which is becoming more extensive all the time, along Route 1 and over the state line in Kittery. There are restaurants in all categories, from the Blue Strawbery and Strawbery Court, which are fancy and fine, to down-to-earth places like the State Street Saloon, whose low prices and great Italian food have been drawing crowds of late.

Even though Portsmouth's population is not large — under 30,000 — it has the tight, congested feeling of a real city, but one that is small enough to be accessible. Frankly, it's one of our favorite places.

Getting There

Portsmouth is located at New Hampshire's most northerly seacoast point. It is easily reached by automobile via coastal Route 1 or Interstate 95. C&H Trailways, headquartered in Dover, N.H., runs buses from the seacoast area to Boston. The closest major airport is Logan International in Boston.

Where to Stay_____ ⟋ＣＣＣ

A full range of accommodation options serves most tastes and pocketbooks. A major hotel, small bed-and-breakfast inns and motels are to be found.

The Sise Inn, 40 Court St., Portsmouth 03801. (603) 433-1200 or (800) 873-2392. A welcome addition to the lodging scene in Portsmouth when it opened in the late 1980s, the Sise Inn is a small luxury inn with amenities favored by business travelers. It is owned by Someplace Different Inc., a Canadian company that buys historically interesting buildings and converts them into inns. This place has an in-town feel, but a walk of a few blocks would take you to the waterfront. Innkeeper Carl Jensen says the large Victorian-era house was built in 1881 by businessman John Sise as a family home. Ten of the inn's 32 rooms are in this original building, the remainder in a handsome addition. All have private baths, air-conditioning, wall-to-wall carpeting and color TVs hidden in armoires; a few have non-working fireplaces. Several bathrooms have whirlpool tubs. The mood is Queen Anne Victorian and there are grand oak beds, skylights, overhead fans and a different, usually flowered, wallpaper in each room. The inn's most striking feature is the amount of richly varnished butternut wood in the lobby. There's a comfortable, Victorian-style parlor, and the breakfast room offers a continental-plus breakfast with such items as fruits, English muffins, bagels, croissants, cereals, muffins and yogurt. Doubles, $115 to $150; suites, $175.

The Sheraton Portsmouth Hotel and Conference Center, 250 Market St., Portsmouth 03801. (603) 431-2300. Opened in 1988, the Sheraton Portsmouth is the only major urban hotel between Boston and Portland — and a popular addition to the city. Designed to blend with the architecture of the historic waterfront, or so they say, the hotel is actually a bit imposing with its solid brick exterior. But inside, all is soft and welcoming, done in tones of soft green and celery, peach and mauve, and with reproduction mahogany furniture in the spacious lobby area from which you get a view of some waterfront activity, including the boats which take off on whale watches and for the Isles of Shoals. There are 148 guest rooms plus 29 two-bedroom condominium suites that sometimes can be rented for short stays. Facilities include an indoor pool, a sauna and exercise room. Guest rooms have kingsize beds or two double beds, cable TV and HBO, and traditional furnishings like wingchairs. The hotel's dining room, **Harbor's Edge,** features contemporary American cuisine and seafood; the **Riverwatch Lounge** offers a view over the busy Piscataqua River waterfront. Doubles, $100 to $125.

Martin Hill Inn, 404 Islington St., Portsmouth 03801. (603) 436-2287. Paul and Jane Harnden run a high-quality B&B with seven rooms in two buildings and a charming city garden connecting them. The inn is on a main thoroughfare, a fifteen- to twenty-minute walk from the downtown historic section, and a world of its own once you are there. Guest rooms are nicely decorated with Williamsburg wallpapers, oriental rugs and sometimes canopied beds. They also have private baths and air conditioning. The garden area leading to off-street parking has been expanded and cultivated over the years and now is a restful oasis where guests like to sit and chat or have an iced tea or a glass of wine in the late afternoon. Breakfast is served in a lovely, traditional dining room with Sheraton furniture; it includes such treats as blueberry-pecan pancakes, Belgian waffles or vegetable omelets. The inn has become a no-smoking establishment, which may be why it always smells so good — although potpourris aid in that. A suite in the Guest House has rattan furniture and a greenhouse area and is a little different. Doubles, $75 to $95.

The Inn at Strawbery Banke, 314 Court St., Portsmouth 03801. (603) 436-7242. Sarah Glover O'Donnell and her two young daughters are in charge of this pleasant B&B quite close to Strawbery Banke itself, which means it's not far from the water. Seven guest rooms, three on the first floor and four upstairs, have private baths and some have non-working fireplaces. Sarah's family ran the Colby Hill Inn for many years in Henniker, N.H., and she more or less grew up in the business. "You really have to know what you're getting into," she says of her purchase of this inn in 1990. Strawberry stenciling in one room and shuttered windows — instead of curtained — are individual touches. The breakfast room is particularly sunny and bright; it is here that the innkeeper serves full breakfasts, the piece de resistance perhaps being sourdough blueberry pancakes. A centrally located parlor has TV and floor-to-ceiling bookcases full of volumes begging for guests' perusal. Doubles, $70 to $85.

The Inn at Christian Shore, Maplewood and Northwest Streets, Portsmouth 03801. (603) 431-6770. Three former antiques dealers, Tom Towey, Louis Sochia and Charles Litchfield, have run this attractive B&B since 1978 in the Christian Shore section of town. Of the six rooms for guests, three have private baths; one has a half bath and two share. A tiny room accommodates just one person and rents for $30. All rooms are comfortably furnished with wall-to-wall carpeting and TVs. The unusually attractive breakfast room has a large central table and several deuces with wingchairs by the windows. The fireplace here is cheering on chilly mornings or evenings and guests are welcome to enjoy the room at cocktail time. The owners take turns cooking the breakfast, which sometimes features steak. Lately, Lou has been whipping up the muffins: cranberry, blueberry, pineapple-orange and so on. Doubles, $65 to $75.

The Bow Street Inn, 121 Bow St., Portsmouth 03801. (603) 431-7760. Advertising itself as "Portsmouth's only waterside inn," this establishment occupies the fourth floor of a brick building that also has a theater and cafe. Forced into foreclosure, the inn was being operated in 1990 by a resident manager under the aegis of the bank that holds the mortgage; check the status if you book. The twelve rooms are exceptionally pretty and two have a view of the harbor activity. All have private baths and are decorated in pastels with Victorian touches. The location is good; you can walk to downtown attractions and the waterfront is right here. Doubles, $80 to $100.

Susse Chalet, 650 Borthwick Avenue Ext., Portsmouth 03801. (603) 436-6363. This motel in the economically priced chain is well-run by local managers Steve and Betty Wells. Located just off the Portsmouth Traffic Circle and I-95, the four-story motel offers a variety of accommodations including two double beds, queens and kings. In the lobby, donuts, muffins, coffee and juices are served from a cart at reasonable prices; you can munch there or take a mini-breakfast back to your room. There is an outdoor pool. Doubles, about $50.

Howard Johnson's, Portsmouth Traffic Circle, Portsmouth 03801. (603) 436-7600. An especially attractive lobby, nicely appointed rooms and an adjoining restaurant open 24 hours a day commend this member of the chain. Doubles, queens and king beds are available in 135 rooms. An outdoor heated pool is a real draw and there is often entertainment in the lounge. Doubles, $60 to $90.

Seeing and Doing

The historic restorations in Portsmouth are part of its appeal. We suggest seeing the restoration-in-progress that is Strawbery Banke plus another — or several, if you are so inclined — of the individual house museums. A boat ride out to the Isles of Shoals is interesting and a whale watch might be fun. Walking in Portsmouth is one of its pleasures; its crazy traffic pattern and one-way streets will confuse you if you drive. You'll want your car, however for a trip out to Newcastle and some nice sea views.

Harbor Happenings

The riverfront is easy to get to. Down on Ceres Street you can stroll past lots of nifty little boutiques (see Shopping) and get a view of the busy river, with the signature red tugboats docked here.

Another place from which to view the water is **Prescott Park,** a piece of land salvaged in the 1930s by two civic-minded Prescott sisters. Formal gardens with lighted fountains are a major attraction. The Prescott Park Arts Festival from early July to early August has all sorts of special events. The gardens — a joint venture between the park and the University of New Hampshire's Cooperative Extension Service — are a place for trying new floral varieties. There are benches for sitting and watching the water activity.

Picnicking is permitted in Prescott Park, but an even better place is **Four Tree Island,** within walking distance from the park across a short bridge that leads from Marcy Street to Pierce Island and then via a causeway to the little island. Here are sturdy picnic tables under shelters, all with wonderful views of the waterfront activity.

BOAT TRIPS. The **Isles of Shoals Steamship Co.** offers a number of trips from its Steamship Dock at 315 Market St., (603) 431-5500 or (800) 441-4620. The best-known are several trips daily in summer to the **Isles of Shoals,** a group of nine rocky islands located about ten miles off shore. Charted by Capt. John Smith when he sailed past in 1614, the islands were originally used in the summer by European fishermen who were attracted by the "shoals" or schools of fish. In the 1800s the islands became famous as summer resorts, especially the two largest, Appledore and Star islands. Since early in this century, Star Island has operated as a religious conference center under the Congregational and Unitarian churches. The legends and lore of these barren islands are fascinating and you can hear them aboard the ships operated by the steamship company. The trips include early morning cruises, a Star Island stopover at 11 a.m., which allows passengers to spend an hour exploring the island and which is highly recommended, dining and dancing excursions in the evening, and a lobster and clambake cruise. Adult fares range from $7 to $30.

Whale watch cruises and **fall foliage cruises** also are offered by the Isles of Shoals Steamship Co.,

Portsmouth Harbor Cruises, 64 Ceres St., (603) 436-8084. These cruises take passengers on tours of the harbor, inland up the river as far as Dover and Great Bay, along the shore at night to see the lights and, a couple of times a week, out to the Isles of Shoals. They run four or five times daily from early June to Labor Day, with a reduced schedule in effect to the end of October. Adults $5 to $12, children $4 to $6.

FORTS. Several forts are found along the Atlantic Coast and the banks of the Piscataqua. One of the most pleasant vistas of sea and coast is gained from **Fort McClary** in nearby Kittery Point, Me. The site contains a six-sided blockhouse commanding an impressive view of the coast and the river's mouth. The fort and grounds are maintained as a state park. Attractive paths lead to the edge of the bluff looking down on the sea. Picnicking is permitted. To reach the fort, take U.S. Route 1 to Kittery, then Route 103 or Kittery Point Road to the fort.

U.S.S. Albacore, Albacore Park, Exit 7 off I-95, 436-1331. This 1,200-ton research vessel was built at the Portsmouth Naval Shipyard in 1952 and retired from service in 1972; it was an experimental sub carrying a crew of 55. The exhibit, with the Albacore in permanent drydock, opened in 1986. A short documentary film is shown prior to a tour of the submarine. Open daily, 9:30 to 5:30, to 4 in winter. Adults $4, children $2.

SWIMMING. Portsmouth does not have a good beach. You must go south to Hampton and Rye for excellent state beaches. Six in all reach from **Hampton Beach** in the south to **Wallis Sands,**, a smallish state beach in the town of Rye. All charge a small admission fee or have metered parking. Of the six, **North Hampton State Beach,** with 1,200 feet of beach and parking for 108 cars, is considered one of the best. There are also **Jenness State Beach,** the Rye Picnic Area with a view of Rye Harbor (but no beach per se) and, in Hampton Beach, both **Hampton North Beach** and **Hampton Beach State Park,** which together stretch nearly three miles along the ocean's edge.

Odiorne Point State Park, at the northernmost point of the Seacoast area on Route 1A — before you drive around to the island of New Castle — is great for walking and exploring, although its rocky shore is not conducive to swimming. Picnic tables are located near the water's edge, offering a fine view of the ocean and the boating activity offshore. The 137-acre site offers a system of pathways popular with joggers and nature-lovers. On a steamy July day, we went to Odiorne and noticed the dramatic difference in temperatures. When you arrive, check in at the Nature Center to get park maps and information on naturalists' walks. Park admission, $1.

The Town of New Castle is a great place to drive to. It is very old and many of the houses sport dates in the 1700s. Riding or biking through offers endless visual treats. Stop at **Great Island Common,** a large, recently developed seacoast park with a vista of the open ocean, walking paths and picnic areas. The late, great Wentworth-by-the-Sea resort was in New Castle. Now just a big white hulk, it hovers ghostlike over the activity as plans are made to turn the site into something else. A restaurant (see Where to Eat) and marina have been developed so far.

SHOPPING. Much of the shopping is along the waterfront, on Ceres Street, around the corner on Bow Street, or a block away on Market Street.

The Cat House has every sort of feline item imaginable, from stuffed cats to refrigerator magnets in the shapes of cats to notepaper, jewelry and clothing adorned with cats. **Macro World** on Market Street offers all sorts of items for the ecology-minded; we especially love the stuffed and huggable globes, the bird's nests, the shower curtains with the night sky, even the radon home testing kits. There is so much stuff here you must give yourself plenty of time to poke through it all. Nearby, **Salamandra Glass** is the one retail outlet for a glass-making company in nearby Greenland, N.H., many of whose items are in museums around the country. The colorful glass objects include pitchers and drinking glasses along with huge discs that can be hung just for decoration.

Jester's Collectibles on Market Street is an unusual shop, filled with harlequin dolls, masks, marionettes, dolls in the shape of Laurel and Hardy, comedy and tragedy masks and other items of a theatrical bent. **E. Richard Ltd.** has elegant men's clothing. **Le Cadeux** is a gift shop with unbelievably nice items; we especially loved the apple tapestry hanging in the window. **Peavey's Hardware** might be the best of its kind we've seen. Husbands get lost in here.

Good **factory outlet shopping** is all around, primarily on Route 1 north of Kittery, where you'll find Dansk, Bass, Dexter, Villeroy & Boch, Royal Doulton, Etienne Aigner, Ralph Lauren and much more.

Historic Restorations

Strawbery Banke, Marcy Street, Portsmouth. (603) 433-1100. Saved from the wrecker's ball just in the nick of time in the 1950s, this ten-acre area is one of New England's larger outdoor history museums. Size, however, is not the point. With its 42 historic homes, 37 of which are on their original foundations, Strawbery Banke offers an opportunity to see just how architectural and restoration experts recreate a site such as this. Every time we visit there is more to see. New in 1990 was the **Rider-Wood House,** built around 1800, restored and furnished to interpret the daily life of the widow Mary Rider in the 1830s. The lady was quite something; childless herself, she brought nine nieces and nephews from England to start new lives in the New World and launched them all from this house. She also kept a small store, which is restored on the site, and had a tiny, contained back yard, also restored to the period. The strawberry-decorated china in the cupboard is reminiscent of some found during excavations.

The **Goodwin House** portrays the life of New Hampshire's Civil War-era governor, Ichabod Goodwin, and his family. The **Chase House** displays furniture and other decorative arts owned in the early 1800s by the Wendell family of Portsmouth.

And so it goes. There are workshops, such as the **Gorman Garage** where a boat-builder was at work on a sprit-rigged twelve-foot dory as we visited. When finished, all by hand, it would sell for about $3,000 and might be a very good buy. You can see weaving at the **Marden House** and barrels and casks being made in the **Dinsmore Shop.** There are archaeological and restoration exhibits and there's an extensive gift shop, the **Dunaway Store,** where you can pick up all sorts of neat gifts, among them strawberry-scented soaps, candles, candle-sticks and table linens. The site is close enough to the water to get the tang of the salt air when the wind blows right.

Lunch (or breakfast) can be enjoyed at the **Washington Street Eatery** in the Conant House where homemade soups, sandwiches and, especially, desserts are scrumptious. Picnic tables out back also allow you to tote your own.

Strawbery Banke is open daily 10 to 5, May-October, and evenings the first two weekends in December for Candlelight Strolls. Adults $8, children $4.

The Portsmouth Trail. Several historic houses are part of what is known as The Portsmouth Trail. While tickets may be purchased individually for the houses, a combined ticket, valid through the entire season, offers a substantial discount. For information call the Chamber of Commerce at (603) 436-1118.

Moffatt-Ladd House, 154 Market St., Portsmouth. (603) 436-8221.
This is the one to visit if you can only visit one historic house in Portsmouth. A copy of an English manor house built in 1763, it is situated high on the banks of the Piscataqua River and it is not hard to imagine lawns extending to the water's edge as they once did. Extensive English gardens remain much as they originally were and are on display during the annual Candlelight Tour of historic houses each August. Visitors are treated to three floors of 18th-century furnish-ings. Next door is the 1823 Counting House where cargoes were laded. A used-book sale is conducted in the barn out back. Open Monday-Saturday 10 to 4, Sunday 2 to 5, mid-June to mid-October. Adults $3, children 75 cents.

John Paul Jones House, 43 Middle Street, Portsmouth. (603) 436-8420.
John Paul Jones, the naval hero, made this lovely yellow, gambrel-roofed house his headquarters during two lengthy stays in Portsmouth. The house has been headquarters of the Portsmouth Historical Society for many years and has rich local collections. You'll love the costumes, the canes in which weapons are concealed, and items from ships that were dismantled in Portsmouth. Open daily 10 to 4, mid-May to mid-October. Adults $3, children $1.

Wentworth-Coolidge Mansion, Little Harbor Road, Portsmouth. (603) 436-6607. Situated on a point of land with a view of Portsmouth Harbor, this rambling yellow clapboard structure has 42 rooms. It was originally the home of Benning Wentworth, New Hampshire's royal governor from 1741-1767, and contains the council chamber where the state's first provincial government conducted its affairs in the turbulent pre-Revolutionary War period. The house's many subsequent owners made changes and added rooms that contribute to its eclectic but not unattractive appearance. The grounds contain the oldest lilacs in the United States. There's relatively little furniture in the house, which is primarily viewed for its construction and its history. Open daily 10 to 5, June 20 to Labor Day; weekends only, May 23 to June 20. Adults $2; children free.

Wentworth-Gardner House, Mechanic Street, Portsmouth. (603) 436-4406.
Considered one of the most nearly perfect examples of Georgian architecture in America, this house had an interesting succession of owners, beginning with a member of the Wentworth family. Among items of interest are the interior carving, the great fireplace in the kitchen, original Dutch tiles that ornament many of the fireplaces, and the spinning attic on the third floor. Open Tuesday-Sunday 2 to 4, June to mid-October. Adults $3, children $1.

Warner House, 150 Daniel St., Portsmouth. (603) 436-5909. This house is considered the finest example in New England of a brick urban mansion of the early 18th century. Among its features: six mural paintings on the staircase wall, an early example of marbleization in the dining room and a lightning rod on the west wall, said to have been installed under the supervision of Benjamin Franklin in 1762. Open Tuesday-Saturday 10 to 4:30, early June to mid-October. Adults $3, children $1.

Where to Eat

From the very elegant to great values, you can be sure to please your palate in Portsmouth. Bostonians, in fact, quite regularly drive up for dinner. Here is a sampling of our favorites.

Strawbery Court, 20 Atkinson St., Portsmouth. (603) 431-7722. Pretty, elegant and with excellent food, this is considered Portsmouth's best. Classic French and nouvelle cuisine are offered in an understated atmosphere by chef Douglas Johnson, a Culinary Institute of America graduate, and partner Frank Manchester, a dentist. Located in a brick 1815 Federal house on a side street, the restaurant is not far from Strawbery Banke. Soft, platinum-colored walls, heavy silver-plated flatware and crystal goblets all shimmer beautifully in the main dining room and two smaller, fireplaced rooms upstairs. Dinners are prix-fixe ($38) or a la carte. Appetizers in the $6.50 range include highly acclaimed escargots served in a garlic butter flavored with pernod, shallots and almonds in a puff pastry. Among entrees ($21 to $25) are tournedos grilled with a sauce of brandy, pistachio nuts and blue cheese or a roast rack of lamb with sauce of lamb stock, rosemary, curry powder, chutney and yogurt. A curry bread served the night we visited was memorable. The desserts are great; most famous is the "unbaked cheesecake." Dinner, Tuesday through Saturday, 6 to 9.

The Blue Strawbery, 29 Ceres St., Portsmouth. (603) 431-6420. Celebrating its 20th anniversary in 1990, this restaurant, in a narrow, brick-walled former warehouse along the riverfront, is still run with panache by one of the three original owners, Gene Brown. This is a dining experience: a two-and-a-half hour, six-course, eight-item meal with a choice of entree from fish, fowl or meat selections. Some of the favored items over the years include sauteed shrimps with radicchio on apricot brandy and corn relish, smoked salmon in tarragon and caper butter, tomatoes stuffed with eggplant and potato puree, roasted red pepper pesto, and tenderloin of beef in a gingered, brandy, dijon mustard and mushroom sauce. The prix-fixe dinner is $38 and diners must reserve ahead. On Mondays in summer an a la carte menu is available; entrees are in the $20 range. Dinner nightly, seatings at 6 and 9 (Sundays at 3 and 6) in summer; Thursday-Sunday in off-season.

Anthony's al Dente, Custom House Cellar, 59 Penhallow St., Portsmouth. (603) 436-2527. Ruth Rutherford's excellent northern Italian restaurant in the stone-walled cellar of a historic building continues in high popularity after more than ten years. The brick and stone walls are decorated with reproductions of Italian paintings; gray slate floors are softened with small oriental rugs and dark wood tables are complemented by windsor-style chairs. All is rather dark and romantic and we have had wonderful meals here. Appetizers ($3 to $6) might be sweet Italian sausage in tomato sauce or sauteed mushrooms with garlic and parsley. Primi (the first course, ($10 to $16) is pasta and might be spinach fettuccine and scallops with a wine, cream and parmigiana sauce or baked lasagna with four Italian cheeses. Secondi (main courses, $13 to $20) can be sauteed veal scaloppine in marsala wine with mushrooms, or sauteed with prosciutto and black olives in a sauce of tomato, white wine and cream, or scampi diablo on fettuccine. Finish with zuppa inglese or a creamy chocolate mousse torte topped with whipped cream. Dinner, Tuesday-Sunday 6 to 10.

The Oar House, 55 Ceres St., Portsmouth. (603) 436-4025. Situated just across the street from the river — where there is a deck for dining in summer — this fifteen-year-old restaurant is ensconced on two floors of what was once a major warehouse in the early to mid-1800s. The brick walls, candles in hurricane lamps and eclectic furnishings (believe it or not, one table features the brass headboard and footboard of a bed) add charm and intimacy. Photos of ships on the walls and stained glass lamps over the bar are other touches and there is lots and lots of varnished wood. Always on the menu are clam chowder and onion soup au gratin. Other appetizers ($2.50 to $8.50) include baked brie in puff pastry and shrimp cocktail. You can have sandwiches, say curried turkey salad or charburger (a hamburger on an English muffin), as well as entrees such as seafood fettuccine at lunch ($5.50 to $9). At dinner, try broiled scallops, the Oar House Delight (shrimps, scallops and fresh fish topped with sour cream and seasoned crumbs and baked), bouillabaisse or lobster (entrees average $17). A meat entree or two can also be found, but seafood is definitely emphasized here. Lunch daily, 11:30 to 2:30 or 3; dinner, 5:30 to 9 or 10.

The State Street Saloon, 268 State St., Portsmouth. (603) 431-4357. This humble corner restaurant became the hottest place in town in 1990 after chef Tony Catalina moved into the kitchen from Anthony's al Dente. The combination of Tony's great cooking, low prices, and no reservations meant that lines would form as early as 6 p.m.; we got a table at 5:30 one Saturday and the place was filled within fifteen minutes. The atmosphere is simple: mostly gray, pink and black with formica tables, hanging plants and high tin ceilings in an old building. There is a bar complete with sports events on TV on one side, and the dining room is on the other. One of us had the dinner special: sauteed pork tenderloin topped with provolone and with scallions and roasted red peppers in a wild mushroom sauce for $9; our other choice was fettuccine with white clam sauce, which was superb for $6. Entrees range from $4.50 for spaghetti with meat sauce to $9 for veal dishes, and the quality is great. You will have to wait patiently as Tony cooks each entree to order; fortunately, good bread and salad help to stave off hunger. Lunch, Monday-Friday 11:30 to 2; dinner, nightly 5:30 to 10. breakfast, Saturday and Sunday, 8 to 11.

The Codfish, Top of the Hill, Portsmouth. (603) 431-8503. Charles and Doris Richmond have taken over this popular spot in an area where lots of old houses have been renovated into law offices and the like. The bar is on the first floor and the dining rooms upstairs. The decor is most attractive with wood tables, dark green napkins stuffed into large goblets, pink flowers and floral curtains at the windows. On Sunday afternoons there is jazz, but usually people are drawn for the food, which is offered in a great range, including what the menu says is "the Seacoast's Best Pizza" with more than twenty items to top it. You also can get sandwiches, salads, pastas, fish, vegetarian dishes, poultry and meat. Prices are reasonable, from $5 or $6 for sandwiches to $9 to $12 for most entrees. Among the possibilities: seafood lasagna, shrimp scampi, chicken marsala and London broil. Open daily, 11 to 11.

Karen's, 105 Daniel St., Portsmouth. (603) 431-1948. Karen Weiss's restaurant is becoming a fixture in town; we love her friendly spot with the narrow brick patio for sunny lunchtime dining and the cozy Colonial interior with fireplace. Breakfasts are great, lunches superior and dinner, well, very good.

There is an emphasis on vegetarian items, things like "Karen's Favorite" sandwich of sauteed spinach, mushrooms, tomato, red onion and artichoke hearts on Syrian bread with melted cheddar, for example, or a "Mountain Climber," an open-face sandwich of tuna, avocado, tomato and melted cheddar on pumpernickel. Hummus and a vegetable salad plate, Greek salad and fresh fruit salad with spiced yogurt are other luncheon choices. At dinner, entrees ($9 to $12) include more meat: beef medallions served with a sweet red pepper puree or a spicy Indian-style lamb stew, perhaps. Breakfast (7 to 11:30) and lunch (11:30 to 3) Monday-Friday; from 8 Saturdays; dinner, 6 to 9 or 10, Thursday-Saturday, Memorial Day to December; Sunday brunch, 8 to 2. BYOB.

The Stockpot, 53 Bow St., Portsmouth. (603) 431-1851. This charming two-level spot overlooks the water, but that's not the only good thing about it. "Reliable" is the way Portsmouth residents describe it. Having moved recently to its waterfront location, it serves an all-day menu and if the day is warm and fine and you are lucky, you might even eat outside on the deck off the main restaurant on the lower level. Upstairs at street level are a bar and lounge, plus a few tables by the windows. Soups are especially favored: our beef barley and chowder were excellent and can be ordered in mugs with a half sandwich as a special. You can get almost anything here: burgers, Syrian bread sandwiches including grilled marinated lamb patties, salads like hummus plate or crab salad, and sides of feta cheese. Dinner entrees ($8 to $10) include mustard chicken, broiled scallops, cheese stuffed shells and three-cheese vegetable casserole. Open daily, 11 a.m. to 11:30 p.m.

Sakura, 40 Pleasant St., Portsmouth. (603) 431-2721. This popular Japanese restaurant is in the old post office building in the heart of downtown. Marked by burgundy awnings and an old gray stone facade, the restaurant has the simplicity of the Orient inside with blonde wood chairs and tables and simple settings. Sushi and sashimi have been added to the offerings. At lunchtime, you might try chicken, seafood or beef teriyaki, pork or chicken katsu (breaded and deep-fried cutlets) or tempura of shrimp or codfish, ranging from $5 to $8. At night, tempuras and teriyakis are augmented by chicken or beef negima — broiled and served in a teriyaki sauce — with entrees priced from $9 to $14. Lunch, Tuesday-Friday 11:30 to 2; dinner, Tuesday-Sunday 6 to 10.

Marina Cafe, at Wentworth-by-the-Sea, Wentworth Road, New Castle. (603) 433-5019. With a book about water, we could hardly leave out this newish restaurant on the waterfront site of the once grand resort. And for posh surroundings and a great view of the ocean, you can't beat it. We would try for a nice, warm day and sit out on the deck, although the inside with its rosewood dining room is intimate and romantic. Luncheon entrees ($9 to $15) include Maine parsley crab cakes in a tomato-mint vinaigrette, a vegetable frittata with mozzarella and filet of beef with marinated tomato and cucumber salad. For dinner ($15 to $22), try steamed lobster in a vanilla-basil sauce, breast of chicken in a balsamic-rosemary sauce or aged New York sirloin, a mushroom ragout and fried oysters. Sunday brunch brings such possibilities as sauteed scallops with black olives, sundried tomatoes and wilted spinach. They are reaching for the stars here, but if location will make it happen, they are in the right spot. Lunch daily, noon to 2; dinner, 6 to 9 or 10; Sunday brunch. Open late spring to December.

FOR MORE INFORMATION: The Greater Portsmouth Chamber of Commerce, 500 Market St., Portsmouth, N.H. 03801. (603) 436-1118.

Ogunquit Beach is a favorite of swimmers and sunbathers.

Ogunquit, Me.

The Indians who were its first summer visitors called it Ogunquit, meaning "beautiful place by the sea."

Today's visitor, who is merely passing through or trying to find a room at peak periods, calls it crowded. Thousands of tourists pack its streets and motels, its beaches and Perkins Cove, to the point where the Chamber of Commerce became one of the first to run a trolley service to shuttle people back and forth.

Which is fine, for you can't really get to know — much less enjoy — Ogunquit's myriad water pleasures by car. You're better off abandoning ship, as it were, and setting off by trolley or foot.

Ogunquit is a walking town, a paradise for people on parade. They walk hand-in-hand on the Marginal Way, tote shopping bags along the Shore Road, and wear bikinis and not much else along Beach Street.

The broad white-sand beach, three miles long and flanked by dunes, is one of New England's finest. Perkins Cove, studded with fishing and pleasure boats, has inspired artists and intrigued tourists for decades. The beach area and Perkins Cove are linked by the Marginal Way, a paved footpath atop the cliffs.

Ogunquit offers boat cruises, art galleries, fine shops, one of the original summer playhouses, and an inordinate number of restaurants and places to stay. In summer, many lodging establishments require four-night or week-long stays, which is fine for the regulars who make this their vacation base. The passing overnighter may not find it to his liking, but will find the off-season is less crowded and, in many ways, just as or even more appealing.

Even in season, however, you can get away — away from the wall-to-wall development and crowds, and into relative seclusion along the Marginal Way, at a hidden beach or on the rockbound cliffs, or at one of the special places to stay beside the water. More than most Maine resorts, Ogunquit is an ocean place, and makes the most of it.

300

Getting There

Ogunquit is located about twenty miles north of the New Hampshire border, 35 miles south of Portland. Take the York or Wells exits from the Maine Turnpike (I-95) and follow Route 1 to Ogunquit.

Where to Stay_____ _ʃʃʃ_

The number of choices is staggering and the variety of lodging places increases annually. Some would say that Ogunquit is overbuilt. Sheila Stone, manager of the Beachmere, reports that "every time I see another one going up, I don't believe it — and yet we're filled constantly." Four-night and seven-night mini-mum reservations are the rule in summer, although shorter stays are granted on the spot, based upon availability. Route 1 has numerous motels and the Shore Road some established inns. We think the more interesting are lesser known and often hidden along the waterfront.

The Sparhawk Resort, Shore Road, Box 936, Ogunquit 03907. (207) 646-5562. This is Ogunquit's top of the line, and conveys it from its large swimming pool and tennis court to its new Ireland House suites and the deluxe penthouse apartment fashioned from the old Barbara Dean restaurant. "Happily filled," said the sign outside the office when we visited — a nice touch, as is the complimentary continental breakfast served in the old Sparhawk Hall, site of the first Sparhawk hotel built more than 80 years ago. The hotel has gradually been replaced by the main Sparhawk motel units, perched right on the seawall overlooking the ocean, the fancier Ireland House suites and the inn-style suites and apartments in the Barbara Dean, which resort owner-operator Blaine Moore is particularly proud of. Each of the 51 Sparhawk units has a private deck, two Queen Anne-style chairs facing the window, two beds and a small refrigerator in the dressing area. The twenty suites in the two-story Ireland House are nicely angled, so that each has an ocean view from its private, handsomely furnished patio or balcony; the upstairs front corner is most desirable (and you can take a look at it from the Marginal Way, which cuts across the property). Each has two queen beds and a separate sitting area with sofa and two chairs. Doubles, $114 to $124; suites, $124 to $140. Weekly minimum stay in summer. Open mid-April to late October.

Cliff House, Shore Road, Box 2274, Ogunquit 03907. (207) 361-1000. For the ultimate in seclusion, you can't beat the historic Cliff House. One of the grand old resorts, this is spectacularly located amid 75 forested acres of oceanfront headland atop Bald Head Cliff. Greatly altered from its original 1872 status as the area's first hotel, it lately has been expanded into a complete resort and conference center by innkeeper Katherine Weare, whose family has owned the inn since its beginning. The new main building houses a circular dining room serving three meals daily, a modern lounge with outdoor patio above the ocean, an indoor pool, sauna, whirlpool and game room. It is attached to the new Cliffscape, an L-shaped building with 68 new guest rooms on six levels, where it's easy to get lost. Our room in the newest section had a great private balcony right over the rocky surf. But we found it surprisingly austere and dark, with burlap wallpaper, green print bedspreads matching the draperies and rug, and two small pictures of the Cliff House over the beds. Rooms on higher floors are away from the ocean behind the dining room or on the side overlooking parking areas. Quite adequate — and closer to the attractive outdoor pool — are the original Cliff Top and Ledges motel units dating to the '60s, nicely perched at cliff's edge. Altogether there are more than 150 rooms, each with two double beds, color TV, phone and a large bathroom. Doubles, $110 to $145. Three-night minimum stay in summer. Open April to mid-December.

The Aspinquid, Beach Street, Ogunquit 03907. (207) 646-7072. Within easy walking distance but off by itself from the hustle and bustle is this lodge-style resort, all quite contemporary and with a condo look not often seen hereabouts (the complex was fashioned gradually from the old Aspinquid Hotel). Sixty-one spacious rooms are offered by owner Lily Andrews and her two sons in three buildings separated by a heated pool and lighted tennis court; all have private balconies with water views. The carpeted rooms have television, phones and good-looking rattan-wood furnishings. Doubles, $90 to $100 in motel, $105 to $175 in efficiencies and apartments. Weekly minimum in summer.

The Beachmere, Beachmere Lane, Box 2340, Ogunquit 03907. (207) 646-2021. The village's grandest location, without doubt, is occupied by the Beachmere, an inn since the 1920s with 27 efficiency units and apartments, plus a sixteen-room motel built in 1970. They rest on the outermost bluff along the Marginal Way, facing Ogunquit Beach and with the open ocean to the east. It's easy to see why most guests are repeat; the lawns and private decks enjoy magnificent views away from the hubbub. The inn rooms retain old-fashioned touches, but each is up-to-date with outdoor deck, color TV, modern bath and kitchenette. Newer rooms and suites are quite luxurious. We like Room 16 with a deck, an enclosed porch-sitting room, a turreted alcove with a dining table, a queensize bed and corner kitchenette with combination sink and stove. Rooms vary in size and price, sleeping two to four. The motel units are angled the way they should be for privacy and ocean views. Doubles, $75 to $190; weekly, $496 to $1,260. Open mid-April to early December.

Terrace By the Sea, 11 Wharf Lane, Ogunquit 03907. (207) 646-3232. Forty deluxe motel units (some with loft sitting areas), a four-unit efficiency motel overlooking the ocean, a one-bedroom apartment and fifteen inn rooms with private baths are attractions at this relatively secluded and nicely landscaped establishment. Its assorted buildings have been spiffed up in recent years by new owners Donna and Gordon Lewis and Daryl and John Bullard, who also are involved in Sea Chambers and the Grey Gull restaurant. From the lineup of lawn chairs or from the picture window in the green and rose living room of the Colonial-style inn you can see the river and ocean. Most rooms are air-conditioned and have color TV and phones. A complimentary continental breakfast is served, and there's a small angular pool. Doubles, $74 to $170. Four-night minimum in summer. Open mid-April to late October. No credit cards.

Sea Chambers Motor Lodge, 37 Shore Road, Ogunquit 03907. (207) 646-9311. This L-shaped 43-room motel isn't angled toward the ocean like Sparhawk or the Beachmere on the theory that nothing should block the public's view. Most of its rooms (and those of many motels we're not including) face sideways toward the parking lot and a smallish pool. Second-floor rooms have the best views, and six deluxe rooms and a few ocean-end units face the water. Rooms are comfortable with two beds, two chairs, a large dressing area with sink and an architecturally ingenious, partly open wall behind the beds that creates cross-ventilation from all the windows. A complimentary continental breakfast is served in the Sea Bell, the oldest stone building in Ogunquit and decorated in Williamsburg style. Doubles, $98 to $125. Four-night minimum in summer. Open April-October. No credit cards.

Anchorage By the Sea, 55 Shore Road, Box 2406, Ogunquit 03907. (207) 646-9384. An attendant at the front gate watches over this resort property, the largest in town with 204 deluxe units in a couple of two-story motel buildings beside the ocean and newer, three-story Towers across the road. Windows and chairs are angled toward the water. Twenty end units closest to the shore face the ocean head-on, as do a couple of walk-out oceanside efficiencies. Rooms have two double beds or queensize beds with pullout sofas, plush chairs and refrigerators, and a few have fireplaces. Facilities include tennis courts, an outdoor pool and hot tub, an indoor pool with sauna and whirlpool, and the poolside **Cafe Cabana** for light breakfast, lunch and drinks. Doubles, $100 to $150; studios and efficiencies, $150 to $170. Three- to five-night minimum stay in summer.

Also On or Near the Water

Riverside Motel, Shore Road, Box 2244, Ogunquit 03907. (207) 646-2741. As we've wandered through Perkins Cove, we've always envied those who were sitting on their balconies at the motel on the far shore. The Riverside is booked far ahead, as you might imagine, and has a three-night minimum but we lucked into a one-nighter and reveled in the location, a foot-drawbridge walk across the cove to the action (actually, it's quiet at night — the real action is in the beach area). Each of the 37 units has a private balcony with cove view; rooms are standard motel, but the large white towels are extra-thick and the shady grounds spacious and attractive. The renovated 1874 House on the property has four guest rooms with private baths and television. Free continental breakfast of donuts, juice and coffee is set out in the Colonial lobby; you can eat at three tables for two inside or at small round picnic tables on a rear deck outside. A few stuffed animals here and there grace the lobby's plush sectionals and sofas. Doubles, $85 to $100. Three-night minimum in summer. Open May-October.

The Trellis House, 2 Beachmere Place, Box 2229, Ogunquit 03907. (207) 646-7909. In beachy Ogunquit it's kind of refreshing to come across a non-beachy place. Such is this B&B, built as a private cottage in 1907 and converted in 1987 by Jim Pontolilo. It's an appealing B&B with three upstairs bedrooms with private baths, a carriage house suite with kitchen, and a guest cottage. The large and comfy Maine Suite has a queensize bed, an alcove with a sofa and a view of the ocean, and nice artworks. Check out the pitched ceiling, the old mantelpiece, and the shutters screwed together to make a headboard behind the bed in the Barberry Cottage out in the shady gardens. The common rooms are outfitted with antiques and oriental rugs. Rockers with chintz cushions are at the ready on the wraparound porch, where Jim serves a continental breakfast in summer. In the off-season, he's likely to prepare french toast and hot fruit compotes to serve at the dining-room table. Doubles, $90. Closed January and February.

Hartwell House, 116 Shore Road, Box 393, Ogunquit 02907. (207) 646-7210. Located near Perkins Cove, Ogunquit's most sophisticated inn has been run with panache for fifteen years by Jim and Trisha Hartwell. Trisha did the splashy decorating in the main inn's enclosed front porch with arched windows and French chintz on the loungers. She also is responsible for the decor in the inn's more recent acquisition, a house across the street. It has four rooms and three suites, including her favorite James Monroe Suite, a two-level affair all in white. The posts are made of birch on the four-poster beds she designed to match the rooms done in English wax pine. The suite has two sofas, a wet bar, kitchenette, a huge bathroom with a skylight, and a small patio with white furniture. Other bedrooms contain two chairs and a writing desk, and all are furnished with English and American antiques. Altogether the two houses have twelve rooms and three suites and two apartments, all with private baths. Lush lawns and sculpted gardens at the rear of the main house provide the profusion of flowers inside. Homemade muffins and blueberry coffee cake are typical fare for the continental breakfast. Doubles, $100 to $175; suites and apartments, $700 to $1,100 a week. Closed two weeks in mid-January.

Marginal Way House and Motel, Wharf Lane, Box 697, Ogunquit 03907. (207) 646-8801. Try for one of the six motel units perched above the water at this superbly located place where the lawns slope toward ocean's edge. Twenty-nine rooms are offered in the motel, in the venerable main hotel or in efficiency apartments in three other buildings. Rooms are individually decorated in New England style in the main inn and each has private bath, television and a refrigerator. "All the pretty gardens are our claim to fame," says the manager. Doubles, $106 in motel, $64 to $98 in hotel, $840 to $1,015 weekly for efficiencies. Open late April to mid-October.

The Beachcrest Inn, 16 Beach St., Box 673, Ogunquit 03907. (207) 646-2156, The Andrews family of the Aspinquid took over the Beachcrest Inn just up the street in 1986, improved its accommodations and eventually closed its dining room. The turreted inn has eight rooms, each with a small refrigerator. Five on the second floor have private baths and TV, while three on the third floor share baths and a common TV room leadling to a deck with a great view. Lily Andrews showed us "a typical New England room" with twin beds spaced far apart, and wicker furniture, curtains and spreads all in white. Guests enjoy a library on the main floor. Doubles, $80 to $90. Open year-round.

Norseman Motor Inn, Beach Street, Box 896, Ogunquit 03907. (207) 646-7024 or (800) 442-7024. For those who want to be near the beach, you can't get closer than in the beachfront units of this 95-room establishment in four buildings also facing dunes, river and street. A typical room has knotty pine walls, shower, phone, color TV, two plasticized chairs and good reading lamps. A long balcony overlooks the beach; the third floor is best for sunning. Doubles, $89 to $130. Open April-October.

Above Tide Inn, Beach Street, Ogunquit 03907. (207) 646-7454. You want to be near the water? The decks outside the rooms at this summery little beachhouse affair thrust right out to the Ogunquit River basin, and you can see around the end of the beach to the ocean. Take the upstairs corner room with its wraparound windows and you'd almost think you were on a boat. The eleven air-conditioned units on two floors have carpeting, TV and one or two double beds; two are suites with two bedrooms and two baths. A complimentary continental breakfast is offered. Doubles, $85 to $120. Open May to mid-October.

The Dunes, Dunes Road off Route 1, Box 917, Ogunquit 03907. (207) 646-2612. One of Ogunquit's more secluded and quiet places is this twelve-acre refuge with seventeen motel and nineteen cottage units. The motel is a bit of a misnomer, since only six units are in a small two-story motel; the rest are nice-looking, well-spaced white cottages with one or two bedrooms, kitchen, bath, TV, screened porch and most with fireplaces. Youngsters like the beach, rowboats, pool, shuffleboard court and croquet layout. Popular with families, the cottages are rented for a minimum of two weeks in summer. Doubles, motel, $64 to $100; cottages, $85 to $110. Open mid-May to mid-October.

RENTALS. A number of houses, cottages and apartments are available. Realtors who deal with rentals include Perkins Real Estate, 7 Beach St., (207) 646-5535; Shore Realty, 67 Shore Road, (207) 646-9345, and Tidewater Property Management Ltd., Box 1600, (207) 646-8989.

Seeing and Doing ⟋⟋⟋

THE BEACHES. From the basin where the Ogunquit River meets the sea, **Ogunquit Beach** stretches three miles north to the neighboring town of Moody. The beach is broad and the surf strong; most summer days we've been there the ocean temperature is posted at 58 degrees. The Ogunquit River separates it from the mainland, and provides a back beach for more sheltered swimming. The point where the tidal river enters the ocean is most popular; on the ocean side you have surf swimming and, on the river side, calmer waters good for children. Beach signs are in French as well as English and, on our latest visit, fully two-thirds of the conversations we overheard in the beach area were in French-Canadian. The beach is free, but parking is $2 an hour from 7:30 to 4:30. Less crowded is the **Footbridge Beach** section of Ogunquit Beach, reached by a footbridge from Ocean Street (you can wade across the river at low tide) or from Ocean Avenue in Moody. Other beaches are **Littlefields, River Side** and **Ontio** on the Marginal Way.

BOAT CRUISES. Finestkind, Barnacle Billy's Dock, Perkins Cove, 646-5227. With three boats, Finestkind runs the most tours, daily from July 1 through Labor Day and a limited spring and fall schedule. Most popular are the 50-minute lobstering trips to see lobster traps hauled amid a running commentary on lobstering. They leave hourly from 9 to 3; adults $6.25, children $4.25. A scenic 90-minute cruise heads south seven miles along the coast to Nubble Lighthouse in York every two hours from 10 to 4:30; adults $9.50, children $6.50. Finestkind also has a breakfast lobstering cruise at 9, four cocktail cruises from 4 to 7:45, and a starlight cruise at 9.

Also at Perkins Cove, **Syd's Sailing,** 646-3524, offers private charters from Perkins Cove on the new sloop Jon B; free sailing lessons are included. **The Silver Lining,** a 42-foot sloop, gives two-hour sails four times daily for up to six passengers at $25 each.

DEEP-SEA FISHING. The Town Dock at Perkins Cove is the launching site for at least two deep-sea fishing boats available for individuals and charters. Capt. Tim Tower runs a 40-foot fiberglass boat, the **Bunny Clark,** a full day for $35 each and a half day for $25. Ken Young gives half-day trips for $25 on the **Ugly Anne.** The fishing is mostly bottom fishing for cod, haddock, pollack, hake, cusk, wolffish and occasionally bluefish and tuna.

The Marginal Way. We never tire of walking this mile-long paved footpath along the rocky cliffs beside the sea. It starts inauspiciously enough as a narrow path heading toward the ocean beside the Sparhawk Resort. Then you climb to a point, which affords a glorious view of Ogunquit Beach, and turn to go gently up and down along the ocean to Perkins Cove. Memorial benches provide resting spots along the way; the rocks and what locally are called "the little beaches" offer seclusion or fun for young and old alike. Arches of trees frame views of the sea; the surf pounds into a crevice at one point, and you can admire the wildflowers and private homes all around. This is the best way to savor the majestic Ogunquit waterfront. A leisurely walk takes 45 minutes; you can retrace your steps for a different perspective, or return past the shops and galleries along Shore Road (keep an eye out for the old cemetery full of Perkins family gravestones). Or take the trolley (25 cents), four of which run every ten minutes between the beach and Perkins Cove with stops in downtown and side trips to major motels and inns.

Ogunquit Playhouse, Route 1, Box 915, Ogunquit, 646-5511. Billed as America's foremost summer theater, this started in a Shore Road garage as a workshop for aspiring actors and actresses. Now the graceful white barn structure with 700 seats on the southern edge of town is the stage for top Broadway shows and straw-hat talent. Its 58th season in 1990 started with "Seven Brides for Seven Brothers" and finished with "Fiddler on the Roof," the five plays running for two weeks each from June 25 to Sept. 1. Performances are Monday through Saturday at 8:40; matinees Wednesday and Thursday at 2:45. All tickets are $17.

ART GALLERIES. Ogunquit and especially Perkins Cove have been a mecca for artists since the late 19th century, and the galleries along Shore Road are known for quality fine art. The **Museum of Art of Ogunquit,** Shore Road, shows contemporary American paintings and sculpture daily in summer; free. Artists from across the country exhibit at the **Ogunquit Arts Center,** Hoyt's Lane. The Art Galleries of Ongunquit brochure has a map and details on twelve galleries. The **Shore Road Gallery, Hoyt's Lane Art Gallery** and the **Barn Gallery** are among the more notable.

SHOPPING. It seems as if everyone is shopping in Ogunquit, especially along Shore Road. The shops get more esoteric as you turn into Perkins Cove. One of the best is the **Country Shop,** a house full of kitchenware, colorful glassware, jewelry, Maine products and neat summery things; we picked up a nifty tray bearing a seagull. **Brass Carousel & Kite Galleries** offers an odd combination of jewelry, brass items, kites and toys. Farther along in the cove is **Camp Ogunquit,** a mix of gourmet foods, wines, books and games for rainy-day activities. In town is the **Whistling Oyster Gift Shop,** the last remnant of the Whistling Oyster restaurant empire with an interesting selection of cards, candles and gifts. **Fancy That,** a gourmet food shop at 7 Main St., offers fresh pies, breads and "sandwiches for the beach" — one is the Happy Flipper, dolphin-free tuna for $3.99 — and all kinds of T-shirts. If you've forgotten any beach paraphernalia, you can pick up suntan lotions and sundries and rent floats, surfboards, beach chairs and umbrellas at the **Norsemen Bathhouse** at the beach.

Where to Eat

Although numerous restaurants abound in town and along Route 1, again we concentrate on those near the water.

Fine Dining

Arrows, Berwick Road, Ogunquit. (207) 646-1100. Some of the most exciting food in Maine is served in this exceptional restaurant in a 1765 Colonial farmhouse in a rural area just west of the Maine Turnpike. Clark Frasier and Mark Gaier, who worked with Jeremiah Tower at Stars in San Francisco, are the personable young chef-owners. Theirs is not for everyone: the fried-clam and boiled lobster set should go elsewhere, as should those on a tight budget. But for anyone who wants creative, assertive food, this is the place. The menu changes nightly. At our latest visit it featured six entrees from $19.95 for grilled yellowfin tuna with wild rice, red and yellow bell peppers, deep-fried green beans and aioli to $23.95 for steamed Maine lobster (yes, they do have that) with a summer vegetale nest, chapati, vanilla and green curry sauces. Start with chilled lentil and eggplant soup with mint and tomato creams, a salad of watermelon and red onions with raspberry vinaigrette and orange creme fraiche, or roasted chile pepper stuffed with cheese, tomatillo salsa and lime creme fraiche. Finish with our favorite dessert, a sampling of pineapple, peach-plum and mango sorbets, each atop a meringue and each with its own distinctive sauce. The setting amid white linens, candlelight and fresh flowers with windows onto the spotlit gardens is as beautiful as the fare. Dinner nightly, 6 to 10. Open late April through late October.

Hurricane, Oarweed Lane, Perkins Cove. (207) 646-6348. This trendy "seafood bar and broiler" is owned by the people who run the Horsefeathers restaurant chain (Portland, North Conway). There, the resemblance ends. Some locals dismiss it; others think it's the best in town, and we know a Kennebunkport innkeeper who urges her guests to make the trek for the best food on the south coast. Every seat has a fabulous view in two small summery rooms beside the ocean; most favored is the enclosed but breezy porch. Jazz was played quietly in the background as we munched on complimentary marinated peppers, served in a jar on every table. The halibut with pecan sauce was missing the advertised coriander, but the seafood primavera was superb. The changing menu ranges from $15.95 for breast of chicken margarita to $23.95 for lamb chops with a minted hollandaise. Creole grilled mahi-mahi and penne pasta with four cheeses are other choices. Appetizers include Hunan lamb salad and soft-shell crab on linguini with a tomato and roasted garlic concasse. Pecan banana fritters with caramel sauce make a good dessert, and most of the wines are priced in the teens. We regretted that a place so serious about food did not accept reservations, and that one could wait for hours for a window table. Lunch daily, 11:30 to 3; dinner, 5:30 to 10:30; in-between and late-night menu; open fewer days in winter.

The Grey Gull at Moody Point, 321 Webhannet Drive, Wells. (207) 646-5701. New owners including Ogunquit hoteliers Donna and Gordon Lewis and chef Roberta Pomeroy from Ogunquit's Clay Hill Farm have upgraded this old favorite by the ocean in Moody. Inside the front entrance of the weathered shingled building is a sitting room with a piano and a comfortable, small cocktail lounge. The rest of the renovated main floor also is elegant with cane and chrome chairs, oriental rugs and paintings in a couple of dining rooms, and the sought-after tables have water views across the road. Robbie Pomeroy's menu emphasizes fresh seafood (pecan-broiled haddock, roulades of sole), but you can get Yankee pot roast, maple walnut breast of chicken, and veal chop with grilled veal sausage ($13.95 to $19.95). The haddock baked with a spicy crabmeat souffle is a specialty. Most popular desserts are lemon freeze and ice cream puff. Breakfast in summer, daily 8 to 11, Sunday to noon; dinner nightly, 5 to 9. Open mid-April through December.

The Laura W. Tanner House, Shore and Pine Hill Roads, Perkins Cove. (207) 646-5090. After being closed for a couple of years, the elegantly restored 1784 Tanner House was reopened in 1990 by chef-owner Ned Grieg, formerly of Hurricane and the Black Swan. Locals have always been partial to the setting: Hitchcock chairs at beige-linened tables in interior rooms surrounding the bar and a small screened porch. Although it seats up to 120, all is serene as guests dine on such entrees ($14.25 to $17.25) as braised mahi-mahi with fresh fennel and plum tomatoes, quilted salmon and sole baked in parchment paper, oven-roasted bouillabaisse and grilled chicken with citrus salsa. Grilled pizza, chimney-smoked lobster stew, warm pate in a hazelnut pastry crust and smoked salmon with marjoram creme fraiche are among the starters. Rhubarb bread pudding with whiskey sauce and rum cake are among the desserts. The Sunday brunch is popular and a good value, featuring things like lobster benedict, Brooklyn bagels and chicken hash with poached eggs, $6.95 to $7.95. Dinner nightly from 5; Sunday brunch, 10:30 to 2:30. Closed Monday-Wednesday in off-season.

The Cliff House, Shore Road, Ogunquit. (207) 361-1000. The new dining room at the venerable Cliff House is as appealing as ever, with windows onto the ocean and white-linened tables rather close together. Brass oil lamps reflect in the windows as you munch on hot rolls and sample the tossed salad with walnut chutney and champagne vinaigrette that's ample enough to skip an appetizer. Among entrees ($12.95 to $19.50), we enjoyed the award-winning and healthful escalops of Atlantic salmon with a champagne vinaigrette and the lobster saute in hazelnut crust. These came with rice or baked potato and a choice of snap peas, broccoli with cheese and corn on the cob. Other possibilities were lobster newburg, veal oscar, chicken pommery and tournedos au poivre. Desserts include white russian pie, chocolate truffle cake, peach melba and strawberry shortcake. Interesting sandwiches, salads and entrees are available at lunch ($5.95 to $9.95) and also on the oceanside terrace. Lunch in summer, Monday-Saturday noon to 3, Sunday 1 to 2; dinner nightly, 5:30 to 9 or 9:30. No smoking.

The Cove Garden, Shore Road, Ogunquit. (207) 646-4497. The green roof atop this eccentric-looking pagoda on a hill reflects its beginnings as a teahouse. It also boasts the best view of Perkins Cove and the sea from windows and deck overlooking lovely rock gardens. A tree grows in the middle of the restaurant; it's lighted at night, and is surrounded by shelves with wines on display. The lattice ceiling, interesting art and a red, white and black decor add to the setting. Northern Italian cuisine is presented by three chefs who lease the place from original chef-owner Oswaldo Coolidge of Genoa. "He was our mentor figure and we wanted to continue what he was doing," said one. The limited menu (three appetizers, four pastas and three entrees) is reasonably priced — $13.50 for fettuccine with olives and heavy cream to $15.95 for veal marsala or sirloin steak with fresh herbs. There are an equal number of nightly specials, perhaps lasagna with pesto and bechamel, sauteed sea bass with champagne sauce and veal saltimbocca. The wine list is all-Italian, priced mainly in the teens. Homemade cakes and ice cream are served for dessert. Dinner nightly, 6 to 10.

Away from the Water

Clay Hill Farm, Agamenticus Road, Ogunquit. (207) 361-2272. "You've found it!" declares the sign near the end of a winding rural road. Built in 1780, the rambling white farmhouse with black awnings is elegant and formal, right out to the deck with umbrellas and gazebo. The lawns and gardens are gorgeous, and bird-lovers come from afar to view the goings-on at bird-feeders outside each window. Executive chef Robbie Pomeroy is overseeing the kitchen at this 220-seat restaurant as well as at the Grey Gull. Maine crab cakes, Cajun sausage-stuffed mushrooms and a smoked fish plate with dill sauce are popular starters. Entrees ($14.50 to $20) include herb and pepper haddock, sole florentine, scallops marsala, seafood imperial, breast of duckling with orange-horseradish sauce, prime rib and filet mignon with bearnaise sauce. Chocolate mousse, peach melba and raspberry pie are favored desserts. Dinner nightly, 5:30 to 9.

Gypsy Sweethearts Restaurant, 18 Shore Road, Ogunquit. (207) 646-7021. Breakfasts are the main attraction in this old house with an upstairs lounge in the heart of town. Sit on the front porch and watch the world go by as you revel in Mexican eggs baked with salsa and cheddar cheese ($3.65) — they're hot enough to make the eyes water. We also liked the poached eggs with artichokes and tomato halves on an English muffin with hollandaise ($5.50). You can get anything from cinnamon toast to buttermilk blueberry pancakes. Seafood is the star at dinner, when prices range from $12.50 for glazed breast of chicken with herbed goat cheese to $15.95 for filet mignon with gorgonzola butter. Lobster comes out of the shell, sauteed with lime-ginger butter. Breakfast daily, 7:30 to noon; dinner, 5:30 to 10. Open May-October.

Jonathan's, 2 Bourne Lane, Ogunquit. (207) 646-4777. Everyone loves Jonathan's with its crazy red sign and a houseful of rooms, all different and intriguingly decorated, most in blue and white. There's a 600-gallon aquarium with all kinds of colorful irridescent fish in the middle of the main dining room. One room has pictures of flowers, another has all cobalt blue glasses, and a third has captain's chairs at tables covered with green and white linens beneath the skylights. Jonathan West's fifteen-year-old establishment is whimsical and chef John Fortin's wide-ranging menu has a few surprises, though the once-contemporary menu has been toned down "because my clientele wanted continental," Jonathan advised. About 250 people can partake at one time. Entrees ($12.95 to $22) include shrimp scampi, haddock stuffed with shrimp, jaeger schnitzel, chicken dijon, veal and lobster bearnaise, and four presentations of filet mignon. Among pastas are lobster ravioli, seafood cioppino and garlic pasta primavera. Jonathan's location right around the corner from the Ogunquit Playhouse makes it *the* place to be for after-theater snacks and desserts. Huevos rancheros is offered at breakfast on weekends. Lunch, Monday-Friday 11:30 to 2; dinner nightly, 5:30 to 9:30 or 10.

Vincent's Steak & Lobster House, Route 1, Ogunquit. (207) 646-5115. People start lining up at 5:30 for the prime rib dinners in the expanded dining room at this well-regarded establishment run by the Lobello family. Prime rib goes for $15.95 and $17.95. The basic menu is priced from $12.95 for baked haddock or baked scallops to $17.95 for fisherman's feast (lobster, shrimp, haddock and scallops). Surf and turf for $19.95 pairs prime rib and lobster, steak and lobster or prime rib and king crab. Italian selections on the menu include baked manicotti, baked stuffed shells and linguini. There are a number of international coffee concoctions. Omelets are made to order at the breakfast buffet, bargain-priced at $5.95 and guaranteed to "get you to the beach on time." Breakfast daily, 8 to 11; dinner from 5:30.

Ogunquit Lobster Pound, Route 1, Ogunquit. (207) 646-2516. Countless picnic tables in the pine grove and many more in the log main house are filled day and night at this institution run by the Hancock family since 1944. About 250 people can be seated inside, but we'd opt for one of the tables suspended beneath little shelters outside. Pick your lobster ($6.95 for soft shell, $9.75 for hard shell at our last visit), have it weighed and watch as it's cooked in outdoor steamers. This is fancier than the usual lobster-pound menu: eight entrees go from $8.95 for baked chicken with maple barbecue sauce to $15.95 for lobster supreme. You can get seafood kabob or sirloin steak, a lobster roll or a hot dog. Finish with one of the homemade blueberry, apple or raspberry pies. There's a full liquor license. Open daily from 11:30, Mother's Day to Columbus Day.

Tops for Water Views

So you really want to eat beside the water, and the proximity to the sea is more important than the food. Ogunquit has its share of places that fill the bill.

Jackie's Too, Perkins Cove. (207) 646-5177. An outgrowth of her original breakfast restaurant on Shore Road, this is the inspiration of Jackie Bevins, who converted an old fish market into a contemporary restaurant with a smashing oceanside deck. The surf laps at the shore as you sit on either the canopied or open-air decks; the dark green and white color scheme is striking. As we savored the ocean setting, we enjoyed a hearty lunch of a lobster roll with potato salad ($7.95) and a cold seafood plate ($9.95), preceded by a Coors Lite and a peach daiquiri topped with a piece of melon and a dollop of whipped cream. Dinner prices run from $9.95 for scrod to $15.95 for scampi over linguini. Breakfast daily, 7 to 10:30; lunch and dinner, 11:30 to 10.

Blue Water Inn, Beach Street. (207) 646-5559. An L-shaped open porch with canopy looking onto the Ogunquit River is colorful with pink and green; an old white boat for cocktails is moored beside. With a setting like this, who cares whether the food is microwaved? There's something for everyone from salads to baked ham, lasagna, fresh seafood and lobster served five ways. Dinner prices range from $9.95 to $17.95. The bar and lounge in blues, peaches and yellows with stuffed parrots on perches is quite charming, but we'd settle for the porch anytime. Upstairs are seven serviceable guest rooms, three with private bath, for bed and breakfast (doubles, $70 to $95). Breakfast, lunch and dinner daily from 8 a.m.

Barnacle Billy's, Perkins Cove. (207) 646-5575. This is an institution, what with its quaint setting along Perkins Cove and a casual approach whereby you place your order as you enter, take a number, find a table (outside by the water if you can, although many seem to prefer the inside) and then dig in. Lobster is the main attraction, $10.45 for a pound and a quarter to $18.25 for a two-pounder; the lobster roll for $9.45 and a crab roll for $6.75 washed down with a couple of beers, made a pleasant lunch. You can feast on steamed clams, barbecued chicken, hamburgers or homemade blueberry pie, on premises or for take-out. Open from 11 to 10 daily, mid-April through October.

Barnacle Billy's Etc., Perkins Cove. (207) 646-4711. Acquired in 1989 at auction, the once-famous Whistling Oyster was taken over by Billy Tower after a failed effort by the Channel Crossing restaurant from Portland. Here, in glamorous splendor (the Oyster was rebuilt following a fire), the new Barnacle Billy's branch next door to the original serves light fare, basic seafood, and some more elaborate entrees ($9.95 for fried chicken to $22.95 for baked stuffed lobster). The lobster saute ($18.25) is a standout, and you can't beat the view from any of the seats in the upstairs dining room or the small outdoor deck. Strawberry cheesecake and key lime pie are good desserts, and the short wine list is nicely priced in the teens. The food and prices are a far cry from the old Whistling Oyster, but that wonderful contemporary ambiance is the same. And they still have valet parking, a necessity we remember from years ago. Open daily, noon to 9, mid-May through October.

Lobster Shack, Perkins Cove. (207) 646-2271. Lobster, clams and chowder have been dispensed from this rustic shack near the end of the cove since 1947. You feel like you're beside the ocean at oilcloth-covered picnic tables, even if you can't see the water. Lobster was going for $7.25 at our last visit, a lobster roll was $6.95 and a hot dog, $1.50. Beer and wines are available. Open daily.

FOR MORE INFORMATION: Ogunquit Chamber of Commerce, Box 2289, Ogunquit, Me. 03907. (207) 646-2939.

Boats wait to pass through hand-operated Songo Lock into Sebago Lake.

Sebago/Lakes Region, Maine

Maine's waterfront is more than the Atlantic. Its inland lakes offer low-key, outdoor vacations — often at bargain prices. While the coastal visitors are apt to be an inn and hotel crowd, a gift-buying, sightseeing and antiquing crowd, visitors to the Maine lakes are often hardy hunters and fishermen, boaters, campers who want to get away from it all, and families who are looking for a vacation on a shoestring.

The Sebago/Lakes Region is happy to oblige. The second largest of Maine's lakes (after Moosehead), Sebago is a crystal-clear, spring-fed lake that is hundreds of feet deep in some areas. Nearby are Long Lake, beautiful Highland Lake, and several other lakes and ponds known for fishing, swimming and boating.

In fact, during the summer of 1990, when many areas of New England, including the Maine seacoast, were feeling the effects of an economic downturn, Sebago was singing a different tune. The innkeepers and restaurateurs had a banner season, the campgrounds were full and one of the longest traffic jams we'd ever seen occurred over Labor Day weekend on the Naples causeway. Perhaps all of this was because visitors know they can get good value here.

The mountains of western Maine, which serve as foothills to next-door New Hampshire's giants, rise just northwest of the Lakes Region, presenting an especially pleasing backdrop to the shimmering waters. Maine's famed pine trees add another dimension; they cluster near the lakeshores and along the roads, deep green sentries, cool and majestic. When you hike, it is often on a soft carpet of pine needles.

311

Sebago and Long Lake are busy: powerboats, parasailers, seaplanes, paddleboats, canoes, sailboats and swimmers all take to the water during the summer season. The Songo River, which ties Long Lake to Sebago, allows passage of boats through a hand-operated lock. Highland and Keoka are quieter but no less attractive; Moose Pond and several others deserve attention.

Because the lakes offer such marvelous recreation opportunities, private owners have snapped up much of the good shorefront property. The main routes (302 and 114 in particular) afford but brief glimpses of Sebago and public beaches are hard to find. Sebago Lake State Park is the happy exception; its supervised beach is long and lovely and there are waterfront campsites as well.

Getting to know the area takes a little doing. There is no one central metropolis but rather several small villages, ranging from commercial and not-very-pretty North Windham to charming little Waterford. Naples is as central as any, and its causeway on the south shore of Long Lake hums with waterfront activity. But of all the towns we like Bridgton best because of its offerings: good restaurants, excellent gift shops, antiques stores, pretty houses (especially on High Street) and its proximity to beautiful Highland Lake.

The Sebago area is one in which the best restaurants, inns and resorts are rather distant one from the other. Expect to spend time driving, for you will be rewarded when you do. An outstanding glass and ceramics museum awaits discovery on a hillside well off the main road in Sebago; the last operating lock of the Cumberland-Oxford County Canal is off the beaten path along the Songo River in Naples, and the splendid Shaker Museum at Sabbathday Lake is a half hour away, near Poland Spring. There are antiques and crafts shops and at least one outstanding gift shop for those who want to browse.

The mood is mellow, so most visitors are happy to spend their time fishing, sunning or paddling slowly across a lake in the waning hours of daylight. The season is short, beginning late in June and ending, quite abruptly, on Labor Day. But for the two summer months these lakes of Maine are cool, relaxed oases, well-priced and welcoming.

Getting There

The Sebago/Lakes Region starts about fifteen miles northwest of Portland. From the Maine Turnpike (I-95) in Portland, head for Route 302 west, which goes through North Windham, Raymond, Casco and, finally, Naples — as centrally located as you can be. On the causeway between the southern end of Long Lake and the Bay of Naples (from which the Songo River leads down to Sebago) are shops, restaurants, the dock for the Songo River Queen paddlewheeler, places to rent boats and the embarkation point for seaplane rides and parasailing. From here you can travel to Bridgton or Waterford, pick up Route 114 to head down the western side of Sebago, or go into Naples.

Where to Stay _____ _ССС_

Migis Lodge, off Route 302, Box 40, South Casco 04077. (207) 655-4524. Its spectacular 100-acre lakefront location, attentiveness to guests'comfort, and extra touches (such as a weekly cookout on its own offshore island) make this 70-year-old lodge a standout. Significantly, it's had only four owners in all that time. The latest are Tim and Joan Porta, who took over full innkeeping responsibilities from his parents about twenty years ago. Twenty-five fireplaced cottages clustered around the main lodge have great views of Sebago Lake. The 1,600 feet of shorefront offers a variety of waterfront activities: waterskiing lessons, sailboats, canoes and rowboats free for guests' use and motorboats for a slight additional charge. There are three clay tennis courts, a shuffleboard court, three hiking trails and other low-key activities like ping-pong and bingo games. Cabin boys deliver wood and lay a fire in each cottage every afternoon, and guests can have their own cocktail hours or join others on the flagstone porch of the main lodge. Cottages vary in size from one to three bedrooms; a few larger ones have two bathrooms. They are separated by low fences of stacked firewood. Spruce, Sunset and Stone's Throw are closest to the water. Five of the seven guest rooms in the main lodge have private baths. This is one of the few remaining full American Plan resorts in New England, and meals in the lodge's rustic dining room overlooking the water become events in themselves (jackets are requested at dinner). Menus change nightly but always offer a choice of five entrees, two of them lighter meals. A typical evening's choices might be poached salmon, roast leg of lamb, sauteed veal and eggplant parmigiana, cold sliced roast beef with vegetables, and apple and cinnamon omelet. Three cookouts a week as well as optional box lunches vary the meal routine. Cost per person ranges from $85 to $104 daily, AP; weekly minimums in summer, although last-minute cancellations may allow for a few days' stay. No credit cards. Open mid-June to mid-October.

Inn at Long Lake, Box 86, Lake House Road, Naples 04055. (207) 693-6226. New in 1988, this sixteen-room, four-story square inn — gray with burgundy accents like an awning leading to the wicker-filled front porch — is so close to the lake and the Naples Causeway that you can park the car and forget it for a while. A Portland native who spent summers in the area, Maynard Hincks and wife Irene left the corporate life to become the innkeepers here in 1990. The building has had an innkeeping history: it was opened as the annex to a place called The Lake House in 1906; that place burned down but the annex stayed, going through a series of lives including that of being a private home. The huge fieldstone fireplace in what the Maynards call the Great Room off the porch is favored on chilly days and especially during the off-season. A buffet-style breakfast is set out at one end of the room. Accommodations are located upstairs on three floors and stairs are a bit steep, but once you're there, the climb is worth it. All rooms have been beautifully renovated with private baths and sport decorator quilts and linens; most have queensize beds. They are named for barges that once plied the Oxford-Cumberland canal nearby. Doubles, $73 to $79; two-room suite for four, $92.

The Noble House, Highland Road, Box 86, Bridgton 04009. (207) 647-3733. Located off Route 302 above Highland Lake, this B&B is the most attractive of its type in the area. The fabulously furnished, gracious old house provides lake views from most of its rooms and there's a separate waterfront lot across the street with a dock and boats, a raft and a hammock for guests' use. You can barbecue your supper on a grill and eat it at a lakeside picnic table. Dick Starets had summered on Highland Lake as a young man and finally persuaded his family (wife Jane and three teenagers) to relocate year-round. They offer eight guest rooms — three in the house and five in an attached Carriage House, which is reminiscent of a done-over barn. The new rooms have wall-to-wall carpeting, porches, water views and quilted bedspreads with matching draperies (Jane's decorative touch). Private baths come with the rooms in the Carriage House, including the second-floor Honeymoon Suite; those in the main house share. Jane serves full breakfasts in a Victorian dining room or a larger fireplaced family room. She cooks, but the rest of the family pitches in. When we visited, the fare included juice, a fresh fruit salad, cheese strata and croissants. Another favorite is "Noble House eggs," a fancy scrambled egg dish. Doubles, $68 to $84; suite, $110.

Tarry-a-While Resort, Highland Lake, Bridgton 04009. (207) 647-2522. The Swiss influence of Hans and Barbara Jenni, innkeepers for 25 years, and Highland Lake, to our taste the area's prettiest, combine to make a dynamic and special retreat. Four chalets (most with four rooms and private baths), the Schloss, a large stone house a bit farther away, and the main Gasthaus with its old-world bedrooms, many of which share baths, offer accommodations for 65 to 70 guests. The resort is located above the lake with good views; a road descends to the secluded waterfront area. Here are picnic tables, a beach, lounge chairs and boats (canoes and rowboats are free; fees are charged for sailboats, windsurfers and water-skiing). A tennis court is next to the main lodge, where guests gather on the porch to enjoy the views and fresh air (it somehow seems particularly invigorating here). The resort operates as a bed-and-breakfast inn, serving a continental Swiss breakfast; Barbara makes all the breads, muffins and apple strudel; Swiss cheese, yogurt and fresh fruit are available as well. For 1991, son John and his young wife, Lisa, were to be in residence, overseeing the **Switzer Stubli,** the famed dining room that had been closed for a couple of years. John spent two years training in Switzerland to present the cuisine of his father's native land. Resort guests and the public may dine here. Doubles, $80 to $100 B&B, $430 to $450 weekly. Open mid-June to end of September.

Sebago Lake Lodge and Cottages, White's Bridge Road, North Windham 04062. (207) 892-2698. Right on the water with its own dock and a view of boat traffic from many rooms, this place scores points for location alone. In addition, Debra and Chip Lougee, the young innkeepers, work hard to make guests comfortable. They rescued two big old houses from apartment-house status in 1985; a couple of years later they annexed cottages to the property. The main lobby has a large fieldstone fireplace and ice-cream parlor tables, plus sofas and chairs. A continental breakfast, set out there in the morning, might include muffins, croissants or even french toast. A steep hill leads down to the dock and there are picnic tables and barbecue grills. Rowboats are free; motorboats may be rented by reservation. There's a bait and gift shop on the property. Doubles, some with kitchenettes, $50 to $95; cottages, $400 to $600 weekly.

The Lake House, Routes 35 and 37, Waterford 04088. (207) 583-4182. While most guests come here to dine (see Where to Eat), the four guest rooms have been handsomely restored and redecorated by Michael and Suzanne Uhl-Myers. The Grand Ballroom Suite is especially stunning and spacious. It really was the old hotel's grand ballroom and has seven windows, plus a raised, carpeted dais that serves as the bathroom; there's a clawfoot tub center stage with a printed shower curtain for modesty. The canopied bed opposite, lovely wood floors and plants make this quite luxurious. The other three rooms, all with private baths, are simpler, country-style hideaways, although the Waterford Suite has its own library-reading room. Guests enjoy a comfortable parlor and full breakfast. Keoka Lake nearby is good for swimming. Doubles, $69 to $79; suite, $89.

Wind in Pines, Route 302, Box 65, Raymond 04071. (207) 655-4642. The Burnham family operates this idyllic and quite private cottage colony on the shores of Sebago Lake. The same families tend to reserve the eleven cottages with their own clay tennis court and 400-foot sandy beach year after year. The location is superb and the owners are congenial. Cottages range in size from little Hillcrest, which accommodates two, to Maineholm, which can take eight. Some are two-story and many have fireplaces. Weekly rates, $350 for two to $700 for eight. Open June to mid-September.

Sloan's Round Table Lodge and Cottages, Route 114, North Sebago 04059.

(207) 787-2101. With its own 200-foot private beach and its knotty-pine-finished cottages, plus a lodge with TV, piano and large fireplace, this is a popular cottage colony. Many cottages have full views of the water, but for those that don't there's a screened porch from which you can watch the lake activity. The beach is equipped with Adirondack chairs, and rowboats and outboard motors may be rented. All cottages have full kitchens and electric heat. In the lodge, three attached units with kitchens and one to four bedrooms have picture windows overlooking the lake. These plus the ten cottages rent by the week only in the summer and on weekends off-season. Four rooms in the lodge sharing one bath rent for $30 a night. Cottages, $240 to $570 weekly; lodge units, $300 to $600 weekly. Open mid-May to mid-October.

CAMPING. Reservations must be made at least two weeks in advance for campsites at **Sebago Lake State Park** by phoning or mailing a reservation form to the Bureau of Parks and Recreation, Station 22, Augusta 04333, or calling the reservation phone numbers from January through mid-August, (207) 289-3824 or (800) 332-1501 in Maine. Sebago Lake State Park has a four-night minimum and a fourteen-day maximum. Facilities include sandy beaches, flush toilets, hot showers and an amphitheater where ranger programs are offered. Nightly fees are $9 for state residents, $11 for out-of-staters.

Private campgrounds abound. One of the more popular is **Bay of Naples Campground,** Routes 11 and 114, Box 240, Naples, (207) 693-6429. The waterfront campground with a beach on the Bay of Naples has playground equipment and a lodge with ping-pong tables and such. The 125 sites cost $17 a day without hookups, $20 with electricity and water and $22.50 with a full hookup. Three-day minimum stay is required.

Seeing and Doing ⟋𝒞𝒞⟍

On the Water

The Songo River Queen II, Route 302 at the Causeway, Naples, 693-6861. A replica of a Mississippi River stern paddle-wheeler, this boat gives the most popular sightseeing rides in the area. Two-and-a-half-hour narrated cruises are offered twice daily from Long Lake south through the Bay of Naples (also known as Brandy Pond), down the Songo River and through the Songo Lock to Sebago Lake. Passage through the manually operated lock is a highlight of the trip; sightseers stand on the banks to watch the maneuvering of the boat. Trips leave daily at 9:45 and 3:45, July-Labor Day, and weekends at 9:45 in June and September. Adults $8, children $5.

The boat also offers one-hour cruises around scenic Long Lake, daily at 1, 2:30 and 7. Adults $5, children $4.

A **U.S. Mail boat** takes passengers on its rounds daily except Sunday and postal holidays, leaving from the Naples Causeway, Route 302. The three-hour trip on Sebago Lake departs at 2; adults $7, children $3.50. A two-hour trip on Long Lake leaves around 10 a.m.; adults $5, children $3.

Long Lake Marina at the Naples Causeway, 693-3159, rents paddle boats and party boats as well as power, ski, pontoon and fishing boats. **Naples Marina** at the bridge in Naples, 693-6254, offers a complete line of marina services including boat rentals. The **Sporthaus** on Main Street in the center of Bridgton, 647-5100, rents canoes and water skis, sailboards and sailboats. **Sailboards** for windsurfing may be rented from **Sunny Breeze Sailboards** on the Naples Causeway, 693-3867.

Seaplane rides are offered by the Naples Flying Service at the west end of the Naples Causeway, 693-6591. It's a 25-minute scenic flight over the Sebago-Long Lake-Songo Lock area.

Parasailing goes out from the Naples Causeway and costs $30 a ride — the ride ranging from seven to fifteen minutes, depending on how long you want to stay up, high above Long Lake.

BEACHES. These can be tough to find unless you are staying at a place with its own. The **Songo Beach** area in Sebago Lake State Park is a glorious, long, sandy strand with lifeguards, backed by a shady picnic grove. There are rest rooms with changing areas and a good snack bar. Cost is $1.50 per person and on a hot summer Sunday the park sometimes is filled by mid-morning. There are also boat launch areas. **Nason's Beach** on Route 114 in North Sebago is a small sandy beach with a parking fee. The water seems exceptionally clear here.

Songo Lock, Sebago Lake State Park. The lock on the Songo River, which connects Brandy Pond (or the Bay of Naples) to Sebago Lake, is still hand-operated and fun to watch. Take the road into the state park from Route 302 and follow the signs to the Songo Lock Camping Area. You'll see the lock just before the bridge that crosses the Songo River. Park and walk across a small footbridge to a grassy island next to the lock where you can watch the action and even help to close or open the lock. On the Saturday morning we were there, a crowd of small pleasure boats was waiting to go downstream. The state attendant saw that as many boats as possible packed themselves into the lock, collected the round-trip fee for each boat, and began to raise the water level slowly by opening one of the gates. After several minutes, when the level was equal to that of the downstream side of the lock, the gates were reversed, and the boats left.

Frye Island, located south of Route 302 in Sebago Lake, is mostly private. Its 260 homeowners aren't crazy about having sightseers wandering about, but there's a public golf course. Small ferries make the trip about every half hour. Take the road to Point Sebago.

Other Attractions

The Jones Museum of Glass and Ceramics, off Route 107, Sebago, 787-3370. This is something of a sleeper if you're not knowledgeable about glass and ceramics. For those who are, it is a hallowed place. A rambling, dark green country house holds an exceptional collection of pottery and glassware from around the world. Founder and curator Dorothy-Lee Jones began to collect glass as a child; her collection forms the core of the museum. Exhibits change periodically, although there are many permanent displays. When we visited, a most informative special exhibit on Sandwich glass was being shown. Tutorial in nature, it sought to teach viewers the difference between true Sandwich glass and the many copies. The museum has an entire case of glass paperweights, including some from 20th-century China and one from the Innsbruck Olympics in 1976. A large case is filled with Chinese export porcelain, among them extravagantly decorated 18th-century teapots; you'll also see a fine Tiffany glass collection. Even an old green Coke bottle finds its way into the displays.

The museum shop here is special — all pieces are antiques and collectibles, priced from a few dollars to several hundred. You also can pick up books on glassware, or sit in a comfortable corner and peruse magazines and books on the topic. Outside is a lovely terrace with tables and chairs where you can contemplate the scenic hillside setting. Open Monday-Saturday 10 to 5, Sunday 1 to 5, mid-May to mid-November. Adults $2.50, children 50 cents.

ANTIQUING is big in the area. Some twenty shops are listed in the Bridgton environs, most of them off Route 302. While most aren't so tony as those along the coast, they are wonderful for browsing and the area around the Naples Causeway is particularly rich in numbers.

SHOPPING is basically low key. That is, except for such gems as **The Call of the Loon** on Route 302 in South Casco, one of the finest gift shops we have seen. Whoever selects the wares has exceptional taste; things are not cheap but they are beautiful, from the handmade quilts (we rather liked a $1,600 one in the front room when last we stopped) to the jams and jellies made in Maine. Stuffed loons are whimsical, and loons show up on cocktail napkins and other items. At **Emphasis on Maine** on Main Street, Bridgton, you'll find Maine-made items like pottery lamps with a blueberry motif. **Craftworks** in Bridgton shouldn't be missed. This huge old church building on the main drag houses several shopkeepers, with sporty clothing, jewelry, gifts, books and toys.

Where to Eat _____ _ᴄᴄᴄ_

The Epicurean Inn, Route 302, Naples. (207) 693-3839. When we first visited this inn in 1986, it was conservative in look — white clapboard with green shutters — but making a statement for itself in the dining area. Now its looks — bright salmon paint with black shutters — match its high culinary profile. Despite the breakup of the partnership that founded the inn, chef Paul Charpentier and his wife Andrea continue to give lake dwellers and visitors a fine, inventive dining experience. Classical music plays in the background and the tantalizing food aromas fill the air as you enter the Victorian-furnished lobby. Brandy Pond can be seen in the distance from the dining porch, a cozy back room with wood paneling and hanging plants. Two other dining rooms on the main floor, and one upstairs for "overflow," are pleasantly intimate; tables have white cloths and a single white candle. With soft salmon walls and an oriental rug on the floor, the middle room on the first floor especially appeals; it has just one dining table, so it is rather like dining in your own home. Chocolate bread with chocolate butter — the only place we've had this — is served along with French bread; sorbets and ice creams are made on the premises, and a tray of assorted cheeses and fruits caps the meal in fine fashion. And, oh, the meal. Among chef Paul's most popular entrees ($15.95 to $18.95) these days are tournedos Aida (beef tenderloin topped with shrimp in a sauce of parmesan, brandy and cream) and chicken praline, boneless breast of chicken coated with pecans in a sweet bourbon glaze. Two to four entrees change each week; specials when we stopped included salmon and wild mushrooms Napoleon, served in a puff pastry, and sole sauteed with bananas, brandy and honey. You'll note the sweet touches but with the chef's deft hand, they are not cloying. Appetizers (from $4.50 for veal pate to $7.95 for cold seafood sampler) are quite creative; among salads are caesar and the Epicurean with smoked shellfish. A wine special is always offered in a tasting portion, by the glass or the bottle. Hidden Cellars' sauvignon blanc was featured when last we checked. Dinner nightly except Monday, 5 to 9; also closed Tuesday in off-season.

The Lake House, Routes 35 and 37, Waterford. (207) 583-4182. The restaurant at this old New England inn, built as a tavern in 1797, has maintained a fine reputation since it was acquired in 1984 by Suzanne and Michael Uhl-Myers. Suzanne, whose previous career was in selling fine wines, is the chef. Her husband acts as host and spearheads room renovations and the like. There are two dining rooms, plus a screened front porch where we enjoyed sitting one rather muggy evening at the end of summer. Alas, there's no view of the lake, but Michael said the inn's name derives from the time when guests came to Waterford for the curative powers of nearby waters, including Lake Keoka, which is at the end of Main Street. For a summer dinner, two in our party who weren't particularly hungry split a caesar salad (available only for two), expertly prepared tableside by our efficient waitress. The others chose a house specialty, roast duck, served with a raspberry sauce, and veal medallions sauteed with two varieties of mushrooms in a brandied cream sauce, both quite good. Other entrees ($14.95 to $19.95) include seafood pasta; boneless lamb loin sliced thin and served on a curry sauce with crisp bacon bits, shallots and vodka, and Sicilian filet mignon, served on a sauce of red wine, garlic, fresh tomatoes, mushrooms and Italian seasoning. Appetizers include duck pate seasoned with apples and grand marnier, a cornucopia of smoked salmon and a sausage medley. A sweet piece of chocolate and orange bread is served each diner first; with the dinner comes French bread. Salads are served after the entrees. On the dessert menu are some decadent chocolate choices; we shared a milk-chocolate shell filled with white chocolate and chocolate mousse, which was like candy. Dinner, Tuesday-Sunday 5 to 10; closed Tuesday and Wednesday in off-season.

Venezia Ristorante, Routes 302 and 93, Bridgton. (207) 647-5333. This location, at the fork of the two main roads, was once occupied by an antiques shop. It was taken over in 1989 by Toni Orlandella, an Italian who came to the lakes area in 1983 after living for years in Boston. Her son, Vinnie, and a nephew, Joe Fabiano, join forces in the kitchen and from the reports of the locals, are doing just fine. The small dining room, with murals of Venice on the walls, seats 30 at tables with white cloths and deep red napkins. Chairs are black lacquer and gold trimmed and there's almost a nightclubby elegance about the place. Vinnie says the chicken and broccoli with ziti is extremely popular, but the menu offers a full range of Italian specialties from fettuccine alfredo and spaghetti puttanesca to shrimp cacciatore, veal marsala and veal saltimbocca (priced from $10.50 for a pasta to $18.95 for some of the veal dishes). Diners may begin with fried mozzarella marinara, shrimp cocktail or clams casino; they may end with cannoli venezia stuffed with homemade ricotta, ice cream pies, cheesecake or tartuffo, a mound of oreo cookie ice cream in bittersweet chocolate served with whipped cream. Out in the foyer, tiny white lights glow on ficus trees and there's another mural of Venice. Dinner, Wednesday-Monday 5:30 to 9 or 10.

The Lobster Pound, Route 302, Naples. (207) 693-6580. Other restaurants in other towns go by the same name but are not related to this excellent spot where schoolteachers Bonnie and Steve Edwards dished up 12.7 tons of lobster in their two-month summer season of 1990. That's not all. They also serve fried clams, clam cakes, fried haddock, surf and turf, shrimp rolls, onion rings and a special: two clam cakes and chips for $3.50. Prices range from $9.95 for one boiled lobster to the Lobster Pound special (clam chowder, steamed clams, french fries, coleslaw, lobster, beverage and ice cream) for $16.95. Diners sit at large, varnished picnic tables in this highly regarded spot run for twenty years by the Edwards family, who steam the lobsters in kettles out back. Beer and wine are available. Open daily, noon to 10, July and August only. No credit cards.

Red Sands, Route 302, North Windham. (207) 892-9877. He's Red, she's Sandy. So they put their names together to come up with the moniker for this low-key, family spot twenty years ago. The Donnellys met in New Jersey, but he had summered in the Sebago Lake area and they decided to make the move to Maine while their own kids were still young. Now, they print their grandchildren's photos on the menu and son Bob manages the place. Another son, still in high school, is a waiter. Red Sands has a little bit of everything, but

318

the homemade oatmeal bread, the chicken salad with huge hunks of chicken and the lobster stew are especially touted. Diners sit on windsor chairs in one of two dark-paneled rooms at tables set with placemats beside windows decorated with Cape Cod curtains. We're not talking fancy, but we are talking honest, and the prices — filet mignon at $11.50 is the highest-priced entree and when have you last seen a fresh fruit cup as an appetizer for $1.70? — make dining here a bargain. Open Wednesday-Monday, 11:30 to 9.

Black Horse Tavern, 8 Portland St., Route 302, Bridgton. (207) 647-5300. This largish gray structure — house out front, barn in back, joined by what turns out to be the bar — came to the area in 1987, a welcome addition. It's a bit commercial for our taste, with lots of equine paraphernalia in the rear tavern room, but the formula seems to work. The menu offers steaks, Mexican and cajun specialties, seafood and prime rib, although the blackened swordfish and scallop pie are probably the most requested. Entrees are priced from $10.95 to $17.95 for "beef and reef." For appetizers in the $5 range, try deep-fried mozzarella sticks, crabmeat-stuffed mushrooms or barbecued pork ribs. Open daily from 11 to 10, Sundays from 12:30.

Gorham Station, 29 Elm St., Gorham. (207) 839-3354. The former Gorham railroad station was converted into this fun spot more than ten years ago with Mike Colerick at the controls. He has maintained a good reputation and following. While it is not located directly in the lakes region, the restaurant is near enough for those who want to make the trip. Gray with blue trim outside, the station boasts old railroad timetables and posters on the walls inside. A greenhouse addition, used for lunch and brunch, adds light and charm. Prime rib is the most popular item, and the menu leans toward good old American food — steaks, seafood, a little veal and chicken, all priced from $10.95 to $17.95. Examples include chicken cordon bleu, shrimps scampi, lobster pie, teriyaki steak kabob, and two cuts of prime rib. Lunch, Monday-Friday; dinner, Monday-Saturday; Sunday brunch.

Rick's Cafe, Route 302, Naples. (207) 693-3759. "We overlook nothing but the lake" proclaims Rick's bright pink menu and location has to be one of its principal attractions. "Sunsets and cocktails" is another phrase used at Rick's, which, since our first visit, has expanded with an upstairs outdoor deck, a larger outdoor dining area on the main level, and even a little outdoor bar where they sell T-shirts. There are lots of mixed metaphors here; palm trees and tropical birds, neon signs, South of the Border drinks, Mexican specialties and such, but the location allows you to accept almost anything. This is the crossroads and you'll catch what action there is in Naples from this vantage point. Burgers, sandwiches, tacos, salads, and steaks and seafood entrees offer a full range. We sipped beer and indulged in Buffalo wings, with a hot and very vinegary sauce, and nachos gringos as we enjoyed a colorful sunset in early September. Rick's is open until October and it's the place to go for lunch, dinner or drinks.

The Barnhouse Tavern in North Windham draws a faithful crowd for lunch or dinner with the emphasis, again, on steaks and seafood. **Tom's Homestead** in Bridgton appeals for dinner with down-home cooking and fresh ingredients. Owner Tom Dobiak had the place up for sale after ten years, but locals hoped it would continue similarly. Also check out the reopened **Switzer Stubli** at the Tarry-a-while Resort on Highland Lake, for it is special.

FOR MORE INFORMATION: Naples Business Association, Naples, Me. 04055, (207) 693-3285 or (207) 693-6365. Bridgton Chamber of Commerce, Portland Road, Bridgton, Me. 04009, (207) 647-3472. Windham Chamber of Commerce, Box 1015, Windham, Me. 04062, (207) 892-8265.

Lobster traps are a picturesque sight in Boothbay Harbor area.

Boothbay Harbor, Me.

The Boothbay region calls itself "the boating capital of New England" and its harbor will tell you why. On the special weekend known as Windjammer Days (early to mid-July each year), dozens of passenger-carrying schooners add their majesty to the hundreds of smaller boats that crowd around. Even on non-holiday weekends, boating is king. The water is such a compelling presence in Boothbay Harbor that you won't rest until you get out onto it; happily there's a long list of excursion boats from which to choose.

Settled in the 17th century by English fishermen, the Boothbay area was the one the Pilgrims turned to for help their first winter; they sent a vessel to obtain supplies. Indian hostility eventually caused those first European fishermen to leave, but by 1729 many returned and the area began to flourish.

Fishing has been the major industry throughout the years, although shipbuilding, shipping, ice-cutting, lumbering and farming were important. The way the fingers of the land stretch out into the ocean reveals the story of a sea-dominated society. Fortunately for the visitor, it was one that turned to the tourist trade quite naturally.

The waterfront area of the town of Boothbay Harbor is amazingly small and congested; you really have to park your car and walk. What's good about it is the access that the inns and restaurants have to the harbor; here it is easy to find a spot where you can dine and watch all the activity. To cross from one side of the harbor to the other, you can walk across a wonderful, long footbridge, which adds to your appreciation of the waterfront.

While Boothbay Harbor will offer many hours of relaxation — dining, walking, watching the harbor activity, and browsing in a wide array of shops — you'll want to drive down Southport Island to Newagen, southwest of Boothbay proper, and then all the way around to Ocean Point, southeast of the harbor, to obtain spectacular inlet and ocean views, set off by the pine tree-lined, rockbound coast. There is a relationship between land and sea that fascinates the viewer; we could spend hours perched on a rock at Ocean Point, watching the waves crash against the shore and the pine trees bend in the wind.

While Boothbay Harbor proper is one of the most popular of Maine's coastal areas, we prefer the nearby harbors around and beyond for their remoteness, their peace and quiet, their sense of Maine as it used to be.

Getting There

The Boothbay Harbor area is located about a third of the way up the Maine coast, about 60 miles east of Portland. It is reached via the Maine Turnpike (I-95) and Route 1. From Route 1 near Wiscasset, Route 27 dips down into Boothbay.

Where to Stay_____ _⌒⌒⌒_

There are terrific possibilities here from full-scale, oceanside resorts to bed-and-breakfast inns and waterside motels. Rarely do we find it so hard to choose.

On The Water

Newagen Seaside Inn, Box 68, Cape Newagen 04552. (207) 633-5242. There is a wonderful sense of being away from everything when you are at Newagen, part of a land trust in a spruce forest on a point at the end of Southport Island. You don't feel a part of the Boothbay Harbor scene, although you can drive into town in about twenty minutes, and the 85-acre property has an astounding number of resort amenities for a place its size: a large saltwater swimming pool, a heated freshwater pool, a gazebo, two tennis courts, shuffleboard, croquet and horseshoes, rowboats and charter sailing, plus a 1.5-mile nature trail. The inn has been in business since 1923, but has been upgraded since 1988 by new owners Heidi and Peter Larsen. The handsome, two-story white inn is simply decorated with rattan furniture and hooked rugs on the polished floors of the lobby where the fireplace is ablaze almost every evening; there are also a cocktail lounge, a game room with a small TV and a good dining room (see Where to Eat). When we last visited, about half the inn had been renovated as part of a five-year plan. All 22 rooms have private baths and cottagey furniture, puffy comforters and colored sheets; most offer ocean views. Most deluxe are three new suites, each with queensize four-poster bed, full bath, sitting area, wet bar and refrigerator. An international flavor is lent by the staff, some of whom come to the inn through a British university exchange program and quickly learn all the ropes of innkeeping and present a weekly Thursday-evening show. One pre-med student who waited on our table at breakfast got his start at Newagen scrubbing pots; as we left, he was practicing on the piano in the lobby for his entertainment debut. A full breakfast buffet is included in the rates, and a sandwich-buffet lunch is available in the lounge. Doubles, $85 to $95, B&B; suites, $150. Open late May through September.

The Lawnmeer Inn, Box 505, West Boothbay Harbor 04575. (207) 633-2544. Adirondack chairs and lobster traps are on the lawn and colorful banners line the facade of this appealing inn, motel and restaurant just past the drawbridge on Southport Island and directly on the water. Best known for its dining room (see Where to Eat), its thirteen inn rooms and suites, all with private baths, have recently been renovated. There are twenty more modern rooms in two motel buildings on either side, and there's a charming cottage for two with a kingsize bed and a sundeck at the water's edge. All accommodations have oversize or two double beds and TVs; most have water views. Co-owner Lee Metzger did the stunning, free-flowing stenciling that graces many of the rooms and bathrooms as well as the diverse wreaths and stenciled pillows in each room. She and husband Jim and co-owners Sylvia and Frank Kelley are very much in evidence. Breakfast is extra, but we found the roast beef hash topped with two poached eggs and the tomato and herb omelet with wholewheat toast (both $3.95) well worth the tab. Doubles, $55 to $85 in inn, $85 to $110 in motel, suites and cottage. Open mid-May to mid-October.

Five Gables Inn, Murray Hill Road, East Boothbay 04544. (207) 633-4551. Perched on a hillside overlooking Linekin Bay, this 125-year-old inn is the last-remaining summer hotel in the area. You'd scarcely know its heritage, thanks to its grand renovation by Ellen and Paul Morissette in 1989. The Morissettes, who'd come from Vermont to run the Kenniston Hill Inn in Boothbay, saw the old Forest House as their dream inn by the water. The public landing across the street offers swimming and moorings for boats, and the inn's location is at the end of a quiet street. A super wraparound veranda with a hammock and abundant sitting areas takes full advantage of the bay view beyond neighboring rooftops. Inside, good-looking wing chairs and bouquets of field flowers grace the common room, where brandy is out on the side board and at the side is a little library with games and books. Fourteen of the inn's fifteen rooms on three floors have water views, four of them from the gables. All have modern modern baths, most have queensize beds and five have fireplaces. Lace curtains and bedspreads color-coordinated to the striking pictures on the walls enhance the decor, all of which is light, airy and new. Room 14, the largest, is outfitted in plum colors with a king bed and two pretty stuffed chairs by the fireplace. The Morissettes offer afternoon tea or lemonade, and serve a hearty breakfast buffet in the common room, with always an egg dish, quiche, chili-cheese strata, homemade granola, cranberry muffins, blueberry cake and fresh fruit. Doubles, $80 to $120. Open mid-May to mid-November.

Treasure Island, East Boothbay 04554. (207) 633-3333. What is this Adirondack-style lodge doing on a Maine tidal island with practically a 360-degree water view? John and Phyllis Washington, retired teachers from New Jersey, found this extraordinary island house built entirely of logs, inside and out, twenty years ago and knew it was just what they wanted. They run a B&B that is downright superior — as long as you're the kind of guest who can appreciate a pipe-smoking moose named Myron above a huge stone fireplace, and the innkeepers' very personalized style. The lodge has a two-story, 50-foot living room with the fireplace, the moose head, and some comfortable sofas and chairs.

A steamer chair from the Queen Mary occupies a booked alcove with a view of the ocean — but there are views of the ocean from virtually everywhere. A stairway to one side takes guests up to the book-lined mezzanine that overlooks the living area and from which three of the five guest rooms are entered. The others are in a small building, where John stores his boating gear for the winter. One is a very private, dark-paneled room with a kingsize bed and a great view from the bathroom. Upstairs is an airy efficiency with kitchenette and two day beds. Ships are on the curtains, trees are carved on the doors and bouquets of wildflowers are in the simply furnished rooms, all of which have private baths. There's a century-old glider on the porch across the front for watching the endless parade of water activity; a binnacle is positioned, as if on a ship's bridge, on the lawn out front. Along one side of the island, the Damariscotta River meets the Gulf of Maine; on the other side, little Ocean Harbor has lobstering activity. Guests can use a dinghy as well as a float for swimming and sunbathing, and the property has two tidal beaches. Phyllis serves a continental breakfast that often features her own popovers and Norwegian spiced blueberry jam in a cozy breakfast nook or at the dining-room table beneath a silver chandelier. You leave the world behind when you cross the tiny bridge that takes you to Treasure Island, six miles from Boothbay Harbor. Doubles, $65; efficiency, $75. Open late June to Labor Day.

Spruce Point Inn and Lodges, Boothbay Harbor 04538. (207) 633-4152 or (800) 553-0289. Since 1958 the Spruce Point Inn has been pampering its well-heeled guests with the ultimate in an oceanside vacation. Everything is on this 100-acre wooded peninsula: a saltwater and a heated freshwater swimming pool, two clay tennis courts, boating, wooded paths for walking, and a fine dining room. New owner James Mackey took over in 1989 from the daughter and son-in-law of the founders and maintained their tradition. The inn has 64 rooms, including thirteen suites with fieldstone fireplaces, plus ultra-modern ocean-house condominiums with less of a view. Twelve rooms are located in the main inn, the rest in four lodges and in cottages of two to four bedrooms spread across pine tree-covered point of land surrounded by water. Photographs of famous visitors line the walls of the inn's large oceanfront living room. Highly rated meals (breakfast and dinner) are served to inn guests and the public in a large, airy, pine-paneled dining room. Two or three times a week meals (like lobster bakes or special breakfasts) are served at Sunset Point, an exceptional oceanside dining terrace across the road from the main inn. The saltwater swimming pool is built into another terrace right above the crashing surf. There's a small pagoda for sitting and watching the water activity. Honeymooners love this place, especially a tiny cottage called Retreat tucked into the hillside near the water. Although Spruce Point still has a degree of formality that's vanishing these days, jackets are no longer required for dinner. Activities also include movies, sing-alongs and dancing in the evening, as well as exercise programs in the pool and piano entertainment in the cocktail lounge. Doubles, $212 to $266, MAP. Open Memorial Day to mid-October.

Ocean Point Inn, Shore Road, Ocean Point, Box 409, East Boothbay 04544. (207) 633-4200. Since we first stayed in a large, white duplex cottage here in 1970, the Ocean Point has grown, adding twenty motel units and an eleven-room lodge, enlarging the main inn and updating the cottages scattered around on the property. And what a piece of property! Located on yet another point with water all around, Ocean Point attracts repeat vacationers who can't get over the views, attentive service and a good dining room (see Where to Eat). All 61 rooms have private baths, electric heat and color TV. Some are decorated in a traditional Colonial style; others are modern. Many have ocean views (for example, those in the lodge, in Seawinds and Westwind, and in the inn); be sure to ask when reserving. A heated pool is located on the property, and there are rocks out front for sitting and sunning. Because the inn property is at the entrance to Linekin Bay, there's usually a parade of boats back and forth. Doubles, $68 to $99, EP. Open Memorial Day to Columbus Day.

Albonegon Inn, Capitol Island 04538. (207) 633-2521. You want a room with a view? How about an entire inn? This 115-year-old hostelry is smack dab against the water, the waves at high tide lapping its pilings on three sides. It faces the town from a suave, residential island reached by a one-way bridge. "Determinedly old-fashioned" is the inn's motto, which is at once both a warning to expect what one innkeeper said is a primitive, camplike setting and something of a misnomer. Young owners Kim Peckham, who summered on the island, and her husband Bob took over in 1987 and have upgraded the fifteen rooms — twelve simple rooms upstairs in the inn with shared baths, and three in an annex with private baths. The nicest is the annex suite with full bath, kitchenette and a private deck beside the water; the annex also has a smaller bedroom with bath and a single room off it, and another little room, a bit musty, that Kim calls "a glorified campground." She understates the appeal, for if you want to be right by the water, you can hardly do better. The inn's wide and narrow breakfast room, where a continental breakfast is served, has picture windows onto the water and a porch all around, the better for viewing the osprey encamped on the channel marker outside. The large parlor has all kinds of furniture, a piano and a small TV. Guests have use of a refrigerator and a grill, and the Peckhams offer sunset cocktail cruises on their 42-foot Grand Banks trawler. Doubles, $62 to $75; suite, $100. No smoking. Open Memorial Day to mid-October.

Hodgdon Island Inn, Barter's Island Road, Box 492, Trevett 04571. (207) 633-7474. Tired of motel-keeping, Sydney and Joe Klenk gave up their Pines Motel in 1990 to renovate and open this old sea captain's home into a six-room B&B. Renovation is an understatement; they put in six private baths, new kitchens, new walls and ceilings, wallpaper and carpeting and added an instant lawn the day before their first guests arrived. Rooms are furnished simply but attractively, and five face the water at the end of a sloping lawn, two from a shared porch. We'd gladly be ensconced in Room 6 at the end of the house, with twin spool beds, the only full bath (with tub) and use of the wicker-filled porch. Downstairs are a parlor with TV, a sunny dining room, and a new front porch with a wooden glider and a refrigerator full of soft drinks. Sydney serves a full breakfast, starting with fresh fruit and homemade granola and including a hot dish like strata, frittata, blueberry pancakes or french toast. Joe, a lively conversationalist and ardent fisherman, presides over the lovely swimming pool at the side and takes guests fishing from a community dock near his property. Doubles, $65 to $75. No smoking. Open March-December.

Ship Ahoy Motel, Route 238, Southport. (207) 633-5222. The view is right and so are the prices at this 54-room motel with a pool beside the water. The original motel rooms are dark and smallish but cost a mere $39; splurge for one of the 30 larger units with private decks down by the waterfront. They have full baths, two double beds, TV and views that won't quit, and go for $45 to $49. Those in the Ship Ahoy Waterfront building, as opposed to the Far East Motel, are even larger and have vinyl chairs facing the TV and tiled entrances with separate vanity areas. The two buildings are separated by an old house, which has been divided into six rooms with private baths. Owner Jim Norman, who's said to own much of the waterfront hereabouts, started the place 38 years ago when "all that was here was trees and chipmunks." Doubles, $39 to $49. Open Memorial Day to Columbus Day.

Ocean Gate Motor Inn, Route 27, Box 240, Southport 04569. (207) 633-3321 or (800) 221-5294. The Boothbay area's best-looking motel building — in a Florida condo kind of way — is located at water's edge in a n 85-acre woodland setting away from the road. The 72 rooms are attractive and comfortable, with the usual motel accoutrements, but the angling of the contemporary waterfront units gives each a lovely, private balcony. Less appealing are the rooms facing the pool or the woods. There are two tennis courts, row boats and a putting green, as well as a dining room and a lounge. Doubles, $65 to $110. Open May-October.

Fisherman's Wharf Inn, Rocktide Inn, Tugboat Inn and **Brown's Wharf Motel & Marina** are large waterfront facilities that are a bit commercial for our tastes, but they have in-town locations for those who want to be near the action. All have large restaurants.

Other Choices

The Anchor Watch, 3 Eames St., Boothbay Harbor 04538. (207) 633-2284. People who stay here tend to be coming to or from the Monhegan Island ferries. Which is to be expected, since the owners of the two ferries also operate this four-room B&B next to their waterfront home. Ships are on the curtains and pillows, and quilts and pretty sheets are on the beds in the guest rooms, the nicest of which are the two new ones on the third floor — especially the front room, which shares a deck and a wonderful view over a rock garden to the sea. One new room has a queen bed; the other a double and a twin. All rooms have new baths. Downstairs are a sitting room with TV and a breakfast room, featuring a continental breakfast of popovers and blueberry muffins. Some guests prefer to take it to the shore to watch the lobster men hauling their traps. Diane Campbell tends to the home front, while husband Bob and their son and daughter-in-law operate the ferries. Doubles, $62 to $75. Closed Dec. 15 to Feb. 15.

Topside, McKown Hill, Boothbay Harbor 04538. (207) 633-5404. This almost could be listed as "on the water;" it isn't, but its hilltop, in-town location offers fantastic water views all around. A handsome gray, 19th-century sea captain's house with white trim and a large, lawn-level porch, plus two two-story motel buildings (Windward and Quarter Deck) a separate cottage and a house amid lush lawns and flower beds form the complex. When we first visited, a watercolor class at one end of the lawn was painting the magnificent view. All rooms have private baths, heat, wall-to-wall carpeting and refrigerators. Those in the main inn have antique furnishings; Number 8 on the third floor is done in gold and blue and has an extraordinary view of the harbor. Coffee is served on a sunny sunporch in the morning. The Quarter Deck has rooms with two full-size beds, and a long balcony/deck with deck chairs for sitting and watching harbor activity. Windward also has two double beds in the rooms, and the views are great. A small cottage accommodating four has two bedrooms, a complete kitchen and full bath. Faye and Newell Wilson, who have run the place for 34 years, recently added microwaves and refrigerators to some of the motel units for the budget-conscious who want to eat in. They also acquired the yellow house in front to preserve their view; it sleeps six and rents for $1,200 a week. Doubles, $95 to $100. Open mid-May to late October.

Welch House, 36 McKown St., Boothbay Harbor 04538. (207) 633-3431.

Martha and David Mason have vastly improved this fifteen-room B&B next door to the Topside and sharing its water view. Theirs has the virtues of intimacy and taste, from the carved wood sign, sculptures and fountain out front to the observation deck off the third floor, where people start sunbathing at 10 and may stay the day. All ten inn rooms have private baths, but some are down the hall. Five more rustic rooms are in the adjacent Sail Loft. Martha crocheted the afghans that adorn the beds; David did the driftwood sculptures out front. Rooms have black and white TV, except for a larger room geared for families with color cable TV. Cereal and homemade muffins are served in the breakfast room; there's also a pleasant solarium-sitting room, where three ladies were playing cards late on a sunny morning as we toured, and a wraparound porch outside. Doubles, $55 to $85. Open mid-April to mid-October.

Admiral's Quarters Inn, 105 Commercial St., Boothbay Harbor 04538. (207) 633-2474. "I am the original," says Jean Duffy of her status as Boothbay's first B&B innkeeper. She came to the task naturally, first remodeling Captain Sawyer's Place just up the street and then moving here for a better view. "I've probably remodeled 52 houses in my life," says she, as if to say that she's not through yet. This is a grand old sea captain's home, set on a knoll with an unobstructed view out to sea. It has six rooms and four loft suites, all with private baths, queensize beds, cable TV, wall-to-wall carpeting and access to decks. One has a living room and bedroom with french doors onto the deck, while two others have bedrooms above the sitting rooms. Cereal and muffins or biscuits are served for breakfast in the dining room. Doubles, $65 to $80; suites, $70 to $90. Seasonal.

Captain Sawyer's Place, 87 Commercial St., Boothbay Harbor 04538. (207) 633-2290. This big yellow sea captain's house in the center of the harbor is for those who like to be in the thick of things. Known as the Yellow House, the inn has a comfortable common room where sherry, beer and wine are available in the afternoon. A continental breakfast of blueberry-oatmeal bread, bran muffins, banana-chocolate chip bread, fresh fruit and homemade granola is served in the morning. The ten guest rooms are notable for wicker-basket chairs beside round glass-topped tables in little bay-window alcoves, stenciling, bold colors, private baths and cable TV. The Captain's Suite has a kitchen, queen bed and private balcony with a panoramic view across the rooftops. Two rooms are in a new addition. Doubles, $70 to $110. Open May-October.

Kenniston Hill Inn, Route 27, Boothbay 04537. (207) 633-2159. Away from the water on the main route between Boothbay and Boothbay Harbor, but set back from the road in a grove of trees with lovely gardens, this white clapboard inn with black shutters and a huge American flag hanging from the front is most appealing. Ellen and Paul Morissette came from Brattleboro, Vt., where he was chef at the Country Kitchen restaurant, to open this elegant B&B in 1983. While Ellen oversees their new waterfront Five Gables Inn, Paul serves a full country breakfast in the fireplaced dining room; among his specialties is peaches and cream french toast. Guests gather anytime after 8 for coffee in the fireplaced living room; breakfast is served at 9, family style. The dining room mantel is a treasury of elephants in every material; the living room has a collection of birds. Each of the eight bedrooms with private baths is distinctively furnished; antiques, oriental carpets and braided rugs make them most attractive. We especially like the Victorian room with its queensize mahogany four-poster bed and working fireplace. The Country Room with king bed, fireplace and private entrance also appeals. Doubles, $60 to $80. Open April-November.

CAMPING. **Shore Hills Campground,** Route 27, Box 448, Boothbay 04537. (207) 633-4782. One hundred sites carved out of the woods — several on a tidal river where there's a float for swimming — have town water, fireplaces and picnic tables. Electricity is available at most, although several are reserved for tent camping only.

Little Ponderosa Campground, Route 27, Boothbay 04537. (207) 633-2700. Miniature golf and a mini-church service Sunday mornings at 9 are attractions at this campground, located in a treed area also on the main road to Boothbay Harbor. There are 90 pine-shaded sites and 30 shore sites.

Gray's Homestead, Route 238, Box 334, West Southport 04576. (207) 633-4612. A forested entry leads from the road into this lovely, more secluded spot, which has a cottage overlooking the ocean and 40 open or wooded campsites beside the water. Hiking and swimming are featured.

RENTALS. These are both available and affordable. Start by ordering the official Chamber of Commerce booklet that describes cabins and cottages available for rent. A number of real-estate agencies also list rentals, among them Colburn Realty Co. at 67 Townsend Ave., 633-2222, and Harbor Realty, 2 McKown St., 633-4803. The going rate is $200 to $1,000-plus weekly. August is the busiest month.

Seeing and Doing

This is a busy area and there's lots to do. Excursion boats go out from the town pier on about 40 trips a day. There is shopping at all sorts of gift stores and boutiques. A railway village with a train ride, an aquarium, deep-sea fishing, art studios and antiques shops, plus a chance to see the rocky coast and its dramatic lighthouses are among the attractions.

Boat Rides

Cap'n Fish's Boat Trips, Pier 1, Boothbay Harbor, 633-3244. A variety of cruises aboard the Pink Lady or the Goodtimes include everything from "Puffin and Coastal Wildlife" to "Cap's Special" for lighthouses, seals and busy harbors. Tours are priced from $7 for a 75-minute seal watch cruise or sunset sail to $17 for the three-hour puffin cruise; children about half price.

Argo Cruises, Pier 6, Fishermen's Wharf, 633-4925. Eight trips a day throughout the region are offered. Itineraries and prices are similar. A 41-mile trip up the Kennebec River to Bath passes seven lighthouses and sails beside the Bath Iron Works, builders of famous Navy destroyers. A two-hour cruise to Damariscove and other outer islands guarantees views of seals and waterfowl.

The Balmy Days, Pier 8, Chimney Pier, 633-2284, visits primitive Monhegan Island. This all-day trip from 9:30 to 4:30 has a four-hour layover on the remote island. The **Maranbo II,** Pier 8, 633-2284, gives one-hour cruises of the harbor islands seven times daily starting at 7.

In what many say is the best excursion of all, the **Appledore III,** Pier 6, 633-6598, an 85-foot windjammer, departs five times daily for two-and-one-half-hour trips to Seal Rocks. Adults, $18, children $9.

The **Friendship Sloop Eastward,** East Boothbay, 633-4780, is a charter boat with no regular schedule, carrying six passengers at $20 each for a half-day sail.

Breakaway Cruises, East Boothbay, 633-4414, offers daily sightseeing trips from Fisherman's Wharf and Ocean Point, as well as custom sportfishing charters by the day or half day. The latter are priced at $25 for adults, $15 for children or non-fishermen just along for the ride.

BOAT RENTALS. Harbour Boat Rentals, Pier 1, 633-4817, offers power and sail boats by the hour or day. **John Ames Associates** has power boat rentals at Pier 8, 633-4188.

FISHING. The Sheepscot Bay area is a fisherman's paradise for tuna, bluefish, sharks, mackerel, cod and pollock. Charter fishing is popular. Walk the docks at Brown Brothers wharf and you'll see many sport-fishing boats lined up, waiting to be chartered. The general range is $180 for a half day and $300 for a full day. Most boats can take six people. The phone at the dock, where you can get information about many boats, is 633-5440.

Other Attractions

SWIMMING. The beaches are few and private. In fact, the waters here are so chilling much of the time that it's not a deprivation to pass up the swimming. However, there are a few places where, on a hot day, you might want a quick dip. Visitors may swim in Townsend Gut. Follow Route 27 toward Southport, beyond the Townsend Gut bridge to a circle; turn right and follow Beach Road to the beach where there's calm, shallow water. You might also try Grimes Cove, a little beach with rocks for climbing at the tip of Ocean Point. A few locals head for the sandy beach at the end of Beach Road in Southport.

Railway Village, Route 27, Boothbay, 633-4727. Here's something for the children. The village consists of 30 display buildings, 55 antique vehicles, picnic areas, a gift shop, and a steam train giving fourteen-minute rides throughout the complex. It is the only steam-powered narrow-gauge train left in Maine. The one-and-a-half-mile excursion recreates the type of ride that would have been popular in such areas as served by the Wiscasset, Waterville and Farmington Railroad. The train operates daily at half-hour intervals, and visitors are then welcome to stroll through the turn-of-the-century village, complete with carriage display, fire equipment, an automobile display, blacksmith shop and doll museum. Open daily 9:30 to 5, mid-June to mid-October. Adults $5, children $2.50.

Marine Resources Aquarium, McKown Point, West Boothbay Harbor, 633-5572. Although small, the aquarium run by the Maine Department of Marine Resources is lots of fun. An enormous lobster, a tank of sharks, two blue lobsters (statistically, they're only one in a million), two seals named Saturna and Trumpet who love to frolic in an outdoor pool, and a chance to watch the residents being fed entertain the entire family. There are picnic benches on the shore. Open daily 8 or 9 to 5, Memorial Day to Columbus Day. Free.

Boothbay Region Historical Society, 70 Oak St., Boothbay Harbor, 633-3666. The museum, housed in the Elizabeth Reed House, is good to visit for a little perspective on the area. Exhibits include a collection of 2,000 photographs, a file of local newspapers, an historical library, and artifacts and memorabilia — many of them relating to the fishing in the region. Open Wednesday, Friday and Saturday 10 to 4 in summer, Saturday 10 to 2 in off-season. Donation.

The Brick House Gallery, Oak Street, Boothbay Harbor, 633-2703. This community-supported public gallery presents the contemporary work of outstanding artists of the region and of Monhegan Island. Most works on display can be purchased, and there are three juried shows each summer. Open daily 11 to 5, Sunday noon to 5. Adults, 25 cents.

Maine Maritime Museum, 243 Washington St., Bath, 443-1316. Relics from Maine's 400 years of seafaring heritage are preserved at this must stop for those with marine interests on their way to or from Boothbay. The showcase is a handsome brick building that opened
in 1989 along the Kennebec River just east of the massive Bath Iron Works complex. The facility, appropriate for a town known for boat-building, occupies a fifteen-acre site where large sailing ships were built at the turn of the century. The new maritime history building contains permanent and temporary exhibits and collections showing prominent shipbuilding families, sailing memorabilia, navigational tools, ship models, artifacts, paintings and interpretive exhibits of life at sea and maritime technology. "Lobstering and the Maine Coast" is one of the interesting displays. Visitors can see boats in the making at the apprentice boatbuilding shop, board the 142-foot Grand Banks schooner, Sherman Zwicker, or take a 50-minute cruise aboard the M.V. Argo on the Kennebec River. Open daily, 9:30 to 5. Adults $5, children $2.50.

Driving Around. Most people who get to Boothbay Harbor go no farther. That's a pity, for they don't know the real Maine they are missing — although if too many do go farther, that real Maine eventually could be spoiled. Every local has his favorite drive; innkeeper Frank Kelley of the Lawnmeer Inn shared his: Drive on Route 27 across Townsend Gut through "downtown Southport," which consists of a post office, town hall, fire department and general store, as well as a new historical museum. Detour to the beach at the end of Beach Road for a look at the lighthouse and skittering sandpipers. Follow the signs for Cozy Harbor and the Southport Yacht Club, whose members patronize the E.W. Pratt General Store, an emporium from yesteryear with a duck-pin bowling alley on one side, some shelves in the middle, and a counter on the other, at which the elderly Mr. Pratt dispenses remarkable hamburgers ($1.55). A fresh crab roll ($4.50) was the special of the day when we visited. On the way to Pratt's Island (also owned by Mr. Pratt), you'll pass Elderkin Studio (advertising paintings, puffins and note paper), Guy Rondlett's boat yard and homes typical of Southport Island's utter lack of pretension. Many are the fishing boats in Christmas Cove, a working harbor. Near Cape Newagen, look for the Lobster Shop (where you can get a lobster roll or a whoopie pie), the homes in the Newagen land trust and the town landing, with a view of Cuckold's Lighthouse. Follow the signs for Albonegon Inn to see Capitol Island. Poke down other side roads to find boat-filled harbors and inlets and your own discoveries.

SHOPPING. The **Basket Barn** on Route 27 in Boothbay has countless baskets (New England hardwood splint baskets, fish baskets, potato baskets) plus wicker furniture, grass rugs and bamboo shades. The **Huckleberry Bookstore** in Boothbay Harbor has a fine selection of Maine authors, as does **Sherman's Book & Stationery Store** on the square. **Hand in Hand** on Oak Street offers splendid crafts and jewelery and you can find Edgecomb Pottery here. But for the best selection of this exquisitely glazed pottery, visit the **Edgecomb Potters** at their complex on Route 27. It's expensive, but there's a shelf of seconds at good prices.

The **Smiling Cow,** a gift shop also located in Camden, is a landmark. All sorts of gifts can be found here and a back door leads to the wharf. The **Village Shop** has room after room of sophisticated cards, kitchen gadgets, cookbooks, table linens, china, children's clothing, and lots of Maine food products. **House of Logan** purveys traditional clothing. **Slick's** sells flashy women's apparel; we were amused by the beach sandals called Fruit Loops, decorated with bunches of grapes.

At **Abacus** we admired the homebody cats done by Solveig Cox, with mice in their mouths. **Beans Corner Corn Co.** has popcorn in every conceivable flavor. An incredible selection of cannisters to put the popcorn in starts at $4.95. **Treasured Crafts of Maine** has nifty red cedar birdhouses and plant hangers; we also liked the Goose Pond Christmas ornaments here. **The Mung Bean** on Upper Townsend Avenue has good cards, pottery and jewelry, birchbark baskets, spruce sachets, chart clocks and such. We also liked the chintz animals, cotton rugs, kinetic sculptures, and silk flowers at **Lupine,** just across the street. The "jumping jacks" for the wall are works of art and many people collect them.

Where to Eat

The emphasis is on fresh seafood, expecially lobster, at a variety of dining spots, many of them perfect for the location. Prices are quite reasonable, too.

Water Views

Lawnmeer Inn and Restaurant, Route 27, Southport Island. (207) 633-2544. There's a water view from virtually every table in this long, narrow dining room with high-back chairs and linened tables that's dim and romantic by candlelight at night. Chef Patrick Dorr prepares an appetizing array of specials — things like stuffed yummies (shrimp in tomato, crab in mushroom caps and lobster in a lemon half, $6.95 as an appetizer) and a trio of fish (haddock with lobster butter, tuna with garlic butter and swordfish with hollandaise, $15.95 as an entree), both of which proved exceptional. When one of us chose the fish trio over the lobster Johnny Walker but missed sampling the sauce, the chef obliged with an extra sauce on the side. We also can vouch for the shrimp in parchment with new potatoes and crisp yellow squash and zucchini, and the poached salmon with dill hollandaise sauce among entrees priced from $9.95 to $15.95. Blueberries in puff pastry with grand marnier and chocolate-covered praline ice cream truffles with strawberry sauce were terrific desserts. Dinner nightly, 5 to 9; Sunday brunch, 8 to 1. Open mid-May to mid-October.

Newagen Seaside Inn, Cape Newagen, Southport. (207) 633-5242. White linens and pretty china bearing a little branch of a spruce tree and pine cones dress up this simple, deceptively large dining room with water views on both sides. The menu has been dressed up lately by chef Alan Milchick, who's known for some of the best meals in the area and considers sauces and soups his specialties. For dinner, start with oysters rockefeller, seafood chowder, cream of broccoli or a hot German potato soup. Fans say they've never tasted such good salmon, poached in its own little pan with julienned vegetables and court bouillon. Crisp roast duckling with a spirited orange sauce and haddock with sesame seeds and parmesan cheese are well thought of, too. Other entrees ($12.75 to $16.50) range from chicken cordon bleu to grilled lamb chops with minted hollandaise sauce. Desserts might be apple strudel, creme de menthe parfait, amaretto cheesecake or chocolate-banana chip cake. The limited wine list is pleasantly priced. Dinner nightly except Tuesday, 6:30 to 8:30 or 9. Open June-September.

Ocean Point Inn, Shore Road, Ocean Point, East Boothbay. (207) 633-4200. The Ocean Point provides the diner with a delightful seven-mile drive from the harbor along Linekin Bay, culminating in a good dinner with an ocean view. The dining room stretches along the waterfront side of the inn, with large windows and two different levels in the main garden room, allowing for water views from most tables. The room is divided into various sections by decor; we sat at a table with black floral print tablecloths and pink napkins; other sections are done in white or earth tones. There are ladderback chairs in one area, white bentwood chairs in another. We lucked out with a window table, even though we didn't have reservations, and our hearty appetites were immediately soothed by an herbed cheese spread that arrived with crackers. Specialties of the day change (roast leg of lamb on Fridays, prime rib on Saturdays). We skipped Sunday's roast turkey for chicken breast with fresh basil and shrimp in white wine sauce ($12.75) and broiled swordfish ($13.95), thick and moist. Appetizers included mussels steamed in wine, crab cakes and smoked trout pate. The clam chowder ($2.50) was creamy and full of clams. Large, fresh salads with a fine creamy dill dressing were extra. Other entrees ($9.95 to $19.95) included broiled scallops, seafood platter, shrimp scampi, fried chicken and charbroiled sirloin steak or filet mignon. Fresh rolls, potatoes or rice, and vegetables of the day — in our case, summer squash — fill out the meal. If you have room left, try a pistachio bombe ($2.95) or cheesecake with strawberries ($2.75). After dinner, it's fun to walk out by the waterfront and Town Pier, to watch the twinkling lights in houses and on boats, and hear the surf as it hits the rocks. Dinner nightly, 5:30 to 9; closed Thursday in off-season. Breakfast is also served from 7:30 to 10. Open Memorial Day to Columbus Day.

Lobsterman's Wharf, Route 96, East Boothbay. (207) 633-3443. Located in a commercial fishing area on the small but picturesque harbor at East Boothbay, this spot captures the flavor of boat building and repairing, fishing, and most importantly, good waterfront dining on the Damariscotta River. The umbrellaed deck overlooking the water is the place to be if it's nice; our lunch on a warm, sunny July day was perfect and we enjoyed watching the small boats (even a canoe) in which people arrived for a meal, even if the construction noise from the boatyard beside did intrude (this is a working harbor, after all). The restaurant is in a low building with booths and nautical memorabilia inside; out front where the deck is, a tugboat-like facade is painted red. You sit at picnic tables and — if it's as glaringly sunny a day as ours — try to get one with an umbrella (we didn't succeed, but what pink cheeks we sported later). For lunch you can have a lobster roll ($7.95), sandwich ($8.95) or club ($9.95); crabmeat, shrimp or tuna in the same guises, a crabmeat melt ($7.25) or a bowl of lobster stew ($8.25). We savored a really fine cup of clam chowder ($2.50) and an enormous spinach salad with an especially good pepper-parmesan dressing ($4.95). Steamed clams and boiled lobsters are available all day, at the market price. For dinner ($10.95 to $16.95), you can also get broiled halibut, grilled swordfish, a broiled fisherman's platter, broiled scallops and the like. Steaks, chicken, barbecued ribs and mixed grill are there for the landlubbers. Big glasses of iced tea or beer or inexpensive wines wash it all down, and the blueberry pie, carrot cake, strawberry shortcake and cheesecake are homemade. Lunch daily, 11:30 to 4:30; dinner, 5 to 9.

Lobsterman's Co-op, Atlantic Avenue, Boothbay Harbor. (207) 633-4900. This is supposed to have the best values around, and its outdoor deck, with rows of picnic tables (a two-story pavilion is protected from the weather) is always full, it seems. Certainly the view of Boothbay Harbor can't be improved upon. You're given a number when you order at the counter, and these are blared out via loudspeaker for pickups. The prices seem right: steamed clams for $6.50; a one-pound lobster for $9.95 hard-shell or $8.95 soft-shell; corn at 85 cents an ear; fried clams for $9.95 and fried scallops for $8.25. The white board might advertise seafood chowder, "made fresh today, yum-yum!" for $3.95. Service is on paper goods; there are large garbage barrels for disposing of the debris. Beer, wine, coffee, tea and soft drinks are available. Open daily from 11:30 to 8:30.

Robinson's Wharf, Route 27, Southport. (207) 633-3830. Dozens of long communal tables are everywhere — inside and out, under cover and on the open wharf — at this bustling, rustic spot beside Townsend Gut and what's said to be the busiest drawbridge in Maine. The food is as basic as the atmosphere: fish chowder ($3.50) and lobser stew ($5.50); lobster rolls ($6.85), sandwiches from hamburgers to fishburgers, and lobster, to eat here or to go, $16.50 for a lobster dinner, plus $1 deposit for the nutcracker. When we visited, Robinson's was out-valuing the Lobster Co-op, charging $4.50 for steamers, 65 cents for corn and $2.80 for mussels, which weren't available that day at the Co-op. Homemade pies and brownies and Round Top ice creams are featured desserts. Beer and wine are available, the latter at $7.25 for a carafe. Open daily, 7 a.m. to 8:45 p.m. Seasonal.

Chowder House, Granary Way opposite the footbridge, Boothbay Harbor. (207) 633-5761. Robert and Sally Maroon opened this attractive waterfront restaurant-cum-shopping arcade a decade ago. It has lots of atmosphere, from the weathered look of the building to the white mismatched chairs at bare wooden tables and an open kitchen area with a serving bar in the shape of a dory. A deck overlooking the harbor is enhanced by flower-decorated lampposts and piled lobster pots. The building's origin as a grain mill and then a plumbing warehouse remains intact, all of the reconstruction done by Robert, who is a woodworker with a small shop on the premises (his specialty is carved signs). Other shops that can be visited before or after dining include Harmony Hill yarn shop with wool from Boothbay area sheep, Maine-le Crafts, the Spider's Web for lace and ribbons, and C.J. Sprong & Co. for antique quilts and country clothing. On the chilly night we first visited, we were lucky to snag one of the eight rough pine-plank tables indoors. Fresh flowers in milk glass vases and flickering candles in red glass containers are just the right touches. Sandwiches and salads are always on the menu, but specialties included baked stuffed haddock and sauteed scallops (both $13.95), and a bowl of clam ($4.95) or fish ($3.95) chowder, creamy and brimming with seafood. A glass of the house wine provided a good accompaniment, or you can start with one of the specialty strawberry or banana daiquiris. We all saved room for dessert: the strawberry-rhubarb pie was excellent, the carrot cake a bit dry. There's a small, convivial bar. Open daily, lunch from 11:30, dinner from 5. Open mid-June to Labor Day.

Andrews' Harborside Restaurant, At the footbridge, Boothbay Harbor. (207) 633-4074. Formerly the Blue Ship, this jauntily awninged and decked restaurant with its exceptional location is much in demand for breakfast, lunch and dinner — especially by tourists browsing through the shops and locals who know the hands-on owners, Lisa and Craig Andrews, he the son of a town physician. We had breakfast at one of the wood-look formica tables, set with blue chairs. Floors are bare wood, pillars are white, and there's a fresh, nautical feeling in blue and white. Tables with blue umbrellas on the deck overlook the harbor. The huge cinnamon rolls fancied by the former restaurant's clientele are still on the menu; at $1.25 they cover a breakfast plate and are the piece de resistance in a $2.75 continental breakfast. Another favorite choice is blueberry pancakes for $3.50; you can also get yogurt, fruit and eggs in all guises. For lunch, lobster and crab rolls and the Harborside salad garnished with lobster ($11.95) or crab ($8.95) are featured. Dinner ($8.50 to $15.25) emphasizes seafood such as lobster pie, scallops and mushrooms in puff pastry, broiled haddock and fried oysters. A country-style chicken pie, sirloin steak and "today's pasta plate, new this year" satisfy the non-fish eaters. Breakfast daily, 7:30 to 11; lunch, 11:30 to 4; dinner, 5 to 9. Open May-October.

McSeagull's, On the Wharf, Boothbay Harbor. (207) 633-4041. The spacious waterside deck is the place for a drink or a casual lunch and dinner, but get there early — it fills up with a young crowd, and the entertainment gets loud after 9. Popular with local characters, it has a large bar and a couple of dining rooms. We'd lunch on sandwiches or salads in the $7 to $8 range. The dinner menu ($10.95 to $19.75) is much more ambitious, perhaps too ambitious to succeed with such exotica as three veal dishes and four shrimp dishes. Stick to the basics like chicken teriyaki and baked stuffed lobster. Frozen grasshopper pie is a good dessert. Lunch daily, 11:30 to 3:30; dinner, 5:30 to 10. Closed January and February.

Clambake at Cabbage Island, East Boothbay. (307) 633-7200. The Moore family hosts clambakes twice a day on this 5 1/2-acre island. Activities include fishing, games, walking and relaxing; a 1900 lodge seats 100 guests in a rainstorm. Lobsters, clams and corn on the cob are cooked in seaweed, covered with tarpaulins and rocks. This is very basic, popular and said to be quite good. Wear casual clothes; it's messy. The full clambake costs $22.80, depending on price of lobster, and chicken is a substitute at $18.95. The boat costs $6, and leaves Boothbay Monday-Saturday at 12:45 and 5, Sundays at 11:30 and 1:30.

Other Choices

Russell House, Route 27, Boothbay. (207) 633-6656. Jocelyn Oakes runs a stylish restaurant in this New England farmhouse on the main route leading from Route 1 to Boothbay Harbor. Bluish gray carpeting, blue calico tablecloths atop pink cloths with white napkins, fresh flowers, blond wood chairs and tiny white lights on potted plants all blend softly in a sophisticated manner. The gigantic menu is no less so, though it's too extensive to bring off with total success. Appetizers in the $3.95 to $5.95 range include oysters Rockefeller, pistachio pate and smoked seafood sampler. The ten pasta dishes go from $10.95 to $16.95 (for lobster Russell). Entrees ($11.95 to $21.95) include many lobster, veal, beef, duck, lamb, chicken and seafood dishes, including ginger scallops, bouillabaisse, maple-bourbon chicken and lobster with pernod. The Russell House has five attractively refurbished upstairs guest rooms, all with private baths, dark green carpeting, stenciled walls and dark pine beds with quilts. Dinner nightly except Sunday, 5:30 to 9:30. Closed Monday in winter.

Ristorante Black Orchid, 5 By-Way, Boothbay Harbor. (207) 633-6650. Very un-Boothbayish and rather New Yorkish in a seaside kind of way is this intimate Italian trattoria run by chef-owner Steven DiCicco, a Culinary Institute of America grad. The unpretentious interior is done up in black and white, with pink stenciling on the walls, beams strewn with odd-looking grapevines and baskets of hanging fuschias. The upstairs Bocce Club cafe and raw bar overlook the downtown harbor scene. The highly rated food includes ten pasta dishes with salad, from $8.95 for fettuccine alfredo to $19.95 for fettuccine with lobster and mushrooms. Shrimp and scallops saute, pork tenderloin marsala, petite filets diavolo and six veal dishes head the entrees ($10.95 to $23.95). Fried shrimp and fried scallops are offered under "traditional fried seafoods" for who-knows-what-kind of traditionalists. Desserts include amaretto bread pudding and chocolate-chambord torte. Raw bar daily 3 to 5, dinner nightly, 5:30 to 10. Open mid-May to mid-October.

Maxfield's, Oak and McClintock Streets, Boothbay Harbor. (207) 633-3444. This five-year-old establishment bills itself as "the prettiest little dining room" in town. That it is, with woven mats on pine tables in a wainscoted dining room and in a cocktail lounge. But we prefer the two-level canopied porch with little round tables, which is even more popular for lunch and dinner. Regulars praise the quaint and quiet interior with light music that, one said, could lull you to sleep. Dinner entrees, priced through the teens, include pork chop au poivre, sole Italiano, shrimp florentine, honey-crumb scallops and lobster pie. Soups and salads are highlighted at lunch, when you might try chilled tomato-cucumber soup, Gramma Ginny's chicken and grape salad ($6.25) or a Mediterranean spinach salad ($6.95). Sandwiches, burgers and crepes are other possibilities. For dessert, how about chocolate marble cheesecake or a fresh fruit medley with raspberry sherbet in the middle? Lunch daily, 11:30 to 2; dinner, 5 to 9. Open Thursday-Sunday in off-season. Closed mid-December through January.

No Anchovies, 4 Todd Ave., Boothbay Harbor. (207) 633-2130. Fantastic metal sculptures, one an anchor, are outside this little house that's a glorified pizza parlor. White lights twinkle in the window and flowers are stenciled all over the walls. There are a few tables for eating in, but most take out, particularly the two dozen versions of pizza, hot and cold submarines and calzones. Those who do miss some of the best Italian cooking around, from spaghetti and meatballs ($5.25) to shrimp alfredo ($11.95). Linguini with pesto and shrimp, Cajun shrimp and chicken primavera are other possibilities. All dinners come with a small antipasto and garlic bread, but you might want to start with fontana fritters or a crock of shrimp stew. Open daily in summer, 11 to 2 and 4:30 to 9 or 10.

The Lobster Shop, Route 27, West Southport. (207) 633-4611. A couple of picnic benches outside and a few tables inside. That's about all at this little roadside stand run by Beverly and Brenda Tibbetts, mother and daughter. Locals rave about the lobster rolls ($6.50), and the Newagen Seaside Inn buys its dessert pies here. The fare is limited: fried fish, hot dogs, BLTs, and fried shrimp or scallop dinners ($7.25 and $8, respectively). Or stop in for the homemade ice cream cookie bar and the whoopie pie, chocolate chip cookies stuck together with ice cream. Open daily except Monday, 11 to 7 or 8.

Cavoli's, 15 McKown St., Boothbay Harbor, is the place to go for takeout food. Most sandwiches are $3.95 to $4.95 and there are a couple of tables on the front porch if you want to eat there. Several interesting salads, splits of wine and cookies (heath bar cookies are 80 cents) are available, as are pates, cheeses, coffee beans, flavored oils and salsas. The staff here will prepare and pack picnics to go. If you are craving something cold, drop in at the **Ice Cream Parlor** almost across the street for a cone; Round Top and Deering ice creams are served here and the owners are known for their large portions. The blueberry cheesecake and peach flavors are especially good.

FOR MORE INFORMATION: Boothbay Harbor Chamber of Commerce, Route 27, Box 356, Boothbay Harbor, Me. 04538. (207) 633-2353. The information booth is on Route 27 just before the harbor area.

Old boats and waterfront structures are typical of Vinalhaven.

Vinalhaven-Camden, Me.

Penobscot Bay is Maine's largest and most interesting. Dotted with islands and busy with lobster boats and windjammers (more sailing trips leave from Camden than from any other port in Maine), it presents an ever-changing picture to visitors.

Lobster is king here. Lobster buoys dot the water and those sturdy lobster boats head out early in the morning, not to return until the end of a hard day. The result is both picturesque and palate-pleasing; lobsters are offered up by area restaurants in guises ranging from roll to newburg, with the standard New England boiled lobster probably first in popularity.

We love lobster but it isn't that alone which draws us to the Penobscot Bay area. The sea is magnificent, tumbling toward a rocky coast edged with the dark and fragrant pines for which Maine is famed. The skies are alternately brooding and bright, clouds scudding across the blue or forming into thunderheads with little warning.

Sailors must know their stuff, and they do. Windjammers ply the waters with graceful sails unfurled, their bows rising and falling with the rhythm of the sea. The tang of salt air fills our nostrils; we breathe deeply and feel energized. There is something about this part of Maine that beckons us back again and again.

Here we sample two places in or on Penobscot Bay: the island of Vinalhaven, and the picturesque seaside village of Camden. Both are do-able in one trip, and each has a special flavor.

Vinalhaven

One of the more populated island communities off the coast of Maine (some 1,200 year-round residents) and larger than most in size (five by eight miles), Vinalhaven is home to an active fishing community. The harbor is very much a working harbor and the island fishermen are busy setting and hauling traps much of the time.

Fishing wasn't always the main industry. Quarrying was, and Vinalhaven granite can be found in the Museum of Fine Arts in Boston and the Cathedral

335

of St. John the Divine in New York City. In the center of the village of Vinalhaven is a large, bright blue "galamander," a wheeled vehicle drawn by oxen and used to haul huge pieces of granite from quarry to boat. Two abandoned quarries have new lives as spring-fed, freshwater swimming areas; you can sunbathe on the rocks surrounding these clear pools. The rocky coast and cold water aren't conducive to ocean swimming, and few attempt it.

Vinalhaven's distance from shore (90 minutes by ferry) and the size of its ferry (maximum of ten to twelve cars and trucks) have helped to limit commercialization.

There's only so much to do here. It's enough for day trippers — who love to visit — and enough for weekenders. If you want to stay longer, know that this will be a low-key vacation. The village, where you'll be likely to stay, is interesting. Neat Victorian houses are mixed among the simpler fishermen's homes. A short Main Street has a variety of small stores and eating places. It's only a short distance from the ferry landing to the village.

Getting There

Vinalhaven is reached by ferry from Rockland, Me. One innkeeper describes it as "the best boat ride, for the money, in the state of Maine." It's a scenic ride on a clear day, across Penobscot Bay and through islands rimmed in spruce and granite, with the possibility of spotting seals (we did). On a foggy day, the passage is eerie as the captain threads between the islands, thanks to radar and his thorough knowledge of the channel.

The Governor Curtis, Rockland Ferry Terminal, 517 Main St., Rockland. (207) 594-5543. The schedule varies, but the latest in summer has been four trips daily on Monday, Wednesday and Friday, leaving Rockland at 8:30, noon, 3 and 6; leaving Vinalhaven at 7, 10, 1:30 and 4:30. There are three trips on Tuesday, Thursday and Saturday, leaving Rockland at 8:45, 1 and 4:45; leaving Vinalhaven at 7, 11:30 and 3:15; leaving Vinalhaven. Sunday also has three trips, from Rockland at 9, 1:30 and 5, from Vinalhaven at 7:30, noon and 3:30. Reservations for cars should be made one month ahead, but are scarce due to heavy summer traffic. Round-trip cost for adults is $3.50, children $2, bicycles $3.25 and cars $15.

The village of Vinalhaven and all its services are a short walk from the ferry terminal. In addition, the Coastal Trans van, 596-6605, a government-subsidized transportation service, meets most ferries and can be hired for trips to the grocers or to and from your cottage. Bikes are useful for short trips, but the narrow island roads are unsuitable for pleasure biking.

If you come in your own boat, you'll find gas, diesel fuel and water at Calderwoods Wharf on the harbor. You can stock up with groceries, wine, beer or liquor there. Moorings are also available.

Where to Stay

The Fox Island Inn, Carver Street, Vinalhaven 04863. (207) 863-2122. This is a short distance from the village center on a side street lined with island homes. Guests enjoy a living room and a game room off the kitchen. Three doubles and one single on the first floor share a bathroom and two bedrooms upstairs share another bath. Buffet-style breakfast includes homemade breads and muffins wih coffee, tea, hot chocolate and orange juice. Owners Anita and Peter Sandefur house overflow guests in an annex set high on the other side of the village. Muffins and coffee are the breakfast fare there. Doubles, $45 and up. Open May-October.

Tidewater Motel, On the Harbor, Vinalhaven 04863. (207) 863-4618. The location of this ordinary looking motel at the foot of Carver's Harbor in the heart of the village cannot be surpassed. All but two of the eleven units have a wide view of the busy harbor. Two units have small kitchens. The motel, owned by Elaine and Philip Crossman with Ellen Adams as the genial manager, rents bikes by the day. Doubles, $65 to $79; open year-round.

RENTALS. A few summer cottages are available. Check with realtors Lorraine Walker, (207) 863-4474; George Harrison, (207) 863-4987, or Wesley Reed, (207) 863-2554. The Wind, the local news sheet, often carries For Rent ads.

Seeing and Doing

To tour the island *and* learn all about it, hire George Harrison, 863-4987. He will give you a 90-minute ride to the island parks, quarries and scenic sights, and relate the history of quarrying granite, the fishing industry, as well as point out the striking architecture of many old homes. The tour is $25 for a party of one to five.

Life goes at a slower pace on the island, but there's much to do. Each summer the **Fox Island Concert Series** brings outstanding musicians for three or four concerts. Townspeople and summer visitors often put on original shows at the ARC (Arts and Recreation Center), where dances and concerts are also held. At least once each summer a visiting band gives an outdoor concert on Armbrust Hill, a town park. Friends of the Library also provide one or two programs, both educational and amusing.

Visit the **Fog Gallery** at Harbor Wharf, where the work of local and visiting artists is displayed. Shows change every week.

The **Vinalhaven Historic Society Museum** on High Street, 863-4969, is well worth a visit. In one large room are gathered memorabilia from island families, ranging from Cantonese china plates to an old foot-pedal-powered dentist's drill. We enjoyed prints of the Lane-Libby fishing factory, a photo of a 155-pound lobster, a codfish skin and samples of granite quarried on the island. Copies of all yearbooks from the island's school give a taste of the place. Open daily in summer, 11 to 3.

For simple pleasures, wander along Main Street in the heart of the village. Visit the **Paper Store** to buy a souvenir, pick up a newspaper or fax a message home. Stop in the **Island Crafts Variety Store** and step back in time. Your children will want to pick out penny candy from the row of glass jars. Check out the handmade articles for sale. Admire the massive **Odd Fellows Lodge,** now the home of nationally known artist Robert Indiana. Finally, stop in either the **Village Center** shop or the **Night Hawk** for a reviving snack.

On Saturdays at 10 a.m., there's a flea market up by **Union Church.** On Sunday, go to church and see the exquisite stained-glass windows contributed by well-to-do families and organizations a hundred years ago. Enjoy the music of the equally old organ, still in excellent condition. Thursday night, return to church for a baked-bean supper, followed by the best pies you've ever eaten.

Bring your camera. The photo opportunities are endless from the time you leave Rockland on the ferry. Bring a heavy sweater; it's usually cooler on Vinalhaven than on the mainland. Stop at the Town Office Building to pick up a guide to island parks. Finally, be warned that there are only three public restrooms in the village: at the ferry terminal, the Town Wharf building and the Town Office building.

Those with cars have 38 miles of roads to drive, not all in good condition. Many people drive to the island's northern end to look out at North Haven, a neighboring island with a pretty seafront village, where IBM's Thomas Watson has a place. The lighthouse, Brown's Head Light, is not particularly picturesque, but beyond it you can see the bay, usually studded with sailboats. We liked Tip Toe Mountain, off Crockett River Road. It's an easy climb, and you're rewarded with magnificent views of Crockett's Cove and Dogfish Island.

Where to Eat

There are two restaurants, an upscale snack shop, several grocery stores and several casual, basic-food places. Wine and beer are sold in groceries. Calderwoods Wharf, on the road to the ferry, is the state liquor outlet.

The Haven, Main Street, Vinalhaven. (207) 863-4969. Located on the waterfront, this has two small dining rooms and a varied menu, and is the only place on the island with a license to serve alcoholic drinks. Co-owner Roy Heisler calls the food of his partner, chef Esther Bissell, creative eclectic American with a Mediterranean and Asian influence. Lobster is always available but is not a specialty. Prices range from $9.95 to $14.95. Dinner at 6 and 8, reservations advised. Open Memorial Day weekend to Columbus Day.

The Mill Race, Main Street, Vinalhaven. (207) 863-9366. This local haunt has a melange of chairs at mismatched tables covered with red oilcloth. Seafood dishes are the speciality and steak is available. Dinner prices range from $9 to $14. The Mill Race is also a popular breakfast and lunch meeting place. While there, browse through the small gift shop up front. Owners Barbara and John Morton also operate the aptly named **Harbor Gawker.** This is a window opening on Main Street where you can get a lobster or crab roll, hamburger or fish chowder and a beverage to go. Take your purchase ($2.50 to $5) across the street, where you can sit on a bench and survey harbor activity. Both open daily, summer only.

The Night Hawk, also on Main Street, is open year-round. Owned by Mary Hurtubise and Cynthia Day, it serves homemade muffins, cinnamon rolls, croissants, sandwiches on homemade bread, salads and chowder; $3.95 will buy a bowl of scallop chowder or a roast beef sandwich; for $2 you get coffee and a croissant. The small shop is located in an old drug store with its paneling, shelves and tiny drawers for storing pharmaceuticals unchanged. Several ice-cream-parlor tables and chairs provide seating. On shelves at one side of the room are eye-catching gourmet and health foods, jars of Maine wild blueberry syrup, dried fruit, sunflower seeds and herb tea. The food is good and the ambiance is a mixture of old and very new. Open Monday-Saturday, 7 to 7.

Camden

Compared with Vinalhaven, Camden is civilized, commercial and touristy. It got that way because it possesses extraordinary natural endowments. The long, narrow harbor is crowded with tall-masted schooners. Behind the town, the Camden Hills form a kind of natural amphitheater. Who wouldn't love it?

Thousands do. They come year-round, but especially in the summer. Consider the opportunities: Shakespeare in the park, rental boats of all sizes and shapes in the harbor, dining on the wharf, shopping in boutiques, staying in one of the many B&Bs and inns, eating lobsters and steamers and blueberry everything.

Camden serves as an embarkation point for windjammer cruises. Most leave town Monday morning and return the following Saturday. Passengers arrive late Sunday afternoon. If you're around, walk the docks and watch the action.

Where to Stay

The Whitehall Inn, High Street (Route 1), Box 558, Camden 04843. (207) 236-3391. Run by various members of the Dewing family, this comfortable white inn with green shutters on the edge of town has a distant view of Penobscot Bay. A Camden classic dating to the mid-1800s, it is associated with poet Edna St. Vincent Millay, who grew up in the area and gave a poetry reading here in 1912. Off the main parlor, a Millay memorabilia room displays her high school diploma and several photos. Huge old rockers with rush backs and seats are lined up along the front porch and guests sometimes carry breakfast coffee there to sit and stare out to sea. This is an old-fashioned place, upfront about the fact that most of the original fixtures are intact, there have been no major renovations since the early days and there are no TVs in the 50 rooms; you're welcome to work on puzzles in the parlor. There are a shuffleboard court and a tennis court. Two Victorian houses across the street are part of the inn. All accommodations are twin or one double bed, and half have private baths. Breakfast and dinner in a country elegant dining room are included in the room rates. Doubles, $125 to $155, MAP. Open Memorial Day to late October.

Norumbega, High Street, Camden 04843. (207) 236-4646. One of the great late 19th-century villas along the Maine coast is this treasure, opened in 1984 as a B&B and run with panache by Californians Murray and Elisabeth Keatinge. The cobblestone-walled mansion looks like a castle. Inside are endlessly fascinating public rooms (the woodwork alone is priceless) and twelve large bedrooms and a new penthouse suite, all with private bath. Most are sumptuously decorated by Elisabeth (the ones in back of the house have breathtaking views of Penobscot Bay). A little porch with two deck chairs and a fabulous view of the ocean, a circular black tub with pillows and big enough for two, a wet bar and a see-through, three-side fireplace are features of the penthouse suite, a bit of a hike up a circular staircase from the third floor. Flower-laden decks go off all the other floors, and expansive lawns slope down to the bay. Wine and hors d'oeuvres are served in the afternoon, but breakfast is the day's highlight. Served at a long table in the formal dining room or a round glass table in the conservatory, it is a feast of juices and fruits, all kinds of breads and muffins, and, when we stayed, the best french toast ever, topped with a dollop of sherbet and sliced oranges. Doubles, $175 to $195; suite, $350.

Edgecombe-Coles House, 64 High St., Box 3010, Camden 04843. (207) 236-2336. This classic Camden summer home has been restored to its original style and furnished with country antiques and original art by Terry and Louise Price. They offer six rooms, all with private baths, and three with ocean views. We're partial to Sea Star, a large room with kingsize brass bed, working fireplace, small TV and a stunning view through the front windows. Others fall for all the stuffed lambs and pastoral paintings in the Herdwick Room and the collection of bunnies in Flopsy's Room. All guests relish the views across the lawns to the bay from the wraparound front porch, restored to its original look and furnished in wicker. Two sitting rooms are full of antiques, samplers, decoys, wreaths, oriental rugs and such. Gourmet breakfasts are de rigeur in the expansive dining room. Doubles, $100 to $145; two-night minimum in summer.

Camden Harbour Inn, 83 Bay View St., Camden 04843. (207) 236-4200. This large white inn with 22 guest rooms high on a hill has a magnificent vista of the harbor below. A late 19th-century establishment, it has been updated and enlarged; there are four new guest rooms and a solarium dining room with great water views. The renovated main parlor has comfortable chairs and couches plus tables for games and puzzles. Two front guest rooms overlook the bay and have their own decks; a fireplaced suite has a lounge area and private porch with a view. Otherwise the eighteen guest rooms in the original structure are of 19th-century vintage, with clawfoot tubs, period antiques and Victorian wicker. Breakfast is included in the rates. Dinner in the solarium offers a varied menu with emphasis on seafood, priced from $12.95 for broiled scallops with honey-lime butter to $16.95 for a shore dinner. Half the menu changes weekly to offer treats like three-mustard veal and whole wheat linguini with monkfish and cilantro. You can have a drink at the **Thirsty Whale Bar.** Doubles, $145 to $185.

Hawthorn Inn, 9 High St., Camden 04843. (207) 236-8842. Classical music wafts through the Victorian parlors of this stately 1884 mansion. Five guest rooms, three with private baths, radiate from the second-floor hallway. Downstairs in the basement are two new garden bedrooms furnished in contemporary style, one that struck us as rather strange with a freestanding clawfoot tub and a semi-partitioned toilet right in the room. Best are the four new rooms in the adjacent carriage house; they can be rented separately or as townhouse apartments with kitchenettes. The balconied bedrooms have queen beds, pretty stenciling and huge jacuzzis under skylights. All carriage house rooms have private decks with views of Camden's harbor. A full breakfast, often including eggs florentine or spanakopita and fruit salads, is served in the inn's fireplaced dining room or on the sunny outside deck. English innkeeper Pauline Staub and her husband Brad also serve tea or lemonade in the afternoons. Doubles, $75 to $85; carriage house, $105 to $135; townhouse apartments, $200.

Lord Camden Inn, 24 Main St., Camden 04843. (207) 236-4325 or (800) 336-4325. You're right in the center of town, above the shops, when you stay at this recently restored brick inn with an elevator. Rooms are on the third and fourth floors (some of those to the rear have cheerful little decks with a view across the rooftops to the Megunticook River and the hills; those in front on the fourth floor have small balconies with a view of the harbor). All 28 rooms are furnished in period style and all have private baths, TV sets and phones. A continental breakfast is brought to the room. Doubles, $118 to $158.

The Owl and the Turtle, 8 Bay View St., Camden 04843. (207) 236-9014 or 236-8759. Book lovers will like these three guest rooms located over an exceptional bookstore of the same name. Each room has a balcony with a panoramic, close-up harbor view; the pleasant, paneled rooms have private baths and air-conditioning. The location puts you in the center of harborfront activity. And all those books to choose from for bedtime reading! Continental breakfast is served in your room in the morning. Doubles, $70 to $75.

The High Tide Inn, Route 1, Camden 04843. (207) 236-3724. This manicured waterfront complex of seven acres north of town has all sorts of accommodations: five inn rooms in the main house, two motel-style buildings totaling seventeen units, two units in a duplex and five individual cottages. It is one of the few places with its own, albeit rocky, beach; we felt like ballet dancers trying to negotiate the rocks for a swim. There are chaises and chairs for sunning on a velvety lawn as well. Popovers, homemade blueberry and bran muffins, and banana bread like your mother used to bake are served buffet-style at a complimentary breakfast in the inn's enclosed porch facing the water. New owners Jo and Steve Freilich took over in 1990; a decorator from New Jersey, she said she was "chafing at the bit" to upgrade the common rooms and guest rooms starting in 1991. We're looking forward to it, for we felt our oceanfront room priced at $115 was a bit steep — it was a quite ordinary if not drab motel room, except for the view and its location away from the road. Inn rooms, $55 to $75; cottages, $80 to $90; motel, $85 to $115. Open late May through mid-October.

The Spouter Inn, Route 1, Box 176, Lincolnville Beach 04849. (207) 789-5171. Three guest rooms and a suite with private baths and ocean views are offered in the B&B opened by Paul and Catherine Lippman and their two youngsters in 1989. Across the highway from the ferry landing, it's popular with those taking the ferry to or from Islesboro. Stained-glass windows, stenciling, antiques and country touches abound in both guest rooms and common rooms. A hearty breakfast is served in the dining room at a magnificent table and chairs that we recognized as having come from Norumbega — Paul picked them up at a Rotary Club auction. The suite, with bedroom, living room with sleeping accommodations, eat-in kitchen and private deck, is a good value for a family. Doubles, $75 to $85; suite, $125.

Water's Edge Motor Inn, Route 1, Lincolnville Beach 04859. (207) 04849. One of the area's few motels with water views, this is fairly primitive. There are five motel rooms with sliding doors onto private decks overlooking the swimming pool and seven cottages rather close together along the road. The decks behind the cottages are as big as the rooms, which are outfitted with TV and a double bed or a double and a twin bed. The pool out back is an asset here, and you can stroll down a dirt road to a private beach. Breakfast is available for guests and the public in a little open-air restaurant between the motel and the cottages. Doubles, $60; cottages, $45 to $75.

CAMPING. Camden Hills State Park has 112 sites, none with electrical hookups. Hot showers are available from June 15 to Labor Day. You're advised to arrive early in the day to claim a site.

Seeing and Doing

Windjammer cruises. Several gorgeous schooners take passengers on six-day sailing trips along the coast of Maine, leaving Camden Monday and returning Saturday. Activities include swimming, sunning, helping to sail the boat, and eating hearty meals. At night there's often a songfest or time to explore the shore. Typical of the windjammers is the Angelique run by Mike and Lynne McKenry, 236-8873 or (800) 282-9989.

Sail aboard the schooner **Surprise,** 236-4687, a 55-foot-long hulk departing four times daily from Camden Public Landing on trips of two or three hours, $20 per person, including snacks. Barbara and Jack Moore, former teachers who educated their four children on their ketch during seven years of voyaging between Maine and the Caribbean, are said to give the best trips around. Another 55-foot schooner, the **Olad,** 236-2323, also gives four two-hours trips a day for $12 to $15 each.

Also highly rated is the 87-foot **Appledore,** 236-9353, the only windjammer and largest vessel offering two-hour trips and daysails out of Camden from Sharp's Wharf, next to the town landing. Reminiscent of the commuter yachts of the 1920s, the **Black Swan,** 236-4449, takes up to six passengers on two-hour wildlife and scenery cruises among the islands of Penobscot Bay ($50 each) and special champagne and lobster stew lunch cruises ($65).

Lobster fishing trips aboard the **Lively Lady** leave four times daily from Sharp's Wharf, adults $10 and children $5.

Sea Touring Kayak Center of Maine, 123 Elm St., 236-9569, rents kayaks and canoes and sponsors daylong paddle trips on Penobscot Bay. Canoes, sailboards and bikes also are rented by the day or week from **Maine Sport Outfitters,** 236-8797, in Camden and Rockport.

The **Rockport Apprenticeshop,** Sea Street, Rockport Harbor, a school of wooden boatbuilding, has a visitor's loft that is open daily from May 30 to mid-October.

TOURING AND HIKING. Some of the East Coast's best hiking is available on 25 miles of trails in **Camden Hills State Park. Mount Megunticook** is the second highest point on the Eastern Seaboard. If you don't feel like hiking, drive the toll road up **Mount Battie,** an easy one-mile drive; the view is worth the $1 per person toll. Another scenic drive is out Route 52 to **Megunticook Lake.** A walking tour of Camden and a bicycle or car tour of Camden and Rockport are available through the Camden-Rockport Historical Society.

Cultural Attractions. The **Camden Shakespeare Company,** founded in 1978, gives four plays in repertory in the summer in the natural, stone-tiered Bok Amphitheater near the harbor. The sylvan setting adds a lot to matinee or evening performances. The **Farnsworth Museum** in nearby Rockland ranks among the finer regional art museums in the country. The collection focuses on American art from the 18th century to the present, with many prized works by the Wyeth family. The **Shore Village Museum,** also in Rockland, has an intriguing collection of lighthouse and Coast Guard memorabilia.

SHOPPING. Sophisticated shopping is available in Camden. **The Smiling Cow,** a large and venerable gift shop with a great collection of Maine items, has a view from its rear porch over a river that ripples down rocks toward the harbor. **Unique 1** specializes in natural fiber sweaters, but also has pottery, baskets and gifts. **Heather Harland** offers interesting kitchen items and cards. **The Admiral's Buttons** specializes in preppy clothing and sailing attire. **Once a Tree** has good wooden items. **Haskell & Corthell** and the **House of Logan** are nice women's apparel stores. **The Winemporium** has a good selection of wines and food products, many of them, like the local goat cheese, from Maine.

Where to Eat

The Waterfront Restaurant, Harborside Square off Bay View Street, Camden. (207) 236-3747. There is no nicer waterside setting in Camden than this establishment with a large outdoor deck shaded by a white canvas tarpaulin that resembles a boat's sails. Blue canvas director's chairs at bare wooden tables continue the nautical feeling. Bread sticks with a crock of cheese and grapes and celery appeared on the table as we were seated; next came a basket of good warm bread. Salads in glass bowls are dressed with any of four outstanding dressings: sweet-and-sour bacon, lemon-parmesan, vinaigrette and blue cheese. Among appetizers are mussels, calamari and shrimp, baked brie and soups. Dinner entrees ($11.95 to $14.95) include cioppino, New England crab cakes, cajun barbecued shrimp, linguini with salmon and sundried tomatoes, filet of beef with a sweet red pepper salsa and a special of swordfish grilled over applewood with rosemary, which was juicy and succulent. Mint chocolate chip pie with hot fudge sauce and whipped cream proved to be the ultimate dessert. All sorts of shellfish, including a smoked fish sampler, and light fare from hamburger to lobster roll are available at the oyster bar and new outdoor grill, open from 2:30 until closing. Lunch daily, 11:30 to 2:30; dinner 5 to 10.

The Belmont, 6 Belmont Ave., Camden. (207) 236-8053. The menu changes almost daily at this inn and restaurant, which has a pristine dining room with well-spaced tables dressed in white and a handful of tables on a summery sun porch at the side. Chef-owner Gerry Clare took over in 1988 from the folks who had given this quite a culinary reputation as Aubergine. He's into regional American cuisine, and some of it is inspired, like an appetizer of grilled oysters in pancetta with two sauces (a triumph, as it should have been for $8.50) and a white gazpacho with delicious homemade croutons. They outshone our entrees, grilled chicken with polenta and a tri-pepper compote and a special of poached salmon with a citrus sauce, chosen among half a dozen entrees priced from $11 to $21. The thick sour cream blueberry cheesecake was sensational, the strawberries Luxembourg with champagne sabayon not so. There's a small bar off the reception room. Upstairs are six guest rooms and suites with private baths, all dressed up a bit with new wallpapers and fresh flowers by Gerry and partner John Mancarella and renting for $95 to $125 a night. Dinner nightly except Monday, 6 to 9:30. Open May-October.

Cassoulet, 31 Elm St., Camden. (207) 236-6304. In its former incarnation, this was the Secret Garden, so named for the hidden garden in the back. Owners Sally and Bob Teague enclosed the garden in 1990 with a screened porch that's summery as can be with pink deck chairs and dusty pink table cloths, an abundance of hanging plants and fresh flowers all around. One of the cooks was picking mint and flowers to garnish the desserts when we peeked in one afternoon. On a pleasant evening, the porch-garden is heaven, but that's not to denigrate the intimate and colorful interior dining room with cacti in the windows, flowers in little carafes and striking pictures of flowers on the walls. Bob Teague, the chef, oversees a small, creative menu supplemented by nightly specials. You might start with mussels mariniere, caponata (chilled eggplant relish served with crostini) or oysters broiled with pesto and move on to entrees ($13 to $18) like shrimp a la grecque, a French cassoulet, a changing Mediterranean seafood stew, baked halibut with pesto and fresh tomatoes, or broiled filet mignon with a rich cognac sauce. For dessert, how about divine decadence (a fudgy cake with brandy-soaked apricots), frozen lemon mousse, or a fresh blueberry tart in a pate sucre with a pecan streusel? Dinner nightly, 6 to 9. Closed Sunday in off-season.

Cappy's Chowder House, Main Street, Camden. (207) 236-2254. Right in the center of town, Cappy's is *the* place for breakfast, and is in demand for lunch and dinner, too. Lobster traps hang above the bar, one wall is exposed brick, and green billiard-room lamps hang above bare pine tables. Your placemat is your breakfast menu ($2 to $4) and offers "pure eggstasy" (country eggs prepared any style), the "omelette shoppe" and pancakes including Maine blueberry and apple spice. The grapefruit is do-it-yourself; a knife comes with it. Soft rock plays in the background and young servers rush around. For lunch or dinner you can have the Penobscot, a grilled crab salad sandwich with swiss cheese, tomato and dijon mustard ($5.25) or pasta and shrimp salad served on greens ($5.95). The Crow's Nest with a raw bar is a good spot for happy hour; it has a similar menu and a view of the harbor. Dinner includes seafood stir-fry, skewered scallops and blueberry chicken in the $9.95 to $12.95 range. Buy goodies at the bakery below, where the morning special might be an apple croissant and coffee for $1.10. Open daily, 7:30 to midnight.

Peter Ott's, Bayview Street, Camden. (207) 236-4032. This steakhouse and tavern is favored by locals, who pack a rather dark, nautical dining room almost every night. Black angus sirloin steaks are featured in the $11.95 to $13.95 range, but you also can get chicken barbados or teriyaki, pasta of the day, and specials like filet of haddock with avocado garnish and lime caper sauce. The chef's steak special might be charbroiled ribeye with brandy, mushroom and tarragon cream ($15.95). The salad bar comes with. Dinner nightly, 5:30 to 10.

O'Neil's, 21 Bayview St., Camden. (207) 236-3272. A shady outdoor deck off the rear of the second floor is popular at this informal restaurant on two levels. Pastas and Mexican dishes are featured on the dinner menu ($6.95 to $14.95), black bean burrito and pasta with scallops and sundried tomatoes mixing with a grilled ribeye steak with sauteed vidalia onions and fresh salsa. Hefty salads and trendy appetizers are available at dinner as well as at lunch. Lunch daily, 11:30 to 3; dinner, 5 to 10.

Harbor View Tavern, 1 Water St., Thomaston. (207) 354-8173. You want good food with a water view? Try to find this hard-to-find, funky eatery with a darkened dining room/tavern that's too atmospheric for words and, beyond, an enclosed porch overlooking the water. A Camden innkeeper said it's a favorite with locals, and only locals could find it down an unmarked roadway next to the Pier gift shop (just keep asking and you'll eventually get there). An upside-down perambulator on the ceiling greets the visitor, who's immediately immersed in a melange of old masks, license plates, photos, books, signs and such. But there's much up to date in this old boat-building facility, from the day's sports page from USA Today posted in the men's room to the garnishes and artful presentations of our lunches. The chicken basil pasta salad ($7.95) was garnished with sliced strawberries, oranges and watermelons; ditto for the fries and coleslaw that accompanied the crab cristo ($5.95). Two candies came with the bill. Dinnertime brings a limited menu of appetizers, light fare and entrees ($10.95 to $14.95) like stuffed haddock, scallops au gratin and filet mignon. Lunch daily, 11:30 to 4; dinner, 5 to 10.

Chez Michel, Route 1, Lincolnville Beach. (207) 789-5600. A water view across the street is offered at this simple country French restaurant opened in 1990 by Michel and Joan Hetuin, he a former chef at the Helm restaurant in Rockport. It's a simple room crowded with formica tables and pink-painted wooden chairs with green upholstered seats. At lunchtime, we enjoyed an avocado-tomato-cheddar melt ($3.95) and a fried clam roll ($4.95), plus Joan's fantastic raspberry pie with a cream-cheese base and an extra-good crust ($2.50). Fried fish and local seafood also are available at night, when the chef offers such entrees as vegetarian couscous, scallops provencale, mussels mariniere, bouillabaisse, beef bourguignonne, lamb kabob and steak au poivre ($9.95 to $13.95). So taken was one long-term guest that his Camden innkeeper reported he went there for dinner seven nights out of ten. Open daily except Monday, 11:30 to 9.

Lobster Pound Restaurant, Route 1, Lincolnville Beach. (207) 789-5550. Three generations of the McLaughlin family run this enormous place, a landmark along the waterfront with a cocktail lounge, a jaunty waterside deck and lobsters at rest in salt-air tanks outside. Whole boiled lobster is available by the pound, $9.75 for a one-pounder and $18.50 for a two-pounder last we knew. Seafood dinners, mostly fried or broiled, range from $10.95 to $20.95. You also can get fried chicken, ham, roast turkey and steak. An inexpensive breakfast menu includes pancakes and Belgian waffles. Open daily, 11:30 to 9; breakfast in summer, 7:30 to 11.

FOR MORE INFORMATION: Rockport-Camden-Lincolnville Chamber of Commerce, Public Landing, Box 919, Camden, Me. 04843. (207) 236-4404. For the islands, contact the Maine Publicity Bureau, 97 Winthrop St., Hallowell, Maine 04347. (207) 289-2423.

Historic John Perkins House overlooks the water at Castine.

Castine, Me.

Poised on a peninsula jutting into East Penobscot Bay, Castine is an enclave of peace and quiet.

Therein lies a certain irony, for this sedate little town was forged from a military heritage and a maritime disposition. Founded in 1613 as a French trading colony that evolved into the first permanent settlement in New England, Castine was a major battlefield through the French and Indian wars, the American Revolution and the War of 1812. No fewer than sixteen fortifications have been built on the peninsula since 1635, so it comes as no surprise that the town's only through street is named Battle Avenue.

Its maritime bent is evident in the windjammers in its harbor and by the Maine Maritime Academy, the dominant presence in Castine today. In their rowdier off-duty moments, academy cadets may tie one on in the boisterous waterfront Quarterdeck Tavern when their enormous training vessel *State of Maine* is tied up at the town dock.

Otherwise, all is prim and proper in this quietly prosperous town, which local historian Gardiner E. Gregory says was the second wealthiest per capita in the United States in the 19th century. Long a summer colony, Castine is evolving into a year-round community. Culture thrives in a quaint summer theater and an impressive museum, and visitors are well cared for in four inns.

History is more noticeable here than in most such places, if only because there's a large historical marker at almost every turn. You can marvel at them all on a couple of walking tours, climb around the embankments of Revolutionary forts, tour the pre-Revolutionary John Perkins House and watch a blacksmith at work. You can see the inside of the State of Maine ship, look for seals on a harbor cruise, thrill to the windjammers near the yacht club and feast on seafood at one of the more atmospheric waterside restaurants in all of Maine.

345

Castine is a haven for rest and relaxation, blessedly off by itself and away from the mainstream.

Getting There

About 40 miles due south of Bangor, Castine is located at the tip of a peninsula, opposite Belfast across East Penobscot Bay. From Route 1 at Orland, take Route 175 and Route 166 to Castine.

Where to Stay_____*ᏗᏗᏗ*

Pentagoet Inn, Main Street, Box 4, Castine 04421. (207) 326-8616. Owners Lindsey and Virginia Miller from Arkansas — he a physician and she a nurse — have upgraded the venerable Pentagoet since acquiring it in 1985. Their downstairs parlors (one a well-outfitted library and the other with a nifty windowseat looking toward the harbor) are smashingly refurbished in seafoam shades, and the shaded verandas are made for rocking. The pristine dining room has an addition looking out over terraced gardens, and there's a sparkling new kitchen. Two-night minimum stays, MAP meal requirements and a cocktail hour with the innkeepers are intended "to make this a highly desirable experience for our house guests," in Virginia Miller's words. Quiet and sedate, the turreted main inn has twelve guest rooms, all with private baths, and antique furnishings. From a large armchair near the brass bedstead in the third-floor turret you can glimpse the harbor; outside the door, some of Virginia's collection of teddybears are seated on a sofa. We thought the bathroom off our kingsize room — with color-coordinated wallpapers, curtains and patterned rug and a basket of towels in shades of pink — a work of art. Perhaps the nicest rooms are in the 200-year-old house (called 10 Perkins Street) behind the inn. All six rooms there with oriental rugs on wide-planked wood floors have private baths; two have church-pew benches and one has a small sitting room with fireplace. Guests who don't want the nightly turn-down service are advised to hang the special "napping" sign on their door while at dinner. The changing breakfast menu might include cantaloupe, homemade granola, sourdough blueberry pancakes and Canadian bacon. The toast, made from homemade whole wheat bread, is delectable. Doubles, $170, MAP. Open April-November. No smoking.

Castine Inn, Main Street, Box 41, Castine 04421. (207) 326-4365. Perfect for people-watching, a pleasant front porch with polka-dot covered seats and a profusion of flowers welcomes guests to the Castine Inn, built in 1898 and operated continuously since. Owners Mark and Margaret Hodesh have redone the front parlor and spiffed up fourteen guest rooms, now all with private baths, opening hotel-style off a long wide corridor. They also opened six more on the third floor. All rooms are carpeted and comfortable with a double or two twin beds; the newer ones have bright wallpapers and colorful accents. Recently, they added a sunny side deck with a view of Mark's elaborate new gardens and the harbor in the distance. The gardens draw almost as many raves as do the striking murals of Castine, beautifully done by artist Margaret, in the dining room. The talented couple have infused their inn with their vibrant personalities. A wood-burning fireplace warms the front parlor, and the dark cozy pub tucked away in a hidden corner is inviting indeed in English hunting green. A table in the spacious entry foyer contains all manner of local brochures, sometimes including the inn's own informative guides to diversions and shopping. Complimentary breakfast includes hash every day, pancakes, sausages and fresh muffins. Doubles, $75 to $95. Two-night minimum in summer. Open mid-April through October.

The Holiday House, Perkins Street, Box 215, Castine 04421. (207) 326-4335. Paul and Sara Brouillard, who got their innkeeping start at the Manor (see below), realized their dream of opening an oceanfront inn in 1990. And oceanfront it is: an Edwardian mansion built in 1893 with nine guest rooms, all with water views — even from some of the seven private bathrooms. At the rear, a lovely wraparound porch full of wicker and another open porch with deck chairs take full advantage of the view, as do a couple of enormous living rooms (one part has a gigantic sectional sofa facing the fireplace). Even the platforms for the new fire escapes in front have chairs for afternoon lounging, which seems a bit of overkill with all that view out back. The Brouillards spent several years renovating the place, which had deteriorated over the years as a lodge of the same name, and added prominent fire escapes and fire walls to bring it up to code. When we visited, Sara was gradually whipping the guest rooms into shape; those with new wallpaper and paint looked the best, of course. "This place didn't have a stick of furniture," she reported, "so we trade and buy and every day add a little more." Guests report that staying in the second-floor corner room is like being on a ship — all you can see from the bed is water. The inn also has an efficiency cottage right on the water, $750 to $895 a week. While Paul is at the Manor, Sara oversees the Holiday House, preparing a similar continental-plus breakfast of smoked meats, cereals and sometimes quiche. She was toying with the idea of changing the name to Castine Harbor Inn. Doubles, $75 to $115.

The Manor, Battle Avenue, Box 276, Castine 04421. (207) 326-4861. The sprawling turn-of-the-century summer cottage designed by Mead, McKim and White for Commodore Fuller of the New York Yacht Club in 1895 looks the way a big old Maine lodge should. You arrive up a long driveway to an edifice of brown wood and stone, a flower-bedecked terrace and an entry archway tunneling between the main house and a wing with the second floor overhead. Sara and Paul Brouillard run an inn with a laid-back spirit. Sara grew up in the house, which they have restored since saving it from demolition in 1980. Paul, a chef of note, oversees the Manor's restaurant, which he changed in 1990 from an off-again, on-again high-style dining room to a seafood bar and grill. Among the public rooms are a large sitting room with three velvet sofas to sink into, two small dining rooms (and a table in the library for intimate private parties), and an enclosed cocktail porch with a magnificent green marble and mahogany bar. All twelve guest rooms have private baths and some have fireplaces. With five acres of lawns near the end of a dead-end street, the inn is so quiet that the only sound we heard at night was made by the melodic harbor bell. The Manor serves a continental-plus buffet breakfast of smoked meats, cheeses, cereals, pastries and muffins, all decorated with fruits and nasturtiums. Doubles, $75 to $135.

Seeing and Doing _____ ⟋⟍⟋⟍

WALKING TOURS. "Welcome to Castine," a brochure you find everywhere, with maps and a history by Elizabeth J. Duff, gives specifics for a walking tour of most of Castine. You can stick to the central area, which covers Main and Water steets and the quaint, out-of-the-mainstream village common that's as picturesque as any in New England. Or you can drive, though we prefer to poke along on foot, to see a larger area embracing Perkins Street and Battle Avenue. Included are the major fortifications (Fort Madison consists of a few embankments with two picnic tables beside the water; Fort George is larger with earthen ramparts and ditches), historic sites, a public path to the water from Dyces Head lighthouse, tree-shaded Georgian and Federalist houses, buildings of the Maine Maritime Academy, and such unexpected pleasures as a tiny circular shorefront house and the enormous stucco summer home, Guerdwood. You encounter more historic markers denoting more sites than the tour map designates.

HARBOR TOURS. Castine's colorful harbor always has been dotted with yachts, sailboats, the tall-masted windjammers (usually tied up on Mondays and Tuesdays) and the ultimate incongruity for a small and sedate harbor, the towering and massive State of Maine ship. Two- or four-hour cruises and sunset cruises depart from Castine Harbor on a 31-foot wooden yawl under auspices of Captain Walter J. Harrington of Orland, 326-8588. Boat rentals frequently are available from Eaton's Boat Yard, Sea Street, 326-8579.

Swimming and Other Sports. Swimming off a long, stony beach is available to the public (no facilities) at Wadsworth Cove. The Castine swimming pool provides saltwater swimming in a pool nearby. A nine-hole golf course is open for a fee at the private Castine Golf Club, one of America's earliest (1897); its first five holes were originally on the site of adjacent Fort George. The club also has four tennis courts. The Maine Maritime Academy offers its gymnasium, pool, weight room, and squash and racquetball courts for a daily fee.

The State of Maine Ship, MMA Dock, 326-4311, Ext. 254. The 534-foot-long, ten-deck-high Maine Maritime Academy training vessel is open to the public when it is in port. MMA cadets give tours on the half hour or as desired on this combination passenger-freighter built in 1949 and in service during the Korean and Vietnamese wars. It's a hulk of a sight on the Castine waterfront, and a sight inside as well. You'll see the vast engine room, the steering mechanisms, some of the cabin rooms used by 300 cadets, the mess hall and kitchens (complete with gigantic hot food vats used one night as hot tubs by the "foodos" and from which no one would eat afterward on the cruise, our cadet guide informed). You might be told more than you want to know and climb more stairs than you want to ascend, but touring a hands-on ship used every spring for ocean training cruises is an unusual experience. Open daily, 9 to 3. Free.

The Wilson Museum, Perkins Street, 326-8753. Built in 1921 to house the extensive collections of anthropologist and geologist J. Howard Wilson, this is a highly personal place reflecting the tastes of Dr. and Mrs. Wilson and their world travels. "There's a bit of the whole world here," said the woman on duty; "the way it's laid out tells you the history of mankind back to Cyprus in 3000 B.C." Included are everything from remarkable beaded Indian moccasins and ceremonial leggins, ship models, an Indian pueblo model, firearms, stone artifacts and pottery to modern paintings by 21 artists spilling onto a rear porch above the harbor. The Wilsons' daughter, Mrs. Norman Doudiet, is the museum director and guiding force. The property also contains a working blacksmith shop, a hearse house with funeral vehicles from a century ago, and the 1763 John Perkins House, the area's oldest house, which was moved to the site in 1970. Museum is open free daily except Monday, 2 to 5, Memorial Day through September. Open Sunday and Wednesday 2 to 5 during July and August are the Blacksmith Shop and Hearse House, free, and the Perkins House, $2.

Cold Comfort Summer Theater, Delano Auditorium, Box 259, Castine, 326-4311. For more than a decade, a local theater company has been staging delightful summer productions in a low-key style. Once, a stray tomcat stole the show during "Carousel" as he sauntered across the stage in the Maine Maritime Academy dock area. After appearing in "The Mikado," the editor of the weekly Castine Patriot newspaper explained in a column why he would "put on silly clothes and sing 19th Century patter to a room full of people, when you can make a fool of yourself just as easily in print." Residents and visitors are charmed by the summer's five productions, which ranged in 1990 from "Annie" to "Medea" to "Our Town." Shows generally are Tuesday-Saturday at 8. Adults, $10.

SHOPPING. Downtown Castine consists of few but select stores. The Bragdons' **Four Flags Ship Chandlery** offers nautical equipment as well as gifts from around the world, books, jewelry, Gordon Fraser cards and, just in when we were there, a novelty scent called Eau de Low Tide. At the **Water Witch,** tall, dark and striking Jean de Raat, the water witch herself, sells a variety of fine clothing (placemats, napkins, pillows, too) made of cotton Dutch wax batiks and Java prints, as well as British Viyellas and Maine woolen fabrics; she also has an interesting mail-order catalog. **Oakum Bay Ltd.** offers antique furniture and accessories along with contemporary crafts and collectibles. **Compass Rose** has books and prints and a special section of Penguin books. Castine transplant Chris Murray sells his award-winning carved wildfowl at his **Wildlife Art Gallery.** New in 1990 was the **McGrath-Dunham Gallery.** The corner **Castine Variety Store,** called Gail's for one of its owners, carries everything from sewing machine bobbins to camera batteries; it's the place where the locals congregate starting at 6 a.m. for coffee and gossip — be advised, the counter stools are "reserved" by local custom and a visitor who sits down to order coffee is apt to be politely but firmly admonished, "that's to go."

Where to Eat

Castine Inn, Main Street, Castine. (207) 326-4365. The dinner menu changes daily but the specialties remain the same in this grand dining room, its pristine aura enhanced by the remarkable murals of Castine done by artist Margaret Parker, innkeeper with husband Mark Hodesh. The murals grace the walls, pillars and even a new service area. The plates are graced by some mighty good fare, including such specialties as crabmeat cake with mustard sauce ($4.50 as an appetizer, $13 as an entree), billi-bi, roasted eggplant and garlic soup, roast pork loin with black beans and barbecue sauce, chicken and leek pot pie, and broiled Atlantic salmon with shelled peas and egg sauce, and baked Indian pudding, almond torte with sweet and sour cherry sauce, and fresh fruit cobblers and crisps for dessert. Featured the night we were there were broiled Stonington scallops with tomato-basil butter sauce, special because the scallops were caught that day by a Stonington fisherman whose wife is a waitress. The price of the meal ($12.50 to $18) includes biscuits, potato or rice, vegetable and salad. Although Mark Hodesh is in the kitchen, he demurs to chef Richard Langsner, "who has taken us to new heights. I'm a cook; he's a chef." Dinner may be taken on the side deck and, later in the evening, desserts and nightcaps are served in the living room or on the front porch. Dinner nightly except Tuesday, 5:30 to 8:30; Sunday brunch, 10 to 1. Open mid-April through October. No smoking.

The Pentagoet Inn, Main Street, Castine. (207) 326-8616. All is serene and sophisticated in Virginia and Lindsey Miller's refurbished and expanded dining room. Virginia did the decorating; her rose-colored walls are a backdrop for bare wood floors and well-spaced tables draped in white linens, each formal place setting containing two wine glasses and a crystal water glass. To the rear, a new dining area has six tables beside a small deck with gardens beyond. Meals are prix-fixe ($25) and begin with a cocktail hour with the innkeepers in the library at 6. Our dinner started with cold smoked quail with cranberry compote, followed by a smashing barley and mushroom soup. Tournedos of beef with sauteed shrimp and pesto and sauteed lobster with sherry were winning entrees. A salad of fresh mixed greens with raspberry vinaigrette came after the main course. Fresh strawberry pie with whipped cream and chocolate sour cream cake with fudge frosting were dessert choices. Lobster is always one of the three entree choices; others could be poached salmon with lemon dill sauce, filet mignon with green peppercorn sauce or baby lamb chops with red wine sauce and chanterelles. Occasionally there is live violin background music. Dinner by reservation, nightly at 7. Open April-November. No smoking.

La Conque, The Manor, Battle Avenue, Castine. (207) 236-4066. Billed as a seafood bar and grill, this is the latest inspiration of owner Paul Brouillard, a talented chef whose other pursuits too often kept him out of the kitchen. Now he's at the grill nightly at the end of his manorial bar, cooking up a storm of light and varied fare — "sort of like Dennett's Wharf when we had it," according to wife Sara. Dining is casual — seafood from the raw bar and steamer, perhaps sea urchins, Portuguese mussels, steamed picky toe crab, a bowl of periwinkles or a steamed sampler ($14.50). To go with, how about a Jamaican conch salad, scungilli, fried clam cakes, herring in wines or Mother Brouillard's homebaked beans? "From de grille" come such skewers as a very spicy chicken mango jerk, tuna lime jerk or assorted vegetables. Grilled entrees (all $14.50) include yellowfin tuna, filet of salmon, duck breast with apricot glaze and lamb tenderloin with rosemary garlic, each accompanied with a vegetable skewer. Tables in the library and porch dining room are topped with blue and white checked cloths and an assortment of olive oil, balsamic vinegar, olives and "sauce of the dog" to accompany all the delectables. Chocolate silk and bourbon walnut pies are among the good desserts. You may want to end your meal with cordials at the elegant bar, surrounded by all kinds of carved birds. Dinner nightly, 4 to 9.

Dennett's Wharf, Sea Street, Castine. (207) 326-9045. Paul Brouillard of the Manor started this seafood emporium and lobster pound right on the water below Sea Street. The former sail and rigging loft built in the early 1900s has been upscaled, sort of, by his brother Gary, with a shoulder-high partition dividing what had been the world's longest oyster bar from the dining area and separate (as opposed to communal) tables in the dining room. We still prefer to eat outside at the hexagonal or regular picnic tables on a large deck right over the water. The menu has been downsized, the dozen or so dinner entrees ($9.95 to $14.95) running from broiled haddock to grilled swordfish and ribeye steak. Seafood lasagna and seafood linguini are house specialties. The house muscadet wine is bone dry, and about the priciest item ($14) on a cheap but good little wine list. The dessert list is a groaner: six kinds of cheesecake, pecan praline truffle and pina colada cake. Many prefer to pick their own lobster at **Dennett's in the Rough,** an outside section where lobster was going for $7.95, a lobster roll for $4.50 and a shore dinner for $14.95, last we knew. On a sunny day the deck is glorious — alas, it gets too buggy for use at night. In season, there's a busy schedule of live entertainment. Lunch daily, 11 to 3; in the rough, 11 to 5; dinner, 5 to 9. Open April-October.

Gilley's Family Restaurant, Water Street, Castine. (207) 326-4001. This place is aptly named and run by a couple who are very much in evidence. The decor is simple with a few booths, ice-cream-parlor-style tables and nautical decor. Also simple is the fare. Entrees run from $6.95 for beef liver with onions or chicken cutlet with gravy to $10.95 for a ten-ounce steak. Seafood and chowders are the rule, and at lunchtime you might order a veal parmesan sandwich. Lunch daily, 11 to 4; dinner, 4 to 8.

FOR MORE INFORMATION: Castine has no tourist information center and no Chamber of Commerce to contact. The Town Office is in Emerson Hall, Court Street, Castine, Me. 04421. (207) 326-4502.

Stonington harbor is on view from deck at Captain's Quarters.

Stonington/Deer Isle, Me.

Turn south off busy Route 1, which is apt to be filled with a steady stream of cars between Belfast and Bar Harbor, and prepare for a different pace in a timeless place.

From the scenic lookout atop Caterpillar Hill as you head down Route 176 is one of the best views in all New England. Blue waters, green islands and mountains meld into one astonishing panorama as far as the eye can see.

Cross the high, unexpectedly imposing suspension bridge over the fine sailing waters of Eggemoggin Reach to Deer Isle and enter another world: one of little traffic, no neon, no fast food, few residents and fewer tourists.

Deer Isle, the second largest island off the Maine coast, is far different from its busy and larger neighbor, Mount Desert Island. It is more like Isle au Haut, its offshore island that embraces a remote portion of Acadia National Park, whose better known section surrounds Bar Harbor.

Back in the mid-18th century, Deer Isle ranked second only to Gloucester,

Mass., as a fishing port. Later, it was the source of granite for New York's major bridges, Rockefeller Center and the John F. Kennedy Memorial in Arlington National Cemetery. At its height, Stonington, its biggest village, had 3,500 people, steamer service, a theater-opera house and something of a boomtown atmosphere.

Today, the commercial fishing fleet remains active, and lobster traps are piled all around a town permeated by the odor of fish. But Stonington's population has dwindled to 1,300 hardy souls who, we're told, rise with the sun and retire when it gets dark. "We used to have beer joints but they were nothing but trouble," reported the clerk in the state liquor store. "You'd need two trained gorillas for bouncers." So the town, commercially at least, is dry and ever so quaint and quiet.

A sign outside the island's little information center says it's open from "10 til ?" on weekdays and "11 til ?" on Sundays. But it was closed every time we passed on three successive July days.

Never mind. The appeal of Deer Isle is not in the tourist attractions (there aren't many). It's in the endearing charms of tiny towns like Deer Isle (the name of the second biggest community, as well as of the island), like Sunshine and Sunset, which remain much as they were 50 or more years ago. It's in the wonderful views that appear at every turn of the island roads that meander hither and yon around bays and inlets. It's in the remarkable crafts turned out by artisans attracted by the seaside Haystack Mountain School of Crafts and a simpler lifestyle.

As potter William Mor's wife Carolyn suggested when we visited: "Out here we have a peaceful way of life — a community where you can live and let live."

Getting There

Deer Isle is about 50 miles south of Bangor, at the end of a peninsula crossed at its top by U.S. Route 1 between Bucksport and Ellsworth. From Route 1, take Routes 175, 15 or 172 to Little Deer Isle, and Route 15 out to Stonington.

Where to Stay

A few choice inns and B&Bs are available (including one offshore in a lightkeeper's station), plus a few motels of older vintage.

Motels

Beachcomber Motel, Little Deer Isle 04650. (207) 348-6115. This twenty-unit motel has a convenient waterfront location right at the foot of the Deer Isle suspension bridge. Our quarters were small but had wall-to-wall carpeting, TV and outside chairs looking onto Eggemoggin Reach. Picnic tables are scattered across the treed lawn leading down to the rocky shore, where you can gather mussels at low tide and swim at high tide, but can't really do either in between, so great is the difference in tides here. The adjacent Beachcomber Restaurant was closed at our latest visit, and owners Nancy and Butch Soo Hoo were uncertain as to its future. Doubles, $42 to $48. Open June-September.

Captain's Quarters Inn & Motel, Main Street, Box 83, Stonington 04681. (207) 367-2420. Another fine waterfront location and a quaint, large deck with a mix of picnic tables, loungers and a little wooden church perched atop a post commend this ramble of rooms, efficiencies and apartments. You enter through a gift shop, office and coffee bar. Sixteen rooms on two floor vary from small doubles with shared baths to two-bedroom apartments with kitchens and living rooms. Best are the eight facing the water, especially a couple with their own private decks. Here, as opposed to the street side, you're lulled to sleep by the sounds of gulls and foghorns. All rooms have black and white TVs and electric blankets; some have unexpected touches like modern fireplaces and one has a spiral staircase. It takes a diagrammed map to figure out what you want and to find your way there. All the prolific flowers in pots and gardens result from the gardening talents of owner Robert Dodge, who also owns the Bayview Restaurant. Doubles, $38 to $80. Open year-round.

Boyce's Motel, Main Street, Box 94, Stonington 04681. (207) 367-2421 or 367-2253. With our children, we once stayed in this small motel, which back then had seen better days. The five original units remain, but Barbara Boyce has added six new rooms in outbuildings to the rear, including a two-story structure with three units and decks. The biggest has a living room, kitchen and two bedrooms, while two others have a sitting room and bedroom. All rooms have color TV and, while not on the water, Boyce's has the next best thing: a small private waterfront deck for guests' use across the street. Doubles, $30 to $50; kitchen units for four, $55 to $60.

Inns and B&Bs

The Pilgrim's Inn, Deer Isle 04267. (207) 348-6615. This striking, dark red 1793 house occupies a grand location on a spit of land between Northwest Harbor in front and the Mill Pond in back. Innkeepers Jean and Dud Hendrick have refurbished the rooms in sprightly Laura Ashley style. Eight of the thirteen guest rooms have private baths; all have wood stoves and are furnished with antiques, oriental rugs, quilts and artworks appropriate to each room. The new main-floor library has an exceptional collection of books; another parlor is a showroom for local artists. A stairway leads down to the cozy common room, its bay window overlooking the Mill Pond; a tap room where Dud Hendrick mixes a neat raspberry daiquiri upon request and, beyond, an attached barn in which Jean Hendrick oversees exceptional dinners (see Where to Eat). For us, the Hendricks' prime attraction is No. 15, a sweet seaside cottage, perfect for honeymooners, a block down Main Street. It has a living room with cathedral ceiling and open beams, fireplace and an intimate window seat, a full kitchen and dining area and an upstairs bedroom. A rear deck overlooks terraced gardens and the water. Meals may be made here or taken in the inn. Homemade granola, scones, fresh melon and omelets are served at breakfast in the inn. Doubles, $130 to $150 MAP; cottage, $180; three-night minimum in August. No credit cards; no smoking. Open mid-May to mid-October.

Goose Cove Lodge, Goose Cove Road, Sunset 04683. (207) 348-2508; winter, (207) 767-3003. A 1.5-mile long dirt road leads to the End of Beyond — the loveliest sight in the world, according to the lodge brochure. This 70-acre preserve marked by trails, wide sandy beaches and tree-lined shores is a paradise for nature lovers; at low tide, you can walk across a sand bar to Barred Island, a nature conservancy full of birds and wildlife. Innkeeper George Pavloff offers seven secluded cottages and four attached cottages, each with ocean view, sundeck, kitchenette or refrigerator and fireplace, plus ten rooms or suites in two annexes off the main lodge. The hillside main lodge is the epitome of a Maine lodge: an enormous stone fireplace and a mishmash of lodge chairs, benches, sofas and bookcases. The shiny pine tables in the paneled, wraparound dining room — with windows onto the water below — are graced with stoneware by local potter William Mor and bud vases holding field flowers. Guests gather for hors d'oeuvres and BYOB drinks in the lodge before dinner at 6:30; counselors entertain children, who have their own dinner beforehand. Weekly rates starting Saturday, $450 to $495 per person MAP in annexes, $535 to $600 per person MAP in cottages; twelve to fifteen percent higher in August. Shorter stays possible in June and September. Open June to mid-October.

The Inn at Ferry Landing, 108 Old Ferry Road, RR 1, Box 163, Deer Isle 04627. (207) 348-7760. A more perfect waterfront location — at a point along Eggemoggin Reach where the ferry from Sargentville once landed — could scarcely be imagined. And the 1850s farmhouse for sale, which we eyed longingly the previous summer, was nicely renovated in 1987 into a trim B&B by young Bostonians Stephen and Donna Gormley, who now offer seven guest rooms, four with private baths. Rooms are nicely furnished with period pieces and antiques, and patchwork quilts top every bed. Two rooms are on the main floor, one with a private entrance and deck. We're partial to the airy second-floor suite with angled queensize bed, a huge tub and separate shower, a loveseat and chair in crushed velvet, wood stove, TV and skylights in the pitched ceiling; others like the third-floor loft. Actually, the showplace is the large, contemporary-style living room with large windows onto the water on three sides. Donna will hand you a pair of binoculars to view seals asleep on the rocks by the shore. Guests relax on a side deck facing the water; the intrepid can swim or dig mussels. The Gormleys serve a hearty breakfast — perhaps blueberry bread pudding, apricot strudel, orange-cranberry crepes or apple-brie omelets — in the homey dining room. Doubles, $50 to $75; suite, $90.

The King's Row Inn, King's Row, Box 426, Deer Isle 04627. (207) 348-7781. A rambling old white Victorian mansion that had seen better days, this was renovated with T.L.C. and great elan for opening in 1990 by Kate Olson, a New Yorker who summered here for years and is into interior decoration and restoration. Obviously, for even as she prepared for a grand opening reception we could see great style in the making. Most striking are refinished floors, gold bathroom features and vivid, hand-screened William Morris wallpapers and borders everywhere — on the walls, on the ceilings, on the stairwells. Five bedrooms include private baths and fishnet canopy beds; a honeymoon suite on the third floor has a small icebox and TV with films from a VCR library. From a huge, professional kitchen with a gold-plated ceiling, Kate serves a continental breakfast (with plans for additions like quiche and eggs benedict) in a dining room like none we ever saw: a two-story library with lavender balustrade around the mezzanine and an incredible wallpapered ceiling. Guests relax in a huge sitting room, also with a wallpapered ceiling and double fireplaces, on a front deck, or in a rear garden with a rebuilt lily pond, taking in harbor views in the distance. Doubles, $75 to $85; suite, $100. No smoking; no children.

Laphroaig, Route 15, Box 67, Deer Isle 04627. (207) 348-6088. The Scottish name means "beautiful hollow by the broad bay," and it's also the name of a little-known (in this country) single-malt scotch whiskey. John and Andrea Maberry bill theirs as "the extraordinary ordinary," one that caters to adults in two-going-on-three small suites. Fresh flowers from a greenhouse in the basement, special soaps, private baths with fluffy towels, TV sets, flannel sheets, handmade afghans and quilts on the beds, and striking Maine photos by Andrea grace the rooms, which appear to be a bit of a mishmash in color and style and a showcase for the owners' collections of dolls, little shoes, handmade period furniture and the like. This is, after all, a very much lived-in 1854 house. There's a well-stocked library-parlor with a pressed-tin ceiling. Beneath a brass chandelier, the long table in the dining room is the setting for gourmet breakfasts: perhaps fresh orange juice and fresh-ground coffee, melon balls with West Indies spicy sauce and oven-cooked pancakes with wild blueberry compote, herbed scrambled eggs or croissants with crabmeat, poached eggs and bearnaise sauce. Doubles, $70. No smoking; no credit cards.

Pres du Port, West Main Street and Highland Avenue, Stonington 04681. (207) 367-5007. The gray cat is appropriate at this gray house on a hill overlooking Stonington harbor. Rockers in a semi-circle face the water in a side sun porch; Adirondack chairs do the same on an upstairs sundeck. Charlotte Casgrain, a Connecticut resident who's summered on the island since 1955, offers three guest rooms sharing two baths. Beau Rivage is a large room with a panoramic view of the harbor, old oak furniture and a small vanity sink to match. Beau Ciel, also with a vanity and a view, is done in pale azure; note the tiny silver-plated faces on the Victorian drawer pulls. The wine harvesting depicted on the wallpaper gives the smallest room its name, Beaujolais. Breakfast, served buffet style, consists of fresh fruit, cereals, yogurts, muffins and breads, sometimes with bacon or sausage and eggs. Doubles, $40 to $50. Open July-August.

Ocean View House, Main Street and Sea Breeze Avenue, Box 261, Stonington 04681. (207) 367-5114. Jack Custer took a glass-blowing class at nearby Haystack Mountain School of Crafts and liked the area so much that he and his wife Christine, who live in a Detroit suburb where he is a teacher and she a physical therapist, bought this turn-of-the-century inn about fifteen years ago for a summer home. They have fixed up the house, originally built to board quarry workers employed on nearby Crotch Island, and have opened it to the public as a B&B. Simple and fresh, the Ocean View has eight bedrooms sharing two baths on the second and third floors. Colorful hooked rugs are on painted floors, curtains are tied with multicolored ribbons, and there are nice touches like shell soaps, Kleenex in little houses with the tissue coming out of the chimney, and Poland Spring mineral water in every room. Colorful thick towels, pretty linens on the beds and lots of fresh flowers are other attractions. A couple of the rooms have fine views of the water; for the best view climb up to the cupola, with its 360-degree panorama. There's a small sitting room where Christine sells jams and syrups; in the sunny breakfast room, she serves fresh orange juice, muffins and sweet breads, strawberry sorbet, and (trust us, we tasted one) the best tart ever, with a seashell of pastry filled with raspberries, cream cheese, whipped cream and a blueberry glaze — the berries are local, of course. Doubles, $50. Open July-August.

The Keeper's House, Box 26, Isle au Haut 04645. (207) 327-2261. For a change of pace, how about staying in a restored lightkeeper's station? You take the mailboat from Stonington to this remote, six-mile-long island, part of Acadia National Park and eight miles offshore from Deer Isle. Innkeepers Jeff and Judi Burke came upon the 1907 Coast Guard lightkeeper's house atop the craggy sea cliff for the first time in 1985 and "immediately saw that it was the most wonderful possibility for an inn anywhere." After pouring $300,000 into acquisition and renovations, the Burkes feel they now offer "a living museum where guests step back in time." No cars, no electricity, no phones nor commercial development mar the simplicity of an island containing a few Acadia Park campsites and 50 residents. The light tower still operates, and beacons from five other lighthouses can be seen at night. The main house offers four large guest rooms, all with water views and furnished with painted antiques, sea chests, rocking chairs and coastal memorabilia. Two modern baths with hot showers (water is heated by a wood stove) are shared. For more rusticity and privacy, the Oil House right on the water has a wood stove, secluded deck and outdoor shower. It shares a "backhouse" with the Wood Shed, the Burkes' newest quarters on the upper floor of a small barn with a gable, a long glass dormer and a winding wood staircase. Judi bakes breads and pastries, and serves a variety of native seafood and chicken dishes (no red meat) and complimentary wine at candlelight dinners; afterward, guests chat amid the glow of gas lights. The daily rate includes all expenses from parking on the mainland and round-trip passage on the mailboat to all meals and a tour of the island. Doubles, $210 AP; out buildings, $192. Two-night minimum in summer; no mailboat on Sundays or postal holidays. No smoking. Open June-October.

RENTALS. Listings may be available from Green's Landing Realty, Box 500, Stonington, (207) 367-5140; Doubleday Realty, Box 346 Stonington, (207) 367-2728, or Shepard's, Box 115, Stonington, (207) 367-2790.

Seeing and Doing

Boat cruises among the islands off Deer Isle are a must, if only for a mailboat ride to Isle au Haut. Among the choices:

Palmer Day IV Excursions, Stonington, 367-2207. The best trip is offered by Capt. Reginald Greenlaw, who conducts daily cruises on his 49-passenger boat in the waters off Stonington. He is as entertaining as is his excursion, which offers closeup views of untold varieties of birds, deer and even an island full of seals, one of whom leaps beside the boat to get the raw fish the captain brings along. The seal-feeding session is more fun than any aquarium's, and we particularly enjoyed the five-mile ride along the shore of Isle au Haut. It's one of the most interesting nature cruises we've taken, as well as the most informative. Only a meanie would take the captain up on his offer to refund the fare of anyone "who will stand up in front of my guests and say they're not happy with the trip." Daily at 2, July 4 to Sept. 1; adults $8, children under 10, $4.

On Wednesdays, the Palmer Day sails to Vinalhaven and North Haven, with stops on each island, leaving at 8:30 and returning at 1:30; adults $10, children $7.50. Captain Greenlaw also offers charters and bird and whale-watch excursions, the latter from 6 a.m. or earlier for those who want to see the auks and puffins at Matinicus Rock and whales off outer Isle au Haut. The cost is $15.

Isle au Haut Co., Isle au Haut, 367-5193. Passengers can ride the U.S. mailboat from Stonington to Isle au Haut and-or Duck Harbor. The trip out takes about 40 minutes, with a fifteen-minute stop, and Duck Harbor is twenty minutes beyond. Trips run two to five times daily except Sunday and postal holidays. One-way trips in summer are $7 adults, $4.25 children. The company also runs scenic excursions aboard **Miss Lizzie,** which departs from the Atlantic Avenue Hardware Dock, Stonington, at 2:30 daily between June 18 and Sept. 8 for cruises among the islands of Penobscot Bay; adults $9, children $4.50.

The Eagle Island Mailboat, Sunset, 348-2817, gives two-hour trips by reservation Monday-Saturday, leaving Sylvester's Cove about 8:30 a.m. Adults $8, children $4. Sightseeing and bird-watching trips around the islands are available by arrangement.

Tillicum, Bucks Harbor Marina, 326-8839 or 326-9562. Capt. Max Middleton's 40-foot fiberglass sailboat gives three-hour cruises daily at 9 and 1 for $35 per person.

Explorers at Sea, Main Street, Stonington, 367-2356, a sea kayaking shop and service, offers a variety of kayaking excursions through the Bay of Jericho and East Penobscot Bay. Most involve instruction and group expeditions, starting at $50 for a half-day trip.

Other Attractions

The Island Country Club on Sunset Road, Deer Isle, offers "friendly golf and tennis," according to an advertisement. It has a nine-hole golf course and a tennis court, and lunch is available from 11 to 2.

Crockett Cove Woods Preserve, Crockett Cove, Stonington. If Deer Isle has a tourist attraction, this is it, we suppose. It's hard to find, off Whitman Road at Burnt Cove on the Stonington-Sunset Road. The persistent will be rewarded with a pleasant quarter-mile walk through part of a 100-acre coastal rain forest maintained by the Maine Nature Conservancy. The self-guided tour is enhanced by a brochure that helps the already knowledgeable identify what they're seeing. Even the uninitiated will be impressed by the beautiful shades of greens, the exotic mosses, a bog, the lush growth and huge rocks. It really is like a rain forest. Free, parking for three or four cars only.

SCENIC DRIVES. You'll need to follow the Chamber of Commerce map, but the rewards are great for those with wanderlust. We particularly enjoy the little Sand Beach Road along the channel known as the Deer Island Thorofare, with a stop for rock climbing or a hasty swim at Fifield Point or Burnt Cove. To the east of town is Ames Pond with some rare pink water lilies. There is a particularly scenic drive out to Oceanville, where you stumble upon a tiny beach with calm waters beside a bridge. Another drive goes way out past the hamlet of Sunshine (at the opposite side of the island from Sunset) to Haystack Mountain School of Crafts, where the waterfront vistas from on high are something else. Follow almost any side road and you'll come to a dead end at the water.

Crafts and Shopping

Haystack Mountain School of Crafts, Sunshine Road, Deer Isle, 348-2306. A long gravel road finally brings you to this noted crafts school, perched on a hillside with wondrous views through deep green spruce trees of sparkling blue waters below. The hardy can descend what seem like endless wooden stairs to the rocky shore. We found the various artists' studios and the school's layout interesting but were surprised not to find any crafts on display. This is a working school, however, and no items are for sale. Visitors welcome Thursday-Sunday 10 to 4 only.

Ronald Hayes Pearson, whose jewelry is exhibited across the country, has a shop in his striking home along Reach Road in North Deer Isle. Pearson works in silver and gold; his twist earrings at $65 for silver and $230 for gold are especially in demand. He and his wife Carolyn Hecker, executive director of the growing Maine Crafts Association which started locally, welcome visitors Monday-Saturday from 10 to 5.

Farther along Reach Road, which parallels Eggemoggin Reach, is the home and studio of potter **William Mor.** His handsome, functional stoneware is neatly displayed in a sheltered outdoor sales area surrounded by flower gardens and a pond. Nearby is a studio showroom in which you may view work in progress and see the potter's gas-fired kiln. Carolyn has been known to offer delicious fresh-baked cookies as you browse. The sales area is open daily from 10 to 5, and we predict you'll come away with a purchase or two.

The **Deer Isle Artists Association** conducts a series of four-person shows all summer in its gallery on the second floor of the old Deer Isle High School, open from 1 to 5 daily. Items are for sale at moderate prices in the Little Gallery, housed in the former library.

Also in Deer Isle, the **Blue Heron Gallery** exhibits contemporary American crafts, featuring works by the Haystack faculty. The **Turtle Gallery** has changing exhibits of watercolors, oils, drawings, photographs and wood carvings by area artists. **The Periwinkle** stocks books, cards, knit goods, stuffed animals and local crafts. The **Gifted Mermaid** has ecology and children's books, native masks, scarves and South American hangings.

At **Once Upon an Island,** a country gift shop of note, Cathy D'Errico offers neat Maine things, from axes and fireplace tools to jewelry by a neighbor, Ronald Hayes Pearson. She makes her own jams and jellies, and will bake her cheesecakes, blueberry cakes and whipped cream cakes to order.

Out the Sunshine Road east of Deer Isle, a must stop is **Nervous Nellie's Kitchen & Mountainville Cafe.** Michal McKeown, a.k.a. Nellie, and her partner Peter Beerits put up 50,000 jars of jam each year in the little house with a big kitchen. So many people began stopping in that they decided to serve refreshments as well. The new cafe offers morning coffee and afternoon tea with homemade breads and pastries, including a frozen drink called a Batido, a refreshing but caloric mix of cream cheese, freezer jam and crushed ice cubes ($2.50). Peter's quirky sculptures outside make this worth a visit, not to mention all the wonderful jams (we especially like the hot tomato jelly). Open Tuesday-Saturday, 9 to 11 and 2 to 5.

STONINGTON SHOPS. For a remote and isolated town, Stonington has a disproportionate number of interesting galleries and shops along Main Street.

The **Eastern Bay Gallery,** its rear windows providing a harbor view for an arty backdrop, features local artists. We were struck by the colorful quilts, hooked rugs, one-of-a-kind clothing, the wall hangings, and some remarkable pottery.

Island Supply Co. has exotic clothing from the Far East, Greece and Mexico, especially things appropriate for summer by the seashore. It's connected with a shop of the same name in South Norwalk, Conn. Out back is **Coast Side Books and Gourmet,** stocking cheeses, Maine jellies and, of course, books. **The Dry Dock** is another fine shop with imported gifts — pottery from Portugal, glassware from Mexico and cooking utensils from across the world — plus colorful clothing from India, handknit sweaters, wool, cards and a children's corner. **Dockside Bookstore,** right beside the water with chairs for reading on a little deck, specializes in Maine and marine books and nautical gifts.

Climb up the granite stairs to **The Overlook,** an imposing restored structure housing **Honeysuckle Books, The Gallery** and the **Hoy Gallery,** colorful with the fantastically vibrant paintings of Jill Hoy.

The jumble of stuff in front of the second-hand shop on Sea Breeze Avenue is such that we passed several times before deciding to stop. A ten-cent box is crammed with gadgets, as are the fifty-cent table and the $1 table. Go inside and you'll find everything from clam rollers to whale trivets to furniture. The owner said the shop's name, which we otherwise wouldn't have known, is **Chairs, Chairs, Chairs.** We're not sure why.

Where to Eat _____ ✧✧✧

Pilgrim's Inn, Deer Isle. (207) 348-6615. Inn guests as well as about ten lucky outsiders feast on the island's best meals at Pilgrim's Inn. Following cocktails and appetizers at 6 p.m. in the common room or by the barbecue, Jean Hendrick and her chef, Terry Foster, offer a single-entree, prix-fixe dinner for $27.50 at 7 in the former goat barn, where you're surrounded by candlelight, fresh flowers, farm utensils and quilts on the walls, mismatched chairs and ten outside doors that open to let in the breeze. Depending on the night, you might be served roast tenderloin with cornichon-tarragon sauce, grilled lamb with herbs, chicken breast stuffed with pesto, ricotta and pinenuts, or stuffed sole mousseline. The salads may contain Japanese greens; vegetables from the backyard garden might be fresh peas or new potatoes. We had a remarkable Sunday night dinner of a salad with goat cheese, homemade peasant bread, a heavenly paella decorated with nasturtiums, and a raspberry chocolate pie on a shortbread crust. The wines are good and exceedingly reasonable. Dinner nightly except Thursday at 7, by reservation only. Open mid-May to mid-October.

The Clamdigger Restaurant, Route 15, South Deer Isle. (207) 348-6187. New owners took over in 1989, spiffed up the facility and hired away the chef from the Lucerne Inn in Bangor. Dining is at tables covered with paper mats in a front room dressed with artifacts; there are a bar and a function room to the rear. The menu is a cut above: at dinner ($11.95 to $17.95), seafood fettuccine, shrimp marinara, lobster stuffed with seafood mornay, lobster saute, chicken cordon bleu and prime rib. For appetizers you'll find cajun shrimp, chicken wings and mozzarella sticks amid the prevailing lobster stew and steamed clams. Desserts are basic. Lunch and dinner, Tuesday-Sunday 11 to 9.

The Fishermen's Friend, School Street, Stonington. (207) 367-2442. The outside is unprepossessing, to say the least, and the interior is zilch: a front room with booths and tables, a small middle room, and a new back room with windows onto a field, and tables covered with oilcloth, paper mats and bouquets of field flowers. Hanging plants are the only "decor." But this fourteen-year-old restaurant now run by Susan and Jack Scott doesn't really need any. It's got down-to-earth food at the lowest prices around. For lunch, two of us had a wonderful clam chowder and a shrimp stew, plus an overstuffed crabmeat roll and great fried clams for $14.50, and the prices haven't really gone up in the four-year interim. For dinner, start with scallop stew ($2.50) or Port Clyde brand sardines, packed in Stonington and served on lettuce with saltines ($1.95). Entrees come with a huge house salad at lunch and a salad bar at night, hot rolls and "real mashed potato" or french fries. They range from $6.50 for haddock to a fisherman's platter for $10.75. Broiled Atlantic salmon steak is a bargain $7.25. Friday's fish fry is $4.99 with "seconds on us," according to the menu. Non-fish eaters like the roast beef dinner with gravy ($6.95), ham steak or perhaps just a hot dog (85 cents). Open daily, 11 to 9. BYOB. No credit cards.

Bayview Restaurant, Sea Breeze Avenue, Stonington. (207) 367-2274. Again there's not much in the way of decor — pressed-tin ceiling and walls, linoleum floor and mismatched Scandinavian cutlery, blue mats and an arrangement of wildflowers at each table (at night, the mats give way to tablecloths and candlelight, we're told). And, despite the name, there's not much of a water view except, perhaps, from the rear kitchen. But the food is fresh and reasonably priced, from $8.95 for fried shrimp to $11.95 for broiled salmon. A seafood platter goes for $13.95. You can get almost any of the local fish fried, broiled or baked, and the "no-frills boiled lobster" is $10.95 at lunch. Breakfast from 6, lunch 11 to 3, dinner 5 to 9 or later. BYOB.

Rainbow's End, Main Street, Stonington. (207) 367-5806. New in 1990 was this little seafood cafe with leather booths and a salad bar. Fresh local seafood is featured at dinner, priced from $8.75 for broiled scallops to $15.95 for double lobster tail. Offerings include chicken kiev, broiled sirloin and lobster thermidor. For lunch, try a lobster croissant ($5.85) or a broiled haddock sandwich. Breakfasts are in the $1 to $3 range. Hours vary, but generally open from 6 a.m. to 7 or 8 p.m.; closed Tuesday.

Eaton's Lobster Pool, Blastow's Cove, Little Deer Isle. (207) 348-2383. It was dark by the time we reached this cavern of a restaurant, with bare tables covered with "how to eat your lobster" paper placemats, bare light bulbs hanging from the ceiling beams, a fireplace in the middle and lobster cut-outs in the doors. We got the manager to unscrew the very bright light bulb right over our heads, drank wine from water glasses, poured our own water from a pitcher, helped ourselves to dressings from a couple of bottles brought along with our iceberg-lettuce salads, and settled in for a lobster feast like everyone else. The lobster dinner ($15) was fine, and the steamed clams some of the most succulent we've tasted. We didn't have room for the only dessert, a homemade blueberry pie. Not til the next day when we returned to take a picture did we realize that tables near the windows had wondrous water views, or that there was a wraparound outdoor deck by the water with, inexplicably, no tables. Dinner, Monday-Saturday 5 to 9; Sunday, noon to 9. Seasonal.

Eaton's Pier, Sunshine Road, Deer Isle. (207) 348-6036 or 348-2489. For your basic lobster, you can't do much better than this family institution (no relation to Eaton's Lobster Pool), which has been around for a quarter century but only took a higher profile a few years ago when it moved off the pier and into a small building overlooking the water. Inside and out, there are a few picnic tables equipped with mallets. Place your order for the basic lobster dinner (a bargain $5.95). Or splurge on the shore dinner (with clams, mussels and corn, $10), the hungry man special (with two lobsters, $16) or the belly buster (three lobsters, $19). Also available are lobster rolls ($6.95), steamed shrimp, corn on the cob, soft drinks, and fresh blueberry pie and chocolate chip cookies, baked every morning. You may even get to see Jim Eaton unload his catch for the day when you're there. There's no alcohol allowed and the place is closed on Sundays; many of the folks in Sunshine are Advent Christians. Open Monday-Saturday, 11 to 7. Open mid-May through October.

Austinwoods, Water Street, Stonington. (207) 367-5871. In what was an ice cream shop with seven tables, the owners expanded the menu, and now one can lunch very pleasantly inside or down the stairs on an outdoor deck over the water. The Austin family, who also operate Austinwoods in Machias, make their chowder from scratch with butter, cream and salt pork from a family recipe, they poach their own turkey at night, obtain their rye bread and bagels from a deli in Bangor, and import their water from Burnt Cove. For a quick lunch, we passed up the day's special of roast-beef hoagie for a good cup of chowder and a delicious hot dog with kraut ($1.25) and a vegetable pocket ($2.25). Most people come for the ice cream, especially the numerous ice cream concoctions (fresh island-grown strawberry sundae, $2.75). The ice cream is made by a cooperative of Hancock County farmers, has a high butterfat content and is absolutely delectable. Open daily, 11:30 to 8, June-September.

Finest Kind Dining, Joyce's Crossroad, Deer Isle. (207) 348-6865. A log cabin houses a counter on the left and tables and booths on the right. A lobster dinner is $10.95, but you also can get barbecued ribs, crab salad plate, sandwiches, pizzas and calzones. Dinner plates run from $5.95 for chopped steak to $13.25 for seafood platter. Grilled ham with pineapple, sliced turkey with gravy, and chicken cordon bleu are among the offerings. For dessert, how about homemade pies, bread pudding or a hot fudge sundae? Open daily, 8 a.m. to 9 p.m.

FOR MORE INFORMATION: Deer Isle-Stonington Chamber of Commerce, Box 268, Stonington, Me. 04681. (207) 348-6124.

Sand Beach offers ocean swimming for the hardy in Acadia National Park.

Bar Harbor/Acadia National Park, Me.

Anyone who has succumbed to the enticements of Acadia National Park can believe full well its claim to having more scenic variety per square mile than any other part of the national park system.

Rugged ocean coastline first comes to mind when one thinks of Acadia, which occupies the better part of Mount Desert Island — the country's third largest (after Long Island and Martha's Vineyard).

There also are towering cliffs and mountain summits (including Cadillac Mountain, the highest along the East Coast), the East's only natural fjord, fresh-water lakes, sandy beaches, and wetlands and forests full of wildlife.

Such scenic diversity produces the widest range of outdoor activity in one place in Maine, if not the East. The visitor can explore the jagged shoreline, climb mountains, swim in the ocean or lakes, go sailing or lobstering, canoe through salt marshes and kayak along the coast, watch for birds and whales, walk along nature trails and through exotic gardens, hike or bicycle or go horseback riding on 50 miles of carriage paths, and camp near the sea, among other pursuits.

They used to call it "rusticating," when thousands of city folk descended in the 19th century on Bar Harbor — the island's largest town — to pursue the active outdoor life, eschewing what they considered the pretentious activities of such summer colonies as Newport, Lenox and Saratoga. In the 1880s, Bar Harbor's eighteen hotels could accommodate more than 25,000 guests, and the elite began building fashionable cottages that were the largest in Maine.

Residents like John D. Rockefeller Jr., fearing commercial encroachments, bought up vast tracts of land. In 1919, they donated them to the federal government for the first national park in the East. The advent of the automobile made the island more accessible, the hotels disappeared and the Great Fire of 1947 destroyed many of the large homes remaining from Bar Harbor's heyday.

Today's visitors find vestiges of the island's Golden Era in the mansions of

361

West and Eden streets, and the enclaves at Seal Harbor and Northwest Harbor. But they're more likely to find campers and hikers and bicyclists who appreciate the outdoor wonderland that led the residents who settled Bar Harbor in 1796 to name the town Eden.

With more than four million visitors annually, Acadia ranks second only to the Great Smoky Mountains National Park as the country's most visited national park. Most are rusticators — the kind of people whom local publisher Frank Matter describes as "more bohemian than sophisticated." After all, he says, the old Bar Harbor was the bohemian resort for the wealthy. Although elements of high-living and luxury creep in this far Down East, Acadia National Park gives the island a sense of rugged individualism in sync with nature.

Getting There

Bar Harbor and Acadia National Park are about 180 roundabout miles northeast of Portland and 45 miles southeast of Bangor. Take coastal U.S. Route 1 to Ellsworth or Interstate 95 to Bangor and Route 1A to Ellsworth. Route 3 from Ellsworth leads to the park entrance and, beyond, to Bar Harbor. An airport just off island in Trenton is served by airlines from New England cities. The Bluenose ferry connects Bar Harbor with Yarmouth in Nova Scotia.

Where to Stay _____ ⟋ᑕᑕ⟍

About 950 rooms were added in Bar Harbor in one year alone, bringing the total to 6,400, according to local innkeepers. The options are so varied and numerous that we can offer only a choice sampling of those near the water.

Cottages and Camping

You'll find more old-fashioned cabins and cottage colonies (and motels) along the approaches to Acadia National Park and Bar Harbor than you thought existed. Even in high season if you arrive without a reservation, with luck you'll be able to find room in one. A few of the better choices:

Emery's Cottages on the Shore, Sand Point Road, Box 172, Bar Harbor 04609. (207) 288-3432. Many cottage colonies aren't near the water, are decrepit and packed close together. This complex is one of the best; it has fourteen housekeeping and eight sleeping cottages, the latter closest to the water. All have electric heat, color TV and private baths, some with new tub-shower combinations. Efficiency cottages vary in size. The sleeping cottages have one double or queensize bed, a refrigerator and coffeemaker. A pleasant lawn leads to a gravel beach; lawn chairs, picnic tables and grills are provided. Weekly rates, non-housekeeping $335; efficiencies, $390 to $465; daily rates off-season and when available. Open May to late October.

Hinckley's Dreamwood Motor Court, Route 3, Box 1180, Bar Harbor 04609. (207) 288-3510. It's not on the water, but its location among the pines is the next best thing. Twenty-nine rooms are available in duplex motel units and cottages, sixteen with kitchenettes. All are carpeted and have cable television; several have screened porches and fireplaces, and there's an appealing small pool. Three two-bedroom and two four-bedroom cottages are available. Housekeeping units require a three-day minimum in season; weekly rates are available. Doubles, $42 to $58. Open May to mid-October.

Seaside Cottages, Clark's Cove, RD 1, Box 2340, Bar Harbor 04609. (207) 288-3674. Fully equipped cottages of one to three bedrooms are offered by the

Leland family beside the waters of Clark's Cove. A wide lawn leads to a private beach for swimming and clam digging, and free rowboats are available for fishing. Weekly rates for two, $500.

Edgewater Motel and Cottages, Salisbury Cove, Box 566, Bar Harbor 04609. (207) 288-3491. A cove-front location well off the highway commends this 23-unit mix of efficiency cottages and a two-story motel, four of whose spacious, paneled rooms have fireplaces, kitchens and kingsize beds. Each cottage has its own deck facing the water. Doubles, $57 to $80 in cottages, $79 to $89 in motel. Open mid-April through October.

CAMPING. Mount Desert Island is a paradise for campers, and five private campgrounds are happy to oblige in Bar Harbor. Closest to town in Salisbury Cove is **Bar Harbor Campground,** whose rates of $12 to $18 a night for a party of four are typical. **Mount Desert Narrows Campground** is the only one on the ocean. Purists prefer the two campgrounds in Acadia National Park — **Blackwoods,** five miles south of Bar Harbor off Route 3, and **Seawall,** near Southeast Harbor. Both are in woods near the ocean, and offer naturalist talks and special activities. Fees are $8 to $10 a night, for a maximum of two weeks. Sites can be reserved at Blackwoods; Seawall is first-come, first-served. Contact the National Park Service, Acadia National Park, RD 1, Box 1, Bar Harbor 04609.

RENTALS. Many cottage colonies rent by the week or longer. Realtors such as Island Realty, 110 Main St., 288-9778, and the Bar Harbor Chamber of Commerce can advise on house or cottage rentals.

Inns/Motor Inns

Bar Harbor Inn, Newport Drive, Bar Harbor 04609. (207) 288-3351 or (800) 248-3351. The Bar Harbor Motor Inn's name was changed in 1986 to reflect the extensive restoration of the original inn building, which now looks and feels as its predecessor (the private Oasis Club's Reading Room) must have at the turn of the century. It also better reflects owner David Witham's upgrading of what has to be the most watery spot in town — on eight landscaped acres with the sea on two sides. The 51 rooms in the main inn have been beautifully refurnished in Colonial elegance, but possessing such modern accoutrements as cable TV, clock radios and pushbutton phones. Some inn rooms have views of the harbor, and some over the lobby are enormous. Part of the older motel section was moved uphill to make way for a deluxe oceanfront lodge in 1988. Fifteen motel units remain, but the grandest accommodations are those in the lodge, where 64 spacious rooms on two floors have fantastic private balconies with a stunning view of rocks, water and islands. White lounge furniture outside, deep green draperies that match the dust ruffles on the beds, moire wallpaper, rose carpeting, good art, and big bathrooms with pink fixtures and fluffy towels characterize these rooms. We didn't know there was such a pleasant public walk around the point along Frenchman Bay until we stayed there. There's a large heated pool, as well as a small public beach adjacent. A complimentary continental breakfast is served. Three meals a day are available at the newly landscaped, outdoor **Gatsby's Terrace** or the striking, windowed **Reading Room** (see Where to Eat). Doubles, $95 in motel, $120 to $195 in inn, $179 to $199 in lodge. Lodge open year-round.

Bayview Hotel & Inn, 111 Eden St, Bar Harbor 04609. (207) 288-5861 or (800) 356-3585. In 1983, Texas businessman John Davis converted his family's 30-room white brick Georgian-style summer home built in the 1930s into a smashing inn (with five spacious and opulent guest rooms) and restaurant overlooking Frenchman Bay. He then added condominium townhouses, set well back from the water, and a 26-room three-story "chateau" hotel next to the inn and, some would say, made it into Neiman-Marcus North. We think the hotel a bit glitzy for Bar Harbor, and are partial to the elegance and seclusion of the inn (it's like staying in a private mansion). Unfortunately, the rooms in the hotel have only fake balconies, but everything else is fit for a visiting Texan, from the crystal lamps and TVs hidden in the armoires to the bubblebath presented in a silver swan. The hotel has a waterside bar and lounge, looking out onto a terrace above a small swimming pool and large whirlpool. The adjacent dining room is the site for a buffet breakfast, when it's not being used as a conference room. For dinner one may go to the inn, where the setting is unforgettable. Doubles in hotel, $215 to $235; in inn, $95 to $250; townhomes, $375 to $425. Open mid-May through October.

Holiday Inn/Bar Harbor Regency, 123 Eden St., Bar Harbor 04609. (207) 288-9723. Most of Bar Harbor's hostelries were Mom-and-Pop operations until the Regency was erected by a Florida outfit and landscaped almost overnight for a late opening in 1986. Taken over by the Holiday Inn in 1990, this is the newcomer with which oldtimers now compete, and compete they do (see above). It occupies the site of the former home of Dr. William Procter of Procter & Gamble, who'd never recognize the four-story hotel with 224 rooms, all rather too sophisticated for Down East Maine (there's even a glass elevator from which one can view Frenchman Bay). Half the rooms have water views, most have tiny balconies and all are tastefully furnished in soft greens or pinks with kingsize or two double beds. The grounds include tennis courts, a walking path, a small pool, two hot tubs and a sauna. There's a **Tiki Bar** in a gazebo by the pool overlooking the bay. The **Edenfield** dining room has canopied windows onto the pool and water. It offers a standard menu from $13.95 for fried clams or pasta with clam sauce to $18.95 for Bar Harbor lobster bake, and lobster is available in five different dishes. Doubles, $119 to $149.

Atlantic Oakes By-the-Sea, Route 3, Bar Harbor 04609. (207) 288-5801 or (800) 336-2463. Until the newcomers arrived, this 109-room resort motel beside the Bluenose Ferry Terminal on the ten-acre estate once owned by Sir Harry Oakes was one of Bar Harbor's most deluxe and expensive. Each spacious room in this brown-shingled low-rise has large windows onto a balcony or patio with a grand ocean view. The attractive grounds include five tennis courts (two of them lighted and with a tennis pro in residence), a heated pool and a pebble beach with a float and a pier, where boats may be rented and sailing lessons are given. In season, a complimentary breakfast is served in the mansion each morning, and lobster cookouts and clambakes are available several nights a week. Doubles, $96 to $125.

Atlantic Eyrie Lodge, Highbrook Road, Bar Harbor 04609. (207) 288-9786 or (800) 422-2883. The owner of Atlantic Oakes By-the-Sea opened this four-story motor inn high atop a hill above Cleftstone Manor in 1986. From their lofty perch, most of the 58 rooms with private balconies have great ocean views (the top two floors carry higher prices). All rooms have cable TV and two double beds except for larger kitchenette rooms that have one king bed and a sofabed. A continental breakfast is provided in the lobby. The swimming pool has a slide, which youngsters like. Doubles, $99 to $117. Open mid-May through October.

Park Entrance Motel, Route 3, Bar Harbor 04609. (207) 288-9703 or (800) 843-2627. Located on a manicured hillside opposite the main park entrance, this established motel is almost always booked and we're disappointed when we call too late, which is usually. It's a low-key kind of place, away from town and with a quarter mile of coastline to enjoy. It advertises "an ocean view from every room," and the lawns slope down to a pebble beach graced by a pier and the biggest mussels we ever saw, ready for gathering by the handful at low tide. Rowboats are free, the outdoor pool is heated (there's a new hot tub as well), picnic tables and grills are available for cookouts, and there are an eighteen-hole putting green, croquet court and volleyball area. The 56 rooms on two floors are comfortable, and five efficiencies are available. Doubles, $110 to $125. Open mid-May to mid-October.

Golden Anchor Inn & Pier, 55 West St., Box 46, Bar Harbor 04609. (207) 288-5033 or (800) 328-5033. Don't be deceived by the name; this is a sprawling 88-room motel of some years, right in the heart of town. It does have a large pier and it's right on the water, all but six rooms with sliding doors onto private balconies with water views — as close as 25 feet to the ocean, our guide pointed out. Best of the two buildings is the one farther from the street and facing directly onto Frenchman Bay. Rooms have two double beds, TV and modern baths, and look like those in any older motel, except for the view. There's a large outdoor pool, and coffee and donuts are served in the morning. Cruises leave from the pier, which is the site of the **The Pier** restaurant (see Where to Eat). Doubles, $85 to $125.

Inns/Guest Houses

The Inn at Canoe Point, Route 3, Box 216, Hulls Cove 04644. (207) 288-9511. One of Mount Desert Island's few small inns right on the ocean, this is a stunner of a place. After getting his feet wet with a couple of B&Bs in Southwest Harbor, Don Johnson provided the crowning touch by turning this Tudor-style home hidden from the highway in an acre and a half of woods into a stylish B&B. A large, L-shaped deck takes full advantage of the location beside Frenchman Bay. Five guest rooms, all with private baths, have water views and are decorated in exquisite taste. For 1992, Don was planning to extend the Garden Room by twelve feet to add a fireplace and windows on three sides, as well as expanding the room above. From the Garret Suite consisting of the entire third floor, one can lie in the kingsize bed and look out at an endless expanse of water. Top of the line is the Master Suite, handsome in grays and neutral colors with two easy chairs and a chaise lounge in front of the fireplace, a queensize bed, good art prints and a private deck. Check out Don's collection of Life and Esquire magazines dating from the 1930s and '40s in the upstairs hall. Guests enjoy a pleasant living room, where an elegant grouping of seats faces the fireplace, and the waterfront Ocean Room with a huge sectional, fireplace and stereo. The latter is the setting for a breakfast of fresh fruit and a main course like eggs strata, blueberry pancakes, cinnamon french toast or spinach and cheddar quiche. Port or sherry is in all the guest rooms, and iced tea and lemonade are served on warm afternoons on the waterfront deck, which is seductive enough to keep guests from touring the rest of the island. Don also can be persuaded to take guests out on his boat. If you can't stay here, be advised that Don also owns two inns in town, the Maples and Ridgeway, run in his style by on-site inn-keepers. But those who want to be near the water won't settle for anything less than Canoe Point. Doubles, $95 to $170. No credit cards.

Nannau-Seaside Bed & Breakfast, Lower Main Street, Box 710, Bar Harbor 04609. (207) 288-5575. Built in 1904 as a summer cottage, Nannau is a fine example of shingle-style architecture and is listed on the National Register.

But that's not the half of it. It's a low-key, sprawling place with three guest rooms, a large and lovely secluded property leading to the sea, and many pampering touches by personable innkeepers Vikki and Ron Evers. Original William Morris-designed wallpapers and fabrics decorate most rooms, and large couches and armchairs contribute to a feeling of elegance and spaciousness. Down comforters and feather pillows dress the bedrooms, all with queensize beds, private baths, fireplaces and distant ocean views. One is a suite with sitting room, colorful wallpaper called Blackberry, and its own screened porch with water view. Caswell & Massey toiletries are in the bathrooms, which have marble sinks, clawfoot tubs and hand-held showers. Guests have the run of two enormous parlors, one with a multitude of books and magazines and the other dressed in chintz. There's a great side porch with casual furniture. Outside are Adirondack chairs and a croquet course. A trail leads to a small sand beach at Compass Harbor, where a few neighbors were swimming in water in the low 60s at our visit. "Scuba divers go nuts in our harbor," says Vikki, and nature-lovers appreciate the wildlife. Eagles nest all year on Bald Porcupine Island, just offshore, which looks like its name. From her professional-size kitchen with its 1904 Edwardian Aga stove, Vicki and Ron prepare a lavish breakfast. It could begin with granola and Ron's Danish fresh fruit compote, followed by German apple pancakes or an egg entree. Breakfast is served at a large table in the dining room, with its heavy draperies, burgundy wallpaper and gold-outlined black chairs. Doubles, $75 to $95; suite, $145. Open May-October. No smoking.

The Tides, 119 West St., Bar Harbor 04609. (207) 288-4968. Listed on the National Register, this classic 1887 Greek Revival mansion faces Frenchman Bay head-on. A sensational wraparound veranda is full of upholstered wicker furniture that's Laura Ashley and all-matching to the max. Complete with its own fireplace, the veranda encloses a dining room with what must be a twenty-foot banquette along the window and a picture of the similar view over the fireplace, plus a formal living room and an entry foyer. Guests have use of an upstairs living room with a huge sofa in front of a fireplace. Our room, the master bedroom, was the epitome of class, from the wing chairs, the queensize four-poster bed, and coordinated Laura Ashley prints to the large dressing room with makeup table, the arrangement of daisies and mums, and the attention to every detail. There was even a small porch off the bathroom where we could sit and enjoy the salt air. And in the bathroom were Caswell-Massey toiletries and thick towels of deep burgundy. A welcoming sparkling cider came in a silver ice bucket with two crystal champagne glasses. The two other bedrooms are not as large but are equally well-equipped and outfitted in varied Laura Ashley prints. Breakfast in the dining room is a feast — fresh fruit, homemade cinnamon popovers with strawberry jam, various breads, and a main course ranging from vegetable strata and spinach quiche to stuffed french toast with blueberry sauce and cranberry-walnut pancakes. Afternoon tea brings cookies, brownies or scones, served on the veranda in summer or in front of the living room fireplace in cool weather. New innkeepers Katy and Jed Wood (she a protege of Don Johnson, who she says "taught me well") were planning interesting weekend packages in the off-season; the 1991 Valentine's package included a harpist and a flutist playing for afternoon tea and Sunday brunch. The one-and-a-half-acre property, with lovely rolling green lawns and landscaped with old lilac trees and Japanese maples, has 156 feet of bay frontage. You couldn't ask for a nicer place to unwind. Doubles, $150 to $175. No smoking.

Balance Rock Inn, 21 Albert Meadow, Bar Harbor 04609. (207) 288-9040. This gray-shingled masterpiece, built in 1903 and facing the ocean across two acres of lawns and gardens, was opened lately as a B&B by the folks who run the Ledgelawn Inn in town. Because of local zoning laws, only three rooms can be rented, but what rooms they are! A gorgeous staircase leads to the first of the three, with a sofa, fireplace, kingsize four-poster bed, deep green carpet and a jacuzzi bath. Nicest is the master bedroom with an adjacent deck for enjoying the view. All rooms have fireplaces, TV, antiques and whirlpools or steam baths. A full breakfast with a choice of eggs is served outside on a flagstone patio with white wrought-iron furniture. Wine and cheese are put out in the afternoon in a smashing sitting room. Doubles, $185 to $250. Seasonal.

Bass Cottage in the Field, off Main Street, Bar Harbor 04609. (207) 288-3705. A huge, glassed-in front porch full of wicker lounges and rockers greets visitors to this Victorian inn that shows its age at the edge of downtown Bar Harbor. Anna Jean Turner is running the place first opened to guests by her mother and her aunts in 1928. She offers ten guest rooms, ranging from singles to family quarters and accommodating an average of fifteen people. Six have private baths and three share. Well-worn oriental rugs and most of the original appointments date from 1885. "We don't serve breakfast because we're right downtown," says Anna Jean. Doubles, $50 to $90. Open Memorial Day to Columbus Day.

Seeing and Doing _____ ᏟᏟᏟ

Acadia National Park, the largest national park in the East, is Mount Desert Island's big draw. The 38,000 acres encompass 44 miles of dramatic coastline, all the island's major mountains, part of the Somes Sound fjord, all or part of every major lake shore, 120 miles of trails and bike paths, and a scenic twenty-mile Loop Road and Ocean Drive that allow drivers to see the highlights.

The **Visitor Center** on Route 3 south of Hull's Cove is a must for orientation purposes (you also can tune your car radio to a special frequency detailing park events and highlights). Up a two-minute walk from an expanded parking lot is a rustic contemporary building in which a fifteen-minute movie is shown on the half hour from 8 a.m. to 6 p.m., park rangers offer advice about trips and naturalist programs, and you can rent a self-guiding cassette-tape tour of the park (rental of player and tape, $9.95; tape only, $6.95). Here also you get your first panoramic view of Frenchman Bay from on high.

Admission to the park is by weekly pass, $5 per car or $2 per person. Annual passes cost $15.

PARK LOOP ROAD. Starting from the Visitor Center, this twenty-mile loop can take three hours (with stops) or a day. The two-lane, limited-access roadway can be entered or left at several locations, but the Ocean Drive segment is one-way outbound. The first two overlooks provide good views of Frenchman Bay, Bar Harbor and the area burned in the 1947 fire.

Sieur de Monts Spring, covered by a small octagonal structure but still bubbling water from a fountain in the adjacent nature center, is a favorite stop. The **Robert Abbe Museum of Stone Age Antiquities** tells most of what you could want to know of the area's history, especially of the Indians (adults $1.25, children 25 cents). The wonderful **Wild Gardens of Acadia** has more than 300 plants indigenous to the area's forests, mountains and shores labeled and grouped in thirteen sections, from deciduous weeds to dry heath and bog. Well-maintained gravel paths lead past some rare specimens, with benches placed strategically along the way. (If the Wild Gardens whet your appetite, stop later at the showy **Asticou Terrace and Thuya Gardens** in Northeast Harbor.)

367

The 1.4-mile **Precipice Trail** rises sharply from the Champlain Mountain overlook. The males in our family climbed it and returned with the report that it took 90 minutes to get up, 40 minutes to come down, and that there were two tunnels and countless firemen-type ladders to traverse, with sheer drops to contemplate. The wild blueberries along the way and the view from the barren summit made the hike worthwhile.

Going from the sublime to the ridiculous, cool off after your climb at **Sand Beach,** the only saltwater beach in the park and an arc of sand between two cliffs. You may notice hundreds of people on the beach and only a few brave souls in the ocean. Feel it and you'll know why; the water temperature rarely tops 55. If you like to get numb, head for the changing room, don your suit and c'mon in, the surf's fine. Otherwise, soak up some sun — if it's not obliterated by fog — or hike the easy 1.8-mile Ocean Path along the water.

Thunder Hole is where the waves rush into a small cave and roar out with a thunderous sound, if tides and surf coincide. At **Otter Cliffs,** look out to sea from the highest headlands on the East Coast. Beyond is **Otter Point,** a rocky place good for sunning and picnicking.

Leaving the ocean, the Park Loop Road turns inland toward **Jordan Pond.** Stop for lunch or tea at the venerable Jordan Pond House (see Where to Eat) and admire the view of the two rounded mountains known as the **Bubbles** (named by a long-ago youth for the bosom of his amour). At the end of Jordan Pond is a huge boulder balancing atop a cliff.

Pass beautiful **Eagle Lake,** which gets smaller and bluer as you drive the 3.2-mile side trip up **Cadillac Mountain.** The road is excellent and gradual (an eight percent grade, which our son bicycled up) and the view from the top is incredible in all directions. A short summit trail has interesting interpretive signs. The Sunset Parking Area near the top is where everyone gathers to watch the sunset — the mountains and waters to the west a changing rainbow of greens, blues, oranges and reds. It's an enlightening sight to anyone who thinks Key West or Carmel sunsets are the ultimate.

Descend Cadillac Mountain and you've completed the loop. Follow the signs to Bar Harbor or other destinations.

OTHER DRIVES. So far, you've seen only a portion of the park, albeit the most popular part. Head for Northeast Harbor and **Sargent Drive,** which borders the fjord-like **Somes Sound.** There are spectacular views all the way around to quaint **Somesville.** Down the west side of Somes Sound is **Echo Lake,** which offers a fine beach, changing rooms, and water far warmer than the ocean. It's a short hike or a long drive around Echo Lake to **Beech Cliff,** which has a great view of the lake below and where if you holler, you may hear your echo. Farther down the peninsula past Southwest Harbor is a section of the park containing **Seawall, Wonderland,** the **Ship Harbor Nature Trail** (which is well worth taking), and the **Bass Harbor Light.** These are the high spots of Acadia National Park on Mount Desert Island; other sections of the park are off-island on Isle au Haut and on the mainland Schoodic Peninsula.

It's a long way around, but don't miss **Schoodic Peninsula.** As far as civilization goes, most of this is a world apart from Bar Harbor (the only accommodations of note are in the fine new **Bluff House at Osprey,** Route 186, South Gouldsboro 04678, (207) 963-7805. It's breathtakingly situated across Frenchman Bay from Cadillac Mountain, and offers eight rooms with private baths, breakfast, and dinner Tuesday-Saturday; doubles, $65 to $75, B&B). Drive around fashionable **Winter Harbor** to see how the other half lives before heading down the one-way loop around **Schoodic Point,** where the crashing surf is awesome. We could spend hours here watching gulls, climbing rocks, viewing Mount Desert Island across the way, admiring passing lobster boats and generally chilling out. The park offers plenty of space for picnics and privacy.

CARRIAGE PATHS. Fifty miles of carriage paths were planned and built by John D. Rockefeller Jr. in the 1920s to provide a refuge for carriages from the intrusions of the auto. The ten-foot-wide paths follow the land's contours, protected by stone culverts and retaining walls and notable for thirteen interesting, hand-cut stone bridges. About eighteen miles of the paths have been specially surfaced for bicycles; the rest are better for hikers, mountain bikers and horseback riders. The park offers six different two-hour rides by carriage or haywagon, leaving from Wildwood Stables by reservation (276-3622). One goes to the Jordan Pond House for tea and popovers. Adult rates are generally $10 for carriages and $8 for haywagons, children $6 and $5.

NATURALIST PROGRAMS. The park conducts a remarkable range of programs and tours, from boat cruises to mountain hikes to nature walks to evening activities. They follow a set daily schedule (available from the Park Visitor Center), starting with a three-hour birder's walk at 7:30 and ending at 9:30 with Stars over Sand Beach. Among the more appealing titles are For the Birds, Forests of Lilliput, Mr. Rockefeller's Bridges Walk, Trees along the Trail and Written in the Rocks. The park naturalists or their assistants are personal and enlightening, and we've enjoyed every tour or program we've tried.

Active Pursuits

BIKING. Although the terrain is hilly, biking opportunities abound throughout Acadia National Park and Mount Desert Island. The park visitor center offers detailed maps of roads and trails through the park. Cyclists can take the same routes as listed above on the Park Loop and other drives. They can get away from cars and trailers on the park's carriage paths. The Eagle Lake-Witch Hole Loop is a five-hour carriage park ride with spectacular views of lakes, mountains and ocean. For shore-viewing, bike the road to Seawall and Wonderland. A longer excursion is to take the 40-minute ferry ride from Bass Harbor to **Swan's Island.** We once picnicked in an eerie fog at deserted Hockamock Head Lighthouse high on a cliff with a bell buoy ringing off shore and an abundance of raspberries, blueberries and gooseberries waiting to be picked. Swan's Island seems not to have a level stretch, however, and pedaling up all the hills isn't easy for aging legs. Bicycles are available for rent in Bar Harbor at Mopeds of Maine, 116 Main St.; Bar Harbor Bicycle Shop, 114 Cottage St., and Acadia Bike & Canoe, 48 Cottage St.

HIKING. Besides 50 miles of carriage paths, 120 miles of hiking trails await the hiker. They vary from mountain climbs (naturalists lead hikes up Acadia and Gorham and Huguenot Head) to self-guided walks for casual strollers — the Jordan Pond nature path and the Ships Harbor nature trail.

HORSEBACK RIDING. Wildwood Stables, Park Loop Road near Seal Harbor, 276-3622, offers one-hour guided horseback rides five times daily from 9:30 for $8 per rider. Hour-long horse-drawn mountain carriage tours over the carriage roads leave three times a day starting at 10 (adults $8, children $5). A two-hour sunset hayride to the summit of Day Mountain leaves at 6:30 in June and July, at 6 in August and 5:30 in September (adults $8, children $5).

CANOEING AND KAYAKING. The lakes of Mount Desert Island are considered a canoeist's paradise. Locals recommend Long Pond, the island's largest with three access points; secluded Seal Cove Pond, Echo Lake, Eagle Lake and Jordan Pond. Tidal currents in Somes Sound are dangerous for light craft; you also might be surprised by frolicking porpoises. Canoeing the Bass Harbor Marsh at high tide is quite an experience, especially on a moonlit night when you may hear and see herons, owls, beavers and deer. Canoes may be rented from **Acadia Bike & Canoe,** 48 Cottage St., Bar Harbor (half day, $16; full day, $22), or **National Park Canoe Rental** at Pond's End in Somesville (mornings, $15; afternoons, $18, and full day, $25). **Coastal Kayaking Tours,** 48 Cottage St., Bar Harbor, 288-5483, conducts a variety of tours and rents kayaks.

SWIMMING. The only ocean beach is **Sand Beach** (see Acadia National Park). Lifeguards staff it and the park's **Echo Lake.** Explore or ask around and you may come upon a little beach or swimming area on others of the numerous freshwater lakes. If you're adventurous (some would say foolhardy), you can swim off the rocks or in the coves of Frenchman Bay.

Walk the Bar. For two hours on either side of low tide, you can walk across a sand bar from the end of Bar Harbor's Bridge Street (just west of the Bar Harbor Club) to Bar Island. There are trails and shoreline to explore, and the shallow water is considerably warmer than at Sand Beach. Bring a picnic and a bathing suit, but don't tarry or you may have to swim back against the current.

Boat Cruises

NATURALIST SEA CRUISES. Park naturalists conduct cruises aboard privately owned boats, and these are among the more informative of all the island's cruises. Tours as scheduled in 1990: **Frenchman Bay,** Municipal Pier, Bar Harbor, 288-3322, two-hour cruise in search of eagles, ospreys and porpoises, daily except Thursday at 10, adults $12, children $9. **Bass Harbor,** Swan's Island Ferry Terminal, 244-5365, two hours of Down East scenes related to the lobster industry, daily except Sunday at 1, adults $12, children $9. **Islesford Historical Cruise,** Municipal Pier, Northeast Harbor, 276-5352, three hours through Somes Sound and Cranberry Isles to Little Cranberry Island to visit Islesford Historical Museum, daily except Sunday at 9:30, adults $9, children $6. **Baker Island,** Municipal Pier, Northeast Harbor, 276-3717, four-hour cruise to isolated, storm-sculpted Baker Island, daily except Thursday at 1, adults $12, children $7.

Frenchman Bay Co., 1 West St., Bar Harbor, 288-3322, offers 21 sightseeing, sailing, whale-watching and fishing cruises of Frenchman Bay daily in summer. Costs range from $8.50 adult, $6.50 child for one-hour cruises to $25 adult, $18 child for a four-hour whale watch. Half-day deep-sea fishing tours leave at 8:15 and 1:30, $25 per person. The Bay Lady II gives two-hour windjammer cruises four times daily; adults $16, children $12.

Aunt Elsie's Nature Cruise, 60 West St., Bar Harbor. 288-9505. The Aunt Elsie takes passengers to watch lobster traps being hauled up and to enjoy lobster and crab cooked on board. Ninety-minute trips leave four times daily starting at 9. Adults $15, children $11.

Acadian Whale Watcher, Golden Anchor Pier, West Street, Bar Harbor, 288-9794. Billed as the largest and fastest whale-watch boat on the East Coast, this cruises the open Atlantic for four to five hours twice daily to look for whales, sharks, seals, porpoises, dolphins and birds. Adults $25, children $15. The 149-passenger boat also gives sunset cruises nightly; adults $9, children $6.

Natalie Todd, 27 Main St., Bar Harbor, 288-4585. This traditional three-master schooner offers two-hour sails daily at 10, 2 and 6. It leaves from the Bar

Harbor Inn pier and passes islands, lobster boats hauling their traps, bald eagles and porpoises. Adults $16, children $10.

Other Attractions

MUSEUMS. The Natural History Museum of the College of the Atlantic, Route 3, Bar Harbor, has exhibits relating to the island's marine mammal, seabird and plant life. Visitors are encouraged to disassemble and reassemble the backbone of a twenty-foot whale skeleton and to walk nature trails. Open daily 9 to 5, June to Labor Day. Adults $2.50, children 50 cents. The **Bar Harbor Historical Museum** in the basement of the Jesup Memorial Libary at 34 Mt. Desert St. has a collection of early photographs, hotel registers and a large scrapbook on the 1947 fire. Open Monday-Saturday 1 to 4; free. The **Mount Desert Oceanarium** along the working waterfront off Clark Point Road, Southwest Harbor, offers much of interest to young and old who like the sea, and the Mills family owners are particularly involved in enhancing Maine's lobster industry. Lately they've established a site in Bar Harbor called the **Lobster Hatchery,** One Harbor Place, next to the Municipal Pier, 288-2334. A tour shows how lobsters are raised for release in Maine waters, and visitors can observe young lobsters through a TV microscope. Open Monday-Saturday, 9 to 5; adults $2.50, children $1.50.

MUSIC. Band concerts are presented by the Bar Harbor Town Band Monday and Thursday evenings at 8 on the Village Green. The green also is the site of other events, including a mid-July Dulcimer Festival. The **Bar Harbor Festival** presents weekend concerts during the summer. Live entertainment is offered at **The Casino,** upstairs at 119 Main St., and a musical revue and an original comedy are presented during and after dinner at **The Unusual Cabaret,** 14A Mt. Desert St. The **Acadia Repertory Theater** has a full summer season in Somesville, and always fun is the dinner-show at **The Deck House Restaurant and Cabaret Theater** in Bass Harbor.

SHOPPING. Bar Harbor shops are concentrated along Main, Cottage and Mount Desert streets. **Island Artisans,** a co-op, is owned by the two dozen artists who are represented in the handsome shop by a variety of wares, and we often do a little Christmas shopping here when we're in town. The Bar Harbor headquarters of the **Acadia Shops,** which also are located in the national park and have an exceptional shop at the Jordan Pond House, features the crafts, gifts and foods of Maine. **Cool As A Moose** is where to get a bathing suit or a T-shirt. The **Great Whale** has interesting paintings and gifts, and we like the clothes at the **Town & Country Shop. J.H. Butterfield Co.** is a gourmet grocery store of the old school (and they will put up a delightful picnic for you.)

Where to Eat

With only 7,000 year-round residents to support them in the off-season, most island restaurants operate seasonally — generally from April or May to October or November.

A Waterside Feeling

The Bayview Inn, 111 Eden St., Bar Harbor. (207) 288-5861. Dine as the elite did in days gone by in the formal dining room or the dark paneled library at this mansion overlooking Frenchman Bay. First, however, have a drink on the flower-bedecked rear terrace, to which you might want to return to watch the Bluenose ferry pass as you sip an after-dinner cordial. Entrees are priced from

$14.95 for grilled basil chicken to $24.95 for veal ribeye with seafood mixed grill in lobster cream sauce. Grilled salmon, lobster au poivre, shrimp aioli, chateaubriand and roast baron of lamb are other choices on the continental menu. Among appetizers ($6.95 to $7.95) are gravlax, carpaccio and Maine crab cakes. A grand marnier-soaked orange cake with ice cream and uncommonly good brewed decaf followed our dinners. A small but select wine list is on the pricey side for Maine. Dinner nightly, 6 to 9 or 10; Sunday brunch, 10:30 to 2.

The Fin Back, 78 West St., Bar Harbor. (207) 288-4193. The harbor is on view across the street from this new little restaurant, pretty in pink and green with neon squiggles on the ceiling and white cloth mats on tables with green marbelized tops. Pink and white material billowing beneath the peaked ceiling creates a beachy effect. Chef-owner Terry Preble offers an ambitious menu, from boneless chicken stuffed with goat cheese and cilantro pesto to Maine lobster and asparagus coquille en casserole. Pork tenderloin with Mexican sauce, duck breast with port wine and filet mignon with sundried tomato aioli are some of the other entree choices ($10.95 to $16.95). Start with shrimp and pistachio pate, crab cakes or wild mushroom ravioli. Finish with strawberry strudel, white chocolate mousse or kiwi sorbet. The wine list is extremely affordable; there's no hard liquor and no smoking. Dinner nightly, 5 to 11. Open late May to late October.

The Reading Room, Newport Drive, Bar Harbor. (207) 288-3351. The redecorated circular dining room of the Bar Harbor Inn and Motor Inn is prettier than ever, all in deep cranberry colors accented by pots of yellow and white mums and the finest ocean panorama around. You feel as if you're sitting right over the water as you dine on such American classics as grilled tuna, lobster newburg, baked stuffed shrimp, rock cornish game hen, prime rib with popover and New York strip steak, nicely priced from $12.50 to $19 (for boiled lobster with steamers and mussels). Chilled salmon with apples and poppy seeds and baked artichokes stuffed with seafood and gruyere are among the appetizers. Typical desserts are chocolate-chambord cake and strawberry-amaretto torte. The outdoor **Gatsby's Terrace** is lovely for waterside meals. Lunch daily, 11:30 to 2:30; dinner, 5:30 to 9:30. Open April to Thanksgiving.

Jordan Pond House, Park Loop Road, Acadia National Park (207) 276-3316. A tradition since 1895 (except for a year's absence following a 1979 fire), the rebuilt Jordan Pond House is more popular than ever. The interior is strikingly contemporary, with cathedral ceilings, huge windows and fieldstone fireplace. For lunch, we prefer to sit outside on the "porch," which is more like a covered terrace, where you can look down the lawns to Jordan Pond and the Bubbles, past the picnic tables where afternoon tea with popovers ($5) is a must for residents and visitors alike. The menu is limited but appealing. Our most recent lunch included a fine seafood pasta ($6.50) and a curried chicken salad ($6) garnished with red grapes and orange slices; we shared a popover — a bit steep at $2, considering it was hollow. Popovers come with dinners, priced from $12 for baked chicken with herbed stuffing to $19 for filet mignon and $19.50 for lobster salad. Accompaniments range from fresh lemonade, homemade ice cream and bread pudding to exotic international coffees. Lunch, 11:30 to 2:30; tea, 2:30 to 5:30; dinner, 5:30 to 9. Open mid-June to mid-October.

Galyn's Galley, 17 Main St., Bar Harbor. (207) 288-9706. You can watch half the world go by from the tiny front porch or the upper deck at this establishment sandwiched between Geddy's Pub and the Bar Harbor Cookie Factory a half block from the pier. Fresh seafood is the specialty, outside or in a couple of nautical dining rooms, and lunch is said to be particularly good here. The food is a cut above most of its ilk: fresh fish specials, shrimp saute, sauteed scallops with scallions and garlic, chicken piccata, New York strip steak and pasta tossed with chicken, ham and mushroom. Entrees are nicely priced from $8.95 to $12.95. Lobster stew, stuffed mushrooms and shrimp cocktail are among starters. Finish with homemade Indian pudding, chocolate mousse or New York-style cheesecake. Light fare is offered at the mahogany bar in the new **Galley Lounge,** and live jazz is played Saturday and Sunday nights. Open daily from 11 to 10 or 11. Closed in December.

Duffy's Quarterdeck, 1 Main St., Bar Harbor. (207) 288-5292. Twin lobster tails were going for $15.95 last we knew at this plain restaurant specializing in steaks and seafood, with a nautical decor and windows onto West Steet toward the water. Entrees range from $10.95 for chopped sirloin to $17.95 for "our own version of surf and turf," New York sirloin and half a lobster. Lunch, desserts and drinks are served on Mr. D's Upper Deck, a sunny — make that hot — place with little relief from blue umbrellas over the tables. But the water view is cooling. Open 7 a.m. to 10 p.m., Upper deck from 11 til closing. Open May-October.

The Pier, Golden Anchor Pier, West Street, Bar Harbor. (207) 288-9740. The former Chart Room restaurant on a pier jutting into the harbor has been gussied up by the owners of the Golden Anchor. Two interior dining rooms in pink and gray are flanked by an enclosed wraparound deck, and topped by an open-air deck screened by glass windbreaks on the roof. It's a good place for a drink or a casual meal. Seafood, steaks and typical Down East fare is offered in the $9 to $15 range. Open for three meals daily in season, 8 a.m. to 10 p.m.

Fisherman's Landing, West Street, Bar Harbor. (207) 288-4632. Very casual is this long-established place on a working fishing pier, to which we head whenever we're in the mood for Maine lobster. It was the first outdoor restaurant in a town that suddenly has many. You order in a steamy shack called the Cook House, pick up beer or a carafe of wine from the adjacent bar and find a table under a pavilion or, preferably, outside by the water or on the new Eagle's Nest upper deck with umbrellaed picnic tables. Soon you'll enjoy one of the most succulent lobsters ever to be boiled ($6.25 for a one-pounder, $7.50 a pound for those over 1 1/2 pounds). The french fries are terrific, and a good lobster roll costs $6.50. There are hot dogs ($1.15) and fishburgers ($2) for those who prefer. Open daily in summer, noon to 9. Open June-September.

Other Choices

George's, 7 Stevens Lane, Bar Harbor. (207) 288-4505. Run by a retired high-school history teacher, this summery place in a little Southern-style house off Main Street behind First National Bank doles out some of our favorite food on the island, imaginatively and with a Greek orientation. White organdy curtains flutter in the breeze, classical guitar music plays in the background and everything is served on clear glass plates atop pink-linened tables. On our latest visit, hot crusty French bread and the best little Greek salads ever preceded our entrees ($11.95 to $19.95) — a distinctive plate of smoked scallops on fettuccine and a special of shrimp on a fresh tomato sauce with feta cheese, rice pilaf and New Zealand spinach with orange juice and orange zest. Only a lemon cloud with a slightly soggy crust was not up to snuff. The appetizers are assertive (perhaps artichoke hearts baked in phyllo with bechamel, and kasseri cheese boiled with garlic), and the entrees inventive (mustard shrimps, lamb seared with pepper and onion, veal sauteed with grapefruit, and duck breast sauteed with honey-rum mango). The seafood strudel is a knockout, the house Greek wine tangy, and the desserts usually first-rate. There's dining on an outdoor terrace, and a pianist entertains in the new piano bar from 9 to midnight. Dinner nightly, 5:30 to 10, lighter dishes until midnight. Open mid-June through October.

The Porcupine Grill, 123 Cottage St., Bar Harbor. (207) 288-3884. The hottest dining spot in town since it opened in 1989 is this elegant but casual grill. It's handsomely furnished in antique oak drop-leaf tables and Chippendale chairs with Villeroy & Boch china, testimony to the antiques business run by owner Terry Marinke and her husband. Regulars like the main-floor cafe tables around the bar. We were seated in one of two upstairs dining rooms for a wonderful dinner that began with smoked salmon and caesar salad. Main courses (priced from $12.50 to $17.95) we sampled were grilled chicken with ginger and Maine shrimp on homemade pasta. Peach ice cream with ginger shortbread cookies made a refreshing dessert. The food and stylish atmosphere put this newcomer in league with George's for the best in town. Dinner nightly from 5:30; winter, Friday-Sunday from 6.

Maggie's Classic Scales Restaurant, 6 Summer St., Bar Harbor. (207) 288-9007. Her husband is a fisherman, so Maggie O'Connor is assured a supply of the fresh seafood in which her small establishment specializes. You may be seated on a newly enclosed porch overlooking pretty gardens or in a small room with about eight tables. Here's seafood the way it ought to be, from Boston blue scrod topped with homemade herbed mayonnaise and broiled haddock with ginger sauce to shrimp enchilada, lobster crepes and bouillabaisse, priced from $9.95 to $17.95. Sirloin steak and tandoori chicken are offered for non-fish eaters, as are vegetable and cheese strudel and spinach and artichoke lasagna. Oysters and shrimps from the raw bar, steamed mussels, and spicy phyllo packages filled with chilies and cheese are among the appetizers, and all vegetables are grown organically. Dinner nightly, 5 to 10:30. Open early June-December.

Brick Oven Restaurant, 21 Cottage St., Bar Harbor. (207) 288-3708. A 35-seat coffee shop catering to local families just grew and grew into a two-story affair that billed itself as a turn-of-the-century museum until it burned down in 1986. Rebuilt in five months, it reopened with a much brighter and lighter feeling inside a replica of an old church. But much of the funky charm remains: 1950s music, gasoline pumps, old signs, even a barber shop. Families sit in the old booths and feed their eyes as well as their stomachs. There's something for everyone on the large menu with categories for children, a pasta corner, a fitness center and such. Entree prices go from $8.85 for baked beans with sausage and steamed brown bread to $15.95 for lobster and broccoli fettuccine. Prime rib and lobster and seafood pie are specialties. The fresh haddock heavily flavored with herbs ($11.95) was one of the better fish dishes we've had, the excellent tossed salads contained everything from peas and sprouts to raisins and apples, and the baked sole wrapped around crabmeat in newburg sauce ($12.95) was too rich to finish. We couldn't even think of trying any of the ice cream concoctions or even a wedge of diner-style pie. Dinner nightly, 4:30 to 9 or 10.

FOR MORE INFORMATION: Bar Harbor Chamber of Commerce, 93 Cottage St., Box 158, Bar Harbor, Me. 04609. (207) 288-5103. Visitor centers are located at the entrance to Mount Desert Island on Route 3, the Bar Harbor Ferry Terminal and the Municipal Pier.

Algonquin Hotel is a landmark for visitors in St. Andrews.

St. Andrews By-the-Sea, N.B.

For many Canadians, no resort — not Mont Tremblant, not Banff nor even Jasper — has the mystique of St. Andrews-by-the-Sea. Since the late 19th century, it has been a low-key watering hole for old-money Canadians and Americans attracted by pollen-free air and a protected, picturesque setting surrounded by water on three sides at the southwestern tip of New Brunswick.

In the 1940s, the Canadian among us cherished the summers she spent with a friend whose family from Montreal owned a house in St. Andrews. Lazy days and nights, swimming at Katy's Cove, having sundaes at the counter and listening to the jukebox in the local teenage hangout, going to first-run films several times a week at the local movie palace (they reached St. Andrews even before Montreal), dropping into Cockburn's Corner Drug Store to be sprayed with the French perfume of choice by owner Bobby Cockburn on the way to the weekly dance, and a first summer romance are lasting memories.

Though the dance hall, movie theater and hangout are gone, St. Andrews still looks and feels much as it did in our teenage years. That's probably because this historic town, settled by British Loyalists fleeing Castine, Me., in 1783 — a year before the province of New Brunswick was born — has been passed over, in a way, by time.

The new arterial Route 1 from St. Stephen to St. John skips St. Andrews, ten miles to the south. The Canadian Pacific Railroad, whose founders built summer estates in the area, no longer stops there, and the Grand Manan ferry has moved its base from St. Andrews to Black's Harbour. Today, the traveler has to be aware of and want to visit St. Andrews to make the detour.

Canada's Old Guard resort peaked in the 1940s and lay somewhat dormant into the 1980s, according to M. Jean Stinson, descendant of original Loyalist settlers, who has run a number of visitor guide services in town. "St. Andrews was sort of at the end of the line. But now the town is waking up."

The air of optimism and the improvements for visitors in the last few years are obvious. The Algonquin Hotel has been renovated and expanded, newcomers have moved to town to become innkeepers and shopkeepers or to work for the Biological Station, and St. Andrews is preparing for a period of growth, according to James Frise, the Algonquin's general manager, who is overseeing plans for a major development on storied Minister's Island.

Sensing the town's incipient revival, Connecticut resident Kathleen Lazare purchased the delightful Pansy Patch cottage for an antiques and rare books shop and then opened a B&B. "There's a little bit of heaven here," she claims.

You'll find it along the shady streets dotted with historic homes and churches, along the shoreline forged by tides that rise and fall up to a staggering 26 feet a day, and on the sparkling waters of Passamaquoddy Bay.

But as ex-Bostonian Bill Dalton, a university professor and innkeeper, advises visitors, St. Andrews is "a place where you have to get yourself going. Touristy things aren't laid on you. It's so quiet and private that you really get in touch with nature here."

Getting There

Facing easternmost Maine just across Passamaquoddy Bay, St. Andrews is at the southwestern tip of New Brunswick off Route 1, about 50 miles west of Saint John. Take Route 127 south to St. Andrews. Calais is the main border entry point from Maine. Two short ferry rides provide a more scenic route from Lubec and Eastport, Me., via Campobello and Deer Island to Letete, N.B. They offer a glimpse of the area's maritime flavor, but run in summer only.

Prices are quoted in Canadian funds, which in 1990 represented a discount of about fifteen percent for Americans. But Canada's Goods and Services tax (GST), imposed starting in 1991, takes part of the difference. New Brunswick is in the Atlantic time zone, one hour ahead of Eastern time.

Where to Stay

Accommodations range from the manorial, veranda-swathed Algonquin Hotel to small B&Bs and a Kiwanis-run campground.

The Old Guard

The Algonquin, 184 Aldolphus St., St. Andrews EOG 2X0. (506) 529-8823. (800) 268-9411 (Canada) or (800) 828-7447 (U.S.). One of the grand old Canadian Pacific hotels that span the country, the 187-room Algonquin preserves a tradition of gracious resort life that has nearly vanished. One look at the turreted, Tudoresque hotel surrounded by lavish flower beds atop a knoll overlooking St. Andrews and Passamaquoddy Bay indicates that this is a special place. Add bellhops in kilts of the New Brunswick tartan (with incongruous-looking intercom beepers on their belts), the long lobby with comfortable peach chairs on which people actually are sitting, the enormous 375-seat Passamaquoddy Dining Room with windows onto the grounds, the book-lined Library Bar with nightly piano music, a large pool, tennis courts, a championship golf course and good conference facilities, and the result is a resort of world renown. That the historic hotel that had been started by Boston businessmen in 1883 as a private club had fallen on tough times in the post-war era is no longer of import.

Rescued by the provincial government in 1974 and managed since by CP Hotels, the Algonquin was immediately upgraded. When we visited in 1990, it was completing a five-year renovation program for all rooms. Those we saw had queensize beds with quilts in gray and peach, two upholstered chairs, cable TVs hidden in armoires, and modern bathrooms with baskets of toiletries; the melon-colored towels and sheets are a CP trademark. Rooms on the third and fourth floors have water views. Because the hotel was rebuilt with concrete walls, ceilings and floors after a 1914 fire, the rooms are solid and unusually quiet. Three meals a day are served in the dining room (see Where to Eat). For 1992, the Algonquin was planning an addition with 35 deluxe rooms and a banquet hall, and was working with the provincial government to develop Minister's Island (see Water Attractions). Doubles, $128 to $133; suites, $210 to $338; MAP available. Open mid-May to mid-October.

Tara Manor Inn, 559 Mowat Drive (Highway 127), Box 30, St. Andrews E0G 2X0. (506) 529-3304. A former private estate, Tara occupies twenty secluded acres crisscrossed by sculptured, century-old hedgerows on a hill overlooking Passamaquoddy Bay. Innkeepers Norman and Sharon Ryall started with two rooms in their residence in 1971, opened a dining room in 1980, and recently added what Norman called five "ultra rooms, the best in the Maritimes." The ones we saw had queen or kingsize beds partitioned off from sitting areas containing a sofa, two chairs and a remote-control TV. The three secluded suites with patios overlooking the gardens command top-dollar, but we like better the panoramic view of the bay from the suites off the third-floor balcony. We settled for one of the other twenty rooms in the old carriage house, boat house and servant's quarters, all with full baths and cable TV and comfortable indeed. Decor varies from French provincial to early American. All rooms are different but have striking draperies and Tara's signature collections of plates displayed in bays on the walls. Some have adjoining sun rooms or private balconies. The park-like grounds include a pleasant swimming pool. Doubles, $88 to $98; deluxe rooms and suites, $126 and $149. Open May-October.

The Rossmount Inn, Highway 127, R.R. 2, St. Andrews E0G 2X0. (506) 529-3351. This venerable Victorian manor house also overlooks the bay from a hill, this one at the base of Chamcook Mountain, highest in the area. Behind the inn are woods that are part of an 87-acre wildlife preserve; in front is a rather barren lawn leading up to a square building with yellow awnings that is almost comical-looking. You'd never suspect that the interior is the height of opulent Victoriana. Energetic young Texan Lynda Estes took over in 1986 from longtime innkeepers George and Marion Brewin, devoted Anglophiles who had given the Rossmount a reputation for eccentricity, haute cuisine and luxury lodging. A wide reception hall boasts the chair used by the king of Belgium at the coronation of Queen Elizabeth, a crystal chandelier and a floor covered with oriental rugs. A formal staircase leads to the second and third floors, where sixteen guest rooms (all with private baths) go off central hallways furnished with Victorian sitting areas (fine for sitting, but we had to go to a vacant west-facing room to be able to read in the late afternoon since our room lacked both comfortable chairs and good lights). Though covered with oriental rugs (which sometimes clash with the flowery bedspreads), the floors are thin and so are the doors, and a grandfather's clock in the hall chimed every fifteen minutes all night. Best rooms are those in the front corners with water views. All are furnished with fine antiques and Victorian accoutrements. The main floor has a dining room, a small parlor and an intimate bar in which resides a piano originally intended for Kaiser Wilhelm before World War I. A large raised deck surrounds a swimming pool beside the inn. Doubles, $95. Open early May through mid-October.

Small and Choice

The Pansy Patch, 59 Carleton St., St. Andrews E0G 2X0. (506) 529-3384. A fairy-tale white stucco cottage, with small-paned windows, towers and turrets and a roof that looks as if it should be thatched, stands across the street from the Algonquin Hotel. Built in 1912 by the superintendent of Canadian Pacific Hotels, it was fashioned after a Cotswold cottage. Kathleen Lazare of Connecticut, an antiques dealer, fell in love with it when vacationing in St. Andrews; she and husband Michael bought it and now have the largest rare book store in Atlantic Canada, plus an antiques business and four bedrooms for a B&B. A fire in the huge fireplace glows in the living room with its beamed ceiling; here guests may sit in the evenings, surrounded by the Lazares' 6,000 volumes. In the tiny breakfast room or on the back deck overlooking terraced gardens, she serves homemade blueberry waffles, french toast or cheese strata for breakfast. Homemade granola, local honey and strawberries are often on the docket. Kathleen Lazare also shows a deft touch in special seafood dinners for houseguests ($25 per person, with 24 hours' notice). Upstairs are four bedrooms sharing two bathrooms; the bedrooms are nicely decorated with antique furniture. We're partial to "The Large Room," done up in dark blue fabrics with a beautiful hooked rug and a window seat offering a view of Passamaquoddy Bay. Note the chandelier with wooden prisms over the stairs; it came from a Quebec church. The Lazares also operate **St. Andrews Antiques** at 221 Water St., dealing in primitive antiques and crafts. Doubles, $65. Open May 15 to Oct. 1.

Pippincott B&B, 208 Prince of Wales St., St. Andrews E0G 2X0. (506) 529-3445. Named after the old pippin apple tree that still grows apples like crazy out back, this is the summer home of one's dreams. Bob and Eleanor Parke offer two bedrooms and a suite, all with private baths, in their gray shingled house dating to 1860. Guests have use of a pleasant fireplaced parlor with patterned rugs and oodles of local books and magazines, a gracious dining room and a back porch looking across the lawn and trees. Tea and shortcake may be offered in the afternoon. Eleanor prepares a continental-plus breakfast of fresh-ground coffee, fresh juice and fruit, oatmeal or granola, and homemade breads with a zinger of a lime marmalade, served on fine English china and silver. Upstairs are a suite with a sitting room and bath with a clawfoot tub; a smaller bedroom with a double bed has its private bath adjacent. Another large bedroom was being renovated for guests downstairs when we visited. Rooms are notable for nicely refinished floors, dainty white curtains, sloping walls and super-quality mattresses. Doubles, $55 to $75.

Maxwell Manor, 276 Montague St., St. Andrews E0G 2X0. (506) 529-4170. A lovely pillared veranda leads to this elegant 1912 home, built for gentry of another era, according to owner Joan McDougall. One of nine houses designed locally by summer resident Edward Maxwell, an eminent Montreal architect, it's a spacious affair with interesting leaded and stained glass windows and doors, lace curtains, a fireplaced living room, and a library-TV room. Fresh flowers and bedside chocolates are in each of three large guest rooms, which share two baths. A buffet breakfast includes such hot items as sausage souffle or eggs cooked inside tomatoes. Doubles, $60 to $65. Open June-October.

Sea Garden, 469 Water St., St. Andrews E0G 2X0. (506) 529-3225. Ordinarily a facility with one room and no breakfast does not qualify for mention here.

"We're strictly bed and roof," says John Mackeen, but what a bed and what a roof! It's a charming "garage cottage" with a view — of the Mackeens' fabulous garden and a glimpse of Passamaquoddy Bay. The sweet little bedroom includes a bathroom, a black and white TV in a cupboard, an easy chair, hooked rugs and good watercolors, plus a view through a window that stretches to the floor. Double, $50. Seasonal.

Other Options

St. Andrews Motor Inn, 111 Water St., St. Andrews E0G 2X0. (506) 529-4571. This two-story motel emerged in 1989 along the waterfront and looks and feels new and in need of character. It seems smaller than its 33 rooms would indicate, much of the interior space having been given over to a largish indoor pool with big windows at the water's edge. All rooms are similar and all share a great view of Passamaquoddy Bay, which makes the facility unique in St. Andrews. Rooms have two queensize beds, remote-control TV, white molded chairs on the balconies and small bathrooms with the sinks outside. A few larger efficiency units have private decks. Coffee and donuts are available for breakfast in the reception area. Doubles, $89.95 (weekly, $450); efficiencies, $109.95.

Marcia's Garden Corner, 364 Montague St., St. Andrews E0G 2X0. (506) 529-4453. Marcia Thomson opened this B&B in 1990 after taking in community-college students over the winter. She offers three rooms sharing two baths. The rear room has a brass queensize bed; the other two are twins, one of them with waterbeds. Marcia serves a full breakfast, sometimes including homefries and fried tomatoes, in a room with a wood stove. Doubles, $50 to $60.

Best Western Shiretown Inn, 218 Water St., Box 145, St. Andrews E0G 2X0. (506) 529-8877. Built in 1881, this curbside hostelry in downtown St. Andrews bills itself as Canada's oldest summer hotel, though purists might find the Best Western connection a bit disconcerting. The white clapboard hotel has a pillared veranda that becomes a sidewalk cafe with umbrellaed tables in summer. Waitresses in Colonial garb scurry around two dining rooms with pressed-tin ceilings and lace curtains and tablecloths, and an English-style pub serving "pub grub." The inn's 26 rooms have been modernized to Best Western standards, including color TV, phones and private baths. But the original dressers and tables from the old Kennedy Hotel have been refinished to blend with the atmosphere of the period. Innkeeper Ian MacKay, the town's most active entrepreneur, also owns the Smuggler's Wharf and Lighthouse restaurants, as well as the **Smuggler's Village** efficiency apartments across Water Street with views of the harbor. The fourteen units there vary from one to three rooms; all have kitchenettes, TV and patios, and rent for $85 to $95 daily, $375 to $550 weekly. Doubles in inn, $66 to $90.

Seaside Beach Resort, 351 Water St., Box 310, St. Andrews E0G 2X0. (506) 529-3846. This complex of 22 housekeeping cottages with access to the waterfront is good for families, as we found in the mid-1970s on our first family trip to St. Andrews with children. At that time, we found no one restaurant to suit our varied (make that outspoken) tastes, so ended up barbecuing a steak outside our cottage here. And our older son was kept amused at night playing Scrabble across the street with an elderly guest at the Sea Side Inn, then under joint ownership. The cottages have been upgraded a bit from the state we remember them in; some are quite large, some have two bedrooms, and every unit has cable TV. A spacious lawn leads to the waterfront, where rowboats are available. Doubles, $50 to $60. Seasonal.

Snore by the Shore, 153 Water St., St. Andrews E0G 2X0. (506) 529-4255. Another good place for families is this amusingly named B&B operated since 1984 by ex-Bostonians Bonnie and Bill Dalton, she a goldsmith and he a professor at the University of New Brunswick in Fredericton. Three of the five guest rooms in the bright red structure have private baths. Its rooming house heritage is reflected in small, plain rooms with old beams and lace coverlets, brightened by colorful afghans made by the Daltons' daughter. An adjacent cottage offers kitchen, living room and beds for five. A full breakfast, including ham and eggs and homemade muffins, is served at two big tables set with local china and mats in a rear living-dining area or outside on the balcony, both of which look onto the water. Bill Dalton encourages guests to sail, windsurf or go scuba diving from his beach, which he describes as "very friendly at low tide." His wife keeps busy with her crafts and gift shop on the main floor. Doubles, $60; cottage, $80.

Picket Fence Motel, 102 Reed Ave., Box 424, St. Andrews E0G 2X0. (506) 529-8985. Bright yellow doors, lawn chairs and flowers in log pots make this nineteen-unit motel the most inviting of several at the edge of town. It's across from the Algonquin Hotel golf course, and set back a bit from the road beyond a shady lawn. A housekeeping unit for two is available. Doubles, $65. Open mid-May to mid-October.

CAMPING. Passamaquoddy Park Campground, Indian Point Road, St. Andrews E0G 2X0. (506) 529-3439. The Kiwanis Club of St. Andrews runs this spacious, well-equipped tent and trailer park at Indian Point, which has a clear view across a little-used road to Passamaquoddy Bay. The beach here is fine, and the campground is off by itself a mile from the center of town. It has 76 full hook-up sites, 35 with water and electricity and 46 unserviced sites. Reservations are not required.

Island View, another campground with 140 sites off Route 127 West in Bayside, overlooks St. Croix Island, where Samuel de Champlain spent the winter of 1604-05. It has a pool, but campers can also swim in the St. Croix River from Sandy Point.

Seeing and Doing _____ ✏✏✏

Surrounded by water on three sides, St. Andrews is naturally geared to water pursuits, which are very much affected by the enormous, 26-foot rise and fall of the Passamaquoddy Bay tides (influenced by the Bay of Fundy, which has the highest tides in the world). The area's rich marine life has made it an important center for marine biological research.

Water Attractions

SWIMMING. Katy's Cove, operated by the St. Andrews Swimming Club in cooperation with the Algonquin Hotel at the end of Acadia Road, is a favorite spot. Gates at the old railroad bridge at the mouth of the cove prevent the replacement of water at every high tide, so the cove is warmer than beaches on the bay (a sign said the water temperature was a relatively mild 63 when we were there in early July). Lifeguards staff the sandy beach, and there's a clubhouse where the porches are lined with old Adirondack lawn chairs. Admission is $1 daily. The beach at **Indian Point,** opposite the Kiwanis Club campground, is good for the hardy who like ocean-bay swimming. Beyond Katy's Cove and reached by Bar Road, the bar to **Minister's Island,** across which you can drive at low tide, provides more sheltered swimming. **Chamcook Lake** is a favorite with locals who like its crystal-clear waters and a secluded beach. North of town along the St. Croix River is **Sandy Point,** one of the few expanses of truly sandy beach in the St. Andrews area.

SAILING AND BOATING. Passamaquoddy Bay is protected from the open ocean by Deer and Campobello islands, so the sailing is better than off the open coasts of nearby Maine and New Brunswick. Varied boat cruises and whale-watching expeditions are offered; they can be arranged through **Cline Marine,** Water Street, 529-4188. A six-hour whale-search tour goes past Campobello and Quoddy Point (adults, $36). A 90-minute sunset cruise leaves nightly at 8 from St. Andrews (adults, $10). Island-hopping, an eight-hour tour offered by **HMS Transportation,** 260 Water St., 529-3371, leaves at 9 a.m. Fridays for St. George, Deer Island and Campobello; four to fourteen people are transported via ferries in a mini-van for $60 each. John Prince of **Prince Yacht Charters,** 180 Augustus St., 529-4185, offers a variety of sailing cruises aboard his CS 27 yacht Miss T.

BEACHCOMBING. Because of the enormous range of the tides, a wide variety of marine life can be found in the area between high and low tides. Walk the beaches or explore the shore near Minister's Island to find shells, mussels, sea urchins, starfish, sand dollars and such.

Minister's Island. The bar to Minister's Island, which we remember driving nervously across a decade ago, is under seventeen feet of water at high tide, so you don't want to get stranded out there. Canadian Pacific Hotels & Resorts (The Algonquin) is working with the provincial government on long-range plans to develop the 500-acre island as an executive conference center and a destination site for the public. The first phase includes 25 rooms in **Covenhoven,** the abandoned nineteen-bedroom estate of CP railroad magnate Sir William Van Horne, plus 30 more in outbuildings. The coach house is to be restored as a museum and opened to the public, as are the windmill and the gardener's house and greenhouse. The huge barn is envisioned as an equestrian center, the creamery as a country store, and another building as an interpretive center. Meanwhile, the island can be visited on Wednesdays and Saturdays under auspices of Jeff Holmes of HMS Transportation.

Other Activities

GOLFING. The Algonquin Hotel's famed golf course was not patterned nor named after the "Old Course" in St. Andrews, Scotland, contrary to belief. Algonquin officials say that golfers who have played both find that this has more hazards, is more capricious and requires a greater variety of shots than the Scotland course. Thirteen of the holes are played near or within sight of Passamaquoddy Bay, making it a particularly scenic setting. The first nine holes were constructed in 1894 and an additional nine holes were laid out in 1900. Another short nine-hole course with narrow fairways and small greens was added in 1921. The Algonquin envisions another eighteen-hole golf course as part of its development of Minister's Island.

WALKING TOURS. Settled in 1783 by United Empire Loyalists who floated their dismantled homes here from Castine, Me. (they were rebuilt and three are still standing), St. Andrews is said to have more examples of fine New England Colonial architecture than any other Canadian town. Everything from Cape Cod cottages to saltboxes to large Georgian houses with Federal detailing can be seen scattered across a grid of neatly squared lots laid out by town planners two centuries ago. More than 250 structures, many of them legacies of the prosperous era when St. Andrews was a port of call on the West Indies trade route, are over 100 years old. The 1824 **Greenock Presbyterian Church** looks like any white Colonial New England church, except for the unusual bright green oak tree carved on the exterior beneath its spire; other St. Andrews churches, particularly those along King Street, are architecturally interesting. Two-hour guided walking tours of the town and local sightseeing tours by bus are tailored to individual needs by HMS Tours, 529-4443.

Ross Memorial Museum, 188 Montague St., 529-3906. Here is a true house museum, acquired and given to the town by Henry Phipps Ross and his wife Sarah as a means to display their extensive collections acquired from world travels. Ross, a onetime Episcopal minister in Providence, R.I., and his wife, the daughter of the Bradstreet of Dun & Bradstreet in New York, summered here from 1902 to 1945. The imposing red brick Neo-Classical house was built in 1824 and acquired by the Rosses in 1938 for a museum. Their collection of decorative arts and furniture was accumulated mainly prior to World War I. When we were there, the special exhibit, which changes annually, showed their fascinating photographs and travel mementos from the 1925-26 world cruise of the S.S. Carinthia, the maiden voyage of the Cunard Lines ship. Guided tours, Monday-Saturday 10 to 4:30, mid-May to early October; also Sunday 1:30 to 4:30 from early July. Free.

Huntsman Marine Science Center and Aquarium, Brandy Cove Road, 529-4285. This is a fun spot for youngsters. They'll probably pass quickly through the basic exhibits, a slide show on "Quoddy Seas and Shores" and a movie, "The Sea." Ahead lies a heart-shaped "please touch" pool surrounded by a raised platform where kids can get close to shells, starfish, wolffish and a rare black sea bass. Harbor seals cavort in an open water tank and are fed at 10 and 4 daily. Don't miss Clyde, a stuffed 27-pound lobster, caught in 1962 off Campobello. Open daily, 10 to 6 in summer, 10 to 4:30 in spring and fall. Adults $3, students $2, family $8.

Atlantic Salmon Center, off Route 127, Chamcook. Just east of St. Andrews is the home of the Atlantic Salmon Federation, the newest in a scientific triumverate (also Huntsman Marine Science Center and the Biological Station of the Canadian Department of Fisheries and Oceans). Together they play a leading role in Canada's growing aquaculture industry — indeed, St. Andrews was host for the third annual Atlantic Aquaculture Fair when we visited in 1990. Opened in 1988, the salmon center has displays on the history and biology of "the king of fish," a viewing chamber where visitors can get a close-up look at salmon in a stream setting, and a nature trail that leads past the salmon rearing tanks along picturesque Chamcook Creek. Open daily 10 to 6, spring to fall.

St. Andrews Blockhouse, adjacent to Centennial Park, off Water Street. This restored, two-story National Historic Site was built of hand-hewn timbers in 1813 to protect St. Andrews from American privateers. Of twelve such blockhouses built in New Brunswick, it is the only survivor. Guides and interpretive displays explain the role of the blockhouse in the War of 1812. Open daily 9 to 8, June to Sept. 15. Free.

SHOPPING. The stores of St. Andrews along Water Street range, we think, from the ridiculous to the sublime. Fortunately there are getting to be far more of the latter:

Cottage Craft, on the waterfront at Town Square, with brightly colored skeins of wool draped around its cork fence in front, shows knit goods in lovely colors like robin egg blue, briar rose and yellow birch. The specialty here is a skirt and sweater kit, the sweater yarn exactly matching the skirt length. They also have knitting bags (one shaped like a house in which the door opens), men's tweed jackets and the neatest collection of mittens for kids you ever saw. **Sea Captain's Loft** is suavely filled with English china, ladies' wear including Geiger jackets and woolens, children's books and toys, and John Putnam's Heritage House miniatures. We picked up a couple of tea towels commemorating the 90th birthday of Queen Elizabeth the Queen Mother for gifts to Canadian relatives. The **China Chest** imports English bone china, Welsh and Scottish woolens and Canadian gifts.

Hollyhock & Vine purveys a little bit of everything in exquisite taste, from a shelf of beautiful glass paperweights to baby gifts, glassware, paper goods and charming arrangements of pressed flowers in frames. **Boutique La Balaena** has cute things like stuffed animals, cards, apparel and a large toy section. **Carriage House Studio,** in the same building as the B&B Snore by the Shore, is where Bonnie Dalton sells her gold and enamel jewelry, as well as interesting crafts, gifts and wooden things.

Stickneys Wedgwood Store, founded in 1842, is the oldest Wedgwood store in North America and the oldest store in St. Andrews. Operated by the Stickney family until 1976, it is now expanded with a complete range from Christmas plates to commemorative pieces. We enjoyed browsing in **Blue Peter Books,** which has a large selection of local lore, as well as maps, charts, nautical books and the like.

Artist Tom Smith, who has won many awards, shows his beautiful raku pottery at **Tom Smith Pottery** on Water Street. His wife Ellen, who manages the studio, makes the drawstring bags for Tom's raku teabowls. At the **Water Street Craft Gallery,** which specializes in Canadian crafts, we admired the hooked rugs done by a couple in their 80s who live nearby (she designs them, he hooks them) and the Padraig slippers lined with sheepskin and made in British Columbia (at $42, a little expensive for us). **The Pansy Patch,** across the street from the Algonquin, is crammed with antiques and paintings, and has an extraordinary rare book collection.

Where to Eat ⏤⏤⏤⏤⏤⏤⏤ ↄↄↄ

L'Europe, 48 King St., St. Andrews. (506) 529-3818. Just off Water Street in the heart of town is this rustic low brown building which, it turns out, is a remodeling of the aforementioned dance hall of our teen years. Copper pots and pottery bedeck the white stucco walls of the little dining rooms. Beamed ceilings, hanging lamps covered with fabric, fresh flowers and candles in antique candle holders make you feel you could be in the heart of Europe. Since 1984, Alex Ludwig and his wife Anita, the chef, have been serving up what is universally considered to be the best food in town from an extensive menu. On time for our reservation, we resisted going to the bar to wait, which we hear is a standard ploy here, and promptly got seated. Our dinner started with a good, hearty, complimentary pate and farmer's bread, followed by an interminable wait for salad, a zesty mix of greens, coleslaw, red cabbage slaw and bean salad. Main courses go from $13.95 for wiener schnitzel to $32.50 for filet mignon with morels. We liked the whole pork tenderloin flambeed in brandy, an enormous affair served with small potato balls and cauliflower, and rack of lamb with a superb garlic sauce. For dessert, we chose a chocolate truffle torte, a huge slab of cake topped by one truffle, from a choice that included peach cream cheesecake, butter cream mocha cake and black forest cake. Dinner nightly except Monday, 6 to 11. Closed in winter except for Christmas week.

The Evening Star at Tara Manor Inn, 559 Mowat Drive, St. Andrews. (506) 529-3304. Burgundy draperies and carpeting, pink linens, crystal chandeliers and live piano music create an elegant big-city setting in a country-inn dining room with a fancy name, one that you might not expect to find in little old St. Andrews. Our latest dinner began with a complimentary cheese spread with crackers and crab bisque, followed by good small caesar salads. Entrees were an excellent but bony stuffed trout with crisp carrots and snow peas, and a curried shrimp and chicken dish ringed by rice with little mounds of coconut, chutney and almonds. Curries are a house specialty: on another occasion, we tried the curried lamb and rice (much more rice than lamb), served with a tray of sliced almonds, chutney and bananas in sour cream, and a braised citrus pork with rice, green beans and almonds. A light blueberry cheesecake and Spanish coffee were worthy endings. Other entrees ($13.95 to $22.75) from the extensive continental menu include turkey stir-fry, chicken a l'orange, red snapper, poached salmon, roast rack of lamb and delmonico steak. Start with New Brunswick fiddlehead soup or oyster stew, among other interesting soups and appetizers. We loved sitting by the window as the shadows lengthened on the lawns, watching rabbits hopping around. Dinner nightly, 6 to 9:30. Open late May to mid-October.

Passamaquoddy Room, Algonquin Hotel, St. Andrews. (506) 529-8823. The airy, windowed veranda with large tables overlooking the gardens and pool is the most inviting section of the 375-seat dining room, elegantly appointed with damask linens, lace doilies on the china, fresh flowers and a particularly striking display of breads — one shaped like an alligator — near the entrance. Upwards of 500 people turn out for the Sunday brunch, a bargain at $15.95 for all you can eat. The daily lunch buffet for $6.95 (plus $3.05 for dessert) also is a treat. We enjoyed selecting from a lavish display of salads, cold salmon, peel-your-own shrimp, hot curried pork, halibut and pasta with shrimp, among others. The regular dinner menu ($15.95 to $22.75) ranges from curried filet of halibut to roast rack of lamb with juniper sauce. Prime rib with Yorkshire pudding and native lobster are popular, of course. The pride of the place is the new **Van Horne Verandah,** an intimate section partitioned off from the main dining room specializing in tableside service and leisurely dining. Here you might start with smoked Atlantic salmon or Malpeque oysters rockefeller, and caesar or radicchio salad. Among entrees ($16.95 to $24.95), try grilled local salmon, stuffed breast of pheasant, veal (a rarity in these parts) with fine herbs, or steak au poivre. Desserts range from pastries to flambeed crepes. The wine list is limited, as is the norm in New Brunswick, and rated according to sweetness. Lunch and dinner daily, early May to mid-October.

Rossmount Inn, Highway 127, St. Andrews. (506) 529-3351. Three stained-glass windows from an 18th-century chapel in Great Britain make up the bay window in the elegant, formal Victorian dining room at the Rossmount. Flickering candles in heavy red glass are overpowered by the light from overhead chandeliers, making the room rather too bright for our taste, and we felt almost as if we were eating in a museum. The style set by longtime innkeepers George and Marion Brewin was being maintained by new owner Lynda Estes. Lynda, trained in French cooking, is chef. We started with French onion soup and a green salad with a radish-cream dressing. Our main courses of very lemony but good scallops and poached halibut were served with crisp zucchini slices, plus a baked potato that didn't do anything for the seafood. A fruit trifle and a black forest cake surrounded by strawberries were delicious desserts. Lynda's menu ($13.95 to $21) ranges from Atlantic salmon, sole amandine and baked stuffed haddock to filet mignon. Dinner nightly by reservation, 6:30 to 9. Open early May to mid-October. No smoking.

Lighthouse Restaurant, Lower Patrick Street, St. Andrews. (506) 529-3082. A nicely nautical dining room dressed in brown and white has large windows overlooking Passamaquoddy Bay at a point beside the lighthouse. It's the choicest waterfront spot in town, and tourists like it for its lobsters (a fisherman's feast of salad, seafood chowder, lobster roll and beverage is $14.50). Other possibilities are seafood casserole, baked salmon, baked scallops and stuffed sole, $13.95 to $19.95. Although the food had been consistently inconsistent, local innkeepers were hearing better reports lately. The wine list is not one of the area's better, but the view certainly is. Lunch on weekends and in summer, noon to 2; dinner nightly, 5 to 9. Open May-October.

The Gables, 143 Water St., St. Andrews. (506) 529-3440. A pleasant, three-level deck shaded by a chestnut tree beside the water is the most appealing part of this restaurant, lately under the ownership of Ted Michener, an artist and cartoonist whose works grace the walls and the menu. Inside are a small dining room and bar, a large licensed dart room with pool tables in front, and a pub upstairs. The all-day menu offers casual, contemporary fare like nachos, deep-fried veggies, soups, salads and sandwiches, plus such entrees ($8.50 to $17.95) as barbecued beef ribs, seafood platter and surf and turf. Ted had just changed the menu, but we heard good things about the mussel, scallop and shrimp dishes. Open daily, 11:30 to 10.

Passamaquoddy Fish & Chip, On the Wharf, St. Andrews. (506) 529-4707. Walk out to the end of the municipal wharf to this rustic place with a takeout window and a few picnic tables scattered about. You'll find fish by the piece, fish and chips ($5.50), burgers, nuggets and such. A scallop plate with chips at $7.50 was the most expensive item; the lobster roll with chips was going for $5.75.

Copper Grill, 246 Water St., St. Andrews. (506) 529-4150. A good family spot of the old school, this newcomer is known for the best muffins east of Montreal, thanks to Rose Cleghorn. When we stopped for breakfast, she was whipping up a batch of chocolate chip muffins; we passed in favor of day-old blueberry, which were still good. The "super value breakfast" for $2.75 — two eggs, bacon, fries, muffin and coffee — lived up to its name. In a room with a long counter, booths and tables, you can get a lobster roll, sandwiches and homemade lemon meringue pie. Open daily 7 to 4, Friday and Saturday 7 to 7, Sunday 8 to 6.

The Victorian Lady, 288 Water St., St. Andrews. (506) 529-3473. From 1 to 4 you can stop for tea at this neat little tearoom and gift shop, with its painted green floor, pink walls and balloon curtains. At four tables, owner Dianne Cole serves two styles of tea. A British cream tea (with Devonshire cream, scones and her own rhubarb preserves) is $4. A Canadian tea ($6.50) brings a selection of tea sandwiches like salmon with egg salad, cheese and cherry rolls or turkey and cream cheese, along with little cakes and sweets. On Sundays, Dianne puts out a buffet of fancy desserts like trifle and cheesecake. The gift shop features adorable stuffed toys, elegant clothing and linens, and presents for babies. We picked up a row of stuffed elephants to hang on the crib of an expected newcomer to the family. Open daily 1 to 4 p.m. Seasonal.

FOR MORE INFORMATION: St. Andrews Chamber of Commerce, Box 89, St. Andrews, N.B. E0G 2X0, (506) 529-3000 or 529-3555. Tourist Bureau is at Market Wharf, foot of King Street.

Mahone Bay is on view from terrace at the Galley at South Shore Marine.

Chester-Lunenburg, N.S.

For those who have searched for a perfect seaside shangri-la along the Northeast Coast — search no longer. We've found it, in a place that until a few years ago we never realized was there.

It's the Chester-Mahone Bay-Lunenburg area along Nova Scotia's South Shore, about 50 miles southwest of Halifax. People call it variously Lunenburg County, the South Shore, Bluenose Country, the Lighthouse Trail. We call it wonderful.

Centered around Mahone Bay and its 365 islands, this low-key stretch of rather sophisticated villages upscales an otherwise provincial, seafaring area. Its undulating inlets are tranquil refuges from the rugged Nova Scotia coastline.

The area brings to mind the Maine coast as it used to be — secluded, unspoiled, yet with a welcome air of civility. It's not so isolated that you have to forego the amenities of good restaurants, inns, galleries and shops. But it's unfrequented enough that you have no sense of the crowds that jam similar areas in New England.

Chester, a village of 1,100 settled in 1759 by New Englanders, is on a peninsula at the head of Mahone Bay. Today it is a summer colony for wealthy Canadians and Americans and, perhaps, a resting place for Captain Kidd's buried bounty.

Lunenburg, called the Gloucester of Canada, was founded in 1753 by German Protestants and is Canada's oldest fishing port. With a population of 3,000, it's the colorful home of working fishermen and Bluenose schooners, and is reputed to be the most architecturally interesting town in Canada.

The village of Mahone Bay (population 1,200) is poised at the head of an inlet from the bay, whose sailing waters are considered among the best in the world. "We love the beauty around us and welcome you to share it," proclaim the endearing signs at the village limits.

Here is the one rural area in the Maritimes that matched our expectations for a balance of quaint charm and urbane shops, good dining on outdoor decks, picturesque harbors and peaceful beaches.

Perhaps you'll think like Lunenburg painter-shopkeeper Gail Patriarche, who fell in love with the area and moved from Ontario in 1981. Said she: "I'm an artist, and I felt I'd been cheated all my life until I got here."

Getting There

This area is easily reached in less than an hour via Route 103 from Halifax, Atlantic Canada's largest city and a major air and rail destination. It's about a three-hour drive via Route 103 from Yarmouth, where the ferries land from Bar Harbor and Portland, Me. Prices are quoted in Canadian funds and are subject to the new GST tax. The province is on Atlantic Time, one hour ahead of Eastern.

Where to Stay⎯⎯⎯⎯⎯⎯⎯⎯⎯⎯⎯⎯⎯⎯⎯⎯ _ⁿⁿⁿ_

Lunenburg and Mahone Bay are about ten miles apart, while Chester is about twenty miles northeast of Mahone Bay. The accommodations are grouped here by location.

Lunenburg and Mahone Bay

Boscawen Inn, 150 Cumberland St., Box 1343, Lunenburg B0J 2C0. (902) 634-3325. Perched astride a steep hill, this restored 1888 Victorian mansion has seventeen guest rooms (fourteen with private baths), a couple of formal parlors, an acclaimed dining room and an outdoor deck with a view across treetops and houses of Lunenburg Harbor. New innkeepers Michael and Ann O'Dowd from Toronto, he an outgoing Irishman, have retained the museum-quality pieces acquired by the last owner, an antiques dealer. They also have made the inn more welcoming than we found it on our first visit. Since our small room had space only for twin beds, one chair and a bureau and the Victorian parlors did not afford comfortable seats or good lamps for reading, we put on sweaters and went outside to read on the deck. The much larger upstairs rooms are elegant in a formal Victorian style with canopy or four-poster beds, fancy curtains and upholstered chairs. The top-of-the-line room, with a view of the harbor, has oriental rugs and a working fireplace. Three meals daily are served in the dining room (see Where to Eat). Doubles, $35 to $75. Closed January to Easter.

Brigantine Inn, 82 Montague St., Lunenburg B0J 2C0. (902) 634-3300. Lunenburg's most deluxe new inn emerged in 1990 above a downtown block facing the waterfront. Jonathan and Merle McCann offer five spacious rooms with queensize beds and two single rooms, all with modern baths. Stylishly furnished, each has cable TV, clock-radio and telephone. Those facing the water have bow windows with great views of the water, and one has a balcony. Locally made bed covers and draperies are colorful, and Merle McCann's artistic touch is evident in the striking posters and paintings on the walls. Guests have use of an inviting parlor with four loveseats covered in a pinky beige material. Picture windows frame the colorful waterfront. A full breakfast is served in the downstairs bistro and coffee shop (see Where to Eat), which offers some of the most interesting food in town. Doubles, $75 to $85.

The Compass Rose Inn, 15 King St., Box 1267, Lunenburg B0J 2C0. (902) 634-8509. The striking house painted maroon with cream trim, built for a sea captain in 1825 in the center of Lunenburg, offers five guest rooms for B&B and an excellent restaurant (see Where to Eat). Suzanne and Rodger Pike moved here in 1984 from Vancouver and have turned this into a going concern. The original Georgian facade was later Victorianized, its exterior dressed up in gingerbread style. Since our first visit, Rodger and his father transformed closets into small private baths for each of the five guest rooms. The Pikes also have opened the **Lion Inn** at 33 Cornwallis St., 634-8509, a four-room B&B with shared and semi-private baths, whose guests take breakfast at the Compass Rose (doubles, $45). At their main inn, rooms are charmingly furnished with puffy quilts and plump pillows on the beds, scatter rugs on painted floors, hanging Tiffany lamps and all kinds of colorful accents. One has a loveseat and two white-iron double beds; another has 1920s art deco furniture. A small parlor with a bar at one end is available for guests. A full breakfast is served in the mornings. Doubles, $45 to $55. Closed January and February.

The Rumrunner Inn, 66 Montague St., Box 1090, Lunenburg B0J 2C0. (902) 634-9200. Nine motel-style rooms with private baths were created in this downtown waterfront property in 1987 by Gene and Yvonne Tanner, who formerly owned a couple of local motels and now also run the Docksider restaurant. Rooms vary in size and shape, and four have full water views. There's also a huge apartment with a balcony off the living room, dining area, full kitchen and two bedrooms. Three B&B rooms are available in another building for $40. There's no common room, but a gift shop provides sundries. Down a spiral staircase is a large dining room in pink and burgundy, serving three meals a day. The nautical decor includes ship's models — one of them said to be the largest model of the Bluenose in Nova Scotia — and a 24-pound lobster on the walls. Complete dinners, including bread, cottage cheese, pickles, salad and sherbet, run from $12.95 for a single chop to $16.95 for Atlantic salmon or seafood platter. The seafood antipasto ($8.95 for two) is a sampling of Lunenburg's bounty. The outdoor deck is popular in season. Doubles, $56 to $75; housekeeping units, $85 to $125.

Bluenose Lodge, Falkland and Dufferin Streets, Box 399, Lunenburg B0J 2C0. (902) 634-8851. A local landmark that had seen better days, to put it mildly, this 125-year-old mansion has been nicely upgraded by new owners Ron and Grace Swan, ex-Montrealers for whom this was "a 27-year dream." A former sales manager for Canadian Pacific Hotels, Ron found this on the market on 1989, but Grace didn't see it until the day they moved in. They gave the exterior a magnificent facelift, one for all the townspeople to see at a major intersection, and new landscaping and signs. The dining room was refurbished (see Where to Eat), and the nine large guest rooms with private baths were spiffed up and made more homey. Four rooms go off a long and wide center hallway on each of the second and third floors. The end of each hallway has a little sitting area with a TV set. Soaps from the nearby North Mountain Soapery are in the bathrooms, and bedrooms have been redecorated with new wallpapers, curtains, quilts and knickknacks. The Swans have prepared a guest book detailing local activities and attractions, even where to get stamps. A complimentary breakfast might include stewed rhubarb, quiche and fresh muffins, and locals were crowding in for the all-you-can-eat breakfast buffet for $6.50. Doubles, $62 to $66. Open May-October.

The Lunenburg Inn, 26 Dufferin St., Box 1407, Lunenburg B0J 2C0. (902) 634-3963. Six rooms with private baths are offered by new innkeepers Faith and John Piccolo in this stately Victorian a bit away from the mainstream. The house follows the line of the nearby railroad tracks, and one room is shaped like a wedge as a result, Faith pointed out during a tour. Rooms are decorated with period furnishings and collectibles, "the kind you're not afraid to use," she notes. A third-floor suite has a whirlpool bath, full kitchen and a sitting room with TV. There's a lounge with books, TV and VCR. Rates include a full breakfast in the attractive dining room, where dinner also is open to the public (see Where to Eat). Doubles, $55; suite, $75. Closed in November.

Atlantic View Motel and Cottages, Mason's Beach, R.R. 2, Lunenburg B0J 2C0. (902) 634-4545. Nine motel units (five with kitchens) and five housekeeping cottages date back more than 40 years, but they're thoroughly up to date in terms of furnishings. And, my, what a view! Across the narrow, untrafficked road is the open Atlantic, and this is one of the few places in the area where you get to see it. From the motel efficiency units (kitchenette and living room with cable TV in front, bedroom with two double beds in the rear), each back door leads to a picnic table. Adirondack chairs are scattered out front for gazing at Battery Point Light. Longtime owners David and Betty Steele, who greet most of their guests by name, offer a heated swimming pool and a couple of rowboats for exploring the tidal pond in the rear; a hike along the path through the woods may reveal turtles and muskrats. Obviously, this is a good place for families, although we middle-agers enjoyed its comforts and relaxed pace as well. Doubles, $45 to $55, each additional $5. Open May-October.

Topmast Motel, Mason's Beach Road, Lunenburg B0J 2C0. (902) 634-4661. Twelve rooms and three housekeeping units have recently been refurbished and decks added to take advantage of the super view of the harbor from this hilltop perch across the greens of the Bluenose Golf Club. Rooms are furnished with two double beds and cable TV, and picnic tables and grills are available outside. Doubles, $45 to $55.

Bayview Pines Country Inn, R.R. 2, Indian Point, Mahone Bay B0J 2E0. (902) 624-9970. There's a splendid water view from the hilltop location of this inn opened in 1987 by Curt and Nancy Norklun, former Long Islanders, who fashioned a large barn into rooms with flair and creature comforts. His family were carpenters, and their background shows — from the collection of old molding planes in the dining room to the wonderful barn sitting area with old sleighs, farm utensils on the walls, hooked rugs and cable TV. Curt built the pine bed in the main-floor honeymoon room, which has an oval jacuzzi in the corner and a bathroom with a shower. He also put a soft-drink machine in the chicken coop and a telephone in the old outhouse. Three rooms are available on the second floor of the turn-of-the-century farmhouse, plus five new ones in the barn; all have private baths. Atlantic Canada prints adorn the walls of guest rooms, which are comfortable and abound with interesting touches. Two rooms in the barn have private entrances. The main house has a cute tea room where three meals a day are served (see Where to Eat), a gift shop in which all the crafts were made within five miles of Indian Point, and a cheery parlor in yellow and pumpkin colors with lots of reading material available. A hammock, chair swing and deck chairs await on the front porch. The 21-acre property includes nature trails but few pines; Nancy said they erred in thinking the spruce trees way out back were pines, so they planted a few seedlings near the house so it would live up to its name. Doubles, $50 to $75.

Longacres Bed & Breakfast, Clearland Road, Box 93, Mahone Bay B0J 2E0. (902) 624-6336. Featured in Chatelaine (a Canadian magazine) in 1985, this is a beauty of a house on a rural hilltop with a glimpse of Mahone Bay. New owners Ross and Sandy Hayden, the fourth family to occupy it in 200 years, share their bounty with guests in three spacious bedrooms, two with full baths and one with a half bath. Fine woodwork detail is evident throughout the house and the original quarter-turn stairs are as steep as they come. Interesting artworks and baskets of magazines are in all the rooms. Balloon curtains match the fabric of the pillows in one room, which has a white iron bedstead, two wicker chairs and baskets of magazines. The Bay Room has a queensize bed, a forsythia tree in the corner and cactus plants. Guests gather in a pretty parlor done in pinks and blues. A huge fireplace with a bakers oven is fitted with a wood stove. A full breakfast is served in the dining room, where a stained-glass chandelier hangs above a maple table with a wood swan in the middle. Sandy, a floral designer in Waterloo, Ont., her former home, makes fleecy sheep to sell in her nifty small gift shop off the parlor. Deer and pheasants roam the fifteen rolling acres, which include lovely gardens, a pond with a rowboat and a nature trail down to the Mush-A-Mush River, which borders the property. Doubles, $45 to $60.

Chester Area

Oak Island Inn & Marina, Route 3A, Western Shore B0J 3M0. (902) 627-2600 or (800) 565-5075. This motel with 69 units and four suites has everything, including the area's largest conference center, banquet hall, game room, indoor pool and sauna, hot tub and exercise room, room service, and dancing in the Anchorage Lounge. The best of the large rooms with two double beds and a pink and green decor are the half that face the water. From your waterfront room you can look across to Oak Island and dream of buried treasure. There's a private beach beside the bay, and the marina offers boat rentals, fishing charters and scenic cruises of Mahone Bay. The **Atlantic Room** is open for three meals a day, dinner from 5 to 10. Doubles, $65 to $89.

Windjammer Motel, Route 3, Box 240, Chester B0J 1J0. (902) 275-3567. Built in the late 1950s, this is still the only motel in Chester. Its season is short and "we could rent 100 rooms for 50 days," new owners Richard and Kim Johnson said of their eighteen-room establishment. Each room has two double or one queensize bed, full bath and color TV; deluxe rooms offer refrigerators, mini-bars and VCRs. Although the motel faces the road, its rear lawn slopes down to tiny Stanford Lake, where there are lawn chairs and picnic tables. There are a small pool in back and a mini-golf course out front. The **Windjammer Restaurant,** under separate management, is next door, serving lunch and dinner. Doubles, $45 to $53.

Sheet Anchor House, Central Street, Chester B0J 1J0. (902) 275-2112. Chester got a new and badly needed lodging facility in 1990 when Ronald and Barbara Chenevert moved up from Massachusetts and opened their 1783 house as a B&B. Across from the well-known Captain's House restaurant, this white clapboard house with black shutters and a stone terrace is full of wood paneling. Stenciling, rag and hooked rugs, a worn staircase, a clawfoot tub and an old oriental fireplace are among features. One of the four upstairs guest rooms, furnished in homey style, even has a crib. The Cheneverts serve a full breakfast in the fireplaced keeping room complete with a 1947 jukebox, or outside on the terrace. Doubles, $65. Seasonal.

The Cove B&B, Big Tancook Island, Lunenburg County B0J 3G0. (902) 228-2054. A 45-minute ferry ride from Chester takes people seven miles out in Mahone Bay to Big Tancook Island, three miles long and one mile wide. The island has a general store, gift shop, canteen, church and — hard to believe — a tourist bureau, plus the Cove B&B, just over a mile from the ferry landing (transportation arranged by phone). David and Martha Farrar offer two double rooms, two singles, two baths and bunkhouse facilities, plus ample lawn space for tenters. A hearty breakfast is included in the room price, and other meals from picnics to high tea may be arranged. The beach and nature trails are nearby. There are special rates for families and extended stays (once you get out here you may not want to leave). Doubles, $40; children $5 each.

Camping

Risser's Beach Provincial Park, Route 331 south of Bridgewater, 688-2034, is a beautiful park with an ocean beach and 90 unserviced campsites, both open and wooded; $8.50 nightly. The **Lunenburg Board of Trade,** Box 1300, Lunenburg, 634-8100, offers twenty serviced and eight unserviced sites in an open area beside the Tourist Bureau on Blockhouse Hill Road; nightly, $9 to $11. **Ovens Natural Park,** Box 41, Riverport, 766-4621, has 85 serviced and 75 unserviced sites near the ocean and scenic caves; nightly, $11 up. Two miles east of Chester, **Graves Island Provincial Park,** Route 3, 275-9917, has 64 unserviced sites in an open and wooded campground beside the ocean; nightly, $7.50.

Seeing and Doing

Lunenburg

Situated on a peninsula between "front" and "back" harbors, this historic fishing and boat-building village is the county's principal business center. It is also becoming an arts center of note.

The **Lunenburg Craft Festival,** the largest in Nova Scotia with more than 100 participating craftsmen, is held annually in mid-July. Since 1986, Lunenburg has staged a **Folk Harbour Festival,** inspired by a similar event in Gloucester, that attracts leading folk musicians for a long weekend in August.

The visitor's first stop should be at the tourist bureau, located in a lighthouse atop Blockhouse Hill. Climb to the top for a panoramic view of the village and its front and back harbors.

The schooner Bluenose, depicted on the back of the Canadian dime, was built here in 1921 and was the racing champion of the North Atlantic fishing fleet. The Bluenose II, a replica of the original, was built here in 1963 and is berthed here when it's not in Halifax. Also built here in 1960 was the HMS Bounty, used in the filming of "Mutiny on the Bounty." It caused quite a stir when it returned in 1986 for only its second visit in 26 years to its birthplace. Moored along the wharf, it lived up to its billing as "the last of the full-riggers — the near ultimate in man's creation of beautiful ships." The Rose, based in Connecticut, was in town during our visit in 1990. Along the front harbor are the shipbuilding yards and commercial fisheries that give Lunenburg its title, the Gloucester of Canada. Today, the fleet of modern trawlers and scallop draggers makes Lunenburg a major fishing port on the North Atlantic seaboard.

The Fisheries Museum of the Atlantic, Foot of Duke Street, Lunenburg. (902) 634-4794. The bright red buildings of a former fish processing plant — typical of the rich and varied colors all over town — commemorate the fishing heritage of Atlantic Canada. Inside are an aquarium with 25 tanks and three floors of exhibits. You might see a fish being filleted in the demonstration room. Boats are on display in the Hall of Inshore Fisheries. In the Dory Shop, you can watch a dory being built. The Bank Fishery/Age of Sail, a Parks Canada exhibit, traces the 400-year history of fishing along the banks of the continental shelf off Canada's East Coast. Another exhibit portrays the triumphs of the Bluenose. On the third floor are the Rum Runners exhibit, reflecting the Prohibition era when fishermen trafficked illicit liquor to the U.S.A., a sailmaker's exhibit, a typical fish company office from the 1920s, ice harvesting equipment, photographs of old Lunenburg and the Ice House Theater, which shows half-hour films on fishing. Outside the museum you can board the Theresa E. Connor, built here in 1938 and the last Lunenburg schooner to fish the Grand Banks with dories, and the steel-hulled side trawler Cape Sable, built in 1962. Beyond is the wooden side trawler Cape North, first of the fresh fish draggers to sail out of Lunenburg. The museum has a restaurant and a gift shop. Open May 15-Oct. 15, daily 9:30 to 5:30. Adults $2, children 50 cents, family $5.

Schooner tours of Lunenburg harbor and deep-sea fishing expeditions leave from the Fisheries Museum Dock. The S.S. Timberwind, 634-8966, a traditional Lunenburg schooner, sails daily at 10:30, 12:30, 2:30 and 4:30. Adults $12, children $8.

WALKING TOUR. The bright colors of the buildings will impress you as much as the architecture along the historic streets on the hillside above the harbor. They're particularly striking against the background of blue harbor and the lush greens of the Bluenose Golf Club on the hillside beyond. St. Andrew's Presbyterian and Zion's Lutheran churches are the oldest of their denominations in Canada. St. John's Anglican (1754) is the second oldest Protestant church in Canada; guided tours are given daily in summer. The hilltop Lunenburg Academy built in 1894, visible for miles around, is a Provincial Heritage Property still used as an elementary school.

ARTS AND CRAFTS. Lunenburg's galleries and shops are relatively few but exceptional. **Montague Woollens,** at Montague and King streets, is a choice shop purveying 100 percent Icelandic wool sweaters and lovely angora sweaters among a wide selection of handwoven and handknit wearing apparel for men and women. Upstairs is **Teddy Bear Knits,** which has knitted outfits for children and a selection of children's gifts. Framed on a wall up the stairway was a wonderful two-tone down vest with sweater and turtleneck, size 6, for $31.95. Owner Gail Patriarche shows her original watercolors at **Montague Gallery** in the back of the store. She and husband John also have the new **C.J. Buck & Co.,** subtitled Lunenburg Outfitters and featuring rugged outdoor casual clothing. They formerly owned the **Morash Gallery,** 55 Montague St., still going strong with paintings, gifts and great pottery in a restored 1876 house that is among the most photographed in Lunenburg.

Houston North Gallery, 110 Montague St., specializes in folk art and Inuit (Eskimo) art on three fascinating floors with views of the harbor. Owner Alma Houston and son John spent many years in the Arctic, an experience reflected in their selection of works and exhibits. We were intrigued by handpainted chairs portraying local scenes, larger-than-life sea birds carved of wood, a porch on which dwelt a gigantic moose, and a yellow bird perched on a giant sunflower. Featured at our latest visit was a special collection of primitives by Maud Lewis, Canadian folk artist. This is a gallery you could spend hours in.

The **Black Duck Handcrafts Cooperative,** 8 Pelham St., is Nova Scotia's first craft cooperative. Now nearly two decades old, it's a showplace for members to display their wares, including clothing, eye-catching kites, toys, pottery, baskets and local books; all the herbal items smelled great. A craft cooperative, **The Lincoln Reef** at 218 Lincoln St., features paintings, pottery, smocking, stained glass, weaving and embroidery. The **Lunenburg Art Gallery** at 19 Pelham St., sponsored by the local Heritage Society, shows works of local artists.

Goods and gifts from the British Isles are sold at the **Admiral Benbow Trading Co.** at 84 Montague St., a new branch of a favorite shop of ours in Mahone Bay. From jars of baby stilton dressing to lacy white nightgowns to Guernsey sweaters to Darington crystal, everything is good-looking here.

Great breads, meats, Maritime jellies and pickles, traditional willow baskets and local produce from her Bonnie Lee Farm in Chester are purveyed by Heather May Sanft at the **HMS Market,** 116 Montague St. Next door is the small **Lunenburg Pottery.**

Mahone Bay

Mahone Bay is the dominant bay of the area, and ringing the head of a harbor is the small town of the same name. It's known for three landmark churches facing the waterfront side by side and, lately, for some fine crafts shops and boutiques along Main Street, the shore Route 3.

Amos Pewterers has been operating from an old boat building shop beside the bay since 1974. You may see Greg and Suzanne Amos at work; you'll certainly see some amazing pewter pieces — many of them surprisingly sleek and contemporary — from bowls to picture holders to jewelry. Across the street at the **Birdsall-Worthington Pottery Ltd.,** Tim Birdsall and Pam Worthington make Nova Scotian earthenware pottery with a decorating technique known as slip trailing. Their delicate floral painting over clay vases and dishes is exquisite. **The Teazer,** named for the legendary ghost ship said to haunt Mahone Bay still, has five rooms of crafts, sweaters, kitchenware, children's items and fine clothing and accessories from the British Isles.

There's an explosion of colors at **Suttles & Seawinds,** 460 Main St., the headquarters of the distinctive Canadian clothing, gifts and accessories empire started by Vicki Lynn Bardon and her husband Gary (brother of Alma Houston of Lunenburg's Houston North Gallery). Vicki designs everything from potholders to quilts. The clothes are expensive (one cotton skirt we admired cost more than $200) and you'll see her efforts on some of the best-dressed women in Canada.

Old and new join at **Mader's Wharf,** a new little shopping complex on the water. **P.G. Joost and Co.** specializes in maritime and local books, **Southern Exposure** in neat Guatemalan cotton clothing and **Heart's Desire** in giftware.

At the eastern edge of town is **Kedy's Landing,** fashioned from a couple of restored historic buildings facing the bay. Our favorite store here is **Admiral Benbow,** where everything is from the British Isles — all the clothing and gifts "and even us," volunteered the owners from Cornwall. Fishermen's smocks from Wales or Cornwall are particularly attractive.

Up a road behind the Tourist Bureau is **North Mountain Soapery,** where the aroma of soaps is almost overpowering. You can buy some of the natural handcrafted soaps produced therein.

Chester

Called "possibly the prettiest village in Nova Scotia" by the Windjammer Motel brochure, this looks like a typical New England coastal town, thanks to its rolling green topography and the houses of its early New England settlers. Located on a hilly peninsula, it has a front harbor, a back harbor and various inlets, all emanating from Mahone Bay for a pervasive water presence. It's a summer refuge for the affluent, including, we're told, Phyllis Diller and Pierre Elliott Trudeau. The summer population doubles, most of them regular visitors and many of their cars bearing American license plates.

Sailing is the village's principal preoccupation. Mahone Bay is a rainbow of colorful sails during **Chester Race Week,** an annual event in August (as is **Old Home Week**). Just west of Chester is South Shore Marine, billed as Atlantic Canada's largest marina complex. All the coves and inlets with which the Chester area abounds are mooring places for fine powerboats and sailboats, quite in contrast to the old fishing boats one sees in most Maritimes harbors. A good place to view the yacht races is from what villagers call the **Parade Grounds,** a green hillside with lawns and flowers. Here on a spit of land separating the front and back harbors (connected by a canal) is the Chester Yacht Club founded in 1901, the War Memorial Monument, the Victorian gazebo bandstand still used for concerts by the Chester Brass Band and a bridge across the canal to Peninsula Road.

An **Historic Walking Tour** brochure guides visitors past landmarks you might not otherwise recognize or find, including several examples of what it calls "Picturesque architecture, an interpretation of Gothic Revival," using decorative trim, steeply pitched gables and lapped siding. Water Street along the front harbor leads to Government Wharf, where ferry service is provided several times daily to Big and Little Tancook islands. Chester has a golf club, tennis courts and a saltwater pool near the Canal Bridge on the back harbor.

Changing art shows are presented by local artists at the old Heritage Station. Local and traveling shows are presented nightly except Monday in summer by the **Chester Theater Festival,** operating out of the Chester Playhouse.

Come-a-Long II, a 40-foot cape boat owned by South Shore Marine, 275-4700, operates harbor and bay tours out of Chester, evening cruises and charters. Scheduled Mahone Bay cruises take 25 people at 10 and 1 daily except Tuesday and Thursday in summer from the Parade Grounds in Chester. Evening cruises depart from South Shore Marine at 7 nightly except Tuesday and Thursday. Adults $10, children $6.

Oak Island. Out in Mahone Bay just off the community of Western Shore is an eerie island of buried treasure. Long a haven for smugglers and privateers, it has a money pit discovered in 1795 by three Chester youths on a camping expedition; they started digging, and treasure hunters have been digging in vain since for what is believed to be Captain Kidd's bounty. Six lives and more than $2 million have been spent on the most expensive treasure hunt in the world. All agree that the designer of the pit was a genius, for the treasure has defied discovery. Since 1969, Triton Alliance Ltd. — a syndicate of Canadian and American businessmen — has been conducting a highly technical hunt on the island. You can tour the island under auspices of Triton Alliance, which has a small museum and gift shop at the entrance, where you listen to a ten-minute tape before getting in a guide's car or a bus for a 25-minute tour. A number of digging sites, shafts, a bore hole, the 100-foot-deep cave-in pit and the money pit heighten one's interest in the Oak Island tale, subject of three books. By the time you finish you may share the guide's optimism that the treasure will be uncovered soon. It's hokey, but fascinating. Tours daily, June 1-Sept. 15. Adults $3.50, children $2.

SHOPPING. Probably because Chester is less tourist-oriented and its residents are busy sailing, the village lacks the number of choice shops found in Lunenburg and Mahone Bay. Queen Street, the main street, has the **Needle's Eye,** featuring machine-embroidered Nova Scotia scenes, quilted tea cosies, pillows and appliqued children's hangings. **The Owl and the Pussy Cat** offers books, toys, handicrafts and imported gifts. Two good shops are beside the harbor on Water Street. **The Warp and Woof,** at the venerable age of 64, is one of Nova Scotia's oldest gift shops, featuring handcrafts, wood carvings, apple dolls, an art gallery and gift items from around the world; its **Sweater Annex** has imported woolens and accessories. Jim Smith's **Nova Scotia Folk Pottery,** charmingly housed in the old Corner Store, features especially colorful plates and pitchers in striking purples and greens. New in 1990 were his appealing dishes shaped like shells for $25. We also liked the Persian blue candlesticks.

Other Attractions

BEACHES. You have to go off the main roads to find them, but if you do you'll love their tranquility and relative privacy. Some of the best are to the southwest of Lunenburg along the scenic shore Route 331 from East Medway. **Beach Meadows,** almost a horseshoe of white sand and clear water, is a beach lover's dream. A long dirt road leads to **Cherry Hill Beach,** where you're rewarded by beaches facing both west and south, and you may find shells and driftwood. **Risser's Beach** is a superb provincial park with a wonderful beach where the breakers roll in neatly in single lines, a 1.5-mile boardwalk traverses a salt marsh, a canteen dispenses food, and there are picnic areas. East of Lunenburg, there's a lovely little unnamed beach on a bay four miles down Second Peninsula. East of Chester is **Graves Island Provincial Park,** which has a small stony beach and picnic tables. Out the next peninsula is **Bayswater Beach,** with a view of the open ocean near Blandford. Queensland, on St. Margaret's Bay, is the home of three beaches, **Cleveland, Queensland** and **Black Point.**

Poking and Browsing. A particularly scenic route leads from East Medway along Route 331 to LaHave and Lunenburg. Besides visiting beaches (above), you'll want to make side trips. A road from Petite Riviere leads to the interesting summer colony of **Green Bay.** Turn right at Crescent Beach for the quaint **LaHave Islands;** stop at the free Marine Museum housed in a tiny church after crossing a strange one-lane, wood-floor bridge. **LaHave** is an appealing town, where a ferry crosses the LaHave River — known as the Rhine of Canada — on the hour to Lower LaHave. The unusual ferry is drawn by cable; the ride takes five minutes and costs 50 cents.

The **Ovens Natural Park,** near Riverport, has 200 acres of caves and rock formations that are spectacular, we're told, but is a tad over-commercialized for our taste. Gold was found here in 1861, and a miniature Klondike started when gold miners arrived in hopes of striking pay dirt; their town was soon abandoned, but tunnels and pits remain. Cunard's Cove, named for the founder of the Cunard Lines, is where his son conducted a successful venture gathering gold from the beach. This is essentially a private campground with a swimming pool, and there's a day-use charge of $2, which discourages a quick look at the caves but friends say it's worth it. Open daily, May 20-Sept. 10.

Several scenic roads lead from Route 3 toward the ocean between Lunenburg and Chester. Everyone heads out to **Blue Rocks,** a tiny weatherbeaten fishing village somewhat like famed Peggy's Cove before it was overrun; it's a favorite with artists and photographers. Drive beyond Blue Rocks around a section called **The Point.** Also follow little signs for Stonehurst South to wend your way past picturesque coves and hamlets to **Stonehurst,** where the road dead-ends at a footbridge leading to an island owned by Americans who summer there.

The road down **Second Peninsula** hugs the shoreline and we saw a cormorant spreading its wings and a big blue heron feeding in shallow water at low tide. **Second Peninsula Provincial Park** has picnic tables beneath a stand of tall fir and spruce trees beside a rocky shore. You can take a circle tour around **Indian Point,** where Micmac Indians once lived, and out to **Martins Point.** Beyond Chester on the other side of St. Margaret's Bay is storied **Peggy's Cove,** which we enjoyed on a May weekday over twenty years ago — the latest time at noon on a September Sunday we felt almost claustrophobic with the many busloads of tourists. But the awesome rocks, the lighthouse and the crashing surf are must sights to see, if you can avoid the hordes.

Where to Eat _____ *CCC*

This is one of the few areas in the Maritimes that we have found to have a concentration of interesting restaurants, both in terms of cuisine and setting — a result, no doubt, of the sophisticated tastes of residents and summer visitors.

Near the Water

The Captain's House, 129 Central St., Chester. (902) 275-3501. Folks from Halifax and even farther away flock to this imposing Georgian house, built in 1822 on a lot owned by one of Chester's first settlers. The draw is the famed Sunday brunch, with seatings at 11:30 and 1:30 — price $19.95. On several long tables are displayed smoked and fresh fish, oysters, pates, seafood crepes, roast beef, apple and rum crepes and just about anything else good to eat you could think of. The three classic dining rooms downstairs are done up in rose linens, heavy draperies and lots of fresh flowers. The dining rooms in back have a grand view of the front harbor, and there's a pleasant outdoor deck with umbrellas on two levels. New owner Nicki Butler, whose son Stephen is the chef, planned to inaugurate traditional Sunday carvery lunches in the off-season to reflect their Yorkshire background. The dinner menu lists entrees from $12.95 for fish pie topped with a creamy potato puree to $17.25 for poached salmon or medallions of pork served on a pool of apple and calvados sauce. Halibut steak sauteed with almonds, shrimp thermidor and toasted duckling with a sweet blueberry sauce are other options. Start with a lobster timbale or a frisse salad with hot lardons and walnut dressing. Finish with key lime pie or Mexican mocha cheesecake. A short bar menu includes a lobster sandwich and a ploughman's lunch. Open daily at 10 for coffee, lunch 11:30 to 3, afternoon tea, dinner 5 to 10.

The Rope Loft, Water Street, Chester. (902) 275-3430. Would that every restaurant could have such a felicitous setting. This popular place at water's edge has a second-story deck with rustic wood furniture, a lower deck with spiffy white tables and chairs, a soaring upstairs Rope Loft dining room and a timeworn, timbered 1815 sea shanty downstairs. Obviously it can handle scores of people, so we were surprised to be the only diners when we arrived about 9:30 on a July weeknight. We wished we'd been earlier to have enjoyed a drink on the upper-level deck right beside the front harbor, with boats moored all around. The candlelit dining room was casual and the service solicitous (after all, we were the only ones there, but the help probably wanted to go home). We shared an appetizer of solomon gundy (Nova Scotia pickled herring) before digging into our entrees of grilled halibut ($13.25) and Digby scallops marinated in vermouth ($14.75), generously served on huge plates filled with carrots and either rice or new potatoes. The limited menu is priced from $10.50 for fettuccine pesto to $18.75 for sirloin steak. Pasta Atlantic, blending smoked salmon and artichoke, and lamb chops marinated with garlic and herbs are other possibilities. A Maritime parfait with dark rum and maple syrup is the specialty dessert. We returned to the upper deck on a breezy day for a good lunch of seafood chowder with a spinach salad and the shrimp salad sandwich special from a pricey menu that did not strike us as particularly lunchy. Open daily, noon to 10, May to mid-October.

The Galley at South Shore Marine, off Route 3, Chester. (902) 275-4700. Part of a large marina at Marriott's Cove, this contemporary restaurant with an outdoor deck and picnic tables overlooks Mahone Bay. The view from the two-level dining room is pretty as a picture, as is the entire restaurant in its nautical setting full of ropes, plants and netting. The dinner menu comes in a canvas cover, offering something for everyone from $10.95 for stir-fried chicken and vegetables over rice to $17.75 for twin filet mignons. Fresh fish from the blackboard can be baked, broiled, poached, grilled or panfried, and you have a choice of eight sauces. Desserts are to groan over: banana royale, chocolate rum mousse, chocolate grand marnier cheesecake and lemon yogurt ice cream pie. The lunch menu, from fish cakes to marina's pasta, is unusually appealing. The wines are limited; the fancy "fog-cutter" cocktails and "hot grog" liqueured coffees are not. In front is **The Loft,** a marine store stocking nautical clothing, equipment and gifts, and outside are tables and chairs under graceful birch trees. Open daily, noon to 9. Closed mid-December to mid-March.

Seaside Shanty, Route 3, Chester Basin. (902) 275-2246. The open rear deck looks right over the water, and we lingered to watch a loon — "one of two who live with us," said a staffer, who also reported that minks live under the rocks and seals visit two or three times a year. Occupying the site of the former Chester Basin Coffee House, this is the new venture of Kim Johnson, who also owns Chester's Windjammer Motel. Pink mats and rose and blue wood tables and chairs create a summery setting inside and out. The menu is centered around homemade chowders, sandwiches on homemade white or wholewheat breads, salads, pastas, steamed mussels, lobster suppers and homemade berry shortcakes. The five chowders, from mussel to broccoli and served with homemade rolls, are $4 to $5 and make a small meal. A couple of entrees in the $8 range are pan-fried scallops and haddock, served with side salad, baked potato and homemade rolls. Enjoy it with half a carafe of the house wine ($5.25). Open daily, 11:30 to 10, from 8 a.m. in summer. Closed November-May.

Zwicker's Inn, 662 Main St., Mahone Bay. (902) 624-8045. This is a special place, run with panache until lately by Jack and Katherine Sorenson, who in 1980 restored to its original use the first posthouse between Chester and Lunenburg, circa 1800. They "retired" to open the Innlet Cafe (see below), yielding to Harold and Iris Hagreen and family, who knew a good thing and kept everything the same, including the chef and the menu. The inviting interior has several small dining rooms with soft yellow walls hung with local art works, red cloths over white linen, lace curtains and begonias in the windows. British music plays in the background. It's a homey setting for some imaginative food, like our lunch of an outstanding mussel soup from a Maxim's of Paris recipe, piping hot and served with wonderful thick herb bread; a delicious mushroom-almond pate served with a small crock of potato salad, raw veggies and crisp rye toast; a seafood chowder and a Danish-style open-face roast beef sandwich with horse-radish sauce. Accompanied by a couple of bottles of the local Keith beer, this was a memorable meal. For dinner, we'd start with the mussel soup again and perhaps soused shrimps or smoked salmon and then try the seafood Skibbereen, poached halibut or maybe skewered pork or broiled lamb chops ($11.95 to $17.95). We might try Zwicker's own noodles with chicken or shrimps, the lemon-steamed mussels or shrimp Louis. Desserts run the gamut from lemon-honey cheesecake monogrammed "Z" for Zwicker's to homemade ice creams to potted cheese, whipped with butter and sherry and accompanied by a few grapes. These people do have fun and serve interesting food at fair prices. The wine list is one of Nova Scotia's most extensive. Open daily, 11:30 to 9 or 9:30.

The Innlet Cafe, Kedy's Landing, Mahone Bay. (902) 624-6363. This got its start as the Silver Spoon Terrace Restaurant, founded by Deanna Silver of the Halifax restaurant and dessert group. It was taken over lately by Jack and Katherine Sorenson, who'd put the nearby Zwicker's Inn on the culinary map. Their new, more casual effort has a small terrace for dining out front by the bay and a spiffy licensed cafe inside. For lunch, we enjoyed a great mussel chowder with a vegetable salad plate and a super cream of halibut-potato-parsley soup with a knockwurst sandwich. The limited dinner fare includes grilled halibut and salmon, steak with mushroom caps, beerfest and banger sausages with kraut and herb-fried chicken, $7.95 to $10.95. The snack menu offers everything from buttermilk biscuits and rice cakes to nachos, welsh rarebit and tofu marinated in orange-tamari sauce. Ginger cake, ginger shortbread and Belgian waffles highlight the dessert list, but the special board might add orange-hazel-nut cheesecake and apricot creme blondie. Open daily 10 to 8, March-December.

The Mug & Anchor Pub, Mader's Wharf, Mahone Bay. (902) 624-6378. Mahone Bay's first pub opened in 1989 as the cornerstone of the Mader's Wharf complex, with an outdoor deck over the water, a fireplace in the corner and, of course, the requisite bar and a dart board. Co-owner Gregg Little says people come here not just for the extensive selection of beers and sherries but for the food, all made on the premises and served on the deck or in a dark and pub-like hunter green room. The menu is short but sweet, from seafood chowder and B.L.T. to ploughman's lunch and mussels with scallops. Among "entrees" are a mugburger, a scallop burger, quiche, meat pies, steak and a seafood platter, priced right from $2.50 to $7.95. Open Monday-Saturday, 11:30 a.m. to 12:30 a.m., kitchen to 8:30 p.m.

Bayview Pines Country Inn, Indian Point, Mahone Bay. (902) 624-9970. The dining room is tearoom-cute at this inn with a bay view. Calico cloths cover the tables and owners Curt and Nancy Norklun offer a limited menu at three meals a day. For lunch from a blackboard menu, you might find french onion soup, solomon gundy, Lunenburg pudding and various sandwiches on homemade brown bread. Solomon gundy and Lunenburg pudding also show up as dinner appetizers. Seafood mornay, chicken divan and old-fashioned spaghet-ti dishes make up the entrees ($9.50 to $12.50). Accompany with peach juice or pear juice, and finish with pineapple-walnut cake or bluebottom cheesecake. Lunch in season, dinner nightly at 6:30 by reservation.

Brigantine Inn Bistro & Coffee Shop, 82 Montague St., Lunenburg. (902) 634-3300. This is the wonderfully innovative and nicely priced venture of Jonathan and Merle McCann. Their airy little bistro with a nautical atmosphere and colorful sails painted on the gray walls overlooks the harbor, and window tables and a small deck take full advantage. We first discovered this for breakfast, and enjoyed the light and flavorful strawberry pancakes ($3.75), the Welsh rarebit with bacon ($3.95) and unusually good coffee. The breakfast menu was so appealing that we returned for dinner, sampling the smoked goose appetizer served with raspberry-orange liqueur on toast points, the spicy rum and fish chowder, and entrees of beef bourguignonne and chicken in wine. Most entrees are in the $7 to $9 range; filet mignon tops the list at $14. One of the five chefs works all night preparing the desserts, which prove so popular that many come late in the evening just for rum cake, chocolate flan, french crunch peach pie or, that Canadian goodie, a Nanaimo bar. Whenever you come, be sure to try Henry's fish cakes ($2.95 for two cakes), based on a recipe from a local sea captain. Open daily, 7 a.m. to 10 p.m.

Dockside Lobster & Seafood Restaurant, 84 Montague St., Lunenburg. (902) 634-3005. Local lodging impressario Gene Tanner runs this large seafood emporium with a carpeted outdoor deck, a pizza and donair (the Maritime version of a gyro) takeout restaurant below, and two sections inside, one for family dining and the other for "fine, tablecloth dining" with a cocktail lounge. The no-nonsense nautical decor is striking for the large pictures made of carved wood in bright colors by woodcarver Stephen Outhouse of Brighton, who signs them with a tiny outhouse. The dinner menu, priced from $12.95 to $22.95, includes an original lobster in a blanket dish, featuring a broiled seafood blanket stuffed with lobster filling. The homemade seafood sausage also is highly rated. Cajun shrimp, Lunenburg scallops and seafood casserole au gratin are other possibilities. The wine list is good and exceptionally low priced for Canada (all but two are in the teens), but the four champagnes run as high as $169. Gene bills the Dockside as "an old town inn and restaurant — people can come in for just a cup of tea, a bottle of champagne or breakfast in the afternoon." Open daily, 9 a.m. to 10 p.m.

Away from the Water

Campbell House, 321 Lacey Mines Road, Chester Basin. (902) 275-5655. You get a distant view of Mahone Bay and many of its islands from this rural house on a rise just off Highway 103. But it's the food that draws the cognoscenti from Halifax and beyond. Don Campbell, former chef at Captain's House, and his wife Judy have a couple of fresh and country-ish dining rooms with a fieldstone fireplace, a screened porch in back, green draped curtains, and white linens and napkins standing tall in the wine glasses. At dinner, entrees ($12.95 to $17.95) include haddock en croute, salmon grenoble, lobster au gratin, pepper steak, rack of lamb and roast Brome Lake duckling. You might start with salad mimosa or smoked Atlantic salmon and end with a chocolate truffle torte, turtle cheesecake or bumbleberry pie, a concoction of apples, raspberries, blackberries and rhubarb. Or try cream crowdie: oatmeal with drambuie and cream. At lunch, caesar salad is the local favorite; when we were there, two ladies sat down and didn't even want to see the menu or hear the specials, simply ordering caesar salad ($3.25). They missed the grilled halibut with fresh lime, the mussels mariniere, the oyster stew and the lamb medallions ($4.95 to $8.25). Lunch daily, noon to 3; dinner, 5 to 9, Sunday to 8. Closed in winter.

Compass Rose, 15 King St., Lunenburg. (902) 634-8509. Music, candlelight and all kinds of art and little mementoes on walls and shelves transform three small dining rooms into romantic, intimate settings for fine fare. Delicious rolls, both white and herbed, preceded a good appetizer ($4.50) of pickled mussels and marinated herring with sour cream and a summer salad. Among entrees from $12.95 for finnan haddie to $16.95 for pepper steak or lobster newburg, we were happy with the fettuccine with scallops and the spicy Lunenburg sausage, a local favorite served with diced potatoes, tangy sauerkraut and hot dijon mustard, a good and hearty dish that would be a real winner in winter. On another occasion we tried the garlic peppered shrimp, a house specialty, and lemon chicken, which tasted rather like chicken McNuggets. The dessert recitation intrigued enough that we shared a yummy creme de menthe ice cream pie with chocolate wafer crust, topped with whipped cream and chocolate sauce; the recipe for the Bavarian torte was requested by Gourmet magazine. A bottle of the house Grand Pre dry white wine was more than adequate. While husband Rodger handles kitchen duties, Suzanne Pike usually oversees the dining room and makes sure her guests feel welcome. At lunch, try the mariner's plate with German-style potatoes ($6.95) or some of the other items we sampled at dinner. Lunch daily, 11:30 to 2; dinner 5 to 9. Closed January and February.

Boscawen Inn, 150 Cumberland St., Lunenburg. (902) 634-3325. The downstairs dining room in light wood is simple and pretty with linens, candles, fresh flowers and sheer curtains on the windows and a high shelf for decorative plates. Since we dined here, a new chef from Halifax has upgraded the fare, according to reports. The dinner menu ($12.95 to $15.95) includes a poached seafood platter, halibut amandine, chicken sauteed in a brandy-wine cream sauce, salmon fettuccine and entrecote bordelaise. Appetizers are typical of the area (smoked salmon, steamed musssels, Lunenburg pudding, solomon gundy and stuffed mushrooms). Desserts run to chocolate mousse, gingerbread with whipped cream and blueberry shortcake. A limited lunch menu offers a few sandwiches, fish cakes with rhubarb relish, steamed mussels, Swiss quiche, and scallop and mushroom crepes. Breakfast daily, 8 to 10; lunch, 11:30 to 2; dinner, 5 to 8:30 or 9. Closed January to Easter.

Bluenose Lodge, Falkland and Dufferin Streets, Lunenburg. (902) 634-8851. The spacious dining room at this inn on the way back has been redone and divided into smaller sections with trellises for intimacy. It's also pretty with big windows all around, lace curtains and lace tablecloths over pink undercloths. Classical music plays as customers partake of a limited menu, usually seven choices ($13.50 to $15.95) like poached scallops, lobster newburg, salmon wellington and strip steak. Lobster mousse is a favorite appetizer, as is Lunenburg pudding. Carrot cake, ice cream sundae pie and pecan pie are featured desserts. At lunch, try the curried chicken salad or a scallop burger. Breakfast, 8 to 9:30; lunch, noon to 2; diner 5:30 to 8:30. Closed November-April, although staying open through December was under consideration.

The Lunenburg Inn, 26 Dufferin St., Lunenburg. (902) 634-3963. John Piccolo, innkeeper with his wife Faith, is the chef in this 24-seat dining room with floral overcloths, lace curtains and rose wallpaper. Faith says the baked scallops are an inn specialty, though you'll find half a dozen other choices ranging from $9.75 for spaghetti with all-pork meatballs to $15.25 for steak au poivre. Among appetizers, she suggests the Spanish shrimp cocktail tossed with cilantro and the steamed mussels. Fruit tarts, death by chocolate and cannoli with strawberries are favored desserts. One percent of the bill is donated to Care Canada to feed starving children. Dinner by reservation, nightly 5 to 9, June-October; weekends only December-May.

Magnolia's Grill, 128 Montague St., Lunenburg. (902) 634-3287. The walls are covered with '50s memorabilia and loud music blares at this lively bistro known for conviviality and creative food. The locals pack its eight booths and two tables to partake of such lunchtime treats as creole peanut soup, nachos, panfried cod cheeks, mussels and Greek salad ($3.50 to $4.50). Melissa Gallant, who hails from Tennessee, teamed up with Nancy Lohnes to create this culinary happening amidst collections ranging from postcards to salt and pepper shakers. At night, you might try the fish cakes, "Zorba the breast" (chicken stuffed with feta cheese), seafood pasta, cajun shrimp or jambalaya, priced from $6.95 to $14.95. The dessert selection might include fruit cobblers, brownies, and pecan and key lime pie. Lunch, 11:30 to 2:30; dinner, 5 to 9 or 10. Closed in winter.

FOR MORE INFORMATION: South Shore Tourism Association, Box 82, Bridgewater, N.S. B4V 2W6, (902) 543-5391. Lunenburg Board of Trade, Box 1300, Lunenburg B0J 2C0, (902) 634-8100.

View of downtown Halifax is afforded from harbor excursion boat.

Halifax, N.S.

Imagine a waterfront city served by two competing bus-tour lines, two excursion boat tours, commuter ferries, half a dozen sailing cruises, Rolls-Royce and rickshaw tours, and even a sightseeing helicopter. A city with eight downtown hotels and a World Trade and Convention Center. A city with half a dozen downtown shopping complexes, five colleges and universities, and countless pubs, nightclubs and restaurants.

You'd think such a city would have to be a major commercial and destination center like Boston or New Orleans or San Francisco. This particular city, however, is Halifax. With barely 100,000 inhabitatants, it is a commercial and destination center far out of proportion to its population.

It happens to be the largest city on Canada's East Coast and "the city" revered and visited by more than one million outlanders from throughout the Maritime Provinces. The world's second largest natural harbor and a heritage as the first English settlement in Canada have granted Halifax an importance beyond its size.

Situated on a hilly peninsula, Halifax is very much geared to the water. Its historic dominance as a seaport has brought it military vessels, freighters and ocean liners; these share the waters today with an inordinate number of private sailboats and yachts.

The once-decrepit waterfront has been rejuvenated into a model unmatched along the Atlantic coast. Considered the leading North American city in historic building renovations, Halifax has restored its waterfront to maximum advantage and not much gets in the way of access to the water.

"We've strived for a balance between commercial and people-oriented activities," said Gerald G. Etienne, president and chief executive officer of Waterfront Development Corp. Ltd., the fourteen-year-old provincial crown corporation that oversees restoration efforts.

All Halifax, indeed, is a people-oriented city. Downtown office workers jog or

401

take their lunch breaks beside the harbor, in the heart of the restored area called Historic Properties, or on the slopes leading to the hilltop fortress, the Citadel. Downtown sidewalks and connecting skywalks are crowded by day, in the evening and on weekends. Eight major parks in this "City of Trees" are fully used and off-limits to cars. Cars stop for pedestrians at crosswalks, which may prove unnerving for Americans who pause at curbside to get their bearings, unintentionally stopping all traffic in the process.

Halifax also is a city of plaques, befitting its history and proud tradition. You can seldom go far on any of the city's walking tours — or anywhere else, for that matter — without pausing to read a commemoration.

The daily blast of the Citadel cannon at noon accentuates the city's military past, inviting the visitor to explore a fascinating, lively area replete with history and water activities.

Getting There

Halifax is a major point of entry to the Maritimes by rail and air. Nova Scotia's major highways — Routes 101, 102 and 103 converge on Halifax from all directions. You can sail from Maine to Yarmouth via an eleven-hour overnight ferry trip from Portland or a six-hour daytime ferry trip from Bar Harbor, and from New Brunswick via a two-and-one-half-hour ferry trip from Saint John to Digby. Or you can drive all the way around on express (though not necessarily four-lane) highways through New Brunswick to Truro and Halifax. Each way has reasons to commend it, and we lean to driving around one way, taking the Bar Harbor ferry shortcut the other.

Prices, subject to Canada's new GST tax, are quoted in Canadian funds. Halifax is on Atlantic Time, one hour ahead of Eastern.

Where to Stay⎯⎯⎯⎯⎯⎯⎯⎯⎯⎯⎯⎯⎯⎯⎯⎯⎯⎯⎯⎯⎯⎯⎯⎯ ⨏⨏⨏

Since this is a city-oriented area, you'll probably want to stay at a downtown hotel or inn. Be advised there are outlying motels and small B&Bs as well.

Halifax Sheraton Hotel, 1919 Upper Water St., Halifax B3J 3J5. (902) 421-1700. Superbly located beside the harbor, this new-in-1985 hotel is the most convenient to all the waterfront goings-on. About half the 350 guest rooms on six floors have partial harbor views; ours was literally perched over the water and fortunately had a small window that could be opened to let in the water sounds. Others face the city or an indoor pool-courtyard. The hotel's award-winning design is based on the military ordinance building that formerly occupied the property. It includes an historic clock tower and is so low-rise and in harmony with its surroundings that you would not suspect it to be a modern hotel. **The Grand Banker,** crowned by a skylight, is the open-to-the-lobby restaurant specializing in fresh seafood, served grilled, sauteed, poached, baked or blackened. The most interesting menu of any Halifax hotel restaurant (dinner entrees, ($17.45 to $32.50) also includes lobster fricasse, grilled supreme of pheasant, grilled quails a la grecque and roast saddle of rabbit. We chose instead to eat supper at the **Boardwalk Grill** outside beside the water, a lovely setting but a comedy of service and kitchen errors — our mussels appetizer never arrived, and the grilled salmon and the seafood brochette were mediocre at best. But with a carafe of wine and a harborside table, we didn't really mind. Doubles, $145 to $185.

The Halliburton House Inn, 5184 Morris St., Halifax B3J 1B3. (902) 420-0658. Taken by the lifestyle of Nova Scotia, Yale University graduate

William McKeever moved his family from Colorado to Halifax in 1987 to open Atlantic Canada's first European-style urban inn. Its 34 rooms and suites have been grandly refashioned from three adjoining heritage townhouses, named for a chief justice of Nova Scotia, and one of them the former home of the Dalhousie Law School, at the edge of the fashionable uptown Spring Garden area. Most rooms are spacious, have comfortable chairs and TV, and are nicely decorated with period antiques and soft, contemporary colors. All have private baths, some rooms on the third floor have skylights, and six have fireplaces. Those we like best in the rear have balconies onto a garden courtyard, where tall shade trees and colorful flowers provide an oasis in a busy city neighborhood. There's a well-furnished library-sitting room near the front entry, which has marble floors and a grand stairway. There are also three small, pleasant dining rooms, where partner Charles Lief oversees one of the premier food operations in the province (see Where to Eat). Complimentary tea and an assortment of excellent pastries and cookies are served in the late afternoon; a continental breakfast is included, and a full breakfast menu is available. Doubles, $105 to $120; suites, $135.

The Delta Barrington, 1875 Barrington St., Halifax B3J 3L6. (902) 429-7410. Just a couple of blocks above the harbor and blending in with the Historic Properties renovation (its east side looks onto the Granville Pedestrian Mall), this well-located hotel sometimes calls itself the Barrington Inn and rightly so. The most requested of the 202 rooms on three floors face onto two inner courtyards; they're quieter and away from the street. Ours was comfortable and spacious, and you couldn't do better for the price, $69 for two any summer night in 1990. Rooms have mini-bars and large baths; the 35 Signature Service rooms offer Gucci accessories and complimentary Perrier as well as continental breakfast. A Nautilus fitness center, indoor pool and children's playground plus a supervised weekend children's center are attractions. Doubles, $114 to $129.

Chateau Halifax, 1990 Barrington St., Halifax B3J 1P2. (902) 425-6700 or (800) 828-7447 (U.S.) and (800) 268-9411 (Canada). Across the street and uphill from the Delta Barrington, the 305-room Canadian Pacific hotel built in 1974 is part of the Scotia Square retail complex and rests atop a five-level parking garage, with a lobby beneath. One-third of the rooms have views up the harbor to the north. All have been recently renovated to produce long credenzas with built-in TVs and mini-bars, marble bathrooms and dressing areas with vanities. The indoor-outdoor pool area is Halifax's nicest; there's an enclosed dome with a jacuzzi. The **Crown Cafe** is considered one of the better hotel dining rooms, and Sunday brunch in the rooftop **Bluenose Room** offers a fantastic view of the harbor and city. Doubles, $155.

Prince George Hotel, 1725 Market St., Halifax B3J 3N9. (902) 425-1986. This spiffy 213-room hotel opened in 1986 across the street from Halifax's World Trade and Convention Center to cater to the business trade — it's linked to the center by underground tunnel. There aren't many water views, our guide conceded, but the sixth-floor rooms have a perfect view instead of the historic town clock on Citadel Hill. All is luxurious, from the art deco lobby with neon lights and gray and plum decor to the spacious guest quarters, all with two phones in the room, remote-control TV, large work tables and dressing areas with hair driers. The Prince George boasts Halifax's only deep-end hotel pool, plus a landscaped garage roof for walking and relaxation. The hotel is part of a small local chain embracing the former Citadel Inn (see below) and the new **Cambridge Suites,** which offers 200 "travel suites" ($95 to $115) at Brunwick and Sackville streets. Doubles, $130 to $140.

The Citadel Halifax, 1960 Brunswick St., Halifax B3J 2G7. (902) 422-1391 or (800) 565-7162. The closest hostelry to the Citadel, this two-tower complex variously called an inn and a hotel has 270 rooms, half facing up the harbor. Strangely, only the lower floors have balconies, which look onto highrise apartments across the street. Rooms have refrigerators and mini-bars, and a solarium contains a swimming pool and jacuzzi. The hotel restaurant, **Arthur's,** features a prime rib dinner buffet with Yorkshire pudding, seafood newburg and salad bar. Doubles, $100 to $130.

Lord Nelson Hotel, 1515 South Park St., Halifax B3J 2T3. (902) 423-6331. A classic older hotel with ornate lobby and a front porch sporting a lineup of chairs facing the Public Gardens, the Lord Nelson is favored by bargain-seekers and people who like the fashionable uptown Spring Garden location. The early section was built in 1928 and the North Towers were added in 1967. "A good majority of our guests prefer the older rooms of some distinction," said the desk clerk. A swimming pool and health spa for the use of guests are adjacent to the hotel. The lower-priced among the 312 rooms lack air-conditioning and cable TV. Doubles, $65 to $108.

Hilton Nova Scotian, 1181 Hollis St., Halifax B3H 2P6. (902) 423-7231. Another hotel of the old school, the Nova Scotian was built in 1930 as part of the railway station complex, and announcements of train departures were still heard in the vast lobby last we knew. A newer section with 175 air-conditioned rooms was added in 1960. After a Toronto company poured many millions into renovations, the Nova Scotian was acquired in 1990 by Hilton International, and the long lobby with its fancy seating and exotic trees is a sight to behold. All rooms are now air-conditioned and each has remote-control TV, telephone, minibar, windows that open, and a hair dryer. Some rooms have ficus trees, fresh flowers, sofas and wicker furniture. At the southern fringe of downtown, the hotel is a long way from the action, but half its 310 rooms have harbor views. An indoor pool, whirlpool, sauna and outdoor tennis court are assets. Doubles, $104 to $124.

Inn on the Lake, Route 102, Box 29, Waverley B0N 2S0. (902) 861-3480. Forty-four rooms, including eight deluxe new suites with fireplaces and refrigerators, are available at this motel-style facility being gradually turned into a Victorian country inn by new owners Ron and Sue Nelson. On the shores of Lake Thomas, it's a good suburban location eleven miles north of Halifax, not far from the airport. From the renovated front you'd never suspect this started as a roadside motel in 1971. The motel units are being upgraded, most with two double beds and three with kings. Most have little balconies looking onto the lake or onto an attractive deck with a licensed gazebo beside the pool. Canoes, paddle boats, tennis courts, shuffleboard, lawn games and a private beach make this a good spot for families. The dining room and outdoor deck serve three meals daily (dinner entrees, $12.95 to $20.95), and folks packed the place for the $13.95 brunch the summer Sunday we were there. Doubles, $73 to $78; suites, $125 to $225.

Seeing and Doing _____ ⏜⏜⏜

There's much to do in and around Halifax, and a variety of tours and excursions are designed to acquaint you with the city, its history and harbor. For quick and easy orientation purposes, start with an auto drive around the Citadel, a walk through the Historic Properties and a passenger-ferry ride across the harbor to Dartmouth and back.

On the Water

THE HARBOR. The world's second largest natural harbor extends inland from the open Atlantic past downtown and through the Narrows into Bedford Basin; a fjord appropriately called the Northwest Arm juts into the northwest residential areas, creating a peninsula for Halifax and a sheltered waterfront haven for the fortunate. The harbor is exceedingly busy, what with traffic above on two soaring suspension bridges connecting Halifax and Dartmouth, commuter ferries, ocean-going ships, numerous sailboats and yachts, and often military planes buzzing overhead. We even saw several parachutists falling through the air trailing red smoke in a military operation. You can get a feel for it all by boarding the Dartmouth Ferry, North America's oldest saltwater ferry service in continuous operation, which takes passengers back and forth between downtown Halifax and Dartmouth on eight-minute trips for 50 cents. This is a commuter ferry and they really know how to move people, with red lights blocking entrances until green lights allow passengers to board and a series of escalators, walkways and parks at the Dartmouth end.

WATER EXCURSIONS. Best is the **Haligonian II,** Privateer's Wharf, Historic Properties, 423-1271. On our trip, the beginning and the end of its two-hour narrated cruise were inexplicably silent, but there was a running commentary in the middle. The cruise goes up-harbor to the McKay Bridge, with a view of the Bedford Institute of Oceanography, the world's second largest. It proceeds back past the 1917 Halifax Explosion site (the world's worst manmade explosion before the atom bomb — caused by the collision of a ship and a munitions ship), the oldest naval dockyard in North America, ocean-going ship piers and the continent's second-largest container loading freighter piers (we saw both a Soviet freighter taking on grain and a passenger liner about to leave), two deep-sea oil-drilling rigs, and McNab's and George's islands. As the boat turns into the Northwest Arm, you may see a mounted policeman among the joggers in Point Pleasant Park. You'll certainly see plenty of pleasure craft at the Royal Nova Scotia Yacht Squadron, North America's first yacht club and the terminus for the noted Marblehead to Halifax Yacht Race, several other private clubs and an interesting array of waterfront homes. Tours daily June-September, 10 and 2 (also 4:15 and 7 in season). Adults $10, children $5.

When in port, the **Bluenose II,** 422-2678, Canada's most famous racing schooner, takes passengers on three two-hour sailing cruises daily except Monday from its berth beside the Halifax Sheraton.

Murphy's Boat Tours, 420-1015, include the Harbour Queen, a 200-passenger paddlewheeler with morning, afternoon, dinner and dancing cruises. Gerard Murphy's 75-foot Danish sailboat, the Mar II, offers daily one- or two-hour cruises as well as lunch cruises and moonlight excursions. **Airlie Sailing & Fishing Tours,** 477-5135, **New Dawn Charters,** 479-2900, and **White Heather Yacht Charters,** 425-0060, offer excursions from deep-sea fishing charters to harbor tours.

Particularly popular with Haligonians is the **McNab's Island Ferry,** 422-9523. The Vera III transports passengers to McNab's Island at the entrance of the harbor for hiking, swimming or a visit to the Island Tea Room, where lobster, seafood, sandwiches and afternoon tea and corn boils are served in a stone cottage set in a century-old garden overlooking the ocean. Round trips are $6.75 for adults, $3.50 for children. Ferry departs hourly daily in summer, weekends only in spring and fall.

On the Shore

LAND TOURS. A different Halifax is seen on any number of city tours. "Ride the Real McCoy," advertises **Halifax Double Decker Tours Limited,** 420-1155, which gives two-hour tours on red British buses daily from Historic Properties; adults $12, children $6. Similar prices are charged by **Gray Line,** 454-9321, which offers city-wide tours daily with stops at the Citadel and the Maritime Museum of the Atlantic. Private tour guides offer such options as Rolls-Royce tours and rickshaw tours, the latter quite an experience to watch, to say nothing of the partaking.

WALKING TOURS. A good walking tour map guides you in some detail through historic Halifax. Other walking tours are outlined in the Halifax Visitors' Guide. Obviously you'll want to explore the waterfront, the central **Grand Parade** (former militia drilling ground) between the Old City Hall and **St. Paul's Anglican Church** (1750), the oldest Protestant church in Canada, and the fashionable **Spring Garden** area.

The Halifax Citadel, 426-5080. Canada's most visited National Historic Park commands a steep hill overlooking downtown and the harbor. Considered one of the finest remaining examples of a bastioned fortification of the 19th century, it is a maze of period barracks, garrison cells and museum rooms, including the independent **Army Museum of Canadian and British Militaria.** To get the most out of it, take a free 45-minute guided tour; otherwise you're on your own and signs and information are notably lacking. A 50-minute audio-visual presentation, the "Tides of History," begins every fifteen minutes and tells the history of Halifax and its military defenses. In summer, the fortress is garrisoned by university students who portray British military personnel of the 19th century Royal Artillery and 78th Highlanders. You'll hear the crack of rifle fire and the skirl of bagpipes as they drill in the parade, patrol their beats, and hoist signals on the masts. The slopes and greens called Halifax Commons around the Citadel are great for lounging. At the foot of Citadel Hill is the **Town Clock,** Halifax's best-loved landmark. It was given to the town in 1803 by Prince Edward, son of King George III — he had been head of the garrison in Halifax from 1794 to 1800. Citadel open daily 9 to 6 in summer (adults $2, children $1), 9 to 5 and free rest of year.

RESTORATIONS. Much of Halifax's rejuvenation has been guided by Waterfront Development Corp. Ltd., a government-backed corporation providing land and planning services for private development. "The whole waterfront area was a disaster not long ago," recalled Gerald G. Etienne, its president and CEO. "Nobody would come down here." Fourteen years later, this public-private partnership is credited with making Halifax the North American leader in historic restorations — from the rebirth of the oldest waterfront wharf complex to St. Paul's Church, Canada's first Parliament Building, Government House, the Brewery Market, Granville Pedestrian Mall and lately the historic City Hall. Next, Waterfront Development planned to complete a walkway along the waterfront from the Sheraton to the Brewery, add a waterfront park next to the Maritime Museum and seek an aquarium. Halifax's downtown, which has shifted north from the Spring Garden focal point of two decades ago along Barrington Street to Historic Properties, is edging back along the waterfront to Spring Garden once again.

Historic Properties, a once-abandoned four-acre waterfront site, is the keystone of Halifax's restoration efforts. Recipient of a Heritage Canada Award for historic preservation, it is a mix of boutiques, restaurants, lounges and the facilities of the Nova Scotia College of Art and Design, as well as a good visitor information center and launching point for tours. The **Brewery Market,** a newer anchor to the south end of the waterfront, was fashioned from the old Keith's Brewery and offers an interesting little farmer's market that attracts many of the locals Friday and Saturday mornings in summer. Somewhat dwarfed by the towering Maritime Center overhead, it's otherwise a food and drink emporium with a few stores and offices.

PARKS. This city of parks offers some special places: the **Grand Parade,** a pleasant place to relax in the historic heart of the city, is the scene of many a noontime entertainment extravaganza and is perhaps the best people-watching point in Halifax. Segments from the annual Nova Scotia International Tattoo were enacted when we were there in 1990. **Point Pleasant Park,** 186 acres of forest surrounded by water at the southern tip of the city, is great for boat-watching, hiking, picnicking, horseback riding, exploring nature trails and the seawall, as well as swimming (the sandy Black Rock Beach is sheltered by a rocky point at Harbour Lookoff). This is a pedestrian's park; no cars are allowed and even bicycling is banned on weekends and holidays. **Fleming Park** along the Northwest Arm offers swimming at another sheltered beach and views of the city from the top of the imposing stone Dingle Tower. The **Halifax Public Gardens** is a shady, sixteen-acre oasis at the edge of downtown. The oldest Victorian formal gardens in North America offer lovely walks, bridges, a gazebo for Sunday band concerts, a free-form pond with an island and, of course, ample flower beds, few of them identified. We were struck by the gardens' Southern air, enhanced by gnarled old trees and an exotic cactus garden, and the friendly ducks and geese seeking handouts from one and all.

Maritime Museum of the Atlantic, 1675 Lower Water St., 429-8210. This is the marine history branch of the decentralized Nova Scotia Museum. Housed in a former shipchandlery and warehouse with a modern addition, it has plenty of room for well-displayed exhibits, among them a collection of boats including Queen Victoria's Royal Barge under a three-story vaulted ceiling. We were especially taken by the inside of a vessel cabin in which the cabinet door was swinging and the horizon tilting through the window, giving one a dizzying sense of sea motion. We also liked the gripping audio-visual program detailing the 1917 Halifax explosion as told by those who lived through it; it debuted as a special exhibit and remained as a permanent fixture. The Canadian scientific ship Acadia is docked outside for exploration. Open daily most of the year, 9:30 to 5:30, Tuesday to 8, Sunday 1 to 5:30. Free.

SHOPPING. As in other cities, most of the large department and chain stores are in the suburban malls. Halifax is blessed, however, with a number of new and restored downtown shopping complexes, some of them connected by pedestrian skywalks. **Scotia Square** is the largest; **Barrington Place** is more fashionable.

An uptown section around Spring Garden Street is both funky and upscale, filled with university students, yuppies and the Old Guard. The adjacent **Blowers-Grafton Street** area is an offbeat area of pubs, yogurt shops, ethnic boutiques and even a Philippine restaurant. **The Pepper Pot** at 1549 Birmingham St. is an unusually fine kitchen and gift store. A three-story atrium at **Park Lane** is surrounded by good shops, with an emphasis on clothing; we particularly like the distinctive gifts and wares at **A Step Up,** a larger offspring of the original at Barrington Place. A waterfall plunges to the food court below. **Spring Garden Place** has more chic shops, a Texas-style galleria with hanging white lights, and a good basement market. Outside, **Jennifers** is a large gift and craft shop that carries almost everything that's made in Nova Scotia. **Mills Brothers** is Halifax's leading women's specialty shop in the British tradition. **Zwicker's Gallery** is worth a look for works of well-known as well as promising Canadian artists.

We like the wide variety of shops in Historic Properties, especially **A Pair of Trindles Bookshop,** which has about every book ever written by a Canadian author. We picked up a couple of the Anne of Green Gables paperbacks and Hugh MacLennan's classic novel about the Halifax explosion, *Barometer Rising.*

Where to Eat

Although Halifax has traditionally been considered a meat and potatoes or fried seafood town, many of its restaurants are changing their menu horizons with the times. Today, its dining establishments offer some of the best, most interesting food to be found in Eastern Canada.

Gourmet Favorites

Upper Deck, Historic Properties, Halifax. (902) 422-1289. The Privateer's Warehouse and Wharf was one of the first buildings to be restored in Historic Properties, and this three-decker sandwich of restaurants has been going strong since 1975. The Upper Deck is the culinary gem of the operation. Although it lacks a water view, "we make up for it with our food and service," the manager told two tourists who were ready to eat at 6 o'clock but wanted to be beside the water. After dark, of course, it doesn't matter all that much. The Upper Deck is captivating indeed with its original stone walls and timbered ceiling, heavy wood tables topped with dark leather mats, brocade runners and candles in etched-glass hurricane lamps on the main level, tiny table lamps on the loft level. Mussels bourguignonne, mussel soup flavored with rosemary and gin, and lobster bisque laced with armagnac are good starters. Among entrees ($14.95 for filet of sole amandine to $24.95 for Privateers' brochettes — shrimp, scallops and beef), we savored the rack of lamb persille and the filet mignon. The accompanying vegetables (roesti potatoes, tiny brussels sprouts, cauliflower and tomatoes) were exceptional. Our only regret was that the special venison with bourbon sauce (around which we'd planned our choice of the sommelier's special Wynns Oven Australian cabernet for $18) turned out to be unavailable. Like the food, the wine list is fairly extensive and on the pricey side for Halifax, but the dining experience is generally considered to be consistently the best in the city. The **Middle Deck Lounge** serves up nightly entertainment as well as lunch, while the lively **Lower Deck Pub,** packed at night with young Haligonians enjoying singalong entertainment, offers pub snacks. Dinner, Monday-Saturday 5:30 to 11, Sunday 5:30 to 10.

La Perla, 71 Alderney Drive, Dartmouth. (902) 469-3241. When we first visited this then two-year-old northern Italian restaurant across the street from the Dartmouth Ferry Terminal, there was not even a sign to identify it. But word of its excellence preceded it everywhere we went, and the quick ferry trip across the harbor to Dartmouth for lunch rewarded us with one of our best meals in Nova Scotia. Pearl MacDougall started with an upstairs cafe, expanded downstairs to the main floor, and added a larger seafood restaurant with the name **San Remo** next door. With the departure of her original chef-partner Maurizio Bertossi, she's running it herself with son James and three chefs. La Perla's decor was designed around the distinctive tall red upholstered seats acquired from a railroad car; they form four booths along one wall on the first and second floors, and the rest of the seating is at four tables for two on each floor. Since the restaurant started upstairs, the kitchen is there, and the staff maneuver back and forth to the main floor along a narrow stairway they share with customers. But what food the kitchen produces! There are intriguing salads like one with thinly sliced marinated veal, heavenly pastas and exceptional entrees ($11.50 to $15.95) such as veal scaloppine with a pecan, mustard, brandy and cream sauce, quail with buttered polenta and rabbit stewed in herbs, tomato and wine. Delicious hot rolls served with butter squeezed through a pastry tube, fettuccine in basil cream sauce and penne with peas and salami made a memorable lunch, topped off with cappuccino and an ice cream crepe smothered in hot orange sauce. And, crowning glory, our crisply linened table happened to be the only one with a water view. Lunch, Monday-Friday 11:30 to 2; dinner, Monday-Sunday 5 to 10.

Da Maurizio, 1496 Lower Water St., Halifax. (902) 423-0859. Acclaimed chef Maurizio Bertossi and his Dartmouth-born wife Stephanie returned from a trip to Italy to open this instant-winner of a place in the restored Brewery building. All in brick, burgundy and green, the theme is Venetian. A fabulous collection of Venetian masks and paintings adorns the walls, and a high counter is lined with bottles of antipasto ingredients, including pickles and vinegars made by Maurizio. Lacquered black chairs and black banquettes are at formally set tables. The wine list is mostly Italian. The antipasti are inspired, such things as scampi baked with garlic butter and brandy or focaccia brushed with garlic and topped with bocconcini and fried tomatoes. We'd go for one of the dozen pastas ($5.95 to $7.95), perhaps penne with pesto and parmigiano or tagliolini sauteed with shellfish, brandy and garlic. For main courses ($11 to $14.50), how about scallops sauteed with chilies, veal saltimbocca or sirloin of pork stuffed with a mushroom duxelle and friulano cheese? Seafood stew and grill specialties are other possibilities. Desserts, including tirami su, are equally worthy of the restaurant's billing, "esperienze gastronomiche." Lunch, Tuesday-Friday 11:30 to 2; dinner, Tuesday-Saturday 5:30 to 10.

The Halliburton House Inn, 5184 Morris St., Halifax. (902) 420-0658. This elegant new inn, which started at the top in terms of lodging accommodations, is making its mark on the culinary scene as well. Partners William McKeever and Charles Lief — he with a restaurant background — backed into the dining operation by offering dinner to attract the winter business trade. Later they added lunch and breakfast. Several small, hushed dining rooms are graced with old prints and Rosenthal china. Chef John Weir is known for his ways with seafood, especially the planked salmon baked on cedar shingles, a success to which we can attest. Our dinner began with a fabulous smoked salmon pate with caviar on a crispy potato pancake and a generous caesar salad. Among entrees ($11.95 to $19.50), the stuffed chicken with brie and walnuts was served on a sauce of raspberries and champagne and the planked salmon came with crisp summer vegetables. One in our party pronounced the kahlua white chocolate mousse cheesecake the best he's ever had, and the Belgian chocolate sack filled with red currant ice cream was another triumph. Many like to adjourn to the library for specialty coffees, hot cider with calvados, blueberry tea with amaretto and grand marnier, or cordials. Lunch, Monday-Friday 11:30 to 2:30; dinner nightly, 5:30 to 9:30.

The Silver Spoon Restaurant, 1813 Granville St., Halifax. (902) 422-1519. Although this establishment is noted for desserts, we recommend it for lunch and dinner as well. Such is its success that when we last visited, it was about to move around the corner from Hollis Street into expanded quarters on Granville. We were assured the food would remain the same, but owner Deanna

Silver planned "a new look for a new place." The main-floor dessert-cafe remains, but the bigger site also has an upstairs holding bar, a dining room and a function room. At lunch, we enjoyed a spicy mussel pasta ($7.95) and Nova Scotia fish cakes with silky leek and smoked salmon sauce ($6.75), topped off by a Swiss mocha-almond truffle. But the spanakopita was so tough we could hardly get a fork through it. On the dinner menu, entrees run from $15.95 for shrimp with caramelized pecans in dijon sauce or roast pork tenderloin with raspberry-orange sauce to $20.95 for veal normande or beef tenderloin with five-peppercorn sauce. Halibut in cashews with a fresh mango-lime sauce and loin of lamb with cinnamon-port sauce are other intriguing possibilities. Even more intriguing are the desserts served here and down below at **Silver Spoon Desserts,** where it seems that half of Halifax comes at night to indulge a sweet tooth. Listening to classical music, perched at little glass-covered tables, you can hardly choose among a couple dozen fabulous truffles, cakes like Queen Mother gateau or, our downfall, a raspberry-hazelnut swirl cheesecake. There are all kinds of coffees and teas, and the glass of water comes with a slice of lemon. Dinner nightly, 5:30 to 10 or 10:30; dessert-cafe, 11:30 to 11 or 11:30.

Scanway, The Courtyard, 1569 Dresden Row, Halifax. (902) 422-3733. If you like Scandinavian food as much as we do, you'll head for this nifty place off Spring Garden Road. Unni Simensen from just outside Oslo owns it, and when you dine here you almost feel you are in Norway. The 150-year-old house has been done over with pine walls and track lighting but the six original fireplaces remain, and the two second-floor dining rooms and adjacent outdoor decks ringed with purple petunias contain lots of nooks and crannies. The comfortable chairs are made of local pine, and red candles and white cloths on the diagonal are at every table. Everyone flocks to Scanway at lunchtime for the wide selection of open-face sandwiches, 22 in all, from $4.95 for Norwegian cheese with fruit to $8.95 for "tartarbiff." Smoked salmon with scrambled egg is one of the most requested. Among salads is an excellent plate of smoked salmon, shrimp on egg and marinated herring. At night, entrees ($13.75 to $16.95) include lobster and shrimp in a white wine sauce and sole stuffed with crab. You could start with smoked eel and end with one of Scanway's fabulous desserts — perhaps marsipankake, a delightful creation of light cake layered with fruit and whipped cream and covered with a layer of marzipan. Aquavit comes right from the freezer, as it should; there are Tuborg beer and a quite decent wine list. Downstairs is **Scanway Gourmet** for snacks, desserts and takeout. Lunch, 11:30 to 3; dinner, 5 to 10. Closed Sunday.

Soho Kitchen & Cafe, 1582 Granville St., Halifax. (902) 423-3049. All Halifax seems to hang out at this eclectic place — even Halliburton House Inn chef John Weir, who was whipping up creative lunches here on his day off when we stopped in. Owned by Tom Russell, who started the Good Egg and Alberta's Cafe in Portland, Me., Soho has grown like topsy and now has an open kitchen and a book and gift shop separating the smoking and non-smoking sections. The dining rooms are a melange of black and white linoleum, different chairs, folk art, and yellow and red squares painted around arches. The food is foremost: a changing blackboard menu that might list hummus and Greek salad, sticky maple chicken, Asian shrimp with ramen noodles and coconut rum pie at wallet-pleasing prices. The cuisine is international, lately with an emphasis on Mexican, and the staff takes turns waiting tables and working in the kitchen, where they cook whatever they want for specials. Select wines, espresso and cappuccino are featured. The laid-back atmosphere is just right for snacking and whiling away an afternoon or evening. Lunch, Monday-Saturday 11:30 to 4; dinner, 5 to 10; Sunday brunch, noon to 4.

410

Other Choices

Clipper Cay, Historic Properties, Halifax. (902) 423-6818. Local detractors contend that this lives up to the first part of its name and sells windows to tourists rather than food, and we admit we were so put off by a haughty maitre-d' who failed to produce a window table as requested that we gave up our coveted dinner reservation. There's no denying that Clipper Cay has the best water view in Halifax, its expansive windows taking full advantage. The main second-floor dining room is supremely elegant, pink and pricey. Dinner entrees run from $15.95 for filet of sole to $21.95 for filet of beef stuffed with escargots in garlic butter. The popular downstairs **Cay Side** lounge offers snacks, salads and pastas, as well as light entrees like tourtiere, seafood casserole and shrimp stir-fry. Cay Side, open daily 11:30 to 10; Clipper Cay, dinner nightly from 5, Sunday brunch 11:30 to 2:30.

Five Fishermen, 1740 Argyle St., Halifax. (902) 422-4421. The tourists also pack this place, and when we stopped by one weeknight we overhead a party of two being told they would have a two-hour wait until 9 for dinner as eight conventioneers were ushered upstairs. Although Haligonians think it has slipped under its recent ownership, out-of-towners like the nautical decor with a statue at a ship's wheel atop the stairs, high-back chairs, bare wood floors and window seats beside the Grand Parade. They also like the complimentary salad bar and seafood bar with steamed mussels and clams. Fish from the restaurant's own boat appears in many forms, from Arctic char and mako shark ($15.95) to house specialties like prawns with cheese, lobster thermidor and Digby scallops with fettuccine ($23.95). Lunch is offered in the **My Apartment** lounge next door, one of nine beverage rooms launched by owner Gary Hurst along Argyle Street. Dinner nightly, 5 to 10 or 11.

Birmingham Street Grill, 5511 Spring Garden Road, Halifax. (902) 420-9622. Everything is in shades of black and white except the yellow lighting behind the glass blocks at the bar of this trendy eatery with an open kitchen lined in glass blocks and black and white tiles. White cardboard clouds hang from the ceiling, and strips of mirrors on the walls make the room seem bigger. The with-it menu offers everything from crepes to pastas to stir-fries ($6.95 to $9.95). For heartier appetites, entrees ($10.95 to $16.95) include duck with pears, chicken with cassis, pork in an apple-grape sauce, braised rack of lamb, and chicken and lobster with cognac. Black cherry ravioli with sour cream sauce is a tempting dessert. The wine list is short but international. Lunch, Monday-Saturday 11 to 2:30; dinner nightly, 5 to 11 or midnight, Sunday 4:30 to 10.

Ryan Duffy's, Spring Garden Place, Halifax. (902) 421-1116. This is the latest incarnation of Le Grand, Duffy's Bar and the Rainbow Grill. Recently expanded, it's formal yet casual and attractive with well-spaced tables flanked by brocade upholstered arm chairs and soaring windows onto the street. The specialties are corn-fed beef and steak carved to size. The uncooked meat is brought to the table, you choose your portion, it's carved and weighed, and you pay by the pound — "the record so far is 28.6 ounces," the maitre-d' informed us. A few seafood dishes complement the beef, and run from $14.95 for catch of the day to $21.95 for lobster. The week's "fresh sheet" offered pan-fried halibut with pecan caramel sauce, baked lemon sole and snow crab topped with swiss cheese, and jumbo tiger shrimp and apricot saute mixed with vegetables. Lunch, Monday-Saturday 11:30 to 3; dinner, 5 to 11 or midnight, Sunday to 10.

L'Bohema Restaurant, 1541 Birmingham St., Halifax. (902) 423-0568. Gypsy music plays in this long, narrow cafe in an old house with pretty blue molding and a pleasant outside garden for dining. This is the newest creation of Pavel Jockel, a Czechslovakian who also owns the Czech Inn and the Hungry Hungarian and is a television cook of some note in the Maritimes. The menu ($6.95 to $14.95) is an interesting mix of Eastern European specialties like schnitzel, pierogi, Hungarian chicken crepes and McPavel's European hamburger and more traditional items like chicken California and seafood fettuccine. The soups, salads and appetizers intrigue, and you can finish with poppyseed strudel or chocolate malakov cake. Lunch and dinner daily.

Le Bistro, 1333 South Park St., Halifax. (902) 423-8428. Don't let its location in the main-floor corner in the high-rise Park Victoria apartment building deceive you. This is as French a bistro as you'll find this side of the Left Bank. An enclosed atrium has umbrella-covered tables looking onto the street; the interior is dimly lit, candles drip over Perrier bottles and the hanging lamps are covered in red and white to match the tablecloths. The inexpensive food appeals to the nearby Dalhousie University crowd. We were stunned to find a Sunday brunch with eggs benedict and crepes florentine for $7.95, including champagne or bloody mary (the latter, served in a mason jar, was one of the biggest we've seen). A classical guitarist played as we brunched on shrimp creole and chicken livers with poached eggs. The regular menu appeals as well, and people rave about the caesar salad garnished with grilled scallops, Icelandic shrimp, crab and mussels. Open daily from 11:30 to 1 a.m.; Sunday brunch, 11 to 3.

MacAskill's Dining Room & Lounge, Dartmouth Ferry Terminal, Dartmouth. (902) 466-3100. This large establishment seats 285 atop the Dartmouth Ferry Terminal, with a glorious view of the Halifax skyline and water on three sides. A statue of the Cape Breton giant for which the restaurant is named stands beside the oven, called Angus' Mill and Bakery, where four kinds of bread are baked. The standard meat and seafood menu runs from $13.95 for pan-fried haddock to $19.95 for filet mignon or seafood skewer over rice. The airy dining room is contemporary in pink and blue; nicely angled tables have large spindle arm chairs. Lunch, Monday-Friday; dinner, Monday-Saturday.

McKelvie's, 1680 Lower Water St., Halifax. (902) 421-6161. "Delishes Fishes Dishes," proclaims the menu of this casual place with an intriguing interior in a restored firehouse across from the Maritime Museum. A pleasant hodgepodge of lattice work with rope dividers, arches and hanging lamps, it's centered by a long boat, which is flanked by seats for large parties or those who want drinks while awaiting dinner. The mussels are extra good here, the halibut and swordfish are blackened with cajun spices, and there's a strip steak for those who don't want seafood. Dinner entrees run from $8.95 for fish and chips to $19.95 for steak and scallops or shrimp. Roasted salmon steak, Digby scallops and shrimp Louisiana are favorites. Lunch daily, 11:30 to 3:30; dinner from 5.

The Sandwich Tree, Xerox Building, Purdy's Wharf, Halifax. Part of a local chain, this is where office workers go for a healthful breakfast or a bargain lunch, inside in a sleek gray, cane and chrome setting or outside on a vast upper deck with harbor view beyond. We marveled at the breafast specials, eggs benedict and eggs florentine, both $2.99, ordered cafeteria style but brought to the table with coffee refills. There are six kinds of muffins, several other egg dishes, and many sandwiches, soups and salads for lunch. The Tree is connected to **Pastamimi,** another local chain, and across the walkway from **Yogen Fruz.**

FOR MORE INFORMATION: Tourism Halifax, P.O. Box 1749, Halifax, N.S. B3J 3A5. (902) 421-8736. It operates a Visitor's Information Center in Old City Hall, Duke and Barrington streets The province runs a handy waterfront visitor center in Historic Properties.

Marker denotes points of interest along Cabot Trail.

Cabot Trail/Cape Breton Island, N.S.

Cape Breton Island — and particularly its Cabot Trail — has long been a destination for knowing travelers who like breathtaking oceanfront and mountain scenery, interesting history and customs, and a distinct change of pace.

Although internationally known, its location away from the mainstream and its distance from the rest of civilization leave Cape Breton a delightful world unto itself. Yes, Americans and off-island Canadians can get there and do, but it's no quick trip.

The 184-mile-long Cabot Trail, Cape Breton's best-known claim to fame, is a sharply rising and falling highway that hugs the most scenic oceanside cliffs this side of California's Big Sur. It alone is worth the five-hour drive from Halifax or the day's drive from eastern Maine.

But there's much more. For scenery and sailing, the shimmering Bras d'Or Lakes make up an inland sea which so captivated Alexander Graham Bell that he made the lakeside resort village of Baddeck his summer home for 35 years. Today, visitors find Baddeck a good base for exploring the island.

The partly restored Fortress of Louisbourg, the largest national historic park in Canada, is an absorbing re-creation of the 18th-century village known as the Gibraltar of Canada. Here you relive the history of the costly site that helped cause France to lose its empire and Britain her American colonies, changing the destiny of North America.

To the French legacy at Louisbourg and the Acadian heritage still dominant at Cheticamp, add the Micmac Indians at four reservations along the Bras d'Or Lakes and the prevailing Scottish presence for a unique mix of cultures.

413

Nowhere in Nova Scotia (which means New Scotland in Latin) is the Scottish influence more pronounced than in the Cape Breton Highlands, which resemble those in Scotland. "Scotland on a Nearer Shore" was the headline on a New York Times article on Cape Breton. You quickly recognize the Scottish dialect and place names, the preponderance of last names beginning with "Mac," and the fondness for the foods and traditions of Scotland.

So isolated are parts of Cape Breton that they remain much as John Cabot found them when he landed, it's believed, in 1497 at Aspy Bay on the northernmost tip of Cape Breton.

Fishing and tourism are the principal occupations. Both are quite different from what you might expect, however. The fishing is done as of old from weatherbeaten boats of many hues; they are moored in picturesque harbors or can be seen at work off the soaring coastline. The tourism scene is straight out of the past as well — no chain motels or fast-food eateries here. Instead you find mom-and-pop motels and a few traditional lodges, fried-seafood restaurants, Scottish and Acadian souvenir stands and shops, and offbeat surprises everywhere.

Cape Breton is a world apart — a place of history, tradition and scenery so powerful that you can't help but yield to its allure.

Getting There

Although there is air service from major cities to Halifax and Sydney, most travelers drive (or rent a car) to see Cape Breton Island. The island is large and, unless you go by tour bus as so many do, it's difficult to get around without wheels. Although great for hiking, we saw few cyclists, probably because of the mountains and distances involved.

The island is easily reached via the Trans-Canada Highway (Routes 104 and 105), which meets the Cabot Trail in the vicinity of Baddeck.

Prices are quoted in Canadian funds and are subject to the new national GST tax. Cape Breton is in the Atlantic time zone, one hour ahead of Eastern time.

Where to Stay

Your choice of accommodations depends on time, budget and personal preferences. Those in the Cape Breton Highlands run the gamut, with the exception of chain motels. Several fine resort lodges are located in or near Cape Breton Highlands National Park. Baddeck, beside Lake Bras d'Or at the beginning and end of the circular Cabot Trail, is the best interior location for exploring all of Cape Breton. The Margarees, Cheticamp and Pleasant Bay are close to the park on the northwest coast; Ingonish is close to the park on the east coast. As in the rest of Nova Scotia, toll-free reservations can be made at most places through the provincial reservations service, Check Inns, from the U.S. (800) 341-6096, from Maine (800) 492-6043, and from Canada (800) 565-0000.

Resort Retreats

Keltic Lodge, Box 70, Ingonish Beach B0C 1L0. (902) 285-2880. World-famous as a full-service resort operated by the provincial government, Keltic Lodge couldn't be more superbly situated. It's off by itself in an idyllic setting, commanding a smashing view of the ocean on two sides from its perch astride a long promontory called Middle Head. You'll likely see it from the road, long before you pass the renowned Highlands golf course and enter the grounds through graceful birches arched over profuse flower borders and, in early July, surprising-to-see rhododendrons. On your right is the resort's newer and more motel-like White Birch Inn; on the left is the Atlantic Coffee Shop and gift shop, and beyond is the striking white, red-roofed Main Lodge. We booked one of the 40 rooms in the White Birch Inn, which had two picture windows overlooking a narrow lawn beside the cliff and nothing but ocean and the craggy shoreline opposite. At least that's what was in view when we arrived; shortly after, it began raining and the next morning we and everything else north of Baddeck were enveloped in fog and a howling gale. Under those conditions, one night was enough; had the weather cooperated, even the most driven traveler might have lingered to laze beside the heated saltwater pool, hike around Middle Head, play golf or tennis and enjoy the usual resort amenities. Before the deluge, we did manage a 90-minute hike out Middle Head to Tern Point, spotting cormorants, viewing the pounding surf below and picking wild raspberries for sustenance. Our spacious room had a double and a twin bed, pale blue walls and carpeting, two yellow rocking chairs beside a red table, a telephone and a small AM-FM radio for company on a rainy (make that torrential) evening under circumstances that best could be described as lonely. All rooms now have color TV. Downstairs are two large lounges, where movies are shown at night. Why the White Birch Inn is air-conditioned we don't know (seldom did the temperature approach 70 during the weeks we were in Nova Scotia either in July or early September). It's also heated and remains open in winter for skiers at the nearby Cape Smokey ski area (a site for Canada's 1987 Winter Games hosted by Cape Breton). Thirty-two more rooms with private bath are located in the Main Lodge. Twenty-six rooms are available in cottages, some with fireplaces and sitting rooms. The lodge has large, comfortable sitting rooms, a downstairs bar and a long main dining room with windows onto the ocean on both sides. Three meals a day are served (see Where to Eat). Doubles, MAP only, $220 in Main Lodge, $215 in White Birch Inn, $230 in cottages. Main Lodge open June to Oct. 20.

The Normaway Inn, Egypt Road, Box 106, Margaree Valley B0E 2C0. (902) 248-2987 or (800) 565-9463. Although not on the water, this out-of-the-way 1920s resort with 30 rooms is perfect for those who seek tranquility and a welcoming atmosphere. "We get people who want to get away and have peace and quiet," says innkeeper David MacDonald. The 250-acre property is in a wooded valley two miles off the Cabot Trail, and we saw a deer as we drove in the long driveway lined with pines. Three meals a day are served in the dining room, considered one of the island's best (see Where to Eat). A fiddler entertains at night in the huge living room, equipped with a fieldstone fireplace, old stuffed sofas and lots of books; a connecting sun room is cheery by day. Downstairs is a gathering room, where red chairs are lined up for local-interest films at night. The inn's nine rooms, each with private bath and located so no two are adjacent, are comfortable with one or two double beds and decorated in lodge style. Extra privacy is afforded in six cabins, plus eleven new one-bedroom pine chalets clustered near the tennis court. Breakfast ($8.50), with Scottish and Canadian music playing in the background, was one of the best we ever had, from the real orange juice and stewed rhubarb with thick cream, through the excellent homemade granola, muffins so hot the waitress burned her hand on the pan, and french toast dipped in oatmeal and cinnamon. The piece de resistance was Eggs Hughie D, a local creation of a poached egg on a toasted Margaree muffin and Canadian back bacon, topped with a light tomato sauce and cheddar cheese. Extraordinary! Doubles, $90 to $100 EP, $155 MAP. Open June-October.

Inverary Inn Resort, Shore Road, Box 190, Baddeck B0E 1B0. (902) 295-2674. An expanding resort with a Scottish theme beside Lake Bras d'Or, this has 114 (g... g on 164) guest rooms, two restaurants (see Where to Eat), a new indoor pool and a gift shop. The MacAuley family have operated it since 1971, and their Scottish heritage is evident from the names of the diverse buildings to the salty kippered herring and untoasted bonnach served at breakfast. The eight original rooms in the inn are appointed with antique furnishings, but they've been dwarfed by a succession of newer buildings, including 50 more rooms planned to open in 1991. Our lakefront room in the two-story Argyle Lodge, the old main motel unit, was comfortable with pine paneling and furniture (the pine chairs, made near Halifax, are especially handsome), autumn-patterned draperies and bedspreads, flowered sheets and cable TV. Other rooms are in Culloden House, lodges and eight pine-paneled cottages. Twenty-four new rooms in the Glasgow House, with an indoor pool and jacuzzi, are open all year. They're thoroughly up to date in pink and blue with comforters on the beds, thick carpeting and bar-refrigerators. Three fine tennis courts are beside the lake, as is The Fish House restaurant and a blue-canopied pontoon boat that takes guests on lake cruises. Between the bustling restaurants, the interesting gift shop and the many bus tours, Inverary is apt to convey a busy feeling; at least we found it so, our car and only two others being sandwiched between four tour buses. Doubles, $80 to $120. Glasgow House open year-round.

Glenghorm Resort, Cabot Trail, Box 39, Ingonish B0C 1K0. (902) 285-2888 or 285-2049. Chris and Clarence Meisner claim to be the deans of seasonal resort operators in the province, having started Glenghorm in 1952. Since then it just grew and grew. They now have 950 feet of beach frontage, a restaurant, gift shop, and 90 motel units, efficiencies and housekeeping cottages in two separate complexes. The first and original is close to the shore and dining room; the newer complex is a bit more distant but near the pool. Picnic tables and some cottages face the water, as do a couple of the six motel buildings with private balconies; we liked them better than the newer motels away from the water. The 130-seat dining room has a view of the ocean at the foot of the 22-acre property. The dinner menu runs from $9 for New York strip steak or pork chops and applesauce to $12 for deep-fried scallops. Says Chris Meisner: "These local ladies know how to cook fish, and people tell us ours are the best meals they've had since leaving home." She has printed her recipe for oatcakes to share with guests. Doubles, $60 to $68; cottages, $60 to $88, usually booked weekly. Open May-October.

The Markland, Cabot Trail, Dingwall B0C 1G0. (902) 383-2246 or (800) 565-7105 (from the Maritimes). This new "coastal resort" on a bluff seemingly near the end of the world was very much in the making at our 1990 visit, according to Ann MacLean, manager for her brother, the owner. Located at the east or top end of the island where the mountains meet the sea, twenty log cottages and suites smelled nicely of fresh knotty pine. Described as typical, the suite we saw had a cathedral ceiling, modern bath with lots of towels, a sofa, bare floors and a bed facing the door toward the ocean. Nearly all the furnishings were made of wood. The rest of the 70-acre property includes a nice beach, a pool to come, nature trails and a sense of remoteness. The main lodge has a reception area and a peaked-ceiling dining room that was not yet open when we were there in July 1990. Well-traveled young chef Donald MacInnis came home to plan a mix of European and Canadian fare. His changing menu might start with seafood terrine, oyster stew with fresh julienne of vegetables, a warm lobster salad, and a local seafood chowder with mussels bouillabaisse that he called "an energetic combination." Entrees could be panfried grey sole, spicy halibut with pepper and vinegar sauce, and blackened chicken with lime sauce. The restaurant is open daily from 7:30 a.m. to 8 p.m. Doubles, $90 EP; efficiencies, $115.

416

Baddeck Bases

Gisele's, Shore Road, Baddeck B0E 1B0. (902) 295-2849. What started as a few efficiency cottages blossomed into a motel and sprouted in 1990 into a luxury high-rise with Baddeck's first elevator. Helen and Hans Sievers took over the complex in 1975 from his mother (Gisele, who retired to Florida) and have added on to the point they think theirs is the best on the island. Forty-three deluxe rooms are contained on three floors of the new building, which stretches perpendicular from the road so that only the end suites get head-on views of the lake. The rooms are pretty in roses and teals, Helen's favorite colors, and have one queensize or two double beds, TVs hidden in armoires, a loveseat and a chair in rose velvet, reproduction period furniture and bathrooms outfitted with hair dryers, toiletries and sewing kits. Three corner suites have jacuzzis and fireplaces. A spa offers saunas, whirlpool and a gym room, and a solarium is used for brunches. "We're going after the European market and conventions," says Helen, who's a leader in promoting Cape Breton tourism. She's removed the original cottages from the complex, which also includes an expanded restaurant of note (see Where to Eat) and a pleasant front dining terrace beside a fountain. Up a hill out back remains a two-story motel with 26 units, each with two beds, color TV and unusual bow windows that let you see more of the distant lake and provide some solar heat on cool days. Rooms here are nicely outfitted with local pine furniture designed by Hans and made by an Indian cooperative. Gisele handpainted the plates hanging on the walls and the tiles on walls and tables. Doubles, $75; suites, $125 to $150. Open May-October, weekends in spring and fall. Closed January and February.

Duffus House, Water Street, Baddeck B0E 1B0. (902) 295-2172. A dear little 1850 house filled with antiques, an annex house next door, extensive English country gardens with the most amazing oriental poppies we ever saw, and a waterfront location. What more could one ask? New innkeepers Judy and John Langley have put it all together to create Cape Breton's most interesting B&B. The two houses have room after little room of period furnishings and nice touches. All told, there are nine guest rooms, three with private baths and the rest with wash basins, in a variety of configurations, including a suite with a wood stove in the sitting room, windows onto the garden and water, a paneled bathroom and a bedroom. There are antiques and curios everywhere you look — ditto for pleasant sitting areas inside and out, in living rooms, on verandas, in the gardens, on the new wharf facing Kidston Island. And the lavish gardens, fashioned by the previous owner, must be seen to be believed. From a galley kitchen in the second house, Judy serves a continental breakfast of scones, muffins and oatcakes with strawberry-rhubarb marmalade. Doubles, $40 to $65. Open June to mid-October.

Silver Dart Lodge, Shore Road, Baddeck B0E 1B0. (902) 295-2340. Despite its name, this is a modern motor inn with 88 units (twelve of them chalets and 24 with kitchen facilities) and a bar and dining room. Although we had expected it to be on the water, it is across Shore Road and up a hill. Our room with two double beds and TV was fine and the view of Lake Bras d'Or from the balcony was inspiring, even though we had to ask for chairs and then had to dodge a thunderstorm; the ensuing rainbow was a colorful substitute for the missing sunset. The bright red lighting in the chalet-style dining room called **McCurdy's** would compete with the sunset anyway. What we thought was a rather strange dinner — our first in Nova Scotia — turned out to be not so strange for Cape Breton. Our entrees of lake trout and salmon with egg sauce came with cubed turnips, carrots, two scoops of lumpy mashed potatoes, one piece of iceberg lettuce and a tomato slice. An $18 bottle of pinot blanc helped. An accordion-playing Scotsman in a kilt entertained. For big-spenders, the Silver Dart offers its **MacNeil House,** a 19th-century mansion up the hill out back, with six suites, each with living room, fireplace, kitchen, private bath and jacuzzi. Furnished in dark cherry wood and four-poster beds, two have balconies and three face the lake. Dinner, 5:30 to 9:30. Doubles, $85 to $100; efficiencies and chalets, $95 to $110; suites, $185. Open mid-May to October.

The Point Bed & Breakfast, 4 Twining St., Baddeck B0E 1B0. (902) 295-3368. A small front deck and the front lawn look onto the water at this new B&B on the point where Twining and Water streets meet. Susan Phelan and family share their home with guests, who have large bedrooms sharing a bath. The two large front corner rooms have great water views, as does the living room with a wood stove and a dining table in the corner. Susan has "a lot of fun with healthful breakfasts," serving fresh fruit, granola and perhaps salmon quiche, cheese strata or pancakes with maple syrup from Black River near Mabou. Doubles, $40 to $60. No smoking. Open spring-fall.

Telegraph House, Chebucto Street, Box 8, Baddeck B0E 1B0. (902) 295-9988. Built in 1861 in the midst of tiny downtown Baddeck, the main building contained the office of the first Trans Oceanic Cable Co. Some of the first telegraph messages in North America were sent from here, and part of the original cable can be seen. Alexander Graham Bell's Room No. 1 is preserved in much the same style as when he stayed here in the 1880s. Other rooms in the three-story inn are furnished in Victoriana and a number share baths. Out back is an L-shaped motel. All told there are 43 guest rooms, 37 with private bath, a pleasant common room in which a fire is lit on cool mornings, and a beamed and paneled dining room serving three home-style meals a day. Owners Buddy and Mary Dunlop are the fourth generation of the founding innkeepers. Doubles, $87 to $95.

Motels along the Cabot Trail

Since the preferred direction around the Cabot Trail is clockwise from Baddeck, lodging is listed in that order.

Duck Cove Inn, Margaree Harbour B0E 2B0. (902) 235-2658. This is not an inn, but a motel, although one with a restaurant and smashing vistas of the harbor. The dining room is comfortable and homey with paper mats or blue cloths on pine tables, captain's chairs and nothing too striking to detract from the view. Dinners (from $9.95 for grilled haddock to $14.75 for grilled or poached salmon) include juice or soup and vegetables. The 24 motel units are standard with two double beds and TV. The twelve newer units in the two-story motel closest to the water have balconies or sliding doors onto a terrace. Canoes are available for rent in a little park beside the river; friends report they were trucked several miles up the Margaree for an enjoyable paddle back that produced sights of deer and otters. Doubles, $58 to $60. Open June-Oct. 20.

Laurie's Motel, Main Street, Box 1, Cheticamp B0E 1H0. (902) 224-2400. Laurie McKeown's father started this growing lodging and dining complex in 1938 with five cabins in the heart of French-Acadian Cheticamp. The cabins are long gone, replaced by an eleven-unit motel behind the restaurant. A later ten-room section was double-decked in 1985 to provide 31 units. Off at an angle without much of a view is a new 24-room wing with a bridal suite boasting a kingsize bed, sofa, ceiling fan and a double jacuzzi with pillows. Laurie refurbished the older units in 1985, and acquired a liquor license (permitting a suave upstairs cocktail lounge) for the restaurant (see Where to Eat). He's proud of the five family suites with sitting areas in the new motel section, especially the large second-story end suite with a view of the Gulf of St. Lawrence from the sofa and chair grouping by the window — "you'll have a hard time finding a better room in all of Nova Scotia," he claims. Doubles, $59 to $80; suites, $85 to $125. Open year-round.

Park View Motel, Box 117, Cheticamp B0E 1H0. (902) 224-3232. Located five miles north of Cheticamp at the West Gate of Cape Breton Highlnds National Park, this is exactly what its name says. The low one-story red building has seventeen units with wall-to-wall carpeting and color TV. There's an oval outdoor pool with a diving board. A licensed dining room serves three meals a day. Doubles, $55. Open May 24-Oct. 15.

Mountain View Motel, Pleasant Bay BOE 2P0. (902) 224-3100. Better looking than its neighboring Beachside but away from the water is the Mountain View. Formerly the Bonnie Doon, it has eighteen motel units with TV and radio, four efficiency cottages and three cabins. A swimming pool, tennis courts, shuffleboard and volleyball are attractions, and the licensed dining room serves three meals daily. Doubles, $50 to $70. Open May 15-Oct. 15.

Amber Gate, Box 177, Ingonish Beach BOC 1L0. (902) 285-2525. A large TV satellite dish is the first thing you notice at this small place in the trees near the beach. "We're the only ones with satellite TV," the office staffer explained. The rooms in the six-unit motel up close to the road have one or two double beds and TV. Near the sand beach are four efficiency cottages and two beachfront houses, the latter with fireplaces and accommodating six or seven people. Doubles, $55 to $80 in motel, $70 to $155 in cottages.

Other Options

Cape Breton Bed & Breakfast. More than 60 homes that take in travelers are marked by distinctive small signs across the island and listed in a brochure prepared by the Cape Breton Tourist Association, 20 Keltic Drive, Sydney River B1S 1P5, (902) 539-9876. Most have one or two rooms and charge $25 single, $30 double for bed and breakfast.

CAMPING. Numerous campgrounds are detailed in the Nova Scotia Tourism Department's travel guide. Two private ones that appealed are the **Baddeck Cabot Trail KOA,** Box 417, Baddeck, 295-2288, with 115 serviced and 36 unserviced sites, and **Bras d'Or Lakes Campground,** Box 392, Baddeck, 295-2329, with 56 serviced and 33 unserviced sites and 500 feet of shoreline on the lake. The National Park has eight campgrounds, some on the ocean, with varied facilities and rates.

For an usual experience, head out to **Meat Cove Camping,** Meat Cove B0C 1E0, (902) 383-2379, "at the end of the road where the Saint Lawrence Seaway meets the Atlantic ocean." The brochure doesn't tell the half of it. You get there by going up and down a hair-raising dirt road to the end of the world, where at the edge of the last hamlet on Cape Breton are ten campsites with services nearby, spectacular views and sheer privacy. Rates, $10.

COTTAGES. Among the choices are **Cape Breton Highlands Bungalows,** Box 151, Ingonish Beach, 285-2000, with 25 good-looking cottages built by the National Parks Service on a lake overlooking Ingonish Beach, doubles $49, and **Whale Cove Summer Village,** RR 1, Margaree Harbour, 235-2202, 30 housekeeping cottages with porches on a bluff beside the ocean, $50 to $75 daily.

Seeing and Doing _____ ♫♫♫

Because Cape Breton's weather is fickle and you can get socked in by fog, it's best to allow two or three days there in order to pick the clearest day to drive the Cabot Trail. Plenty of diversions are available for marginal weather.

The Cabot Trail

The 184-mile-long trail around the outermost tip of Cape Breton Island embraces some of North America's most spectacular scenery. The road is good and the complete trip easily can be done in a day, or you can linger and retrace your steps.

Pick a clear day — preferably sunny, although even cloudy days can yield good visibility. The most breathtaking scenery (and slowest driving) is along relatively short stretches in Cape Breton Highlands National Park, up and down cliffs on the eastern and western shores and in the mountainous northern interior near Big Intervale. Although you might choose as we once did to go counterclockwise against the prevailing traffic and for right-hand access to scenic pull-offs, don't. The other times we went clockwise and concluded that that direction offers better vistas.

Cape Breton Highlands National Park, Ingonish Beach. Established in 1936, this is Eastern Canada's largest national park and the heart of the Cabot Trail. The park's main feature is an extensive plateau, criss-crossed by rivers and valleys between mountains and a rugged coastline of bold headlands, steep cliffs, hidden coves and sandy beaches. To us, it's a cross between Scotland's Highlands, Portugal's Algarve and California's Big Sur, and the wilderness is so vast and the signs of civilization so different that you could imagine yourself in a foreign land.

Naturalists appreciate the many varieties of wildlife and vegetation. Hikers like the 140 miles of trails leading to the interior plateau, the rugged coast or to 1,000-foot viewpoints overlooking it all; the 28 trails are detailed in a special brochure. Swimmers will find two supervised beaches and any number of salt and freshwater beaches. Picnicking is offered at numerous "picnic parks." The eighteen-hole Highlands Links near the Keltic Lodge is one of Canada's more challenging golf courses. Three tennis courts are available at the Ingonish Beach Day Use Area. In winter there's skiing on Cape Smokey. The park's interpretive program includes a variety of roadside markers and exhibits, self-guided trails and, in summer, guided walks and evening talks by park rangers.

Information centers are open from mid-May to mid-October at the Cheticamp and Ingonish entrances to the park. Park admission is $4 per car daily or $25 annually.

Trail and Park Highlights

The Cabot Trail and the park have as many interesting (if not quite as diverse) attractions as Yellowstone or Yosemite. Going clockwise, we were particularly struck by the colorful old boats and the loons in the harbor at **Grand Etang** and the austere, barren Acadian fishing village of **Cheticamp** (pause to view the ornate interior of **St. Peter's Roman Catholic Church),** the ride up **French Mountain** (with views behind) and then down the switchbacks to **Pleasant Bay.** Atop French Mountain are the **Skyline Trail,** from which you peer down on the Cabot Trail and see fishing boats and maybe a whale, and the **Bog Trail** where signs along a boardwalk attempt to make the bog interesting.

As you head into the interior, stop at the **Lone Shieling,** a replica of an open Scottish sheep crofter's hut dwarfed by 300-year-old sugar maples. The descent down **North Mountain** provides awesome views toward Aspy Bay. Take the one-mile side trip on a dirt road to **Beulach Ban Falls,** a 50-foot-high waterfall and picnic area that's worth the detour.

At **Cape North,** leave the trail to head out to the northernmost tip of Cape Breton. Stop at **Cabot Landing,** where English explorer John Cabot and his son Sebastian are thought to have set foot on the sandy beach in 1497. The view across the church spire and colorful houses as you descend the hill into the harbor at **Bay St. Lawrence** is unforgettable. The intrepid can continue out past Capstick and up and down a winding dirt road to **Meat Cove,** a hamlet sequestered seemingly at the end of the earth, where the views and the seclusion are awesome.

Back in Cape North, leave the Cabot Trail to take the alternate coastal route off to **White Point** and **Neil's Harbor.** It provided even more spectacular views than some of the Cabot Trail, and so unexpectedly. We liked the multi-colored bluff near Smelt Brook, which ends with a formation that looks like the profile of Richard Nixon. Drive down to White Point, a working dock reeking of fish, with colorful boats and lobster traps all around. Neil's Harbor is as picturesque a fishing village as you'll find.

Rejoin the Cabot Trail and stop at **Black Brook Cove,** one of the many picnic parks in the area and this one with grass, a sandy beach and a bluff on one side. Go into the Keltic Lodge grounds and hike, if you have time, out to the end of **Middle Head. Ingonish Beach** is long, sandy and reminiscent of Ogunquit's, except when the surf is crashing in a storm. The beach is actually a spit of land with the ocean on one side and a freshwater lake on the other. The Cabot Trail climbs **Cape Smokey,** which may be clouded in mist, for the most hair-raising part of driving the trail. At **North Shore,** you may be able to see in the distance the famous **Bird Islands,** home of the Atlantic puffin and a favorite with bird-watchers (who can visit by tour boat from Big Bras d'Or). At the **Gaelic College** in St. Ann's, the only one of its kind in North America, is the **Great Hall of the Clans,** which depicts the history and culture of the Scots. It's open daily, June-Oct. 15 from 9 to 4:30, July-August 9 to 8, adults $2.

Stops and Shops along the Trail.

Starting clockwise, note the Margaree River, one of North America's most beautiful (and prolific) salmon rivers. It offers twenty fishable miles of crystal-clear water and an abundance of salmon pools. Visitors are welcome to view salmon and trout at the **Margaree Fish Hatchery** in Northeast Margaree; there's a new salmon interpretation center nearby. Also at Northeast Margaree is the **Margaree Salmon Museum,** operated by the Margaree Anglers Association, a diverting experience for anyone interested in salmon and fishing; open June 15-Oct. 15, daily 9 to 5, adults 50 cents.

The sandy ocean beach at Margaree Harbour, as well as others along the west shore, are said to have the warmest waters north of the Carolinas. At Belle Cote, one of us found a small cave formed by rocks in which to change clothes for a quick dip in the ocean. **Schooner Village** is a must stop for anyone with an ounce of Scottish blood and a taste for the offbeat. It's a crowded indoor complex of five gift shops with British facades, where you can find anything from kilted tartan skirts and Hudson's Bay coats to Quebec wood carvings, owner Stephanie May's sculptures, Beatrix Potter figures, T-shirts and souvenir spoons. (You can also get a snack at the coffee shop, eat at the Schooner restaurant and go below decks to the Schooner Museum.) As you head north toward Cheticamp, you'll spot **Joe's Drive-in Theater of Scarecrows,** a bizarre outdoor stage near Cap

LeMoine where about 80 scarecrows, all dressed differently, flap in the breeze. The butterflies you see decorating many houses are for sale in the shops.

Around Cheticamp you'll come to **Flora's,** a vast emporium of souvenirs and Cheticamp hooked rugs and smaller pieces made by more than 100 local women. You may get to see Flora, dressed in her Sunday best, at work; asked how many rugs she'd hooked, she leaned back and said, "I've been doing this for 58 years and have no idea." The Cooperative Artisanale de Cheticamp runs a small **Acadian Museum,** featuring a craft shop with locally hooked rugs, and a **Restaurant Acadien,** a homey spot that's a good choice for breakfast or lunch with a difference and all dinners are under $10. **Les Trois Pignons** (The Three Gables) is a highly touted center of Acadian history with a rather overpriced museum and gallery of hooked rugs and tapestries by Elizabeth LeFort, the Cheticamp native whose works are in the Vatican, Buckingham Palace and the White House (open May-October, daily 9 to 5, summer 9 to 9). Beyond, the world's largest lobster trap catches your eye as it envelops **Le Gabion,** a gift shop with more hooked rugs, souvenirs and local crafts.

Whale cruises leave the Government Wharf at Cheticamp, 224-3376, on the 42-foot Bonnie Maureen daily at 9, 1 and 6 in July and August. The three-hour cruise shows sea caves, unusual rock formations, cormorants, perhaps a bald eagle and an average of twenty Atlantic pilot whales (adults $25).

Whales also are spotted from the 43-foot Gail Marie, run by **Pleasant Bay Boat Tours,** 224-2547. Capt. Ariland Fitzgerald, a native with a wonderful twang, points out bald eagles, dolphins, porpoises and pilot whales and even a Buddhist monastery on his two-hour tours at 9, 2 and 6 from Pleasant Bay (adults $20). He says his sunset cruises are best for those who want calm waters and beauty.

Other boat trips: Minke, pilot and fin whales are spotted on 2 1/2-hour cruises by **Bay St. Lawrence Boat Tours,** 383-2981, along seven miles of uninhabited coastline to the Money Point Lighthouse from Bay St. Lawrence Wharf. Summer tours leave at 10, 1:30 and 4:30 (adults $20, children $10). **Margaree Harbor Boat Tours,** 235-2848, offers tours and deep-sea fishing.

Near Cape North you'll find **Arts North,** a small two-story contemporary building selling local pottery, woven items and especially nice jewelry.

Ingonish is one of the oldest settlements on the Atlantic coast. Today it's a golfing, beach and ski resort. Works of award-winning local painter Christopher Gorey, an American emigre, are shown by his wife at **Lynn's Craft Shop and Art Gallery** in Ingonish. We loved them all and finally parted with some hard-earned cash for a small watercolor of lupines, the Maritimes' gorgeous wildflowers that grow in profusion along the roads, which are at their colorful height here in late June and early July. Chris Gorey put in a word for the works of William Rogers, who has **The Brush and Easel Art Gallery** at Wreck Cove.

Baddeck and Bras d'Or Lakes

Baddeck is on a hillside beside Lake Bras d'Or, and world-class sailboats dock in its harbor while cruising the inland saltwater lakes. From a park near the Bras d'Or Yacht Club you can see where Alexander Graham Bell's Silver Dart flew off the ice in 1909 to become the first manned flight in the British Commonwealth and where his hydrofoil set a world speed boating record in 1919. You also can see **Beinn Breagh,** the mountain he owned and the roof of the 1892 summer estate he built there.

In 1990, the town was abuzz over its new waterfront boardwalk, a landscaped walkway in two sections with park benches. It opens up the harborfront area, which is sheltered from the broad lake by Kidston Island.

In an old warehouse at the government wharf is **Seawinds Chandlery,** a smart shop with thick-knit Prince Edward Island sweaters, local handcrafts and nautical gifts. From here, a free boat run by the Baddeck Lions Club takes swimmers back and forth in summer to a beach on **Kidston Island.** Up on Chebucto Street, Baddeck's main thoroughfare, is Seawinds' newer and bigger sister, **Kidston Landing,** billed as a Cape Breton country store; it has a fine collection of local handcrafts, woolens, tableware, cookbooks, jams and lots of clothes. Just east of town is **Bute Arran Gift Shop,** which offers fine British woolens, Nova Scotia tartans, blankets, china, local crafts and books. In 1990, Camilla McDonald opened the **Rose Cottage Gallery,** stocking one-of-a-kind crafts items and gifts, and **Lynwood** offered more shopping pleasures in a typical red Nova Scotia gabled house. The **Bras d'Or Festival** presents a lively, summer-long series of music and theater at Baddeck Rural High School.

Boat tours seem to come and go in Baddeck. When we were last there, the schooner **Amoeba,** 295-2481, was about to go into operation at Government Wharf. Also advertised were boat tours by Capt. A.C. Rose, 295-2346, at 2 and 6 p.m. daily and mornings by appointment. **Paddles Unlimited** on Ross Street, 295-2631, rents paddleboats, a good way to explore the sheltered waterfront.

Alexander Graham Bell National Historic Park, Route 205, Baddeck, 295-2069. If when you think of Mr. Bell all you think of is the telephone, think again. This fascinating place shows the extraordinary range of his inventive genius, from genetics and medical science to the Silver Dart airplane and the hydrofoil. Through films, audio displays and such you'll learn of his romance with his deaf pupil Mabel, whom he later married, hear his famous "Dr. Watson, Dr. Watson" phone message, enjoy his early telephones and airplane models, view hundreds of historic photographs and see the remains of the hydrofoil. The priceless collection that makes up the museum was donated by his family, some of whom still summer at Beinn Breagh, which you can see from the roof of the striking tetrahedon-shaped museum. Open July-September, daily 9 to 9; rest of year, 9 to 5. Free.

Bras d'Or Lakes. Anyone coming this far to Cape Breton ought not to miss the majestic, mountain-ringed sprawl of inland lakes. Their reach is 50 miles long and 20 miles wide, creating 600 miles of shoreline. The tides flow in from the Atlantic through two narrow passages at the north end, Great Bras d'Or and Little Bras d'Or. Boats can get to the Atlantic from the southern end via St. Peters Canal. The drive up the lake's east side along Route 4 affords spectacular hilltop views. Returning south toward Baddeck from Sydney around Great Bras d'Or at sunset was unforgettable, matching in its own way the grandeur of the Cabot Trail. You may cross through the middle of the lakes via a five-minute ferry ride (50 cents a carload) at Grand Narrows. Stop at Iona to see the **Nova Scotia Highland Village Museum,** a recreated Scottish village overlooking the Barra Strait (June 15-Sept. 15, Monday-Saturday 9 to 5, Sunday noon to 6, adults $2.50). A good place to eat or stay here is the **Highland Heights Inn,** Route 223, Iona, 622-2360, an attractive hilltop building with 26 units, private baths and color TV, doubles $56 to $62; serving three meals daily in season.

A Side Trip to Louisbourg

Fortress of Louisbourg National Historic Park, Louisburg. (902) 733-2280. We don't know when we last were so surprised and impressed by a restored village as here. We expected to spend a couple of hours and ended up having to drag ourselves away after six.

Louisbourg, for the uninitiated (which included us), is the Canadian government's $26 million re-creation of the abandoned 18th-century walled city established by the French between 1713 and 1745 to defend their possessions in the New World. Until it was ambushed by Americans in 1745 and destroyed by the British in 1760, it was the mightiest fortress on this continent, the third busiest seaport (after Boston and Philadelphia) and the center of French civilization in North America. It is the only colonial town of import without a modern city superimposed on top, so one-fourth of it has been authentically restored as it was in 1744.

After orienting yourself in the visitor center via a five-minute slide show as you proceed through four small theaters to a bus loading area, you are transported two miles out to the fortress, poised on a point beside the ocean. Outside is a scene of melancholy desolation; inside, the physically austere fortress masks a lively working village of soldiers and seafaring families. Here, 175 costumed guides, most of them in their 20s and unusually articulate, interpret the town as it was in 1744, and the intriguing story of the rise and fall of Louisbourg gradually unfolds.

Although guided tours are offered periodically, you're on your own as you go through guardhouses, barracks, vegetable gardens, warehouses, homes, taverns, the military bakery, government buildings and the elegant Governor's Quarters. Guides will volunteer information if spoken to (they and their stories are fascinating). Take the time to chat and also to listen (by telephone) to exceptionally interesting recordings detailing facets of Louisbourg life pertaining to the building you're in.

Stop for a meal or snack at the **Hotel de la Marine** or **L'Epee Royale.** At the former, you'll be seated communally and served by waitresses in 18th-century garb. For $7 each, we had a lunch of pea soup, chicken fricassee and bread pudding, plus a pewter container of red wine. You sit on low chairs at a table covered with a sheet and huge serviettes, using a single pewter spoon for the entire meal. Quite an experience, we thought, as did our tablemates from Arizona and a California man whose wife was lunching in L'Epee Royale because she liked the sound of the stew there better.

There's so much to see and absorb that you could easily spend an entire day. Don't miss the building detailing the restoration of Louisbourg; that story is almost as interesting as the story of Louisbourg. Usually between 600 and 1,800 people a day visit for a yearly total of about 125,000, which isn't many considering the significance of the site. It's apt to be windy, lonely and cold out there (wear something warm and windproof), and you'll understand why Louisbourg — planned as the New World's capital — didn't make it. Open daily, July and August 9 to 7, June and September 10 to 6. Adults $6, children $3, family $15.

The village of Louisbourg, as opposed to the fortress, has a handful of restaurants, shops and motels, but most visitors prefer to stay in Sydney or commute from Baddeck. One shop not to be missed is the **Louisbourg Craft Workshops,** an airy building on four levels showing exceptional crafts, many made next door. Here also you can get tea, coffee and local oatmeal and molasses cookies and relax in a glass enclosure or outside at tables by the water.

Where to Eat _____ ♫♫♫

The food of Cape Breton was not, with exceptions, what we had hoped for: interesting seafood, simply yet imaginatively prepared, served with fresh vegetables and produce at small restaurants beside the ocean. Instead, the fish is generally deep-fried, the vegetables heavy-handed, the salads cost extra and almost everything is geared to tour buses. We found only one oceanside seafood shanty and two outdoor decks on the water in all our travels. Some of the Scottish specialties were fun, however.

Baddeck Area

Gisele's of Baddeck, Shore Road, Baddeck. (902) 295-2849. One guest wrote that its food is "an oasis in a gourmet desert," and we had a fine dinner here. The curved dining room has some tables at windows with a view of Lake Bras d'Or across the road. The striking blue tile tables were designed by owner Hans Sievers; more tiles and local art are on the walls. Until the place grew too big for her, Helen Sievers did the cooking after her mother-in-law Gisele retired to Florida. Now she has a Swiss chef, of whom she praises: "I was a cook; he is a chef." We shared the house terrine with aspic and melba before digging into our entrees, a good poached salmon with a delicate maltaise sauce, roasted potatoes and carrots, and a special of poached haddock with three caviars and rice. Other choices ($15.95 to $17.95) included veal scaloppine with wild mushroom sauce and wiener schnitzel, thanks to the Swiss chef, plus sauteed Digby scallops with green peppercorns, rack of lamb, beef wellington and cornish game hen. Desserts, baked on the premises, include pies, tortes, cakes and cheesecakes, and you might finish with Gisele's special flambeed coffee with creme de cacao, grand marnier and whipped cream. The wine list features good French, German, Spanish and Nova Scotia wines; we opted for a liter of the Nova Scotia Jost chablis, as we did frequently when faced with far pricier choices on our latest trip to Nova Scotia. Dinner nightly, 5:30 to 10.

Inverary Inn, Shore Road, Baddeck. (902) 295-2674. Old bottles of all colors are lined up on the windowsills in the airy outer dining room looking across the lawns to Lake Bras d'Or. Gone are the Royal Stuart tartan overcloths whose pattern was repeated in the waitresses' skirts. They now are color-coordinated with the beige and green tablecloths in the main room, or the white linens in a newer room. The short dinner menu (entrees $10.95 to $17.25) had been upscaled at our latest visit: pan-fried filet of haddock seasoned with coriander and fennel, medallions of pork charcutiere with sliced gherkins and breast of chicken forestiere. We settled for a prime rib that tasted better than it looked and a New York strip steak that was too thin and rather fatty and tough. The steak came with mashed potatoes and frozen peas, the prime rib with coleslaw and horseradish. A basket of oatcakes and buns was served first, and a side caesar salad ($4.25) was very good. A tangy lemon snow made a nice, light ending. Dinner nightly, 5 to 9.

The Fish House, Shore Road, Baddeck. (902) 295-3155. This is the casual, waterside restaurant at the side of the Inverary Inn property, opened by Scottie MacAuley, son of the innkeepers. And while we wished we had eaten here rather than in the main dining room, friends who preceded us had dinner at Scottie's Fish House and thought the inn would have been a better choice. Such are the vagaries of eating on Cape Breton. The red-linened interior has generous windows overlooking the water, but (unless it's too buggy) we'd choose the outside porch beside the cove, where luxury sailboats and yachts are moored. This is the kind of outdoor place we'd been looking for, where you can watch the waterfront goings-on as you sample seafood chowder, steamed mussels or clams, fish and chips, lobster croissant or filet of salmon ($5.95 to $17.95 for a seafood platter). Open daily 11 to 10, June 15 to Oct. 15.

Taj Restaurant, MacLeod Street, Baddeck. (902) 295-2915. Who'd ever expect to find an Indian restaurant on Cape Breton, much less one in an ordinary brick house facing the parking lot behind the Alexander Graham Bell Museum? Otherwise you might never know it was there, and even so it's hard to get to, but for those of us who crave Indian food, it's a treat. The Mathur family from New Delhi (he's a teacher at Baddeck Rural High School) serves sandwiches, seafood and standard dinners as well as East Indian specialties at prices not to be believed. How about chicken curry for $7.95 or tandoori murgha for $8.95? That's the same price as for grilled halibut or poached salmon, and a roast beef dinner is $7.05. Accompany with pokoras or samosas. Those irresistible Indian breads like poori and paratha are 50 cents or $1.25. End with mango pulp and ice cream, $1.50. The Mathurs started with a gift shop and expanded with their licensed restaurant a decade ago. Open daily 9 to 9, June-September.

Bell Buoy, Chebucto Street, Baddeck. (902) 295-2581. An expansive room with glass tops over gray and red tablecloths and windows onto the water beckon at this new steak and seafood restaurant, a pleasant mix of rusticity and contemporary. The menu starts with nachos, Buffalo wings, peel and eat shrimp and potato skins, then gets traditional in such entrees ($8.95 to $15.95) as fried clams, scallops in a wine and cheese sauce, stuffed sole, beef liver with onions and pork chops with applesauce. The chowder ($6.50) is said to be a meal in itself; you also can go full bore for the shoreline harvest, $19.95. Finish with hot gingerbread or bread pudding, both with brown sugar sauce and cream, homemade pies or ice cream. Wines from Jost Vineyards are featured on the wine list. Lunch daily, 11:30 to 5; dinner, 5 to 10 or 11. Open June through mid-October.

Baddeck Lobster Suppers, Ross Street, Baddeck. (902) 295-3307. The former Royal Canadian Legion Hall has been turned into a pleasing site for lobster suppers in the Prince Edward Island style. Dining is casual at tables covered with plastic and red and white checkered cloths, with window tables offering a semblance of a view. When we visited, a one-pound lobster in the shell was $16.95. It came with unlimited seafood chowder, steamed mussels, homemade rolls and biscuits, potato salad, assorted desserts and beverage. Cape Breton salmon ($14.95) and ham ($12.95) were offered as alternatives. There's a full liquor license. Open daily, 4 to 9, June-October.

Highwheeler Cafe, Chebucto Street, Baddeck. (902) 295-3006. Finally, a cafe-deli-bakery with inspired food and a casual outdoor deck. And not catering to busloads of tourists. This highwheeling winner was opened in 1987 by Heidi and Dan Atkins, he a transplanted American, who had been partners in the Herring Choker Deli down the road in Nyanza. Here they offer oversize sandwiches served with salad of the day ($3.50 to $4.95), soups like gazpacho and french onion, individual pizzas, intriguing salads and, for breakfast, great muffins, bagels and cinnamon rolls. The desserts in the pastry showcase are too good to resist. We picked up gazpacho and some salads for a picnic and it was one of our best lunches in the Maritimes. Open daily in summer, 7:30 a.m. to 9 p.m.; closes between 4 and 5:30 rest of year. Closed mid-January to mid-February.

Around the Cabot Trail

Normaway Inn, Egypt Road, Margaree Valley. (902) 248-2987. Big windows on both sides of the charming, country-fresh dining room look out onto a tranquil rural landscape, and as the sun sets and the room is totally lit by candles, it's quite lovely. With tables covered with dark green cloths, Wedgwood china and fresh flowers, it's a simple but pleasant setting and the food is considered the best on Cape Breton. Complete dinners are $30 for four courses with a choice of selections changing nightly; meals also can be ordered a la carte. We started with sherried mushrooms and shrimp-filled salmon rolls and a good salad with excellent dressings. The accompanying oatcakes and porridge bread were fabulous and came with real pats of butter, not the aluminum-foil miniatures foisted on diners in most Maritime restaurants. The butterflied leg of lamb tasted more like a roast with gravy and could have been rarer; the filet mignon with herb butter was more successful. Halibut with pecan butter, cornish hen with apricot stuffing and coquille of scallops and shrimp were the evening's other choices. Dinner ended triumphantly with an apple-rhubarb crisp with ice cream and an ice cream pie on a chocolate coconut crust. Vegetables and salads are fresh from the inn's gardens. The wine list is better than the norm in Nova Scotia. Afterward, a stroll down the lane to watch the horses frolicking was a pleasant interlude before the fiddler started entertaining in the inn's living room. Lunch daily in summer, noon to 1:30; dinner nightly, 5:30 to 8:30, to 9:30 in summer. Open June to Oct. 15.

Schooner Restaurant, Cabot Trail, Margaree Harbour. (902) 235-2317. You can dine aboard the schooner Marian Elizabeth, built in 1918 and one of only two remaining Lunenburg fishing schooners, listen to cocktail music played on the piano by Stephanie May and perhaps chat with John May, who's unmistakable in long gray beard nd MacDonald tartan kilt. The May family moved here in 1974 from Hartford, Conn., where she was a widely known political activist and he a comptroller for Aetna Life & Casualty. They reopened the Schooner Restaurant and have vastly expanded the rambling Schooner Village Gift Shop complex of five boutiques with half-timbered facades under one roof, a coffee shop and the Schooner Museum. Dinners run from $6.50 for two chicken dishes (Acadian chicken and pork pie or chicken marengo) to $12.50 for broiled scallops. A small boiled lobster was going for $10 when we were there, and other reasonably priced choices included grilled halibut, poached salmon, cod Portuguese and Margaree River trout. Chowders, sandwiches, salads and smaller dinner entrees are the fare at lunch, and among desserts are strawberry shortcake and hot gingerbread with applesauce and whipped cream. Lunch daily, 11:30 to 3; dinner, 6 to 8 or 9. Open July to Oct. 15.

Harbour Restaurant, Main Street, Cheticamp. (902) 224-2042. The pleasant, rustic dining room in beige and brown tones looks onto the harbor beside a lighthouse, but the best view is from the new enclosed sun porch, with mauve chairs at butcherblock tables beside the water. We could see cows grazing along the shore of the island across the cove, near a spit of sand covered with birds, as we lunched on a spicy noodle soup (which contained everything but the kitchen sink), a lobster roll and a plate of fried clams with coleslaw (both $6.95), washed down with the local Oland beer. The menu offered a variety from egg rolls to salads to butterscotch meringue pie. Dinner entrees go from $7.95 to $19.95 for seafood platter or surf and turf. Open daily, 7 a.m. to 10 or midnight, Sunday from 8; winter, 7 a.m. to 8 p.m.

Laurie's Dining Room, Main Street, Cheticamp. (902) 224-2400. Laurie McKeown has been upgrading his family's motel and restaurant operation, obtaining a liquor license, adding an upstairs cocktail lounge, and planning to open a second-story deck for waterview dining in 1991. The main-floor dining room seats 60 at oak tables covered with Cape Breton paper maps. The upstairs lounge is unexpectedly chic with plush rust velvet chairs at good-looking ash tables; you'd almost think you were in a city hotel. For 40 years, Laurie's father John has reigned in the kitchen, where his homemade soups and chowders, breads and pastries, and seafood obtained from the wharf across the street have won acclaim. The halibut, haddock and grey sole fillets are broiled in foil and served with tartar sauce ($10.95 to $12.95) — not exactly the way we like them, but better than the deep-fried and heavily breaded treatment indigenous to the area. The salmon is steamed Acadian style (again served with tartar sauce), and other choices might be baked ham with scalloped potatoes and pork chops with apple jelly. Prices range from $10.95 to $21.95. Some say the mince pie is the best they've ever tasted. Dinner, 5 or 10. Closed in winter.

The Black Whale, Cabot Trail, Pleasant Bay. (902) 224-2185. We'd seen the publicity and drove quite a distance — which you often have to do on the Cabot Trail — to have lunch at this "internationally famous" seafood restaurant. The only problem was that it had no lunch items, just a few seafood dinners chalked on the blackboard and served in the local (heavy dinner) manner. We longed for a lobster roll or chowder and salad, so moved on after glancing at the homey interior of the unusual pine and log building seating 150 in several sections. The owners say their aim is to provide good seafood to thousands of travelers at a fair price. The tourists respond in droves, and are especially fond of the fish and chips. Open 11 to 10, July-September.

Keltic Lodge, Ingonish Beach. (902) 285-2880. The food in the famed lodge's 200-seat dining room is good if unremarkable, and the public is welcome by reservation. In resort style, the menu changes daily and meals are prix-fixe. Our dinner for two started with solomon gundy (four pickled herring, a local specialty) and a ham and asparagus feuillette, followed by Ingonish clam chowder and cream of vegetable soup, and good salads. For main courses we chose cornish game hen, which came with a large baked potato and red braised cabbage, and a rather dry poached salmon doused with raspberry sauce. Desserts of assorted sherbets and a fresh plum tart were the best part of the meal; we also appreciated the good rolls and oatcakes which arrived, mercifully, with butter that you didn't have to unwrap. Although we skipped the porridge and kippered herring, the next day's breakfast was filling as well: a fresh fruit cup (more canned than fresh, we regret), cream of wheat, a poached egg on English muffin with good Canadian sausage, and scrambled eggs with ham. Prix-fixe, $35 for dinner, $17 for lunch and $10 for breakfast. Jackets required for dinner. Breakfast, 7 to 9:30; lunch, noon to 2; dinner, 6 to 9. Open June to Oct. 20.

The Lobster Galley, Cabot Trail, St. Ann's Harbor. (902) 295-3100. Newly renovated and expanded, this old-timer dressed in blue and white offers a lovely view through balloon-curtained windows up St. Ann's Bay. It claims to be Cape Breton's largest seafood restaurant, and it's unexpectedly handsome in its refurbished digs. Nova Scotia music plays as you feast on seafood (strip steak was the only salve to meat eaters on the latest menu). A lobster dinner went for $14.95, but you could also sample stuffed sole, dilled salmon, grilled halibut and a cold salmon plate with potato salad, watercress and dill yogurt sauce ($11.95 to $15.95). Three vegetarian items and numerous appetizers are available. Many people make the trek up from Baddeck just for the lobsters and the view. Open from 7 a.m. to 11 p.m., May-October.

Special Treats

The Gingerbread Man, Cabot Trail, Cape North. (902) 383-2942. A mile west of tiny Cape North in the 1876 Middle Ridge Schoolhouse is a quaint Scottish bakery, gift shop and restaurant run by Roseanne and Don MacInnis. The restaurant, like none we ever saw, resembles a camp building with screened windows that can be covered from the outside on cool days; a portable heater was going on the September afternoon we dined alone, sitting on black stools at round pink tables. Three complete dinners are served for $9.50: a Scottish baked fish roll, Forfar Bridie or seafood chowder. All include carrots and three-bean salad, bonnach, white and brown bread, oatcakes, Scottish jam, beverage and dessert, perhaps a gingerbread man or woman. Breakfasts are $4.45 for egg and Canadian bacon pie or oatmeal raisin cinnamon porridge, accompanied by juice, coffee and all those marvelous breads and oatcakes. If you can't be there at mealtime, stop in for a chocolate chip cookie (75 cents) or an apple turnover ($2.75). Open 8 a.m. to 6 p.m., June to mid-October.

Neil's Chowder House, Lighthouse Road, Neil's Harbor. Hidden just past the lighthouse on the point at Neil's Head, this is the kind of eatery we'd expected to find all over the island. You place your order and pick it up at the counter, then sit at red picnic tables inside or out on a deck on a point beside the ocean. Even though we'd had a light lunch at the Gingerbread Man less than two hours before, we had to split a bowl of seafood chowder ($4.50), which was the essence of fishiness, chock full of lobster, haddock and clams, and served with a biscuit. Other choices ranged from a fried clam plate ($5.95) to scallops and chips ($8.95). Another time we tried clam chowder and a lobster burger for $6.95 and for dessert, oatcakes and ginger cake. The owner told us there once were four such places across Cape Breton, but they were the only survivors. Open summer, 11 to 9; fall, 11 to 4.

FOR MORE INFORMATION: Superintendent, Cape Breton Highlands National Park, Ingonish Beach, N.S. B0C 1L0. (902) 285-2270. Or write Tourism Nova Scotia, Box 456, Halifax B3J 2R5. (902) 454-5000 or (800) 341-6096.

Index to Major Accommodations, Attractions and Restaurants

434

438

440

Also by Wood Pond Press

The Restaurants of New England. The newest book by Nancy Webster and Richard Woodworth, this is the most comprehensive guide to restaurants throughout New England. The authors detail menu offerings, atmosphere, hours and prices for more than 1,000 restaurants in the same informative style that makes their other books so credible. Published in 1990. 394 pages of up-to-date information. $12.95.

Weekending in New England. The best-selling travel guide by Betsy Wittemann and Nancy Webster details everything you need to know about eighteen of New England's most interesting vacation spots: nearly 1,000 things to do, sights to see and places to stay, eat and shop year-round. First published in 1980; fully updated and revised in 1988. 290 pages of facts and fun. $10.95.

The Best of Daytripping & Dining. Another book by Betsy Wittemann and Nancy Webster, this is a companion to their original Southern New England and all-New England editions. It pairs 25 featured daytrips with 25 choice restaurants, among 200 other suggestions of sites to visit and places to eat, in Southern New England and nearby New York. Published in 1985; updated in 1989. 186 pages of fresh ideas. $9.95.

Getaways for Gourmets in the Northeast. The first book by Nancy Webster and Richard Woodworth appeals to the gourmet in all of us. It guides you to the best dining, lodging, specialty-food shops and culinary attractions in 22 areas from the Brandywine Valley to Montreal, Cape May to Burlington, the Finger Lakes to Monadnock, Saratoga to Nantucket. Published in 1984; fully revised and expanded in 1991. 474 pages to read and savor. $14.95.

Inn Spots & Special Places in New England. Much more than an inn guide, this book by Nancy Webster and Richard Woodworth tells you where to go, stay, eat and enjoy in the region's choicest areas. Focusing on 32 special places, it details the best inns, restaurants, sights to see and things to do. Published in 1986. Fully updated in 1989. 394 pages of timely ideas. $12.95.

The Originals in Their Fields

These books may be ordered from your local bookstore or direct from the publisher, pre-paid, plus $1.75 handling for each book. Connecticut residents add sales tax.

Wood Pond Press
365 Ridgewood Road
West Hartford, Conn. 06107
(203) 521-0389